The Community of the Weak

The Community of the Weak

Social Postmodernism in Theological Reflections on Power and Powerlessness in North America

Hans-Peter Geiser

WIPF & STOCK · Eugene, Oregon

THE COMMUNITY OF THE WEAK
Social Postmodernism in Theological Reflections on Power and Powerlessness in North America

Copyright © 2013 Hans-Peter Geiser. All rights reserved. Except for brief quotations in critical publications or reviews, no part of this book may be reproduced in any manner without prior written permission from the publisher. Write: Permissions, Wipf and Stock Publishers, 199 W. 8th Ave., Suite 3, Eugene, OR 97401.

Wipf & Stock
An Imprint of Wipf and Stock Publishers
199 W. 8th Ave., Suite 3
Eugene, OR 97401

www.wipfandstock.com

ISBN 13: 978-1-61097-634-3

Cataloguing-in-Publication data:

Geiser, Hans-Peter.

The community of the weak : social postmodernism in theological reflections on power and powerlessness in North America / Hans-Peter Geiser.

xx + 534 pp. ; 23 cm. Includes bibliographical references.

ISBN 13: 978-1-61097-634-3

1. Postmodernism—Religious aspects—Christianity. 2. North America—Church history. 3. Power (Christian theology). I. Title.

BJ1275 G45 2013

Manufactured in the U.S.A.

to
Urban Spirit www.urban-spirit.net
www.urban-spirit.ning.com
Facebook www.facebook.com/urbanspiritch

my mom
for having opened up to me
the North American continent

my wife
in love ever since California

in longtime memory
of Klauspeter Blaser
University of Lausanne

thankful to

Denis Müller and Marc Boss
Nancy Bedford and Pierre Bühler
a most graceful jazz combo

Contents

Foreword ix

Intentions xiii

1 Trilemmas 1

   Power, Writing, Project, Social Location 3

       Power in Postmodern Times 4
       Writing in Trilemmas 7
       The Project of the Dissertation 8
       Finding Your Social Location 9

2 The Social 12

   Difference 12

       Social Postmodernism and Oppression 14
       Fragment, Ambiguity, and Difference 33
       Postmodern Theology and Power 67
       Dogmatic Relevance : Violence and Creation 79

3 Power 98

   Experience 98

       Sacrificial Logics and the Abuse of Power 99
       Geographies of Exclusion 106

   Memories 115

       Hermeneutics of Powerlessness 115
       Trajectories of Violence: Hagar and Jesus 126

   Closure 139

       In the Beginning a Cry 140
       The Crucified God and Crushed Humanity 152

Contents

- 4 North America   159
  - *Landscape*   159
    - Traveling to a Different World   160
  - *Contexts*   169
    - Thematic Backgrounds   169
  - *Treading*   184
    - A Kaleidoscopic View   184

- 5 Real Life   220
  - *Method*   220
    - Finding the Real   221
    - Context, Lived Experience, and Practical Action   233
  - *Reflection*   244
    - A Fundamental Theology of Experience   249
    - Biography and Situation   272

- 6 Postmodern   283
  - *Grounding*   283
    - Theology, Art, and Messy Texts   283
    - Socially Imagining a Better World   290
    - "Everything Starts With a Good Cry"   292
    - Communal Knowing from Experience   299
    - Whose Experience Counts in Theological Reflection?   307
    - Theology as Autobiography   315
    - Contextual Theology and Multicultural Identity   326

- 7 Culture   334
  - *Koinonia*   334
    - Building Postmodern Communities   339
    - Cultural Studies and Theologies of Culture   357
    - Ecological Theology and Power   375
    - Dogmatic Relevance: Oikos and Koinonia of Cultures   402

- 8 Music   428
  - *All that Jazz*   428
    - New Themes, New Tunes, New Chords   429
    - A New Fundamental Theology   437

Bibliography   451

Foreword

"There's no doubt anymore that the church of the West is clearly in some form of long-term, trended decline that is now reaching critical level—witness the demise of Christianity in Europe and Australia, for instance. Furthermore, the number of people who will be in a church in the United States has shrunk to just more than 18 percent, the lowest level in the history of a once very religious country. And if that isn't alarming enough, we need only look to the major cities of the U.S., where leading cultural indicators are birthed. In these, only 10 percent of the population attends church. This is just a precursor to what has already taken place in Australia, where less than 10 percent attend church, and Europe, where no more than 2 percent of the population will participate in church life this weekend." (Hirsch and Ferguson 2011, 204)

"Geneva, Zurich, Basel. What will the future be like? For the local churches, spirituality, and its urban vision? A young generation is leaving most of the classical institutions. In many places out of a lack of creativity. Maybe many things have to be restarted in radically new ways. More jazzy, more artistic. City chill-out. Urban arts. Streetwise creativity. Inclusive. Emotional. To the rhythm of dance." (Urban Spirit www.urban-spirit.net, 2 and www.urban-spirit.ning.com, a Swiss—US emergent global & urban Gen-XY project 2011, FB www.facebook.com/urbanspiritch)

"Even though immediately prior to the Edict of Milan, the church was developing forms, theology, ritual, and structure, when Constantine co-opted Christianity, he fundamentally altered the way we saw and experienced ourselves as God's people. What was largely an illegal, underground people-movement was now given money, status, power, and legitimacy. Everything changed . . . This was a radical shift, and we've never escaped it. Constantine is still the emperor of our imaginations, of the way we see and

Foreword

> *experience ourselves as church, seventeen centuries later." (Hirsch and Ferguson 2011, 33)*
>
> *"Being Christian is like being a pumpkin. God lifts you up, takes you in, and washes all the dirt off of you. He opens you up, touches you deep inside and scoops out all the yucky stuff—including the seeds of doubt, hate, greed, etc. Then He carves you a new smiling face and puts His light inside you to shine for all the world to see." (Anonymous—E-Mail from California 2011)*

I am sitting right now in *Burger King* in the city of *Basel, Switzerland*, writing on my laptop a foreword to a *dissertation* of almost 550 pages I wrote over the long and extended lifetime and research period of 8 to 10 years—depending on how you count—, and which I finally finished 6 years ago. *It seems like yesterday*. Looking over the text, revising references, updating literature, choosing the format for the publication, all this and more *keeps memories and old feelings coming back*. Reading what I wrote over all these years of *pastoral-theological reflection* in a *most organic form of intellectual work* (my big heroes in this are *Antonio Gramsci* and *Cornel West*)—working as a *local pastor* in various places in Switzerland, while at the same time getting plunged into *action-reflection* every day on what I experienced in the most intense moments of joy and pain, ecstatic beauty and death-dealing ways, leading ultimately to a dissertation—makes me marvel at how much is still *contemporary*. Every word in it has a ring of *cutting-edge*, envisioning some *permanent revolution* (Hirsch and Catchim 2011).

I've been reading *Alan Hirsch* and *Michael Frost* lately (Hirsch 2006, Hirsch and Frost 2006, Frost 2006, Frost and Hirsch 2009, 2011, Hirsch and Hirsch 2010, Hirsch and Ferguson 2011, Hirsch and Catchim 2011). It's not just *Fuller Theological Seminary* which connects us at a most deeply felt level. It's also a creative and *daring reframing of the future* which joins us in some very similar musical standards played out in the latest gig of improvisational and future-oriented *jazz visions*. Sometimes people play *theological jazz* on God's magnificent globe without knowing each other. And yet, deep hope and creative dreams seem to intergalactically converge across global and continental limits. Fortunately, *Steve Jobs* (who had just died before writing this) and others networked a whole new generation into the next truly *global village*. This dissertation, now in the form of a book publication, intends nothing less than joining a *global vision*—to connect with other *visionaries*.

Foreword

Over the last three years different people in *Switzerland* have been working at envisioning a *new dream* for how church could be done differently. Switzerland is the *birth place* of one strand of the *Magisterial Reformation* in Zurich, Geneva, Berne, Basel—connecting power, wealth, and societal *pole positioning*. At the same time, a *historical memory* is still scarred by an *unresolved story* which led to the *new vision of a new continent*. North America in many ways inherits from this story—the story of the *Anabaptist Left Wing Reformation*. This dissertation—revised in book form—comes out of this still *unresolved story*. Its vision comes out of a *soul-friend spirit* which has learned a great deal from those who *lost the game* times past, many centuries ago. And yet, as it seems, the *losers of old times* and centuries seem to be coming back calling the *new time* by its name. As *Stuart Murray* from the *Anabaptist Network* in *England* calls it, we now live in a *postchristendom world* (Murray 2004). Losing power, losing influence, losing money, losing members, losing societal status. Losing on all sides, and yet still being called to be *God's people*.

This dissertation may be like the *Magna Charta* of a *new vision*. Theoretical, academic, complicated, messy, and even *openly jazzy postmodern*, with lots of books and references in a *linked-in style*—the way the new generation reads the Web nowadays. And yet, this dissertation undergirds a *practical vision*—a vision in the form of a *project* three years old—under the name of *Urban Spirit*. A new *Generation-X-Y project* which attempts to reach out in new and creative ways to a new generation which is no longer part of an *old Christendom model*. Open, liberal and evangelical, post-evangelical and postmodern, pious, socially activist and spiritual, creatively engaged for a new generation of *cultural creatives*—following *Richard Florida*. The *city of Basel*, where this book is being prepared for publication, according to the latest statistics has over 40% of its city population in 2011/2012 *radically unchurched*, with a majority under the age of 40. The *Genevan Reformed Church* in Switzerland - John Calvin's church—is facing institutional bankruptcy some years from now, as the majority of the population no longer has any connection to church. Out of Geneva's 460,000 inhabitants just about 10,000 still pay to support the Genevan Reformed church—a marginal minority of under 3% with an age average of 61-years old. A Reformed population in the *city of Zurich* has declined over the last 40 years from over 280,000 to now 98,000. A *recent national research study* calculated the Swiss participation in regular local worship services in Reformed churches all over Switzerland at exactly the same number of 98,000, with a general population of over 7 million.

Foreword

Free churches in Switzerland gather more than double this number on Sundays, also younger in average age—over 180,000 in worship in Baptist, Methodist, Mennonite, or *newly emerging churches* for the *next generation*. In the city of *Zurich* weekend worship participation for a whole city of a little less than half a million is down at 2,000 in Reformed churches, age average 60+, while a *new Generation-X church* www.icf.ch—now 17 years old—collects more than 2,000 young people between the ages of 20–45 in just one location. *Swiss churches* are dying, the slow way, but still losing the next generation.

Alan Hirsch, as an Australian adjunct connected to *Fuller Theological Seminary* in LA, California—my theological home base—and *Dave Ferguson* in Chicago (Hirsch and Ferguson 2011) are right. The *Constantinian age* of the church is over—all over the globe. Even *Chicago*, where I spent most of the last 5 years setting up an *International Exchange Project* for new models in *urban-global church thinking* www.urban-spirit.net and www.urban-spirit.ning.com, lives up to Alan Hirsch's and Dave Ferguson's church figures. Less than 10% of the population visits local churches on any given weekend—in over 8,000 churches, 80% with no more than 100 members. Willow Creek, Salem Baptist, Moody Bible, Park Community, Church Community Christian, Apostolic, and a more liberal Roman Catholic Saint Sabina or Obama's former church Trinity UCC—gathering 2,000 to 20,000 people each Sunday—are remarkable exceptions. This dissertation in book form, revised and adapted to a different and new public, attempts to offer a *theological base grounding* in postmodern and even at times *jazzy ways* to a different vision of what *church as a community of the weak* could be. In this, it stays *cutting-edge*.

Basel, Zürich, Geneva, Lausanne/Switzerland
linked in with Chicago, Los Angeles, Philadelphia 2011/2013
www.urban-spirit.net
www.urban-spirit.ning.com
Facebook www.facebook.com/urbanspiritch

Intentions

"It is this perspective, the ambivalent, multivalent way of seeing, that is at the core of what is called critical theory, feminist theory, and much of the minority critique of law. It has to do with a fluid positioning that sees back and forth across boundary, which acknowledges that I can be black and good and black and bad, and that I can also be black and white, male and female, yin and yang, love and hate . . . Nothing is simple . . ." (Thistlethwaite and Cairns 2003/1994, 158, quoting Williams 1991, 130)

"For many years I have been interested in the arts of improvisation, which involve recombining partly familiar materials in new ways, often in ways especially sensitive to context, interaction, and response . . . Jazz exemplifies artistic activity that is at once individual and communal, performance that is both repetitive and innovative, each participant sometimes providing background support and sometimes flying free . . . Just as change stimulates us to look for more abstract constancies, so the individual effort to compose a life, framed by birth and death and carefully pieced together from disparate elements, becomes a statement on the unity of living. These works of art, still incomplete, are parables in process, the living metaphors with which we describe the world." (Pederson 2001, 1, quoting Bateson 1990, 2–3, 17–18)

"Jazz provides an alternative way to think about creativity in contrast to the tight, precise, and controlled music of many Euro-American composers and musicians. Jazz focuses on a community of conversation, in which the give-and-take creates ongoing fresh statements . . . Montuori applies the musical model to the academic community. For knowledge to be creative, one must be willing to take risks in a trusting community. The old 'battleground' model wages war and reinforces distrust among colleagues. The jazz model encourages trust, community, and an enthusiasm for the process of creating music together." (Pederson 2001, 37)

Intentions

Prefacing this dissertation with a few thematic notes, I would like to introduce the reader to the main purpose and the general intention of this dissertation. I will choose a few semantic and associative words to summarize the general intent of this work.

Playing Jazz . . . This dissertation proposes to write theology in the way *Keith Jarrett* plays the piano, be it in cities like Köln, Bremen, Lausanne, Geneva, New York or Paris. *Playing jazz* in formulating deep belief is one way to compose one's most personal and intimate theology. Belief may be like jazz, inviting to the communal beat (on leadership and jazz De Pree 1992, on creativity and jazz Pederson 2001, Perkinson 2005, Gelinas 2009). Theology, even the kind that calls itself *systematic—systematic theology—*, most definitely has recurring and rebirthing elements of jazz, whether we hear it and like it, or whether we prefer to overhear it. *Jazz* and *creativity* go together, as do the birth of life and the sound of music. Theology as well can become more musical, crisscrossing and jam-sessioning along some of the most diverse North American systematic theologies—mixing generous post- and/or younger evangelical orthodoxy (McLaren 2006), postmodern Calvinism (Smith 2006), Rastafari Jamaican liberation theology (Erskine 2005), African American religious traditions (Murphy 2000), and post-denominational spiritual jazz practices (Perkinson 2005) to tell our personal and communal lives in alternative rhythms and melodies to the North American groove (Gelinas 2009). As younger evangelical and postmodern post-evangelical *Brian B. McLaren* describes the artistic-poetic and musical side of doing theology: "Perhaps this . . . means that serious theologians in the years ahead will more often, along with their scholarly work, write poetry, or make films, or compose music, or write plays and novels—not as their avocation, but right along with their primary theological vocation . . ." (McLaren 2006, 173, on musical evangelicalism Webber 2002, McDermott 2010).

Improvisational . . . This will mean that theology, in this dissertation as well, becomes more *improvisational*, the way jazz improvises on standard themes in ever new ways. Improvisation in theology is no stranger to the systematic or even ethical endeavor, as new monographs show (Pederson 2001, Wells 2004, Welch 1999, 2005, McClintock Fulkerson 2005, Perkinson 2005, Gelinas 2009). Putting together melodic tunes and varying rhythms of alternative theological and ethical worlds in North America and elsewhere (Jones 1989, Wells 2004, Livingston and Schüssler Fiorenza 2006, De La Torre 2004, Higgins 2009, Dyrness, Kärkkäinen, Martinez, and Chan 2008) may be a new way to describe our theological endeavor.

Intentions

This dissertation attempts to play after such tunes and rhythms adding to the new sound.

Fluidly Pneumatic . . . The text of this dissertation will be more *musical*, less analytic, more *symphonic*, less tight, precise, and controlled. It will be more *narrative*, less composed, more meandering and searching, less arrived. *Keith Jarrett* has a way to play the piano in *fluid form*, beginning at the beginning, ending at some unknown moment. In between melodies like colors get painted, added, composed, repeated, developed, as the flow of creativity takes its course. A certain structure is given and prepared, but the way to be taken is *pneumatic* (Bedford 2006, 39), if a word like this can be used for a concert or a gig. In some ways, this dissertation invites the reader to a concert. Once intonated in tunes, developed in rhythms, varied in choruses, endlessly repeated while modulated, and finally concluding, it may never again be played or written in the same way.

A Community of Conversation . . . In 1999 the *University of Lausanne* approved the *basic outline* of this dissertation project, still with *Klauspeter Blaser* as its mentor and director. For the last eight years this dissertation has been written and crafted, rearranged and recomposed, on and off, sometimes in peaceful times, at other times interrupted through painful life experiences. In its basic outline it has followed its vision. Today the concert is ending. With a few remaining tunes and notes to be added, modified, attached, inserted, up-dated, re-arranged. The way *Keith Jarrett* plays jazz—not just in individual solos, but also in group quartets—*creating music together*. The solo expands into a trio, a quartet, a *trustful community*, a give-and-take of a *community of conversation* (Pederson 2001, 37). The way a jury acts in working out the last stages of a project as a dissertation.

Bibliographically Multiglobal . . . Some *bibliographical references* have been added, taking into account the flux of time which moves theology further and deeper in the course of its flow. Getting an overview of the multivalent and multifaceted variety of *systematic theology* across the many and divers cultures and continents over the last hundred years since the beginning of the *twentieth century* up to our ever new and most fragmented *twenty-first century* is now accessible in many new places, in a global move beyond Eurocentric myopia of theological vision, covering French, African, Asian, Latin/Central American, African American, Latino/a, Asian American, and Native American theologies alongside an age-old European dominance (Ford and Muers 2005, Livingston and Schüssler Fiorenza 2006, Davey 2002, Macquarrie 2002, Musser and Price 2003,

Intentions

De La Torre 2004, Higgins 2009, Dyrness, Kärkkäinen, Martinez, and Chan 2008). At the same time, the history of theology for the last 2000 years has become a lot more *intercultural* as well (Collins and Price 2003, Cory/Landry 2000, Keen 2004, Tomkins 2005). The *Christian tradition* (Cory/Landry 2000, Keen 2004, Webb 2004, Gonzalez 2005, Lane 2006) in its history and contemporary presence has become *multi-global*, especially in view of the radical changes in the *global South* (Jenkins 2002, 2006). At the same time, *North American systematic theology* over the last half-century has become a most respectable and *indigenous theology* of its own kind, whether we look at the *liberal tradition*—as in personalist theology, secular theology, process theology, liberation theology, pragmatist theology, black theology, feminist theology, post-feminist theology, postmodern theology, neo-historical theology, postliberalism, and Neo-Barthianism (covering a vast range of liberal North American theological developments from 1950 to 2005 Dorrien 2006)—, or whether we look at other more *evangelical theological currents* in North America (Grenz and Franke 2001, McDermott 2010, viewed from a European perspective Pally 2010).

The Next Christendom . . . This *global vision* and reality of a *next Christendom*, with ever new voices coming from the *global South* and the *local and ethnic margins* of *North American society*, profoundly changing our systematic, ethical, and pastoral theologies, has been most prominently placed in recent North American systematic theologies, in particular in the most *recent textbooks* (McGrath 2001, 2001a, Thomas/Wondra 2002, Jones 2002a-b, Flynn 2000, Hill 2003, Migliore 2004, Inbody 2005, Jones and Lakeland 2005, Webster, Tanner, and Torrance 2009). Especially *Latino/a* or *Hispanic North American systematic theologies* have become more prominent in the last several years (De La Torre and Aponte 2001, Gonzalez and Perez 2002, Valentin 2003, Pedraja 2003, Padilla, Goizueta, Villafane 2005). *Postcolonial theologies* (Keller, Nausner, and Rivera 2004, Keller 2003, 2005, Kwok Pui-lan 2005) as well have taken a prominent place in the theological center, together with recurring and expanding discussions on *postmodern theologies, radical theologies,* and *postliberal theological ethics* (Ward 2005, Bradstock and Rowland 2002, Long 2001, Wells 2004, Oki Ahearn and Gathje 2005, Hauerwas and Wells 2006). *Cultural* and *popular culture studies* as well have taken a central place in theological-anthropological monographs, interwoven with questions on *race and culture* (Cobb 2005, Murphy 2000, Young 2002/1983, Thistlethwaite 2004/1989, Erskine 2005, Hopkins 2005). And even *evangelical systematic theologies* have not been untouched by all these new and recurring concerns in North America (Vanhoozer 2002, 2005, McGrath 2002, 2004, Kärkkäinen 2002a-2004, McLaren 2006, Penner 2005, Smith 2006, 2008, McDermott 2010).

Postmodern Communal Living Together . . . The dissertation itself is an attempt to formulate a *fundamental* and *systematic theology* of a *new and postmodern kind of communal living* in this world. How to *live together in peace as community* (Banks 1994 following a social-science perspective on the Apostle Paul) in this highly complex and ever more fragmented world is the bottom-line concern, vision, and deeply felt need and social hunger of this textual mass of verbiage and imagery, emotive description and reflective theological synthesis (Clapp 1996, Grenz 1994, 1998, Sawyer 2003, Kirkpatrick 2001, Childs 2006). The dissertation follows the dream of a "beloved community" in social history of community organizing in North America—engaging vital issues of *social justice* and *social change* (Harmer 1998, Dudley 2002, Marsh 2005). In this, I have personally learned from one model of community living in the tradition of the *radical Anabaptist movement* of the 16th century—the intentional Mennonite community *Reba Place Fellowship* in Evanston near Chicago (Jackson 1987). The pastoral experience of *communal living*, broken and aborted, torn and uprooted, after a communal and social crisis facing a local community with 14-year-old teenagers taking heroin in some local village in Switzerland, serves as a recurring backdrop and *hermeneutical horizon* to the variously reflected concepts in this dissertation. Theology in the opinion of this author should never lose touch with *everyday moments of human pain*. Theology should stay *immersed* in the daily pain and laughter of the *global* and *local*, as exemplified in the *Plowshares Pilot Immersion Project PIP* of local and global theological education of the *four theological seminaries* in the South Side of Hyde Park in Chicago, in which CTS Chicago Theological Seminary, McCormick Theological Seminary, Lutheran School of Theology at Chicago, and CTU Catholic Theological Union were involving faculty, administration, board members, and students with *local and global partners* in the *Chicago metropolitan area* (Thistlethwaite and Cairns 2003/1994).

Interdisciplinary Theology . . . The dissertation pleads for a new kind of *interdisciplinary theology*. Theology profits from a *new language*, combining and coalescing with the social sciences, ethnographic studies, cultural studies, art theory, critical theory, postmodern theory, narrative theory, feminist theory, cinema theory, postcolonialism, popular

Intentions

culture studies, music theory, (auto)biographical theory, global theory, vocational theory, and many other human, social and ecological sciences as perspectives on the commonly *human, earthly* and *global*. Formulating a systematic theology in a *new language*, playing it in a *new key*, getting more musical about it, while rapping over variously rearranged and recomposed melodies like a DJ would play music, this may be the future for a theology deeply conversant and familiar with the language of the common people on the street, in bars, pubs, shopping malls, on school benches. *North American biblical and systematic theology* is leading the way for this *new vocabulary* (retelling biblical narrative Bandstra 2004, Van Voorst 2004, engaging pop and ethnic culture Cobb 2005, Neafsey 2006, Murphy 2000, Hopkins 2005).

North American Systematic Theology . . . Guiding thread of this dissertation are theological reflections on *power and powerlessness* in *North American systematic theology*. Systematic theology in North America is multifaceted. Dogmatic, fundamental, ethical, cultural, and pastoral issues combine in a different kind of *theological method* which unites the often separate. In comparison to *European usage* where dogmatic and systematic theology are often understood to be a purely theoretical and academic endeavor, most often untouched by the impurities of daily life, *North American systematic theologies* very often combine the *fundamental* with the *practical*, the *dogmatic* with the *pastoral*, the *systematic* with the *ethical*. The lines get blurred, the disciplines intertwined. This dissertation follows the same basic conviction that theology should come out of the pastoral, the practical, the ethical, the social, the ethnographical, the *autobiographical*. Theology will then become most *personal*.

Comparing Continents . . . *Europe* and *North America* seem to produce different kinds of systematic theologies. An important part and proposal of this dissertation is a *contextually comparative perspective* on two very differently developing *theological worlds* (Jennings 1976, 1985a, Jones 1989, Ford and Muers 2005, Livingston and Schüssler Fiorenza 2006, Higgins 2009, Dyrness, Kärkkäinen, Martinez, and Chan 2008) which meet only quite irregularly across the vast and impenetrable distance of the Atlantic. The interchange and conversation between North American and European systematic theologies are still very rare, exceptional, haphazard, and most often just one-sided (Volf, Krieg, and Kucharz 1996, Volf and Welker 2006, following in the tradition of Jürgen Moltmann). This dissertation is an attempt to open up new perspectives and a new vision for a *global conversation*. Fully aware of the contextually very different historical and social worlds in which North American and European theologies are formulated, this dissertation invites to a more global awareness.

Some Limitations . . . This dissertation is a modest attempt at a *first comparison* between geographically and theologically very vast and limitless worlds and most often still very divided continents. Not everything written could be included. Works of authors are used selectively. The dissertation focuses mainly on *monographs* and *basic textbooks* used and discussed in debates and discussions on two theological continents. Articles are mostly left out. This would require another full attention to the small print of theological reflection across continents in its most refined minutia. Most students and faculties get introduced to other worlds—theological and otherwise—through basic textbooks and leading monographs. Intellectual debates in and across specialized journals and collected essays remain secondary to the primary vision and perspective that a fully crafted book offers. The primary comparison of books helps quite often to see the obvious *contrast*. In articles perspectives get blurred, as it opens up some endless and formless reflection. Books and monographs are more like concerts with a clear tone and shape and ending.

Autobiographical . . . The dissertation offers a *theology as autobiography*. Text and project of this dissertation will provide its own justification. A certain audacity is involved in the way this dissertation is presented. Not every dissertation attempts to be so thoroughly and extensively *personal*, mixing and messing up some common disciplinary categories. And yet, the choices in method and style, personal conviction and theological vision are very conscious and intentional.

Joining somehow words and experiences of other *contextual theologies* where moments in common and real life seem to *mess up* common distinctions for an uncommon and new creativity:

> "Virginia Azcuy articulates this pneumatic agency and its consequences for an ecclesial and social ethos in a narrative fashion, by situating in (auto)biography some of the theological conversations that have helped to give shape to her own theological method . . . Latin American and Latino/Latina theology which emerges in great part through a biographical interweaving of conversation and interchange . . . the semantic field of *entreverar* is that the richness and ambiguity of the word reflects an openness to factor in the *messiness* involved in living out theology in the quotidian in the materiality involved in the intersection of the global and the local that is reflected in each of our lives . . ." (Bedford 2006, 39)

Intentions

This dissertation will try to *make friends* with the everyday world of *pain* and *laughter*, hope and sorrow, envisioned dreams and broken communion, in a world in which *power* and *powerlessness* are often quite unequally distributed, but where *friends of Jesus* are invited to live a *new vision* for a *new world*. A new world, more communal, creative, pneumatic, narrative, messy, (auto)biographical, ecclesial, social, ethical, conversational, rich, ambiguous, and *deeply involving* in the everyday world of 14-year-old teenagers and others—looking for some healing *peace*.

1

Trilemmas

Theology may be nothing more than the attempt to make sense of deep-wounded pain and memory. At the crossroads of the past, the present, and the future, theology is trying to speak some word, write some text, compose some symphony of sounding music that heals the soul. Theology for me has always been this kind of a healing word or a soothing sound. Certainly, not everything would qualify in this way. Some verbiage of words and pages, bulks of books and papers, may be put to rest as endless talk. But some books, some texts, some phrases and images, poetry and singing in words can touch your soul. Especially if they touch the wounds of broken souls.

Souls break in the violence of power. Violence can turn powerful and overpowering. Ever since I have been a pastor over the last twenty-eight years in various local churches, ministering to people, places, souls, the question of power and powerlessness has haunted me. Power seems to be a double-bind. Inviting and breaking. Healing and wounding. Embracing and excluding. Giving birth and creating death. Power engenders powerlessness, distributes spaces and places, hands out approval and engraves judgment. Power has blown away whole cities, nations, habitats, faces, stories, biographies, creatures, flowers, pastures, valleys. Power has separated a whole people into the rich and the poor, male and female, white and black, the conqueror and the native, the old and the young, the healthy and the disabled, humans and creation, the one who belongs and the one who is excluded. Power works this way in a most cruel way. Power can become the

The Community of the Weak

death-dealing distributor of violence and destruction creating the broken and wounded in vulnerable places.

Power creates the powerless, distributing the geography of space and place, life and death, along the lines of power and powerlessness. Powerlessness usually is no way to live. It creates permanent seclusion, retreat, enclosure, starving souls, thirsting eyes, demolished visions, as people and nature long for more. And yet, being powerless breaks your back, blocks your soul, smashes your bones, keeps you from moving, living, hoping, laughing, dancing.

To grant the gift of power. To empower. To find one's own inner and outer power in powerlessness. And to invite others to get in touch, to feel, to sense, to uncover, to let power flow again, so that movement and hope may be possible one more time, this may be theology's most honorable call. Theology could become such an empowering vision, letting power flow and flourish, meander and seek its way again. The kind of power that is healing, enlivening, opening up new vision, soul, mind, heart, and faith.

In a world full of violence, because people no longer seem to gather, to commune, to communicate in a way that creates the bonding of hearts, souls, minds, lives, visions, colors, desires, tastes, projects, communal dreaming. Power could empower in a way that this bonding, this dreaming, this uniting of souls into community where people can live and flow, flourish and grow, may become possible again. If power is used differently. In a new way. In a tender way. In a careful way, empowering those without power, the powerless, and calling those with power, the powerful, to a new and different way, more peaceable in its queen- and kingdom-faith and ethics (Hauerwas 1983, Long 2001, Stassen and Gushee 2003, Wells 2004, Hauerwas and Wells 2006). The Jesus way.

Theology, empowering the powerless, may need a new language for a new way. This work is trying to speak a new dialect, walk some new paths. Listen to a new song. A new tune, color, melody, shape, vision. Behind it stands a personal experience that broke my soul, next to many others still breaking. It is an attempt to speak theology in a most personal tone, most autobiographical, most experiential, most vulnerable, most transparent, and yet also most longing for a different vision. A different way.

This work—may it be called an essay in systematic theology— will be strolling along the complexity of our postmodern world where violence and healing are twins always dancing around us as tempting choices in a broken or breaking world. We are thrown into the mix and mess, the crossover and border-crossing, the intermingling and colluding of power and powerlessness, plurality and understanding, violence and healing, the breaking of souls and the creating of community. All this in a world in desperate need of a new kind of power to make life livable. To create an ecology of power letting people and all living things live and grow, flow and flourish, together, being able to breathe its own breath and heartfelt drum to the rhythm of its own beat. Heartfelt in the innermost circle of our most hopeful power.

To find ways and words and emotions and images for this kind of power and vision empowering and envisioning the powerless and broken in an ever more violent world called to live in modern and postmodern communities may be the deepest and most honorable reason for writing any kind of a social and postmodern theology in a new way. This work is one modest attempt at envisioning this kind of a different world as well.

POWER, WRITING, PROJECT, SOCIAL LOCATION

"'Post' means 'after' and 'modern' is 'up to date' or 'now'. Thus, the term 'postmodern' could be translated as 'beyond the now'. What does it mean, or feel like, to be 'beyond the now'? It is fast, on the go, ever-changing, just like life. It flows. To be 'beyond the now' is to live on the edge. This sounds rather Zen-like, and that is not far from the mark. Postmodernism is concerned with non-linear, expressive and supra-rational discourses that have been marginalized and atrophied under the influence of the Enlightenment. To explore the postmodern is to explore ourselves again and to link up with a partially forgotten past." (O'Donnell 2003, 6)

"They propose that society, culture, and lifestyle are today significantly different from what they were a hundred, fifty or even thirty years ago . . . They are concerned with concrete subjects like the developments in mass media, the consumer society and information technology . . . They suggest that these kinds of development have an impact on our understanding of more abstract matters, like meaning, identity and even reality . . . They claim that old styles of analysis are no longer useful,

The Community of the Weak

and that new approaches and new vocabularies need to be created in order to understand the present." (Ward 1997, 5)

"In the postmodern world, people are no longer convinced that knowledge is inherently good. In eschewing the Enlightenment myth of inevitable progress, postmodernism replaces the optimism of the last century with a gnawing pessimism. Gone is the belief that every day, in every way, we are getting better and better. Members of the emerging generation are no longer confident that humanity will be able to solve the world's great problems or even that their economic situation will surpass that of their parents. They view life on earth as fragile and believe that the continued existence of humankind is dependent on a new attitude of cooperation rather than conquest . . . The emphasis on holism among postmoderns is related to their rejection of the second Enlightenment assumption—namely, that truth is certain and hence purely rational. The postmodern mind refuses to limit truth to its rational dimension and thus dethrones the human intellect as the arbiter of truth. There are other valid paths to knowledge besides reason, say the postmoderns, including the emotions and the intuitions . . . Finally, the postmodern mind no longer accepts the Enlightenment belief that knowledge is objective. Knowledge cannot be merely objective, say the postmoderns, because the universe is not mechanistic and dualistic but rather historical, relational, and personal. The world is not simply an objective given that is 'out there', waiting to be discovered and known; reality is relative, indeterminate, and participatory . . . In rejecting the modern assumption of the objectivity of knowledge, postmoderns also reject the Enlightenment ideal of the dispassionate, autonomous knower. They contend that the work of scientists, like that of any other human beings, is historically and culturally conditioned and that our knowledge is always incomplete . . . The postmodern worldview operates with a community-based understanding of truth. It affirms that whatever we accept as truth and even the way we envision truth are dependent on the community in which we participate." (Grenz 1996, 7–8)

Power in Postmodern Times

Power in postmodern times will be the *question* posed by this writing of a dissertation. The experience or suffering, confronting or colluding with power will be the guiding theme all along. People have all kinds of experiences of power, both *healing* and *wounding*. At the same time, power in postmodern times opens a variety of *accompanying themes* popping up as one peels away the outer surface to get to the inner kernel of that which power in postmodern times could mean. *Diversity, plurality, ambiguity, violence, ecology, empathy,* and *community* in postmodern ways are such *concomitant themes* circling around the issues of power. Power participates in the *complexity of a postmodern world* that no longer seems to be so clear, so transparent.

Postmodern life is set and moving in various *trilemmas,* in addition to many dilemmas. This may be the most permanent signature of the postmodern times. Trilemmas have a way to make life active, pulsating, constantly being pushed and pulled backward, forward, to the sides, circling and searching left and right and back and forth in many possible and impossible places. Trilemmas make life *complicated*, and yet enlivening, empowering, energizing, and constantly *moving*. *Dilemmas* have a way to stop the action, to immobilize, to make people startled and *indecisive*. Some turn inactive, others despairing, a third party gets sarcastic or ironic. But nothing moves.

The *trilemma* of *power, powerlessness,* and the *gift of empowering* humans and creatures and all living things of this earth, seen and blessed through God's eyes and vision, will be one fundamental theme guiding this dissertation work. It is a trilemma to live in between these three realities encountered by most people somewhere and sometime in life. *Power* is a reality coloring everything in life. The human arrangements of communal living, the skills and possibilities of individuals and whole communities and nations. At the same time, wherever there is this *power*, there is also *powerlessness* as a twin.

Some people, some creatures, some places, some natural habitats, rocks, flowers, birds, ants become *powerless* when the *powerful* stomp over them. This is one way to experience the consequences and aftermaths of *power*, used in detrimental and life-destructive ways to erase the living from among the living. Power can be used this way, abused, misused, overused. Used against the living, the moving, the dancing, the singing. Power can be used to silence the most beautiful voice. Power can be taken in to eradicate all living things. Power can destroy, break, abuse, wound, bruise, break somebody's back. Then, the *gift of power* turns into the *nightmare* of destruction and the demolition of souls and lives, habitats and dreams.

Power, however, can also be used *differently*. More tenderly, more carefully, more in symphony, more in tune with all living things. Some

The Community of the Weak

would call this *ecological*. An *ecological sensitivity* for the way power paints and rearranges, composes and re-composes the world on canvas, on paper, in musical notes, in the global of the earth. Power is part of life, whether we see it or not, whether we become aware of it or not. Our own power. The power of others. The power of institutions, traditions. The power of nature, the living, the ocean. The power of human relations. The power of our relating to the earth and the sky, the waters and the colors. Everywhere power is greeting us at the door inviting us in to use it or abuse it.

The *powerless* know the effect of *power*. The *dilemma* of being *stuck* in between the *powerful* and the *powerless*, creating a stalemate between the two. Most of the time, nothing changes in arrangements like this. Some turn hopeless, others victorious. Others again resign and turn ironical or despairing. But *nothing changes*, nothing moves, nothing lives in the tension of split and clearly distributed places of power, and the powerless. The *powerless* live on one side of the fence, in the ghetto, in the inner city, in the slums. The *powerful* live somewhere else, in the outskirts, in the suburb, in the rich place, where the power dwells. In between, there is no relating, no communicating, no sharing, no learning *how to live together in peace*, in *shalom*.

A *third element* in the *trilemma* introduces the *movement*. The *gift of empowerment*. Sometimes it just happens. At other times it has to be searched for, called for, awakened, opened, encouraged. Sometimes it arrives as a gift. At other times people have to fight for it. Battles, demonstrations, oppositions, social movements. At all times, however, it may change some things in life. It may make life *moving* again. The *trilemma* that keeps life moving. Slaves in the South of North America did change some things by *singing*. American Natives all over the stolen earth of their homes and habitats did change some things by *dancing*, while publicly *protesting*. *Martin Luther King* did change some things by *dreaming*. Women of all colors, like *Rigoberta Menchu* in Guatemala, and all over the globe, did change some things by *finding their own voices*. Gays and lesbians did change some things by colorfully *parading*. And the poor and the broken, the tortured and the excluded, the exiled and the shunned, the power-stricken and power-smashed did change some things in this world by *weeping and crying*.

Writing in Trilemmas

This dissertation will try to *write in trilemmas*, addressing some fundamental themes and issues in *contemporary North American systematic theology*. The project itself will try to write within such *trilemmas*. Writing in trilemmas may be more confusing, less composed in a polar architecture, less structural, more flowing, twirling, circling. And yet, there is structure and movement in such writing.

One element in the *trilemma* haunting contemporary North American systematic theology nowadays in its attempt to speak a *word of hope* to the people living on this global planet is the *given past* in tradition, handed over to every new generation in texts, memories, and theologies of our foremothers and forefathers from biblical times to the most recent moments. The given past is our calling. At the same time, this given past has also become our *problem*. In need of reading, understanding, listening, interpreting. The given past is no longer such an easy road to travel on without some redirecting of how we take the route.

Another element is the recognition of a *radical plurality* of anything spoken, written, preached, proclaimed, sung, sculpted, crafted as *theology* in all these times ever since the past to the most recent moment. This has made theology most careful, most suspicious, most indecisive, most tentative, most playful, most serious, most indeterminate about many things, avoiding most often a loud and proclaiming voice. Most often, theology has become more whispering, more suggestive, more textual, more meandering in between various positions, names, currents, proposals, leaving things open for the peaceful and reading eye.

However, a third element, seems to intrude and upset the most peaceful writing of any contemporary theology, the *voices of the suffering*. Those who cry, scream, yell, being bruised, wounded, hurt, abused, those voices of the suffering seem to interrupt the playful game calling us to some more earnest questionings of everything we do, in theology as well. The tension is uprooted in a *third way*. No longer are we allowed to remain stalemate in a situation of immobility and restful reading. *Action* and *decision* are called for. Whoever sees someone suffer will not be able to remain indecisive, indeterminate, even tentative, or only suspicious. At the face and vision of the suffering theology will have to *oppose*, to *resist*, to *speak out*, to call for *action*, to live in *discipleship*, even to the *Cross*.

Theology in this kind of a *human trilemma* between the *given past*, the *present mess*, and the *future of all those suffering and aching* among and next to us will never be able to remain just some verbal game. Theology in this postmodern day and age will have to write in trilemmas leading to some new word and action that heals the broken, soothes the wounded, frees the fearful, and empowers the despairing.

The Project of the Dissertation

This dissertation will try to write in a *human trilemma* getting theology *moving*. It could be looked at as an *essay in systematic theology* in postmodern times, trying to keep things together in relationship and community that usually are kept in tension or balance, even split apart and kept separate. It will try to integrate more so than separate. It will try to find coalitions, common or mutual understanding. The dissertation will try to propose an *ecological vision* of things, even for theology itself. Ecology being the *art of living together*. In all diversity, in all biodiversity of living things.

Theology could be more *ecological* in writing as well. Therefore, the *autobiographical* takes up a large space and importance in this dissertation, always connected, tied to, related, put in context, serving as a background melody to things written about. The experience of a local pastor who had to bury a 14-year-old young girl—still a kid, a young teenager—dying of a heroin overdose in 1993 somewhere in a small village in Switzerland will serve as an autobiographical anchorage to everything written. In an experience like this, *power* and *powerlessness*, and the dream of a different world *empowering lives* in the midst of death become most visual, most experiential, and most personal.

Theology will then become jazzier. Improvising on common *standards* of what life brings in terms of *joy and laughter*, but also in terms of *pain and wounding* in moments like this. Methodologically, this dissertation will be *autobiographical* in a *jazzy way*, addressing some of the most current and promising themes in *North American systematic theology today*. Theology understood in this autobiographical way may even be *therapeutic,* most definitely *practical* in guiding the way. Theology in this way may be more like a musical melody, a song, a symphony, a gig, playing as we walk along our Christian way. Giving us tunes, notes, colors, melodic lines, tones, in order to survive some pain. *North American systematic theology* quite often has understood itself in this way, accompanying the walking, the struggling, the searching, the dreaming.

Themes like *power, plurality, violence, ecology,* and *community* will be at the center of my dissertation. Always in relation to some concrete experience made in pastoral ministry. *North American systematic theology* offers many *hopeful visions* for a different kind of world. This dissertation will try to join the sound of music with one more melody in the North American composing of *jazzy symphonies*. As such, it is *one voice* playing along, contributing to the sound, to the jam-session in the course of composing. At the same time, it is a most *personal voice*, recalling many personal moments.

This, to me, would be the best kind of *theology*. Theology speaking from your own most personal moment, laying out the innermost *soul* and *blues* of melodies singing inside of your own most personal dream. Writing in these *postmodern trilemmas*, calling on us for some *new melody* that may empower and enliven *dreams*. Then, theology may again become colloquial, everyday, passing up and down the streets or the alleys somewhere in small villages, larger cities, and even global mega-cities or landscapes wherever people meet, pass by, and are looking for some word of *hope* in the midst of *pain.*

Finding Your Social Location

Theology in this way would find its own *social location*, as any theology speaks out of a particular location. To get in touch with your own most *personal moment*—where your memories are aching, are hurting, where your images of the past and the present are shaking or rejoicing—may be one way to get a feel for where you are. Any sentence spoken or written comes out of the coloring of some personal moment, whether painful or joyful. To become more conscious of theses moments would be the beginning of *good theology*, in academics as well as on the street.

As Swiss and French Christian ethicist *Denis Müller* from the University of Lausanne in Switzerland (Müller 1992, 1998, 1999, 1999a, 2005) recalls and asks of any theology passing along the *rue du Bourg* in the city of *Lausanne*, without forgetting the stairs of the church at *Saint-Laurent* where some of the excluded of society—drug addicts, the poor, the left-alone—quite often find their only public place and sanctuary in an inhospitable world: "Doing theology in the everyday, is this not foremost and first to join the rue du Bourg—without forgetting Saint-Laurent . . . ?" (Müller 1999, 66). With the critical modern and postmodern note: "Is it not, first of all, to join the city, civil society, urban and cosmopolitan, irreducible to our old schemes? And is it not to force ourselves to think the margins which the center cuts off, in formulating the first hypotheses of a 'theology of marginalization'? . . ." (Müller 1999, 66).

This dissertation will be an attempt to think the world—*modern and postmodern*—from the *margins*, highly sensitive to our *social locations* in theology (on social location in theology connecting with Lausanne's rue du Bourg and Saint-Laurent Müller 1999, 63–66). It may be one among many possible hypotheses of a *"theology of marginalization"* in a small and modest way. To experience marginalization close at hand, even in your soul, in your body, in your mind, in your longings for another world, makes you more sensitive to its dynamics. Theology coming out of these engraved, written-in, and *incarnated* and most *physical* moments of *pain* and *hope*, resistance and surrender, survival and breaking down—the Jewish rootedness of Christianity (Reijnen 1998, 215, on the social-scientific Jewish origins of Christianity in New Testament times Duling 2003, 33–51, in systematic theology Williamson 1993, 1999, in Christian ethics Maguire 2004/1993, 2005)—changes your language the way you write theology. It makes it more personal, more social, more *concrete*, more emotional, more physical, more *hands-on* and basic in a simple way.

Therefore, and foremost, most personally, this dissertation will also be an essay in *systematic theology* along *social postmodern ways*, with the *systematic, fundamental, dogmatic* or *doctrinal, ethical, practical,* and *pastoral* joining hands, minds, and hearts, in trying to understand joyful and painful moments in a *personal (auto)biography*. Along these lines, the author speaking in writing will become quite *transparent*, quite vulnerable, quite open. Many vignettes and passages through life will be laid open. A *window into experience* will be opened, even in the midst of pages full of concepts, debates, words, kilobytes and megabytes of dots and letters, sentences and paragraphs, chapters and headings.

Writing in this *personal way* can be a different approach to *do theology* (on theology becoming more polyphonic in Europe Sedmak 1999, 2002, 2003, 2003a, Hilpert/Leimgruber 2008, in North America Taylor 2008, Taylor 1990, 2011), even for a *dissertation*. The *narrative quality* of the text may be judged on its own and vulnerable tone. The *witnessing vision* may not always look, if ever, for validation, but it may invite into a *convictional world* (McClendon 1990, 2000, 2002, McClendon and Smith 1975, 1994, De La Torre 2004) full of good *reasons* for *acting* and *believing* out of *discipleship-faith in Jesus* (on systematic theology as discipleship-faith Yoder 1972/1994, Hauerwas 1983, McClendon 1986, 1990, 1994, 2000, 2002, Finger 2004, for a spirituality of discipleship in the Anabaptist radical tradition Augsburger 2006, following Yoder, Hauerwas, and McClendon). The *cry of the wounded* may be validation on its own. As an academic contribution to *systematic theology* it invites to a different place, and yet still a place set in the theological landscape of words and images, calling for *action* and *social change* while giving a reason for its deepest *hope* (1 Peter 3:15).

2

The Social

DIFFERENCE

"The preoccupation with difference is as central to political activism as it is to current theoretical debates. While mainstream politicians, both Democratic and Republican, deny the validity of difference in their critique of 'special interest groups', a resolute embrace of difference marked the populist Rainbow Coalition of Jesse Jackson. Iris Young, for example, contrasts the Enlightenment ideal of the civil public 'in which persons unite for a common purpose in terms of equality and mutual respect' with the public created in the Rainbow Coalition . . . While the Rainbow Coalition 'includes commitment to equality and mutual respect among participants, the idea of the Rainbow Coalition specifically preserves and institutionalizes in its form of organizational discussion the heterogeneous groups that make it up' . . . The aims of equality and respect are met by highlighting differences, not by transcending them or looking beneath them for a common foundation." (Welch 1991, 83)

"Consider, for example, Michel Foucault's analyses of different discourses in our history: . . . the discourses of penology, medicine, law, sexuality, madness, and reason, indeed the discourse on discourse itself in the modern development of disciplines and specializations. What these analyses show is that every discourse bears within itself the anonymous and repressed actuality of highly particular arrangements of power and knowledge. Every

discourse, by operating under certain assumptions, necessarily excludes other assumptions. Above all, our discourses exclude those others who might disrupt the established hierarchies or challenge the prevailing hegemony of power . . . And yet, the voices of the others multiply: . . . the hysterics and mystics speaking through Lacan; the mad and the criminals allowed to speak by Foucault; the primal peoples, once misnamed the primitives, defended and interpreted by Eliade; the dead whose story the victors still presume to tell; the repressed suffering of peoples cheated of their own experience by modern mass media; the poor, the oppressed, and the marginalized—all those considered 'nonpersons' by the powerful but declared by the great prophets to be God's own privileged ones. All the victims of our discourses and our history have begun to discover their own discourses in ways that our discourse finds difficult to hear, much less listen to. Their voices can seem strident and uncivil—in a word, other. And they are. We have all just begun to sense the terror of that otherness. But only by beginning to listen to those other voices may we also begin to hear the otherness within our own discourse and within ourselves. What we might then begin to hear, above our own chatter, are possibilities we have never dared to dream."
(Tracy 1987, 79)

"Giving singular attention to domination alone can also entail unfavorable consequences. First, a program of resisting domination, without the other two postmodern emphases, easily fails to actualize its own envisioned strategies for achieving justice and freedom from oppression. Without developing a sense of plurality, the struggle to be free from domination can founder on the divisiveness that springs up among agents for change who work with different visions of 'the just' and from different experiences of oppression. Moreover, without a sense of tradition (some tradition of myth and ritual, at least, not necessarily the established Traditions), the struggle is impoverished, lacking the resources of communal memory and symbolic heritage that often provide some minimal dialogical consensus for marshaling critique and action." (Taylor 1990, 41)

The Community of the Weak

Social Postmodernism and Oppression

Postmodern Variations

This work will present some first proposals and preliminary sketches in *systematic theology* in a *social and postmodern new way*. Prophecies and predictions of the *post-modern* in theology may be as old as 1964, or even 1948, when Dutch theologian *Johannes Christiaan Hoekendijk*, working 1949–1952 in the unit for Evangelization of the *World Council of Churches* in Geneva in Switzerland, teaching mission theology years later from 1965–1975 at the Union Theological Seminary in New York City, already predicted a *postmodern future* for the churches, or more precisely, predicted the *end of the churches* in their traditional form (on the first uses of the word postmodern in theology Hoekendijk 1964, 9).

Theology will be introduced both as *social* and *postmodern*, closely in touch with hurting *bruises* and aching *wounds* engraved and stricken by *power*. Power and its twin brother or sister in the distribution of *powerlessness* in this world are the guiding thread leading through everything. Sometimes addressed, sometimes just hinted at, sometimes taken into the limelight in its most vocal outspokenness, sometimes just silently humming along. Juxtaposing *power* and the *postmodern* in this world which is our own, while at the same time searching for *new visions* how theology, in particular *North American systematic theology*, is humming along these new melodies in this *postmodern world* (in social science perspective Ritzer 1997, Ward 1997, Berger 2003, Featherstone 2007, Mouzelis 2008, in theology Hart 2004, Ward 1997, 2005, Penner 2005), will be the general intent of this theological essay in search of some common new ground.

Postmodernism in North American systematic theology in these days is omnipresent, having taken a central and all-determining place in most recent publications (Tracy 1987, Taylor 1990, Tilley 1995, Grenz 1996, Lakeland 1997, Grenz and Franke 2001, Riggs 2003, Musser and Price 2003, 392–394, Vanhoozer 2003, Ward 2005, Penner 2005, Smith 2006, 2008). And yet, the definition of the term is as elusive and confusing as the constantly changing use of terminology from *postmodernity, postmodernism, late modernism, hyper-modernism*, or *the postmodern*. The postmodern seems to be as *varied* as the postmodern itself.

In addition, terminology gets highly confusing, as both *process theologians* use it, mainline and feminist, classical *liberals* use it and even *evangelicals* use it. The distribution between *Roman Catholics* skirting the word and social phenomenon and *Protestants* dancing around it seems to be about even in score. Definitions vary, but the omnipresent challenge of *the postmodern* seems to be acknowledged and omnipresent.

African American *Cornel West* is called *postmodern*, together with Roman Catholic *John Paul II*, formerly secular and radical theologian *Harvey Cox* turns postmodern, as much as feminists like *Mary Daly* or *Sallie McFague*. Some are radically *purifying*—Mark. C. Taylor—or *politically liberating*—Cornell West, Mary Daly, Sallie McFague—in being postmodern, others more *preserving* - George Lindbeck, Paul Holmer, Brevard Childs—as a distinguishing quality of the *postmodern* (Griffin/Beardslee/Holland 1989, Riggs 2003, Penner 2005). The sheer variety of postmodern theologies is mind-boggling and concept-confusing. But this may be the nature of the definition of the postmodern.

Roman Catholic systematic theologian *Terrence W. Tilley* in his helpful overview *Postmodern Theologies* (Tilley 1995) edits playfully contradictory categories and contributions to get a first taste for the presented general menu of a confusing variety of *the postmodern* in *contemporary systematic theology*, fundamental and dogmatic—, thereby juxtaposing people and trends, authors and theological representatives that at first glance seem to be surprising to be joining the crowd of postmodernity.

Helmut Peukert, Paul Lakeland, Francis Schüssler Fiorenza, and *Edmund Arens* join the first crowd of *constructive postmodernisms* in *post-Habermasian* fashion for a theology of communicative action, followed by *process theology* with *David Ray Griffin*, and *David Tracy's revisionism*, while among the next crowd, the *postmodern dissolutions*, we find memories of death-of-God *Thomas J. J. Altizer*, as well as the radical deconstructivism and a/theology of *Mark C. Taylor*, redeemed a little in its ground-smashing radicalism by the saintly narratives of *Edith Wyschogrod*. An intermediary position is taken up by *George Lindbeck* as *intertextual postmodernism* of the postliberal sort, with critical thoughts by *John Milbank* pointing out the dangers of being too much in love with some form of postmodernism for the wrong reasons. *Political theologies of communal praxis* finish up the *postmodern roundabout*, with *Gustavo Gutierrez, Sharon Welch*, and *James McClendon* making up a surprising and concluding crowd, in spite of obvious differences, but united in the communal approach to a political and practical theology that could be looked at as being of the *postmodern type* (Tilley 1995).

The Community of the Weak

Postmodern Defining

To *define* the postmodern is almost impossible, and yet various attempts at *defining* may give a first impression what we are getting in, or for that matter, what we may be getting out of. As *post-expert* and Roman Catholic *Terrence W. Tilley* puts it succinctly: "Manifestos appear with disheartening regularity, announcing that our era is postmodern, postchristian, postreligious, postcolonial, postindustrial, postideological, postmoral, postanalytic, postliterate, postnarrative, postauthorial, postpersonal, poststructuralist, postliberal . . ." (Tilley 1995, vi). After the inflation of everything being *post-*, there may be nothing more to say. But we are definitely living in some age that is *post everything else*, if we believe it. And what we may agree on, is quite minimally but certainly the general and widespread feeling: "Ambiguity and uncertainty stamp the post-age" (Tilley 1995, vi).

Art historian *Richard Appignanesi* and cartoonist *Chris Garratt* in their co-authored and highly picturesque *Postmodernism for Beginners* (Appignanesi and Garratt 1995), a good place to begin with if one does not know how to enter into the vastly confusing new world of the postmodern, phrase it quite mystically, leavening things as open as the postmodern future may be. Playing with the *word "post-"*, asking the entering question what postmodernism may actually mean, they come up with a few suggestively leading possibilities, like "a result of modernism", "the aftermath of modernism", "the afterbirth of modernism", "the development of modernism", "the denial of modernism", and last, but not least in the mind-mapping list, "the rejection of modernism" (Appignanesi and Garratt 1995, 4). After this, we probably do not know any more what it may mean. However, a basic agreement seems to be that we do live now, because of postmodernism, in a "mix-and-match of some or all of these meanings", in other words, as anyone could see, "a confusion of meanings", but most definitely in a time and age where the modern "has been surpassed by a new age" (Appignanesi and Garratt 1995, 4), whatever this may mean.

Others give a more *poetic definition*, leaving it to the reader to figure out what it may mean. Like Anglican priest and philosopher-theologian *Kevin O'Donnell* in his easy and accessible primer on postmodernism:

> "'Post' means 'after' and 'modern' is 'up to date' or 'now'. Thus, the term 'postmodern' could be translated as 'beyond the now'. What does it mean, or feel like, to be 'beyond the now'? It is fast, on the go, ever-changing, just like life. It flows. To be 'beyond the now' is to live on the edge. This sounds rather Zen-like, and that is not far from the mark. Postmodernism is concerned with

non-linear, expressive and supra-rational discourses that have been marginalized and atrophied under the influence of the Enlightenment. To explore the postmodern is to explore ourselves again and to link up with a partially forgotten past." (O'Donnell 2003, 6)

The concept may still be as elusive as before, but you get some more feeling and intuition for what the new sentiment of living in a new time and age may be. This feeling and intuitive premonition with a taste for the *new times* is further intensified by art und music theorist *Glenn Ward* in his *Teach Yourself Postmodernism* (Ward 1997), explaining to us the postmodern in the way some small pocket-philosophy and cultural theory, political science and sociology can be carried along in a *Teach-Yourself* booklet to quickly look at. The *new themes* of postmodernism describe to us a *new world* in which we already live in these present times:

". . . They propose that society, culture, and lifestyle are today significantly different from what they were a hundred, fifty or even thirty years ago . . . They are concerned with *concrete* subjects like the developments in mass media, the consumer society and information technology . . . They suggest that these kinds of development have an impact on our understanding of more *abstract* matters, like meaning, identity and even reality . . . They claim that old styles of analysis are no longer useful, and that new approaches and new vocabularies need to be created in order to understand the present." (Ward 1997, 5)

Postmodernism has entered all the fields of academic teaching and researching, writing and publishing, even in biblical studies and theology. As evangelical systematic theologian *Kevin J. Vanhoozer* observes: "In fact, 'postmodern' has become a gregarious adjective, and can often be seen in the company of such respectable terms as 'literature', 'philosophy', 'architecture', 'art', 'history', 'science', 'cinema'—and ,yes, even 'biblical studies' and 'theology'" (Vanhoozer 2003, 3). And yet, to make things a little bit more complicated, Roman Catholic fundamental as well as postmodern theologian *David Tracy* can claim that "there is no such phenomenon as postmodernity" (Tracy 1999, 170), as there is more than one, there are several "postmodernities" (Vanhoozer 2003, 3).

Baptist evangelical Stanley J. Grenz talks about a *postmodern mind,* a *postmodern mood,* or a *postmodern consciousness.* This captures better the general feeling and life attitude behind confusing concepts that nevertheless are shaping contemporary approaches to daily as well as academic life.

"In the postmodern world, people are no longer convinced that knowledge is inherently good. In eschewing the Enlightenment myth of inevitable progress, postmodernism replaces the optimism of the last century with a gnawing pessimism. Gone is the belief that every day, in every way, we are getting better and better. Members of the emerging generation are no longer confident that humanity will be able to solve the world's great problems or even that their economic situation will surpass that of their parents. They view life on earth as fragile and believe that the continued existence of humankind is dependent on a new attitude of cooperation rather than conquest . . . The emphasis on holism among postmoderns is related to their rejection of the second Enlightenment assumption—namely, that truth is certain and hence purely rational. The postmodern mind refuses to limit truth to its rational dimension and thus dethrones the human intellect as the arbiter of truth. There are other valid paths to knowledge besides reason, say the postmoderns, including the emotions and the intuitions . . . Finally, the postmodern mind no longer accepts the Enlightenment belief that knowledge is objective. Knowledge cannot be merely objective, say the postmoderns, because the universe is not mechanistic and dualistic but rather historical, relational, and personal. The world is not simply an objective given that is 'out there', waiting to be discovered and known; reality is relative, indeterminate, and participatory . . . In rejecting the modern assumption of the objectivity of knowledge, postmoderns also reject the Enlightenment ideal of the dispassionate, autonomous knower. They contend that the work of scientists, like that of any other human beings, is historically and culturally conditioned and that our knowledge is always incomplete . . . The postmodern worldview operates with a community-based understanding of truth. It affirms that whatever we accept as truth and even the way we envision truth are dependent on the community in which we participate." (Grenz 1996, 7–8)

Put this way, the *postmodern mind* seems kind attractive, contemporary, and to the point. One final aspect, underlined over and over again, is the *mixing* of everything that normally is not put together. The postmodern mind is less concerned about systematic thinking, but rather likes "mixing elements of what traditionally has been considered incompatible . . ." (Grenz 1996, 7–8). Mixing the incompatible, like a DJ at the music desk getting his grooves going. Artistic *collage*, *pastiche*, and "*messy texts*" (on the cultural-ethnographic and social-scientific concept of "messy texts"

Denzin 1997a, XVII–XVIII), combining what is usually not visually seen or audibly heard, seriously considered or naturally built together, messing up a neat and tidy world a little bit, are called for. In *theology—systematic, fundamental,* and *dogmatic*—as well.

With the poetic and deconstructing words of North American Roman Catholic *David Tracy*, pointing out the potential for *resistance* in the postmodern collage of the unruly and unsystematic mixing of everything:

> "In postmodernity, resistance may take the form of a breaking of all the codes of traditional narratives in order to allow language and history to disrupt the self of the reader. Resistance may be Nietzsche's joyous affirmation of plurality itself, alive again in the unstable ironies of Barthes, de Man, and Derrida, alive as well in the encyclopedias become labyrinths of Borges. Resistance also may take the form of Foucault's 'dry-as-dust' archival research on the institutions and almost impenetrable codes of power and knowledge in all historical and scientific discourses."
> (Tracy 1987, 83)

Playing with the unsystematic, the joyfully plural, the upcoming ironies and laid-out labyrinths, willfully mixing und messing up things, being untidy in academics, even a little in a dissertation, may be one way too to be politically *resistant* to the unspoken and outspoken codes of power and knowledge that assume how things should be done. Here, the postmodern is turning *political, social,* and *critical,* in spite of, or because of itself.

Postmodernism Turning Social

Quite regularly, the postmodern is accused of being *unpolitical,* and at its worst *neoconservative* (Habermas 1987 and 1989 describing postmodern thinkers as neo-conservative). Roman Catholic theologian and critical theorist *Paul Lakeland* (Lakeland 1990) can say: "The postmodern sensibility, let me suggest, is nonsequential, noneschatological, nonutopian, nonsystematic, nonfoundational, and, ultimately, nonpolitical" (Lakeland 1997, 8). Pleading for a theology and ecclesiology of protest and emancipatory communicative action, following *Jürgen Habermas, Helmut Peukert, Charles Davis,* and *Johann Baptist Metz,* the vision is more that of a clear political and social stand as regards to a suffering world than on postmodern playfulness, often seen and witnessed in postmodern circles. Facing the horrors of this world, there may not be time for intellectual deconstructions and postmodern play. "In the late capitalist Western world that is most responsible for the set of circumstances that make up postmodernity, the Christian church remains the prevalent religious tradition. Its potential to be both a protest and an alternative may thus be crucial, not only for those who live in this world, but also for those upon whom this wealthy world visits even greater horrors" (Lakeland 1990, 242).

However, the postmodern seems to be more than just playful deconstruction and ironic but non-committal affirmations of pluralism, as Roman Catholic fundamental theologian *David Tracy* points out. The critical potential of postmodern questionings touches the deepest level of all our common and social arrangements of *power* and *knowledge*. Thereby, the postmodern can become highly *political, social, critical,* even *prophetic*, uncovering discourses and practices of exclusion, hegemonies of definitions, and repressed sufferings of the marginalized, the powerless, the poor, the cheated, the mad, the mystics, the criminals, women, children, Natives, Coloreds, the oppressed and left-asides from common life and acceptance definitions, as *the others* that nobody considers as human persons. There may be a *prophetic kind of postmodernism* in touch with the prophetic traditions of biblical literature. In this, in good company with radical deconstructions of common and uncommon discourses by *Michel Foucault* and others, a postmodern theology may turn highly *subversive* and radically *political*:

> "Consider, for example, Michel Foucault's analyses of different discourses in our history: . . . the discourses of penology, medicine, law, sexuality, madness, and reason, indeed the discourse on discourse itself in the modern development of disciplines and specializations. What these analyses show is that every discourse bears within itself the anonymous and repressed actuality of highly particular arrangements of power and knowledge. Every discourse, by operating under certain assumptions, necessarily excludes other assumptions. Above all, our discourses exclude those others who might disrupt the established hierarchies or challenge the prevailing hegemony of power . . . And yet, the voices of the others multiply: . . . the hysterics and mystics speaking through Lacan; the mad and the criminals allowed to speak by Foucault; the primal peoples, once misnamed the primitives, defended and interpreted by Eliade; the dead whose story the victors still presume to tell; the repressed suffering of peoples cheated of their own experience by modern mass media; the poor, the oppressed, and the marginalized—all those considered 'nonpersons' by the powerful but declared by the great prophets to be God's own privileged ones. All the victims

of our discourses and our history have begun to discover their own discourses in ways that our discourse finds difficult to hear, much less listen to. Their voices can seem strident and uncivil—in a word, other. And they are. We have all just begun to sense the terror of that otherness. But only by beginning to listen to those other voices may we also begin to hear the otherness within our own discourse and within ourselves. What we might then begin to hear, above our own chatter, are possibilities we have never dared to dream." (Tracy 1987, 79)

Theology and Social Postmodernism

Postmodernism does not, therefore, have to become by necessity nonpolitical. A *social postmodernism* can be found (combining the social with the postmodern Nicholson and Seidman 1995). Theology most often has associated postmodernism with the *nonpolitical* and the *asocial*, a limitless play and irony of senseless meaning in the endless deconstruction of dissolving meaning, the destruction of subjects and major narratives, political visions and social empowerment, leading to a radical relativism with no real potential for *social change, political resistance*, and *communal action* for a better world. It seems to be high time to look at all this again and to revise some preconceived and false concepts about what *the postmodern* as a new *transforming and liberating social empowerment* may be (Tracy 1987, Tilley 1995, Hodgson 1994, Jones and Lakeland 2005 Taylor 1990, 2011).

A *fundamental theology* for the twenty-first century would be well advised to take up the challenge to develop a *social and critical postmodern theology* in open dialogue with *social postmodernism* (on the postmodern in systematic theology Hodgson 1994, 53–66) that speaks a constructive word of prophecy to the many break-ups, break-downs, and break-aparts in the violent social and personal fragmenting and suffering of this global world. This prophetic-empathic *postmodern social listening* in real life, as well as in theology, my open up new political visions, when those newly heard voices suddenly "discover their own discourses in ways that our discourse finds difficult to hear, much less listen to . . .", since fragmenting and suffering, they may seem "strident and uncivil—in a word, other" (Tracy 1987, 79). And yet, we may listen politically and socially.

Social postmodernism will become the most interesting *dialogue partner* for *systematic theology* in the process of changing to a *new paradigm* for a new century. Paradigmatic changes as major earthquakes in intellectual and scientific thinking have always happened along the history of theology and the sciences (King and Hodgson 1994, 1–34). Now it seems that the time has come to go one step further and cross the seeming line of *the modern into the postmodern*. What this means for *theology— systematic, fundamental* and *dogmatic—*is still to be discovered.

Social Postmodernism Coalitional

Feminist social theorist *Linda Nicholson* and postmodern sociologist *Steven Seidman* have helped to put postmodernism in a different *social setting*, gathering some of the most progressive authors in the social sciences in North America for a new kind of *social postmodernism* (Nicholson and Seidman 1995, Seidman 2008). Radical on all ends, without giving up old allegiances, the postmodern turns *social* in a most comprehensive and creative way, contesting suffering and pain (Giroux 1983, 1991, 1992, 1997, 2011, Giroux and McLaren 1994, McLaren 1995, 2005, Denzin 1989, 1997a, 2003, Featherstone 2007, Mouzelis 2008).

In times for open and true confession, *Steven Seidman* can say: "Before I was a postmodernist, I was a Marxist" (Nicholson and Seidman 1995, 1). The convictional change from Marxism to postmodernism leads through *identity politics,* the *new social movements,* and the politics of the *body, race, gender,* and *sexuality. Linda Nicholson* adds her personal memories of changing social convictions: "As with Steve, Marxism was for me a means of making sense of many of the political and psychological sentiments which came out of my early years" (Nicholson and Seidman 1995, 5). The conversion to postmodernism in later years happened "because it seemed to provide a label by which to name this common problem I saw in Marxism, feminism, and liberal understandings of reason and knowledge: the tendency in elements of all to forget that what they were calling 'reason' or 'history' or 'women' came out of a particular context and were implicated in relations of power . . . As this power was coming into question, so might also the ways of theorizing knowledge which had attended it. The term 'postmodern' seemed to provide a name for this break" (Nicholson and Seidman 1995, 7). *The postmodern* as a radical *break* in one's ways of seeing the world, this may be the best definition so far.

All these disputed topics mentioned—*identity, new social movements, body, race, gender, sexuality,* and we may add *class* and *age, health* and *knowledge—*do certainly not in any way allow for a nonpolitical

The Social

reading of the social in the postmodern. On the contrary. A *postmodern social theory* can become even more *political*, more *radical*, and even more *liberating*, just in a different way (for postmodern social theory/sociology becoming radical and liberating Feagin and Vera 2001). Linda Nicholson and Steven Seidman develop such an approach, even with the awareness of possible pitfalls along the way. Social oppression, global injustice, a society of violence, and the exposing of sites of conflict and inequality are still part of a postmodernism turning social. The move to a postmodern concept of the social will still be "productive for generating conceptual and political strategies that can continue to expose inequalities, oppressions, forms of social injustice, and sites of conflict and change in societies that mix modern and postmodern features" (Nicholson and Seidman 1995, 35).

Postmodernism has its origin in the various *critical traditions* of a Western self-critical reflection looking at itself. "As a way of thinking about knowledge, self, society, and politics, postmodernism has roots in the struggles over social life that have been at the center of many Western societies in the past few decades" (Nicholson and Seidman 1995, 34). A postmodernism turning social will therefore *creatively integrate* these various critical traditions that have moved things, bettered society, and changed the world.

A *postmodern collage* of *creative coalition building* is called for, combining and mixing the best in the various critical traditions in social theory, as a radical and *social postmodernism*, the way *Linda Nicholson* and *Steven Seidman* with many other included authors conceive it, "makes possible a politics of coalition building, a cultural politics of social tolerance and difference, a critical politics of knowledge, and an affirmation of particular, local struggles without disavowing the possibilities of broader forms of social solidarity and political mobilization" (Nicholson and Seidman 1995, 35).

Coalitional thinking (in social theory and fundamental theology Clarke 1989 and Wetherilt 1994) in the postmodern way *turning social* has no real problem with combining things, if it serves the betterment of the world. Seeming oppositions and built-up contradictions may not hold anymore, encouraged by a hopeful and "possible move beyond the antinomy of 'radical modernism' (Marxism, feminism, Afrocentrism, gay liberationism) and postmodern deconstruction: a theoretical perspective which refashions both into a new language of radical democratic theory and politics" (Nicholson and Seidman 1995, 35).

The Community of the Weak

Social postmodernism can be highly sensitive to an aching and suffering world, torn between epidemic hunger and chronic poverty, repeated oppression and solidified inequality, out-breaking violence and up-coming renewals in segregation, purposed social exclusion and systemic radical extinction. All these various forms and analyses of *power*, the *abuse of power, powerlessness*, and the miracle of *empowering people*—coalitional, in moving and changing the world—can be an integral part of a social postmodernism that definitely will not be nonpolitical. On the contrary. Whenever a community is experiencing the break-down of shared values, common beliefs, mutual recognition, and the basic right for everyone *to be*, postmodernism the social way moves in as a basic and fundamental challenge, the way teenagers taking heroin at the age of 14 in some local village in well-protected Switzerland make it happen that social and postmodern questions challenge anyone being part of modernity.

Fundamental Theology Turning Postmodern and Social

Systematic and political theologian *Mark Lewis/Kline Taylor* from *Princeton Theological Seminary* presents in his autobiographical and theological *Remembering Esperanza* (Taylor 1990) a *fundamental theology of cultural-political praxis* for the North American context, pointing to the *postmodern trilemma* that modern and postmodern systematic theology finds itself in (on the postmodern trilemma Taylor 1990, 23–45).

Holding in tension and keeping present the three challenges of modern-day theology—a respectful *sense for tradition*, a conscious *celebration of plurality*, and a convinced *resistance to domination*—, a postmodern theology for the North American context will be *political* and *cultural* at the same time, clearly opposing any form of oppression and violence, domination and social exclusion, enacted most destructively in the various demeaning and dehumanizing forms of classism, sexism, racism, or ageism. A *postmodern fundamental theology* turning *social* does not have to be colluding, condoning, or silently passive towards human oppression. A postmodern perspective of the social, on the contrary, will make systematic and fundamental theology more sensitive, more prophetic, and more outraged at any attempt to break the human soul and the human body.

Even one of the most central aspects of postmodernism, the *celebration of difference*, lends itself to a *stance of resistance* against any form of domination, and does not have to lead to a passive acceptance of the simple fact of pluralistic difference. Postmodernism comes in two possible forms, a "postmodernism of reaction", and a "postmodernism of resistance" (Foster 1983, xi–xii, Taylor 1990, 32, 38).

A *postmodernism of reaction* stays detached, unmoved, lacking any left-over political or social stance, watching the play and endless turnaround of plural worlds with no more guiding perspective, marveling at its aesthetic and artistic variety, complexion, color, but moving nowhere and no one. At the same time, a postmodernism of reaction can also become quite nostalgic, retreating to some paradise lost of times long time gone, pasts overcome, traditions abolished, inviting basically to a new and conservative return to a premodern-postmodern world.

A *postmodernism of resistance*, on the contrary, envisions another and newly created world, still celebrating the pluralism of difference, but also formulating "strategies that are both subversive of and resistant to the status quo . . ." (Taylor 1990, 32).

Mark Kline Taylor refers to North American *Derrida-philosopher John D. Caputo* in his *Radical Hermeneutics*, describing the new *postmodern ethics* of a community celebrating difference in a flux of lacking metaphysical grounds to stand on, but still being able to develop the moral force to challenge "constellations of power, centers of control and manipulation, which systematically dominate, regulate, exclude . . ." (Caputo 1987, 260, Taylor 1990, 39). Celebrating the different, quite to the contrary, can radically enliven and empower a critical and oppositional stance to protect the different, to fight the violence of monomythic logic, to oppose any attempt to make those suffer who do not conform or fit in. Concurring with *John D. Caputo*, and underlining the moral strength of a stance on difference, *Mark Kline Taylor* continues that, "in order to do justice to the special suffering known by the victims of systems", such *a postmodern ethic*, with *John D. Caputo*, needs to "take its stand" with "women, children, the mad, the ill, the poor, blacks, the religious and moral minorities" (Caputo 1987, 264, Taylor 1990, 39).

The Postmodern Trilemma

The *postmodern trilemma* requires the constant attention to all three traits of a social postmodernism, *respect for tradition, celebration of plurality*, and *resistance to oppression*. "In the case of postmodernism's three traits, each presents a demand that invites attention and development: to acknowledge tradition, to celebrate plurality, and to resist domination—all three together" (Taylor 1990, 40). It needs all three to construct a new kind of *postmodern fundamental theology* open for *radical social critique* and *communal social action*. The balance between the three elements is *dynamic*, reflecting the social location in which theology finds itself.

Mark Kline Taylor describes it well, pointing out the detrimental effects of just focusing on one aspect at the expense of the other co-relevant elements:

> "Giving singular attention to *domination* alone can also entail unfavorable consequences. First, a program of resisting domination, without the other two postmodern emphases, easily fails to actualize its own envisioned strategies for achieving justice and freedom from oppression. Without developing a sense of plurality, the struggle to be free from domination can founder on the divisiveness that springs up among agents for change who work with different visions of 'the just' and from different experiences of oppression. Moreover, without a sense of tradition (*some* tradition of myth and ritual, at least, not necessarily the established Traditions), the struggle is impoverished, lacking the resources of communal memory and symbolic heritage that often provide some minimal dialogical consensus for marshalling critique and action." (Taylor 1990, 41)

A *social postmodernism* conceived in this way is no easy posture, both in theology and in the social sciences. And yet, it is a possible-impossible position, constantly at variance with living situations and ethical callings that change and transform previous positions. But the *stance on oppression* remains an integral part of this kind of a social postmodernism wanting to change the world. It is "by no means an easily maintained posture" (Taylor 1990, 40), and yet *Mark Kline Taylor* identifies and enlists a whole crowd of possible companions in *systematic and fundamental theology* trying to follow this narrow path of a social-critical postmodern.

John Cobb, Francis Schüssler Fiorenza, Gordon Kaufman, Sallie McFague, Langdon Gilkey, and *Rosemary Radford Ruether,* among others, join the illustrious and highly ecumenical crowd (Taylor 1990, 40), not to forget *David Tracy,* Mark Kline Taylor's doctoral father, even though not mentioned. All of them classical liberals in the North American theological way of life, but critically aware, like *Langdon Gilkey,* that a postmodernism or radical pluralism so dear to North American academics "is toothless if one faces oppression" (Gilkey 1985, 728, Taylor 1990, 40).

Rainbow Coalitions

It seems that it is time for *rainbow coalitions*, in theology—systematic, fundamental, and dogmatic—as well. A *postmodern fundamental theology* will not lose its identity if it becomes more colorful, varied, the way the world is anyway. Colorful, kaleidoscopic, multivocal, polyphonic. Too often theologies have turned out quite mono-cultural and outright boring in sticking to one color, one focus, one allegiance, one commitment in style. In a postmodern world, this will no longer do. The world is too big, too various, too melodious, too colorful to stick to one particular style.

Jesse Jackson, former candidate for U.S. presidency, African American, Democrat, and radical Christian as well as social activist, change agent and fascinating preacher—as I heard him one time live during a plenary session at the *World Council of Churches* in Geneva—, created a Rainbow Coalition to change U.S. society and the world. Theology as well may be asked in this inaugurating twenty-first century to create a new kind of radical *Rainbow Coalition*—social, political, cultural, theological—to change the world.

North American and feminist theologian *Sharon Welch* in her contribution to postmodern cultural and educational theorist *Henry A. Giroux's* edited *Postmodernism, Feminism, and Cultural Politics* (Giroux 1991) on an "Ethic of Solidarity and Difference" highlights the creative vision and social potential of such a concept of the Rainbow Coalition in modern-day and postmodern society (Welch 1991). Trying to give an answer to her introducing question: "How can the differences that create our particular identities, differences of race, ethnicity, sexual orientation, class and gender, best be recognized, affirmed and understood?" (Welch 1991, 83), she refers to *Jesse Jackson's Rainbow Coalition* as a new model of political and social action with a promising practical as well as theoretical future.

> "The preoccupation with difference is as central to political activism as it is to current theoretical debates. While mainstream politicians, both Democratic and Republican, deny the validity of difference in their critique of 'special interest groups', a resolute embrace of difference marked the populist Rainbow Coalition of Jesse Jackson. Iris Young, for example, contrasts the Enlightenment ideal of the civil public 'in which persons unite for a common purpose in terms of equality and mutual respect' with the public created in the Rainbow Coalition . . . While the Rainbow Coalition 'includes commitment to equality and mutual respect among participants, the idea of the Rainbow

The Community of the Weak

> Coalition specifically preserves and institutionalizes in its form of organizational discussion the heterogeneous groups that make it up' . . . The aims of equality and respect are met by *highlighting differences*, not by transcending them or looking beneath them for a common foundation." (Welch 1991, 83, Young 1987, 76)

Border Crossings

Henry A. Giroux, North American cultural theorist, radical educational scholar and critical postmodern pedagogue emphasizes in his *Border Crossings* (Giroux 1992) the need for new spaces to remap the postmodern world in order to create new human possibilities to resist and change the world. Amazingly open and receptive as a critical and radical theorist in interdisciplinary fashion for what some of the most progressive theologies—feminist, postcolonial, postmodern like *Cornell West* or *Sharon Welch* (Giroux 1992, 20, 248, 132-133)—have to contribute to a critical and cultural theory of human possibilities in a postmodern world, *Henry A. Giroux* presents some of the most hopeful and inclusive concepts in *social postmodernism* available to this day.

A fundamental concept of *Henry A. Giroux* for a *social and postmodern revisioning of the world* is the remapping and border crossing of *new spaces*. The postmodern challenge is the necessity to rearrange our common living, thinking, and believing arrangements in radically new ways, reaching out for new places, new territories, new geographies of the social. Old notions of what may be at the center, what may be at the periphery, what may be crucial and what may be accidental, what may be primary, and what may be secondary, are falling apart. Our whole *cognitive and social map* in the way we have been used to looking at the world needs to be redrawn in new ways.

> "The old modernist notions of center and margin, home and exile, and familiar and strange are breaking apart. Geographic, cultural, and ethnic borders are giving way to shifting configurations of power, community, space, and time. Citizenship can no longer ground itself in forms of Eurocentrism and the language of colonialism. New spaces, relationships, and identities have to be created that allow us to move across borders, to engage difference and otherness as part of a discourse of justice, social engagement, and democratic struggle. Academics can no

longer retreat into their classrooms or symposiums as if they were the only public spheres available for engaging the power of ideas and the relations of power. Foucault's notion of the specific intellectual taking up struggles connected to particular issues and contexts must be combined with Gramsci's notion of the engaged intellectual who connects his or her work to broader social concerns that deeply affect how people live, work, and survive." (Giroux 1992, 82)

The postmodern negates particular views of totality, reason, foundationalism, and the human subject (Giroux 1992, 52–54, 59–61). Even with some critical questions left unanswered, the political relevance of a postmodern approach to *social and oppositional action* allows for a more inclusive and coalitional acting and reflecting. Postmodernism also negates *border cultures* (Giroux 1992, 54–59). Comparing approaches to social space both of *the modern* and *the postmodern*, "postmodernism constitutes a general attempt to transgress the borders sealed by modernism, to proclaim the arbitrariness of all boundaries..." (Giroux 1992, 55), while "modernist culture negates the possibility of identities created within the experience of multiple narratives and 'border' crossings; instead, modernism frames culture within rigid boundaries that both privilege and exclude around the categories of race, class, gender, and ethnicity" (Giroux 1992, 54).

Border crossings may be the new *peace-making activities* in a postmodern world, both in academic *mixing* and *joining* of past incompatibles—like the social sciences, cultural studies, feminist theory, and theology—, and in the day-to-day struggle on the street, in the city hall, at council meetings, in church activities, and in the general public arena to create a better and more social world across old boundaries, past walls of separation, and long-gone classifications.

Social Postmodernism and Feminism

Two bed-fellows that have recently joined the political struggle are *postmodernism* and *feminism*, though not in all discovered partnerships and attempted one-night-stands always for both convincingly. Some have split again, others have never really fallen in love. But some have stayed together, at least for a while (on feminism and postmodernism Nicholson 1990, Hekman 1990, Brooks 1997, Gamble 2001, Mann 2006).

The Community of the Weak

The general climate for this change from the modern to the postmodern, the Eurocentric to the postcolonial, and the patriarchal to the feminist or postfeminist, is again well described by *Henry A. Giroux* in his *Border Crossings* (Giroux 1992) combining all of this in himself as a *modern critical theorist*, a *postmodern postcolonial*, and a *radical (post)feminist*:

> "We have entered an age that is marked by a crisis of power, patriarchy, authority, identity, and ethics. This new age has been described, for better or worse, by many theorists in a variety of disciplines as postmodernism ... It is a period torn between the ravages and benefits of modernism; it is an age in which the notions of science, technology, and reason are associated not only with social progress but also with the organization of Auschwitz and the scientific creativity that made Hiroshima possible ... It is a time in which the humanist subject seems to no longer be in control of his or her fate. It is an age in which the grand narratives of emancipation, whether from the political right or left, appear to share an affinity for terror and oppression. It is also a historical moment in which culture is no longer seen as a reserve of white men whose contributions to the arts, literature, and science constitute the domain of high culture. We live at a time in which a strong challenge is being waged against a modernist discourse in which knowledge is legitimized almost exclusively from a European model of culture and civilization. In part, the struggle for democracy can be seen in the context of a broader struggle against certain features of modernism that represent the worst legacies of the Enlightenment tradition. And it is against these features that a variety of oppositional movements have emerged in an attempt to rewrite the relationship between modernism and democracy. Two of the most important challenges to modernism have come from divergent theoretical discourses associated with postmodernism and feminism." (Giroux 1992, 39)

In a way hardly noticed on the European continent, *North American social theory* (Ritzer 2000, 1997, Seidman and Alexander 2001, Jones 2003, Best 2003, Seidman 2008)—here represented in an impressive way by *Henry A. Giroux* for educational, cultural, and social theory and practice (Giroux 1981–2011, Giroux and Simon 1989, Giroux and McLaren 1994, McLaren 1995, 2005)—has experienced a radical inter-mixing and intersecting over these last several decades.

The joining of *(post)feminism* with *postmodernism* is only one example. Other *radical social movements* and their accompanying social theories have fertilized each other, inter-married, in a playful and serious intercourse between various radical approaches to the social. The sheer amount of endless publications of more and more social-theoretical interchange between *critical theory, marxism, symbolic interactionism, postmodernism, poststructuralism, deconstruction, feminism, post-feminism, postcolonialism, antiracism*, and other ever more radical approaches to the social, is both fascinating and mind-boggling at the same time.

Postmodern, Postfeminist, and Postcolonial

A *social postmodernism* will be *social critical, feminist* and *postcolonial, poststructural* and *deconstructivist, postfeminist* and *anti-racist, post-foundational* and *post-liberal, post-educational* and *post-political* at the same time, if all this is coming out of the daily and painful struggles of people experiencing what it means being excluded from life for being *different*.

Being black, yellow, white, Asian, Hispanic, being handicapped, child, juvenile, female, being leftist, radical, traditional, being atheist, agnostic, believer, being liberal or evangelical, gay or lesbian, pacifist or anarchist, housewife or community activist, spiritualist or artist, all these various social experiences of being *particular* and *different*, with possible communal exclusion and extinction, violence and destruction, qualify for critical attention in a *postmodernism* turning *social*. Here, commonalities outweigh the separating distinctions of particular theories and political convictions, social preferences and philosophical predilections.

Postfeminist sociologist *Ann Brooks* from *New Zealand* puts it well, giving a first panoramic view of the need for a common social agenda for *postfeminism, postmodernism,* and *postcolonialism* (Brooks 1997, Gamble 2001, Mann 2006) out of the hurtful and experiential callings of various subaltern groups that have not been heard in modernity, but now are raising their voices louder than ever before:

> "Postmodernism as an intellectual movement captured a tendency across a range of disciplines and aesthetic practices for a radical reappraisal of modernist normative structures and representations. Debates emerging from within feminism had already challenged feminism's dichotomous frame of reference around biological and philosophical essentialism and historical reification, which had their origin in modernist discourses. Postmodernism's emphasis on 'deconstruction' and 'difference', and its challenge to the idea of a single epistemological truth,

added to the voices of those who had been marginalised by feminism's modernist heritage. Subaltern groups have encouraged both feminism's and post-colonialism's engagement with postmodernist discourses in political, cultural and representational terms. Feminist and post-colonialist theorists have recognised the potential of postmodernism to advance debates around identity, nationality and difference already articulated within these political and cultural movements. The articulation of a 'democratic politics of voice' *(as quoted in Yeatman 1994)* and representation has been given greater authority by the intersection of feminism and post-colonialism with postmodernism . . ." (Brooks 1997, 92)

Social Postmodernism Oppositional

In all these various and creative coalitions, interchanges, and cross-fertilizations in *postmodern social theory*—postmodernism with critical theory, postfeminism, postcolonialism with postmodernism, feminism with postcolonialism—the most important concern should not be forgotten, namely the central conviction that social theory should be *critical* as well as *practical, deconstructive* as well as *oppositional*, ultimately being a guiding theoretical perspective to contribute to a better *real world*. Postmodern social theory has come out of the social struggles and political oppositions, community actions and empowerment envisionings of various and radical *new social movements* (Nicholson and Seidman 1995, Magnusson 1996, Cruikshank 1999, Della Porta and Diani 1999, Mullings 2009) fighting any form of social and personal, communal and global *evil, oppression* or *human destruction* (on a social psychology of destruction Fromm 1973, for a process theology of evil Suchocki 1995). In all its sometimes overdrawn playfulness and ironic detachment, a postmodern social theory is always a critical and oppositional call *for a different world*.

This safeguards theory from getting too much detached from the day-to-day real world. A *theory—social* and *postmodern—*coming out of the *everyday world* of common and shared sufferings, witnessed injustices, experienced segregations, succumbed violence, physically felt abuse, and the daily confrontation with excruciating pain, unbelievable horror, unexpected evil, and the day-to-day problems of hunger, poverty, violation, disregard, disrespect, and intentional destructiveness against humans and life, will turn out *different* than a theory coming out of an academic world that keeps itself off-guard from most of these *everyday experiences*. Social *theory*, like *theology—systematic, fundamental,* and *dogmatic—*, will turn out differently depending on where it comes from.

Fragment, Ambiguity, and Difference

"*The purely autonomous ego was mortally wounded when it was found that if language was not its instrument, then the subject was no longer in control. Furthermore, radical plurality and ambiguity have undermined its once-assertive claims to mastery and domination . . . And yet I write this book, and you read it. How? Who are the 'I' writing and the 'I' reading? The self cannot be that solitary freedom tinged with despair of the existentialists, or the autonomous self of the Enlightenment, or the expressive self of the romantics, or the pretense at no-self of the positivists. The self is somewhere else. But where? Perhaps experiencing the pleasures of irony in the abyss of indeterminacy? Perhaps trapped in the interstices of all the historical institutions and discourses that formed the modern self in the first place? But now, through the new discourse on discourse itself, are we finally witnessing the erasure of this figure in the sand? . . .*" (Tracy 1987, 82, 1993, 121)

"*The implication of the political cross for North American pastoral theology means we cannot hide and cover our ears. We must listen to the cries of suffering in our own neighborhoods and hear what people are saying to us . . . It hardly needs to be stated that we live in a world that is torn and fragmented. Most all of us want desperately to make it different, almost at any price. But do we really stop to consider at what cost? How do we even pause to count amidst the noise and confusion that prevents us from seeing clearly? How can we find a place still enough to hear one another, let alone ourselves? The cross reaches out to hold these conflicts, distractions, and tensions. The cross causes an interruption, a jolt into silence, which can become the stillness where the unimaginable can somehow become possible again.*" (Thornton 2002, 17, 23)

"*Like Mamie Mobley, like the early church, as a teenager I sought to find meaning in the suffering I encountered in the violent death of someone I loved and still love (I believe in the communion of saints). When I entered Seminary in 1987, I brought the questions of my youth with me and learned that structures of oppression exist that generate not only a world of sin but also a worldview of sin that reflects on the moral characteristics of*

The Community of the Weak

individuals or on the presumed shortcomings of God. I learned to reformulate the question, What's wrong with my mammy? into, What were the social and economic factors that led to her alienation and ultimately to her demise?" (Terrell 1998, 144)

"The challenge of the Spirit to the guardians of the dominant culture is the Spirit's celebration of differences vis-à-vis the wider society's increasingly violent attempts to preserve sameness, order, and tradition. The story of Pentecost in the book of Acts, for example, narrates the origins and formation of a Spirit-filled countercommunity that celebrated its cultural and linguistic diversity in the face of an imperial government of occupation that persecuted nonconformists as instigators of social unrest . . .
In Western culture we pride ourselves on championing the values of democracy, but the Spirit calls us to a more radical political vision, a heterocracy of sorts, to paraphrase Foucault's notion of 'heterotopia', in which the unity of common values and commitments is never purchased at the price of scapegoating any person or group as the 'demonized other' who has caused the breakdown in social order." (Wallace 2002, 216)

At the end of November 1997, a whole community in a middle-sized Swiss village broke apart. After years of public conflict, private battle, youthful demonstrations, violent newspaper slander, and hidden political and church hierarchical maneuvers, a community voted to kick out a local pastor. The kick-out happened following legal and decisional preparations by highest local and regional church authorities. At the age of thirty-nine a local pastor had to face the open effect of public leading, secret lobbying, hidden colluding, year-long slander, and intentional political and personal scapegoating.

In the beginning of June 1993 I buried a 14-year-old girl and young teenager of a confirmation class I was leading as the local pastor in a middle-sized suburban village half an hour away from cosmopolitan and metropolitan Zurich. A few weeks before, I had still talked to her outside of the parsonage about smoking grass, taking cocaine or heroin, and life. Weeks later I sat on the preaching pulpit looking down on almost 300 teenagers saying good-bye to a 14-year-old. At the end of the funeral service in the local church in the village, with hardly any adults participating at the ceremony, many of these 300 teenagers kept sitting outside of the church looking down on a village that had left them alone. In the following months, more 14-

year-old teenagers turned out to be in serious and real danger to personally collapse under a social problem this village had never seen or accepted before.

Having been publicly disputed as a local pastor already before I even came to this place, with newspaper articles being intentionally placed before my first and second public election by the people in the village, I decided to get closer to these teenagers and problems. I hardly had any ideas about cocaine, heroin, grass, or any other chemicals entering a whole village. But what I did know was the effect it had on a whole community. Fear, anger, prejudice, violence, ostracism, slander, and public dispute were things I did know all too well, having experienced some of these things before. So I got involved in a messy world with messy people and messy problems.

At the end of it I got messed up myself. Voted out. Slandered. Broken. Ostracized. Stigmatized. Like these teenagers I met along the way.

At the time I experienced some of my most meaningful moments in ministry, but also some of my most painful ones. Personal encounters with hopeful signs of community, most often at the fringe of official Christendom. But at the same time deeply touching, intense moments of solidarity and communion more truthful that most of what church usually proclaims. I found myself being moved in moving to the margins of societal spaces and places to meet teenagers hardly older than the age of 14, but already shooting heroin. This one girl was not the only one playing with fire and her life that she lost. Some other teenagers were just as close to death and radical catastrophes in their lives like this girl. Over the years I got to be a friend, a person to talk to, a companion to be with. But these teenagers taught me just as much, staying alive deep down in personal memories.

On the 18th of August 1994, these teenagers and others experienced the worst kind of public church assembly this village, and this region, if not Switzerland, probably ever had seen or witnessed as a public media event. 70 young teenagers from and outside of the village were standing in front of a local church while demonstrating for the local pastor who was supposed to be the topic of a highly publicized summer evening. The church officials had initially asked security personnel to bring along watch dogs in order to keep the young teenagers from entering the church. The chief responsible security officer, however, had

The Community of the Weak

decided on his own not to take any dogs along, but to let the young teenagers go in so they could peacefully participate at and observe the assembly. About 250 members of the church, with the press and other high church officials present, were going to debate for almost three hours what to think and to do about a local pastor, turning a church sanctuary into a legal court to speak a final and personal condemnation.

During the following years the conflict escalated, got politicized, publicized, legalized, institutionalized, while taking on dimensions hardly ever known before in this region. At the same time, teenagers and young adults got baptized and confirmed, people married and buried, creative worship services transformed, cultural events hosted, social actions started, communities built, fantasies encouraged, solidarities discovered. Something like church was growing somehow, tenderly, always endangered to be destroyed at any time. And it did get destroyed. By a public vote of almost a thousand people with most of these thousand people hardy caring for, let alone knowing, what kind of a tender community had slowly grown.

From 1993 to 1998 news went around and multiplied about some popular youth pastor in the region. Known by many. Respected by teenagers. Called in by adults. Admired even by critics. And yet still secretly hated. Openly opposed. Publicly fought against. Ultimately rejected. Filling newspaper headlines and television news regularly. Providing conversation and story-making material for table talks and pub or public slander. Serving as projection figure for political interests and ecclesiastical new legal intentions. The painful and joyful ambiguity of life all enclosed in one particular turbulent place and fragmenting situation. It all ended brutally in 1997, with some 6 month over-time granted into 1998 to leave a place, hand over a parsonage, move out of town, and hide in a Bally factory nearby trying to write about what just had happened.

Life being broken. A soul fragmented. Still in pain writing about it years later. Images of places and faces, moments and memories that do not erase. Almost 7 years later still the same emotion of breakdowns and break-ups of shattered life moments.

Language Fragmenting

People do get *fragmented* in life. So does the world. Even *language* can break your back and bless or kill. As North American womanist theologian *Cheryl A. Kirk-Duggan* puts it, describing the power of human language to dance or to kill: "We use language to dance and to defy reality. We use language to communicate and compensate, to love, and to kill" (Kirk-Duggan 2001, 114). Language may rub against reality, or it may twist and turn reality. One way or another, reality hits you once in a while. In 1997, reality hit me and a whole village with a full blow. While teenagers were dancing over the years at their confirmation worship services to *Michael Jackson's* rhythms in black and white, *Céline Dion's* vocals on love, and African drums' beating memories of a girl that had just died at the age of 14, others were preparing to kill.

The public and private campaign to get rid of a local pastor happened most of the time through the use of language. Language was turning into a weapon. *Logos* and speech got to be transformed into *radical evil*, ultimately remaining unexplainable and *irrational* (Peters 1994, 9). The human will to destroy, be it people, projects, visions, and life goals of a whole community, will always remain a mystery somehow. Trying to understand why people in a community may put up all their energy into breaking ties of grown friendships, newly born bonds of common understanding, and the enticing beauty of a developing social vision, exchanging it for a violent *breakdown of human community*, will remain a secret.

The *secret* of humans, as North American systematic theologian *Ted Peters* from Northern California's *Berkeley* describes it in his *social and theological phenomenology of radical evil*, intentionally turning "self-destructive and world-destructive. No good reason for such destructive activity can be given. Any reason we find to justify our sin is rootless" (Peters 1994, 9–10). The human skill of language, turning communities into places of *slander*, rumors, stories, fantasies, and projections, was socially constructing a new kind of reality in a local village called *Erlinsbach* in order to serve only one intentional purpose: to get rid of someone. Secret and social workings of language I already knew from the stories of my mom.

All along, *language* in words and expressions turned out to be highly instrumental and influential for an intentional build-up of *social and communal violence*. Words have a way *to create* a different kind of reality somewhat detached from what may seem to be real. Already in 1990 and 1992, when I was first, and in the second round definitely proposed as a candidate for public election for pastoral ministry in this particular village, solicited newspaper articles and letters to the editor on my pacifist background, my political involvement with Central America, and my diverse theological convictions had some public effect. *Words* like "communist", "conscientious objector", "supporter of Switzerland without an army", and "unbelieving pastor" served their intended political purpose to create a particular kind of reality preparing for the outliving of symbolic and possible real violence.

Years later, words like "drug pastor", "driving teenagers around to get some heroin", and "constant trouble-maker" added and finished a concluding *stigmatizing process* never ending ever since (on stigma in interpretive sociology Goffman 1963, Fuchs 1993, in New Testament studies and practical theology Mödritzer 1994, Ebertz 1987, 178–195).

Symbolic Violence

It is amazing how human language can fragment and break things cherished and lives built-up. The postmodern recognition of *symbolic violence* (on symbolic violence in Pierre Bourdieu Jenkins 2002, 103–110, Swartz 1997, 82–94, Schäfer 2004, Bourdieu 1991) in all our attempts at describing reality should become a constant warning to any systematic theology forgetful of its own social power and influence. Too often theologians have been unaware of how the things they say or don't say can destroy people and their life projects. The postmodern feel for ambiguity, open ends, and unfinished dreams may remind us that most past and present communal "master narratives of our time are soaked in the blood of victims" (Wallace 2002, 29). Theology—be it *systematic, dogmatic,* or *fundamental*— in church's history has quite often and willingly participated in some of these most *life-destructive master narratives* destroying people, breaking apart whole communities, smashing visions, and eradicating daring dreams through the use of *wounding* and *abusive power* (as told in old and new social-critical church histories in Kahl 1968, Deschner 1972, 1988, Gonzalez 1999, 2002).

The *social mechanism* of communal *victimization* (as a theological concept Gudorf 1992) can be seen most visibly in communities that keep creating sacrificial victims, a common play and plot still written and performed, modernized and refined over and over again wherever people in communities fall into conflicts over strong and determinative differences. Churches seem to be especially vulnerable to this kind of a social but *deadly play* (Gutmann 1995, Hinkelammert 1989, Janowski und Welker 2000) creating *victims* and *wounding people* and local communities here and there. Churches have always and unendingly kept producing *victims* of violence, exclusion, slander, and prejudice, having to face threats of annihilation, erasure, and deletion.

The *deadly play* or *social drama* of becoming a communal and individual victim, hit and broken by the ominous power of symbols converting into *violence*, turns into the perpetual experience of one's human voice of pain and hurt being silenced (Berger 1999, 167, 1988, 75). A socially sensitive and eye-opening *hermeneutics of victims* (Berger 1999, 167–168, 1988, 21–22, 75–92)—with hermeneutics being the empathic *art of words and understanding*—will need to listen more carefully and attentively to those silenced voices at the communal and theological margins, assembling the *council of victims* (Berger 1999, 167, 1988, 75) right there in its own most social and hermeneutical middle.

As New Testament scholar *Klaus Berger* from the *University of Heidelberg* puts it (Berger 1988, 1999), carefully leading through the creative art of human words and understanding in *hermeneutics* (Seiffert 1992, Hitzler und Honer 1997, Heitink 1999, 178–200) by placing an emancipatory *hermeneutics of victims* (Berger 1999, 41–53, 167–168, 1988, 21–22, 75–92) right at the center of a theological method that gives hope to the socially speechless and physically wounded, the emotionally abused and relationally trampled on to find their own human voice: "The truth is with the victims because only the victims—the real ones and also only the possible ones—can mercilessly uncover which way does not lead to life" (Berger 1999, 167).

Words as Worldmaking

Excluding, excommunicating, banning, burning, stoning, indexing, and many other linguistic forms of symbolic violence point to the ominous power of words that *transform reality* somehow. Suddenly things are seen in a new way, people are looked at differently, whole communities are judged in novel ways.

Whole nations go to war because of words. Words and symbols can change, twist, settle, seduce, and disfigure, disclosing their *"world-making* power" (Swartz 1997, 89, Bourdieu 1991). The power to *define*, the capacity to choose between various worldmaking and community-building or community-breaking verbs, nouns, adjectives, adverbs, sentences and paragraphs, by naming people and projects this way or another—witch, bitch, heretic, lunatic, trouble-maker—, is the power of *defining reality* which becomes social and *political* (as defined in Meyer 2003, 106–108). Whether it is true or not, what is being said, is of no concern.

This subtle or obvious *world-making* and *world-defining* may be self-conscious or unconscious, known or unknown, detectable or secretive, in as much as most social and political workings of power, in the use and abuse of language and elsewhere, have always been more invisible than laid open, in theology as well.

As French sociologist *Pierre Bourdieu* puts it, listing art, religion, and language as prominent places of hidden or open *symbolic power*:

> "For symbolic power is that invisible power which can be exercised only with the complicity of those who do not want to know that they are subject to it or even that they themselves exercise it." (Bourdieu 1991, 164)

Believing some worldmaking and world-defining *words*—witch, heretic, apostate, lunatic, enemy, trouble-maker, drug pastor—may be the beginning of social carnage and *communal destruction* as people have a way to look at words longer than at reality. For some reason, words sometimes receive more credit than what really is. The same happened in a local community years ago where people decided to believe and trust words in newspapers, slander on the street, and made-up fairy tales at the local pub more than real faces and real voices, with silent words speaking wisperingly to them.

Symbolic power (Bourdieu 1991, 163–170) as *violence* has a way to crush any remaining sense of conscience, any left-over sensitivity for what might be right and wrong. What counts, after all, is a new image, a new picture, a new story about how reality should be, if we want to humanly *destroy*.

Monomythic Logic in Constructing Babel

The temptation to *destroy* is omnipresent wherever people decide to believe words and follow seductions of speech. Words turn into myth, and myth turns into a logic that keeps repeating and asking for its toll. A postmodern sensitivity for the violence of the *monomythic narrator* (on monomythic violence Wallace 2002) would be a healthy reminder for systematic theology to look at its own worldmaking and word-making for a while.

The Social

Wherever people gather together the remnants and lumber of past and present narratives to fabricate a newly and humanly erected and even more modern *Tower of Babel* than the one known in the old ages (exegetically narrated in Brueggemann 1997, 494–495, McKenzie 1997, 10–11, Anderson 1994a, Ebach 1998a), reality gets unified by one common and *single goal*, vision, party book, and reflective unity. But at the same time, some people and whole communities inevitably get *crushed* and *scattered* into various incommensurable languages and dialects. The biblical *Tower of Babel*, slave-driving humans and nations into just *one common goal*, creating an omnivorously tyrannical *Empire*, local or global (on empire, the modern and postmodern global Hardt and Negri 2000), while irrespectful of its many victims on the way, is a human and social temptation wherever people try to live and gather in community.

As North American Old Testament scholar *Bernhard W. Anderson* puts it in his commentary on the story of the *Tower of Babel* in Genesis 11:1–9 (Anderson 1994a), describing the human temptation and the divine counter-intervention to congregate in one single language, one single place, one single aim:

> "Taken by itself, the story portrays a clash of human and divine wills, a conflict of centripetal and centrifugal forces. Surprisingly, it is human beings who strive to maintain a primeval unity, based on one language, a central living space, and a single aim. It is God who counteracts this movement toward a center with a centrifugal force that disperses them into linguistic, spatial, and ethnic diversity." (Anderson 1994a, 166)

Too often in human history people have succumbed to this all too human and social temptation to create one common tower outreaching the common ground of everybody else. The seducing whisper or twirling storm of common belief, common goals, common vision, common politics, and common history has kept blowing the needed social awareness of *fragment, ambiguity*, and *difference* (Tracy 1987, 1993, Hardt and Negri 2004) among local people and global nations away, leaving human history with whole battlefields of corpses wounded and communities crushed.

The creative freedom of tower-building humankind is open to creating both human grandeur and social misery, as Old Testament scholar *Bernhard W. Anderson* describes it:

> "This creative freedom is both the grandeur and the misery of humanity. On the one hand, it enables human beings to rise above the limitations of their environment and, with

cooperative effort and technological ingenuity, to build a city that affords unity and protection. There is security for people who are of one kind: who speak one language, live at one center, and share one goal. On the other hand, their 'will to greatness', which also reflects anxiety, prompts an assertion of power that stands under the judgement of the God whose creative purpose includes richness, variety, and proliferation. Human beings are, indeed, 'members of a lacerated body'—a broken, fragmented humanity in which God's will for unity in diversity is transformed into conflicting division between peoples who speak different languages, live in separate territories, and belong to particular ethic groups or nations. The ambition of the builders of Babel for human unity has been refracted into the conflicts of human history. The blessing of God, which produces a rich variety of peoples of different races, colors, tongues, nationalities, and living spaces, has been transformed into antagonistic division between peoples who speak different languages, live in separate territories, and belong to particular ethnic groups or nations. The human drive for unity has fearful possibilities and consequences, as Yahweh's judgmental word in the Babel story indicates: 'Now everything they plan to do will be attainable!' The picture of a million people raising their hands in a single salute is an awe-inspiring—and frightening—vision . . ." (Anderson 1994a, 178)

Thinking in Fragments

North American systematic theology long ago has witnessed its own *shattering* and *scattering* of its *spectrum* (Kliever 1981). Pieces have broken off, whole communities displaced, theological familiarities turned strange and unfamiliar. The contemporary landscape of North American systematic theology through its turbulent history has taken a dissociate and disfigured shape not unlike the one most probably found after the mythological breakdown of old and powerful Babylonian *Babel*. Incommensurable languages, incomprehensible dialects, contextual divisions, cultural antagonisms, and the violent *scattering* after Babel (Brueggemann 1997, 494) of voices and people across irreconcilable differences not unlike old Babylonian times, even if only mythological, have challenged long ago a monomythic logic in systematic theology to become plural in its logics, fragmentary in its system, as well as openly ambiguous in its wording.

The Social

Systematic theology in North America today is facing the upsetting recognition that we live in a preeminently *violent world facing evil* (Peters 1994, Wallace 2002, Swartley 2000, Kirk-Duggan 2001, 2001a, Suchocki 1995, Staub 1989, 2003, Hasker 2008) made up of irreconcilable antagonisms, as the various peoples and nations, theologies and cultures, idiosyncracities and human assurances have scattered all over the globe, on North American soil and elsewhere. Violence between those scattered human exiles *after Babel* is both real and symbolic, ready to erupt at any time (on violence in ethics after Babel Stout 1988). Past understandings disappear, familiar frames of references fall to the side, recognizable metaphors are being displaced, even sent into exile like in old Babylonian times, in a world—theological or other—of "coherence and unity of humanity irreversibly violated . . ." (Brueggemann 1997, 494).

To face this reality is part of a *postmodern trauma* (Farley 1996, Lakeland 1997, Riggs 2003, Hart 2004) that any good theology has to go through. To act as if the world was still modern, unitary, cohesive, rational, logical, and even grown-up, will show to be another civilized illusion just leading to more violence. *Thinking in fragments* (Wallace 2002, Raberger/Sauer 2003, Schupp 1974, Lüthi 1971) will be the new Spirit-mode in which theology has to be put together. Fragmentary as this modern-day world is, in particular its theological world, any good theology—*fundamental, systematic* or *dogmatic*—in the *twenty-first century* will need to learn how to think and construct its new language in theology in *fragmentary ways* (Schupp 1974, 158), reconstructing old phrases, new images, persistent metaphors, and forgotten similes from the shambles of broken down houses of former ecclesial and theo-linguistic authority (Farley 1996, 32) that do not carry its grounding weight and meaning anymore.

To be able to think fragmentarily in theology—*fundamental, systematic*, or *dogmatic*—requires a whole new way of approaching theology in its method. Theology in bits and pieces, *sketches* and *projects* (on theology as a project Klammer 1995) will be more like the haphazard work of an artist filling in space, moving from here to there, following intuition, falling back on previous forms, trying out new territory, sketching the unknown. The picture develops as the different spots and spaces get colored, filled, reworked on, rearranged in order to let a shade turn into form. At the end those bits and pieces make up a whole without ever having intended to become one particular unified form.

Theology *developing* (Klammer 1995) as life and its many projects go on will be the best kind of antidote to the common and recurrent temptation to do theology as if people and events shaping us, rattling us, wounding us, elating us, did not matter. *Theology in fragments*, developing and meandering, reviewing and revisioning along the way, follows the way "Jesus was doing theology as if people matter . . ." (Sedmak 2002, 33).

Fitting In

To be able to think fragmentarily would have meant to think in a local village in a new way about these marginal teenagers that did not fit in during those troublesome years between 1993 and 1995 in *Erlinsbach*. *Fitting in* is the social language of *monomythic violence*, requiring everyone to move around within clearly defined social boundaries of the *acceptable* while shunning the socially *delinquent*. Social thinking about delinquency or deviant behavior was for a while my regular reading material trying to understand why teenagers at the age of 14 would take heroin. Along the way, more prominent themes came to the foreground, like the *allocation of space*, opening up a youth cellar for those teenagers to meet. The *Bunker* turned out to become—only for a very short while, since under the pressure of neighbors it got closed again only a few weeks old—a theological topic for the community as teenagers who were considered *marginal* would at some point become *central* in a church's and a local community's attention.

The local community in *Erlinsbach* in the years between 1993 and 1995 was facing a choice between looking at the world as a *unified whole* or as *broken shambles* after those many and various humanly built towers had fallen, being introduced into a new world *after Babel* (Stout 1988) where things had become a little bit more complicated. The choice was an ethical one, placing before a local community the choice between *life* and *death*, between the possibility to belong and the possibility to fall out of all means of staying a part of it. It was an ethical choice between believing in a world where diversity, fragment, ambiguity, and variety had its natural place, even with teenagers at the age of 14 being so far out of bounds. Or to believe in a world where things had to turn back to the common, the known, the familiar, the one and only *single vision* that would along the way sacrifice a few for the many. The old *sacrificial game* still being in place. As such the choice was a highly theological one.

As North American systematic theologian *Mark I. Wallace* describes it, unraveling the many intricacies of *sacrificial thinking* in communities by developing a postmodern and fragmentary *theology of creation* in the face of violence:

> "The American myth of redemptive violence promulgates the doctrine that the death of a few is often a prerequisite for the salvation of the many. Thus, occasional cycles of purgative violence are necessary for preserving the health and the well-being of the body-politic . . . All those who exist on the fringes of Western culture—whether for economic, ethnic, or religious reasons—are potential victims of the American monomyth's logic that blood forges unity, that death generates life. Many such marginal persons are branded as insidious outsiders who must be quarantined, if not destroyed, in order to preserve the health of the larger whole. The high priests of the myth theologize that the good of the commonweal is best served when certain individuals volunteer, or are 'picked', to sacrifice their lives for the welfare of the system. The postmodern cry against the tyranny of the whole—the cry of thinkers such as Kierkegaard, Derrida, Levinas, Lyotard, and Girard—is the cry for the integrity of the individual life over and against the demands of the totality for more sacrifice and more blood." (Wallace 2002, 29)

Postmodern Crumbling

For this to happen, modern buildings have to fall, modern assurances have to be disassembled, the monolithic being taken down, as thinking is becoming fragmentary. The postmodern crumbling of any Tower-building like the one in old Babylonian *Babel* is a necessary starting point and foundational beginning for the reconstruction of a *postmodern theology in the 21st century*. The *Spirit of life* seems to be coming and going, moving here and there, in the ebb and flow of life, always breaking up in fragments. Fragmentary thinking in theology—*systematic, dogmatic,* and *fundamental*—will need to gather the crowd of those who normally are not put together. Fragmentary thinking is *creative thinking* the way God made the world, taking bits and pieces here and there to make something new.

This can even mean putting teenagers on drugs in a local village into some church building to make the place their own, upsetting the common social mappings of what seems to be appropriate. *Mixing and joining, combining and blending* are the new words in theological method to describe this kind of *fragmentary thinking*. Like an *artist*, dancing across her canvas by filling in colored spots in empty space, like a *musician* moving along his rhythms of notes filling in newly-born melodies in silent space, the *systematic theologian* of the 21st century will be an *artist* and a *creator* at the same time.

To put it in postmodern terms, following North American systematic theologian *Mark I. Wallace's* fragmentary *pneumatology* of the *dancing sun*:

> "Where are the fragments of the Spirit in our world today? I believe the Spirit is present in the eyes of our neighbor, in the green fuse that drives the growth of trees and plants, in the ebb and flow of the life cycle within which all of us live and move and have our being. The Spirit is alive and active whenever and wherever committed persons and communities work to bring reconciliation and healing to members of the life-web that have been denied the basic means for sustaining a fruitful existence. The Spirit is the green face of God, the intercessory force for peace and solidarity in a world saturated with sacrificial violence, the power of renewal within creation as the creation groans in travail and waits with eager longing for environmental justice for all God's creatures. Like the dance of the sun's light across the surface of the earth, the Spirit in fragments shines with bright hope in anticipation of a time when the original unity and integrity of creation will again be realized." (Wallace 2002, 228)

Fragmentary, Ambiguous, Different

North American systematic theology of these days circles around these various *key-words* summarizing the *postmodern condition* (on the postmodern, postmodernity, postmodernism Harvey 1990, Bertens 1995, Ward 1997, Connor 2004, Hart 2004, Vanhoozer 2003, Ward 2005, Penner 2005, Smith 2006, 2008). Whether we like it or not, we are part of this condition. The *fragmentary* nature of our personal knowledge and social wisdom is becoming more and more recognizable as we go on. The *ambiguity* of all our convictions—ethical, religious, political—, and the every-day challenge of people being so radically *different* that global communication and communal understanding, civic consensus and interpersonal comprehension seem to become almost impossible, are the new signatures of these contemporary times.

The *fragmentary* (Hart 2004, 67–86) is one key-note cord that describes our *life in fragments* in the postmodern world (Bauman 1995, Tracy 1999), noticeable not only for the up-to-date philosopher, the newspaper-reading social scientist or the modern-art-familiar cultural theorist, but for the culturally sensitive systematic theologian or Christian philosopher as well who dares to look at how the ever-changing world nowadays looks like (Grenz 1996, Lakeland 1997, O'Donnell 2003, Smith 2006, 2008). Reading the "signs of the times" (Matthew 16:3) (Sedmak 2002, 8, following Sanks and Coleman 1993, Segundo 1993, Haight 2001) is one methodological task facing a *fundamental theology in postmodern times*. Getting in touch with the reality of the fragmentary is a first step.

Fragmentary is everything. Human understanding and comprehension are facing a time and an age that celebrate and bemoan the end of totality and unity, the end of the comprehensive and systematic in human thoughts and moral minds, convinced individuals and normative communities (Hart 2004, 67–86). Nothing holds everything together anymore. Systems seem to appeal to the human mind only to end some day on a dissolving note showing that no system really captures the many parts and pieces of what makes up *real life*. There could almost be talk about a *spirituality in fragments* (Tracy 1999), capturing the spiritual situation of our times where nothing seems to really fit anymore so that people could talk about a unitary whole or perspective, as "the only spirituality that is viable for us these days is one that works from and around fragments" (Hart 2004, 85).

The same is true for theology, *systematic*, *fundamental*, and *dogmatic*, as well. The *shattering of the spectrum* (Kliever 1981) that North America has been experiencing over these last thirty years of contemporary theology scattering into all human directions is a determinative point of no return from which to move on. It seems that the United States in comparison to the European and German-speaking theological continent has experienced this radical acceleration of pluralism and the fragmentary nature of all our theological work even more extensively and rapidly than the old continent where some familiar systems still seem in common place.

Karl Barth still waves his flag at recruits following. *Paul Tillich* still moves people out of their common categories in presenting his complex theological system. *Karl Rahner* continues to appeal to the familiar recital of important references. And even *Jürgen Moltmann* has his own way of seducing succeeding disciples into becoming *Moltmannian*.

The Community of the Weak

Familiar systems and names, however, whether *Barthian*, *Tillichian*, *Bultmannian* or any others, have found their legitimate ending in North America, as a newer generation of young theologians has discovered the *ambiguous*, the *fragmentary* and the *non-systematic*. "The age of systems, including theological systems, is well and truly over" (Hart 2004, 85). In all this the *different* is upheld as the most challenging new systematic.

Systematic theology in North America today is turning cultural, deconstructive, and postmodern in that systematic writing becomes a patchwork of *narrative collage* telling a story. Like the one being told here. Different memories, different stories, different nationalities, different sensitivities, different communities are all telling their story by making up a new one in combining the different elements. Theology written that way becomes a lot more *ambiguous*.

The *ambiguity* of contemporary North American theology is written into its own social story. A cultural and social, individual and communitarian story as diverse and contradictory, contextual and counter-contextual as the embattled *American story* will never produce just one particular type of systematic theology. The radical pluralism is an ingrown part of social biographies telling their theological story.

Life and its story is *ambiguous*, open to a variety of different understandings. *To be different* used to be a social sin. Nowadays it is a common social fact. What used to be the social memory of communal living, people sharing common normative values, has become a bygone memory of having lived some time before *Babel*, but not in this and our time anymore. In our time people break apart out of sheer differences. People go to war, raise their hands against the other, break promises, leave or are made to leave, because of sheer differences. Not one place where people don't seem to be different. Different in language, color, belief, politics, style, culture. Whole communities can break apart by their great differences. Whether we like it or not, we live in this kind of a *pluralistic universe* (Taylor 1990, 36). Even as theologians.

Pluralist Sensibilities

Pluralist and cultural theologian *Mark Lewis Taylor* from *Princeton Theological Seminary* describes the intellectual and social challenges for theologians trying to live in a postmodern world:

> "While historical consciousness and the history of religions were for Christian theologians perhaps the nearest nurturers of

> pluralist sensibilities, current theological reflection is often confirmed in its pluralist convictions by more recent developments in the natural and social sciences. Both clusters of sciences display the impact of a relativizing affirmation of different forms of life, particularly in the debates about the incommensurability of competing paradigms or research programs. In the natural sciences, the discussion is exemplified by debates between Thomas Kuhn, Paul Feyerabend, and Stephen Toulmin ... In the social sciences, the discussion is perhaps best represented as occurring between Peter Winch and Alasdair MacIntyre ... Wittgenstein's reflections on the different 'language games' inquirers play, together with the relativizing impacts of cultural anthropology and the sociology of knowledge, also make it difficult for theologians to live, at least with intellectual integrity, anywhere other than in a pluralistic universe." (Taylor 1990, 35–36)

Our reading of texts, events, and stories remains *ambiguous*. Even our day-to-day conversations and interactions will forever remain ambiguous as long as human language and behavior are open to a variety and *plurality of understanding*. One simple and seemingly obvious behavior of one person can mean something very different done by someone else. What is good for some, may be pure evil for others. What is sheer beauty in one place, may be appalling misery in another. In the course of history various narratives have been replaced by others to explain the great variety of grandeur and misery of the human race, all of them falling in between the ambiguity of "the strange mixture of great good and frightening evil" (Tracy 1987, 70). Ambiguity has to do with this mix of both in whatever we do or the human race can or will do. The life *in-between good and evil, beautiful and ugly* will remain with us, shaping our actions and our language, our everyday world and our theologies.

As Roman Catholic fundamental theologian *David Tracy* from the *University of Chicago* puts it, underlining the intrinsically plural and ambiguous nature of all our stories, moving from admiration to horror, beauty to pure cruelty, in order to finally finish all such human stories with a postmodern and post-narrative good-bye to it all:

> "Ambiguity may be too mild a word to describe the strange mixture of great good and frightening evil that our history reveals. And yet, at least until more adequate and probably new words are coined, ambiguity will have to suffice ... Historical ambiguity means that a once seemingly clear historical narrative of progressive Western enlightenment and emancipation has now

become a montage of classics and newspeak, of startling beauty and revolting cruelty, of partial emancipation and ever-subtler forms of entrapment. Ambiguous is certainly one way to describe our history. At one time we may have believed realistic and even naturalistic narratives of the triumph of the West . . . But these traditional narratives are now overlaid not only with modernist narratives and their occasional epiphanies amidst the mass of historical confusion, but also by postmodernist antinarratives with their good-byes to all that . . ." (Tracy 1987, 70)

Ambiguous Writing

Therefore, *writing* becomes *ambiguous* as well. Denominating concepts get blurred, clarified words used in many and multiple ways, locked-in definitions crisscrossed. The often presumed and expected necessity for systematic complexity and linguistic clarity of definitional precision in endless academic battles with other positions of common prosaic styles of dissertational writing gets replaced by a new and more *narrative style of ambiguous writing*, marveling at the fragmentary, the different, and the ambiguous. Such narrative writing may turn out to be less conceptual, less argumentative, less dissecting, and less combative. It will be less judgmental as well, less qualifying, less distancing or separating.

Narrative academic style and writing in the ambiguous and fragmentary mode is *integrating* more so than separating, *celebrating the different* in true *admiration* (on the "celebration of difference" Taylor 1990, 34–37, 199–208). Whoever has learned how to admire other stories in the course of our postmodern theological story-telling across all nations, cultures, and times will be less inclined, as most often found in normal university settings, to create a theological and analytical battlefield exposing and rejecting, counter-positioning and competing names and concepts, schools and traditions. Instead, a new narrative academic style enjoying *ambiguity, fragment*, and *difference*, will be more like the assembling and gathering narrator of a good story combining the unfamiliar, the juxtaposed, and the contradictory into one fascinating human tale.

This causes not only suspension, but also a feeling of disorientation, a necessary condition for living a life in the *liminality* of narrative *in-between* various cultures and traditions. As North American systematic theologian *Mark Lewis Taylor* puts it, using *Paul Ricoeur* and the New Testament as confirming witnesses to the cause:

The Social

"Both the narrative language of the New Testament that was produced by early Jewish and Christian movements and the communal praxis in these movements contain features that allow us to speak of admiration and liminality as *Christian* reconciliatory postures... Analysis of both the form and the meaning of these narratives suggests that New Testament narratives themselves foster not only the affirmation of others that is intrinsic to admiration, but also the sense of suspension and disorientation that is essential to liminality... Ricoeur and others have stressed that the *form* of the gospel narratives, particularly in the parables, is qualified by a structural trait intrinsic to the narrated action. This trait, or qualifier, is the narrative's tendency to highlight the extravagant, the paradoxical, the hyperbolic... The gospel narratives intensify ordinary experience to the point of the extraordinary, not to distract from the ordinary but to illumine it from within. So, for example, the parable of the Good Samaritan is not only recommendation or illustration of a virtuous life-style. It is extravagant portrayal of compassion without limit... The narrative form, structurally charged with extravagance of this sort, has the particular function for readers of dislocation. Even though the plot of the narrated story of Jesus may culminate in reorientation for readers, our experience of this in the narrative is not without a jarring, disorienting encounter with an intensified vision of the ordinary. The narrative form 'dislocates our project of making a whole of our lives.'" (Taylor 1990, 204)

This fragmenting and dislocating style of narrative writing may also become more prominent in telling our own personal story as *systematic, dogmatic,* or *fundamental theology. Ambiguous, different,* and *fragmentary* as it may be, the postmodern signature of these times will encourage new and different styles of theological academic writing, sensitive to the pluralism of *radical difference* not only in academic writing, but also in academic and human living.

Fragment, Ambiguity, and Difference in a Village

The radical breaking-in of some loose ends, the disrupting unfamiliar, and the disquieting unknown show a basic similarity to the gut-level emotional and intellectual reaction of a local village in the 1990s somewhere in Switzerland to the disruptingly unknown, as a community had to face some 14-year-old teenagers taking heroin. Facing it, both individually as concerned parents, as witnessing friends, as observing teachers, and as a community in solidarity and in turmoil, had the cognitive quality of something so shocking, so threatening, and so disquieting that the intellectual and emotional reaction to it could only be half-way consciously and unconsciously *fragmentary*, putting broken-off bits and pieces together trying to understand.

The *cognitive and dissonant breakdown* (for a social psychology of emotional and social breakdown Aronson, Wilson, Akert 2004, 188–190, 1994, 74–77, Cohen 2001, 98–99) of common reflective categories in trying to understand this new kind of social reality right next door in one's personal neighborhood and village, when most of these stories happen somewhere else, but not around here, had the emotional magnitude and conceptual multitude of a *postmodern trauma*. Common concepts would no longer hold. General experience would not last to guide parents and villagers in what to do. A unitary, common worldview would dissolve into many fragmentary bits and pieces no longer making up a whole. A highly ambiguous plurality of good advice, bad slander, repressive first measures, therapeutic talks, and communitarian growing-together or falling apart made up the new social fabric of a village that had to regroup itself around this breaking-in of the unfamiliar and threatening, the disquieting and dislocating.

Communities Choosing Exclusion or Embrace

Communities in moments like this face an ethical and theological choice between *exclusion* and *embrace* (for a theology of exclusion and embrace Volf 1996), choosing between a kind of communal *new identity* that includes *otherness* by reconciling the radically *different* and even threatening, or the outliving of open and social violence by extinguishing that which does not seem to belong. *Violence* trying to force an old unity on a community falling apart always offers itself to be the most promising first and second thought. At moments like that the nature of true or false *community* shows.

Pseudocommunity (Peck 1987, 86–90) is the most common and established form of human dwellings in social and temporal space. Most of us live somewhere where community seems to exist, but only at some superficial and highly provisionary level. Greeting each other at the street corner, saying hello in the elevator or at the entrance door, helping each other with a smile stepping outside of the bus or the local subway, tossing each other in the crowd, walking with each other for a while before parting into different occupational or non-occupational directions. Inviting each other for casual neighborhood parties, evening chats, and school or party reunions to exchange formalities, small-talk and social preferences.

All this we know. And yet it may create the *tempting illusion* that this is all there is about true community. Most often it is living *by pretense*, acting as if we really do care for each other in community, when actually it is only a form of *pseudocommunity*, not really in touch with who we are, what we believe or don't believe in, and how different, even *radically different* (Jeanrond and Rike 1991, a Festschrift for David Tracy) we really are.

> "In pseudocommunity a group attempts to purchase community cheaply by pretense. It is not an evil, conscious pretense of deliberate black lies. Rather, it is an unconscious, gentle process whereby people who want to be loving attempt to be so by telling little white lies, by withholding some of the truth about themselves and their feelings in order to avoid conflict. But it is still a pretense. It is an inviting but illegitimate shortcut to nowhere ... The essential dynamic of pseudocommunity is conflict-avoidance. The absence of conflict in a group is not by itself diagnostic. Genuine communities may experience lovely and sometimes lengthy periods free from conflict. But that is because they have learned how to deal with conflict rather than avoid it. Pseudocommunity is conflict-avoiding; true community is conflict-resolving ... What is diagnostic of pseudocommunity is the minimization, the lack of acknowledgement, or the ignoring of individual differences ... The basic pretense of pseudocommunity is the denial of individual differences." (Peck 1987, 88–89)

A Fundamental Theology in Community

Theologically, this resonates with the contemporary social challenge of a world—modern or postmodern—in *broken fragments, ambiguous, radically different*, contradictory, in desperate need to commune with each other in order to put the various broken-off pieces back into community to become a newly assembled human whole. There is no way back to a premodern world where everyone sees or is required to see things and live lives the same way. The broken-off parts of social exclusion, communal closure, and individual cognitive dissonance in dealing with those who seem to be radically different from us—like teenagers at the age of 14 taking heroin—are just as much a mirroring reflection of the cognitive and emotional challenge, as disquieting as young teenagers taking heroin, *systematic, dogmatic* and *fundamental theology* are facing in this postmodern and broken-off world.

Theology as well is asked if it has ever really known and experienced *true community* in its century-old human endeavor, with a theological community dispersed nowadays all over a fragmented, ambiguous and radically different globe. *Fundamental theology* may be the prime candidate to function as a therapeutic group leader to get those hot-heads of century-old theological battles and rebuttals, break-offs and break-ups back into a peace-making and peace-mingling attitude, recognizing both globally and communally the basic human reality: "We need each other" (Peck 1987, 17).

Such a *fundamental theology in community* would be *communicative* (for fundamental and systematic theology Scharer/Hilberath 2003) and sensitive to the *postmodern* break-ups of our common worlds. Theology—systematic, dogmatic and fundamental—would become a *community of communication* on a global scale (in fundamental theology Arens 1995a, 145–169) living out and learning how to be a *communio* of universal solidarity in this broken-up world. A *communio* in radical diversity and in desperate need to learn how to become a *true community* that knows how to humanly deal with conflict and division, inequality and difference.

Roman Catholic fundamental theologian *Edmund Arens* describes such a global vision for a *communicative theology* as ecclesial and universal solidarity in a *polycentric global world* where all the global and social players, the poor and the rich, the excluded and the included, the illiterate and the literate, the recognized and the ostracized, those pushed aside and those enjoying still most privileges, those similar and those most radically different from us, know that the human experience of "belonging together, out of the experience of sharing the one bread and wine" (Arens 1995a, 167), will be fundamental both in theology and in a new kind of life in a *true and global community*. For this kind of *theological community-building* across national and global lines there needs to be first the recognition of an *open conflict*:

> "The insight into the necessity of ecclesial solidarity entails first of all the insight that the church itself is divided. It is divided not only into confessions and denominations, but also between North and South. In view of this division the church must take a side. It must act in accordance with the partiality of Jesus and of God. Ecclesial solidarity is often mobilized by means of diaconal, prophetic, empathic, and even suffering support and help

for persecuted Christians and churches in other countries. At a basic level it is guided by the knowledge and the recognition that the 'others'—Christians, ecclesial bodies, and churches—belong to the one body of Christ. This type of ecclesial solidarity grows as christopraxis out of the experience of belonging together, out of the experience of sharing the one bread and wine. Such solidarity contradicts *eo ipso* every form of paternalism. It works against every type of racism, sexism, and imperialism . . ." (Arens 1995a, 167)

Fundamental theology in community lives from the recognition that in order to be able to create a new kind of *true community* world-wide and locally, there needs to be the address of such open conflicts. Embracing the conflict, accepting it, respecting it, and acting on it, is the beginning of a therapeutic recognition that things are not the way they should be. Any attempt at community will only be superficial and pretending, if negating the basic reality of secret violence, unspoken exclusion, hidden segregation, and covered-up pseudo-mutuality that crushes "individuality, intimacy, and honesty" (Peck 1987, 89). Such human solidarity in community has to be learned the hard way, both humanly and theologically.

"Solidarity is fundamentally both human and theological. Human identity is constituted by the recognition of the other and of others as persons who have the same rights, needs, and necessities of life. Solidarity must be learned in a process that transcends existing relations and aims at contextually and globally oriented, communal, and universal attention, respect and responsibility." (Arens 1995a, 169)

Social and pastoral ministry with teenagers taking heroin at the age of 14 in a village confronted with the communal challenge to embrace the threatening presence of the *fragmentary*, the *ambiguous* and the *different*, makes one sensitive to what it may mean to include this experience as a fundamental category in any type of theological reflection, *systematic*, *dogmatic, fundamental,* and *pastoral*. Classical and academic divisions of *theological disciplines* get blurred and mixed up as hardcore and painful realities mingle and shake up human elements in need of some conceptual framework. In critical moments like this theology becomes *inclusive, integrative, fundamental,* valuing the interdisciplinary, the border-crossing, the liminal, connecting and combining, interchanging, reuniting, and intertwining the various disciplines to guide some urgently needed *social* and *pastoral action* in a crumbling postmodern world (on theology as practice Farley 1983, Wheeler and Farley 1991, Chopp 1995, Hodgson 1999, Heitink 1999, Volf and Bass 2002). Universal solidarity in a community breaking apart in social violence poses the fundamental question what theology can contribute to a different kind of thinking and acting in tragic moments of human need.

Fundamental theology—*systematic*, *dogmatic* and *pastoral*—is called upon in situations where people can no longer juggle the *fragmentary*, the *ambiguous* and the *different*, and therefore resort to violence as their only and last possible means. *Building true community* as a step to *communicative world peace* (Peck 1987, 255-334) in a broken postmodern world is a fundamental task for theology in all its many academic disciplines, most preferably for a *practical fundamental theology* (Metz 1980, 1992/1977, Peukert 1984, Arens 1995a, Haight 2001, Taylor 1990, 2011) working out of a concept of universal solidarity where we all "need each other" (Peck 1987, 17), "out of the experience of belonging together" (Arens 1995a, 167).

Then, the modern and postmodern realities of fragment, ambiguity, and difference lose their threatening character, and instead, contribute to a marvelous and creative new kind of mosaic as we recognize and believe in a "God as Communities in Solidarity" (Wetherilt 1994, 145-146, Welch 1985, and Sawyer 2003). "Universal solidarity grounded in this way becomes the central category for a particular kind of fundamental theology" (Arens 1995a, 168).

Peace-Learning in a Safe Place

True community is capable of gracefully embracing and inviting in the *fragmentary*, the *ambiguous*, the *different*, the foreigner, the burdensome, even the threatening. True community is inclusive, liminal and beyond fear. True community refuses to play the all too human game of exclusion and embrace, withdrawal and ostracism. True community will become a *safe place*, turning into a *peace-learning laboratory of personal disarmament* as humans learn how to deal with conflict and differences in a new and nonviolent way (Peck 1987, 67-70). Recognizing that each one needs the other for his or her personal and social, political and global salvation.

As North American psychiatrist and social visionary of *true community* in a world embattled by violence and close to radical extinction M. Scott Peck puts it beautifully in his pragmatic dream *The Different Drum*

(Peck 1987) of a new kind of *peace-making society* for the future as humans learn the challenging art and process of *living in community*:

> "In and through community lies the salvation of the world ... Nothing is more important. Yet it is virtually impossible to describe community meaningfully to someone who has never experienced it—and most of us have never had an experience of true community. The problem is analogous to an attempt to describe the taste of artichokes to someone who has never eaten one ... Still, the attempt must be made. For the human race today stands at the brink of self-annihilation ... Some of the victims of Hiroshima and Nagasaki are described as walking blindly down the street after the blasts, dragging bundles of their own skin behind them. I'm scared for my own skin. I'm even more scared for the skin of my children. And I'm scared for your skins. I want to save my skin. I need you, and you me, for salvation. We must come into community with each other. We need each other." (Peck 1987, 17)

Fundamental theology has a contribution to make to this kind of a *safe place* in the world where people as Christians and others are invited to a peace-learning process building true community. *Postmodernity* is a trendy new word. Yet, as long as there is no better word, theologians will have to reckon with its fundamental social challenge. The challenge being not so much a new apology for fundamentals, a new construction of fool-proof basics, nor a new system of intellectual consistency and evidence. Rather, the challenge will be, theologically and socially, to create a new kind of community in theology that allows people to *feel safe* and to learn peace-making activities to grow into a new kind of *postmodern community* as *spiritual community* - in theology as well (on the postmodern and spiritual in community Hodgson 1994, 295–297, Kirkpatrick 2001, Childs 2006).

As North American and postmodern systematic theologian *Peter C. Hodgson* puts it in his systematic theology of the *Winds of the Spirit* (Hodgson 1994), describing the future social shape, theological definition, and ethical character of an ecclesial community following and going beyond *Jürgen Habermas' communicative action* (Hodgson 1994, 4) in a postmodern communicative freedom in a global world:

> "The definition incorporates several biblical images of the church—people, body, communion, Spirit—allowing these ancient symbols to help establish the lineaments of a new ecclesiology. Ecclesia is the people of God, one people, yet drawn from a

plurality of peoples and cultural traditions. It is the body whose unique intersubjectivity is shaped by the life, death, and resurrection of Christ. It is a transfigured mode of human community, a koinonia of faith, hope, love. And its source of vitality is the creative, upbuilding work of the Spirit of God . . . Ecclesia has a peculiarly self-surpassing character: It knows no ethnic, spatial, or temporal boundaries and is intrinsically nonprovincial. There are no absolute strangers, for God's redemption has no specific cultural conditions . . . Ecclesial community is human community transfigured in the direction of liberation—liberation through Christ from all provincialisms and oppressions based on race, sex, sexual orientation, class, dogma, ideology, location, culture . . . Freedom is the critical mark of ecclesia in our time." (Hodgson 1994, 298–299)

True community understood in this way would include instead of exclude, letting *free communication* and *living together* flow, even in the midst of our many and various conflicts of interpretation *(Paul Ricoeur)*, as "it is above all conditions of systematic exploitation that block communication" (Hodgson 1994, 295). True community understood in this way is still something to be *progressively learned*, in hard work and sensitive listening, engaging belief, and stubborn trust that peace is after all *possible*, in spite of everything acting and speaking against it. True community is a *gift*, since it does not come to us naturally, but only spiritually (Peck 1987, 73–76). Like peace, true community cannot be fabricated, programmed, managed by objectives, forced into existence, ordered by decree. "The spirit of true community is the spirit of peace" (Peck 1987, 74). And *peace happens*, somehow quite miraculously.

Revisioning Community

Revisioning *true community* in this way, as a new kind of *postmodern and fundamental ecclesiology* (for a postmodern ecclesiology Welch 1985, Hodgson 1988, 1994, 293–304, Page 2000, Kärkkäinen 2002a, 221–230, Mannion 2007), will speak to a community in desperate need for some humanly *redeeming word*. Like a community in a local village facing teenagers taking heroin at the age of 14. In moments like this you recognize that we still have not learned how to really live in community. New models of *living* and *peace-learning* in *true community* (Doyle 2000, Kirkpatrick 2001, Fuellenbach 2002, Sawyer 2003, Marsh 2005) are desperately needed, especially in a radically postmodern, over-digitalized, and under-emotionalized world (Beaudoin 1998, Harvey 1999, Sweet 1999, 2001, 2007, Staub 2008, Frost 2006, Frost and Hirsch 2009, Hirsch 2006, Hirsch and Ferguson 2011, Hirsch and Catchim 2011).

As *José Comblin*, Belgian systematic theologian having lived in Latin America for many years, puts it in his visionary ecclesiology of the *people of God*, calling for new and creative ways of living in community in a postmodern as well as post-Western world:

> "The Christian message is that they are called to form peoples, according to the image of the people of God: people means collaboration and covenant between free and equal people in family bonds. That is the goal . . . All peoples will have to achieve peoplehood by themselves. The people of God can show the way and how to journey, if it wants to. Otherwise, it will stay in church praising God while humankind stumbles along with no clear direction. Given the triumphant individualism that constitutes the power of the West but is destroying the traditional integration of the rest of humankind, forming peoples is going to mean a long journey. Certainly anything that can show models of community life will be helpful. The older forms of community are obsolete: they can no longer function within the social model now imposed by the Western way of life. That is why religious communities have disappeared as communities. New ways of living in community must be imagined and created." (Comblin 2004, 177)

Sometime in the year 1993 at a local community meeting of villagers concerned about what was going on with 14-year-old teenagers in a village, an older woman stood up to use the metaphor and image of a *family* that would unite us all together to care for and look after each other, even with juvenile teenagers taking heroin at the age of 14. The subsequent developments of the story turned a beautiful *family metaphor* as a new kind of possible *community in universal solidarity* (on community and universal solidarity Arens 1995a, 145–169) in a postmodern day and age into the opposite of a premodern and modern *war zone*, playing the habitual game of exclusion and embrace.

Communities and Theologies Turning Postmodern

Systematic theologies in the twenty-first century will have to become *postmodern* in the sense that all our common and established foundations and ground floors of a past *House of Authority*—be it *Scripture, tradition, teaching authority, philosophy* - have fallen (Hodgson and King 1994, 72–77). Some still act as if nothing has happened. Others know very well that the world is no longer the same. Nothing holds anymore the way it used to give some balance, some stability, some place and common ground to stand on. The bottom has been taken out, free-falling into the unknown. What used to give a certain assurance that things are the way they seem, has disappeared. Traditional authorities have lost their convincing power. What used to be unbelievable now seems possible. 14-year-old teenagers taking heroin is only one example for what nowadays does not hold anymore, but still happens.

Communities turn *postmodern*, inasmuch as our theologies, social convictions, village traditions, local narratives, national histories, societal philosophies, lifestyle theories, and even *global worldviews* turn *postmodern* (Smart 2000, Cooper 2003, Tarnas 1991, Armesto 2003). Theologies and communities are deeply connected, as one reflects the other. No common narrative holds people together anymore. The breaking apart of a community is only a symptom of the breaking apart of a communal or global world no longer in agreement on what may hold the center, what may be a common and shared vision, and what may still be worthwhile investing and engaging in so that superficially built-up but not built-together communities become deep-level *true* and even *healing communities* in this global world (Peck 1987, Granberg-Michaelson 1991, Harmer 1998, Marsh 2005).

This global or local challenge touches on the most honorable and pressing calling of what a contemporary *modern* or *postmodern fundamental theology* as a *communicative open forum* (Arens 1995a, 1995b, Waldenfels 2000, 81–90) could be to a world falling and breaking apart. That people are broken, that communities fall apart, that human communication is ending, that nations go to war, that global poverty breaks up a whole world, that theories and ideologies, policies and sociologies, local visions and global melodies do not go together anymore, but are radically parting, if not falling apart, is the common daily bread of what we are faced with as endless *fragmenting of our world*, every day more. "We live today in a world that is broken by war, injustice, poverty, exploitation, and ill health. Families, homes, communities, nations, and people are broken" (Granberg-Michaelson 1991, xi).

As North American feminist theologian *Gloria Albrecht* puts it, describing the *postmodern fragmentation* of a contemporary and "postpositivistic" world, where "there is no stable place to stand" anymore (Albrecht 1995, 27), with its deepest challenge, "the question of the meaning and

The Social

possibility of 'community' in the midst of a fragmented and secular society" (Albrecht 1995, 19), the pressing need for a new kind of basis for human community—social and theological—may be a promising calling for theology in new days. Fundamental theology could become something like the new therapist of a world in need of a *peace-making* and *community-building* thinking and acting along and across humanly constructed and deconstructed old and new *border crossings* (on border crossing in the social sciences Giroux 1992, Giroux and McLaren 1994, Soja 2000, 2011, in theology Arens 1995a, 1995b, Schreiter 1997, Taylor 2011). Border crossing *fundamental theology* could become a creative and *world-crossing midwife* for *peace-building thinking and acting* in an open "*communicative freedom*" (Hodgson 1994, 131–132), border crossing across all common and uncommon human boundaries and theoretical partings, mental territories and social dividing walls, so that people from all walks of life may start to understand and learn how to live with each other again.

Theology Healing Communities

Karin Granberg-Michaelson from the *Christian Medical Commission* of the *World Council of Churches* in Geneva puts it beautifully in her little suggestive book *Healing Community* (Granberg-Michaelson 1991), underlining the creative healing mission of community building, both socially and theologically, in our wounded world: "In the act of creating a caring community, one finds that the community has become a place of healing" (Granberg-Michaelson 1991, 14). Theology could become a place like that too. *Fundamental theology* as the entrance hall and window pale for interested outsiders and convinced insiders, firm believers and grown agnostics, casual visitors and faithful tenants, violent critics and sweet relatives, long-time companions and temporary bystanders, scathing commentators and vivid narrators, as well as hard opponents and soft skeptics, could become something like a creative therapy place for a new kind of theology healing the world. Thinking, acting, and living out of a *critical social reason* (Haight 2001, 46-47) combined with *community social action* (Haight 2001, 47–48), *fundamental theology* conceived in this way could even *change the world*.

Building community and theology as an *open and therapeutic forum*, encouraging consensual communicative rationality, creative communicative action, and postmodern communicative freedom, combining Europeans like *Jürgen Habermas, Helmut Peukert,* and *Edmund Arens* with North Americans like *Peter. C. Hodgson, Gloria Albrecht*, and *Francis Schüssler Fiorenza*, may be more than just an academic and intellectual game. If, like North American postmodern, systematic, and political theologian *Peter C. Hodgson* puts it in his systematic theology of the *Winds of the Spirit*, the "telos of communicative rationality is free and liberated human community, based on unrestrained dialogue, mutuality, solidarity, and equality", the utopian ideal of "communicative freedom" (Hodgson 1994, 131), and if, like feminist liberation theologian of community and "embodied reason" *Gloria Albrecht* reminds us, pleading for a theology that embodies itself in concrete embodied experiences, we "must literally place ourselves in the midst of concrete justice struggles and live in such a way that we participate in the building up of just communities of nonviolence" (Albrecht 1995, 139), then the therapeutic and political pertinence of such a *fundamental theology of community* becomes visible.

The Collapse of the House of Authority

The *fragmentary*, the *ambiguous*, and the recognition of *radical diversity* in our common and uncommon *differences* in everything we believe and live by in this radically postmodern world has globally and literally flooded the human consciousness. An information overkill has left us in our human software and hardware philosophically and theologically helpless in sorting out what may still be right and wrong, true and false, worthy our belief and ready for abandonment. Everything that used to be certain has turned out to be simply a *perspective*, one among many possible and impossible ones. In life, as well as in systematic theology. Whole houses of safe belief and certain assurances seem to be falling.

North American systematic theologians *Peter C. Hodgson* and *Edward Farley* vividly describe already in 1985 and 1994 (Hodgson and King 1985, 1994) in an ecumenical-collaborative *basic textbook introduction* to the different *loci* of *systematic or dogmatic theology* the radical *collapse of the house of authority* (Farley 1982 and Hodgson and King 1994, 72–77), affecting not just systematic theology, but all of human life:

> "The house of authority has collapsed, despite of the fact that many people still try to live in it. Some retain title to it without actually living there; others are antiquarians or renovators, attempting in one way or another to salvage it; still others have abandoned it for new quarters or no quarters at all." (Hodgson and King 1985, 76, Hodgson and King 1994, 76)

Once authorities collapse, common narratives disappear, shared visions recede to the background, mutually agreed upon covenants are broken, *violence* creeps in as the most natural response to the different, or *denial*. Violence in postmodern society is always a form of denial. The dream of by-gone unity, enforced conformity, ordered cohesiveness, and wished-for universality of what we believe, live by, act on, dream of, as the only way and path how people should live, is always the beginning of the subtle temptation to *violence*.

Accepting the radically disquieting *challenges of postmodernity*, both socially and theologically (on postmodernism in systematic theology Hodgson 1994, 53–66), may be the most therapeutic thing to go through, making people more humble, careful, and listening. After the collapse of all our houses of authorities, we may start building up something new from scratch. Something new has to come, because the break has been too final and definite. Pleading for a new kind of systematic theology sensitive to a radically changed postmodern situation, *Peter C. Hodgson* from *Vanderbilt University* concludes: "The foundations of modernity are too deeply shaken to allow for any simple continuity" (Hodgson 1994, 55).

Feminist theologian *Ruth Page* from Scotland puts it theologically and pastorally in her reflections on a new pastoral existence in a postmodern world:

> "Who are we, with whom God has these relationships? In pluralist, postmodern times, that is almost an unanswerable question, except in terms of diversity. There is diversity even in the degrees of postmodernity people 'flow' with. They may still adhere to more or less of modernity, while a few have chosen to return to, or may never have removed from, aspects of premodernity (before the Enlightenment) . . . Yet to describe the 'us' with whom God is in relation now, at the point where the church is and acts at the moment, postmodernity has to be taken with full seriousness." (Page 2000, 30–31)

Denial in Postmodernity

However, to accept such a radical diversity in postmodern conditions with full seriousness is not necessarily self-evident. Most often, the disquieting fact of worlds breaking apart, common perspectives falling, shared values disintegrating, is *violence* in the personal and social form of *denial*. Whether in theology, or in communal life.

The Community of the Weak

Some villagers in 1993 in *Erlinsbach*, at the high point of irruption of some of the most threatening juvenile social problems in a local village, actually suggested to put teenagers taking heroin at the age of 14 against a wall to get rid of them. Such beer-table statements were quite common signs of a helpless social envisioning in view of more possible nightmares than those that had already been experienced. Simple mechanisms of *social denial* moved in. Denial became a communal way of dealing with things in a world having turned *different, ambiguous, broken into fragments,* where there was "no stable place to stand" on anymore (Albrecht 1995, 27). Afterwards, when the openly violent and secretly slanderous exclusionary and scapegoating mechanisms had done their work - not just getting rid of some teenagers on drugs, chasing them around from here to there, but also getting rid of a local pastor who had taken their sides - the village fell back into classical *states of denial* (on a social psychology and critical theory of states of denial Cohen 2001).

Meeting other people in need, suffering, but also upsetting our common social fabric by seemingly improper or even dangerous behavior, quite often challenges us with the simple question asked by sociologist of denial *Stanley Cohen*: "what do we do with our knowledge about the suffering of others, and what does this knowledge do to us?" (Cohen 2001, X). Some people look away, others start blaming those who seem to be suffering, some again try to fix the problem, and some try to get rid of it. Various forms of *social denial*, repression, dissociation, and exclusion seem to be first responses to the in-breaking of the unfamiliar, the cognitively dissonant, the socially upsetting. Only after the first cognitive and social, emotional and communal shock or trauma do people usually regroup to figure out some new ways of responding to what is happening.

The first social reaction to the *different*, the *ambiguous*, and the *fragmentary* in the local village of *Erlinsbach* in 1993 was *denial*, even though everybody could read about it in the national and local newspapers. The young teenager that had died filled newspaper articles all over Switzerland. The girl, 14-year-old, was a confirmation class member of mine. A few weeks before we had still talked about soft drugs, hard drugs, and the knowledge to know when to stop. I still remember those moments just outside the parsonage where I lived. Only some weeks later the news hit the village that *Cornelia* had died of a heroin overdose not far from the village at an open drug scene in a city nearby. At the time, Switzerland was even internationally known for several such openly tolerated drug scenes, one the widely known "needle-park" in metropolitan Zurich, the other

The Social

one about 15 minutes by bus away from our local village. And some other teenagers, 14-year-old, were in danger too. Another one of them being again one of my confirmation class members.

Sociologist *Stanley Cohen* describes the *states of denial* in any community that faces the in-breaking of the traumatically shocking:

> "One common thread runs through the many different stories of denial: people, organizations, governments or whole societies are presented with information that is too disturbing, threatening or anomalous to be fully absorbed or openly acknowledged. The information is therefore somehow repressed, disavowed, pushed aside or reinterpreted. Or else the information 'registers' well enough, but its implications—cognitive, emotional or moral—are evaded, neutralized or rationalized away." (Cohen 2001, 1)

Ambiguity, fragment, and *the different* hit me as well. The temptation to let the in-breaking of the shock pass away was there too. The possibility to let the *ambiguous* and *fragmentary* stay there without any *different* change of heart and action remained. I had no experience whatsoever with drugs. Never had I even seen how teenagers prepare a joint. Neither did I know how you sniff heroin. Nor did I know what to do if you have a 14-year-old confirmation class member about whom you know he is taking drugs, but he will not tell you. Only after months of friendship and shared crises, common trips to amusement parks and weeks of clandestine hosting in the parsonage after having run away from a juvenile home, with many hours of simply being there, did *Adrian*—or *"Adi"*—once tell me at some quiet lake near evening sunset he was taking heroin. My world as well needed some regrouping trying to understand what was happening.

Facing the Postmodern

The reader may question what all this experiential recalling of concrete moments in a story of tragic and communal break-ups around some 14-year-old teenagers taking heroin has to do with fundamental and systematic debates as regards to the *postmodern signature of our times*, extensively treated both in the *social sciences, cultural theory, political science, feminist thought, radical philosophy,* and *systematic theology* (for the social sciences, cultural theory, political theory, and feminist theory Ward 1997, Best and Kellner 1991, Nicholson and Seidman 1995, Sim 2001, for systematic theology Vanhoozer 2003, Hart 2004, Ward 2005, Penner 2005, Smith 2006, 2008).

The Community of the Weak

And yet, these concrete and visual-tactile examples of day-to-day living, worrying, witnessing, sharing, and facing exhilarating moments of peace-making *community healing* as well as traumatic memories of communal *war-making* and *people-wounding* point to the most omnipresent signature of our times in which the confusing and de-confusing *postmodern* (Anderson 1995), portable even *for beginners* (Appignanesi and Garratt 1995, Berger 2003), in easy and digestable form so that you can, if needed, even *teach yourself* (Ward 1997), can be tasted and felt at any time, witnessed and seen as it goes by, heard and remembered right down at the most basic and day-to-day level of some dinky little local village somewhere in this global world at some time past or present that was and is, in this postmodern time, violently *breaking apart*.

The postmodern is as *basic* and *ordinary* as well as *everyday* as the telling of this story of some 14-year-old teenagers taking heroin in a local village suggests. At the same time it is most elusive and slippery. To quote communications and art theorist *Arthur Asa Berger* from *San Francisco State University* in his *The Portable Postmodernist* (Berger 2003): "Postmodernism is like a piece of whet soap that keeps slipping out of your hands; you think you have it and then it slides away from you" (Berger 2003, vii). The postmodern can be found *in everything*. Most definitely it has changed our whole human way of life, even if we may not recognize it. So it comes, that everything can be conjoined within this phenomenal and global description of the postmodern, "romantic love in postmodern societies, advertising and postmodernism, therapy and postmodernism, Disney and postmodernism, punk and postmodernism, African Americans and postmodernism, and a number of other analyses, all of which suggest that life in postmodern societies is radically different than it was before..." (Berger 2003, xii).

The postmodern is *all-inclusive*, in that it affects everything in our personal and social life. From the smallest trip to the shopping mall right next door to the biggest political debate at some hot-shot summit on world peace, the postmodern creeps in from all sides, through the backdoor, from the front screen, along the sides and in the midst of those who commune and try to communicate with each other in a world that is no longer the same as before. A global world, a confusing world, a world where nothing holds anymore, everything being invented anew or torn down to the ground. As *Glenn Ward* in *Teach Yourself Postmodernism* puts it: "Postmodernism is everywhere" (Ward 1997, 1).

The *postmodern challenge*, most prominent for a new kind of fundamental and systematic theology in this global world, touches on all aspects of the human soul, the *cognitive* and the emotional, the *historical* and the contemporary, the *political* and the cultural, the *socioeconomic* and the musical, the *ecological* and the artistic, the *sexual* and the spiritual, the *religious* and the philosophical (on cognitive, historical, political, socioeconomic, sexual, spiritual, and religious challenges of postmodernism Hodgson 1994, 53–66). All this can be seen even in looking at some simple story of some 14-year-old teenagers in some local village taking heroin.

North American *Peter C. Hodgson* in his basic introduction to systematic theology for a postmodern world *Winds of the Spirit* (Hodgson 1994) leads us right into the outspoken or only intuitively felt sentiment of a *new time and age* having arrived, one more radical and lasting change of scientific and cognitive paradigms ready to be assumed:

> "What is it today that demands the revisioning of Christian theology? What is the new cultural situation that we face as North American Christians? It seems that it is not that of the 'underside' of history . . ., as is the case with Latin American, African, and Asian theologies, but rather that of the 'passage' of history—the passing of Western bourgeois culture, with its ideals of individuality, patriarchy, private rights, technical rationality, historical progress, capitalist economy, the absoluteness of Christianity, and so on. It *feels* as though we are reaching the end of a historical era since we find ourselves in the midst of cognitive, historical, political, socioeconomic, environmental, sexual/gender, and religious changes of vast importance, comparable perhaps to the great Enlightenment that inaugurated the modern age. Can we speak, then, of a second Enlightenment, a new watershed, a new paradigm in theology?" (Hodgson 1994, 53)

Whether we call it *postmodern* (Hodgson 1994, 54), or any other term, the feeling is there that things have radically changed. And this affects all of our daily walking and academic thinking, right down into our most personal and social *pastoral reflection and action* (Forrester 2000) as *practicing theology* (Volf and Bass 2002)—systematic, fundamental, or dogmatic.

Postmodern Theology and Power

Power and the Postmodern Theological

On the surface, most commentators of postmodernism seem to get lost in a labyrinth of contradictory impressions. Some view it as totally nonpolitical, eschewing any question of power and the political. Others find in it a analysis of the workings and *faces of power* (Boulding 1990) much more complex and intricate than in any other comparable approach to the social and personal. *Power* seems to flow *through everything*, both the personal and the social, even the biological, as this undercurrent or exposed river of a "potential for change" (Boulding 1990, 15). Power thereby can be both openly *creative*, transforming, and visionary, or purposefully *destructive*, abusive, and life negating. *The demonic of power*, the force of destruction showing its face everywhere, comes out most visibly especially in this postmodern age.

North American and feminist systematic theologian *Rebecca S. Chopp* describes the end of the modern era with quite vivid images, as our most common and trustworthy concepts of *reason, progress*, and *freedom* have been evaporating in the explosive arrival of a new, maybe postmodern sentiment, mostly facing the abuse and violation of fragile life forces in this world in which we all live, another word for *the postmodern demonic*:

> "How are we to characterize, to describe, no matter how partially, the world in which we live? Death, control, destruction, deviance, force, manipulation, murder. These terms, these words, label the end of the modern era, the era of freedom, progress, and reason. If there are history books in the future, of what will they speak, what events will they find symbolic—the progress of science that leads to Hiroshima or the not-yet nuclear apocalypse that looms to explode us all as dust unto dust, having finally managed unto ashes the fragile force of life? . . . In what manner will future history books speak of the modern state, guarantor of the Enlightenment, with its hatred of the Jew suppressed through reason and representation, finally made manifest in the Holocaust? . . . Such events rupture discourse even in the present situation, they are fundamentally unrepresentable in the magnitude of their horror. The mimetic or even descriptive language used to report such events suggests already an enlightened history in which torture and repression are more common than aid and refuge . . . The demonic power of destruction and force, threatening nature, society, and subjectivity, is co-present with the mania of psychic oppressiveness: failure, suicide, stress, psychosis, drug addiction, depression, and schizophrenia stalk the present age . . ." (Chopp 1989, 101–102)

In distinction to a *nonpolitical reading of the postmodern*, which would leave out most of these *demonic forces* and powers as well as the *creative energies* reflected in the ending of a modern age, some of the most interesting and perspicuous social scientists and critical theorists of *the postmodern* have contributed a great deal to a *political reading* of the little and bigger workings of power in almost everything making up the life of this present age. Language, culture, history, biology, community, identity, subjectivity, the media, communication, the cross-cultural, the personal, the everyday, the artistic, the spiritual, the emotional, the erotic, the sexual, the political, or simply the social, are all soaked by this invisible and visible reality or fluidity flowing in and through most everywhere called *power* (for a sociology and critical theory of power Wartenberg 1990, 1992, Kreisberg 1992, Westwood 2002, Kahane 2010).

Theology—systematic, fundamental, and *dogmatic*—shows a similar tendency of outright confusion in view of evaluating and integrating postmodern dealings with the question of *power*. As the topics of investigative concern have multiplied endlessly—language, culture, community, subjectivity, the personal, the social, the political, the artistic, the erotic—, to find a common entrance door to the vast field of possible shared interests is not easy. And yet, theology may do well in opening up to the limitless questions on *power and the social* (Westwood 2002). The theme of power may be the most important contribution of postmodernism to a *new kind of systematic theology in the twenty-first century*. *The postmodern* as well as *power* as a *basic category* of the theological will need to become more central in the revisioning of *constructive theologies—systematic, fundamental* and *dogmatic*—in the future (Taylor 1990, Hodgson 1994, Chopp and Taylor 1994, Peters 2000, Ward 1997, 2005).

Language and Knowledge

One area of common concern where power is entering the central stage both in *postmodern social theory* and in *systematic theology* is in the question of *language and knowledge,* as authors on both ends of the social and theological spectrum are drawing attention, as North American systematic theologian *Peter C. Hodgson* puts it—following *Rebecca S. Chopp*— to the close "connection between knowledge, power, and language" (Hodgson 1994, 65, on power, language, and knowledge in theology Chopp 1989 and Schmalstieg 1991).

Language and knowledge are *fundamentals* of theology, as well as basic constituencies of human living. Whoever controls human language— *theological* and *social*—has a certain control over human life. As theology has traditionally been a highly *linguistic endeavor* of the human word, of human phrases, narratives, definitions, descriptions that do make a big difference on how people see things and live in the world, the self-critical analysis of its own use and abuse of language is most pertinent. Language creates a *social-symbolic order* (for deconstructing power in literary feminist theory/theory of science Weedon 1997 and Rouse 1987) that determines what people may feel free to think or not to think, how people may feel free to feel or not to feel, and how people may feel free to act, or not to act. Language has a way of being precognitive, pre-subjective, being there already *before* we even think and act.

In that sense, North American and Lutheran post-liberal *George Lindbeck* (Lindbeck 1984) makes his point of a *cultural-linguistic presupposition* of all our modern or postmodern theologies in that we are all born somehow into our cultural-linguistic cradle that determines even our most personal identities and subjectivities. Depending on what kind of a cultural-linguistic map we have been born into and grown up in, some things just seem to be out of vision, out of perspective, out of reach and possibility, out of the perusing question. Even though it may not be so. The sudden shake-up of radical break-downs—*modern* or *postmodern*—may be the most healthy and transforming thing to go through in culturally-linguistically determined lives like that.

Looking at the *politics of language* and the *symbolic order* may be the beginning of *personal transformation*, as feminist and deconstructive systematic theologian *Rebecca S. Chopp* puts it: "Language, subjectivity, and politics: these three realms, dimensions, common places, form today the structuring of the dominant social-symbolic order and provide the problems and possibilities of transformation" (Chopp 1989, 103).

Feminist poststructuralist *Chris Weedon* describes the potential of deconstructive analysis of language, knowledge, and power in a postmodern, poststructural world:

> "Feminist poststructuralism, then, is a mode of knowledge production which uses poststructural theories of language, subjectivity, social processes and institutions to understand existing power relations and to identify areas and strategies for change. Through a concept of *discourse*, which is seen as a structuring principle of society, in social institutions, modes of thought and individual subjectivity, feminist poststructuralism is able, in detailed, historically specific analysis, to explain the working of power on behalf of specific interests and to analyse the opportunities for resistance to it. It is a theory which decentres the

rational, self-present subject of humanism, seeing subjectivity and consciousness as socially produced in language, as sites of struggle and potential change." (Weedon 1997, 40)

Theology—systematic, fundamental and *dogmatic*—may well need the therapeutic shock of poststructural analysis of its linguistic distribution of power and powerlessness over centuries on behalf of specific interests and interest groups in order to start to reinvent a whole *new language* in tune with those that have historically and socially been left out as whispering and small voices to be heard again for the reconstruction of *theological language*.

Whispering small voices most often have been *shut up*, pushed to the side, hit over with a bat, bullied into silent existence. Some of these voices are starting to trust in their social importance again—women, children, Natives, African Americans, Hispanics, Asian Americans, non-Europeans, the globally and locally excluded from the *history of church and world theology* (Kee/Albu/Lindberg/Frost/Robert 1998, Hastings 1999, Norris 2002). *Social postmodernism*, in its radical questionings in social poststructuralism, feminism, postfeminism, and postcolonialism, may be that long-awaited and needed cultural shock for theology—*systematic, fundamental*, and *dogmatic* as well (Taylor 1990, Schüssler Fiorenza 1996, Welch 1985, 1999, 2000, 2004, 2005, Kwok Pui-Lan, Compier and Rieger 2007, Rieger 2007, Taylor 2011).

Postmodern Empowerment

Another topic of common concern may be the social and communal vision of *postmodern empowerment* (Weissberg 1999, Cruikshank 1999, Mayo 2000, Adams 2003) in a world of crisscrossed solidarities, mixed-up identities, and messy social or political, personal or ethnic loyalties. In spite of some harsh criticism about the inflationary use and abuse of *empowerment language* (for a critique of the concept of empowerment Weissberg 1999), the personal and social need for everyone to be able to change some things, and maybe even a lot of things, in one's personal and social life, remains a lasting and transforming political vision.

Jesse Jackson's Rainbow Coalition symbolically represents this postmodern condition of political and social involvement in a nevertheless still painfully *violent* and *unjust*, outright *dismembering* and *extinguishing* world. Some people just get totally *erased*, as it seems, from the surface of the earth or out of anybody's perceiving social vision. Others just get minimally tolerated on the side lines, waiting for life. Millions still keep waiting for their daily bread. Millions keep hoping for some lasting peace on earth. Millions keep looking for protection, a home, shelter, empathy. Millions keep waiting for the right to be.

Community developer and cultural theorist *Marjorie Mayo* (Mayo 2000, Craig and Mayo 1995) describes the creatively political potential of such *new social movements* (Della Porta and Diani 1999, Mullings 2009) as *Rainbow Coalitions* celebrating postmodern variety and diversity, alternatives and difference, while at the same time, as *communities of a new kind of identity*, trying to change the world:

> "However problematic, the notion of 'communities of identity' has been central to the discussion of New Social Movements such as those campaigning for Black Liberation, Women's Liberation, and Gay and Lesbian Liberation, together with movements of older people and movements of people with disabilities . . . These movements have been concerned with contesting the negative identities which have been associated with the prejudices of racist, sexist, homophobic, ageist and ableist societies—aiming to promote positive identities, alternative communities based upon shared cultures and values. The celebration of diversity and difference has been a central theme in debates about community politics, and indeed in debates about alternative approaches to politics more generally . . ." (Mayo 2000, 3)

Postmodern Empathy

To this world, a *postmodern empathy* (Bauman 1993, 143–144), filling some of these hurting and alternative social spaces with human warmth, spacious hearts, and all those human emotions that transform modern pathological society, like "love, sympathy, compassion, or care . . ." (Bauman 1993, 144), may lead to a new experience of *feeling* and *finding some power*, a radical new way of *personal, social, cultural, and political empowerment*, something, for instance, to be learned culturally and theologically from African American narratives and stories (on empowerment in African American systematic and ethical theology Walker 1991, Sanders 1995).

African American and womanist theologian and ethicist *Cheryl J. Sanders* portrays such an *empowerment ethics* (Sanders 1995), leading the people to believe in and take charge of their most *personal and social power* in their *capacity for empathy*. Both are needed for *political action* in this postmodern world, with *theological reflection* being called to provide social as well as theoretical models for "promoting empowerment and empathy in community-building ministries" (Sanders 1995, 123).

> "The willingness of African American Christians to retain an open moral and spiritual commitment to empathy may prove to be the key to this nation's ability to marshal its moral and fiscal resources to liberate the poor within its own borders. The ethics of empowerment challenges religious leaders to embody creative approaches to personal growth and collective resourcefulness for meeting human need, and to resist the temptation to follow the path of 'cheap justice' that demands repentance and restitution from the oppressing group on behalf of the poor without engaging in a self-critical assessment of the full cost of the equitable sharing of one's own power and resources. It is hoped that increasing numbers of religious and moral leaders will step forward who are willing to prod themselves toward cultivating character-producing structures that embody the noblest ethical ideals being preached and taught in the name of Christ. The distinctive calling of the African American Christian community at the close of the twentieth century is full implementation of the ethics of empowerment, so that the disinherited can be motivated to hope, and the privileged can be challenged to do justice." (Sanders 1995, 123–124)

This commitment to *empathy* is central for beginning and ending any *fundamental ethics of social empowerment*. Theology—*systematic, fundamental, dogmatic* and *ethical*—can then be looked at in the tradition of *biblical holiness* (Gammie 1989) as a "remoralization" in the "interrelatedness of personal and social transformation" attentive to "social justice, personal piety, and wisdom or intellectual purity" (Sanders 1995, 105). All three should be basic categories for *fundamental theology*. *Social justice, personal piety*, and *wisdom* provide the ingredients with which theology is being built. An attentiveness to these three ingredients will change the way theology is being developed, right from its *fundamental start*.

Postmodern Creativity

Making *social justice, personal piety*, and *wisdom* as the old theological *habitus*—with theology as a holistic concept, instead of a fragmenting and dissipating conglomeration of ever more self-containing specialties—

basic even in *fundamental theology* provides a new framework from where to build the new architecture of encyclopedic theology (on social justice, personal piety, and wisdom as habitus in an encyclopedic theology Farley 1983).

The basic theme of *power* (Schmalstieg 1991, Griffin 2004, and Keller 2005)—in *modern and postmodern ways*—will then be addressed more often, inasmuch as fundamental theology considers itself "as a critical project of 'enlightenment' that resists those systems engaged in amassing power . . . ," as Roman Catholic fundamental theologian *Edmund Arens* (Arens 1995a, 31, referring to Metz 1980, Peukert 1984) summarizes the critical project of a *practical fundamental theology* in the tradition of *critical theory, Jürgen Habermas, Johann Baptist Metz*, and *Helmut Peukert*. Fundamental theology intentional on *empowering people* in *empathic learning* and *community acting* (Sanders 1995, Walker 1991) will make a difference in this modern and postmodern world, encouraging people to "stand over against the mechanisms for amassing power," by "breaking through these mechanisms" in order to give space for a kind of hopeful *social creativity* that *Helmut Peukert* and *Edmund Arens* describe as an "ethics of intersubjective creativity" (Arens 1995a, 32).

Both a *social ethics of empowerment* (Sanders 1995, Walker 1991) and a *fundamental ethics of intersubjective creativity* (Arens 1995a, 32)—while being reminded by *action-oriented social sciences* that human and "temporal, creative, rule-breaking communicative action of subjects" is always "free" (Peukert 1984, 43, on intersubjective creativity in sociology Joas 1996)—converge in the shared social vision and human dream to have people discover their own *inner and outer power* to change the world. *Power* in this sense is *freedom-creating, space-giving, hope-filling*. Power in this sense has nothing to do with most of our common and uncommon concepts of limiting, destructive, coercing power that rules, forbids, and stands *above* people, ruling *over them*.

Power conceived as *intersubjective creativity* (Arens 1995a, 32) *empowers* people, opens up discussion, comprehension, understanding, disagreement, even conflict, but dealt with humanly. Power experienced that way encourages people, lays open spaces and places to play, lets people breathe and see, agree and disagree. Power in these postmodern times will be *postmodern creativity* juggling the *different*, the *ambiguous*, the *fragmentary*, in new and creative ways without resorting to old and modern forms and temptations of violence. Since *violence* is no other than the helpless *ending* of creativity in staying together.

The Social

Postmodern Power as Being Together

North American feminist theologian and Roman Catholic social ethicist *Christine Firer Hinze* (Firer Hinze 1995), after presenting a most thorough and comprehensive general survey of social, political, and theological concepts of social and personal power from *Max Weber* over *Karl Marx, Jacques Maritain, Reinhold Niebuhr, Michel Foucault, Hannah Arendt,* and *Anthony Giddens,* to contemporary *feminist social theory, Paul Tillich, process theology, liberation* and *black theology,* and *feminist social ethics,* gives a beautiful description of this new kind of *empowering power,* infusing both *fundamental theology* and *social ethics* in the experience of *being together*:

> "Power understood in a comprehensive manner illumines features of the social and political landscape otherwise obscured, and lends the necessary starting point and context for a sophisticated Christian social and political ethics. In the end, the particular way of being comprehensive that a Christian ethicist embraces transfuses fundamental theological and anthropological convictions into the heart of ethical thinking about society and politics. For my own part, the evidence of scripture and Christian tradition, social analysis, and especially the historical testimony of peoples' struggles for empowerment and justice, converge in a concluding theological judgment. Most essentially, God's kingdom, God's power, and God's glory bespeak the shining forth not of dominion over the other, but of sheer, overflowing, efficacy of being, and being together. Divine efficacy, graciously reflected in the creative and collaborative features of human agency: here we find the most profound and truthful starting point, motive, and term for comprehending power in Christian social ethics." (Firer Hinze 1995, 290)

Creativity, collaboration, and *being together* as fundamental terms for a *systematic theology—fundamental, dogmatic,* and *ethical—*reflecting its own *power* and *powerlessness* in the many and painful struggles of people all over the world for *justice* and *empowerment* in the postmodern age of the twenty-first century are the new fundamental starting points for constructing future theologies, taking its lead from *God's power* (Case-Winters 1990, Migliore 1983, Pasewark 1993, Rigby 1997, Snook 1999, Dawn 2001, Griffin 2004, Keller 2005) that does not live or act from "dominion over the other", but from "sheer, overflowing, efficacy of being, and being together" (Firer Hinze 1995, 290).

The Community of the Weak

"Sheer overflowing of being together" may be another word for *divine and human creativity*. This kind of divine and human creativity of *the postmodern*, living out *intentionally* and *artistically, reflectively* and *practically*, an "ethics of intersubjective creativity" (Arens 1995a, 32), transfuses through all theological disciplines and changes them all. "Sheer overflowing of being together" may not be the worst experience *theological disciplines* and its central actors could make in learning again and in new ways how to construct theology in *creatively intersubjective interaction* with each other, *border crossing* (Giroux 1992, Giroux and McLaren 1994, McLaren 1995, Welch 1991, 1999, 2000, 2005, Taylor 2011) along and across *interdisciplinary* and *postmodern ways*.

A New Community of Poets

Systematic theology in the postmodern age needs to develop a *new poetics* (Chopp 1989, 73) transforming oppression, violence, monomythic and sacrificial logics, and any other abuse of *human and earthly power* in ways diminishing life and language, vision and desire, creativity and color, by simply destroying people, into a *new "community of poets"* (Chopp 1989, 73). *The poetic* in *power* may come up in those moments people feel *empowered* to *dream again*, to flow, to go with their hidden and open desires, to envision the artistic and poetic in life, to paint, draw, compose, sketch, model, and invent their lives again. Poetics that way is *border crossing* and *community-building*. "Poetics pushes the limits, plays with the boundaries, and allows participation in communion with the Word", sharing with others *life* and "a communion of words which is multivocal and multiform, dense and rich, imagistic and creative . . ." (Chopp 1989, 85).

This *new community of poets* (Chopp 1989, 73) could be the *communio* or *koinonia* of that gathered and mixed, intermingled and thrown-together group of people that *Jesus* had imagined. The *church* could be the beginning of a community of *new poets*, gathering and collecting the broken-of pieces of a postmodern age, bringing them together, creating a new whole of free and transformed people. *Ecclesiology* developed in words and images, pictures and bill-board posters of a *poetic postmodernism* could turn out to be that kind of a place of freedom where people learn to live with each other, in spite of their modern and postmodern diversities.

Then, *postmodernism* as a *theo-poetic artwork* (for theology as theo-poetic and imaginative Jennings 1976, Wilder 1976, Brueggemann 1993,

2001) and an *empathic-social protest* (Bauman 1993) against any form of *oppression*—personal, communal, social, and global—would become the most challenging social conviction to change the world.

> "Is this not the vision of Luke's proclamation: the community who gathers in God's time and space—time of fullness, connection, and rupture, in spaces of solidarity, intersubjectivity, and possibility? As the community which receives the fulfillment of good news, the church is the scene of emancipatory transformation: relations reordered, the church is the community whose texture is made, sustained, and constantly renewed through discourses of freedom. By being a space and time of freedom the church proclaims emancipatory transformation, discovering and creating new ways of speaking freely . . ." (Chopp 1989, 72)

This *new community of poets* will be *multifaceted, multicolored, polyphonic*, and *kaleidoscopic* in all its shattered and broken existence (Kliever 1981). What *Rebecca S. Chopp* reports in her *The Power to Speak* on the marks of the church in *women-churches* (Chopp 1989, 74–78), will be the marks of the church in *postmodern churches* as well (Page 2000, Mannion 2007). The *postmodern churches* will live by a "poetics that nourishes community in the constant play of images", becoming a *community of poets* "that constantly finds new ways to discover and create the beauty and flourishing of life in Word and words." (Chopp 1989, 73)

The *postmodern church* will experience how "the modern church as the cult of individuals and the cult of institutions is replaced by the intersubjectivity of community . . .", "a community of rhetoric by fore-grounding the dialogical nature of life together" (Chopp 1989, 73). *Life together* (Bonhoeffer 1954, Jennings 1992, Page 2000, Mannion 2007) will be the central mark of this postmodern church that "is neither closed nor defined by identity and autonomy, but is open and is constituted by difference and connection and lived in solidarity with the world" (Chopp 1989, 73–74).

Facing the Different

Social postmodernism as an oppositional *"postmodernism of resistance"* (Taylor 1990, 32, 38, Foster 1983, xi–xii), fighting and resisting oppression and violence, social exclusion and societal *evil* (Farley 1990a, Farley 1990b, Peters 1994, Gebara 2002, Gestrich 1996) wherever it sees it and witnesses it, will be *life-transforming* and *life-changing*, for *theology—systematic, fundamental*, and *dogmatic*—as well. The *ethical* will be omni-present. There is no ironic or detached attitude possible in a *postmodern social theology* wanting to transform the world. Pain causes pain, horror causes horror, the witnessing of trauma and break-downs touches soul and heart, mind and body. A *systematic theology of the social postmodern* will not acquiesce to evil, violence, and destruction of human and earthly life. On the contrary, it will become even more sensitive to the exclusion of *the different*, the eradication of *the other*, the negation of *variety* and *diversity*.

The *ethical challenge* in having to confront and look at, look into and meet, feel, and sense the daily *face of the hurting other* (Levinas 1969, 1987, Ogletree 1985, Sponheim 1993, Farley 1996) will make any *systematic theology—fundamental* or *dogmatic*—inherently *socio-ethical*. The classical separation of theological disciplines, splitting the inseparable twins into primary *dogmatics* and secondary *ethics*—sometimes justified out of half-heartedly presented work-economic reasons, at other times out of strong theological convictions—will be over with.

Ethics and systematic theology—*fundamental, dogmatic,* and *ethical*—in a *postmodern social theology*, both *fundamental* (Lamb 1982, Lane 1984, Wetherilt 1994, Haight 2001, Taylor 1990, 2011) and *systematic* (Herzog 1988, Chopp and Taylor 1994 Williamson 1999, Jones and Lakeland 2005), will flow into each other, forever mixing and freely intermingling, wildly interchanging and poetically interlacing in a *discipleship of life together* (McClendon 1986, 1990, 1994, 2000, 2002). *Postmodern theology* that way will even flow into the *pastoral* and *practical* (Jennings 1992 and Volf and Bass 2002).

The most challenging task for a *postmodern social theology* in the twenty-first century will be *facing the different*. Here, theology is still light-years away from it. In a time when a confessional and Lutheran-Roman Catholic peace-making on the *doctrine of justification* still creates a public uproar among theological professors in Germany to debate about what was left out in justifying and pursuing continued separations, in a time when Roman Catholic professors still lose their teaching job because they were participating in inter-communion at the *first ecumenical church-day in Berlin, Germany*, and in a time when *evangelicals* and *liberals*, especially on German-speaking continents, still freeze in an absolute refusal to even recognize each other's legitimate theological and academic existence, in such a time of petty academic and scholarly modernisms the fundamental task of a *postmodern social theology* resisting *evil* (Taylor 1990, 37–40) will be simply the fundamental learning of *social communion*, in facing the different.

On a much bigger scale, making *postmodern social theology* a *poetic force* to change the world (Chopp 1989, 84-98), a *socially resisting postmodernism* baptized in this radical and new way may encourage and create *new and true communion* in local and global worlds and communities, socially sensitive, politically oppositional, artistically visionary, where "communion—the participation, the overflowing, of grace—revokes, rends, renews, and restores us into human life and transforms us anew in the horizon of all hope. The community of poets in gentleness and unconstraint will speak forth of community in many ways and spaces, including the imaging of universal community, community with the living and the dead, community with the future" (Chopp 1989, 89). A social as well as postmodern vision of this kind, uniting *the different* with *the peaceful*, in a most radial way, is highly *political*, making *theology—systematic, fundamental*, and *dogmatic, ethical, pastoral*, and *practical*—highly *political* as well.

Dogmatic Relevance : Violence and Creation

Postmodern Social Dogmatics

That *dogmatics* can be *theological and political*, is not all too surprising anymore (Glebe-Möller 1987, Herzog 1988, Williamson 1999, Migliore 1991, 2004, Rieger 2007, Taylor 2011). That dogmatics could be *political* and *postmodern*, *social* and *postcolonial*, *(post)feminist* and *antiracist*, is somewhat more startling. Some first, even global proposals have been made (Hodgson 1994, Chopp and Taylor 1994, Barr 1997, Thistlethwaite and Engel 1998, Jones and Lakeland 2005).

On the *European continent*, few comparable attempts have been made so far, with only beginning probings into the *the postmodern* in prolegomena (a first attempt to treat postmodernism in prolegomena can be found in Biehl und Johannsen 2002, 49–59). Systematic theologian *Michael Welker* from *Heidelberg* gets closest to it in his *postmodern pneumatology* on *God the Spirit* (Welker 1994), as he develops a systematic theology of the *Holy Spirit* with "new insight into primarily 'premodern' experiences by cautiously employing 'postmodern', relativistic forms of thought that have been developing for over fifty years, particularly in North America" (Welker 1994, xii).

As European *Michael Welker* puts it, pleading for a new and *postmodern* or *realistic systematic theology* of *radical plurality*, interconnected

The Community of the Weak

differences, and placed together incompatibilities in a *doctrine of the Holy Spirit*:

> "Authoritarian theologies of one-upmanship have sought to grasp and expound God and God's revelation in numerous abstract formulas: God always comes 'from above', God always 'precedes', God is the 'all-determining' reality. The theology of the Holy Spirit will challenge us to replace these formulas or to render them superfluous. It will teach us to concentrate in a new way on seeing God's reality make its appearance in tension-filled interconnections of different realms of experience that are not necessarily compatible with each other." (Welker 1994, xi)

Systematic theology in this way will become more *creative* again, *cultural*, and *artistic*. *Cultural workers* in these *postmodern social times*—with *systematic, fundamental*, and *dogmatic theologians* being cultural workers of their particular kind—desperately need a new kind of social and *sociological imagination* (on sociology as sociological imagination Mills 1959) reinventing and repainting the modern world, wavering between the barbaric temptation of absolute destruction and violence, and the hopeful new possibilities and human capacities of discovering new *borderlands*.

As *cultural worker* and postmodern critical theorist *Henry A. Giroux* puts it, describing the creative potential of any *cultural art work—theology* being such a cultural art work too—in rephrasing the modern and postmodern world:

> "Finally, cultural workers need a language of imagination, one that both insists and enables them to consider the structure, movement, and possibilities in the contemporary order of things as well as how they might act to prevent the barbaric and develop those aspects of public life that point to its best and as yet unrealized possibilities. This is a language of democratic possibilities that rejects the enactment of cultural difference structured in hierarchy and dominance; it is a language that rejects cultural, social, and spatial borders as shorelines of violence and terrorism. In opposition to this view, the concepts of democracy, border, borderlands, and difference must be rewritten so that diverse identities and cultures can intersect as sites of creative cultural production, multiple resources, and experimentation for expanding those human capacities and social forms necessary for a radical democracy to emerge in this country." (Giroux 1992, 248)

Any word or phrase mentioned could be just as well applied to the creative new task of *systematic theology—fundamental, dogmatic, ethical,* and *practical*—for the twenty-first century. Theology in the *global world* will need to engage in a hard and most painful learning process rehearsing and practicing *radical democracy* as if it were for the first time and only just recently discovered. Theology in a postmodern world will need to learn how to create spaces and places, launches and seminar rooms, lecture halls and book-filled jackets where those most "diverse identities and cultures can intersect as sites of creative cultural production, multiple resources, and experimentation" (Giroux 1992, 248).

Systematic theology will need to become a *borderland* of its own kind where people, convictions, cultures, confessions, and nations intersect with each other in a *community of theology* newly discovered. In this community we will need *peace makers* as well as *hermeneutical artists* who know how to interpret one to the other so that war and violence, barbaric extinction and the terror of hurt will no longer prevail. Then, only then, theology may actually become a *therapeutic medicine* to heal the nations.

A *postmodern political dogmatics* includes its own *conflict* and *conversation, living together* and *fighting together—creatively*—right in its own theological middle and does not exclude it. Some collaborative first efforts have been made to write a new kind of systematic theology *in many, even conflicting voices* (Chopp and Taylor 1994, Barr 1997, Thistlethwaite and Engel 1998, Placher 2003, Jones and Lakeland 2005). Creating a *community of theology* right in its own middle may be the future task of systematic theologies written in a postmodern age. What will be most challenging for future projects, is to grow into a real and *true community* (Peck 1987).

In this kind of a *communitarian work*, fights and hurts, stubbornness and hard-nosed closures are just as much part of the postmodern journey as are play and love-making, retreat and forgiveness, softness and wildness in a limitless horizon. Theology written in this postmodern mode may be more *chaotic*, less systematic, more *poetic*, less structural, even more *argumentative*, but less hurtful, more *playful*, less serious, more *musical*, less literal, more *rhythmical*, less general, more *colorful*, less straight-lined, more *noise-filled*, less monotone, more *emotional*, less serene, more *haphazard*, less teleological. Theology out of *living together in many voices* will be more real, but also more difficult.

The Community of the Weak

Living and Modeling Creation and Violence

Then, the dogmatic topics of *creation* and *violence* will be lived and modeled right there. *Creation* bespeaks and invites the *creative life spirit* (Moltmann 1992, 1997 and Keller 2003) flowing and blowing, moving and lifting, encouraging and empowering, as an "undreamed-of love for life awakens in us" and we "begin to flower and become fruitful again, like the plants and trees in the spring of the year" (Moltmann 1997, 81). Creation serves here as a *poetic symbol* for the *creative* over against the *destructive,* as we all know it. Creation as a continuing *narrative* and *poem* telling about the ever repeated *beginnings of life,* regardless of what falls and breaks apart all around us. *Creation* also as that which is *simply there,* my neighbor, my home, my life, my patio, my city, my friendships, my dreams.

And *violence* as that which makes things *simply disappear,* my dreams, my visions, my hopes, my belief, my trust, my day, my job, my food, my future, my life. Living in between violence and creation, the *disappearing of things* and the *birth of new things.* And in all this, the ominous human and earthly recognition, that *we all hold life in our hands,* our own, that of others, their dreams, their hopes, their home, their place, their job, their food, their friends, their future, their life. And that we better watch *whether we handle life with care,* as we *"let it be* or let it come" (Moltmann 1992, 177)

German systematic theologian *Jürgen Moltmann,* much-traveled, internationally all-over respected, highly sensitive, beautifully poetic, and most vividly and clearly *political* in all his *dogmatics,* describes the *Spirit of Life* against death most passionately as well as realistically, pleading for *handling life with care,* as it is *holy*—"'whole', 'hale', 'heal' and 'holy' . . . meaning . . . entire, healthy, unhurt, complete, and 'belonging especially' to someone" (Moltmann 1992, 175):

> "Today life itself and actual survival are called into question. Death is threatening life on earth, not just here and there but universally. So 'the passion for life' . . . must be awakened and the numbing spell of apathy must be broken. Before the earth dies its nuclear and ecological death, men and women will die the death of apathy in their hearts and souls. The powers to resist are paralysed if the passion for life is lacking. People who today want to live and want their children to live must consciously *desire* life. They must learn to love it with such passion that they are not prepared to adapt to the forces of destruction, and to let

the trend to death take its course unchecked. The 'Holy' Spirit is the Spirit who sanctifies life, and he sanctifies it with the Creator's passion for the life of what he has created, and with the Creator's wrath against all the forces that want to destroy it. At the edge of the abyss, the integrity of creation and rebirth to life become so intermingled that it is as the life-giving Spirit that the sanctifying Spirit is experienced." (Moltmann 1992, 178)

Creation and *violence* are the two ethical callings tempting and enticing, inviting and luring, seducing and leading to one or the other. The choice is ours. Every day again, at every moment we choose between *letting life be*, even *letting life come* (Moltmann 1992, 177), or letting life *die*, letting life *disappear*. The *creative act*, both in the beginning *God's act* (Anderson 1984, 1994) fashioning, molding, forming, modeling, painting, drawing, sketching, carving, sculpting this our existing world—God the great creative *first artist* (Fox 1983, 1991, 1995, 2002 and Keller 2003)—, and at every new moment both *God's* and *our* own sculpting, forming, painting, inventing, dreaming, enacting, performing the continuing and ever renewable world, is at its most fundamental level pertinent to *the doctrine of creation*. This seems to become a theological consensus uniting even the most diverse linguistic, cultural, and global continents (Moltmann 1993/1985, 1992, 1997, 2003, Trigo 1991, Sponheim 1999, Bouma-Prediger 1995, 2001, Keller 2003, Edwards 2004).

Biblical Poetics

North American Old Testament scholar *Bernhard W. Anderson* summarizes the *biblical doctrine of creation* in succinct distinction to how it is usually misunderstood: "To understand creation biblically one must abandon the premise on which the 'science-versus-religion' battle has been waged . . .", as the doctrine is not primarily a statement on past or present worldviews or cosmologies, but rather a *poetic image* for *the creative* in the here and now, "since it is not dealing with a speculative question but with *human life here and now*" (Anderson 1994, 1).

As an *affirmation of faith*, the doctrine is *poetic*, musical, artistic, rather than scientific, prosaic, literal. "The affirmation that God is Creator arose originally out of the worship experience of Israel, not out of the reflections of a systematic theologian or a philosopher" (Anderson 1994, 1). *Creation* and *violence* belong to *the poetic* of life, even though they are as real as any prose.

The Community of the Weak

Violence in God's creation (Anderson 1984, 161–165) is as real as *the creative*, but at the same time just as poetic. At its most earthly level, *violence* is disruption, destruction, denial, dissolution, disregard, disrespect, disarray, dispersal, displacement, and after all the disappearance of any remaining sign of life, as life gets erased and eradicated in an ultimate act of lasting destruction, "the disruption of the goodness and order of God's creation through violence" (Anderson 1984, 161). As such it is an *all-powerful* and *all-de-creative* dismembering and disordering of human life, human community, human living. "In short, violence is a disease, as it were that affects all those living in the same *oikos* (house)" (Anderson 1984, 164).

Violence is always *social* and *ecological*, affecting a whole *community* and *communio* of human and non-human life. Violence is like a broken mirror disfiguring the whole picture. A lot more, than usually and intentionally aimed at, most often breaks and disfigures under the limitless blow and weight of specific or unspecific violence.

Violence is that *disruption of things* having turned out *"very good"*, but now—out of envy, jealousy, misery, theodicy—being torn apart, broken down, smashed and dismembered into disintegrating pieces. It is the opposite of great art, messing up the creatively crafted work of the *Book of Genesis' Great and First Artist*. It is *power*—the creative, musical, poetic, artistic—turned suddenly and somehow irrationally *destructive*.

> "Translated into the terms of traditional theology, we are dealing here with the problem of power in a 'fallen world', or perhaps better, in a marred creation. What is the source of the corruption? The narrator does not interrupt the flow of the narrative to raise this question or to reflect on the problem of evil (theodicy). We can only say that the creation story itself does not allow one to trace the source of the problem to the creator. The marvelous order of creation, in which every creature, celestial and terrestrial, plays a role in a harmonious whole, receives the Cosmic Artist's imprimatur: 'very good' . . ." (Anderson 1984, 165)

Creation as a marvelous melody, harmony, poetry, ecology. *Violence* as that which violently interrupts, disrupts, and breaks it all apart.

Creation and Violence in Postmodernity

The *different*, the *ambiguous*, and the *fragmentary* seem to have a tendency to lead people and the world—theology as well—into temptation. The

The Social

temptation of *violence*, in order to create unity and order, comprehensiveness and closure. *Creation* suddenly and most irrationally can turn *violent* and *against itself*, while the *artistic act of creating* is usually freeing, opening, leading people and the world into a wide open space. For some wild reason people sometimes choose the *act of destroying*.

Swiss and North American systematic theologian *David J. Krieger* in his *The New Universalism* (Krieger 1991), reported by *Peter C. Hodgson* in his systematic theology *Winds of the Spirit* (Hodgson 1994), distinguishes three particular ways of *discourse* the people in this world can talk to each other (Hodgson 1994, 310–311, Krieger 1991, 124–162). One way is simple *matter-of-fact argumentation* about facts of life within the boundaries of what we know about our own particular world. Another way is *diachronical*, setting and crossing the boundaries along time and tradition to determine the unity of one's world and worldview. Most often it includes excluding other aspects of our life. A third way of communicating in this world is the most challenging one, but also the most promising one. *Diatopical discourse* is discourse across, beyond, and in between various places and spaces, not just in time, moving along from one place to the other, both back and forth, as a radical "discourse of 'disclosure'" (Krieger 1991, 125), whereby "radically different horizons (or *topoi*) of meaning may encounter one another" (Hodgson 1994, 310). Some would call it *border crossings* across *time* and *space* and any *common locality* (Giroux 1992, Giroux and McLaren 1994, McLaren 1995, Welch 1991, 1999, 2000, 2005, Taylor 2011).

The most challenging task for *systematic* or *global theology* (Krieger 1991, Schreiter 1997, Dyrness, Kärkkäinen, Martinez, and Chan 2008), in this postmodern age is to find a language that helps create a *universal community* of people living a "diatopical hermeneutics in a *pragmatics of cosmotheandric solidarity*" (Krieger 1991, 123). In contrast to any discourse that favors closure, unity, totality, even universality, *Peter C. Hodgson*, following *David J. Krieger*, portrays a way of talking and learning how to live with each other where people remain *ambiguous, fragmentary*, and *different*, using interreligious dialogue as an example relevant just as much for any other living in *ecclesial and liberated human communities* like the church and other ways of living together, both locally and globally, in learning a *diatopical discourse* across borders and boundaries, spaces and places, times and identities:

> "Diachronic discourse, by projecting unity, totality, universality, is a discourse of closure. Interreligious dialogue occurs primarily

at the third level, in the diatopical space that precedes all identity, a space of difference, of dis-continuity, of dis-closure. On the one hand, it is a discourse of *difference,* which lets the difference between transcendent faith and particular beliefs appear (corresponding to the ontological difference between Being and beings). On the other hand, it is a difference of *discourse,* a discursive difference, a difference that issues in dialogical solidarity rather than apologetic antagonism. It moves beyond primal violence and social resistance to a pragmatics of nonviolence, a horizon of encounter that transforms the violence of exclusion into a solidarity from which speech may arise. It opens human existence to the cosmic and the divine, thus grounding a cosmotheandric solidarity . . ." (Hodgson 1994, 310–311, based on Krieger 1991, 124–162)

Violence in this global and postmodern world is the *death-creating* temptation for absolute and radical *closure. Creation* will be the *opening* and *artistic invitation* to join in the *life-creating* working and painting, composing and drawing, crafting and modeling, playing and performing of *the power of the Spirit* (Moltmann 1992, 1997, Fox 1983, 1991, 1995, 2002, Keller 2003). A Spirit of nonviolence, *letting life be* and *letting life come* (Moltmann 1992, 177), giving space, time, and a place to be, a place in which the *different,* the *ambiguous,* and the *fragmentary* are honored and celebrated (Taylor 1990, 34–37). This Spirit of Life is the *soul force* of all existing things, opening up closed doors, locked-in people, frozen attitudes, and stiff structures. The Spirit is moving to twirl everything around and make new kinds of human communities with the living possible. Like the Spirit of God hovering over the chaos and the waters at the beginnings, the Spirit of Life is hovering over our world to make everything *creatively new* (Moltmann 1993/1985, 9–13, Fox 1983, 1991, 1995, 2002, Keller 2003).

Creation is the inflow of Spirit that wants to live, move, dance, sing, craft, write, play, and change the world, again and again wanting *to make all things new.* "Everything that is, exists and lives in the unceasing inflow of the energies and potentialities of the cosmic Spirit. This means that we have to understand every created reality in terms of energy, grasping it as the realized potentiality of the divine Spirit" (Moltmann 1993/ 1985, 9). Creation is more than just the first universal act, the beginning moment of some past cosmology, the first movement in a play called world existence. Creation, *dogmatically,* is the flowing of life, at all times ever new. It participates in the moving of the *Holy Spirit.* As *Jürgen Moltmann* reminds us of the *dogmatic tradition*: "The Holy Spirit, 'the giver of life' of the Nicene Creed, is for Calvin 'the fountain of life' (*fons vitae*). If the Holy Spirit is 'poured out' on all created beings, then 'the fountain of life' is present in everything that exists and is alive. Everything that is, and lives, manifests the presence of this divine wellspring" (Moltmann 1993/1985, 11).

Continuous creation is what goes on every day. *Being creative*, dreaming up new ideas, new projects, new visions, is part of God's creative act every day. In that sense, the doctrine of creation in systematic or dogmatic theology is part of a bigger picture describing the world. The constant *renewal* of creation is what it is all about. Therefore, *the artistic* belongs most intimately to the doctrine of creation as traditionally conceived. "From the continual inflow of the divine Spirit (*ruach*) created things are formed (*bara'*). They exist in the Spirit, and they are 'renewed' (*hadash*) through the Spirit" (Moltmann 1993/1985, 10).

Every *act of creation* in the renewal of creation partakes in this Spirit being Holy, whole, healed and healing. This may be a local artist painting a facial structure, coloring or sketching an empty canvas, this may be a poet composing past moments, retrieving present impressions, this may be a musician playing, a jam-session congregating, a performance artist uniting people, a local church gathering races and genders, a community activist reconciling opponents. Many more moments of a creative act contribute to God's creation and contradict the annulling and erasing of *violence*. Somehow, violence has a way to *dis-create*, making things and people, hopes and dreams, projects and celebrations, moments and places, stories and memories disappear for ever. There is a dismembering and disintegrating power in violence *that makes life disappear*, even whole communities and nations, worlds and ecospheres.

Creation, in contrast, weaves and moves people and lives together into a new kind of a *community of life* where people feel safe, where all living things rejoice, laugh, move and have their being. A community of life where everyone is dependent on the other, and yet safe, vulnerable, and yet embraced, healing, recovering.

A Fellowship of Creation

Jürgen Moltmann describes in his *God in Creation* (Moltmann 1993/1985) such an *ecological fellowship of creation* where every living thing, where every particle, light wave, moving wind, staying rock, hardened soil, born child, jumping horse, resting worker, expecting mother, protesting demonstrator, and performing play artist is moving and living in the Spirit that is holy, healing, and making all things *creatively whole*, since "very good" again:

> "If the Holy Spirit is 'poured out' on the whole creation, then he creates the community of all created things with God and with each other, making it that fellowship of creation in which all created things communicate with one another and with God, each in its own way. The existence, the life, and the warp and weft of interrelationships subsist in the Spirit: '*In him* we live and move and have our being' (Acts 17.28) . . . For nothing in the world exists, lives and moves *of itself*. Everything exists, lives and moves *in others,* in one another, with one another, for one another, in the cosmic interrelations of the divine Spirit . . . The patterns and the symmetries, the movements and the rhythms, the fields and the material conglomerations of cosmic energy all come into being out of the community, and in the community, of the divine Spirit." (Moltmann 1993/1985, 11)

In a *fellowship of creation* (Moltmann 1993/1985, 11, Rasmussen 1996, McDaniel 1989, 1990, 1995, 2000, Keller 2003, Edwards 2004) the in-breaking of *violence* is the end of any life creating spirit. Violence is that breaking and breaking-up of the most fundamental relationships in a community, tearing and breaking up everything living and growing. Whether in its smallest form of personal prejudice, social disrespect, emotional abuse, group slander, communal hatred, neighborly exclusion, or in its largest form of nuclear destruction, global hunger, ecological extinction, violence is always the breaking-up of the fragile, beautiful, and vulnerable "*interconnected web of life*" (McDaniel 2000, 150)—*life in all its life-giving relations.* In that sense, violence is always *social* as well as *ecological*, affecting everything else as well, calling for a *social and ecological spirituality* (Fox 1983, 1991, 1995, 2002 and Keller 2003) honoring and safeguarding the *ecological world-wide community of creation.*

> "Creation in the Spirit is the theological concept which corresponds best to the ecological doctrine of creation which we are looking for and need today. With this concept we are cutting loose the theological doctrine of creation from the age of subjectivity and the mechanistic domination of the world, and are leading it in the direction in which we have to look for the future of an ecological world-community . . . The progressive destruction of nature by the industrial nations, and the progressive threat to humanity through the pile-up of nuclear armaments,

have brought the age of subjectivity and the mechanistic domination of the world up against their definite limits. Faced with these limits, we have only one realistic alternative to universal annihilation: the non-violent, peaceful, ecological world-wide community in solidarity." (Moltmann 1993/1985, 12)

Developing *true communities* (Peck 1987) like this, living and learning an ecological spirituality of a *non-violent community of poets* (Chopp 1989, 84–98), now even on a world-wide and global scale, seems to be the fundamental task of any *new theology—systematic, fundamental* or *dogmatic*—in this postmodern age, trying to find its way in between the human temptation of *violence* and the divine celebration of *creation*. In this, systematic theology could learn from a whole tradition of *non-violence*, as even *discourse*—theology being one form of human and social discourse changing the world in one way or another—can make the world violent or peaceful, colorful or totalitarian, closed or open, destructive or creative.

North American postmodern systematic theologian *Peter C. Hodgson* suggests that theology could be learning—not just for interreligious dialogue—from the spirituality of someone like *Mahatma Gandhi*, developing a kind of *spiritual soul force* and attitude in all our human talks and actions communicating and living together with others:

"Mahatma Gandhi termed the pragmatic conditions of such a universal discourse *satyagraha*, a quiet and irresistible pursuit of truth. *Satya*, truth/the true (God), requires *ahimsa*, nonviolence, and *tapas*, suffering. Nonviolence is necessary because no one possesses absolute truth, only fragments of truth, and thus no one is allowed to force his or her partial truth on others. Nonviolence is capable of instituting community because it participates in the power of truth, a power greater than all violence. Suffering is needed because the only way to break the ideological absolutization of a particular worldview is by solidarity with the enemy and voluntary suffering. Nonviolent resistance and voluntary suffering break the logic of suspicion, condemnation, self-justification, and make it possible for conflicts to be carried on within the domain of discourse. . . . It is significant that Gandhi called this pursuit of truth 'soul force' or 'spiritual force'. It is the power of the Spirit, not the power of weapons and wealth, that engenders a universal community of discourse. Spirit has the power to open a truly global, noncoercive community of communication, of cosmotheandric solidarity, in which differences are honored and all sides are turned toward truth . . ." (Hodgson 1994, 311)

The Community of the Weak

The Postmodern Kairos

A *fundamental theology of the postmodern* will be mostly *christopractical communicative action* (Arens 1995a, Taylor 1990, 151–154, Hodgson 1994, 130–132), with a lot of *soul force* and cosmotheandric learning in human solidarity, combining the search for *truth, nonviolence,* and a special sense for the *suffering* of people and nature in order to create a new kind of *world-wide theological and ecological community.*

North American *Mark Kline Taylor* poses the basic questions facing a *fundamental theology of the postmodern* in christopractical terms:

> "What is the connection between christic living and the postmodern trilemma of North American discursive and extradiscursive affairs? How would christology articulate the Christ symbol in relation to a hermeneutical vision that not only celebrates plurality but also affirms a critical privilege for the voices of those needing emancipation? What particularly must christology become if it is to address the specific oppressions of sexism, hetero-realism, classism, and racism that political and cultural theorists have explored?" (Taylor 1990, 153)

Creating a new kind of *world-wide ecological and theological community* needs new *values* and *methods,* new *presuppositions* and *communicative skills,* both in writing and reflecting, in arguing and narrative telling, in practical living and theoretical assembling. *Fundamental theology* could be such a preparatory entrance door into a new world of *the postmodern,* teaching fundamental and basic *new skills* in order to develop a new theology for the *"postmodern kairos"* (Hodgson 1994, 64). In this new world, *new skills* will be needed right from the start in developing new theologies.

The *cooperative,* the *communicative,* the *multilingual,* the *polycentric,* the *border crossing,* the *intercultural,* the *interdisciplinary,* the *nonstructural,* the *poetic,* the *plural,* the *dispersed,* the *ecological,* the *relational,* the *coalitional,* the *communal,* the *reciprocal,* the *nonhierarchical,* the *empowering,* as well as the *ambiguous,* the *different,* and the *fragmentary,* with other new terms, will guide a different *theological method* leading to a *fundamental theology of the postmodern* trying to take seriously the *kairos of the postmodern,* a "time of opportunity demanding a response—a right time or a special time when momentous things are happening or about to happen" (Hodgson 1994, 64). In this, *the postmodern* could become part of the new task for theology—*Protestant* as well as *Roman Catholic post-Vatican II*—in reading "the signs of the times" (Sanks and Coleman 1993, Segundo 1993, Haight 2001).

The Social

Postmodern New Values

In a world where the cooperative, the communicative, the polycentric, the border crossing, the poetic, the plural, the multilingual, the dispersed, the relational, the coalitional, the ecological, the different, the ambiguous, the fragmentary, and the non-violent have their legitimate place *to be*, teenagers on drugs taking heroin at the age of 14 will also be part of a *postmodern new and true community of cosmotheandric solidarity* in which they experience in a *fellowship of creation* the suffering and empathic Spirit of Life *letting life be* and *letting life come* (Moltmann 1992, 177). A *postmodern fundamental and pastoral theology* will address and face the reality of teenagers taking heroin at the age of 14 in some local village in Switzerland in the 1990s differently than a modern type of theology geared on order, system, dualism, clarity, rationality, unity, boundary, and similarity. The shock of *the postmodern radically different* will be dealt with differently depending on one's basic and fundamental theology.

North American *Peter C. Hodgson* in his systematic theology Winds of the Spirit (Hodgson 1994) refers conjointly to ecological-political process theologian *John B. Cobb* and to poststructural feminist theologian *Rebecca S. Chopp* to describe the *new values* and social visions of *the postmodern*:

> "(1) a wide dispersal of power, contrasted with Eurocentric hegemony, leading to the affirmation of a genuine pluralism of traditions, cultures, religions, and to dialogue among them; (2) earthism, contrasted with nationalism and economism, a refocusing of human activity on the healing of the earth; (3) holistic thinking, contrasted with Enlightenment rationalism and the fragmentation of academic disciplines, the quest for a new way of thinking that is more organic, ecological, relational, communal, nondualist, nonsubstantial, nonanthropocentric; (4) liberation from sexual repression combined with an awareness of new forms of sexual exploitation and the ambiguities of sexual practices; (5) new conceptions of power that are not patriarchal or hierarchical and that have the character not of control but of empowerment, reciprocity, and participation..." (Hodgson 1994, 64–65)

> "openness rather than closure in the face of the experienced ambiguities of life; solidarity through and across radical differences; embodiment as a basis for overcoming fragmentariness; and liberation in the face of systemic oppression." (Hodgson 1994, 65)

The Community of the Weak

In a world like this, teenagers taking heroin at the age of 14 in some local village—and their local pastor—would most probably not be violently *excluded*, but empathically *embraced* (Volf 1996), would not be communally *extinguished*, but socially *included*, with postmodern ecclesial communities living out and witnessing a *cosmotheandric solidarity* , "a holistic, organic vision, especially one that is theanthropocosmic in scope" (Hodgson 1994, 65), an "ethics of intersubjective creativity" (Arens 1995a, 32). A world like that would be *different*, with local and global communities living out and believing in a *fundamental theology of the postmodern* where people are learning the new and *peace-making skills* of *letting life be* and *letting life come* (Moltmann 1992, 177). In *social* and *postmodern communities* like this people would live in a spiritual "openness rather than closure in the face of the experienced ambiguities of life; solidarity through and across radical differences; embodiment as a basis for overcoming fragmentariness, and liberation in the face of systemic oppression" (Hodgson 1994, 65).

And most definitely, teenagers taking heroin at the age of 14 in a local village somewhere in Switzerland in the 1990s in *ecclesial communities* (Hodgson 1988, 1994, 293–304, Kirkpatrick 2001, Childs 2006) like this would not experience the radical outbreak of *violence*, if our *postmodern broken world* had some *new image* and *fundamental theology* or communicative belief in "new conceptions of power that are not patriarchal or hierarchical and that have the character not of control but of empowerment, reciprocity, and participation" (Hodgson 1994, 65) that encourage the building of *true community* (Peck 1987) as "non-violent, peaceful, ecological world-wide community in solidarity" (Moltmann 1993/1985, 12), a *communio* and community of *universal solidarity* (Arens 1995a, 145–169).

Fundamental Theology Transversal

This is where *fundamental theology* joins *pastoral* or *practical theology* and *social ethics*, and this is where *systematic theology* or *dogmatics* intermarries and messes up with *moral theology* or *theological ethics*. The disciplines get blurred, the separating lines get worn out, frizzled and outdated. A *practical fundamental theology* (Lamb 1982, Lane 1994, Tracy 1987, Wetherilt 1994, Arens 1995a, Haight 2001, Taylor 1990, 2011) in the *postmodern age* will have to become *interdisciplinary* and *border crossing* (for cultural studies and feminist theology Giroux 1992, Giroux and McLaren 1994, McLaren 1995, Welch 1991, 1999, 2000, 2004, 2005) not only towards and across the environing *outside* academic world of human and social sciences, political science, literary studies, cultural studies, media studies, art theory, philosophy, but also towards and border crossing the *inner circle* of commonly segregated theological disciplines.

Fundamental theology could actually work at creating a new vision for an *integrative theology* that is *biblical, systematic, realistic,* and *postmodern* (Tracy 1987, Wetherilt 1994, Haight 2001, Taylor 1990, 2011), as well as *social, pastoral, practical,* and *actional* (Browning 1991, Groome 1998, Heitink 1999, Volf and Bass 2002, Markham 2003), crisscrossing in *transversal manner* all disciplinary boundaries (Widl 2000).

When 14-year-old teenagers in a local village somewhere in Switzerland in the 1990s are starting to take heroin, and one of them in 1993 dies of it, then *theology* in pastoral ministry—*systematic, fundamental,* and *dogmatic*—becomes *transversal* (in philosophy Welsch 1996b) and *border crossing* (Giroux 1992, Giroux and McLaren 1994, McLaren 1995, Welch 1991, 1999, 2000, 2004, 2005). Living as a pastor, as a cultural worker, and as an *organic* or *integrated intellectual* in the tradition of *Antonio Gramsci* (Widl 2000, 185–186) in a situation like this—totally unexpected, utterly new, strange, *different,* scary, threatening—blows you out of your cognitive mind and makes you rethink what life and the world may be all about. The cognitive dissonance blurs common concepts, breaks open old securities, moves you outside of protected areas, both cognitively and locally.

The postmodern moves in, not playfully, not ironically, but deadseriously. The challenge then is to redraw your cognitive map and to act in new ways. The fundamental task then is to become *transversal* (Widl 2000, 192–202) to let the most diverse and contradictory concepts and realities mess up, mix up, crisscross, interrupt, reshuffle your whole theology. And then you start to *act*.

In that sense, the *postmodern shock* in *theology* (Hodgson 1994, 53–66)—*systematic, fundamental, dogmatic, ethical,* and *pastoral*—is a healthy one. It reflects back and prepares for the many little and big shock waves that we witness, experience, and have to face in this modern and postmodern life anyway. A *fundamental theology* that is becoming *socialpastoral,* trying to make theology *change the world* (Lamb 1982, Lane 1984, Arens 1995a, Haight 2001, Taylor 1990, 2011) and having survived the postmodern shock of *reality* (McGrath 2004, 93–169) knocking at our ministerial door, will have to become more *integral* (Widl 2000, 226), combining, crisscrossing, and integrating *systematic, fundamental, dogmatic,* and *pastoral theology*.

As much as life in these present and future days seems to become more and more messy, a *fundamental theology* in the postmodern age, trying to understand reality in order to change the world, will also be more and more *messy*, writing, thinking, living, and acting out human life in these many and various literary and everyday *"messy texts"* (Denzin 1997a, XVII–XVIII) that people—teenagers at the age of 14, and others—daily live in.

This world of teenagers should become the *everyday material* of theology, as messy and as real, as it is. Then only will systematic theology in the postmodern time become *real*.

Creation, Violence, and the Postmodern in Pastoral Care

The *dogmatic relevance* of the topics of *creation* and *violence* shows itself in simple and everyday experiences like these virulent moments with teenagers at the age of 14 taking heroin in some local village in Switzerland in the 1990s. In moments like this, people in a community show what they believe or don't believe in. The theological *doctrine of creation* has a lot to do with *reverence, life-protection,* celebration of *the different,* and respect for *human dignity* within an utmost variety of colors, shapes, forms, tones, rhythms, and musical melodies, artful pictures and painted scenic realities. Whoever believes in the boundless *creativity of creation* (Fox 2002 and Keller 2003) will approach teenagers at the age of 14 taking heroin *differently*. Certainly not in any way condoning it, certainly not looking away, or simply walking by, turning the human face elsewhere, ironically moving on to well-protected philosophical distances, with left-over human concern or horror drowned in general societal callousness and carelessness. On the contrary, whoever believes in the beauty and marvel of creation, in the life-giving and heart-moving *Spirit of Life* among us, will not go by, will not look away, will not remain untouched, but will stay and try to do something about it.

Pastoral care then gets *social, political,* and *ecological* (Clinebell 1984, 1996, Clements and Clinebell 1995, Smith 1982, Gerkin 1991, Graham 1992, Couture and Hunter 1995, Schipani 2003, Way 2005, Chinula and Clinebell 2009, Clinebell and McKeever 2011), recognizing in reading "the signs of the times" (Shanks and Coleman 1992, Segundo 1993, Haight 2001) the *social-pastoral* and *ethical calling* in pastoral moments like this. To reach out as a pastor of a local village to young teenagers taking heroin at the age of 14, with one of them having just died, means developing a *new set of values*, maybe *postmodern values*, in order to be able to deal with the initial shock. Only when we have slowly faced and accepted the *radically different*, the unexpected, the unusual, the unheard of, can we start to redraw our coordinating map and figure out what to do next. In a sense, it is like *creating a whole new world out of chaos*.

The *creative part* of it is the ethical question how to respond to it. As a community, as an individual, as a local pastor, in a *social network* of parents, families, friends, school, church, local authorities, by-standers, commentators, newspapers, television stations, and gossip producers. And then the big temptation of *violence* moves in, the violent solution to get rid of the problem in its most simple way. At the same time, everybody knows, or at least should know, that problems like this are always part of a bigger problem, that the personal in this is always part of a bigger world. Teenagers taking heroin at the age of 14 in some local village in Switzerland in the 1990s need, as anybody knows being familiar with pastoral care of systems, the "care of persons" as well as the "care of worlds" (Graham 1992), as the problem is most definitely *ecological and communal* (Clinebell 1996, Clements and Clinebell 1995, Chinula and Clinebell 2009, Clinebell and McKeever 2011). Ecological in the sense that everything in this problem has to do with the way the interdependent and codependent, the independent and over-dependent *others* are dealing with it. In other words, everything depends on how the *created other world* around us is dealing with it, *creatively* or *violently*.

Finding *the postmodern* in it is the social challenge of the day. Safeguarding *creation* in it is the *theological calling* of the moment. And working at keeping *violence* out of it is the *great creative art* of every particular second. What is needed in *pastoral care situations* like this—systemic, organic, communal, interdependent, in need of radical change and a whole new social conscience—is the *sense for the postmodern*, befriending the *ambiguous*, the *fragmentary*, the *different*, while acting in empowering people as a *social change agent* and *artistic local Creator* with others of a *whole new world*.

North American pastoral theologian *Larry Kent Graham* describes it well in his *Care of Persons, Care of Worlds* (Graham 1992) what is needed in moments of *pastoral care in society* when novelty, creativity, and a new just social order are called for in trying to change the many and various systems of this world:

> "In a psychosystemic view, change is not simple, automatic, or predictable. It is rooted in the nature of God, who desires and

seeks to promote a new thing of beauty, characterized by an increase of love, justice, and ecological partnership. Since the psychosystemic matrix is simultaneously stable and unstable, both the basis for change (and resistance to it) are built into the nature of reality, including the reality of God. For change to occur, there needs to be a stimulus upon the system as a whole, or from pressures between subsystems. When these pressures mount and create dissonance, symptomatic crises result, which threaten the stability of the system and require a response . . . For change to occur, therefore, there must be dissonance, in the form of symptomatic crises, followed by a strategic influence that engages the symptomatic situation . . . There are several operational goals of change, and numerous interlocking strategies to realize these goals. These goals and strategies reflect the principles of organicity and simultaneity, inasmuch as they recognize that everything is connected—including the pastoral caretaker—and that change in one area coincidentally leads to change in another, at least in part. The goals and strategies reflect the principles of conscientization and advocacy inasmuch as they require an illuminating interpretation of the total situation in which the symptoms function, and push for public efforts to bring about new structural models of organizing the institutions of our world. These goals and strategies reflect the principle of novelty inasmuch as they promote the possibility of surprising change, which increases the values of love of self, God, and neighbor, and promotes a just social order and a more livable world." (Graham 1992, 110–111)

Creating a New World

Creating a new world in which in the midst of systemic organicity and simultaneity, with the awareness that everything in this world is connected, people and teenagers at the age of 14 can experience in *pastoral care, conscientization*, and *advocacy* a new novelty and a surprising change so that their lives may increase in love of self, God, and neighbor, leading to a more just social order and a more livable world, could be another way to describe the creative potential of *the doctrine of creation*.

And *creating another world* in which in the midst of social prejudice, local slander, and communal exclusion, in spite of the awareness that everything in this world is connected, people and teenagers at the age of 14 experience the most violent rejection so that their lives are systemically deprived of an ecclesial community in which people believe in a "God, who desires and seeks to promote a new thing of beauty, characterized by an increase of love, justice, and ecological partnership" (Graham 1992, 110), will be another and unforgetable way to describe and inscribe in people's and young teenagers' soul the destructive potential of *the reality of violence*. In that sense, *dogmatics* living in between *creation* and *violence* gets most pertinent at the deepest level of one's enlivened or embittered soul.

Power in our modern and *postmodern age* in between the alluring *doctrine of creation* and the tempting *myth of violence* will need to ponder for a moment on what it wants. Both ways are open. Both invitations sent. Both possibilities more than evident and visible in what humans can succeed in. The decision is an *ethical one*.

Systematic theology—fundamental, dogmatic, and *pastoral*—may contribute to a more sensitive dealing with *the postmodern* in some of the most contradicting and conflicting worlds—like in a local village with teenagers at the age of 14 taking heroin, or in any other place—in need of a *healing word* and *lasting action* to help people and whole communities to *creatively* and not *destructively* move on in the face of God, the earth, and each other to a "joyful transformation of persons and worlds, and of the interplay between them" (Graham 1992, 239). And this will be, most certainly, a *systemically postmodern interplay.*

3

Power

EXPERIENCE

"A small boy is said once to have remarked: 'People are the words with which God tells his story.'" (Schillebeeckx 1989, XIII)

"Power, in the first place, is simply that: can-ness . . . , capacity-to-do, the ability to do things. Doing implies power, power-to-do. In this sense we commonly use 'power' to refer to something good: I feel powerful, I feel good. The little train in the children's story . . . that says 'I think I can, I think I can' as it tries to reach the top of the mountain, has a growing sense of its own power. We go to a good political meeting and come away with an enhanced sense of our own power. We read a good book and feel empowered. The women's movement has given women a greater sense of their own power. Power in this sense can be referred to as 'power-to', power-to-do . . . Whereas power-to is a uniting, a bringing together of my doing with the doing of others, the exercise of power-over is a separation. The exercise of power-over separates conception from realisation, done from doing, one person's doing from another's, subject from object. Those who exercise power-over are Separators . . . , separating done from doing, doers from the means of doing. Power-over is the breaking of the social flow of doing. Those who exert power-over the doing of others deny the subjectivity of those others, deny their parts in the flow of doing, exclude them from history." (Holloway 2002, 28–29)

Sacrificial Logics and the Abuse of Power

> *I remember quite vividly those tears on the telephone, telling me of the pain of personal rejection. It happened after a typical group meeting, following the course of events not unfamiliar to me. Some participants in the meeting turned out to be winners, some losers. Power was ordered according to classical and political concepts of decision making. And yet, in spite of the apparent and obvious legitimacy following familiar democratic rules in the distribution of power, there remained a deep feeling of uncomfortable ambiguity. Even if one side in the debate did finally win, there was a feeling of increasingly breaking relationships between individuals, leaving us happy and sad at the same time.*

> *These tears reminded me of past images. Years of memories in winning and losing. Up to the month of November 1997 which turned out to be the beginning of the last chapter of a long and painful story of almost a decade. A story with high media curiosity and interest for almost 10 years, here and there filling television and radio headlines and pages of articles in local and national newspapers and magazines. That half-way concluding press-covered month in November stays with me in my memories as the official und final breakdown of years of work und vision, hope and creativity. I lost my job. My home. The place where I had lived for over 8 years in parish ministry. I lost friendships and contacts to many faces and people, I lost a home and place in a community. Some of my deepest roots in life were violently pulled out. Things that meant a lot to me in my work, in my ministry. Illusions had been smashed, illusions about people, about the church, as I was slowly waking up to a political theater play that secretly had been played with me already since the beginnings. Relationships broke apart. The world took on the dark and light shades and figures of divided enemies and friends, by-standers and violators. With uncontrolled tears all along a country road for quite a while, washing away ideals as I was driving away some month later for the last time from a place that had somehow become home for me.*

Power as a Double Bind

Power is as omnipresent as it is difficult to catch its tail. The moment you may point at it, it disappears behind closing doors. The moment you may encircle it with your definitions, it already evades closure in various ways.

The Community of the Weak

And yet, *power* calls for a partial description. *North American systematic theology*, especially following *social postmodernism* of its various kinds, touches on many aspects of the reality of power. Power can be found in the social, the geographical, the distributional, the economic, the political, the educational, the cultural, the global, between races, gender, ages, abilities, sexual orientation, social location. Between the rich and the poor, black and white, Hispanic and WASP, Native and alien, educated and illiterate, arrived and homeless. Power in the *everyday life of people* is written into the *geography of exclusion and embrace* (Volf 1996, Gundry-Volf and Volf 1997), as *social space* and *living places* are distributed according to *grace*, for some, and according to a *curse*, for others.

The intent of this chapter is an *everyday description* of *power* and its twin brother or sister, *powerlessness*, in *social-science categories*, with *biblical* and *theological reminiscences* to fill the blank of social categories that need some *human flesh* and *pain* to get a feel for what power may be and do to *people* and to the *earth* in its manifold ways. Power can turn into sacrificial logics, into the bruising of people, breaking of stories, *wounding* most deeply the vulnerability in open souls. Power can also empower, enliven, embracing the tender living dreams of anything living, *healing* the broken, making spacious and hospitable our hearts for those in pain. Power in its *healing* or *wounding effects*, is most basically *experienced* in the day-to-day dealings of people in these many and earthly places.

Power and its distribution seem to be a *double bind* (Osborne 2002b, Brooker 2001, 177–178, Holloway 2002, 19–42, Haugaard 2002, Kahane 2010). "Power is two-edged", as North American and Roman Catholic systematic theologian *Francis Schüssler Fiorenza* would say (Schüssler Fiorenza and Galvin 1991a, 70). Power invites people in to be seated in the circle of life, welcoming people with new beginnings, open doors, new places and charming homes. At the same time, power can forever end a particular future, break up the present, destroy the past, wound the soul, incurably, leaving traces of violence that will never heal. *Power acts in both ways* (on power empowering and disempowering Schmid 1998, 146–156, Korte/Schäfers 2002, 161–181, Herriger 2002), silently or with words.

Giving life, or *taking life*. Inviting in, or chasing away. Speaking up or remaining silent. Looking for someone or leaving him alone. Like some of my colleagues in pastoral ministry—both male and female—who repeatedly chose to remain silent before and after 1997, with no human interest in someone else's broken destiny, while teenagers in puberty, unfamiliar with the dirty work of politics and power strategy, were biking after a kicked-out pastor even months later, looking for him in a nearby factory.

Eye-opening experiences like these made me seriously rethink *the basis* of my *systematic theology*. "The plausibility of faith (the topic of the discipline of systematic theology), its symbols of power and powerlessness—here too most if not all things have to be reconsidered" (Schmalstieg 1991, 9–10). Words spoken and written, becoming eye-opening experiences *ringing so true*, as I read these words in *Olaf Schmalstieg's* marvelous book on *"theological power-shifts"* (Schmalstieg 1991), inviting us to a new systematic theology on *power* and *powerlessness* in a time when everything seems to be moving and shaking to the ground. Everything: faith, theology, church, and politics.

The power to *make things possible* or impossible is a power quite omnipresent, both in systematic theology and ministry. "We recognize the fact that we are enmeshed in power and dominion only when our experiences hit somewhere against a wall and crack" (Schmalstieg 1991, 12). After more than ten years of ministry something did *crack in me* (on dramas breaking souls in the abuse and wounding of power and powerlessness Ménard et Villeneuve 1995). Experiences of power and powerlessness break and crack the ground on which we walk and the soul by which we live. This is not the only lasting wisdom learned already years ago in Geneva from my former mentor and companion in ministry and systematic theology.

Power *makes things possible*, or *keeps things from happening* (Schmid 1998, 146-156, Herriger 2002). Some would like more of it. Others openly curse the abusive violence it usually leaves behind. Neither side knows exactly what to think of it. All we know is that it exists and is fully alive, ordering our *everyday world* between us and all around us (Westwood 2002, Stewart 2001, Kahane 2010). We all have tasted it, this smell of the omnipresent *distribution of power*, equal and unequal, creating a world split between those in power and the powerless. It seems as simple as the everyday pain of tears after a group meeting where some turn out to be winners and others have to leave as losers. It never feels good to be on the losing side. Nor does it feel good to be among those who win the game at the expense of a well-known *sacrificial logic of exclusion* "which represses the connectedness of human beings" (Weir 1996, 1). After that meeting something *broke apart*: the fundamental experience of being connected. The dividing line between those in power and the powerless created a whole new world.

On the one hand, we do not appreciate being overtly *powerless*. And yet, exerting our power sometimes leaves us just as unhappy as being

The Community of the Weak

under the rule of some arbitrary king. As social philosopher *Thomas E. Wartenberg* points out:

> "Power is one of the central phenomena of human social life. Yet no sooner does one begin to reflect upon what power itself means than one is confronted by a fundamental problem: It becomes unclear whether power is a positive or a negative feature of human social relations. The use of the term 'power' within ordinary discourse seems to reflect a basic ambivalence about the nature of power. Sometimes power is spoken of as something that people think of as belonging to them, part of their proper inheritance. They have been 'ripped off' when someone else has *their* power . . . On the other hand, the term also functions to denote negative features of human social relations. When we speak of a dictator's power over the minds of his followers, the concept connotes a sinister aspect of human life . . . " (Wartenberg 1990, 9)

There seems to be no final word on this. Most evidently, what can be seen by all is the overall effect of *abusive power* (Poling 1991, 1996, Farley 2004, Keller 2005). Slavery, torture, witch burning, inquisition, conquest, apartheid, war, genocide, death penalty, child abuse, child labor, sexual abuse, domestic violence, hunger, poverty, social discrimination, communal exclusion, self-inflicting violence and many other forms of the abuse of power remind us of the tempting nature of its use in history (Staub 1989, 2003, Schmookler 1988, Cohen 2001, Shaw 2003).

Sacrificial Logics

The all too common forms of *sacrificial logics* (Weir 1996) and their accompanying *violence* (Williams 1991, Baudler 1992, Bailie 1995, Wallace 2002) in the historical and contemporary experiences of people suffering under colonialism, racism, sexism, classism, and ageism have taught us forcefully for centuries the destructive logics of power intent on destroying life. The old and ancient mechanisms of *ritual scapegoating* (Girard 1986, 2001, Douglas 1995) in the form of the sacrifice of life, people, nature, and communities for some abstract and higher instrumental goal—be it religious, social or political (Schwager 1987, Wallace and Smith 1994, Williams 1996, Wallace 2002)—seem to belong to the primal data of humankind that want to remain with us as long as the earth exists. The *ancient sacrificial ritual* will always continue to be found and reenacted—secretly *secularized* and more refined and developed—in multiple modern and theological forms (on modern forms of sacrifice Baudler 1992, 2001, Huber 1993/1996, Gutmann 1995, Janowski und Welker 2000).

Social psychoanalyst and cultural critic *Erich Fromm* has given us already in the early 1940's a powerful description of *the human desire for destructiveness* as an "outcome of unlived life" (Fromm 1942, 158), portraying individuals and communities caught in the *tragic double bind* of wanting to live and yet being held back by whatever keeps them from opening up to the possibilities of the gifts of life. "The more the drive towards life is thwarted, the stronger is the drive towards destruction ..." (Fromm 1942, 158, on Erich Fromm see Fromm 1973, Burston 1991, Lundgren 1998, Thompson 2009).

In the midst of our own contemporary superficial normalcy, rereading Erich Fromm may help us to diagnose even nowadays a recurrent pathology that seems to enjoy the *simple power to destroy others and their life work*. Whether we see little kids playing rival war games in a sandpit, razing artistically built castles forever to the ground, or whether we hear of all-powerful generals and warlords still playing around with nuclear bombs, all of them seem to enjoy this never-ending human game called the *"thwarting of life"* (Fromm 1942, 156).

Life and Death

Prophetically and *biblically speaking*, we hear the invitation by the ancient Jewish saying *to choose between the fullness of life and the destructiveness of death* (Sölle 1981, Hall 1988, Schottroff und Schottroff 1991, Brueggemann 1996, 2001). A systematic theology proclaiming the gift of life puts before us again and again the decision to choose between the *idols of death* and the *God of life*, as we formulate our dogmatics in our ethics and pastoral theology as a *choice for life* (Richard 1981, Gutierrez 1991, Moltmann 1992, 1997, Keller 2005). A "small tribe was told thousands of years ago: 'I put before you life and death, blessing and curse—and you choose life.' This is our choice too" (see Deuteronomy 30:19) (Fromm 1956, 363). To hear the invitation is a *theo-ethical choice*. To act on it a never-ending challenge, proven to be quite difficult again and again in the history of humankind.

Decisions to destroy life seem to be easier than decisions to enrich life. This mystery of *human evil* will remain as long as humans have the power to choose between good and evil. The omni- and ever-present mystery of evil can only be described as *tragic*, opening and laying bare the *deep wounds* of a *hurting world* (Staub 1989, 2003, Schmookler 1988, Cohen 2001, Shaw 2003), wherever the world's bodies are *violently broken* (on the breaking of bodies Scarry 1985, Cavanaugh 1998). A theology in *physical touch* with the pain and tragedy of evil will be sensitive to the *wounds of a hurting world* (Smith 1992, Townes 1993, Inbody 1997, Brock and Parker 2001). Evil remains forever *tragic*, as no human words can ever take away its excruciating pain and meaningless absurdity. The sacrificial logics engrained in human history and thinking have lead to the most gruesome instances of human destructiveness. The logics of war and sacrifice color all our thinking. Abuses of power in all forms seem to be a natural ingredient of history.

While searching for the signs of power and powerlessness in *the little episodes of our day-to-day lives*, we may see its footprints and marks whenever we dare looking at things more carefully and with open eyes. *Choosing life* (Sölle 1981, Brueggemann 1996) or *choosing death* makes all the difference in our *use or abuse of power*: in the way the world is being crafted, painted, sculpted, imagined, sung and narrated by scientists, philosophers, artists and politicians, imaginatively guided either by a fundamental dream and hope of a world where the social order is "not based on the sacrifice of women, or of any social group or individual by another . . . " (Weir 1996, 14), or guided by the simple desire for pure destruction. This *either-or* stands before us as a *critical choice*. Such a critical and artistic imagination of an all-inclusive hope needs to guide our theo-ethical vision to counteract a *"sacrificial logic, a logic of domination"* (Weir 1996, 3) that keeps on sacrificing life and people out of pure limitation of *visionary imagination* (on theology as social imagination Jennings 1976, Brueggemann 1976, 2001).

Racial extinction, genocidal war, homophobic exclusion, and strategic destruction are part of a *play-station* gambling vocabulary of the human race well trained in a *sacrificial violence* in the name of some instrumental goal. It starts at early age when envy and the shortage of equal access to love and play lead to sibling rivalry acted out in warlike wrestling, in most cases with no major and serious consequences. It ends more dramatically and more seriously in last century's discovery of the ultimate power in the human playground, as little boys now turn out to be grown-up *nuclear players* threatening each other with the multiple destruction of the planet. The play with the nuclear may be the ultimate symbol for the human incapacity to know what to do about power. It's there. It can be used or abused. It leads to love or destruction, hope or devastation, the greening of a planet or the freezing of a nuclear winter, the reconnecting of races, cultures, and ages, or the radical breakdown of understanding, friendship, and peace that was meant to be eternal. The *ultimate power of the earth* is mysterious, ambiguous and *double-sided*. We decide what it will do and how it will be.

Friendship with the Earth

As feminist theologian *Elisabeth Moltmann-Wendel* says in her beautiful book on *the power of friendship* (Moltmann-Wendel 2001) with the earth and each other: "The earth with its mysterious power brings about both dying and becoming new, death and life" (Moltmann-Wendel 2001, 116). Power *transforms*, each way. The way of *destruction* and the way of *giving birth* to something new. Power always transforms what it touches and handles. It changes people, landscapes, politics, and the surface of the earth. Power rearranges things, recreates relationships, rebuilds societies, rejuvenates lives. "A further mystery of the earth . . . is its transforming power. It represents death and life, dying and becoming new. Attention to it can produce a liberating experience of transformation" (Moltmann-Wendel 2001, 115).

Power at its heart has to do with the *envisioning of justice and peace*, the *shalom* of the earth as *biblically* and *pastorally* understood (on shalom in biblical theology Brueggemann 1976, 2001). Remembering in tears a group meeting after losing a vote is not just a question of politically legitimate voting procedures, but is at its core also a question of *peace* and *justice*. Leaving a place of ministry after a violently destructive public election creating deeply wounded and forever scarred winners and losers is a question of peace and justice. Have decisions over power at last contributed to peace and justice to all? Quite often power leaves us with no answer to the searching question. Rather, it leaves us alone, inasmuch as power remains *naked*, brute, as deaf and dumb as definite, with no answer to the effect its use or abuse has had on others.

Power most often is quite willing to remain *blind* and oblivious to the sacrifice of people as well as ethics. The omnivorously *sacrificial logics* in the mechanisms of power define our voting, our behavior, our institutions, our relationships, even our innermost definitions of *personal identities* (Weir 1996, Sibony 1997, Kearney 2002). Very seldom the question is asked, what micro- or macroscopic power has done or undone to nations and communities, relationships and friendships, groups and individuals. Tears usually show some of its effects, but are most often easily forgotten. The brute and naked legitimacy of power overrides the questioning of its many sacrifices in the course of personal and collective history of humankind.

Things somehow turn normal again, at least at the surface, after the many human and inhuman power games in human history are over. Time goes by, as power has spoken and divided between *winners and losers*. Very seldom do we ask, after the game is over, whether or not it is now more true or not: "The central vision of world history in the Bible is that all of creation is one, every creature in community with every other, living in harmony and security toward the joy and well-being of every other creature" (Brueggemann 2001, 13).

The guiding vision, after all, of a *shalom-world*, transformed by a *creative and life-enriching power* cannot be managed, controlled, bombed, and forced through even with our utmost violent human power, as the mysterious Spirit of life-enriching power is not at our disposal. And yet it is meant to be the *ethical goal* and purpose of the smallest of our personal decisions. "*Shalom* is precisely the capacity to yield to the gift of power, which comes unexpectedly and unexplained and, therefore, is neither understood or managed by us" (Brueggemann 2001, 160). Power as ordinarily understood quite often misses this mark.

Geographies of Exclusion

In the spring of 1993 a 14-year-old blond, cute, and lively girl surprisingly died of a heroin overdose just 10 minutes away from the village where I had been a local pastor for more than 3 years. National newspapers and television immediately showed a highly publicized interest, as she had been one of the youngest to die of a heroin overdose. The parents were run over by journalists, the news on Swiss television tried to show the place where it had happened. The openly tolerated drug scene in the nearby city, by bus or motor cycle for teenagers only about ten minutes away from a suburban village of predominantly well-to-do intellectuals, lawyers, medical doctors, professors, and other representatives of a higher social class, had been one of several nationwide constant political and social hot spots for highly disputed debates between politicians, local and regional governments, journalists, social workers, street workers, as well as would-be

Power

problem-solvers who thought they knew exactly what to do about a social "disease"—called drugs—so close at home only 10 minutes away as if around the corner.

Cornelia's death changed everything. She had been a sensitive, lively and independently thinking teenager in a confirmation class I was teaching at that time. I remember a particular afternoon, months before, talking to her quite openly and casually about many things. Among others the question of hard drugs, the possibility to stay away from it, or at least to know when to say no, how far to go, where to set the limit. In that talk she tried to convince me—as a teenager who smoked pot like other teenagers at that age—that she knew exactly when to say no and how far to go. Hard drugs were out of the question for here, she said.

Months later I had to bury her as her pastor in a funeral ceremony with more than 300 teenagers in church. Teenagers who after church were sitting outside on the concrete floor, on the steps entering the church, in the cemetery, most of them personally lost and left alone, unaccompanied by adults, weeping while looking at a panoramic view of a village that had just been brutally hit by reality.

After 1993 things were never the same again. A village lost itself in the fear of looking at its own mirror and shadow. Exclusionary mechanisms started to redraw the dividing lines and borders of an inner and outer social geography in a village scared of itself. More teenagers were taking heroin, more 14-year-olds were playing around with death, lost in a place where they were given no place and space to be. The distribution of space became the most symbolic language speaking and betraying a society with no vision, no bonding, no community, no solidarity. Geography turned out to be the most obvious and visible way in revealing the radical emptiness of a social space with no permitted crossing of boundaries. Boundaries started to redefine who was allowed to live or die.

Social Space

Geographies of exclusion (for a social-geographical description in postmodern terms Sibley 1995, Soja 1989, 2000, 2011) work in many and mysterious ways. Some are more obvious than others. But the distribution of *social space* and *place* in modern society (Westwood 2002b, Osborne

2002c, Brooker 2001, 163–164, 203–204, Giles and Middleton 199, 104–125) along clearly drawn lines, borders, and geographical boundaries is one way humans define themselves, their soul, their body, their vision. Living implies having some particular space and place or territory, *symbolically* or *actually* (in cultural anthropology Nanda 1994, 81–83, Hendry 1999, 25–26, Herzfeld 2001, 78–79, Mach 1993, Isin 2002).

Teenagers who take heroin *have no place to be*. The social construction of reality tells them so. Power distributes space as we determine who we like and who we don't like. Those teenagers in 1993 represented a clear threat to a village afraid of itself. Stories as narratives of hearsay produced a climate of silent fear and open suspicion allowing no crossing of boundaries, no contact, no meeting point. These teenagers were considered to be on one side of life—*"on the dark side of the moon" (Pink Floyd)*, so to speak—, the rest of the village on another, well protected, in need to be safeguarded from possible threat. Preemptive image making and protective prejudice like " those teenagers are going to draw everybody else—friends and others—into their world and place" created a open climate of distrust, aggression, and violence, both symbolically and in reality.

The *social distribution of space* in a village became the most political issue in the years following, leading to a *politics and genealogy of exclusion* well-known in the history of political definitions of citizenship in urban and suburban space.

Social and urban scientist *Engin F. Isin* (Isin 2002), following *Michel Foucault*, describes to us remarkably well how since the time of the Greek *polis* one's place has been the most familiar way to determine who will be considered *political citizen* in human space, the city as *polis* being an all-powerful *"difference machine"* producing *"citizens, strangers, outsiders and aliens"*, dividing up social space along clear social lines. Women, children, peasants, slaves, and mercenaries, knights, merchants, prostitutes, and artisans, humanists, colonists, witches, and vagrants, savages, flâneurs, intellectuals, and Africans, immigrants, the homeless, drug addicts, and refugees, are *genealogically constructed social categories* distributing space up until modern times.

> "The city is the battleground *through which* groups define their identities, stake their claims, wage their battles, and articulate citizenship rights and obligations... The city as a difference machine relentlessly provokes, differentiates, positions, mobilizes, immobilizes, oppresses, liberates. Being political arises qua the city and there is no political being outside the machine." (Isin 2002, 50)

Social Constructions

Social space—the city—*divides* people, families, and neighborhoods, whether in a city or in a village. Even in a small village like Erlinsbach this mechanism of *"the city as a difference machine"* worked to produce categories of the accepted and unaccepted. Some seemed to belong, others got the clear feeling that they do not really belong. Teenagers taking drugs do not really belong. These categories created a *social geography* in which space is clearly divided. Space is "a machine" (Isin 2002, 49) relating people to each other in keeping them from each other, out of fear, out of prejudice. The human psyche needs to divide up the world into the good and the bad, light and darkness, clean and dirty, friend and enemy, not allowing one to move and live next to the other.

The soul of modern man seems to be in need of the creation of *fearful others* in order to feel righteous and good about him- or herself. "The 'history' of citizenship has often been narrated by dominant groups who articulated their identity as citizens and constituted strangers, outsiders, and aliens as those who lacked the properties defined as essential for citizenship" (Isin 2002, IX).

Drug addicts are *"the other"* with no right to political citizenship, therefore with no right to be, to be heard, seen, touched, understood, taken seriously, and no right to put their feet somewhere nearby to find some rest (on hospitality to find some rest Gundry-Volf and Volf 1997, Pohl 1999, Hendriks 2001). Somewhere else, yes. Somewhere far away, yes. In some possible religious-utopian rehabilitation village planned in the years 1993-1995 by the regionally well know pastor for the homeless and drug addicts *Ernst Sieber* from Zurich, yes. But please, not somewhere near us. Actually, rumors spread in some local newspapers that the planning for such an utopian village for about 2000 drug addicts in rehabilitation might be considering a place about 10 minutes nearby. The village council of Erlinsbach immediately published a disclaimer against such possible ideas.

To have a place to be, to be seen, heard, listened to, to be welcomed, included, integrated, recognized, accepted, acknowledged, is part of a *symbolic basic human need* that defines who we are (Thiersch 1992, Böhnisch und Münchmeier 1990, Deinet 1999, Hendriks 2001), our personal *living room* as pedagogical *oikos* to *live in* (on the ecology of social and educational worlds in pedagogy Kleber 1993, Mertens 1998, Hof 2009). Theology will have to become more sensitive to the needs of people for *space and a place to be*. There is a basic anthropological need to draw a personal geography in which we feel at home, our *life-world* in which we move and feel welcome by those around us (on hospitality healing the stranger Granberg-Michaelson 1991, Winklmayr 1993, Hendriks 2001).

Human identities are defined by *space* and the *place* in which they live, grow up, see, hear, feel, and smell the world as it unfolds around them (Keith and Pile 1993, Pile and Thrift 1995, Cavallaro 2001, 167–180, Westwood 2002b). In order to live we need a space and place to be.

> "The complexity of space both as a concept and as a physical reality is testified by the fact that there is no single and universally accepted definition for this term. The multi-accentuality of space has been problematized by the increasing recognition that space is not an immaterial idea but rather the embodiment of cultural, political and psychological phenomena. Space is always, to some degree, social. Its organization and the ways in which it is experienced and conceptualized contribute vitally to the mapping of individual lives and social relations." (Cavallaro 2001, 170)

Space is always *interpreted symbolically and emotionally*. Buildings, places, landscapes, schoolyards, meeting rooms, street corners, and city or village maps take on a *symbolic meaning* depending on the distribution of power between individuals in a particular society (for the relationship between space, power, and meaning Osborne 2002c, Westwood 2002b). These teenagers in 1993 were chased around from one place to the next, no place to be. And yet, in every new place there was some *personal meaning* attached to it. Sitting on a bench, near the village center, where everybody could look at you. Or sitting on more secluded benches in a schoolyard, congregating every night at dawn, talking to each other, hoping that life had some place to stay. A home, an embrace, people who would listen and understand. Even the smallest of places had some particular meaning for these teenagers constantly on the move.

No wonder, did they turn out to be the first official visitors in a newly opened youth club set up in a cellar in the nearby church building, called *"the Bunker"*. A name chosen by those teenagers and others to attach some meaning to this new place, as every place has some meaning to tell. Maybe, it meant a place of protection, maybe it meant a place to retreat. "Concrete, emotional, functional, symbolic" meaning is attached to townscapes and landscapes, buildings and meeting places, street corners and schoolyards in a personal and symbolic interpretation which becomes more important than any spacial attributes (Cavallaro 2001, 171).

Theological Space

Even *God* needs a place to be. *Jürgen Moltmann*—among only a few—beautifully formulates a *theology of space* in his *God in Creation* (Moltmann 1993/1985), underlining God's need for some place and space to be (Moltmann 1993/1985, 140–184). God is no homeless. God created a space and a place in which to be. Theological meditations need to take more seriously the importance of *a place and space to be*, a much neglected and rare topic in mostly disembodied theological reflection (Biehl und Johannsen 2002, 146).

"Ever since Augustine, there have been many theological meditations on time. But meditations on space are rare" (Moltmann 1993/1985, 140). *Time* seems to be more detached from emotion, the concrete, the everyday world. It is rare to find a systematic theologian to deal with life in the daily realities of *space* and *body*. Life, however, is *embodied life*, in need of a wide and open *"living space"* (Moltmann 1993/1985, 148, on living space as a place of open hearts Gundry-Volf and Volf 1997) to put our feet (Psalm 31:9) (Moltmann 2002, Moltmann und Rivuzumwami 2002).

Life needs a place and space to live. We need personal space to freely move around. Sound resonates in space, people hide in protective space, time is prolonged in space. *Jürgen Moltmann's* German word association on the meaning of space is helpful and highly imaginative, as he invites us to move around in our various *"Lebensräume, Freiheitsräume, Wohnräume, Schutzräume, Klangräume, Zeiträume"* preparing us for *"God's wide open space"* and grace "in which we live, weave, and have our being" (Moltmann 2002, 6, Gundry-Volf and Volf 1997).

Space can invite people to come in. *Hospitality* and an open heart and home to share with strangers are part of a *fundamental Christian social ethic* (Ogletree 1985, Sponheim 1993, Pohl 1999, Hendriks 2001) inviting people in who usually are left outside (Luke 14:12–24, on the Parable of the Great Banquet Sigrist 1995) hanging and wandering around in our urban and suburban streets and streetcorners, market places and crosswalks, home-less, space-less, room-less.

Does God share in the human fate of becoming home-less, "in the original sense of the word utopian, space-less"? (Moltmann 2002, 41). Then God would share the lot of millions of people all over the globe. Naked, hungry, homeless, thirsty, locked away, pushed to the side and outside of human space. The *Son of Man* had no place to put his head to rest (Matthew 8:20). The Christian God incarnates in the story of the itinerant preacher and social prophet *Jesus* and the travelling community of his *homeless* (Elliott 1981) disciples as the "House of God in the Spirit" (Ephesians 2:22). The Church as an "Open-Door-Community" opens its "inviting rooms" to strangers, the poor, the sick, the naked, the hungry, the thirsty, the imprisoned (Matthew 25:35–36) creating "a home for God who is homeless in this world" (Moltmann 2002, 41).

Teenagers taking drugs need a place to be. This was true for the teenagers in Erlinsbach. Church could be such a place where people find room and space to be. In 1993 room was created in a small village for teenagers who needed space and a place to be, emotional space, living space, space to resonate and to be listened to. At the same time, the *social distribution of space* worked its way. Rumors spread. Prejudice kept different groups of people at a distance. Space was not shared but only temporarily tolerated.

After a few months the project was stopped, teenagers were again chased away. A pilgrimage began from one place to the next, no place being permanent. Teenagers had to be on the move from one segment of a social geography to the next. Teenagers became *homeless* in many different ways, constantly on the move, never invited to some feast, being left alone in the streets. Hospitality was denied, hearts were closed, space taken away. God's wide open space and grace turned out to be empty and fake.

Christian faith turned out to be home-less, world-less, as it kept on breaking promises. *Theology* took off into some political *no-where*, with no real feet on the ground. Church authorities played along with social violence in a geography of exclusion chasing away not just teenagers but others as well. One teenager had died in 1993, other teenagers had to experience in the following years a Church with no conscience, no ethics, no heart. In 1998 a long story ended, leaving teenagers behind who had learned what a Church might mean that does not follow in what it says, keeping *hands back, feet up, hearts closed*. Theology turned out to be *disembodied*, disconnected from truth and reality, the physical and the real, denying itself three times like *Peter* (Mark 14:66–72, Luke 22:54–62).

Theology in Space

Systematic theology that *follows* in what it says and *walks* on what it talks (Herzog 1988, Biehl und Johannsen 2002, 63–65, Sedmak 2000, 108–162) needs to revive the biblical and old Jewish image and metaphor of *the way* (Acts 9:2, also Herzog 1988, Moltmann 1993/1990, Williamson 1999, McClendon 1986, 1990, 1994, 2000, 2002), getting its feet on the ground *walking* (Boff 1987 and *Vamos Caminando* 1983). It needs to renew the theo-ethical importance of embodied itinerant discipleship, which is more than the static proliferation of linguistic or dogmatic phraseology quite often so dear to academic playfulness or forgetfulness.

Theology, if walking, needs to move, stroll, run, kneel, follow and wander from one place to another, one house to the next, one human place to some other human story, sometimes tired, in need of a place to rest, out of breath, with feet wounded from being *bare-footed* (Rothenbühler 1976), hearts concerned, with hunger and thirst unquenched, uncertain about where to spend the night. Systematic theology will need to convert and be transformed again into a song along a wayfaring *God-walk* following in the steps of the *itinerant charismatic preacher* and prophet it proclaims (Horsley 1994, Theissen and Merz 1998, 185–403, Moltmann 1993/1990, Malina 2001, Jennings 2003, Maguire 2005, 27–40), roaming around with "no staff, no sandals, no knapsack" at hand (Crossan 1994, 102–122). Following Jesus the itinerant preacher who had no place to put his head to lay on.

Theology Materialistic

Theology needs to become more *materialistic* and less idealistic, as good theology does not just simply "fall from the skies" (Casalis 1984), but *post-idealistically* (Casalis 1984, Taylor 1990, 194–242, Metz 1981, 1997, 1998, Bradstock and Rowland 2002) reconnects with the ground and *dirt* (Countryman 1988), and the people and all that is living on earth, feeling the dust on the road, breathing the air, tasting the rain, relishing the freshness of bread, joining ranks with companions in need of a hand or a compassionate soul. Theology needs to become less cognitive and more *embodied* (Taylor 1990, 1–22, Cooey, Farmer, and Ross 1987, Cooey 1994, Biehl und Johannsen 2002, 145–146.), getting in touch with the *everyday-world* of the physical, the sexual, the material, *the body*, in particular the often defiled and repelled female body (Isherwood 2000, Moltmann-Wendel 1994).

As Jesus used to touch people, be it the dead, a leper, a woman, or a child. In the beginning is not the word, as some may misinterpret the Bible, but "in the beginning is the body" (Crossan 1994, 75–101), and "in the beginning is the scream. We scream" (Holloway 2002, 1), as Jesus, the most physical and embodied, incarnate and material Word of God, has taught us in touching and healing our bodies and our *cries*.

The Community of the Weak

Theology worth its prize has to do with real space, daily hunger, recurrent thirst, felt recognition, excruciating pain, overpowering joy, heartbreaking tears, and exuberant laughter. Theology cares about where real people of this real world find a concrete place to be, accepted, invited, welcomed. A Word without Flesh cannot touch the human heart. Teenagers on drugs can only taste and smell God if some concrete human hand touches them, cordially inviting them into the wide open circle of hospitality and grace (Gundry-Volf and Volf 1997). God's grace can only be found in some concrete human form, embodied, bodily living somewhere among us (on grace as embodied Boff 1979).

Theology Visiting

Systematic theology needs to *visit* those real places where God may be, travelling along God's manifold ways of revealing him/herself in the concrete experiences of *everyday walks of life* (Herzog 1988, Williamson 1999, Biehl und Johannsen 2002, 63–78, Boff 1987, *Vamos Caminando* 1983), practicing a life of *secular-monastic discipleship* in combining theory and action, *mysticism* and *prophetic witnessing* (Metz 1978, Eurich 1993, Marsh 2005), getting its feet on the ground *walking*, while meditating on where to go, whom to visit, who to listen to, who to touch as we are travelling along *the way* (Herzog 1988, Williamson 1999, Boff 1987, Sedmak 1999, 157–165, 2000, 108–162, 2003), sensitive to the human and inhuman landscapes and geographies of social space and place.

The *Jewish doctrine* of the *Shekinah* and *Makom*—the indwelling and naming of God in creation—, *Kabbalistic ideas* of the *Zimsum*—God retreating in order to leave space to the world—as well as the Christian doctrine of *God's incarnation* in the life of *Jesus of Nazareth* invite us "to speak of the marvel that the infinite God himself should dwell in his finite creation, making it his own environment" (John 1:14) (Moltmann 1993/1985, 150, on God's indwelling in creation Moltmann 2002, McFague 1987, 1993, Grey 2003). Along the way we may even meet God unexpectedly. This should have an effect on the way any systematic theology is written and spoken today. It should also have an effect on how theology moves and lives *among us*, in good *Jewish-biblical tradition*, as a *shadow* on the *earth* (on the Jewish-Christian image of the incarnation as a shadow of God's presence Reijnen 1998).

MEMORIES

"From the Greek term "emptying" or Kenosis one speaks of a kenotic Christology, and, because one deals ultimately with God's own Kenosis, also of a kenotic theology. Which means: The all-powerful God chooses for himself in Jesus Christ powerlessness. He, who owns the fullness of Godhead, makes himself empty. God himself thereby steps on the side of the poor and the most abandoned and becomes a suffering God." (Waldenfels 2002, 56)

"Organic intellectuals combine theory and action, and relate popular culture and religion to structural social change." (West 1982, 121)

"In the hermeneutics of Christian narrative, theology and ethics are two sides of the same coin." (Stroup 1981, 228–229)

Hermeneutics of Powerlessness

> *It took me five years half-way to get over it. Five years to calm down and get settled, trying to start reconstructing a broken story. Turbulences of memories and woundings of a perpetually bruised soul. Only a few years ago still sobbing-like tears violently erupted like a blocked-up current freed at last from the closed-up inside that had been rationally and intellectually so well protected—being a theologian after all—, muffled, but suddenly and irrespectfully bursting out like a fountain while listening and role playing in the city of Bern and its Kursaal, amidst quite a big crowd of by-standing and perplexed lawyers, theologians, psychotherapists, and social workers.*
>
> *A woman psychotherapist did run after me, wanting to know the story. And yet, I was hit by my own incapacity to tell the story at that particular moment, inasmuch as stories need listeners to really listen. Tradition could be a community of listeners. In Bern in the Kursaal I discovered people with a common language, but who may not want to be listeners. It was only months later, accidentally running into one of the organizers of the conference— a well-known feminist psychotherapist and writer—, that I experienced a little glimpse of sharing traditioning stories. It remained, however, a passing and hardly lasting moment of a highly rare exception.*

The Community of the Weak

Traces of Wounds

Tradition seems to be constantly writing on your body. Traditions get carried on and handed down along the road leading us through life, closing or opening up possibilities. Traditions also seem to carry *traces of wounds* along. Some traditions seem to be forever inscribed in your body, lingering under the deceivingly pacified and solidified surface of a variously well-learned intellectualism and a well-trained protectionism, ready, however, at any time to burst out again, irrespectful of your will or your wishes. *Traditions of hurt and pain* (in biblical theology Brueggemann 1992a, 1992b, 1996, 2001), personal or collective, get burned into your skin, even if memory seems to be forgetting at times. Storied traditions keep reminding you of things that will never erase, inasmuch as *scars* become a way of traditioning.

I never realized until I got hurt myself how much the *Bible* may be a book of *scarring traditions*. I used to like reading passionate theologies like those of *Dietrich Bonhoeffer, Martin Luther King, Ernesto Cardenal, Oscar Romero, Jim Wallis, Dorothee Sölle, Jürgen Moltmann, Johann Baptist Metz*, but I never really knew what it means to get hurt because of reading the Bible. Somewhere along the way it dawned on me that these *compassionate theologies* (Fox 1990, Song 1982, Boff 1999, Metz, Kuld und Weisbrod 2000, Koffler 2001) had a lot to do with re-reading familiar and variously pain-imbued biblical stories. Biblical traditions take on a new color, taste differently, smell unusual, as soon as you start recovering from being *wounded* yourself (on the wounded healer Nouwen 1994, Ford 1999, Hernandez 2006). Before that texts, having been way too often read, preached about, put aside, used, abused, tended to turn into dead corpses touching no one. But suddenly, after personally experienced pain, words begin to speak again, words that used to leave you *silent* and *speechless*.

Hermeneutics

Hermeneutics is the *art of understanding* (Osborne 2002a, 153–155, Brooker 2001, 100–101, Hawthorn 2001, 147–151, Abrams 1999, 127–132), in *philosophy, literature* (Bleicher 1990, Wachterhauser 1986, Mueller-Vollmer 1988), and the *social sciences* (Hitzler und Honer 1997). Theology— systematic and *practical*—as well has become *hermeneutical* (Heitink 1999, 178–200) as it seeks to understand what is being said, written, proclaimed, and finally enacted in human form, as humans live and act on what they mean to understand (Geffré 1983, Tracy 1975–1994, Jeanrond 1988, 1991, Schneiders 1999, Schüssler Fiorenza 2006). Whenever we read a text or listen to a story we need to understand what we are reading, what kind of a message a text, story, novel, epic, poetry, parable, myth, biography, or history may want to tell us. Biblically speaking, we need to understand the message proclaiming the good news. It is a message for the hurting. Only after having being *hurt* can we approach the biblical text in a new way. The same wordings take on a new flavor if the soul reading is in pain. Texts are scars writing a story, some even *texts of terror* (Trible 1984). This can be said of the biblical text as well.

Historical-critical approaches to the Bible quite often tend to miss *emotional and political flavors* of the human text, as "*historical criticism has become a mode of silencing the text by eliminating its artistic, dramatic, subversive power*" (Brueggemann 1992, 64). Hermeneutics as the art of understanding has to become *critical* (Bleicher 1990, 141–211, Smith 1997), dethroning any remaining idols of the commonly assumed, or the normally expected, be it traditional or confessional. It has to become *social* and *political* (Taylor 1990, 46–75) in being *fundamental* (Schillebeeckx 1974, Tracy 1987, Jeanrond 1988, 1991, Schüssler Fiorenza 2006), exposing any remaining idols of the powerful and their self-imposing assumptions on the marginal, be it political or ecclesiastical. Any classic text, any human word, any written book, any spoken speech is embedded in some social or political context that shapes what is being said, influences how people hear, hinders or opens up what readers or listeners can see and understand. The hermeneutical reframing of *liberation* and *political theologies* (Gottwald and Horsley 1993), *feminist* (Schottroff, Schroer, and Wacker 1998, Noller 1995), *African American* (Wimbush and Rodman 2001), and *postmodern biblical studies* (The Bible and Culture Collective 1995, Adam 2000) has open up our eyes and ears to the world of those most often *not listened to*.

Reading and understanding are also *emotional* as well as *communal*.. Reading may trouble, hurt, and scar us. Reading may leave us to a sleepless night. Reading or listening may awaken some deeply felt compassion reaching out to those who speak a word to us. Reading and understanding *literature*—the Bible being literature—involve the *critical* (Barry 2002, Bertens 2001), the *social* and *political* (Jameson 2002/1981, Humm 1994), as well as the *emotional*. The historical and the critical alone will not do. Reading self-implies the reader in a *community art work of interpretation*. Everybody and everything gets involved, reasoning, emotion, memory, the personal as well as the political. Reading and understanding are *relational*, somehow trinitarian, as North American and radical feminist Old Testament scholar *Phyllis Trible* remarks: "Storytelling is a trinitarian act that unites writer, text, and reader in a collage of understanding" (Trible 1984, 1).

Collage of Understanding

This *collage of understanding*—of stories of the present and of the past—lives not without us. We have our own story to tell. Quite often *painful*. Our story intersects with stories of old. Hermeneutics is a *communitarian praxis* (Schüssler Fiorenza 1992, 2006, Richard 1998) in a radical sense. Stories are shared, listened to, unlocking the depth of possible pain inscribed in words and texts.

Feminist and womanist theologian *Elizabeth M. Bounds* invites readers and listeners to such a *deep listening* as they "listen so deeply to another's narrative that their own narrative is changed..." (Bounds 1997, 120). Through sharing our own story we may understand biblical stories in a new way. "If without stories we live not, stories live not without us" (Trible 1984, 1). Hermeneutics invites us on a journey as listening travelers into foreign lands, even lands "of terror from whose bourn no traveler returns unscarred" (Trible 1984, 2).

Embrace of Pain

Feeling the wounds and scars of unsettling hurt and upsetting pain stands at the beginning of reading and listening. *Bible reading* may be described as an *embrace of pain*. North American Old Testament scholar *Walter Brueggemann* uncovers this central faith tradition in *biblical theology* (Brueggemann 1997, 2002) as opposed to an *Ancient Near Eastern common theology*. Such a common theology is at its core "structure-legitimating", offering "a normative view of God who is above the fray and not impinged upon by social processes" (Brueggemann 1992, 4). It tends "to serve the ruling class which regularly identifies the order of creation with the current social arrangement..." as it "provides an ordered sense of life..." (Brueggemann 1992a, 22). It feels no pain, sees no suffering, senses no need for change.

In contrast, a biblical theology of the *embrace of pain* knows of the "full acknowledgment of and experience of pain and the capacity and willingness to make that pain a substantive part of Israel's faith conversation with its God. Such an act of embrace means to articulate the pain fully, to insist on God's reception of the speech and the pain . . . " (Brueggemann 1992a, 25). This pain leads us through the whole Bible up to modern times. "It is this embrace of pain that opens the Old Testament to the future. It is this radical probe of a new way of relationship that runs toward the theology of the cross in the New Testament and that runs in our time toward and beyond the Holocaust . . . " (Brueggemann 1992a, 26).

The embrace of pain is *political*, upsetting and unsettling familiar orderings of *power*. Disregarding hurt and pain serves a political interest. "Where pain is not embraced, critical uneasiness about every crushing orthodoxy is banished" (Brueggemann 1992a, 26). Biblical traditions recall the crucial *minority voices* of all those without a voice, but hurting. Articulation of pain is both private and public, a *political hermeneutics* crying out for change. "It is like *Rosa Park's* refusing to move to the back of the bus in Montgomery. Such a refusal means there can be no more business as usual" (Brueggemann 1992a, 27–28).

The recognition of *personal pain* is a subversive and political questioning of the *empire* (on subverting the Empire Hardt and Negri 2000, McLaren 1995, 2005, in theology Welch 2004, Keller 2005, Maguire 2005, 3–21, Rieger 2007, Taylor 2011)—in recent and in Ancient times—, inasmuch as *hurt and pain* are no longer accepted as normal. "To acknowledge normalcy as hurt is a fundamental act of courage and of subversion, which in the moment of expression delegitimates the claims of the empire and initiates the process of dismantling the empire" (Brueggemann 1992b, 46). Reading and interpreting texts and stories partakes in such a political dismantling of the empire.

Pain cannot remain *silent*, unless it is threatened to do so. Violence requires the silencing of voices. Biblical theology opens up the *cry* (Mark 15:34, Matthew 27:46, Luke 23:46) for the hurting (on the biblical and theological importance of a cry Comblin 1988, Aquino 1993, Aguirre 1997, Sölle 2001). This is a fundamental ethical thrust of biblical traditions all the way from the First to the Second Testament. Expressed *pain* is the beginning of *hope*. In the socially poetic and biblical words of *Walter Brueggemann*:

> "Literary analysis is teaching us that texts are never simply reportorial; all texts are acts of social construction. They are always imaginative proposals, acts of world construction from a particular position of advocacy . . . The texts of hurt and hope

are peculiarly rich instances of such creative efforts because they seek to draw the imagination of the community outside the hegemony of the dominant regime. The dominant regime—social, economic, political, religious—has constructed a world in which hurt is denied and hope is domesticated or precluded. The texts of the dominant regime seem true, established, correct, and authorized. Texts of hurt and hope, to the contrary, demand another world. It is a world artfully voiced but touched by the reality long denied, domesticated, and precluded. This rhetoric of hurt and hope is an affront to established social power. The passionate voices of complaint and lament, the powerful oracles of hope, the narratives of hidden, inscrutable transformation—these are not escapist comments of transcendentalism, but they are acts of power perpetrated by the powerless through the only power available to them." (Brueggemann 1992b, 61)

Advocacy

Reading and interpreting texts from a position of *advocacy* and *powerlessness* becomes *physical* the moment we feel the pain. We may even be *wounded* by it, as feminist Old Testament scholar *Phyllis Trible* (Trible 1984) tells. Texts and stories don't leave you untouched. Memories and images come up in your mind, while reading and mixing the contemporary with the old, connecting emotions and histories.

> "Choice and chance inspire my telling these particular tales: hearing a black woman describe herself as a daughter of Hagar outside the covenant; seeing an abused woman on the streets of New York with a sign, 'My name is Tamar'; reading news reports of the dismembered body of a woman found in a trash can; attending worship services in memory of nameless women; and wrestling with the silence, absence, and opposition of God." (Trible 1984, 1–2)

Reading and interpreting texts and stories may quite often compare with a painful and powerful *struggle*, like the struggle of Jacob: "We struggle mightily, only to be wounded. But yet, we hold on, seeking a blessing: the healing of wounds and the restoration of health. If the blessing comes—we dare not claim assurance—it does not come on our terms. Indeed, as we leave the land of terror, we limp" (Trible 1984, 4–5, on violence in the Old Testament Römer 1998, Dietrich und Link 1995, 2000, Gibert 2002).

Power

In reading and interpreting *social texts* (as narratives in postmodern times Brown 1977, 1987, 1989, 1995, in postmodern ethnography Denzin 1989, 1997a, 2003)—literature, history, or stories of what people may socially narrate and construct to be reality—*power* and *powerlessness* serve as critical lens through which we are led to hear or overhear what texts want to tell us. Sometimes texts and overly familiar ways of reading or listening to what is being said may cover up *silenced and wounded voices* wanting to be heard. Any text is a final and finalized vote on unsuspected and most often well hidden *power struggles*, subaltern, unseen and invisible to the passing ear or eye, only detectable through intense and sensitive listening and looking at what may lie underneath the surface of simple reading (for critical reading in postmodern times Leitch 2001).

Looking at the distribution of power and powerlessness in human texts is a way of critique of ideologies, *criticizing idols and idolatry*. All too often human texts enthrone adored gods allowing no others besides them, installing one particular way reality is to be conceived. Hermeneutics constructs meaning as well as it *dethrones idols*, as *Paul Ricoeur* remarks:

> "At one pole, hermeneutics is understood as the manifestation and restoration of meaning addressed to me in the manner of a message, a proclamation, or as it is sometimes said, a kerygma; according to the other pole, it is understood as a demystification, as a reduction of illusion . . . The situation in which language finds itself today comprises this double possibility, this double solicitation and urgency: on the one hand, to purify discourse of its excrescences, liquidate the idols, go from drunkenness to sobriety, realize our state of poverty once and for all; on the other hand, to use the most 'nihilistic', destructive, iconoclastic movement so as to *let speak* what once, what each time was *said*, when meaning appeared anew, when meaning was at its fullest. Hermeneutics seems to me to be animated by this double motivation: willingness to suspect, willingness to listen: vow of rigor, vow of obedience. In our time we have not finished doing away with *idols* and we have barely begun to listen to *symbols*." (Ricoeur 1970, 27, as quoted in Jameson 2002/1981, 274–275)

Power bows to repeatedly self-proclaimed *illusions* and *idols*, commanding to worship and adore the surface and the superficial appearance of what is being said, but not really heard or understood. The therapeutic effect of *pain* may be such that only through touching the scars of our pain can we finally hear the real meaning and message, the hidden and submerged proclamation and good news of texts. Getting slapped to the face by power, broken down on your knees with a broken back, bent and cracked by sheer violence, may be the only possible narrow gate and eye-opening entrance door to hermeneutical understanding.

Social and Political

A *social and political hermeneutics*—be it in Protestant systematic theologies, in Roman Catholic fundamental and systematic theologies, in Latin American and feminist theologies, or in radical and postmodern biblical studies—will be sensitive to the many and various *faces of power* (Boulding 1990) in *human understanding*, by listening more carefully to what might have been *overheard*, *silenced*, and *left out* (Taylor 1990, 46–75, Schüssler Fiorenza and Galvin 1991a-b, Thistlethwaite and Engel 1998, Adam 2000, Haight 2001, Rieger 2007, Taylor 2011). "On this account, political biblical interpretation occurs all the time. In nearly countless ways people employ biblical texts to make sense of their lives and to defend or question specific social formations" (Adam 2000, 181).

A *social-political reading of the Bible* gets alphabetized in a *sensitivity for powerlessness* (Schottroff and Stegemann 1984, Gottwald and Horsley 1993, Noller 1995, Schottroff, Schroer, and Wacker 1998, Adam 2000, Wimbush and Rodman 2001), knowing what it means to get *hurt*. Hurtful reading allows for a new sensitivity for subaltern wounds and hidden scars that reads and understands with different eyes and ears—*female, queer, Afro-American, South African, Asian, Hispanic, Native American, Latin American*, or simply just *global* and *postcolonial* (Segovia and Tolbert 1995a-b, 1998, Segovia 2000, 2003, Sugirtharajah 2001, De La Torre 2002, 2004, Keller, Nausner, and Rivera 2004, Kwok Pui-lan 2005).

Such political reading is *emotional*, crying with the hurting, laughing with the joyful. *Politics* understood in an emotional way is nothing else but the distribution of joy and pain, life chances and life fallings, openings and closures, welcomings and exclusions. North American radical cultural and literary critic *Fredric Jameson* (Jameson 2002/1981) from *Duke University* describes such a sensitivity for the workings of power in an iconoclastic analysis of the *political unconscious* in human texts as a "political perspective not as some supplementary method, not as an optional auxiliary to other interpretive methods current today—the psychoanalytic or the mythcritical, the stylistic, the ethical, the structural—but rather as the absolute horizon of all reading and all interpretation" (Jameson 2002/1981, 1).

The *distribution of power* is such an emotional *absolute horizon* determining everything: literature, reading, listening, understanding.

Different Readings

Texts are read differently depending on how *powerful* or *powerless* you are. In the words of postmodern systematic theologian *Mark L. Taylor* in his fundamental and hermeneutical theology *Remembering Esperanza* (Taylor 1990), proposing a *cultural-political hermeneutics* for the *North American context*: "Present-day social locations, shaped by diverse cultural practices and different degrees of access to political power, shape readings of the tradition's texts" (Taylor 1990, 46).

Texts of tradition will not be and speak *the same* if you are a *poor Central American campesino* in southern Nicaraguan country sides reading for the first time the *Beatitudes of Jesus* (Matthew 5:1–12, Luke 6:17–26, for Matthew and Luke Betz 1995, Guelich 1982, Patte 1996, Topel 2001). Beatitudes and words of hope so close to home as if proclaimed and spoken just around the corner of some similar social-anthropological neighborhood among the literally *poor and excluded*—as if then as well as now having been waiting for so long for a new spirituality and economy of a coming and *socially subversive kingdom* (Crosby 1981, Galilea 1984, Moxnes 1988, Hanks 2000, Maguire 2005).

Stories as if *just written next door* in our own world though so far, in worlds today somewhere on a continent as if reenacted in words of old of a marginal Jew and *social prophet* called *Jesus* (Malina and Rohrbaugh 1992, Malina 2001, Stegemann, Malina, and Theissen 2002). This rebel of the *poor*, a variously called *prophet* walking on earth and touching people as a possible *radical peasant*, upsetting *cynic*, *social peacemaker*, or compassionate *wisdom child* (Hellwig 1983, Nolan 1992, Crossan 1991, 1994, Herzog 2000, Wink 2002). Reading about the same *text* and the same *prophet* as a university professor in Europe or in the United States with a substantial salary will make you feel *different*. How you feel and what you see is what may or may not touch you in a text or a story, as you allow stories and texts then and now to get close to you.

Hermeneutics joins together *text and experience* (Smith-Christopher 1995), asking the important question, "Whose experience counts in theological reflection?" (Hellwig 1982). In doing so, we decide for a particular option. *What* and *who* we choose to listen to as readers and listeners in the contemporary and global arena of *human conversation* (Tracy 1987) has a lot to do with our *personal and social ethics*. Leaving out the powerless, the muted, the silenced is an ethical choice. In a global world of unequal access to voice and speech, image and news, writing and reading, e-mailing and interneting, knowledge and wisdom, understanding and interpreting basic human hurt and pain, as well as visionary hope and faith, needs to become more conscious of the *political unconscious* (Jameson 2002/1981, Brooker 2001, 220–221) of other voices as an ethical and political urgency.

Reading and listening with open ears and eyes for the subaltern and marginal voices at the outside of the public and global square—as we are confronted with those many modern, trans- and postmodern *outsiders of the underside of modernity* (Dussel 1995, 1998) who are crying out to be let in and listened to—is the beginning of the new Kingdom. We are only slowly becoming conscious of the *politics and ethics of interpretation* (Schüssler Fiorenza 1988, 1999, 2000, Patte 1995, Jennings 2003) all our hermeneutical and theological decisions imply, both locally and globally.

World Conversation with the Other

In a world of ever enlarging possibilities of *conversation* and *communication* between the rich and the poor, between black and white, hispanic and Anglo, North and South, male and female, child and adult, straight and gay, conservatives and radicals, the way we communicate is crucial. The willingness for conversation is not as self-evident, as war and violence—the end of all human conversation—show. As Roman Catholic fundamental and hermeneutical theologian *Werner G. Jeanrond* (Jeanrond 1988, 1991, 1995) points out, "hermeneutical thinking may be able to make the theologian more sensitive towards the need to engage in a world wide conversation . . . " (Jeanrond 1991, 182).

A conversation that needs the courage to face the fear of *the Other*. To face the Other as *different*, threatening, even as terror, as Roman Catholic hermeneutical and political theologian *David Tracy* from Chicago (Tracy 1975–1994, on David Tracy see Jeanrond and Rike 1991) describes the ethical urgency to include those others in human conversations in postmodernity, in North America as well as on the globe:

> "Above all, our discourses exclude those others who might disrupt the established hierarchies or challenge the prevailing hegemony of power. And yet, the voices of the others multiply . . . : the hysterics and mystics speaking through Lacan; the mad and the criminals allowed to speak by Foucault; the primal peoples,

once misnamed the primitives, defended and interpreted by Eliade; the dead whose story the victors still presume to tell; the repressed suffering of peoples cheated of their own experience by modern mass media; the poor, the oppressed, and the marginalized—all those considered 'nonpersons' by the powerful but declared by the great prophets to be God's own privileged ones. All the victims of our discourses and our history have begun to discover their own discourses in ways that our discourse finds difficult to hear, much less listen to. Their voices can seem strident and uncivil—in a word, other. And they are. We have all just begun to sense the terror of that otherness. But only by beginning to listen to those other voices may we also begin to hear the otherness within our own discourse and within ourselves. What we might then begin to hear, above our own chatter, are possibilities we have never dared to dream." (Tracy 1987, 79)

Hermeneutics as *strong hermeneutics* with an *ethical vision* (Smith 1997) that creates "new languages of personal resonance—to disclose matterings in the world and to voice previously inarticulate moral claims . . ." (Smith 1997, 169), does make a social and political difference in *what* and *who* we listen to in the global and noisy orchestra of limitless and endless voices.

Hermeneutics Life-Changing

Hermeneutics done this way will not become, as quite often, a simple linguistic and noncommittal playground for the highly literate and privileged. Rather, it will speak hopeful and *life changing words* to worlds in crisis, torn and divided by muting violence and unspeakable suffering. Worlds in crisis cannot afford the luxury of hermeneutically unending playfulness. Interpretation needs to encourage *changing the world*. Language and meaning need to become practical, embodying and enacting what Christians believe. "When this is done, hermeneutics becomes much more than a professor's playground; it is transformed into a way of thinking about our texts and traditions that has a strategic value for worlds in crisis" (Taylor 1990, 47). Called by those who cannot find words for what they have seen, hermeneutics will start to listen to those who are seldom listened to. The *silent or silenced voices* most overheard may be the most important ones, as God knows.

The Community of the Weak

Trajectories of Violence: Hagar and Jesus

Some 29 teenagers surrounded by nearly 800 churchgoers celebrated in 1997 two creatively and musically colorful confirmation worship services on the theme: "You belong too". The accompanying biblical story was the story of Hagar. Exclusion and embrace—I had just read Miroslav Volf (Volf 1996)—served as a symbolic movement playfully including and excluding parents, godparents, friends, visitors, and by-standers, while playing bingo or lottery on who was going to be locked up in a wooden and clumsy closet, who was going to be sent outside the front church door, who was going to stand in a designated corner stigmatized as visible outsider, and who was going to stay inside as privileged and favorite elected.

A few months later the playground turned into reality. The message remaining unheard. The game starting all over, this time leaving stigmas and wounds that would never heal. Exclusion and embrace distributed. The crossing out of sentences like "you belong too". Violently erasing any remnant memory. Violence making sure that nothing anymore would remind anyone of moments or images of a permanently broken past. This time people could not go home to recover from an artificially virtual game. This time the game was final, leaving many outside church doors, permanently positioned inside with faces against a corner, never again allowed to come out of second hand wooden and clumsy closets. Bingo or lottery no longer as just a momentarily passing moment. But this time as final concluding battle. A political battle excluding many and embracing others.

The highly publicized vote, after 7 years of strategic slander, political maneuvers, open violence, and secretly dirty coalitions, turned out to divide everybody. A division between those who belong, and those who do not belong. A division between those who got embraced and those who got kicked out. Hagar reenacted, symbolically repeating age-old mechanisms as if re-lived over and over again. Teenagers and parents starting to understand what the story of Hagar may have to do with real life. But this time the story never ended.

Exclusion and Embrace

The *story of Hagar* has always fascinated me. A kind of an allegory for what was going to pass, mindful of similar plots while later reading the *story of Jesus*. Stories connected, even though never made as explicit (Galatians 4:24-31, on Hagar and Galatians Trible 1984, 8, Janzen 1991, Troost 1993, Castelli 1994, Hamilton 1995, 95-96). The repetition of stories now and then, rehearsing and practicing *exclusion and embrace* (Volf 1996, Gossai 1995). A picture of statues at the *Sidney Janis Gallery* in New York portrays *Abraham's Farewell to Ishmael, 1987*. One in a series of possible visualizing pictures over the centuries (Kramer 1998a). A powerful picture, telling a story that keeps repeating wherever people go. Some will be embraced, others will stand by, watching the story of multiple exclusion and embrace. Abraham embracing Ishmael. Two women watching. One hidden behind, the other standing aside. One strategically and secretly working at the definite embrace, the other facing the violence of indefinitely being chased away (Genesis 16:1-16, Genesis 21:1-21, Genesis 25:12-18).

New Readings

Feminist and *Afro-American Old Testament scholars* from the Northern and Southern parts of the *Americas* were the first ones to look at this discomforting, while surprising, story more closely, starting with focused biblical studies in the United States and Latin America (Trible 1984, 8-35, 1985, Tamez 1986, Weems 1988a, Waters 1991), but soon picked up in other literary places and political contexts, with both a male and female interest in the story. This has opened up new vistas on *female figures in the Old or First and New or Second Testament*, looking at various forgotten and female narratives with *social-scientific* and *literary eyes* the story of *Hagar* being a particularly promising one, paradigmatic for the fate of a narrative as well as some destiny's child (Newsom and Ringe 1992, 17-18, Berquist 1992, 41-53, Bellis 1994, 67-79, Nowell 1997, 3-20, Meyers, Craven, and Kraemer 2000, 86-88).

European literary and biblical feminists followed soon after in picking up the interest for some seldom well-remembered story, while *general biblical commentators* began to include new readings in view of *radical feminist questionings* (Fischer 1994, 1994b, 2000a, Brueggemann 1982, 150-162, 177-185, Hamilton 1990, 441-458, 1995, 71-96, Fretheim 1994, 450-455, 485-492, Soggin 1997, 257-262, 296-300, Turner 2000, 76-80,

94–97). At the same time, most interestingly, *Hagar* is becoming a powerful and *guiding symbol* for *North American womanist theology* (Williams 1993, Wollrad 1999, Mitchem 2002, De La Torre 2004).

Complicating History

Feminist biblical scholar *Elsa Tamez* from Costa Rica retells the "story of the woman who complicated the history of salvation" (Tamez 1986). She invites us to look at the story of Hagar with *new eyes*. "Bible study from this perspective is full of conflict" (Tamez 1986, 6). The story of Hagar is such a deeply *conflictual story*, leading to equally *conflictual readings*. Looking at the history of interpretation of the text, however, shows how much this conflict has deliberately been overlooked, covered up, and set aside to allow the normal course of reading follow its natural way, undisturbed by the simple but disturbing story of a simple woman, a story quite simply having to do with simple violence, race, and sex. Normally, stories of violence, race, and sex seem to draw a lot more attention from possible readers. Here, it seems, things are left and will be left as if nothing had happened.

And yet, something did happen, at least in the story as being told. Hagar is used by Sarah and Abraham to give birth to a first-born child, as Sarah assumed being barren herself. A practice of surrogate motherhood not unfamiliar in the Ancient Near East of the time. After use, however, and with the subsequent birth of Isaac by Sarah, Ishmael and Hagar are of no more use. The Egyptian slave or servant woman's and Abraham's son are simply chased away. "It is a scenario familiar to domestic servants today. The servant is thrown out of the house because she bears a son to the master of the house, because she is powerless to resist him. She is taken as an object, and thrown out as an object" (Tamez 1986, 10). A plot as simple as that, repeated in history uncountable times. Exclusion and embrace, distributed among *loved ones* and *the rejected* over and over again, reminiscent of various contemporary moments, as Elsa Tamez recalls situations "typical of many poor Latin American women who, abandoned by their husbands, watch over and doubly protect their families" (Tamez 1986, 16). Hagar experiencing something no different from what women experience today, used, abused, thrown out, and left alone. And yet, there is more to it, underneath the simple story.

> "The appearance of Hagar and Ishmael in the patriarchal history is not a simple trick to add suspense or interest to the story. It may appear so from a literary point of view, but that is not its true significance. If this story was gathered through traditions and included in biblical history, it is because it has a lesson for us. The marginalized demand as first-born sons to be included in the history of salvation. They break the order of things. They complicate history." (Tamez 1986, 9)

First-born sons—and daughters—are demanding to be included in the history of salvation. Even more so, black sons and daughters are demanding to be included in the history of salvation. And, surprisingly so, God is speaking a blessing to a *woman*—quite singular in the Old or First Testament—, promising her and her offspring to become a great nation. The story of Hagar is quite some unusual story, breaking many and various orders of things done and heard off as usual.

Texts of Terror

A haunting figure, as radical feminist Old Testament scholar *Phyllis Trible* notes: "Belonging to a narrative that rejects her, Hagar is a fleeting yet haunting figure in scripture" (Trible 1984, 27). A *text of terror*, leaving no one unmoved, describing the familiar in being abused.

> "Kept in her place, the slave woman is the innocent victim of use, abuse, and rejection . . . She is the faithful maid exploited, the black woman used by the male and abused by the female of the ruling class . . . , the surrogate mother, the resident alien without legal recourse, the other woman, the runaway youth, the religious fleeing from affliction, the pregnant young woman alone, the expelled wife, the divorced mother with child, the shopping bag lady carrying bread and water, the homeless woman, the indigent relying on handouts from the power structures, the welfare mother, and the self-effacing female whose own identity shrinks in service to others." (Trible 1984, 28)

The suffering of Hagar is repetitious and *contemporary*. Women all over the globe even nowadays are chased away after being used and abused as surrogate mothers, subservient to a violence unspoken but just as threatening. And yet, there is also some highly *subversive undercurrent* in the story, as Afro-American Old Testament scholar *John W. Waters* points out:

The Community of the Weak

> "It is significant that Hagar is the only Old Testament woman who has a recorded theophany and is a recipient of the promise of possession of land and a large number of descendants . . . Thus, Hagar is portrayed as the first genuine matriarch of the Old Testament. This North African woman, an Egyptian by birth, demonstrates that the divine promise could be given to a non-Israelite or a woman." (Waters 1991, 199)

Womanist Afro-American systematic theologian *Delores S. Williams* remembers Hagar in her powerful book *Sisters in the Wilderness* (Williams 1993) as determining foremother and *symbol* for black Americans since the time of slavery. "The African-American community has taken Hagar's story unto itself. Hagar has 'spoken' to generation after generation of black women because her story has been validated as true by suffering black people" (Williams 1993a, 33). The story of Hagar speaks a word of hope to the many sufferings in black women's biographies which Delores S. Williams unfolds so beautifully in her womanist and autobiographical systematic theology. "I have come to believe that theologians, in their attempt to talk to and about religious communities, ought to give readers some sense of their autobiographies" (Williams 1993, IX). "Interlacing" (on interlacing systematic theology, biblical stories, and contemporary narratives Barnes 1995, 10) biblical stories with personal biographies and autobiographies, womanist theology discovers Hagar as primal mother speaking to all. "As I encountered Hagar again and again in African-American sources, I reread her story in the Hebrew testament and Paul's reference to her in the Christian testament. I slowly realized there were striking similarities between Hagar and the stories of African-American women" (Williams 1993, 3, on Delores S. Williams and womanist theology Wollrad 1999, Mitchem 2002, De La Torre 2004).

Communal Memories

African American and feminist Old Testament scholar *Renita J. Weems* adds some further womanist aspects to the story, staying within the female-female dynamic:

> "It is a story of the social and economic disparity between women, a disparity that is exacerbated by ethnic backgrounds. It is the story of a slaveholding woman's complicity with her husband in the sexual molestation of a female slave woman. It is a story of the hostility and suspicion that erupt between women

over the plight and status of their male sons. It is the story of an enslaved Egyptian single mother who is subjected to the rule of a vindictive and brutal mistress and an acquiescent master. It is a story familiar, even haunting to African American female readers." (Weems 1991, 75, Weems 1988a)

As such it is not just some individual story of some ancient and particular past. It is just as much a communal story of a *community of sufferings*. It is a story continuously rewritten in the lives of countless women along the path of a history of violence suffered, inscribed, remembered. Memories of pain physically inscribed in the bodies of silent screams hardly ever listened to.

"For black women, the story of Hagar in the Old Testament book of Genesis is a haunting one. It is a story of exploitation and persecution suffered by an Egyptian slave women at the hands of her Hebrew mistress. Even if it is not our individual story, it is a story we have read in our mothers' eyes those afternoons when we greeted them at the front door after a hard day of work as a domestic. And if not our mothers' story, then it is certainly most of our grandmothers' story." (Weems 1988a, 1)

Betrayal. Exploitation. Denial. Resentment. Suspicion. Distrust. Anger. Silence (Weems 1988a, 17). The symphonic chapters and shades of color as we experience the radical breaking up of relationships, promises, communities, churches. Politically and in private. The private always being political. We all somehow may at some point in our lives become *sons and daughters of Hagar*. Betrayed, abandoned, banished. In Erlinsbach in 1997, when a whole community consciously or unconsciously re-inscribed and re-enacted the radical violence and breakdown of the story of Hagar, or somewhere else along the way. Then, we would so desperately need some healing hand, quite often, however, absent, unavailable—out of sight, out of mind.

"At some time in all our lives, whether we are black or white, we are all Hagar's daughters. When our backs are up against the wall; when we feel abandoned, abused, betrayed, and banished; when we find ourselves in need of another woman's help (a friend, neighbor, colleague, relative, stranger, another man's wife); we, like Hagar, are in need of a woman who will 'sister' us, not exploit us. In those times we are frequently just a sister away from our healing." (Weems 1988a, 17)

The Community of the Weak

A healing in the midst of pain. The *wounding* of communities and individuals as violence takes its course, with "hidden scars and ugly memories" (Weems 1988a, 16). Here and there. Regardless of the story, black or white, grandmother or grandson.

In all its ambivalence, the story of Hagar remains—now and then—contradictory as a *text and re-text of terror*. European feminist and Roman Catholic exegete *Irmgard Fischer*, having offered the most substantial historical-critical approach to the text so far, interprets the story of Hagar as one of those "biblical texts which in their original form were composed as texts about the liberation of women, but have been reinterpreted repressively", being "an example of how stories of liberation can become stories about oppression" (Fischer 1994, 77, Fischer 1994b, 2000a). "The revision of the texts turns the liberator God who in the basic narratives in Genesis 16 and 21 supports those who are deprived of their rights, oppressed and outcast, and who breaks open the structure of a slave-owning society, into one who preserves the system" (Fischer 1994, 81).

However, the final word on the *historical and tradition-critical development of the text* has not been spoken yet (for the exegetical discussion see Brueggemann 1982, 150–162, 177–185, Hamilton 1990, 441–458, 1995, 71–96, Fretheim 1994, 450–455, 485–492, Soggin 1997, 257–262, 296–300, Turner 2000, 76–80, 94–97).

Suffering Servants

The story of Hagar is reminding theology—biblical as well as systematic—of the *suffering* of servants and those *suffering servants* like *Jesus*, as *Phyllis Trible* dares to make the invisible connection. "She was wounded for our transgressions; she was bruised for our iniquities" (Trible 1984, 8). In the all too familiar triangle of conflictual violence over *exclusion and embrace* (Volf 1996) Hagar served her purpose in making an oppressive system whole. "This Egyptian slave woman is stricken, smitten by God, and afflicted for the transgressions of Israel. She is bruised for the iniquities of Sarah and Abraham; upon her is the chastisement that makes them whole" (Trible 1984, 28). As such it is a story with no redemption. "All we who are heirs of Sarah and Abraham, by flesh and spirit, must answer for the terror in Hagar's story. To neglect the theological challenge she presents is to falsify faith" (Trible 1984, 28–29).

Hagar and Jesus

A small, even though quite uncommon, quantum leap or step to take it seems to move on—for just a moment—to the *story of Jesus*. *Hagar* and *Jesus* are hardly ever put together, meeting somewhere at a possible future table in human history. Let alone are Jesus and Hagar ever seriously compared, or pictured standing somewhere and somehow together, conjoined, and talking.

A thing unheard of, seemingly inappropriate, to imagine *Hagar* sit with *Jesus* at the same eschatological banquet eating a redeeming endtime *messianic meal* (Isaiah 25:6-9, Matthew 8:11-12, Luke 5:27-29, 7:33-34, 7:36-50, 14:1-24, 22:14-30, Revelation 3:20). Meals in Old and New Testament times always had a *social mapping* involved in them, distributing honor and shame, precedence and rejection, social strata and distribution of reverence. But meals in the biblical tradition also served as a hopeful and promising *eschatological and messianic image* of how the world could be newly redefined at the end times, where all the world was going to share in peace the daily bread and those many places of honor, with no more war nor separation between nations and the people (McKenzie 1965, 558-559, Achtemeier 1985, 616-617, Malina 1998, Freedman 2000, 874-876, Smith 2003).

Table Fellowship

Jesus in the *Synoptic tradition*, most particularly in the *Gospel of Luke*, is continuously portrayed as meeting people at a *table* prefiguring the *messianic end times*, enacting the ancient Jewish and prophetic message and vision of an *egalitarian new kingdom* (on Jesus' egalitarian table-fellowship in the Gospel of Luke Evans 1990, 221-227, Johnson 1991, 222-233, Malina and Rohrbaugh 1992, 367-369, Ringe 1995, 193-200, Green 1997, 539-563).

Table-fellowship with *Hagar* might therefore not be so far out of the ordinary for a historical Jesus who surprised many by his dealings with those whom nobody else would ever consider appropriate for a simple meal-time dinner. Later on this part of the *historical memory* about Jesus seemed to fade away a little in the continuing biblical and ecclesiastical tradition, forgetting who Jesus shared predominantly bread and wine at table with, leaving out of the theological picture exactly those kinds of people Jesus did consider *first in the kingdom* (on the economy of the Kingdom

The Community of the Weak

Ford 1984, 101–105, Moxnes 1988, 127–138, Neyrey 1991a, 1996, Smith 2003), proclaiming and enacting an all-inclusive *table kingdom* in anticipation of God's Kingdom.

This, inasmuch as Jesus in his *symbol-enacting lifetime*, crossing boundaries of all social and humanly made *bodily and microcosmic mappings* (Neyrey 1991a, 364–371, Jennings 2003, Duling 2003), quite regularly used to join, communicate, and commiserate with exactly *that kind of a people*, namely *the blind, the lame, the poor, the sick, the socially excluded* (Hanks 2000a, Pilgrim 1981, Neyrey 1991, Green 1995, Roth 1997), thereby reflecting in a social mirror by putting upside-down accustomed social structures and social conflicts of ancient Palestine (Hanson and Oakman 1998, Duling 2003). The *historical Jesus* invites us to redraw our common *maps of people and places, times and things,* so often responsible for our discrimination between the clean and the unclean, the holy and the sinful, the invited and the excluded. As *Jerome H. Neyrey* puts it:

> "Jesus' selection of table companions is no mere lapse of regard for the customs of his day but a formal strategy. Although likes should eat with likes, by eating with sinners and foreigners Jesus formally signals that God extends an inclusive invitation to non-observant and sinful outsiders for covenant membership and for status as forgiven persons . . . The meals of Jesus and his disciples, then, suggest a new map of people who belong in God's inclusive covenant." (Neyrey 1991a, 378, also Neyrey 1996)

New Social Mapping

Theology in tune with the historical Jesus and his *"language of meals"* (Neyrey 1996, 160) will always be in touch with a *new social mapping* inviting those kinds of people, the rejected, the abandoned, the abused, and excluded, the frowned upon, the miserable, the marginal, the left-out, in other as well as in biblical words: *the poor* (Hanks 2000, Malina 2001, Esler 2001, Blasi, Turcotte, Duhaime 2002). The *followers* assembling in *prophetic memory of Jesus* (Espeja 1987) worth his name will be gathering around an *ecclesial communion table* in community with those usually left out, prophetically remembering those many table scenes in the life time of Jesus, creating a new society in open commensality with everyone.

> "Jesus of Nazareth was not a sociologist but a prophet of God. Since he lived in a society which did not know how to be in

solidarity, his experience of the Father led him to the call for radical change. He himself inaugurated this new practice of social relations: in this enclosed society he took the side of the excluded and formed the community of the Twelve as a sign of the 'new society', in other words, of the people of God." (Espeja 1987, 127)

North American Roman Catholic New Testament scholar *John D. Crossan* (Crossan 1991, 1994) has given us a beautiful and powerful description of Jesus' radical-symbolic, communal-rearranging, and political *"open commensality"* (Crossan 1991, 261–282, 1994, 66–74), the *Kingdom of God* being a place where Jesus is eating with all kinds of people at some promising symbolic but present table, drinking and feasting, talking and laughing together with "nuisances and nobodies of society", commonly last on the list of normal invitations to a private and public dinner where everyone is watching very carefully who is going to be invited and who will not be part of it.

Commenting on the socially highly upsetting *Parable of Jesus* on the *Great Banquet* (Sigrist 1995), where the socially privileged who were invited don't show up, but those, who were not invited—the poor, the crippled, the blind, and the lame, the good and the bad, anyone off the streets—do receive and accept the invitation to a great meal (Luke 14:1–24, Matthew 22:1–14) (on Luke 14/Matthew 22 see Braun 1995, Roth 1997, Bartchy 2002, Smith 2003, Sigrist 1995), *John D. Crossan* observes:

> "It tells the story of a person who gives a presumably unannounced feast, sends a servant to invite friends, but finds by late in the day that each has a quite valid and very politely expressed excuse. The result is a dinner ready and a room empty. The host replaces the absent guests with anyone off the streets. But if one actually brought in *anyone off the streets*, one could, in such a situation, have classes, sexes, and ranks all mixed up together. Anyone could be reclining next to anyone else, female next to male, free next to slave, socially high next to socially low, and ritually pure next to ritually impure." (Crossan 1994, 67–68, Crossan and Reed 2002)

The visionary thought alone appears like a *"social nightmare"* (Crossan 1994, 68) in those times and days. *Meals* as places of a new kingdom distributing *new roles* (Malina 1998, Roth 1997, Bartchy 1992, 2002, Smith 2003). Single women of bad reputation sitting with respectable men, tax collectors laughing and joking with sinners, the poor serving themselves at

The Community of the Weak

table next to the rich, the sick eating with the well-to-do, a woman caught in adultery—ready to be put to death by stoning—now relaxing at the feet of her forgiving teacher (John 7:53—8:11, Kreitzer and Rooke 2000). All of them eating one of those many and redeeming meals with Jesus. Meals of reconciliation, forgiveness, acceptance.

Biblical Social Vision

The biblical vision of a new world is always inviting to a luxurious meal where people taste, savor and digest what is being proclaimed. Invited to *meals of justice* proclaiming the *biblical social vision* (Pilch and Malina 1998, Janzen 1994, Long 1997, Pleins 2001, Spohn 2000, Grassi 2002) that puts at its biblical and theological center *justice for the poor*. Sitting down at table for *meals of peace* enacting and prefiguring the Old and New Testament *Shalom for the living*, counter-acting all our spirals of violence in dire need of those healing visions for a peaceful world (Mott 1982, Tamez 1982, Lohfink 1987, Pixley and Boff 1989, Brueggemann 2001, 2002). Reclining at *meals of healing* breaking through all our classical divisions of society and stratification. Healing the broken bodies and minds of societies split among the dispersed and aching. Meals at a table painting and composing a new world. The new world of an *endtime table* where all nations, races, sexes, classes, and ages meet (Isaiah 25:6–9, Revelation 3:20) to be *reconciled and healed to each other* (Martin 1989, Granberg-Michaelson 1991, Schreiter 1992, 1998, Müller-Fahrenholz 1997, Enns, Holland, and Riggs 2004, Farley 2004), gathering at last in a *healing-land*, redeeming and healing all cycles of hatred and violence (Minow, Rosenblum 2002).

The New Testament is presenting to us a picture of Jesus gathering a melting-pot of people around his *table fellowship* in the tradition of a *socially subversive hospitality* as pre-figured already in the First or Old Testament (Genesis 12:10–16, 18:1–16, 46:1—47:12, Exodus 2:11–22, Exodus 22:21, 23:9, Leviticus 19:33, Deuteronomy 24:17–18, Ruth 2:1–23). A biblical hospitality to *strangers* (Janzen 1994, 42–46, 177–178, Brueggemann 2002, 198–199) is radically extended by Jesus to the socially marginal of all sorts, including those who normally would not be included (Luke 14:12–14) (Koenig 1985, Pohl 1999, 20–29, Hershberger 1999, Smith 2003). This social practice of Jesus, turning on its head and *upside-down* (Kraybill 2003/1978, Jennings 2003, Maguire 2005, 27–40) everything of what had been politically as well as socially systematized into acceptable and quasi-eternal societal stratification, eventually and quite naturally would lead either to open and heartfelt admiration or deep-felt enmity.

Open Hospitality

As Mennonite Old Testament scholar *Waldemar Janzen* (Janzen 1994) notes, gathering together the various *social and ethical trajectories* of biblical traditions on *hospitality* from the Old Testament to Jesus (Janzen 1994, 206–209):

> "Central to the message manifested by Jesus in the form of hospitality offered and accepted is the identity of those he invited and those from whom he accepted hospitality. Here lies both the good news and the offense. On behalf of God, Jesus invited all, the only advantage, if any, being that of greater need; stated in a different metaphor: 'Those who are well have no need of a physician, but those who are sick', a word said at a banquet (Mark 2:17; par. Matt. 9:12). Now, a certain indiscriminateness is widely inherent in the customs of human hospitality, including those of the ancient Near East. By the time of Jesus, however, this remnant of divine intention had been heavily overlaid by careful distinctions between the worthy and the unworthy. Social status, religious purity, national origin, wealth and power, and so forth, were well systematized into rules regulating hospitality. When Jesus refused to be restrained by these rules as to whom he invited and visited, he evoked release and joy in some and deep enmity in others." (Janzen 1994, 208–209, for a Christian social ethics and practical theology of hospitality Koenig 1985, Ogletree 1985, Pohl 1999, Hendriks 2001)

Roman Catholic *Robert J. Karris* (Karris 1985), summarizing *Luke's artistic and theological motifs*, points out most observantly that as a recurrent motif in the *Gospel of Luke* "Jesus is either going to a meal, at a meal, or coming from a meal" (Karris 1985, 47, quoted in Culpepper 1995, 283). A motif so strong as to lead to the revealing impression: "The Son of Man came eating and drinking, and you say, 'Here is a glutton and a drunkard, a friend of tax collectors and sinners'" (Luke 7:34 New International Version NIV, The New Jerusalem Bible NJB). Meals are like a musical motif in the life of Jesus, recounted in many instances in the Gospels. Meals as a *symbolic speech act* with a social vision, enacting the socially upsetting stories of *Jesus' parables*. Meals inviting everyone, nobody excluded. There must be, most obviously therefore, some evident basis for all this in the *historical Jesus*.

A *social vision of Jesus* (Malina 2001, Jennings 2003, Maguire 2005, 27–40) painting *another world, another map* (Neyrey 1991a, 1996, Malina 1998, Bartchy 1992, 2002, Smith 2003). An *open world* without exclusion, distinction, discrimination. A newly drawn social map of a world in which the familiar games of *exclusion and embrace* (Volf 1996) are forever turned around *upside-down*, with those marginal ones of society suddenly moving to the center of stage (McKenna 1994, Kraybill 2003/1978, Duling 2003). The *Kingdom of God* as envisioned by *Jesus* in his *subversive parables*, proclaiming a *kingdom and queendom* different from all (Kaylor 1994, Fuellenbach 1995, Herzog 1994, 2000, Maguire 2005) and a place where even *Hagar* will feel at home.

A place where *Hagar and Ishmael* finally might find some rest, some *place to be*. Like teenagers on drugs on the run from one place to the next.

A place of an *open commensality* where anyone is invited to be an equal. Equally welcome, equally embraced, equally a part of it. Regardless of their race, sex, class, age, sins, or salvation history. A social vision as a radical *crossing of boundaries*.

> "What Jesus' parable advocates, therefore, is an open commensality, an eating together without using table as a miniature map of society's vertical discriminations and lateral separations. The social challenge of such equal or egalitarian commensality is the parable's most fundamental danger and most radical threat. It is only a story, of course, but it is one that focuses its egalitarian challenge on society's miniature mirror, the table, as the place where bodies meet to eat. Since, moreover, Jesus lived out his own parable, the almost predictable counteraccusation to such open commensality would be immediate: Jesus is a glutton, a drunkard, and a friend of tax collectors and sinners. He makes, in other words, no appropriate distinctions and discriminations. And since women were present, especially unmarried women, the accusation would be that Jesus eats with whores, the standard epithet of denigration for any female outside appropriate male control. All of those terms—tax collectors, sinners, whores—are in this case derogatory terms for those with whom, in the opinion of the name callers, open and free association should be avoided." (Crossan 1994, 69, Klosinski 1988, Farb and Armelagos 1980, Crossan and Reed 2002, 115–135)

I am quite sure *Hagar* would feel comfortable here. No more running, no more distribution of exclusion and embrace. No more favoritism, power scheming for precedence in place, no more dividing and division according to history, ethnicity, sexuality, gender, class, and age. An *open kingdom* where *the least are the first*, all the world gathering around *Jesus* (as in the missionary call for ecclesia according to the World Council of Churches in *Your Kingdom Come* 1980).

CLOSURE

"The liquidity of power is the new theme that we encounter in our rethinking and reconsidering of texts, dogmas, and inspirations. It is to be heard as an accompanying basic melody when talks of the dominion, power, and omnipotence of God come up. It is to be introduced as a corrective into the language of dogmatics and of the church. A power-shift is required. Power is still not thought through altogether." (Schmalstieg 1991, 228)

"Though the question of power is almost absent from the writings of theologians, in the Bible it figures prominently . . . I argued that Christians and their theologies are always situated in a given field of personal and social forces—drives, desires and interests, struggles for goods and for power . . . Finally I argued that theology in a post-Christian and postindustrial context should celebrate the social space it is forced to inhabit (the margins) and shed all traces of nostalgia for the life in the center." (Volf 1996a, 61, 66)

"Awareness of contextuality leads to the understanding that all knowledge, theology included, reflects not only some general sense of meaning but also specific forms of interests. For instance, it was beneficial to the economic interests of white slave owners to have African-American slaves imaged as inferior, animal-like, and sinful. Given the structural as well as personal character of the crises that new voices are addressing, it is no surprise that what distinguishes the present era of theology is its attentiveness to the political character of theology. Theology is, of course, 'political' in a very broad sense, including also dynamics of sexuality, gender, and culture. In general, though, a contextual approach works at the intersection of the analysis of power, interests, and meaning and is oriented toward the transformation of

The Community of the Weak

the present situation to greater social and personal flourishing."
(Chopp and Taylor 1994, 13–14)

"A mujerista understanding of power, like our account of justice, starts from the underside of history, from those who are powerless." (Isasi-Diaz 1996a, 119)

In the Beginning a Cry

"In the beginning is the scream. We scream. When we write or when we read, it is easy to forget that the beginning is not the word, but the scream. Faced with the mutilation of human lives by capitalism, a scream of sadness, a scream of horror, a scream of anger, a scream of refusal: NO. The starting point of theoretical reflection is opposition, negativity, struggle. It is from rage that thought is born, not from the pose of reason, not from the reasoned-sitting-back-and-reflecting-on-the-mysteries-of-existence that is the conventional image of 'the thinker' . . . Our scream is a refusal to accept. A refusal to accept that the spider will eat us, a refusal to accept that we shall be killed on the rocks, a refusal to accept the unacceptable. A refusal to accept the inevitability of increasing inequality, misery, exploitation and violence. A refusal to accept the truth of the untrue, a refusal to accept closure." (Holloway 2002, 1, 6)

> I used to stand at night outside the dormitory to scream and yell at the stars over the Lake of Zurich. It was the time when I used to speak in tongues, or at least I thought so, and when I traveled from one continent to another to participate in a Catholic charismatic renewal conference with Francis MacNutt talking in front of thousands of people about healing and miracles on the sick. I remember quite well those people in the wheelchairs in Dublin in some big soccer stadium, waiting for some miracle to happen, expectant of some showdown of divine omnipotence, power, and healing.
>
> I remember my own desire and longing for some miracle, some sign, some moment turning things around for my mom. I had become a Christian somewhere around sixteen, joining a Christian youth group of greenhorn intellectuals in high school and later college in a city awakening to deep theological discussions on about everything imaginable all through the night. A real revival

Power

happened around that time, groups of smart and philosophical teenagers getting to some youth group cellar underneath a free church chapel in the town I had grown up. Heated discussions about God, philosophy, sociology, politics, debates and rebuttals, agnostics turning into believers, and later on turning back to some kind of pantheistic agnosticism.

I remained, over the years, intrigued by that field called theology. I read Francis Schaeffer even before I had ever read a history of philosophy. I turned out to be quite some smart fundamentalist and pious evangelical with a soft heart, fighting with my first girl friend about Jaspers, Fromm, Hesse, and the simple problem that she turned agnostic, while I did not. It's at that time, around sixteen or seventeen, I decided I wanted to become a pastor and study theology.

During the first years of seminary—I had deliberately chosen not to go to some liberal and "unbelieving" school of theology at a Swiss state university—in a Baptist Theological Seminary near Zurich I discovered my theological breakdown in everything—a definitely unintended result of a deeply respectful curriculum. It was not so much unending battles and fights on historical-critical methods in theology—to which I always found someone pro and someone con—, but it was simply and surprisingly Church History that broke a pious soul. Somewhere foundations I had assumed stable irrespectfully and irreversibly flushed away like sand, leaving a searching soul already then—I had not yet the term for it—with the feeling of postmodern homelessness.

In the meantime, healing and power had become my strongest generative theme (Paulo Freire) at that time. Scenes at night, with theological table talks moved to the starry sky, empty, silent, unresponsive, useless, lonely. Yelling at someone or something like God that had just disappeared from my soul. Yelling at a universe impotent, callous, cold. Asking the deep theological question what in the heck God was doing or not doing after all. Yelling out of a nostalgic cry for some life- and world-changing power beyond the ordinary. Going to bed with the feeling there was nobody out there, or at least leaving open and unanswered the question for tomorrow—"is there anybody out there?" (Pink Floyd).

At the bottom of a cry the yelling for power. For some change in life, for some healing of a story, for some redeeming of an aching soul, that of my mom and that of myself. Sensing the wounds

The Community of the Weak

> *of stories in my mom. Feeling and seeing the difference between having power and having no power. A story, even though so everyday, hardly spectacular, but still an openly oozing and unredeeming wound of some lack of power. Longing for some final and spectacular showdown—the power of God, the power of people, the power of the unexpected—while reading and feeling Paul Tillich on the shaking of foundations and wondering what in the heck all this theological paperwork was good for after all.*

Systematic Theology Digital

Systematic theology or *dogmatics*—depending on the particular view of a fundamental and theological option for some preferential name—is immersed in all our human games of a quite simple and most obvious *reality of power*. You either have it, or you don't, or at least that's how it feels like it.

All our speech, action, writing, selecting, proclaiming *divides* the world and *distributes* life chances according to *power*, including some and excluding others, be it people, experiences, worlds and words, perspectives and interests, sorrows and concerns. Not everyone who might have something *valuable or life-changing* to say seems to be able to enter the renowned theological halls of a self-proclaimed and even sometimes quite openly self-indulging academic busywork. Busy it seems, if we look at what masses of ink-filled paper and books, articles and monographs, scripts and CD-ROMS, digital bits and bytes and textual dots are still produced on what actually started quite small and rather unpretending as a *simple theological and ethical life journey* of some intrigued and bewildered *disciples* mostly considered *illiterates* and *unawares* of human knowledge and world-encompassing learning.

Learning as wisdom, at the *time of Jesus*, at the time of the *first disciples*, was still small, microcosmic, and *short-range, colloquial* (on learning in the time of Jesus for a postmodern and theological pedagogy Hodgson 1999, 87–124), in comparison to a modern day globalized and limitless *information and knowledge society* (Osborne 2002a, 167, 174–175, Lechte 2003, 123–125, 134–135, Fuller 2002, Lash 2002, Schmid 1998, 297–324) that quite frankly leaves most of us most often disoriented, dispersed, if not altogether fragmented.

In addition, *knowledge* and *information*—with theology being part of it—seem to become the most important *social commodity* for the future, dividing the world between the rich and the poor, the dumb and the informed. As radical philosopher *Richard Osborne* remarks, listing those many and various flashy-trendy *mega-words* (Osborne 2002) for the cyberspacial future: "Wealth can now be seen in terms of information rather than money: you can be information rich or information poor" (Osborne 2002a, 167). *Systematic theology* or *dogmatics* may not be exempt from such a political and social criticism. At least it should think about it.

Life-Changing Wisdom

It should also think about how it can *remember* as well as re-member *life-changing wisdom* (Schmid 1998, 297–303, Alt 2002) within a fragmented and dismembered information and knowledge society, infusing life-changing knowledge and information *out of experience* that enable and *empower* "the transformation of the present situation to greater social and personal flourishing" (Chopp and Taylor 1994, 14), *putting together the pieces* that have been broken, smashed, and spread all over in a disoriented world.

Systematic theology may find a new calling in being the *collector of experiential and liberating wisdom* (Scannone 1992, Grey 1993, Hodgson 1999, Sedmak 2002, Yoder 2007) like in ancient times *the sage* or *the wise woman*, sometimes called witches, sometimes treated as lunatics and fools. And yet, theology may become the only left-over carrier of local and human wisdom in this all too forgetful and fragmented cyber-age, a specific and highly *local and episodic* but *life-empowering knowledge* (Schmid 1998, 299, 303, on knowledge as empowering Grey 1993, Hodgson 1999, 87–124) transmitted and re-narrated over the ages, from one generation to the next, *telling the story* that helps people live.

Franciscan spiritualist and Swiss theologian *Anton Rotzetter* (Rotzetter 2000) describes *sapientia* as a type of knowledge and *wisdom* to be restored to the academic and cultural world: "It has its basis in concrete experience, in the living out of life, in the intuitive-holistic presentiment that everything is inhabited by mystery. 'You only get smart through experience' is a common wisdom saying. This wisdom can be found in all cultures. Over the last decades it has forcefully demanded back its full right to be recognized in a world that since the Enlightenment has been determined by science and technology" (Rotzetter 2000, 13).

This wisdom is inclusive, emotive, emotional, intuitive, as well as cognitive, it is practical, creative, life-changing, as well as abstract and theoretical. Wisdom understood in this *inclusive and holistic way* is puzzle *work* putting things together to make a picture or an image—worldly or theological—of the world *whole* (on theology as wisdom making the world whole Grey 1993).

Putting Things Together

Putting together pieces in order *to help women and men and children live* may be the only left-over and adequate definition of a theology wanting to be *systematic* or *dogmatic*, if dogmatic is understood as artistically composing a pictorial and cognitive *tapestry* or *story* that enables us to *weave together* with "the weaver's shuttle" (Barnes 1995, 10) the dispersed and loose ends and threads of broken off stories or pictures in order to tell again and one more time *the whole story*—turning systematic theology into something like *narrative dogmatics* (Fackre 1984 and 1996, McClendon 1986, 1990, 1994, 2000, 2002, Koyama 1999, Song 1999, Vanhoozer 2005)—to encourage the *taking of concrete and witnessing action* (McClendon 1986, 1990, 1994, 2000, 2002 and Augsburger 2006): healing the sick, feeding the hungry, clothing the naked, visiting the imprisoned, transforming violence, visualizing peace.

Resistance against the World as It Is

Following the words of social philosopher and critical theorist *Max Horkheimer* from the *Frankfurt School* who described more than fifty years ago the critical and public role of the university as an accountable place for wisdom and knowledge, a "place of knowledge, of memory, and of critique ... which at the same time is forming people for resistance against the world as it is", as paraphrased by *Edmund Arens* in his advocate and engaged meditation on the social and political purpose and public vision of education as *life-transforming Bildung* (on the German concept of Bildung—life transforming—Arens 2003, 81, Arens, Mittelstrass, Peukert, Ries 2003, Hof 2009).

Otherwise, theology—as an individual or communal first-order expression of faith and as a second-order university discipline among the sciences—may only be good for the passing but disconnected and wandering or amused eyes of short-term visitors in a historical or natural museum. Any task below that *life-transforming vision* is not really worth the paper or the screen theology is written on. Systematic theology as well may have to ask itself, some day, the simple, but determinative and dividing *theo-ethical question,* holding ethically responsible every single individual, communal, and intellectual biography:

> "Lord, when did we see you hungry and feed you, and thirsty and give you something to drink? When did we see you a stranger and invite you in, or needing clothes and clothe you? When did we see you sick or in prison and go to visit you?" (Matthew 25:37–39 NIV, New International Version)

Edmund Arens (Arens 1988–2010)—as a Roman Catholic and fundamental theologian in the tradition of *Johann Baptist Metz's new political theology* and the *critical theory* of the *Frankfurt School* (Bottomore 2002) of *Theodor Adorno, Max Horkheimer, Walter Benjamin, Herbert Marcuse, Erich Fromm,* and most predominantly in the second generation *Jürgen Habermas* and *Helmut Peukert* (Finlayson 2005, Outhwaite 1994, Peukert 1984)—describes the life-forming and transforming potential of such a politically and socially conscious *narrative theology* in a systematic or dogmatic context, self-critically pointing out the obvious limitations *social location* in theology puts on the classical academic endeavor most proudly, but sometimes quite blindly called the high and venerable discipline of a university science:

> "Narrative theology is done wherever people continue to tell, contextualize, and transform the stories of Jesus and Jesus stories in view of their own situation in order to make relevant in a new way their narrative and theological potential. That this is more easily done in Isolotto, in Bambamarca, or in Solentiname than in Münster, in Regensburg, or in Rome is obvious." (Arens 1988, 26)

Systematic Theology Confessional

Systematic theology understood as a *personal* and *narrative confession of faith* has from the beginnings of *confessions* in the Old Testament (Deuteronomy 5:6, 26:1–10, 6:4) and in the early church been related to special moments in a person's or a people's life, be it *the exodus, baptism, prayer,* or *conversion to a new life* (on confession as an exodus movement to new life Schneider 1998, 29–62, Jennings 1992, Yoder 2007).

Biographical elements are always coloring and directing a confession of faith in a *systematic-dogmatic story* of an individual telling and confessing his or her beginnings, conversions, callings, and changes in the direction of his or her life (on biography and theology Schneider 1997). Without these specific elements theology becomes sterile and unrelated to life. Theology—systematic, fundamental, or dogmatic—had its beginnings in the *beginnings* of a person's and a community's *life* (Moltmann 1980a, 1988a, 1997b, Jennings 1985a, 1982, 1992).

Roman Catholic dogmatic theologian *Theodor Schneider* (Schneider 1985, 1990, 1992a–b, 1998) describes quite well the social and individual location of *the Credo* as a *symbolic basis* for *confessional and narrative systematic theology*, the *symbolon* meaning, after all, putting one's things, all the broken and broken-off parts in one's life *together* (Schneider 1998, 29–62, Müller 2002, 20–23, Boff 1976, 106–113). Theology understood in this way, putting and throwing things together, may be compared to the work of gathering the life-pieces and life-puzzles in one's personal and communal story into *a whole*, telling myself and others *the story* that God, somehow, mysteriously, unexpectedly, has come to us:

> "Its sentences are not our draft of a world interpretation, not a philosophy of religion in short-form, nor the historically concrete expression of a general and all-encompassing transcendental experience, but rather they are the quite simple description of this journey of God to us . . . The sentences of the Credo articulate what the confessing person has experienced from God . . . From its theological architecture the Apostolic Credo is not meant for sophisticated disputation, but as a witness of living faith: faithful life praxis as praising answer to the great deeds of God." (Schneider 1998, 58)

Systematic theology conceived as a *faithful life praxis* (McClendon 1986, 1990, 1994, 2000, 2002, Augsburger 2006) touches your heart, leaves you restless, keeps you going. It may turn out to be the most personal and existential *life experiment*, life journey, and life travel. Meandering, roaming around, travelling and following the *trail* on a *way* (Schneider 1990, 9–12, Schneider 1997, 14–16, *Vamos Caminando* 1983, Herzog 1988, Rieger 1999, 2003, 2011) along a life biography telling its *story* (Schneider 1990, Schneider 1997, McClendon 2002, Yoder 2007). Dogmas, doctrines, and concepts may be looked at as never-ending and never-finished experiments *telling a story*, just as systematic theology may allow itself a more experimental attitude in the uttering of words in search of some place to stay.

Maybe theology is nothing more than *letting words rest* after a long and tiring journey through cities and places, histories and geographies, societies and academies, tossing around playfully and earnestly with human ideas and questionings, checking in at the end of the day in some tourist hotel or lodge to stay for the night before rising the next morning to go on. In this way theology—systematic, dogmatic, and fundamental—may actually become more of a personal *travel log*, tourist guide, and adventure diary telling others where we have been, what places we have seen, and which destinations may be interesting for others *to go to and see*. Books and monographs may be nothing else than friendly and *communitarian* invitations to others to a life-long theological adventure to go and see some of the same or similar places that we have seen.

In the words of *Jürgen Moltmann*:

> "I have never done theology in the form of a defence of ancient doctrines or ecclesiastical dogmas. It has always been a journey of exploration. Consequently my way of thinking is experimental—an adventure of ideas—and my style of communication is to suggest. I do not defend any impersonal dogmas, but nor do I merely express my own personal opinion. I make suggestions within a community. So I write without any built-in safeguards, recklessly as some people think. My own propositions are intended to be a challenge to other people to think for themselves." (Moltmann 1996, XIV)

Looking at Starry Skies

Looking at the starry but silent sky over the *Lake of Zurich* sometime during the nights between 1978 and 1980 had a lot to do with a personal kind of *systematic theology*. Longing for some sign of power in the midst of theological paperwork—writing papers, reading books, browsing through articles—pointed to some *personal beginning* in formulating and trying out first trials in systematic theology. I still remember it so well, because it never left me as a memorable first experience.

Reading *Tillich* and *Pannenberg*, *Bultmann* and *Sölle*, *Brunner* and *Barth*, *Bonhoeffer* and *Robinson*, *Gollwitzer* and *Braun*, *Metz* and *Moltmann*, *Cox* and *Ruether*, all this had no relevant meaning if there had not been this unanswered question in search for some possible answer. The answer did not come, no miracle did happen, the sky remained callously silent, but the feeling stayed as I went further, crossing oceans, travelling on my theological journey from one school and seminary to the next. At some point I had even contemplated to enroll at Anaheim's *Melodyland*

School of Theology not very far from Disneyland, all because of an unanswered question about that simple commodity or miracle called *power*.

Somewhere along the way the feeling seemed to recede a bit, but the theme remained. The more surprising, therefore, to find Pentecostal, evangelical, *Moltmannian* (Migliore 1991, 268–282, 2004), and Yale-systematic theologian *Miroslav Volf* in critical and confrontational conversation with post-liberal *George Lindbeck* describe contemporary systematic theology with the observation that "the question of power is almost absent from the writings of theologians" (Volf 1996a, 61, Volf, Krieg, and Kucharz 1996). Looking at traditional European systematic theologies, this judgement seems somewhat appropriate. Looking at the US and the rest of the world, however, it may have to be revised a bit.

God Dead and Dying

Power and *powerlessness* in *systematic theology* is no unknown among authors and writers describing it (Case-Winters 1990, Schmalstieg 1991, Ritter, Feldmeier, Schoberth und Altner 1997, Bachmann 2002, Keller 2005). However, most often, power and powerlessness get transposed to some far away linguistic, metaphorical, and theological heavenly sky, speculating on metaphysical, post-metaphysical, and transcendental *otherworldliness*.

Trinitarian and christological re-imaging in contemporary systematic theology very often transforms academic talk on power and powerlessness into some aesthetic and idealistic debate on a *theology of the Cross*, on the kenotic-emptying character of the divine, or on the linguistic, philosophical, and post-theistic subtleties of a *becoming* and a *dying God* (Jüngel 1976, 1983, on Eberhard Jüngel see Musser and Price 1996, 244–252). Metaphysical and post-metaphysical imagery and image-making, even though well taken, creatively developed, intellectually soaring quite high, but ultimately unable to touch the earthly human heart. "Useless truth" (Jüngel 1990, as quoted in Schneider 1992a, 2) in the many ways of the wording.

God Crucified

Even a systematic theology of the *crucified God* (Moltmann 1993/1974, Kitamori 1974, Koyama 1976, McWilliams 1985, Tesfai 2001)—as powerful and hopeful as the image may be—may turn out to remain captive to highly otherworldly speculation, not really getting close to where people are *really* hopeless and powerless.

Jürgen Moltmann, author of *The Crucified God* (Moltmann 1993/1974, on Jürgen Moltmann see McWilliams 1985, 25–49, as well as his personal autobiography Moltmann 2009), is probably the most consistent and consequential systematic theologian of the twentieth and twenty-first century creatively and relentlessly to have addressed the fundamental and unresolved question of *power* and *powerlessness* in every single *theological locus* ordinarily taught in the classical school curriculum of contemporary systematic theology covering over 50 years (Moltmann 1959–2010), showing an impressive and kaleidoscopic sensitivity to the many and various workings of *power* and *powerlessness* (Moltmann 1983) in language, in doctrine, in systematic, dogmatic, and fundamental theology.

Jürgen Moltmann has thus moved the minds and hearts of innumerable readers and listeners to a life-changing faith and ethics in concrete action, preaching and teaching *theologically* and *pastorally* in various social contexts all over this globalized and power-stricken world (Moltmann 1980a, 1988a, 1997b, 2000, 2010, followed by Deuser, Martin, Stock und Welker 1986, Volf, Krieg, and Kucharz 1996, Moltmann und Rivuzumwami 2002 and various Festschriften).

God Speculative

Nonetheless, even someone like *Jürgen Moltmann* has not been exempt from criticism about dangers of speculative and world-distanced linguistic playfulness by a variety of commentators as diverse as North American, Australian, British, German, Italian, Spanish, Swiss, and French *Roman Catholic* and *Protestant* sympathetic *friends* and *critics* (in North America Chopp 1986, 100–117, Livingston and Schüssler Fiorenza 2000, 283–287, in Britain Bauckham 1995, 1993, 1997, in Australia Ormerod 1997, 134–143, in Germany Müller-Fahrenholz 2000, in Spain Vilanova 1997, 794–798, in Switzerland and France Blaser 1995b, 189–217, Goudineau et Souletie 2002).

North American and Roman Catholic systematic theologians *James C. Livingston* and *Francis Schüssler Fiorenza* (Livingston and Schüssler Fiorenza 2000, 283–287) paraphrase the vocal protest from theologies in the Two-Thirds-world in view of *Jürgen Moltmann's political eschatology* on the Kingdom of God, the biblical metaphor for *the power of God* (Müller-Fahrenholz 2000):

The Community of the Weak

> "They argue that his conception of eschatology is more Neo-Platonic than Christian to the extent that it presents God's Kingdom mainly as a transcendent reality so that it becomes almost a Platonic ideal standing in contrast to earthly existence. By contrast, the liberation theologians point to the notion of a 'realized eschatology'. By this term they suggest that, just as the Kingdom of God is being realized on earth in Jesus's healings and exorcisms, so, too, the Kingdom of God is being realized on earth whenever justice and love are being realized." (Livingston and Schüssler Fiorenza 2000, 287)

Even as impressive and powerful a dogmatic and systematic image as the *crucified God* (Moltmann 1993/1974, McWilliams 1985, 25–49, Chopp 1986, 100–117) may turn into, what evangelical *Richard Bauckham* (Bauckham 1995, 1993, 1997) warns, "undisciplined speculation" (Bauckham 1995, 167), if systematic theology does not stay in touch and listen to the biblical and human story of *real pain*. At the beginning of good systematic and dogmatic theology is a *cry* (Aguirre 1997). With the poetic and academic words of Argentinian Jesuit *Luis Pérez Aguirre*:

> "This cry we hear we do not know what it signifies nor what is its cause; this is why it is disquieting to us and mobilizes our attention and our sensitivity. Through this cry of pain there is not a doctrine or a theoretical expression that comes to us, but the person itself that pronounces it." (Aguirre 1997, 36)

Theology out of Pain

Systematic or dogmatic theology as *narrative* needs to become a *theology out of pain*, screaming and yelling at starry skies, in daily contact and close encounter with pain and cries. It needs to become *suffering as a theology*. This way, talk—theological or simply human—about God and human pain will not become doctrinal or theoretical, but *confessional* and *personal*, leaving no conventional trinitarian or christological debate hanging somewhere in the noncommittal air, as if taking off with the lightness of being in a balloon with no more ground.

Theology as suffering needs to become *grounded*, implanted in the dirty soil of living pain. *Weeping, confession, resistance*, and *pain* (Smith 1992) make up the necessary and basic ingredients of life-transforming wisdom and knowledge for proclamation in a world in need of radical change.

Radical activist and social scientist *John Holloway* (Holloway 2002) from the Zapatista and Chiapas' Mexico may seem to put things rhetorically and daringly a little upside-down and on its theological head, and yet he remains so impressively and truly faithful to the world-changing biblical truth, basing his *radical social science* on the simple fact of a *human scream* (Holloway 2002, 1–10). This in turn should serve as a healthy and self-critical reminder for *systematic theology*—a radical social science in its own way—that has long ago forgotten to listen to its own human pain:

> "Saint John is doubly wrong, then, when he says that 'in the beginning was the word.' Doubly wrong because, to put it in traditional terms, his statement is both positive and idealist. The word does not negate, as the scream does. And the word does not imply doing, as the scream does. The world of the word is a stable world, a sitting-back-in-an-armchair-and-having-a-chat world, a sitting-at-a-desk-and-writing world, a contented world, far from the scream which would change everything, far from the doing which negates . . . In the world of the word, doing is separated from talking and doing, practice is separated from theory. Theory in the world of the word is the thought of the Thinker, of someone in restful reflection, chin in hand, elbow on knee." (Holloway 2002, 23)

Academic playfulness so often just sitting back in armchairs chatting, writing, and musing, chin in hand, and elbow on knee, would do well—both in the social sciences and in systematic theology—to listen attentively to these words of John Holloway, coming out of a deep sensitivity for human pain. Science and pain go together if they want to become practical and life-transforming in order to *change the world*.

Theology Shifting

Systematic theology becoming *practical* will be preaching and speaking in the midst of such pain. This recognition and awareness, this sensitivity and openness to the in-breaking of pain, changes your whole perspective on life and everything.

As feminist theologian and homiletician *Christine M. Smith* writes: "Once a theologian, a preacher, or a person of faith names the pervasive world reality that permeates the globe as radical evil, her or his entire theological thinking, writing, and interpretation of the word shift" (Smith 1992, 3). Pain makes you *shift* your vision. Pain makes you relocate in social space. Pain makes you rewrite your theology, systematic theology as well. "'Preaching is weeping'. Often when people weep, they are most in touch with the deepest passions, strongest yearnings, and greatest desires ... In a world filled with human suffering, inequity, and oppression, surely preaching is a kind of weeping" (Smith 1992, 4). Systematic theology may become a kind of weeping as well.

Then only, it may happen, that theology—systematic, fundamental, dogmatic, and practical—may reach the top of the mountain in poetic formulations, the way Brazilian Sister of Notre Dame and feminist liberation theologian *Ivone Gebara* (Gebara 2002) finds systematic-theological and dogmatic words for God, higher even, and more beautiful, than most academic abstraction:

> "This is a God mingled with the daily routine of poor women who cry to him/her in the midst of their struggle simply to survive; a baroque God sometimes clement and sometimes stern, present in cloisters and libraries, inspiring love poems and love for poems; a God critical of his own images, images frozen in a patriarchal world, likened to an army, to emperors and kings, to philosophical systems and theological treatises; a God who cries within us to be free from our prisons, who cries to be allowed to be simply God, the One who *is*. From the phenomenology of evil, we have arrived at silence on the mystery that dwells in us and in whom we dwell, Mystery in all and beyond all." (Gebara 2002, 180)

The Crucified God and Crushed Humanity

"The question: does God exist? is an abstract one. Theology is never concerned with the actual existence of a God. It is interested solely in the rule of this God in heaven and on earth. The notion of a divine monarchy in heaven and on earth, for its part, generally provides the justification for earthly domination—religious, moral, patriarchal or political domination—and makes it a hierarchy, a 'holy rule'. The idea of the almighty ruler of the universe everywhere requires abject servitude, because it points to complete dependency in all spheres of life." (Moltmann 1981, 191–192)

"My interest was aroused in the experience of 'the dark night of the soul'. The prison cells of the martyrs and the monastic

cells of the mystics are not very different. Academic critics again complained about my 'one-sidednesses' and pointed out how controversial and confrontational I was . . . Before my eyes is another image. On 16 November 1989 six Jesuits and two women were brutally murdered in the University of San Salvador. The soldiers took the body of brother Ramon Moreno into the room of the absent Jon Sobrino. In his blood was found a book which had fallen down, El Dios Crucificado. Now it lies there under glass as a symbolic interpretation of the martyrdom of the brothers and sisters." (Moltmann 1997b, 19)

> *Memories of crucifixion und pain. Memories of crucified minds, people, projects, dreams, visions, and lives. Eight people in El Salvador crucified. A crucified mind. A crucified person. A crucified people. A crucified life. Crucifixion and crucifying in many various ways and times. Bringing up personal memories and unforgetable cries.*

> *Memories about a young Swiss activist and theologian—working outside of the traditional church context—who was shot in El Salvador in the 1980s. The Swiss government never really took a clear stance condemning it. I used to know Jürg, although not very well, but I remember liking and admiring him. We walked alongside each other sometime in the 1980s in Geneva protesting against the US war in Nicaragua. In between I had met him several times in Bern and Zurich in a Swiss Central America solidarity group.*

> *Some years later I got to know a Swiss Reformed pastor in Zurich who had started a sanctuary movement for refugees fleeing from Pinochet's Chile. Around that time when I got to know him he had just gotten voted out by a public vote by the people, after a most ugly, most destructive, and most hurtful and slanderous public campaign against him. Some years later Peter—who in the meantime had become a friend of mine—died of bone cancer. In a beautiful book with soul-searching and heart-moving prayers— personally written during the time in the hospital—he mentions how that experience of being kicked out of the ministry in Zurich "went into his bones". Words I would never again forget.*

> *Only some little time later I got myself into a similarly disputed vote for a position in a local church in the Zurich region. Accused of simply being a communist, an anti-military pacifist, a non-believer, and a dangerous mind—being still quite young with only just 31—, I provided Swiss newspapers for the first time in*

The Community of the Weak

my life with seemingly entertaining but painful headlines for only a very short time. It took me half a year to get over it, after I had wept all Sunday when I was told the voting results.

Eight years later I spent the night—just as dark as nights of the soul can be—on the lake of my home town waiting for some other results after a public and again highly disputed vote by the people. A vote that had been page-filling and word-inflating news topic never-ending for probably most of the important times during these same eight years. With sometimes almost daily, weekly, and monthly press, radio, and television coverage just for one particular goal of some: to get rid of someone. It took me five years half way to get over it, with scars of pain remaining deep and hurtful as memories and images that will never go away for the rest of my life.

Images of pain and images of elation. Images of solidarity and images of betrayal. Images of a church dying to its own lying, intriguing, and destroying.. Images of silent colleagues and vomiting enemies. Images of cowards and images of hypocrites. Images of rest and images of restlessness. Images of the care of unemployment officers and the abuse of church hierarchies. Images of compassion of teenagers and the betrayed of a youth. Images of homeless drug addicts and homesick runaway-teenagers. Images of confirmation worship services with people dancing and clapping.

Images of the self-righteous wanting to destroy it all. Images of a funeral for a 14-year-old. Newspaper headlines about the death of this girl. Images of 300 teenagers weeping and grieving inside and outside of a mid-size countryside church door. Images of public demonstrations, images of privately caring faces. Images—even newspaper pictures—of 70 teenagers in front of a local church in support of a pastor. Images of 250 adults in a church with some acting out their most shameful behavior. Images of open violence and images of secret slander. Images of painful hurting and images of releasing laughter. Images of country roads and images of rear mirrors, with images and memories in sobbing tears while leaving a place that used to be home for the officially last time.

Crucified

In spite of possible and aforementioned criticism, I do like *Jürgen Moltmann* a lot. And this not just because of a most touching and personal letter hanging on a wall somewhere in our home wishing me all the best for the writing of my dissertation. But also, because of this unforgetable and unredeemable theological image of the *crucified God*. A crucified God as an image for every crucifixion. Crucified minds, people, lives (Tesfai 2001, Kitamori 1974, Koyama 1976, McWilliams 1985, Farley 2004).

Smashed lives, broken people, demolished souls. *Crushed humanity* will not be foreign and unknown to a *crucified God* (Moltmann 1993/1974, McWilliams 1985, 25-49). A systematic theology of a crucified God is continuously and compassionately called to be *in close touch* with the omnipresent possibilities of the *perversion of power* (Poling 1991, 1996, Farley 2004) that we can see and smell, taste and hear, wherever we dare to look. Broken people, abused souls, violated nations, destroyed habitats, endangered species, plundered resources.

Jürgen Moltmann has been one of a few Europeans in systematic or dogmatic theology who has consistently faced and addressed this permanently threatening reality of the *use and abuse of power* (Moltmann 1983), including considerations on power and the abuse of power in all his various and innumerable elaborations and contributions to a *political-dogmatic* and *social-ethical systematic theology* (Moltmann 1959–2010), followed by other companions in systematic theology in *Germany* and other parts of *Europe* (Metz 1980, 1992/1977, 1997, Sölle 1971, 1974, 1990, Gollwitzer 1982, Kraus 1983, Marquardt 1988, Schmalstieg 1991, Volf, Krieg, and Kucharz 1996, Blaser 1997, Biehl und Johannsen 2002).

Theology Crucified

Power plays an *open* or *secret, unveiled or hidden role* wherever we look in reframing and reformulating common *theological disciplines*. Power colors theological epistemology. Power rewrites fundamental theology. Power shows the social location of systematic theology. Power talks in religious language. Power stipulates dogma. Power invites to the critique of ideologies. Power remakes theological ethics. Power starts prolegomena or epilegomena. Power shapes the doctrine of God and creation. Power rewrites theological anthropology and christology. Power revisions soteriology. Power breathes pneumatology. Power determines ecclesiology and the sacraments. Power tells history. And power predicts eschatology. Power creeps up wherever we look and listen as omnipresent.

All along the *classical school curriculum* of systematic, dogmatic, and fundamental theology questions of power and powerlessness, and the use or abuse of power, creep up like a blocked and contained melody wanting to be heard, and yet most often silenced by millions of words. Considering the masses of bits and bytes of papers and monographs, essays and books, dissertations and CD-ROMS, there seems to be a certain most obvious and disquieting forgetfulness for this omnipresent reality. Into this field of quiet acquiescence to the all-determining and all-subservient empire of power and silence the discomforting news of a *crucified God* is like the explosion of a bomb, or the irruption of a volcano, or the silent whisper of a deeply bruised soul in excruciating pain.

God crucified? Not just *God dead* or *dying,* as some may have wanted to proclaim the ultimate deadening and deconstructing of and into silence in a highly abstract God-post-mortem absurdity (as in postmodern and deconstructivist play Taylor 1984, Jennings 1985, Ward 1996, 1997, 2005). But God *really* crucified. Like the children and women in Nicaragua, Guatemala, Mexico, Chile, Peru, Bolivia, South Korea, South Africa, Iraq. Like the six university professors and their housekeeper with her daughter in San Salvador. Like the AIDS-victims and hungry in Africa. Like the homeless in Europe, North and South America. Like the abused and violated. Like the tortured and the imprisoned, bombed and bombarded. Like those on death-row, like those on unemployment checks. Like the forgotten and unnamed, excluded and dismembered. Like the broken souls and aching hearts. Like the betrayed and lied to. Like the demolished and shattered. Like the no-persons and no-people. Like the drugs addicts and social cases. Like the single mother and homeless child. All crucified, like many more. Forever wounded, scarred.

As *Jürgen Moltmann* describes his most personal and biographical background for his belief in a *crucified God*:

> "I found the positive influence of my theology of the cross especially in the christology of Jon Sobrino, who deepened and sharpened it for the Latin American context . . . I have learnt from his theology of the cross, which he not only taught but suffered. A few days ago I received a letter from Robert McAfee Brown, in which he told me the following moving story from San Salvador. On 16 November 1989, six well-known Jesuits, together with their housekeeper and her daughter, were brutally murdered in the university there. The rector of the university,

Father Ignacio Ellacuria, was one of them. Jon Sobrino escaped the massacre only because he happened not to be in the country at the time. The letter continues, 'When the killers were dragging some of the bodies back into the building, as they took one of the bodies into Jon's room, they hit a bookcase and knocked a book on to the floor, which became drenched with the martyr's blood. In the morning, when they picked up the book, they found that it was your *The Crucified God*.' This sign and symbol gives me a great deal to think about. What it says to me is that these martyrs are the seed of the resurrection of a new world. Like Archbishop Oscar Romero, they are the hope of the people: unforgettable, inextinguishable, irresistible." (Moltmann 1993/1974, xi–xii, Sobrino 1978, on Jon Sobrino see Bedford 1995, Musser and Price 1996, 427–433)

Anamnestic Memory

So *concrete*, so biographical, so bloody, painful, and unbelievable is the crucified God. No abstract construction, but a *real human story* told in a letter from one friend in systematic theology to the other, retold and remembered in the midst of those many and millions of useless and empty bits and bytes circulating in a callous and forgetful, information-overdosed and knowledge-overproduced world. A simple and personal story at the beginning of memorable confession and good theology. A story told, felt, *relived*, remembered. *Anamnestic and dangerous memory* (Metz 1980, 184–204, Ashley 1998, 27–58, Jennings 1992, 87–120, Metz 2006, Metz und Reikenstorfer 2011) remembers the stories of such concrete suffering and pain. Only then can dogmatic belief as *martyrial and liberating life witness* in *word and deed* be transformed into a world- and life-changing and life-empowering following and calling of Christians and martyrs in the discipleship of a *suffering and crucified God* (Bachmann 2002, Keller 2005).

In the words of a friend, systematic, and widely-traveled *world-theologian* with a big heart and wide-open eyes for human pain all over the world, *Klauspeter Blaser* (Blaser 1972–2004) who passionately taught systematic and practical theology over thirty years at the *University of Lausanne* in Switzerland until his all too premature death in the summer of 2002:

The Community of the Weak

> "Why speak about God? If the question of God does not change anything in the behaviors of people and of society, then it is finally of no importance . . . Furthermore, the Jewish background, its roots in the Old Testament, rediscovered by contemporary exegesis, encourages current christology to never forget the terrestrial character of salvation and the political dimension of the notion of the Kingdom of God, of its expectation and its coming: this idea revolutionizes history as it inverses our evolutionary and, for that matter, bourgeois conception of time. The end of all sufferings can only be the spectacle of history if the time of God is coming and is taking over our time . . . We should beware, however, of all triumphalism or enthusiasm. The unity of the Resurrected with the Crucified is in effect generating an awareness of the real conditions of the world and time. We are not living in heaven, and our faith can neither escape from suffering nor from struggle." (Blaser 1997, 135, 232, Blaser 2003a)

Systematic theology worth its prize is coming out of *struggle* (Fernandez 1994), pain, and suffering. Theology for the *crucified mind*, remembering and expecting the crucified God. As *Klauspeter Blaser* reminds us, no theology will be able to bypass this reality, as we are not living in some abstract and speculative heaven, but in this—what friend and colleague Christian ethicist *Denis Müller* calls the Rue du Bourg and St. Laurent in *Lausanne* (Müller 1999, 66)—earthly, dirty, messy, painful, and all too often *violently suffering world of today* (Blaser 1997, 232). Theology composed and acted on responsively should never fall back into amnesia and forget human and living suffering—feeling nothing, sensing nothing, seeing nothing—, be it systematic, fundamental, ethical, and dogmatic.

Only then will *systematic theology* become more sensitive to the workings of *power* and *suffering*, both in their destroying and healing presence, and reconnect with the story of the *suffering and healing Jesus* who taught us to *think and act* out of *passion and compassion*, in the context of our *social location* (Müller 1999, 63–66), turning human lives in the midst of suffering and crucifixion into an *exuberant messianic joy* (Moltmann 1973) in a theological and social-ethical *love at first sight* (Blaser 2003b).

4

North America

LANDSCAPE

"... there is no greater public task for theology in North America today than to help to provide a people indoctrinated in the modern mythology of light with a frame of reference for the honest exploration of its actual darkness..." (Hall 1989, 36)

"He was back in May 1973, in a meeting room at the seminary where he taught. A group of faculty had assembled to approve a call to a famous scholar from across the sea. Nothing stood in the way of this action except the known reservations of two persons in the room, one of whom was the theologian himself. He believed the call was futile, that (as it later turned out) the appointee would not accept, and that the faculty's fascination with overseas scholars of fame deflected it from attending to candidates who, with lesser fame, had more pertinence to the theological agenda in America..."(Driver 1977, 50–51)

"By using the word 'contributions', the writer recognizes the conditions and limitations of his own position, and the relativity of his own particular environment. He makes no claim to say everything, or to cover the whole of theology. He rather understands his own 'whole' as part of a whole that is much greater. He cannot therefore aim to say what is valid for everyone, at all times and in all places. But he will set himself, with his own time and his own place, within the greater community of theology. For him this means a critical dissolution of naive, self-centered

The Community of the Weak

thinking. Of course he is a European, but European theology no longer has to be Eurocentric. Of course he is a man, but theology no longer has to be androcentric." (Moltmann 1981, xii)

Traveling to a Different World

I used to read theological books already when I was 18. At that time I had decided to look for some theological training in the US, even though I did not know how to speak let alone how to write a simple and easy text in English. I remember talking to some pastor who had studied at the Westminster Theological Seminary in Philadelphia about which possible graduate schools in the US to consider. For a while I seriously contemplated enrolling at the then only recently founded charismatic Melodyland School of Theology near Disneyland, with no clue whether my studies would ever be accepted back home in Switzerland.

I vividly remember a personal letter from Eduard Schweizer, at that time New Testament professor at the Protestant theological faculty of the University of Zurich, warning me about the US and its theological educational system. To my question as to which degree from different possibly considered theological schools would be accepted in Switzerland as equivalent to the requirements for becoming a minister in Swiss Reformed Churches he refused to give me a definite answer.

Years later, coming back from a personally and theologically highly nomadic and world-discovering journey to the inner linguistic and theological exile at the outskirts of the Lake of Zurich, to the high-rise skyscrapers of the Big Apple, to the green pastures of horse-riding Kentucky, and to the gray-brown smog and the blue-skied sunshine of the City of Angels, the Santa Cruz Boardwalk, and the Golden Gate bridge, I first had to take a Swiss denominational accrediting body to a recourse legal committee to have its decision revoked not to accept my six years of theological graduate training with a Master of Divinity from a US theological seminary as a sufficient requirement to be a minister in a Swiss Reformed State Church.

At the same time, while fighting legal battles with some German-speaking accrediting church body about what some 20 years later would quite naturally become the all-accepted and European-wide "Bologna graduate education reform project", declaring the

North America

> *Anglo-Saxon and US credit and educational system of Bachelors and Masters the future norm for all the universities and theological graduate schools of the European Community, the University of Geneva accepted without any reservations, even with a deep admiration for the material depth and quality of my Baptist, Methodist and interdenominational US-theological training, all my academic credits.*
>
> *Having come back from a big continent in a big world, I keep wondering why things were the way they were, and why things still don't seem to have changed that much.*

Power and Powerlessness in North America

North American systematic theology has developed a keen sensitivity and open receptivity for the issues of *power* and *powerlessness* in theology. Not only do we find intense discussions on the reality of power and powerlessness in *biblical studies*, but also in *systematic theology, ethics, practical theology,* and *pastoral theology*.

At the same time, however, most of these recent debates in *North American systematic theology* have not reached the *European continent*. The two worlds still seem to remain far away and *apart* from each other, one inviting to a *different world*, mostly *unknown* by the other. *German systematic theology* is highly present in North America, especially through its classical names. The new names in *North American systematic theology*, however, are almost absent on European soil. The reasons for this may be many—one of them, most certainly, the absence of the issue of *power* in theology itself.

Power and *powerlessness* in *North American systematic theology* are almost omnipresent in many ways. Issues of *race, gender, sexual orientation, gay and lesbian issues*, but also the new themes of *culture, ethnicity, disability*, as well as old but ever recurring social themes of *poverty, hunger, violence, social exclusion*, and *justice in peace* determine the language, the structure, and the interest of most *North American systematic theologies* in past and present days. *Power* and *powerlessness* are the *underlying melody* playing along in every tune. The present chapter will attempt to give a *first tour* to a vast continent of North American theological thinking and acting in need of some more *global resonance*.

The Community of the Weak

English-Speaking Theology

It used to be that God spoke *German*. At least in theology, so was the joke going around among world-traveling students. Whoever had anything most valuable or at least half way worthwhile to say or write or research in theology, be it systematic, dogmatic, or fundamental, in the only just recently bygone and left behind *20th century* needed to be most fluently conversant and familiar with those few but often recited giants of *European*, predominantly *German or Swiss, theology*.

Would-be and soon to be *scholars and academics from all over the world* followed the much treaded trail of educational pilgrimage to those well-known and much admired *European centers of deep wisdom, knowledge, and theological erudition* demanding every possible awe from traveling disciples struggling with *basic German* for graduate requirements to get some Ph.D. or Dr. theol. from a renown European university.

It still seems to be a commonplace to find in Europe a *history of systematic, dogmatic or fundamental theology in the 20th century* as recent as in the year 2002 (Fischer 2002) as if God's only concern over a whole century had been the voluminous productions of theological books and monographs, dissertations and articles in and of one single continent or country, let alone of only one language, namely *German*.

British evangelical and across a wide range of combating theological currents respected Oxford systematic theologian *Alister McGrath* (McGrath 2001, 2001a, 1997, 2004) captures this amusing as well as revealing theological oddity for the 21st century well in his short and lucid summary of historical description and newly registered *paradigm shift* on a global and linguistic-geographical scale, timidly pointing out that God may, after all, and in spite of hard-dying traditions, not only speak German:

> "One of the most prominent features of western theology during the modern period has been the intellectual hegemony of German-language theology. The German-speaking lands of Europe, above all Germany and northern Switzerland, have long been the source of a rich and fertile theological tradition. Two leading figures of the Reformation, Martin Luther and Huldrych Zwingli, are witnesses to the importance of this tradition to the development of modern western theology. Since the Enlightenment, the prominence of the German-language tradition has become even more firmly established; a list of the leading theologians of the modern western tradition—including Karl Barth, Rudolf Bultmann, Jürgen Moltmann, Wolfhart Pannenberg, Karl

Rahner, and Paul Tillich—has an unquestionably Germanic ring to it. In recent years, however, this situation has changed. A new generation of German-language theologians of truly global significance has not emerged to succeed writers such as Bultmann, Moltmann, Pannenberg and Rahner. Instead, there has been a steady increase in the significance of English-language theology, especially that originating from the United States of America. With the increasing role played by English as the lingua franca of the world (the parallel with Latin in the Middle Ages being of significance), it seems likely that this development will be consolidated, at least in the opening years of the new millennium." (McGrath 2001, 88, McGrath 1997, 99)

Broadening of Horizons

German systematic theologian *Hermann Fischer* (Fischer 2002), writing an impressive and recently revised overview of Protestant systematic theology in the 20th century, hardly mentions any other theological developments outside of the European continent. A broadening of horizons still seems to be out of sight. From *Barth* through *Brunner, Althaus, Hirsch, Elert* via *Bonhoeffer* to *Bultmann, Käsemann,* and *Tillich* we find every possible German name succeeding the founding fathers—fore-mothers except radical feminist *Dorothee Sölle* (on Dorothee Sölle see Pinnock 2003, Wartenberg-Potter 2004) do not appear—of German theological and continental thinking. The author leads us from *Pannenberg, Ebeling, Moltmann, Metz*—the only Roman-Catholic exception—to *Jüngel, Rendtorff, Herms,* and *Wagner,* while reserving just a little more than 10 pages out of over 370 altogether to US-, Latin American, and feminist theologies (Fischer 2002, 158–160 and 195–206).

Women and *non-Europeans* turn out to be the big absentees in the book on almost every page of an overview on systematic theology in the 20th *century*. As such a revealing signal for a seemingly still very basic and symptomatic problem of a missing link in global dialogue.

The theological claim to cover the entire *20th century* in systematic theology is passingly relativized by the author with a personal acknowledgement of a limited competence in covering more than the German continent (Fischer 2002, 6). Sitting through lectures and seminars in different Swiss or German universities in systematic, dogmatic, or fundamental theology in the *21st century* would most probably confirm—with a few notable exceptions—the impression that this globally odd state of affairs of self-imposed limitations in *inter-cultural and inter-gender competence* is more than just simply accidental, but has everything to do with a fundamental and self-conscious *theological decision*.

In Need of a Global Vision

Even more recent accounts in 2004 of the current state of the theological discipline called *systematic theology* seem to stay within a European, in particular a German theological vision, with publications by the *Wissenschaftliche Gesellschaft für Theologie* not really looking beyond national and linguistic borders while reporting on *systematic theology in the contemporary world* (Deuser und Korsch 2004). The *global world* disappears and never really makes an appearance somewhere in the limited in-betweens of a history of systematic theology from the 19th century of *Ernst Troeltsch* to the 20th and 21st century of *Gerhard Ebeling, Wilfried Härle* or *Hans-Martin Barth* (on Ernst Troeltsch, Gerhard Ebeling, Wilfried Härle, and Hans-Martin Barth see Deuser und Korsch 2004, 61–77).

Other European accounts of the story of *systematic theologies* of the *nineteenth* and *twentieth century* on a *global and international scale* seem to end as well, as exemplified by *Munich's* systematic theologian *Jan Rohls* (Rohls 1997a–b), with a description of theological developments in Germany (Rohls 1997b, 740–859). In an otherwise notably open account of *global developments in systematic theology* over these last two centuries, giving more attention than most others to French, British, North American, Scandinavian, Dutch, Latin American, Asian, African and feminist theologies (Rohls 1997b, 14–59, 199–222, 363–390, 512–554, 687–740), the still remaining preponderate space taken up by German theology in almost two-thousand pages upholds a symbolically telling embrace. The limited vision remains. A *global vision* is needed.

Breaking Out of the Eurocentric

European systematic theology even in the *twenty-first century* (European systematic theology as reported in Fischer 2002, Deuser und Korsch 2004, Rohls 1997a–b) still chooses to remain predominantly *Eurocentric*. Whether this is so out of conviction is not clear. However, what is clear is the fact that such *limited visions* have a tendency to preclude any transformations of paradigms. This might be one reason why European academic theology appears more and more caught in old battles over and over again in ever new ways. Breaking out of old familiar ways may actually get a limited vision renewed in a totally new light.

In these limited visions we find a hardly developed sense of the *interconnectedness* of a *global theological world* in this postmodern age, as compared, in more encouraging ways, with the global-cosmopolitan recognition of someone like *Jürgen Moltmann* that theology nowadays can and should no longer be and remain *Eurocentric* (Moltmann 1981, xii). Here, in contrast, we find a self-reflecting and self-critical recognition of one's *limited place* and time, space and story, in writing systematic theology, as Jürgen Moltmann quite openly explains his deep reluctance to write a *dogmatic Summa*, preferring rather sporadic and self-limiting *theological contributions*.

With critical words about his own contextual clientele by *Jürgen Moltmann*, worthwhile to be quoted again, as Jürgen Moltmann reflects on the still dominant temptation of European theology to stay self-centered in itself. Words that serve as a healthy reminder how *global* and *polycentric* the world has become in these relative, postmodern, post-confessional, and, most definitely, *post-European times:*

> "By using the word 'contributions', the writer recognizes the conditions and limitations of his own position, and the relativity of his own particular environment. He makes no claim to say everything, or to cover the whole of theology. He rather understands his own 'whole' as part of a whole that is much greater. He cannot therefore aim to say what is valid for everyone, at all times and in all places. But he will set himself, with his own time and his own place, within the greater community of theology. For him this means a critical dissolution of naive, self-centered thinking. Of course he is a European, but European theology no longer has to be Euro*centric*. Of course he is a man, but theology no longer has to be andro*centric*." (Moltmann 1981, xii)

North American Theology Coming of Age

At the time, *North America* seems to have slowly *emancipated itself* from being focused on the *Eurocentric*. Systematic theologian of culture *Tom Driver* (Driver 1977) at *Union Theological Seminary* in New York describes more than thirty years ago in 1973 a common North American faculty's tempting and comprehensible fascination with European scholars of fame from overseas in view of the academic approval of a call.

> "He was back in May 1973, in a meeting room at the seminary where he taught. A group of faculty had assembled to approve a call to a famous scholar from across the sea. Nothing stood in the way of this action except the known reservations of two persons in the room, one of whom was the theologian himself. He believed the call was futile, that (as it later turned out) the appointee would not accept, and that the faculty's fascination with overseas scholars of fame deflected it from attending to candidates who, with lesser fame, had more pertinence to the theological agenda in America." (Driver 1977, 50-51)

A subtle hint questioning and reconsidering an old and long tradition in New York's liberal and highly progressive *Union Theological Seminary's* practice of calling European scholars, which has seen several of those many names of fame pass by, from *Dietrich Bonhoeffer, Paul Tillich, Dorothee Sölle* to *Edmund Arens*. Most of them eventually retained some particularly US-made coloring in their academic and personal ways of theological thinking and writing, bringing some of it back to the European continent in their own personal way.

Tom Driver most timidly but determinatively points out, already in the 1970's, a slowly emerging and silently growing *self-consciousness* and *coming of age* in a newly discovered theological *American cultural pride*. It takes courage, and pride, after all, to cut the maternal or mostly paternal umbilical cord of a theological and academic dependency on European scholars and Europe-made theologies, crossing the ocean most often just in the direction of one way. Hardly did Tom Driver know at that particular time how pertinent and visionary for the future his hesitations and casual thoughts at the time would turn out to be.

Years later, *the coming of age of North American theology* will become general pattern in a radical *change of paradigms* (Küng and Tracy 1989, Küng 1988) as part of a newly reconfigured and theologically *globalized world* where God would no longer only speak German (on the globalization of theology Gibellini 1995, Blaser 1995a, 1995b, Chenu 1987, Neusch et Chenu 1994, Chenu et Neusch 1995, Vilanova 1997, Ford and Muers 2005, Livingston and Schüssler Fiorenza 2006, Jenkins 2002, 2006). A *shift in power*—with theology always inscribed in a *geography of power*—would rearrange *theology's global landscape* in a *radically new way*.

Unknown Territory

> *It still seems to be that North America remains a mysterious and hardly ever walked on planet to be discovered by some daring astronauts or a powerfully looking telescope. Edmund Arens from the Roman Catholic theological faculty of the University of Lucerne in Switzerland, fundamental theologian and frequent theological visitor, both personally or vicariously in literature, to the US, tells the amusing little but symptomatic story how years ago in a more casual conversation with some well-known systematic theologian in Germany the simple comment on North America got resumed to one ever-meaningful statement: "There is no such thing as a systematic theology in North America".*

North American systematic theology is still, in spite of globally detectable changes of paradigms, for the most part an *unknown territory* for the European continent. For most European theological publications North American systematic theology does not exist, neither as a valuable and important resource for possible translations, nor as a seriously considered partner for university research and dialogue.

One exception to the rule is the geographically comprehensive *university report* of Roman Catholic ethicist *Dietmar Mieth* (Mieth 1995), editor of the international theological journal *Concilium*. In 1995, reflecting on the future directions of theological research in Europe, he points out the underestimated importance of North American theology for *university research in the European context*, a situation to be remedied and changed in the future. A similar conclusion is found in the competent review in 1993 on the latest developments in *systematic theology* in the *United States* in the German theological journal *Verkündigung und Forschung* (Sauter/Welker 1993), reporting on research in various theological disciplines. Outside of these exceptions, we hardly find any mentioning of North American systematic theology in European contexts.

North American systematic theology is a wide and limitless field of academic research. The often conjured-up and confusing complexity or *"Neue Unübersichtlichkeit"* (Habermas 1985, 1989) of our modern and postmodern society shows itself most eloquently and ominously in treading and strolling along this wide and gigantic theological and geographical continent called the USA.

North American systematic theology is hardly known in the European context. The academic and scholarly exchange between the continents is very limited, most of the time only unilateral. European theological names like *Karl Barth, Emil Brunner, Dietrich Bonhoeffer, Paul Tillich, Rudolf Bultmann, Karl Rahner, Edward Schillebeeckx, Jürgen Moltmann, Johann Baptist Metz, Dorothee Sölle, Wolfhart Pannenberg, Gerhard Ebeling, Eberhard Jüngel, Hans Küng*, and several others have been widely received in the United States over the last several decades, most of their works being translated as soon as published in German, Dutch or French.

However, hardly anybody in German-speaking theological Europe would know names like *Cornel West, Serene Jones, Sallie McFague, Rebecca Chopp, Mark Lewis Taylor, Matthew Lamb, Francis Schüssler Fiorenza, Paul Lakeland, Douglas John Hall, Ada Maria Isasi-Dias, Joerg Rieger, George Tinker, Alejandro Garcia-Rivera, Dwight Hopkins, Cheryl Kirk-Duggan, Karin and Garth Baker-Fletcher. David Tracy* may be familiar, but not many others, just or even more pertinent nowadays for a *globally aware and interculturally conversant theological discourse* at the beginning of the twenty-first century. *James Cone, Thomas Altizer, Harvey Cox, John Cobb, Elisabeth Schüssler Fiorenza, Carter Heyward, Rosemary Radford Ruether, Matthew Fox,* maybe *Miroslav Volf,* probably *George Lindbeck* or *Stanley Hauerwas,* would exceptionally find a place in the European hall of fame on twentieth-century and contemporary theology. Other names would remain unknown.

Urgently needed would be a more deliberate *theological bridge building* between these far apart worlds and continents. Theology may become more *cosmopolitan*, introducing and getting people across continents acquainted with each other, even if momentarily only on silent and passively submissive paper.

This dissertation will try to do *beginning bridge building*, connecting people and debates, complementing themes and landscapes that usually lodge alongside each other without even a moment of neighborly recognition in our *global and multicultural village*. I am deeply convinced that the theological discussions and debates in the United States provide some of the most important, intriguing, and relevant themes for a *theology in the twenty-first century*, also for the European context.

At the same time, this dissertation will suggest that issues of *power* and *powerlessness* may explain some of this general neglect in *intercultural theological dialogue* between *Europe* and *North America*. The *Eurocentric focus* in European theological discussions reveals a particular kind of distribution of power and powerlessness in the *global ecclesial world*. Only now are voices from *other parts of the world, North America* being one voice among others, questioning this dominance in theological *world perspective*.

CONTEXTS

Thematic Backgrounds

A Theology in Context

North American approaches to *systematic theology*, or more precisely, to the *plurality of fundamental and systematic theologies* (Tracy 1975, 1981, 1987, 1994, Schüssler Fiorenza 1984, O'Donovan and Sanks 1989, Dulles 1992, Wetherilt 1994, Haight 2001, Taylor 1990, 2011), can only be understood if viewed within its more comprehensive and most particular *historical, cultural, and social context*. Issues of *power* and *powerlessness* are present in all of these social contexts, visible at any time along the way.

Everywhere and at all times the *down-to-earth and day-to-day context* shapes the text, the thinking, the writing, the singing, the poetic reciting or narrating. Stories and metaphors, images and models, paradigms and theological constructions, all of these various attempts at systematic theology are somehow drenched to the skin with the *American story*. Whether black, hispanic, Indian, female, gay, lesbian, WASP, or simply straight, North American theology is always and at all times reflecting some of *who is writing it*, willingly or unwillingly. By that it serves like a mirror looking at itself and at others. *Power and powerlessness*, as well, appear in such a mirror.

Anyone who tries to understand the various discussions and debates on the great diversity of *fundamental themes* in North American systematic theology needs to hear the *undertones* of the *past* swinging or vibrating all along in the most recent *present* (on the history of Christianity in North America Noll, Hatch, Marsden, Wells, Woodbridge 1983, Askew and Spellman 1984, Gaustad 1990, Toulouse and Duke 1997, 1999, Noll 1992, 2000, Wills 2002, 2005). The historical coloring and cultural-social formation of theology through each population group's own *sacred story* and its various *ethnographic themes* (Smith 1994a, 1994b) is ever more present in theological discussions in the United States. Black America produces another kind of theology than gay America or white America.

This makes North American systematic theology basically *kaleidoscopic* or *spectral*, maybe even *shattered* (Kliever 1981), but definitely *multi-colored* right from the start, as each ethnic theological culture starts with another story. Therefore, listening is required, more so than responding or rebutting, as anyone wanting to understand North American theology first has to listen to its story. *Multicultural America* needs first to be listened to as it tells its and *(his/her)story*, placing the mirror and the proportions we look at somehow differently and sometimes even *up-side down* (Takaki 1993, Cenkner 1996, Berthrong 1999, Sawyer 2003, Mitchell Corbett 2000, Neusner 2003).

Digging up the ground, letting the bottom turn up on top, revolving the cultural and social mirror and its memory on its natural head, is a day-to-day part of modern-day systematic theological thinking in the United States thinking *from the margins* (Fernandez and Segovia 2001, De La Torre 2004) and writing from the bottom-up. Sometimes, actually most often, dead corpses come alive again. In a discourse of unfinished North American dreams putting everything past and present upside-down is a necessary work for building the future, as Hispanic-Latino systematic theologian *Eleazar S. Fernandez* describes the necessary and also painful work of digging up the cultural past in order to envision a different kind of future:

> "This discourse on unfinished dreams not only names the pains of the present but also names the past memories of unfinished dreams in order to carry them forward to the future. What was buried is exhumed not simply for its own sake, for there is no joy in exhuming the unfinished dreams of the previous generations as such. The buried is exhumed because it is necessary in forging a new and better tomorrow." (Fernandez and Segovia 2001, 275)

Race, Gender, and Power

My first cross-cultural encounter was an African American roommate in the dormitory I stayed in while studying in Southern California. For almost a year we shared a room as students at Fuller Theological Seminary in Pasadena. Before that I had never really shared a single room with another student, except back in Switzerland at the International Baptist Theological Seminary in Rüschlikon outside of Zurich. There I shared the room with an older Russian family father, but it somehow didn't make the same engaging impression.

Ron was as black as you could be. I was as white as I could be. Good Swiss, a little naive. With hardly any experience or knowledge of North American history, let alone African American culture, memories, stories, sensitivities. I knew a little about Martin Luther King and the civil rights movement way back from confirmation classes. Ron and I got along beautifully. We still get his regular newsletter with pictures of his growing and cute kids, a darling wife, and his pastoral ministry. Only later did I understand what a memorable gift of little or greater grace amidst still torn fabrics of broken communities this had been.

Whether black, or gay, the broken fabric may be the same. About a year earlier I had had the privilege to visit a gay bible group somewhere in the green pastures of horse-riding Kentucky. An evangelical student at an evangelical theological seminary had invited some of us to come and meet gay evangelical Christians. Something probably unheard of, at least at that time. Driving home again, after having been literally saved by some gay Christian in a gay bar from advances of interested by-standers late night, I timidly and curiously asked the student in the car whether he was gay himself. A silent moment of honesty in a world still torn apart. Yet a memorable moment that has ever since remained unforgetable. Unforgetable also his only real concern whether the seminary would find out.

Little glimpses of the possibility of beginnings in community building across experiences of race, gender, and other borders in a theological and social world still violently split apart.

Race, gender, and power (Hill and Jordan 1995, Morrison 1992, Giroux 1991, 2003, McLaren 1995, 2005, Bernasconi 2001, Rieger 2007, Taylor 2011) are still the most fundamental and divisive themes touching all groups in North America, necessary to be constantly exhumed somehow. Race, gender, and power reappear at every corner of the theological agenda, knowingly or not. America mirrors to itself its shattered history, its broken past, its torn fabric that lets all pieces and threads fall apart.

Therefore, the big and moral theme of *community* (Peck 1987 and Kirkpatrick 2006) or how to live peacefully and rightfully in a multi-colored postmodern, postmetaphysical, and cosmopolitical community reappears everywhere. It creeps up as a recurrent and repetitive theme both in the *political and social sciences* (Delanty 2003, Simpson 2001, Marsh 2005) as well as in *theology* (Banks 1994, Albrecht 1995, Clapp 1996, Bounds 1997, Doyle 2000, Fuellenbach 2002, Sawyer 2003).

The Community of the Weak

Community as a *social and ethical vision*, leading beyond just individualistically being religious or pious (on community versus individualism in post-Constantinian ecclesial times Clapp 1996, Baker 1999, Dudley 2002), remains a powerfully mobilizing unfinished dream, a no-man/woman's-land and theological utopia to someday hopefully become real. Dreaming the still unfulfilled promise in the aftermath of *Martin Luther King's* creative vision. The vision of a nation and a people as well as a globe united again, different in culture, race, gender, and power, more fractured, and yet more colorful, but *one,* in order to become *free at last* (King 1992, 101–106).

Social and Cultural History

North America has a deeply fractured *social and cultural history*. This is striking, especially if looked at through the direct witness of the underside of a *people's history* (on the history of North America in the perspective of a people's history Foner 1997, 1998, Zinn 2003). Here we find everywhere and at all times the marking and demarcating lines of *race, gender,* and *power* (for general introductions to North American history Norton, Katzman, Escott, Chudacoff, Paterson, Tuttle, and Brophy 1996, Boyer, Clark, Kett, Salisbury, Sitkoff, Woloch 1996, Jenkins 2003, Axelrod and Phillips 2004).

Multiple painful *breakdowns of communities* (Takaki 1993, Jacquin, Royot et Whitfield 2000) are a determining part of US history, influencing the formulation and social envisioning of theology—*systematic, dogmatic,* or *fundamental*—in these days. Powerlessness, discrimination, violence, and marginalization set the tone of the music or the color of the picture still and even now, reminding everyone of a social and ethical dream, kept alive, but *unfinished* (Fernandez and Segovia 2001, De La Torre 2004). Violence, exclusion, and hatred go on dividing a people and a nation. North American systematic theology reflects and keeps the pain of those past and present memories alive.

Solidified forms of power along the lines of race, sex, and social standing are nowadays carefully retold in a *New American history* (Foner 1997). History writing is now looking through the eyes, the body, and the oral history in stories of the little, the marginal, the invisible. African and Asian Americans, American Indians, Latinos/as, as well as women, workers, gays and lesbians are rewriting American history as well as American theology. *Minority studies* become part of Christian studies, as theological reflection in America is nowadays inconceivable without thinking and writing from the *margins* (on US. theology on the margins Fernandez and Segovia 2001, Cenkner 1996, De La Torre 2004).

Theological thinking and writing conceived this way will never again be oblivious to *the poor, the excluded, the silenced, the illiterate* (Rieger 1998, 2001, 2007). Too often theology has settled in a social world of academic security and status, position and general acclaim. European influences up to the middle of the 20th century have made North *American systematic theology* often *academically detached* from every possible defilement by real people, real stories, and real pain. Theology in North America, however, has been violently and radically forced and coerced over the last decades by its own newly remembered and newly irrupted social and cultural history to go into exile, driven out, chased away, by listening to those hardly ever listened to, as North American systematic theologian *Joerg Rieger* puts it:

> "Theology as a whole is driven out of its secure position when it starts to pay attention to that which is repressed, especially when the repressed are real people, their children, and their environmental 'habitats.'"(Rieger 2001, 193)

Real people, real faces, and *real social worlds* have challenged a complacency in theology to look again through the tear-filled eyes of those on the *cultural and social margins*. North American systematic theology nowadays is inconceivable without the looking glass of such a *broken memory* and *rediscovered past*.

Nation-Forming Experiences

The primal and *nation-forming* experiences of *powerlessness* and *extinction* in the conquest and genocide of a continent and of a people are being rediscovered (on conquest and genocide in the Americas Stannard 1992, Dussel 1995, Wearne 1996, Shoemaker 2001). The deep-acting remembrance of Afro-American *discrimination* and *soul-robbery* in slavery, racial violence, the uprising of black power, black culture, and the fight for civil rights up to the present is being retold (Feagin 2000, Fredrickson 2002, Gates and West 2000, West and Glaude 2004). The never-ending and continuously present *marginalization* and *disempowering* of many and various social groups in the battlefield of postmodern distributions of social power, spaces, and places according to culture, gender, sexual orientation or economic and social standing are becoming visible (on "the other America" Harrington 1962/1981, on the omnipresence of power and empire in contemporary North America Buhle, Buhle, and Georgakas 1990, Buhle, Buhle, and Kaye 1994, Gottlieb 1993, Taylor 2001, Keller 2005, Maguire 2005).

Memories of pain continue to set the *agenda* for *theological reflection* still now. North American systematic theology is thematically and politically soaked and trenched wherever we look with this painful past and all-determining present (Rivera 1992, Tinker 1993, Harding 1990, Hopkins 2000, De La Torre 2004).

Without the *reflecting mirror* of *social and cultural history* most contemporary debates and discussions in the theological academic world in the Unites States are without context. *American history and culture* (for American cultural studies Mauk and Oakland 2002, Duncan and Goddard 2003, Bigsby 2006), always put in the context of a social-critical *everyday-perspective* and *people's history*, are part and parcel of most if not all theological attempts in North America at making sense of God, the world, Christ, the church, and some hopeful future for a nation in a world broken and most often shattered.

Turning Cultural

The conscious or unconscious radical interdependence of *American spiritual culture* and *theology* (Dean 2004) in all academic endeavor is most visible and detectable in the theological debates of a continent constantly reminded of its fractured *prism or spectrum* (Kliever 1981) of colors and its polyphony of melodies. *American cultural studies* are the inescapable entrance door to North American systematic theology today (Campbell and Kean 1997, Breidlid, Brogger, Gulliksen, Sirevag 1996, Crowther and Kavanagh 1999, Bigsby 2006).

Culture, even as *spiritual* (Dean 2004), turns out to be another word or synonym for the dividing, distributing, and disseminating spectrum and socially networking web of *daily power* (on power as network Foucault 1980, Foucault see Miller 1987, Caputo and Yount 1993, Brown 2000). Power has a way of breaking up or bringing together communities and languages, histories and memories that only now are starting to culturally regroup and reconnect in a newly envisioned and highly diverse *community of theology*. *Power* as *culture*, therefore, is at the center of attention in most *North American systematic theology* of these days (Tanner 1997, Hopkins and Davaney 1996, Brown, Davaney, Tanner 2001, Cobb 2005).

Power and *powerlessness* are invisible or visible manifestations in *culture* and *reality* which can be recognized and relived in various past and present forms in the *history of the Unites States*. Thereby we can see that power and powerlessness are in no way just relegated to the limited and *institutional forms of political legitimacy and rule*, as maybe *Max Weber* might have suggested. The old sociological and political debate on the possible use and abuse of legitimate power has been transformed, deepened, and eternally refined in the United States through the concrete experiencing of *various cultural forms of power and powerlessness in its history*. Power and powerlessness flow through *language, culture, narrative, memory, identity*, and continuous violence reminding the voluntary or involuntary participants in this common story called United States history of its deep scars and *remembering wounds*.

Culture could be called the *new vernacular* of communication in North American theology of these days through which people tell each other their personal and social story, either wounded or healed. Power and empowerment are discovered as human possibility to destroy or create, hinder or envision a new kind of *community* that is desperately needed in this modern world. Envisioned is in particular a newly spirited and *theological community* breathing with the *breath of life* (Edwards 2004) as variously hurt and broken theological communities in the US. are starting to reconnect by telling their most particular and hurtful stories. People are starting to tell each other their cultural and institutional *basic narratives in search of a good life*, healing and reconciling, in reorganizing and regrouping stories and life-determining personal and social histories for a newly meaningful *communal narrative* (for a history of popular culture in North America, told as a communal and local narrative Loebbert 2003).

Academic theology can be looked at as an institutional and communitarian networking of new relations of power to be regrouped and reconnected in different ways, rearranged nowadays in fascinating ways in North American theology to contribute to some deep-leveled *communal and cosmopolitan healing* (Granberg-Michaelson 1991) in a *globally cultured and inter-cultured world* (Appiah and Gates 1996, Jenkins 2002, 2006). This can only be done most effectively, it seems, through the *exchange and interchange* of *personal and communal histories and stories*.

The Community of the Weak

Building a Community of Theology

Building a community on the basis of a fractured and shattered social and cultural history is the *fundamental task* North American systematic theology has put before itself as a demanding challenge. The radical deconstruction of an unitary world stands at the beginning of this ethical awakening to a world that still is *divided* and *segregated*, split and broken. *Community-building* may be the most promising and called for task for *systematic theology* in the *21st century*, both in *North America* and elsewhere.

This is true just as well for a global and multi-faceted *home-leaving* and *home-coming* in *intercultural theology* along the many and various geographical trips and travels from and back, as German systematic theologian *Jürgen Moltmann* would say, to our "own time . . . and place, within the greater community of theology" (Moltmann 1981, xii). We do live in a community of theology *worldwide* (Jenkins 2002, 2006), whether we are aware of it or not. This dissertation will be an attempt at community-building across borders and places, languages and convictions, with a belief in a cosmopolitan *community calling* of contemporary theology.

We seem to be only at the beginning of really creating and building such a global and multi-cultural *community of theology* worth its name. *North American systematic theology* is trying to live up to such a social-ethical vision of *theological community-building* by facing a challenge that turns out to be a social and ethical calling for all of theology worldwide. No true community can be real and lasting by excluding the greater part of its many and diverse members.

In *North America* this challenge of a *social and ethical calling to community* has been recognized a lot earlier than in *Europe*, partially through a greater urgency to look into the eyes of one's *closest neighbor* just down the street, be it Afro-American, Asian, Latino/a, gay, lesbian, womanist or American-Indian. Through this daily and inevitable exposure systematic theology in North America has become much more *decentered* and *polycentered* in radical ways than European German theology. The decentering of positions and perspectives turns out to be a highly therapeutic process opening up new worlds.

Theology conceived this way becomes a *polyphony of voices*, past memories, current stories, and *multi-colored faces*. As North American systematic theologian, Jesuit and charismatic *Donald L. Gelpi* (Gelpi 1978) from the *Graduate Theological Union* at *Berkeley* near *San Francisco* resumes his own *melting-pot* of theological influences shaping a new and probably postmodern, if not at least post-traditional identity, truly deserving the more global title of a new way of being *catholic* (on "new catholicity" in a globalized and post-confessional world Schreiter 1997 and McLaren 2006):

> "I had seen too that an 'American' theology that aspired to be Catholic could not be narrowly conceived. I had absorbed Canadian influences from Lonergan. I resonated to the cry for human justice emanating from the Church in Latin America. An American theology, I realized, had to be sensitive to the soul of black religion and to the struggle of blacks and chicanos for their human dignity and rights. It should be sensitive to values that Christian faith derives from Hebrew piety. It should have a word to say to the aquarian religion of the sixties and to the fascination of American romantics with Oriental mysticism. And it should attempt to enter into dialogue with theological thought in Europe and in other parts of the Church." (Gelpi 1978, 17)

A word of truly *catholic* and cross-cultural *world ecumenicity* already spoken by a systematic and fundamental theologian in the 1970s. North America would follow the trail prepared this way. Europe would wait or even forget to move on into a globally cross-cultural world.

Intra- and Inter-Cultural Dialog

That theology has become global, post-national, and most definitely post-denominational, is still a novelty to some. Looking at the general course descriptions of Swiss theological faculties may even be able to prove the contrary. Sometimes however life itself is taking us some other way.

Looking back makes me marvel and grateful at the road—biographical and theological—traveled. Out of a deep fear of liberal theology at any of the Swiss Protestant theological faculties— Berne, Zurich or Basel, Lausanne, Geneva or Neuchatel—I had decided already before the age of twenty to go to the US to study theology. Initially I was strongly determined to get some academic and spiritual support and confirmation of my gut-level fundamentalism or evangelicalism in a North American evangelical seminary. At the same time I had also gotten into contact with charismatic spirituality in Roman Catholic circles. Westminster, Trinity Evangelical Divinity, Asbury, Gordon-Conwell, Eastern Baptist, Southwestern Baptist, Fuller, or any other evangelical seminaries were on my list of possibilities. Melodyland School of

> *Theology was a favorite possible choice. But I ended up, first in a Baptist seminary in Switzerland, then in a Methodist seminary in Kentucky, and last, but not least, in an inter-denominational seminary in Southern California.*
>
> *In the end, I lost most of my evangelicalism, but gained a deep and lasting respect for new evangelicals, social action radicals, Jim Wallis, Ron Sider, Stephen Mott, but also Cornel West, Letty Russell, Carter Heyward, Dorothee Sölle, Mark Lewis Taylor, Matthew Fox, Sharon Welch, Rebecca Chopp, David Tracy, Miroslav Volf, James Cone, Robert McAffee Brown, Frederick Herzog, Albert Nolan, Justo Gonzalez, Rosemary Radford Ruether, Elsa Tamez, and innumerable other highly kaleidoscopic mishmash mixtures of a good postmodern, post-confessional, post-denominational, and therefore mostly messy theology. I got to be inter-cultural, cross-cultural, border-crossing, and polycentric right there, at the most inside of myself. So things appear a little limited back home again.*
>
> *Reason enough to marvel once more, after all this to now be enrolled as a Reformed doctoral student at a Roman Catholic theological faculty with a German fundamental theologian fully conversant with and fascinated by North American systematic and fundamental theologies. Boundaries fall, borders crumble, and new visionary ways of—if not postmodern, at least post-confessional or post-denominational—theological community building seem to become possible and real. Theology the way I keep dreaming of.*

Systematic theology in *Europe* is only now starting to recognize its many and various *global and other-cultural neighbors*. An open dialogue between continents and geographies, languages and nations, cultural groups and social worlds is desperately needed much beyond what has been the limited case so far. Only then will systematic theology all across the globe become *polycentric* the way the world, in particular the Christian world, already and inevitably has become.

Here *Europe* can learn a great deal from the *North American inter- and intra-contextual dialogue* practiced and developed already over many decades. A practice still mostly unknown on the European continent. Here even a simple dialogue between *French* and *German theology*, as Swiss systematic theologian *Klauspeter Blaser* (Blaser 1972–2004) from the *University of Lausanne* points out, is practically non-existent (for contemporary French theology in the 20th century Blaser 1995b, 490–497). The lack of reception of North American theology on the European continent could just as well be repeated for the lack of importance and visibility of French theology in German theological literature:

> "There used to be a time when for European philosophical and theological thinking the intellectual life of the Anglo-Saxon world, and in particular of North America, got resumed, so to speak, to a footnote at the bottom of the page." (Blaser 1995a, 5)

This marginal footnote is getting more prominent and better placed nowadays, with systematic and inter-culturally experienced theologians like *Klauspeter Blaser* and others opening up a whole new theological world to European theological students (covering North American theology Blaser 1995a, in the context of contemporary theology Blaser 1995b, 435–467). It seems symptomatic, however, that predominantly *French theologians* are interested in this larger *international and intercultural world* (Chenu et Neusch 1995, 85–111, on feminist theology Parmentier 1998, on process theology Gounelle 1981, 2000).

German theologians still for the most part remain reluctant to have a serious look at theological developments in North America, with a few notable and most recent exceptions treating *Afro- American, feminist* and *womanist, process,* and *American Hispanic* theology (on North American theology in general Rohls 1997b, 52–55, 217–18, 385–387, 544–554, 728–740, on womanist theology Wollrad 1999, Kalsky 2000, on process theology Faber 2000, 2003, on US-Hispanic theology Fornet-Betancourt 2002). The continuous absence of most other North American systematic theology in an intercultural or intracultural dialogue in German-speaking Europe points to a symptomatic division of fame and name in a worldwide and ecumenical context called *theological world ecclesia* (Barr 1997, Thistlethwaite and Engel 1998, Pittman, Habito, and Muck 1996, Jenkins 2002, 2006).

A Global Quest

God nowadays most probably knows and understands less and less what theologians write and say in *German*. God nowadays may be joining a *global quest,* speaking more *Spanish,* more dialects, more *African French, Latino English* or *Asian American,* more the language and feel of Soul,

Hip-Hop, or Afro-Brazil. God nowadays may be more conversant in the local vernacular of simple people, hardly trained in the metaphysical and philosophical traditions of Eurocentric prominence. The European dominance in systematic theology, fundamental, dogmatic or ethical, may have reached its overdue end as contemporary and global *world theology* (Barr 1997, Thistlethwaite and Engel 1998, Thomas/Wondra 2002, Migliore 2004, Schüssler Fiorenza and Galvin 1991a–b, 2011) becomes *cross-cultural* and *polycentric* in the *21st century* (Blaser 1995b, Schreiter 1985, 1992a, 1997, Arens 1995b, Jenkins 2002, 2006).

The *next Christendom* (Jenkins 2002, 2006 and Koschorke, Ludwig und Delgado 2004) will no longer be *mono-cultural*. The new landscape of a *global Christian world* will radically change the future make-up of theology, faith, and ethics. Christianity will no longer be mainly European, white, predominantly male, nor German-speaking—at least in its theological halls of literary celebrities and cultural-historical fame—anymore. To quote the latest figures about a changing landscape of Christian faith in this global world, pointing out the radical *paradigm shift* this will have for all endeavors of theology in a new day and age:

> "The map of Christianity in this global world has changed dramatically. While around the year 1900 still 82% of the Christian world population lived in Europe or North America, today we find a majority (in the year 2000 almost 60%) living in the countries of the southern hemisphere, and this with an increasing tendency. In the global ecumenical dialogue as well the importance of the churches from outside of Europe is increasing. Like never before in its history, Christianity has become a world religion." (Koschorke, Ludwig und Delgado 2004, V)

As North American systematic theologian *William R. Barr* (Barr 1997) recalls in his *multi- and cross-cultural introduction* to a Christian theology for a *worldwide church:*

> "Constructing—and reconstructing—Christian theology is a work of the whole church. Certainly, academically educated theologians can assist in this effort, but seeking a deeper and clearer articulation of Christian faith in the contemporary setting involves all Christians and the church as a whole. Too often, however, works on theology, and especially works on constructive or systematic theology, do not reflect this global quest for understanding in the church . . . Surely in the future the church's theology and works in theology will have to reflect this global quest more adequately than has been the case to date.

> Increasingly, with new technologies and almost instantaneous worldwide communication, we now have the capability of entering immediately into conversation with peoples throughout the world community. As this global conversation develops also within the church, and with those of other views outside the church, it will include theological understanding formed in many different situations, cultural contexts, and traditions."
> (Barr 1997, xi)

Systematic theology in the 21st century needs to be in *global conversation*, something like the casual or maybe sometimes heated conversations around a family table. For this to occur people and theologians first have to recognize each other as part of the same global household or *oikumene* in need of exchange and debate, learning and listening, feasting and weeping. Systematic theology in Europe as usually taught is far away from sensing such family ties to a bigger world. *Cross- and inter-cultural learning* will become the next frontier for a globally sensitive theology that recognizes its own poverty in keeping others away from the table.

Doing this may also turn the habitual in academics upside-down, allowing other forms of theological thinking and writing to be heard and expressed. As *William R. Barr* points out, not all contributions in such a new global quest for a *cross-cultural systematic theology* "take the form of scholarly essays; some are expressed in songs, dances, stories, and rituals" (Barr 1997, xi). But in all artistic variety of form, text, expression, and reflection, such a new and globally sensitive systematic theology will become something like the conversation "around the family table in which both individual differences and common loyalty and family solidarity bind the members together" (Barr 1997, xii).

Theology at a Round Table or in a Chat Room

The *round table* (on the image of an ethnic round table of all nations in theology Russell 1993, Gonzalez 1992, Barr 1997, 6) of family gatherings or the virtual chat-room of computer networking serve as an inviting metaphor for building a new type of *theological community thinking* worldwide. The *global world* calls for a new kind of communal theological conversation.

Systematic theology is only at the beginning of recognizing this *globalized context* (Castells 1996–1999, Schirato and Webb 2003, Keane 2003,

Anderson 2004), just now learning new languages, new models, *new ways of theological and practical learning.*

Some exceptional places are trying to invite to such a globally theological round table. The international theological journal *Concilium* is one illustrative example for a new type of globalized theological conversation, multi-lingual, cross-cultural, and community building.

The *World Council of Churches* and its various plenary sessions, world assemblies, and graduate academic institutions like the *Ecumenical Institute at Bossey* (on the history of the Ecumenical Institute in Bossey near Geneva, Switzerland VanElderen and Conway 2001), as well as historic events such as the Roman Catholic *Second Vatican Council* (Doyle 1992, Murphy 1999, McBrien 1994, Sullivan 2002), are other occasions and promising visionaries of such a new type of global theological conversation writing a new kind of theology. They remain institutional and academic exceptions, however.

Classical textbooks and *basic classes or courses in systematic theology* in many places are still far from exploring the world as a *single, interdependent,* and *global place.* A challenge to be taken up in the future if theology does not want to become an incomprehensible and folkloristic vernacular of only one particular place. *North American systematic theology* has recognized this challenge in a more fundamental and paradigmatic way.

Visiting the Global Village

A *cross-cultural theological conversation*, coming out of the exchange of biblical, historical, systematic, and practical viewpoints, will write a different kind of systematic theology. Africa, Latin America, Asia, North America, Europe, Roman Catholic, Protestant, and Orthodox, need to sit down at the family table getting ready for some overdue chat. A polyphony of voices may thereby create, if only temporarily, a new kind of *cross-cultural theological community.* Systematic theologies in the *21st century* will profit from becoming visitors and travelers in a *global village* (Taylor and Bekker 1990, Schreiter 1993, 1997, Jenkins 2002, 2006).

Thinking and writing systematic theology in the new century will need to become a lot more globally *communitarian*, leaving behind the solitary and provincial scholar buried under pounds of individualistic and nationalistic papers, books, and articles, leaving scholars lonesome, a-social, and non-contextual. Systematic theology should become a networking *global chat*, virtually or actually sitting around a table joining hands, cultures, and languages. Modern technology has put us closer to each other and virtually next to each other at a global table. *Globalization* is our common new context and destiny in theology as we have to face the *coming next Christendom* of a *new and global Christian faith* (Jenkins 2002, 2006).

As Roman Catholic and North American systematic theologian *Robert J. Schreiter* (Schreiter 1993, 1997) puts it, pointing out the new context in which *theology and ministry in a global world* find themselves:

> "The phenomenon called globalization can be said to have begun when European explorers began their planet-encircling voyages at the end of the fifteenth century. Since that time it has been possible—in theory at least—to think of the world as a single, interconnected place. For that is the essential meaning of globalization: that the world is an interconnected—and increasingly, interdependent—single place . . . But it has really been in the last third of the twentieth century that globalization has become more than a notional possibility. As one theorist of globalization has put it, we are now experiencing a compression of time and space. Nearly instantaneous communication is possible to almost all parts of the globe. Satellite-linked television makes it possible for the entire world to be witnesses in historical events. Fax and computer networks now interlink people around the globe in ways that make hierarchies of communication superfluous. Long-distance air travel has redefined the nature of our perception of space, allowing peoples to move and mingle on an unprecedented scale. Consequently, boundaries of time and space are being radically redrawn, and with them, the boundaries of our cultural, social and personal identities." (Pittman, Habito, and Muck 1996, xi)

Systematic theology has a long and challenging way to go to become a *global conversation, community building* across cultures and languages, times and spaces. *Postmodern*, as this world has become, God no longer only speaks *German*, or, for that matter, *American*:

> "Today and in the years ahead Christian theology will need to be developed through interaction and conversation among Christians around the world in the worldwide church, and with those of other persuasions in the world community . . . Furthermore, the need for global conversation is evident from the fact that creative theological voices are speaking out today from many lands and cultures. The European-American hegemony in

modern Christian theology is rapidly passing as we enter what some speak of as a 'postmodern' era." (Barr 1997, 1)

Whether postmodern, post-confessional, post-traditional, or just simply post-European, contemporary systematic theology—fundamental, dogmatic, and ethical—will need to become *global* in being *local* (on becoming local and global Ambler 1990, Balasuriya 1984, Schreiter 1997, Jenkins 2002, 2006). Here, North American systematic theology is leading the way.

TREADING

A Kaleidoscopic View

> *I lost my evangelicalism not because of historical-critical approaches to the Bible, nor because of some radicalism in systematic theology, but because of Church history. It may seem odd, but it is true. The experience of radical diversity and a conflictual faith history broke my faith, my security, my trust, and my monolithic world. I used to run around in the International Baptist Theological Seminary in Rüschlikon near Zürich shifting between stoic agnosticism and protesting atheism out of sheer desperation over Church history, in addition to the pain over the story of my mom who did not get healed.*
>
> *My involvement in the Roman Catholic charismatic renewal movement in Switzerland had led me to Francis MacNutt's and Morton T. Kelsey's books on healing. But nothing really happened with my mom. God seemed like having lost his voice in the midst of too many conflicting voices. Radical pluralism made in the USA made God appear fall silent.*
>
> *Now it appears adolescent, typically juvenile, yet at that time it was existential and real. The radical diversity of theology broke everything in me, both personally and theologically.*
>
> *And yet, this radical diversity of a theology no longer capable to speak in one voice healed everything as well. My trip to the US turned out to be the most healing road ever taken.*
>
> *Years later I recognized, through this trip to a boundless and limitless country, how diverse and multi-lingual in the all-encompassing sense my own most personal theological world had become. Highly conflictual within, contradictory at its core, plural,*

hybrid and mixed, resonating and jam-sessioning in many tunes, colors, and rhythms. Having become black and white, liberal and evangelical, feminist and womanist, liberationist and mystical, social radical and creation spiritual, a little Baptist, Anabaptist, Mennonite, Methodist, Pentecostal, Episcopal, Presbyterian, Lutheran, United, Roman Catholic and even Unitarian. A little this and a little that. Postmodern and political. African and American. Latino and French. Some Canadian, a little Asian, and American Indian. A little here, a little there, as a globalized citizen in no one place alone any more at home.

This messy and plural, hybrid and globalized state of affairs, right deep down inside of myself, has a way to make life humble and modest, grateful and resting in a kaleidoscopic identity of many and various roads less or more traveled, colors less and more painted, tunes less and more played. Everything gracefully having been given by a trip to the USA.

And as much as roads are taken, road maps sometimes help find the way. At least it helped me as I crossed the Atlantic ocean boarding an airline for the touchdown in USA.

Drawing a Road Map

To resume *North American systematic theology* in a *briefly introducing overview* is an almost impossible and possibly hopeless endeavor. In spite of the impossibility, I will attempt a kind of sketchy drawing of a highly provisionary *road map* with a *bird's-eye view* giving travelers on foot, bike, horse, rental car, airline, ship, or simply cyberspace to a vast continent at least something at hand so they don't get all too lost.

Writing as a kind of *socially constructed road* or *country map*, in good *postmodern style* or *cultural-linguistic ways* (on the cultural-linguistic model of language as map-making Lindbeck 1984, Jennings 1985), may be helpful at times in finding one's way around in a new place, a new continent, a new world. It may help in finding one or several possible *entrance doors* through which we then move on more freely and on our own to discover the last frontier of this big and boundless continent. In such a vast and limitless place like North America some guiding posts in carefully putting our feet on the unknown ground may ease and actually make easier the subsequently more adventurous exploring—*in good old pioneering US spirit*—of this great and fascinating theological continent.

The Community of the Weak

Getting to Know the Unknown

North American systematic theology is hardly known on the *European continent*. With a few exceptions (for North American systematic theology between 1970–1985 Buri 1970, 1972, Ritschl 1981, Bauer 1985), German-speaking Europe seems to be only minimally interested in *theological North America*. The title of a book edited by *Dean Peerman*, translated more than thirty years ago for *German-speaking Europe*, no longer seems descriptive that *North American theology* may have an *important contribution* to make to *modern-day theology* (formulated in the title of Peerman 1968).

Most illustrative of this *absence* of a whole theological continent in *Europe* is the latest translation of a *British and American general introduction to Christian theology* in the twentieth and twenty-first century (for the second edition in English Ford 1997, the third edition in English Ford and Muers 2005), which in the *German translation* and adaptation (in German only one edition Ford 1993) of the *first English edition* (Ford 1989) leaves out the whole chapter on *North American systematic theology* (North American systematic theology being covered in the second edition in English Ford 1997, 307–404). *North American systematic theology* seems to fall and *drown* in the stormy water in its timid and general transmission and translation across the Atlantic.

An only exception to this may be the overall positive or critical reception of *North American feminist theology* on the European continent (Gerber 1987, Jakobs 1993, Volkwein 1999, Kalsky 2000, Leicht, Rakel, Rieger-Goertz 2003). More recently, *Process theology* has been shown a more vivid interest (Welker 1988, Faber 2000, 2003). And lately, *postliberalism* with *George A. Lindbeck* has had some limited impact (translated into German Lindbeck 1994, reviewed in Zeindler 2001, 89–106). Other than that, North American systematic theology has been mostly invisible on the European continent.

French Recovery

Recent publications in the *French-speaking* parts of the theological world have called for a *change of perspective* in this regard (Blaser 1995a, 1995b, Chenu et Neusch 1995, Chenu 1977, 1984, Neusch et Chenu 1994, Gounelle 1981, 2000). *Italian-* and *Spanish-speaking* publications also have added an academic interest in a larger world (for Italy Gibellini 1994,

1995, for Spain Vilanova 1997) where systematic theology in the twentieth and twenty-first century seems to be no longer reduced just to the European, predominantly German continent.

It may be that *family twins* or co-sufferers in open marginalization at the global market of fame and interest in theology seem to take a serious and new look at each other, both having been left out from the glamorous palace of fame and name in historical and theological archives. *French, Italian or Spanish theology* as well have hardly ever been recognized on the free market of *modern-day theology*, at least on the European continent.

Klauspeter Blaser

Many years ago, somewhere near the train station in the city of Berne, the capital of Switzerland, I sat together with Klauspeter Blaser, systematic theologian at the University of Lausanne, to have a coffee and to talk about God and the world and everything else. I remember his friendly openness, his warm, light, and casual approach to life, theology, the US, the state of theological education in Switzerland. He liked wearing something close to a Hawaiian T-shirt. It somehow reminded me of Howard Clinebell from Claremont in my years at Fuller Theological Seminary in Southern California. I still see Klauspeter's wide open eyes shining warm and friendly while talking in great modesty but still intrigued about his recent sabbatical at Yale, getting a taste for North American postliberalism, a Barthian becoming friends with George Lindbeck, and getting a feel for US culture, New Haven life style, and North American postmodernism.

Over the years Klauspeter and I became good friends, like most of his doctoral students. When in the summer of 2002 I got news about his unexpected and untimely death on a mountain hike with students it rekindled many personal memories. When months later the faculty of the University of Lausanne organized a touching memorial for Klauspeter Blaser, with George Lindbeck present, it triggered little and bigger tears about some deep and meaningful moments. Klauspeter Blaser will always be remembered as a most modest, most competent, and most fascinating systematic theologian in touch with a bigger and global world. The common bond with North America somehow got us close, this hidden and still most undiscovered theological planet.

The Community of the Weak

> *Years later, after sitting in different lectures again in Swiss universities, participating in doctoral seminars here and there, in French, in German, reading the latest publications in German, in French, in English, there still remains this basic feeling of closeness reminding me of those personal coffee talks with Klauspeter. Something he always fought against was the narrowing of perspectives, the limiting of thinking and acting in learning to provinces, be it theological or social, be it South Africa or Switzerland, North America or the Swiss Romandie.*
>
> *Klauspeter himself was a Swiss-German teaching in French students from Africa, Latin America, Germany, and of course French and German Switzerland and other places of origin at the University of Lausanne. His deep interest was border-crossing. Getting across bordering languages, places, continents. In its truest sense a missionary theology getting across boundaries. His interest in North American systematic theology underlined this basic general interest in a bigger world of unknown territories. Something rather exceptional in comparison to what is still generally found, with a few minor exceptions, in most other places on an old and still self-enamoured continent.*

Among the most memorable *trendsetters* in a new interest in a bigger world, in particular regarding the *theological developments in the United States*, was *Klauspeter Blaser* (for his publications Blaser 1972–2004), multi-linguist in French, German, and English, formerly, before his untimely death in the year 2002, *systematic* and *practical theologian* with an additional emphasis in *mission theology* at the *University of Lausanne* in Switzerland. He has left a future generation of theologians sensitive to a *global world* an impressive amount of literature opening up systematic theology in the 21st century to its *cross-cultural and missionary task*.

With former teaching appointments in *South Africa*—still in the time of *Apartheid*—(for his dissertation on racism and systematic theology/black theology in South Africa Blaser 1972), with close connections to the *World Council of Churches* in Geneva, regular attendance at the various *mission conferences* of the World Council of Churches, as well as being the *doctoral father* of *Emilio Castro*, former General Secretary of the *World Council of Churches*, for his dissertation in mission theology *Freedom in Mission* (Castro 1985), and of *Elsa Tamez*, well-known feminist and biblical liberation theologian from *Costa Rica*, for her dissertation *The Amnesty of Grace* (Tamez 1993), Klauspeter Blaser has influenced generations of theologians to open up their vision and understanding, interest and sensitivity to a bigger world.

In this there has been no one like him in the *German- and French-speaking world* of an old continent in desperate need to see *the new* in *systematic theology* approaching the contemporary and *globalized world*. The definite high-points of this new vision and reality of an intercultural theological world have been *Klauspeter Blaser's* voluminous overviews of systematic theology in the twentieth century, both in his general history of modern theology in *La théologie au XXè siècle: Histoire-Défis-Enjeux* (Blaser 1995b) and in his textbook dogmatics *Dossier dogmatique: Manuel couvrant les principaux lieux de la doctrine chrétienne* (for students at the University of Lausanne and others Blaser 1997). Each contribution to a globally aware systematic theology in a European and worldwide context is comparable in breadth and width to none, covering theology in this interconnected and interdependent world from North to South, East to West, while getting the *global chat* or family table talk going.

Klauspeter Blaser, close in ecumenical spirit to systematic companion *Jürgen Moltmann's* post-European and post-colonial vision for a new kind of *systematic theology in a global and inter-cultural conversation across continents*, as well as intrigued by *George A. Lindbeck's* (Lindbeck 1984) staunch and countercultural *postliberalism*—after a sabbatical spent with "the *New Yale School*" at *Yale Divinity School* (referring to the visit at Yale, the "New Yale school," and postliberalism Blaser 1995a, 126–139, 1995b, 456–467)—, has kept a basic admiration for *Karl Barth* (Blaser 1987 and Müller 2005), going beyond Karl Barth, however, in various directions. In particular and most intensively Klauspeter Blaser has been dialoguing with various *ecumenical and contextual theologies* challenging the North from the South (Blaser 1990b, 1991), and even, though also critically, *the postmodern* in theology (Blaser 1996, 1999).

The *University of Lausanne*, theological-academic home of Klauspeter Blaser, under his lasting influence has shown in various publications and colloquia a serious interest in what *recent North American systematic theology* has to contribute to modern-day theology. North American challenges to theology in *Marc C. Taylor's* erring and *deconstructing postmodernism* (Gisel et Evrard 1996), *George A. Lindbeck's postliberalism* (Boss, Emery et Gisel 2004), and *Stanley Hauerwas' communitarian ethics* (Müller 1999, 50–52, Troisième Cycle en éthique de Suisse romande, May 4–5, 2006 with Stanley Hauerwas at the University of Lausanne) have been topics of interest across the disciplines. General and *encyclopedic publications* from that institution also show a wide and ecumenically sensitive interest in the global and inter-cultural world in *contemporary theology* and *Christian ethics* leading into the *21st century* (for an encyclopedia of Protestantism Gisel 1995, for Christian ethics Müller 1999, 2005). All this remains true and in debt to the spirit and open vision of Klauspeter Blaser.

French theology seems to assume a leading position in the transatlantic and inter-cultural reception of *North American systematic theology* in Europe.

First Steps

This dissertation would like to invite the reader to *first steps* into a big world with unlimited possibilities to find one's way around on *new ground*. For this, several helpful publications are available for some *introductory first trips* into a new and unknown territory (in short article form Herzog 1982, Cobb 1989, Holifield 1992, Sauter/Welker 1993, Herzog 1999a, Wills 2002, 2005). Easy *backpack excursions* can be taken here and there (Blaser 1995b, 435-467, Ford 1997, 307-404, Rohls 1997b, 52-55, 217-218, 385-387, 544-554, 728-740), with more *extensive and systematic explorations* of a vast and multifaceted theological landscape inviting the general reader to a fascinating place (Blaser 1995a, Peerman 1968, Buri 1970, 1972, Ritschl 1981, Bauer 1985, Kliever 1981, Ferm 1990, 1982, Gill 1995, Badham 1998, Musser and Price 2003, Dorrien 2006). All of this can be *panoramically viewed* and set in the general context of *modern-day contemporary theology* (Bacik 1989, Musser and Price 1996, Ford 1997, Ormerod 1997, Miller and Grenz 1998, Macquarrie 2002, Ford and Muers 2005, Livingston and Schüssler Fiorenza 2006, Higgins 2009).

The literally overwhelming *diversity and pluralism* of *contemporary North American systematic and fundamental theology* is scholarly legitimacy enough to contribute with this dissertation to the exploration of the so far in *European circles* mostly unknown. At the same time it will be an exercise in *cross-cultural theological conversation*, if only on paper, but nonetheless as a beginning dialogue. *Power* and *powerlessness* will thereby serve as *guiding* and *fundamental themes* throughout the chapter.

A Shattered Spectrum

Contemporary North American systematic theology can only be described as a *shattered spectrum*, as *Lonnie D. Kliever* (Kliever 1981) has already put it more than twenty years ago in 1981 in his well-written and colorful survey of contemporary, mostly North American systematic theology. An already then highly picturesque description of the state of affairs, and though dated, still applicable and appropriate today.

Theology shattered as a *spectrum*, broken, fractured, but also *spectral* letting white and boring light split in different interesting colors. A positive as well as a negative image, depending on the value given to *radical pluralism* in a contemporary world. North American systematic theology in the last century has become *radically plural*, and it is getting ever more so as time goes on.

Europe as a formerly dominant theological *foreground* in the picture is slowly being pushed into the gestalt-like *background*, as theological and literary giants like *Karl Barth, Rudolf Bultmann, Paul Tillich*, and others are clearly fading in importance, although one or more revivals of one or several of those former names of fame may be part of a postmodern recycling always possible in the USA (on the recent revival of Karl Barth in North America Johnson 1997, Dorrien 2000, in French Switzerland and France Müller 2005).

More visibly pushed into the spot-lighted and highlighted *foreground* of North American systematic theology today are *constructivist* concerns which are trying to rewrite and *reconstruct* systematic theology in the twentieth and twenty-first century in new and *revisionist ways*, giving it a radically *new form* and shape along an intensified interest for the *social context* and *social location* of all human attempts at doing and writing theology.

Liberation theology (Herzog 1988, Rieger 1999), *political theology* (Glebe-Möller 1987, Migliore 1991, Hodgson 1994, Hodgson and King 1994, Williamson 1999, Migliore 2004), various *contextual theologies* (Hodgson 1994, Hodgson and King 1994, Chopp and Taylor 1994, Barr 1997, Thistlethwaite and Engel 1998, Thomas/Wondra 2002, Migliore 2004, Inbody 2005, Jones and Lakeland 2005), as well as a new *postliberal* mixing of voices (Placher 2003, Jones 2002a–b, Vanhoozer 2005, Webster, Tanner, and Torrance 2009) are becoming the *dominant themes* in modern-day systematic theology in North America. *Non-foundational approaches* combine *Anabaptist and baptist roots* with *social and peace ethics* (McClendon 1986, 1994, 2000, 2002, Finger 1985–1989, 2004, Augsburger 2006). *Feminist and post-feminist theologies* (Ruether 1983/1993, LaCugna 1993, Coll 1994, Carmody 1995, Parsons 2002) in particular have strongly influenced North American systematic theology, having become a kind of respected countercultural *establishment* that any theology has to seriously listen to.

Roman Catholic systematic theology stands out through an open and *creative inclusion* of all these more radical contributions—*political theology, liberation theology, feminist theology, postliberalism, postmodernism*—into a new kind of *creatively revisioning* systematic as well as fundamental theology (for systematic theology McBrien 1994, Flynn 2000, Hill 2003 Schüssler Fiorenza and Galvin 1991a–b, 2011, for constructive fundamental theology Tracy 1975–1994, Haight 2001).

New as well in the colorful crowd of contemporary North American theology are *cultural theologies* coming out of different *ethnic communities* writing their own contextual and local theology. *African American* (Evans 1992), *womanist* (Baker-Fletcher and Baker-Fletcher 1997), *Hispanic* (Gonzalez 1990, Pedraja 2003), *Mujerista* (Isasi-Diaz 1996a), *Asian American* (Phan and Lee 1999), and *American Indian* (Kidwell, Noley, Tinker 2001) systematic approaches to theology are drawing attention to the fact that systematic theology in the twentieth and twenty-first century will need to become a lot more sensitive to the *prismatic coloring* of all our theologies through the place and time where we come from.

Secularity, process, liberation, hope, story, and *play,* the dominant themes in the *1970s* and *1980s* (Kliever 1981), keep being around, fully alive and kicking, as theological catchwords or summaries circumscribing radical changes over the last half century in a theological climate that can only be called exhaustingly *creative.*

Some thirty years later, *new words* can be added to this—like *culture, postmodernism, deconstruction, postcolonialism, postliberalism, non-foundationalism,* but also *African American, womanist, Latino/a, gay, lesbian, Native, Asian* (for Protestant systematic theology Jones and Lakeland 2005, for Roman Catholic dogmatic theology Schüssler Fiorenza and Galvin 2011, on postcolonialism Keller, Nausner, and Rivera 2004, Kwok Pui-lan 2005), to add on to the endless play on words in order to describe what has dramatically and fundamentally changed even more in North American systematic theologies of these days.

A New Generation

Mostly *young* and *newly up-coming theologians* dominate the modern-day North American theological scene, both in publications and teaching positions. An incredible proliferation of theological and religious research

North America

and writing, publishing and lecturing keeps the whole country religiously and theologically most up-to-date, in fascinatingly multi-cultural ways. Something that can be seen most vividly and visibly at the annual meeting of the *American Academy of Religion*, the *AAR*, most probably the largest and most diverse marketplace on religion and theology in the world, appearing to outsiders sometimes more like a show of endless and always improving intellectual fireworks.

New names, new writers, and *new faces* appear regularly on the scene, with a large proportion of women, African Americans, womanist theologians, Latino/as, Asian Americans, American Indians, gay theologians, lesbians. Post-denominational as it has become, North American systematic theology is no longer identifiable according to primarily denominational attachments and loyalties. On the contrary, theological and ethical common interests can be found across old denominational demarcation lines. Theology gets fertilized across various theological and denominational or confessional gardens, with an impressive and open exchange and cross-fertilization from here to there, and back and forth.

Beyond the Liberal-Conservative Divide

> *I used to be evangelical, or even fundamentalist. I read Francis A. Schaeffer's apologetic and militant fundamental theologies or Christian-religious philosophies on the dividing line of despair between Christian faith and human reason, detectable at any corner in the history of art, architecture, music, painting, literature, philosophy, and modern theology, already at the age of seventeen. My girlfriend at the time turned agnostic or even atheist, while reading Hans Küng, Hermann Hesse and Karl Jaspers.*

> *After I had decided, during that time, to take the academic route of university studies in theology, with the professional goal of becoming a pastor, I had to choose where to go. At the time I was very active in a Christian youth group in town. The group and movement was born out of a kind of hippie-aftermath of young, smart, and intelligent college students discussing forever and late into the night everything between God and the world. It had its origin in a major city evangelization of some impressive nomadic philosopher-theologian from Germany, who toured Switzerland with a rock-band while preaching about Christ as the answer to Habermas, Horkheimer, Adorno, Marcuse, Jaspers, and many*

other more or less desperate examples of humanism without a final and plausible answer.

I visited various theological faculties in Switzerland, took a three month pre-theological course with an openly-minded evangelical minister at a theological center near Berne. He had studied for most of his academic training at the Westminster Theological Seminary in Philadelphia and recommended to me a study career in the US. There I got introduced to the bewildering world of books and authors, schools and names that even now seems ever more fascinating, but also overpowering.

After having looked into some private fundamentalist theological faculties in Switzerland and France I recognized that in spite of my great and real fear of liberalism I still was not really made for tight regulations for women to wear skirts, for stipulation of clear divisions between women and men, and for a strict obedience to a particular view in theology that looked down or even demonized my Roman Catholic charismatic sidestepping classical Protestant orthodoxy.

So I ended up not really where I wanted to go. But with hardly any knowledge of the English language, being still quite young to dare the big jump over the Atlantic ocean without knowing where I was going, I enrolled at the International Baptist Theological Seminary in Rüschlikon outside of Zürich in Switzerland. An English-speaking graduate school founded after the Second World War to further intercultural dialogue, learning and Christian reconciliation between different nationalities in Europe.

Initially it was meant to be a stepping stone for me to then move on to the US. Neither being Baptist—I got accepted very cordially even though I was Reformed—nor very keen on its known halfway liberalism similar to that at the universities I shunned I took the courage and enrolled anyway. A beautiful location, with a marvelous view on the Lake of Zurich, with really very special people. Today the school moved to Prague in a cooperative endeavor with the State University there.

As was to be expected, I had my deepest theological crises there. Everything started to crumble. Church history did it. Not even so much historical-critical studies of the Bible, to which I always found some conservative counterpart in the US. But it was Church history that broke my fundamentalist and fearfully-bigoted back.

North America

After two years I really liked it there. The people, their humbleness, their seriousness, their modesty, and their diligently pursued scholarship. At the same time I found out that getting accepted in Switzerland with a full degree from that institution would not be so easy. The irony of it all: I was being told by the Swiss academic and church officials that coming back from outside of Switzerland with a equally valid and accredited graduate degree would make things in terms of acceptance for the ministry easier for me. So old dreams and playgrounds started to come alive again.

To make a long and winding story short. After three months in New York at Columbia University to brush up on my English and to take the TOEFL, the Test of English as a Foreign Language, the entrance requirement for graduate studies in the US, I finally went on from the outskirts of the Lake of Zurich to green-pastured and horse-riding Kentucky and its Methodist-Evangelical Asbury Theological Seminary for one year and then to the West-coast to Fuller Theological Seminary for some three more years to finish with an accredited degree. I got a Master of Divinity that would be accepted—though only after some legal battle with some German-speaking Church officials, the French, in particular the Church of Geneva, accepted it all with no further battlefield—back home in Switzerland.

Along the way I lost what I had started with, and yet I gained a lot more. I lost my fundamentalism, I lost my basic or simple evangelicalism, even though I still now deeply appreciate those life-forming years in classical evangelical schools. I learned a lot more, in particular from evangelical teacher-scholars who kept an open mind, an open heart, an open spirit. There are a lot more of these to be found in the US than Europe can imagine, sticking to old stereotypes. Rüschlikon, Asbury, Fuller, each one in its own way and all three together taught me a wide open horizon and a wide open vision to look at the world.

Along this way, a long way after all, I turned quite messy, multi-identical, crisscrossed, hybrid, mixed, spectral, chaotic, prismatic. Maybe the way good North American theology can and could be. The old cultural and embattled dividing line between conservative and liberal somehow got erased, or just simply disappeared as being no longer so important in life after all. Along the way all these lived-through worlds, and many more I got to see, turned out to become an inalienable part of me. Patchwork or mosaic turned out to be my new metaphor for identity. Postmodern, some would say. Taking from here, listening to there. Seeing

> *something beautiful here, learning some deep council there. Regardless where and from whom it may come after all. Combining in mixing, rearranging and recreating. Softly weaving a new tapestry beyond the old divide to tie some new kind of a pattern in life as well as in theology that turns out to be me in my most personal and intimate history.*
>
> *Theology as art and life-art, the art to paint and compose your own life with new and flashy colors, crooked lines, exotic shapes, touching stories, and clustered tones. Theology joining what usually is not put together. Theology uniting what usually has lived apart or will not want to talk to or even glance at each other. Theology in all this creative and multi-vocal. An image or metaphor for North American systematic theology today. The personal imaging and mirroring a continent equally as diverse, plural, mixed, crisscrossed, multi-identical, hybrid, patchworked, prismatic, spectral, chaotic, and ultimately and creatively beautifully messy.*

Mainline North America systematic theology is most definitely as *radically divided* and *messy* as any other current in North American theology today. *Postmodern theology* questions old *liberalism*. *Left-wing* theologians are still in a *culture or cultural war* with *right-wing* mainline representatives. *Postliberalism* opposes *constructivist* or *revisionist theology*. *Feminist theology* learns from the critiques and warnings of *womanist voices*. *African Americans* meet *Asian Americans* with *postcolonial reservations*. Mainline systematic theologies get cross-fertilized across campuses. A great interchange and exchange of influences and *mutual questioning* happens across and beyond classical denominational lines.

North American evangelicalism as well is deepening its *pluralism, division* and *internal variety*. Most evangelical theologians and their institutions are opening up to seriously interested dialogue with other mainline theologies. *Postliberalism* or *postmodernism* can be found in two currencies, both liberal and evangelical. *Non-foundationalism* and *deconstruction* are being developed on all sides of the liberal-conservative continuum. *Process thinking* is entering the evangelical mind or its God-talk. *Feminism* and *social action* are a common concern to both liberals and evangelicals. *Liberation theology*, be it *African American, womanist, Asian, Latin American, American Indian,* is developed worldwide in the evangelical mode. *Contextualization* in theology turns evangelical as well as *cultural-anthropological*. And even *gay and lesbian voices* have found a more open and graceful hearing.

A world creatively *mixed* and *messed up*, mingled together and separated along new demarcation lines. A highly *creative* if not creatively *chaotic* state of affairs that can be summarized, even today, with the still memorable words of *Lonnie D. Kliever* on the haunting question whether we now live, if looking at this obvious *mess*, more in the time of *Pentecost* or in the time of *Babel* (Kliever 1981, 185–205). Words which remain, though dated, still and even more pertinent for North American systematic theology today:

> "The last twenty-five years of Christian thought have been a period of intense experimentation if not chaotic change. The revered traditions and towering giants of the theological past have been supplanted by a bewildering variety of theological programs and pundits. Theologies of secularity, process, liberation, hope, play, and story have emerged like the overlapping bursts of a fireworks display. First one and then another of these new interpretations of the Christian faith has captured the center of attention only to be succeeded by yet another explosion of theological energy and illumination. As a consequence, an unprecedented pluralism of belief-systems and life-styles is available today under the heading of 'Christian faith' . . . While diversity and conflict have always been a part of the life and thought of the Church, past disagreements usually fell within a clearly defined spectrum of theological options. That liberal-conservative spectrum has been shattered, however, by the turbulent developments in Protestant and Roman Catholic theology in the last half century." (Kliever 1981, 1, 185)

It seems as if we are almost nostalgically led back to where *Richard J. Coleman* (Coleman 1972/1980) in both editions of his telling and hopeful book *Issues of Theological Conflict: Evangelicals and Liberals* used to be already more than thirty and then twenty years ago, advocating a creative and new position *beyond the liberal-conservative divide* as the future *middle ground* of mixing and intermingling, cross-fertilizing each other in mutual and respectful inter-learning. Except that such a middle ground will most probably no longer hold, since nobody knows anymore where the middle may be. It still may be worthwhile to hear and heed again to what was said already years ago:

> "At one time there was considerable resistance to dialogical study between evangelicals and liberals. The former were hardened

by the idea that until there was agreement on basic matters of truth, fellowship with others was dangerous. The latter simply thought they could ignore evangelicals and assumed dialogue was irrelevant. The conservative still tends to be apprehensive about any situation that might compromise his position. But liberals have likewise been reluctant to do any more than meet with evangelicals over an occasional lunch because they, too, hesitate to be challenged. It must be stressed to both liberals and evangelicals that their misgivings are largely unfounded." (Coleman 1972/1980, 55)

North American systematic theology has come a long and moving way getting beyond just occasional lunches to find out about unfounded misgivings. Luckily, these times are partially gone, as interesting *mixing and intermingling* is becoming a new and creative possibility.

Crisscrossing Typologies

In our times, as theological labeling and worn-out typologies get more and more crisscrossed, *evangelical Pentecostals* and former teaching assistants of *Jürgen Moltmann* like *Miroslav Volf* (Volf 1996, 1996a, 2002, on Miroslav Volf and his Pentecostal background Hollenweger 1997, 285), previously teaching systematic theology at the evangelical *Fuller Theological Seminary*, can now be called for a prestigious teaching appointment at the traditionally liberal and now even post-liberal *Yale Divinity School*.

At the same time, evangelical institutions open themselves to cordial dialogue and personal invitations to more liberally, or at least not evangelically known theologians for guest lecturing on their campuses. So it happens that nowadays people and names like *Jürgen Moltmann, Peter Stuhlmacher, James Dunn,* or even *Rosemary Radford Ruether* may end up sitting and chatting with evangelical students.

Liberal institutions like the *American Academy of Religion* give highest awards, for instance in the field of science and theology, to philosophers of religion coming out of a more evangelical background, as for instance the highest award given to *Nancey Murphy* (Murphy 1996), at home both at the liberal *Graduate Theological Union* in *Berkeley, San Francisco* as well as at her evangelical home-base *Fuller Theological Seminary*. These are just two examples to show how whole landscapes and formerly convenient and trustworthy roadmaps may need to be revised.

North American Systematic Theology in Textbooks

Contemporary *North American systematic theology* may best be briefly and succinctly presented by following *textbooks*. Each textbook may represent a particular orientation, a specific interest, a definite distribution of shade and color, topic and concern, vision and reconstruction. In looking briefly at some of the most currently used textbooks in systematic theology in the United States, the full and multi-colored picture painted on canvas in artistic variety and diversity can be easily seen.

Secularity, process, liberation, hope, play, and *story* (Kliever 1981) still play their part in sketching a basic outline, and yet new themes have rearranged common threads. As North American theology's general chronicler *Lonnie D. Kliever* has rearranged various theologies and names around a single and summarizing *word*, the opposite can also be done, rearranging contemporary currents in North American systematic theologies around particular *names*, represented in particular *textbooks*.

Secularity turned out in 1981 in *Lonnie D. Kliever's The Shattered Spectrum* (Kliever 1981), a survey of *contemporary*, mostly *North American systematic theology*, to welcome John A. T. Robinson, Harvey Cox, and Paul van Buren to common tea, *process*—how else could it be—got John Cobb, Teilhard de Chardin, and Thomas Altizer stand under the same umbrella, *liberation* had James Cone, Mary Daly, and Gustavo Gutierrez visualize in unity the coming of freedom from oppression, *hope* let Jürgen Moltmann, Carl Braaten, and Gabriel Vahanian dream together, *play* had Hugo Rahner and, again, Harvey Cox clowning and chuckling and laughing with Robert Neale, and last, but not least, *story* showed John Dunne, James McClendon, and Sallie McFague sitting at the common metaphorical camp fire while telling their parables, biographies, and stories (for the combination of names and themes Kliever 1981). Most striking for readers of today: Nowadays *women* and *Other-coloreds* would most definitely take a more prominent place.

Contemporary *basic textbooks* introducing *North American systematic theology* are for the most part *plural*, multi-cultural, written by one or several authors, while giving a diverse and prominent place to the various voices of *women, African Americans, womanist theologians, Hispanic, Latin American, Asian,* and *American Indian* authors (Chopp and Taylor 1994, Barr 1997, Thistlethwaite and Engel 1998, Placher 2003, Jones and Lakeland 2005), next to covering the usual curriculum on European theological developments in the twentieth and twenty-first century. Recent textbooks in the United States are setting systematic theology in the context of various *cultures*, theological schools, as well as contradictory voices from all over the *globe*. Systematic theology made in the USA has long ago become *global* (Hodgson 1994, Barr 1997, Williamson 1999, Peters 2000, Migliore 2004, Webster, Tanner, and Torrance 2009, Schüssler Fiorenza and Galvin 1991a-b, 2011).

The Difference between Continents

Contemporary *North American systematic theology* shows itself most visibly in a *great diversity of textbooks* introducing the student to the field of systematic or dogmatic theology in North America today. A general comparison with *textbooks* in *German-speaking universities* in *Europe*, however, shows a *telling difference*.

For any beginning student in the study of systematics, *German or Swiss students* may easily exchange their *basic textbooks* (Mildenberger/ Assel 1995, Joest 1995-1996, Ott/Otte 1999, Härle 2000, Frey 2000, Pöhlmann 2002, Leonhardt 2004, Schneider-Flume 2004, Schneider 1992a-b, Müller 1998, Hasenhüttl 2001a-b, Wagner 2003, Pesch 2008-2010), one similar or at least parallel in approach to the other, with some minor or denominational differences, the general outline, content, and range of information for study and exams looking more or less *the same*. Certainly, each theological approach remains unique in its own way, with some authors putting the emphasis more on an exhaustive *history of dogmatic themes*. Others give more extensive prominence to *contemporary discussions and positions*, following only partially the traditional outline of dogmatic or systematic tables of contents.

All of them, however, seem to follow more or less *similar references* in discussing various systematic or dogmatic themes and positions, debates and battles. *Barth, Brunner, Tillich, Bultmann, Bonhoeffer, Gogarten, Braun, Käsemann, Pannenberg, Moltmann, Metz, Rahner,* maybe *Sölle,* more likely *Ebeling, Dalferth, Küng, von Balthasar, Greshake,* and a few others keep regularly coming up as common names and repeatedly visited tourist attractions in a beginner's excursion into the vast and open field of *systematic theology in the twentieth and twenty-first century*. *A clear dominance of mostly males, Caucasians*. References to women, Blacks, Asians, Latin Americans, North Americans, Canadians, British, French, Spanish, Italian, Dutch, and other foreign visitors on the to-be-discovered systematic planet remain rather minor.

Some authors follow a more *idiosyncratic and personal approach*, leaving more or less traditional and classical paths behind. Systematic theology can be written in German-speaking Europe in the theological tradition, for instance, of *Dietrich Bonhoeffer*, the *Barmen Theological Declaration*, and a left-wing-interpreted *Karl Barth*, putting dogmatics in the general context of a strong *biblical theology* and intensified *Jewish-Christian relations*, while at the same time developing systematics as engaging *political theology* concerned about issues of *justice and peace* (in the tradition of Karl Barth, Reformed theology, Jewish-Christian dialog, and a more global and ecumenical social and political ethics Gollwitzer 1982, Kraus 1983, Marquardt 1988, Link-Wieczorek/Miggelbrink/Sattler/Haspel/Swarat/Bedford-Strohm 2004).

Others lay the groundwork, though only sketchy, for a new and *feminist-liberation type* (Sölle 1990, 2002/1990) of a radical and political systematic theology. Still others let other disciplines like religious education in an interdisciplinary intent give systematic theology a new and more *experientially creative form* (in open dialog with literature, cultural studies, religious pedagogy, and social ethics Biehl und Johannsen 2002).

All this points to a *fundamental difference* in perspective on the nature and task of *systematic and dogmatic theology today*. The comparison between North American and German basic textbooks on systematic or dogmatic theology reveals a more fundamental difference in the way *theology as a whole* is being done. As such it belongs to the discipline of *fundamental theology* to reflect on this telling difference.

Meeting Reality

One element in the *fundamental difference* in the way systematic theology is being done in the *United States* in comparison to *Europe* has to do with questions of *power* and *powerlessness*, and the way these questions are being made aware of and consciously recognized. Some of it may be a question of a *hard awakening to reality*.

Reality seems to have jolted around North American systematic theology. Reality has a way to become stronger than any idealistic attempt to keep it out. Reality moved in and changed most if not everything in *North American systematic theology*.

British evangelical and systematic theologian *Alister McGrath* (McGrath 2001, 2001a, 2004, in German McGrath 1997, 2011) has an interesting chapter on *reality* in his *foundational introduction to the science of theology* in a postmodern world (McGrath 2004, 93–169). In a time of *radical social constructivism* and *postmodern playfulness* on whether reality really exists, it may at times be *therapeutic* to be hit by reality. That kind of a reality that does not budge, keeps standing up to us, does not let us get away with repeated excuses and apologies, homilies and theologies, philosophies and theories, as we are closing our eyes, our ears, and our hearts to what is really going on around us and in this world. As *Alister McGrath* puts it:

> "Theology is concerned with knowledge of God and of the world. It is therefore important to give careful consideration to the question of how such knowledge is acquired. The debate goes back to Plato, who attempted to distinguish between 'opinion' and 'knowledge'—in other words, between a weaker and a stronger form of knowledge. My basic position is that knowledge arises through a sustained and passionate attempt to engage with a reality that is encountered or made known." (McGrath 2004, 94)

Reality is an *African American roommate* who lives with you for a year. Reality is a *gay evangelical Christian* and a *gay Christian couple* living together somewhere in green-pastured Kentucky leading evening bible studies. Reality is the *laughter* of a *kid* after having been told in the 1960s or in *South Africa* that segregation and racism are over. Reality are the tears of a *hungry mother* still waiting for a more just and equitable global order. Reality is a *young woman* getting shelter from violence in a presumably Christian home. Reality is an *older single mother* who has never been healed from her wounds and her pain. Reality is being kicked out as a pastor from a village after taking sides for *14-year-old drug addicts* and other scum of society. Reality is living in the *favelas* of *Rio de Janeiro* or *Bogota* and surviving.

Reality is getting to know *social evangelicals* who join in with *liberal radicals* in fighting North American involvement in *Central America*. Reality is meeting some *atheist theologian* who keeps dreaming of the same peace for the world as you are. Reality is sitting in front of a *class* in a *lecture hall* and realizing that you are the only European, the only white, the only rich, the only male, the only straight. Reality is getting challenged by *real faces, real people, real names*, as we travel through this global world.

By reality I mean those *concrete faces*, names, voices, memories, real people, real places, real times, real stories, with real question and exclamation marks challenging ordinary and quite often unreal talk among comfortably well-to-do academia in North America and elsewhere. Writers, teachers, professors, and scholars in the US had to look again as reality moved in. Reality moved in, right into the heart of universities, bookstores, dormitories, lecture halls, cafeterias, student lounges, seminar rooms, copy places, and publishing houses.

Women, African Americans, Hispanics, Asian Americans, American Indians, Latin Americans, Africans, Asians, Europeans, gay or straight Christians, lesbians, evangelicals, liberals, Roman Catholics, Protestants, Unitarians, Orthodox, and other real people suddenly sat at the feet of lecturing theologians teaching classes while having to look again at reality. *Reality* transmitted in history books and camp fire stories, gospel songs and slave narratives, late night talks and personal papers, biographies and student reports, love letters and boards of declarations, newspaper columns and personal confessions, lunch meetings and weekend hikes, Church visits and neighborhood excursions, community projects and peace walks, civil rights protests and anti-nuclear-war marches. All these and many more real marks of *real life* moved in and turned *North American systematic theology* around.

A *multi-cultural, multi-faced, multi-voiced,* and *multi-experienced* student body moved in and changed a whole theological landscape, in theology in general, and in systematic theology in particular. Various conscious or unconscious forms of *affirmative action* and a *melting-pot* steaming and overflowing beyond even its own orderly ghetto mentality made it possible that real people with real faces, and yet radically different stories, are meeting and becoming, by necessity or voluntarily, a new kind of *theologically multi-cultural community* around the *new global, ethnic, and theological roundtable* (on an ethnic and global round table in theology Gonzalez 1992, Russell 1993, Cenkner 1996, Jenkins 2002, 2006).

A process of *transformation* that shows itself and leaves its marks even in the way books and papers, seminar presentations and dissertations, CD-ROMs and internet pages are written today. *Globalization* right at the most elementary level, omnipresent and all-determining, changing *theological education* in North America in ways never seen before. It shows that Europe, at least German-speaking Europe, has not had this privilege yet of meeting and letting *global reality* in (Jenkins 2002, 2006, Koschorke, Ludwig and Delgado 2004, Blaser 1995b), at least not in this compelling and convincing way as North America had the chance and opportunity to experience over these last few decades.

The Community of the Weak

A Mosaic

Multicultural as its own *student body*—and its *faculty*—has become, *contemporary North American systematic theology* has turned into a real *mosaic*. The *multicultural church* as a *mosaic* (Cenkner 1996, Berthrong 1999, Sawyer 2003, Jenkins 2002, 2006) has moved in and radically changed the old academy. North American systematic theology nowadays is mirroring a different kind of reality inasmuch as the North American academy has become a *different mirror* (Takaki 1993 and Jenkins 2003), *multicultural* at its own institutional and educational center. University faculties and teaching appointments, publications, conferences, seminar rooms and lecture halls reflect back to academia in a mirror a new make-up of the contemporary audience and authorship of systematic theology. A formerly *marginal world* is moving in (Fernandez and Segovia 2001 and De La Torre 2004), letting itself being heard, raising a voice for and with those who used to be kept silent or peripheral.

The *shattered spectrum* (Kliever 1981) of contemporary North America systematic theology is best reflected in a variety of textbooks mirroring to itself these radical changes in a newly to be measured and surveyed landscape. Roadmaps or country maps from a few decades ago may no longer serve a helpful orientation guides as reality is changing ever more rapidly and dramatically. Nevertheless, a basic *introductory tour guide* will be offered here.

Denominational Contexts

Denominational textbooks still exist. Textbooks continue to be published in recognizable denominational contexts. *Reformed* and *Presbyterian* (Leith 1993, Guthrie 1994, McKim 2001, Migliore 1991, 2004), *Lutheran* (Braaten and Jenson 1984, Schwarz 1986, Hall 1989, 1993, 1996, Hanson 1997, Jenson 1997–1999, Peters 2000), *Baptist* (Moody 1981, Garrett 1990-1995, Grenz 1994, 1998, 2000, Olson 2002), *Mennonite* and *Anabaptist* (Kaufman 1968, 1993, Finger 1985–1989, 2004, McClendon 1986, 1994, 2000, 2002), *Methodist* (Cauthen 1986, Neville 1991, Jennings 1992, Morse 1994, Williamson 1999, Jones 2002a–b, Inbody 2005), *Episcopal* (Thomas 1994, Thomas/Wondra 2002), and *Roman Catholic* (McBrien 1994, Flynn 2000, Hill 2003, Schüssler Fiorenza and Galvin 1991a–b, 2011) *basic textbooks* continue in more or less pronounced ways to present contemporary systematic theology in the twentieth and twenty-first century from a confessional perspective. However, in spite of particular *publishing* and *confessional contexts*, denominational coloring is becoming more and more faded, leaving only traces here and there of recognizable identity and denominational home of origin.

Some textbooks are openly trying to go beyond old denominational confines to a new and more *ecumenical or inter-confessional* overture (inter-denominational-Episcopal Thomas 1994 and Thomas/Wondra 2002, Lutheran-Reformed Jenson 1997-1999, Lutheran-postmodern Peters 2000, Reformed-inter-denominational Placher 2003). Others are fully conversant with *inter-denominational and inter-theological dialogue* on a *global scale* (Smart and Konstantine 1991, Barr 1997, Thistlethwaite and Engel 1998, Jones and Lakeland 2005), breaking out of traditional categories of theological origin to move into a more *postmodern*, post-traditional, and post-confessional time (postmodern, post-confessional, postliberal, post-colonial Peters 2000, Placher 2003, Jones and Lakeland 2005). Overriding *other concerns* like liberation or political theology, process theology, narrative theology, post-Shoah theology, feminist theology, and interfaith theology are also shaping and changing classical denominational color to such an extent that the confessional place of origin in textbooks is receding in the background (Hall 1989, 1993, 1996, Hanson 1997, Peters 2000, Thomas/Wondra 2002, Migliore 1991, 2004, Inbody 2005) or hardly visible and detectable anymore (Kaufman 1968, 1993, Cauthen 1986, Neville 1991, Morse 1994, Williamson 1999, Jones 2002a–b, Placher 2003). Roman Catholic textbooks as well show a high awareness and impressive openness for *ecumenical and inter-denominational dialogue*, while at the same time fully conversant with political, liberation, and feminist theology (McBrien 1994, Flynn 2000, Hill 2003, Schüssler Fiorenza and Galvin 1991a–b, 2011).

Less easily categorized can be those basic textbooks offering a *compendium* or *world perspective* on systematic theology in the twentieth and twenty-first century (for a global or a compendium style Smart and Konstantine 1991, Gunton 1997, McGrath 2001, 2001a, 2004, Webster, Tanner, and Torrance 2009), or having a highly idiosyncratic and *personal approach*, be it *liturgical*, or *narrative* (for a doxological approach Wainwright 1980, for a narrative style Fackre 1984, 1996, McClendon 1986, 1994, 2000, 2002).

The Community of the Weak

Evangelicals Facing Pluralism

A category of its own, interesting and eye-opening about its own diversity and plurality, are *evangelical systematic theologies* in North America coming from a variety of denominational and theological backgrounds (Bloesch 1978–1979, Grenz 1994, 1997, Erickson 1998, Jinkins 2001, Olson 2002, Vanhoozer 2003, 2005). North American *evangelicalism* has gone through many phases and developments, changes and renewals, alternating between becoming more progressive or regressive, moving from the *old* to the *young* to the *new* and returning again, with some, to the *old* (Coleman 1972/1980, Quebedeaux 1974, 1978, Marsden 1984, 1987, Tidball 1994, Webber 2002, McDermott 2010). North American systematic theology has become an experimental field and lively playground across various denominational boundaries for a variety of *old, young,* and *new evangelicals* (on older, young, and younger evangelicals McGrath 1993, 1996, Wells 1993, Grenz 1993, 2000, Webber 2002, McDermott 2010, from a European perspective Pally 2010). Evangelical theologies are contributing to an additional and impressive diversity in *North American inter-denominational systematic theology.*

The enlivening diversity of a *mosaic* of Christian belief (Olson 2002) seems to be coloring even *evangelical basic textbooks* in North America today, showing how *radical pluralism* and *postmodernism* have not stopped at the doorsteps of new and old evangelicalism (Grenz 1996, Mouw and Griffioen 1993, Phillips and Okholm 1996, Grenz and Franke 2001, Penner 2005, Smith 2006, 2008, Dyrness, Kärkkäinen, Martinez, and Chan 2008).

As evangelicals *Richard J. Mouw* from *Fuller Theological Seminary* and *Sander Griffioen* from the *Free University of Amsterdam* put it (Mouw and Griffioen 1993), poetically juxtaposing human solidarity, social coherence, and radical differences in a plural world:

> "Auden's poetic observation that 'all the real unity commences / in consciousness of differences' eloquently expresses an insight pivotal to our account of pluralism: real unity can only come from a source that transcends the bounds of human society. Only by becoming aware of the 'open heaven' under which society is placed, does it become possible to promote unity without destroying plurality. Christian social thought must provide an account of unity—or, if one prefers, of coherence or solidarity—that does justice to pluralities. whether contextual, associational, or directional." (Mouw and Griffioen 1993, 168)

Inter-denominational *Fuller Theological Seminary* in its institutional and theological history (Marsden 1987) has been closely *mirroring* ever since its beginning most of the fundamental and paradigmatic changes in development in North American evangelical theology over the last several decades. As probably the most *progressive* evangelical institution in the world, Fuller's evangelicalism has done more to open an evangelical constituency to serious and open dialogue and learning with and from other theologies than any other place.

In contemporary North America, even in its diversity of evangelical theologies, and in good *inter-disciplinary dialogue with the social and human sciences*, we are led to a new kind of systematic thinking in dogmatic and systematic theologies based on *solidarity* in *conflict* across various *denominational* and other even more *global* boundaries.

> "These examples lead us to the conclusion that social unity cannot be conceived of in a thoroughly immanentistic manner. This contention is reinforced by Jürgen Habermas's discussion of these topics. To many observers, Habermas's thought epitomizes the contemporary *post-religious* understanding of society. But on closer scrutiny it becomes clear that Habermas himself can only develop his communication theme by introducing religiously laden metaphors, such as 'covenant' and 'atonement' ... One does not find here Rousseau's civil religion, nor Comte's cult of 'Mankind'; rather, Habermas's concern is to demonstrate the need for, as well as the possibility of, a basic solidarity that would exclude neither differences nor conflict." (Mouw and Griffioen 1993, 166–167)

Evangelicalism in North America today is learning a new kind of *living and thinking with others in diversity* in its own and beyond its ranks *on the globe* (Samuel and Sugden 1984, Pope-Levison and Levison 1992, Sugirtharajah 1995, 2001, Küster 2001). *Solidarity* and *theological community building* across cultural and global differences is becoming a new *fundamental task* facing a young and dynamic movement in need of a *conversational culture*.

Multiculturalism and the *globalization of Christendom* (Jenkins 2002, 2006) will become as much a paradigmatic challenge for evangelicalism in the near future as it has already become for other theological currents in the US. Some new and promising authors are already pointing in this future and hopeful direction of a *world-open, ecumenical, and global vision* in evangelical North American systematic theology. Foremost among them seems to be Finnish and Pentecostal North American systematic theologian *Veli-Matti Kärkkäinen*, again to be found at *Fuller Theological Seminary* (Kärkkäinen 2002a, 2002b, 2003, 2004).

Whether *young, new,* or *old evangelicals,* all modern-day *liberal, post-liberal, evangelical,* and *post-evangelical* theologians in North America and elsewhere are challenged by a new basic fact as *common horizon* under which to move around. *Pluralism,* global, cultural, ethnic, racial, sexual, contextual, social, philosophical, political, ethical, and theological, will not pass away but stay as our common horizon. It is a fact in life and in Christian faith. A *reality* (McGrath 2004, 93–169) to rub our nose on or to hit our head against, but *it will not go away.* The extent to which this *radical pluralism* (Jeanrond and Rike 1991) is now changing a whole landscape of *contemporary North American and worldwide systematic theology* has not yet even been estimated or recognized in its fullest proportions.

Textbooks in Collaboration

Collaboration across *theological camps* seems to be moving in lately to *reconstruct* and *remodel* modern-day North American systematic theology. *Basic textbooks* are now written and edited by *several authors,* allowing a great denominational, cultural, and theological diversity of voices to speak. *Liberals, post-liberals,* and even *evangelicals* are starting to inhabit the same literary home in a book gathering the crowd in sharing the room with other roommates. Theological or publishing student and teacher housing is becoming *communitarian* allowing for a new kind of *community building* across the pages between two book covers. As such a fascinating new way of doing theology, starting to look more like the real world.

One important contributor to this *new way of doing systematic theology* has been the *Workgroup on Constructive Theology,* starting out already in the 1980s at *Vanderbilt Divinity School* by bringing together for projects of *collaborative effort* some of the most interesting and diverse systematic, dogmatic, or fundamental theologians in North America today (Hodgson 1994, Hodgson and King 1985, 1994, Chopp and Taylor 1994, Jones and Lakeland 2005). *Close collaboration, writing in community,* and a *high sensitivity for a radically changing world,* torn apart by some of the most violent intellectual and social turmoil ever to be seen in history, showing itself in various forms of radical suffering, have been the basic credo and fundamental theological decisions shaping this new collaborative project.

To quote former President of the *American Academy of Religion* and feminist North American systematic theologian *Rebecca S. Chopp,* introducing the collaborative *basic textbook* on systematic theology together with political and cultural systematic theologian *Mark Lewis Taylor* (Chopp and Taylor 1994):

> "Close collaboration has engendered this volume. In weekend meetings once or twice a year for the last four years, members of the Workgroup on Constructive Theology have attempted to articulate a strategy for introducing theology amid the intellectual and social turmoil that marks the end of Christianity's second millennium ... Although the Workgroup's members themselves exhibited real diversity in theological methods and even disciplines, they sought a pedagogy that would employ concern for today's cultural and social crises and that can inform a praxis of hope. This book is an invitation for students to delve into Christian theology's deep and rich traditions, truly engage in analysis and evaluation of those traditions and contemporary social challenges, and then to bring Christianity's chief doctrines, reconfigured or reconstructed, as hope-filled responses to these 'crises of suffering.'" (Chopp and Taylor 1994, ix)

Collaboration, dialogue, analysis, and common pedagogy, bringing together a *polyphony of voices and viewpoints*, even in conflict, but always engaged in conversation, seem to become *new fundamentals* in doing systematic theology, even in basic textbooks. As such a unique way of doing theology, a *new theological method* (Mueller 1984, 1988, O'Connell Killen and De Beer 1994, Kinast 2000, Sedmak 2002) promising more experimental forms in the near and far future. Others have followed this kind of *collaborative doing and writing systematic theology multiculturally* (Chopp and Taylor 1994, Barr 1997, Thistlethwaite and Engel 1998, Placher 2003, Jones and Lakeland 2005), though not all of the subsequent authors being necessarily part of the Workgroup on Constructive Theology.

Most interesting also in some of these latest developments in basic textbooks on systematic theology are individual chapters in *dialogical structure* around a particular theological topic setting *evangelical* and *liberal* voices right next to each other. So it happens that Jamaican *Noel Leo Erskine* is joining British Columbia's *Stanley J. Grenz* in fundamental theology, or Californian *Richard J. Mouw* may be eschatologically sharing the room with in-state-neighbor *Ted Peters* (Placher 2003, 11–49 and 329–365). A real pleasure wetting one's appetite to join the crowd.

Revisionist and *constructive systematic theology* in North America today, taking in good *ecumenical* and *post-denominational* manner some of its most hopeful and socially highly aware playfulness in *revisioning systematic theology* from Roman Catholic fundamental and systematic theologian *David Tracy* (Tracy 1975–1994, on David Tracy see Musser and Price 1996, 468–478, McEnhill and Newlands 2004, 263–266), has proven itself over the last decade to be one of the most creative and promising developments in *contemporary North American systematic theology in the twentieth and twenty-first century* (Hodgson 1994, Hodgson and King 1985, 1994, Chopp and Taylor 1994, Jennings 1992, Barr 1997, Thistlethwaite and Engel 1998, Jones and Lakeland 2005).

Textbooks Turning Cultural

North American systematic theology in its *latest update* is turning *global* and *cultural* in its *basic textbooks*. *Culture* as being defined as "an interactive process with two main component processes: the creation of shared activities (cultural practices) and the creation of shared meaning (cultural interpretation)" (Greenfield 1997, 303, as quoted in Chryssochoou 2004, xx, on culture Triandis 1994, Delaney 2004).

To put it in a less complicated way: *Culture* and *inter-cultural encounter* are those moments in life, most often more or less upsetting, when your own deeply grown and through life, experience, friends, hometown, neighborhood, skin color, sex, gender, or through other social-upbringing-related side-effects developed values, beliefs, actions, and dreams just don't make sense to someone else you meet on the street anymore.

Most often such small or big *clashes of cultures or civilizations* (Huntington 1996, Gallagher 1997, Hopkins 2005) end up in some minor or major form of a *conflict*. This may in *postmodern* and *McDonaldization society* (Ritzer 1997, 1993, 2000, 432–440) start already and most simply with your very often unquestioned *eating culture*, as some kids may love a late night eating binge at McDonalds while you abhor the Big Mac. Some other *cultural conflicts*, social, ethical, political, sexual, racial, musical, philosophical, religious, and theological, may have a little bit more of a heavy weight than a simple choice in your menu order at the fast-food restaurant counter. People in history have died for their cultural convictions, ethical beliefs, religious visions, and theological dreams.

To quote social psychologist *Xenia Chryssochoou* (Chryssochoou 2004) in her *social psychology of cultural diversity*:

> "Sharing a culture means that people have a common way of viewing their relationship with the social and physical environment, a common way of institutionalizing their relationships,

of communicating their thoughts and emotions, of prioritizing their activities, of dividing tasks and resources, of attributing value, honors, and power. In other words, it means that people have shared views about the world and how it functions, and they are aware that they do. People have a sense of belonging to a collectivity with a common way of thinking about the world. However, having common understandings does not mean that every single person has the exact same view about social reality. What is important from a social psychological perspective is not how many others think like ourselves, but the fact that we believe that others do think that way . . . The idea that others think like us consolidates our beliefs and makes them more powerful. Furthermore, it gives us a feeling of togetherness. Both these things make culture important for people." (Chryssochoou 2004, xxi, also Triandis 1994, Smith and Bond 1998, Delaney 2004)

Belonging to those who for the most part *think and feel and live alike* has always been a powerful temptation. Kings and nobility, races and nations, the educated and the cultured, sexes and ages—or more modern in form—professors and students, the rich and the socially arrived, the powerful and the privileged, the verbally trained and the digitally loaded, have always had the temptation to lose sight of the world how it really may be. Only in stepping down and intermingling with the common people have kings and others sometimes learned about *another world*.

What used to be a generally accepted canon of education and culture is changing. Multicultural as it has become, North American academic education is turning *cultural*. The same is happening today in *North American systematic theology* facing a *multicultural church* (Cenkner 1996, Berthrong 1999, Sawyer 2003, Jenkins 2002, 2006) globally and locally. Old and famous names are fading away, old privileges are crumbling, old bastions of cultural Christendom are falling, old ways of doing things or theology are losing their attraction. What used to be the common canon and territory of theological education, circling around repeated names like *Barth, Bultmann, Tillich, Pannenberg,* or *Moltmann*, is slowly being replaced be a new theological and cultural planet ushering into a whole *new world*. Culture as new thematic melody in North American debates on foundations of systematic theology has open up a whole new vision for the cultural captivity of theology.

The Community of the Weak

Facing Cultural Conflict

The first ones to call attention to this urgent need to maybe reconsider the *cultural captivity of a systematic theology* prisoner and slave to its own *social and cultural history* were narrators of slave narratives and *children of slaves* themselves (Hodgson 1974, Smith 1994a, 1994b, Hopkins 1993, 2000). With the socially explosive outbreak in the 1960s and 1970s of *black theology, African American spirituality,* and *Pan-African cultural sensitivities* (Young 1992, Paris 1995, Stewart 1997, Wilson Bridges 2001), the *open conflict* in North American systematic theology had moved in into the open wound of a still oozing and not really faced nor dealt with *cultural (his)story.* This common story was waiting to be redeemed and brought together finally. *Black America* called North America, its society as well as its *systematic theology*, to finally face its *cultural conflict.*

Contemporary North American systematic theology is living and dealing with these various and fundamental *cultural conflicts* right there in the middle of its *basic textbooks.* Over many decades now, various *ethnic and cultural groups* besides North America's *children of freedom* (Hodgson 1974) have become a lot more vocal in speaking their word about God and the world, while at the same time severely criticizing what has been going on in *theological God-talk* and *church-talk* before.

Textbooks Turning Political

The *ethnocentric*, mostly *Eurocentric* captivity (for a critique in contemporary theology Moltmann 1981, xii, Schreiter 1985, 1992a, Sedmak 2002) of the Christian church *worldwide* as well as in *WASP-White Anglo-Saxon Protestant culture* to just one and only *one particular*, mainly *German theological culture*—Barth, Brunner, Bultmann, Tillich, Bonhoeffer, Moltmann, Pannenberg, Ebeling, Jüngel, Rahner, Metz—has become most evident in its monolithic system of theology. In the course of a slow but steady *coming of age* of a new kind of *cultural and multicultural systematic theology* in the United States fundamental issues on *faith and culture*, or *theology and social context* have become the most prominent topics for fundamental debate.

Politics and *culture* have a lot to do with each other. Culture is becoming *political* the moment it uncovers *workings of power* in the way worlds have been and still are *socially constructed.* Formerly so-called *social or cultural minorities* like African Americans, women, womanist theologians, gay and lesbian theologians, Hispanics, Mujerista theologians, Asian Americans, as well as American Indians and others are starting to look at the world again and in particular at its *distribution of power*. This *social and political turning* in the way the world is looked at is happening right now in the midst of contemporary North American theology.

Predecessors to this *new look* at systematic theology in a newly configured North American social make-up in the *distribution of power* among the different social and cultural groups in theology have been North American systematic theologians like *Frederick Herzog* at *Duke University* (Herzog 1972–1999a, Rieger 1999) and *Peter C. Hodgson* at *Vanderbilt University* (Hodgson 1971–2007) who already in the 1970s and 1980s had an open and *political eye* for the *radical social and cultural changes* that were happening around them, affecting both social as well as theological systems. It is not surprising therefore that both *Frederick Herzog* and *Peter C. Hodgson* have been strongly influenced in the writing of their own *textbooks* in systematic theology by the *civil rights movement* and *black* or *African American theology* (Herzog 1988, Hodgson 1974, 1994, 2001). Others have followed, taking feminist theology, *Jürgen Moltmann*, and black theology as well as important *dialogue partners* for a *political theology* (Migliore 1991, 2004). Systematic theology as revisioning *political dogmatics* (Glebe-Möller 1987, Herzog 1988, Rieger 1999, Jennings 1992, Hodgson 1994, Morse 1994, Williamson 1999, Migliore 1991, 2004, Inbody 2005) had to take a new look at the *real world* as it is. And the real world in North America beginning in the 1960s was racist, sexist, and violent.

It still is that way today, the difference being, that formerly silenced people, also in theology, have started to take the courage to *speak up*, both in society as well as in contemporary North American systematic theology.

Feminist Theology Becoming Establishment

Not to forget in all this is the great importance and lasting fundamental influence *feminist theology* has had in reframing and reconstructing *North American systematic theology*. To a much greater extent, in a much wider scope, *North American feminist theology* has colored and changed almost everything in the way theology is being done in North America today than anywhere else.

That feminist theology in North America somehow has become *establishment* shows itself most visibly in *basic textbooks*, either written or collectively edited by *feminist theologians* (Ruether 1983/1993, LaCugna 1993, Coll 1994, Carmody 1995, Parsons 2002), or covered to a large extent in *basic textbooks* strongly influenced by feminist theology.

Feminist revisions of systematic theology can be found in most *basic textbooks* in *Roman Catholic* (McBrien 1994, Flynn 2000, Hill 2003, Schüssler Fiorenza and Galvin 1991a–b, 2011) as well as in *Protestant* publications (Hodgson 1994, Chopp and Taylor 1994, Thistlethwaite and Engel 1998, Barr 1997, Jones and Lakeland 2005).

Textbooks Turning Multicultural

Multicultural systematic theology in *North America* has a much more *recent history*, only lately becoming a determining influence. Starting with the *African American* movement passing from the *civil rights movement* to a more radical *black theology* (Hopkins 1993, 1999, 2000), followed by *womanist theology* (Hayes 1996, Mitchem 2002), succeeded by the awakening of *Hispanic Latino* theologies (Isasi-Diaz and Segovia 1996, Pedraja 2003, Valentin 2003, Padilla,Goizueta,Villafane 2005), *Mujerista* theologies (Isasi-Diaz 1993, 1996a, 2004), *Asian American* contextual theologies (Ng 1996, Phan and Lee 1999, Matsuoka and Fernandez 2003), and *American Indian* retrievals of past and present history (Peelman 1995, Kidwell, Noley, Tinker 2001), North American *basic textbooks* in systematic theology nowadays are looking at a *different mirror* (Takaki 1993) of a newly told *social history* and *personal or communal story*, both locally and globally.

Looking at this different mirror, facing yourself and your *other-colored, other-cultured*, and *other-storied* neighbor, may change systematic theology in the twentieth and twenty-first century. It certainly does so in the United States. Theological thinking in North American *multicultural society* (Cenkner 1996, Berthrong 1999, Sawyer 2003, Jenkins 2002, 2006) is now coming *from the margins* claiming an *unfinished dream* (Fernandez and Segovia 2001). *Basic textbooks* in North American systematic theology are turning to become *multicultural*, letting in a variety of voices, cultures, races, sexes, and theological backgrounds (Hodgson 1994, Chopp and Taylor 1994, Barr 1997, Thistlethwaite and Engel 1998, Jones and Lakeland 2005).

African American systematic theology is revisioning modern-day dogmatics from the perspective of *the last that shall be first* (Evans 1992, 141–154), always remembering the slave owners' whip and the lynching mob's rope. No systematic theology *written in black* can forget these moments of a people's history that have left scars of violence that will not heal. A systematic theology written out of recurring memories and unforgettable stories of *pain* will come along *differently* than most other *basic textbooks* in systematic theology (Evans 1992).

Womanist and *African American* systematic theology *in dialogue* shows even more potential to rewrite contemporary systematic theology. *Xodus-God-talk* combined with *womanist experience* is searching for a *new language* for most topics in dogmatics, poetic, autobiographical, artistic. The Exodus story of the Old Testament, the death of Jesus on the Cross, and the self-naming designation that *Malcolm X* used for himself are newly combined reference points creating a different kind of *systematic theology* (for a new Xodus-language in systematic theology Baker-Fletcher and Baker-Fletcher 1997).

Hispanic or *Latino systematic theology* is discovering its own language, namely *Spanish*, while still recognizing its highly *plural denominational backgrounds*, letting *Roman Catholics* together with *Pentecostals* and other *Protestants* write a new kind of *collaborative systematic theology* (Espin and Diaz 1999, Rodriguez and Martell-Otero 1997, Padilla, Goizueta, Villafane 2005). *Manana-theology* is dreaming of the final *ethnic roundtable* at which ultimately all people *out of every tribe and nation* will meet to write theology (Gonzalez 1990, 1992, Pedraja 2003). *Mujerista systematic theology*, the feminist expanding of these visions of a *global and multicultural roundtable* in Christian theology, adds the image of life journey, daily struggle, and birthing poetics in liturgy to a *new kind of systematic theology* (Isasi-Diaz 1993, 1996a, 2004e).

Asian American systematic theologies are only starting to rewrite systematic theology while reflecting on the coerced liminality of being marginal in a male-, white-, and suburbia-dominated Anglo-Saxon society in North America (Ng 1996, Phan and Lee 1999, Matsuoka and Fernandez 2003). Doing theology from the *edge*, the *margins*, and the liminal meeting-points of various cultures and places serves as a guiding metaphor and critical hermeneutical principle for revisioning contemporary theology (Lee 1995, Matsuoka and Fernandez 2003, 11–28).

The latest *new revisioning* of North American systematic theology comes from those *most originally* at home and *most primarily* entitled to speak for this vast and beautiful land, having lived on *American soil* ever since. *Native America* is reclaiming its territory, finding new words in theology for space, time, and place, creation, the land, and the *trickster* or *sacred fool*, like Jesus, *reversing the ordinary* (Kidwell, Noley, Tinker 2001,

113–125). A *native hermeneutics* in a new kind of *Native American* theology will need to recover language, culture, and even life, after all this and more has been taken away *violently* by a surrounding and predominantly self-proclaimed *Christian society*.

As *Native American* systematic theologians *Clara Sue Kidwell, Homer Noley,* and *George E. "Tink" Tinker* (Kidwell, Noley, Tinker 2001) put it, opening their systematic theology with considerations on *theological method* and its basic *cultural conflict* right there:

> "For American Indian people, hermeneutics must extend beyond the interpretation of biblical texts. Interpretations of their cultures by government agents and Christian missionaries have led to policies that contributed to loss of language, culture, and even life. We maintain that Indian people must be able to assert their own interpretations of their cultures. These must come not only from an elite group of individuals but should represent a true community viewpoint. This viewpoint extends to interpretations of Christian doctrine from a truly Indian perspective." (Kidwell, Noley, Tinker 2001, 30–31)

The opened *Pandora's box* of *cultural conflict* in a *global Christendom* (Jenkins 2002, 2006) right there, at the *center* and heart of contemporary systematic theology in the twentieth and twenty-first century in North America and elsewhere, could not be more vividly and painfully summarized than this.

A Copernican Change of Perspectives

The *Pandora's box* of *cultural conflict* shows itself even more so in the *comparison between continents*. African American, African, feminist, womanist, gay, lesbian, Asian American, Asian, Latin American, Hispanic, Mujerista, Native, French, Italian, or any other concerns of *contexts* in the *worldwide symphony* of *modern-day systematic theology in the twentieth and twenty-first century* are only marginally of interest to most German-speaking basic textbooks in systematic theology, even today. Most of these contextual issues of global theologies are still relegated to the secondary theological *periphery* in most German-speaking theologies.

While in German-speaking *Europe* the *theological center* of attention still seems to gravitate around the same *names and places*, refreshed in ever new ways, the *microphysics of power* (Foucault 1980, on power in Michel Foucault see Brown 2000) in the social and academic distribution

North America

on what is to be considered *attentional periphery* and *visual center* seem to have dramatically changed in almost *Copernican ways* in systematic theologies of North America today. This brief overview should have given an introducing perspective of this Copernican change, even on its own continent in the USA.

Comparing *basic textbooks* on systematic theology in *Europe* and in the *United States* reveals a striking *difference* and *change of perspectives* in what is being *moved* and *rearranged* in the *microphysical game of discursive power* from the theological periphery to the academic *center of attention*. The way a *symbolic room* or place, its space and vacancies, cluttered middle and empty corners, are being arranged has a way to speak a clear and determinative symbolic language. Academia can also be looked at as made up of many possible symbolic arrangements of space and time, room and clutter. Not always are those corners where the most clutter and noise are to be found necessarily and really the most important ones.

Comparing *North American* and *European* textbooks on systematic theology, a *Copernican change of perspectives* can be easily proven. This *change of perspectives* has everything to do with the way *power relations* between different *social contexts* of theology are being redefined. Theology is not made in heaven, nor does it fall *from heaven* (Casalis 1984). Nor is it formulated in some laboratory with no influence from the outside. Depending on *who you are, where you live, what you have seen*, and *what or who has hurt you or made you laugh*—the *social location* of theology (Müller 1999, 63–66)—, your own theology—systematic, fundamental or dogmatic—may turn out quite *differently*. The *social location* of contemporary systematic theology in the twentieth and twenty-first century will become, as it seems, the most important topic for common attention.

As North American Evangelical *Veli-Matti Kärkkäinen* (Kärkkäinen 2004) puts it, this *distribution of space and importance, power and attention* given to *contextual issues* in systematic theology points to an *open social wound* in the way most theology is still being done in these days:

> "During a time when the majority of Christians lives outside Europe and North America, it is scandalous that African, Asian, and Latin American theologies are hardly mentioned in textbooks, let alone given fair treatment . . . Whereas respected schools seek to hire scholars from third world contexts, amazingly little has changed in the way textbooks are written and classes taught. Yet theology at the international level must give proper attention to these contextual voices and offer opportunities for patient dialogue between Western and non-Western

theologies in light of biblical and historical traditions . . . Much work needs to be done not only in Africa, Asia, and Latin America but also in the West, for example, among women and others whose voices have not been properly heard in the discourse." (Kärkkäinen 2004, 12, 304)

Spacial terms like *center* and *periphery* always point to questions of *power* and *powerlessness*. The way *textbooks* are written has something to do with the way *space* and *power* are distributed in this world, the way voices are heard or not properly heard in our global discourse. Textbooks in systematic theology both in Europe and in North America participate in the *microphysics of power*. Some things are mentioned, other things disappear in the silence of words and pages. Whatever is silenced, relegated to the margin, to the appendix, to the place of lesser or even no importance, may have to become *central* in our future attention.

North American systematic theology has consciously taken up these questions of *power* and *powerlessness* in order to revise and reconstruct systematic theology with these new themes from the periphery, putting them right at the center. Here, North America is taking up a leading role in the *reconstruction of systematic theology for the twenty-first century* in a *globalized context* (Jenkins 2002, 2006, for a reconstruction of systematic theology in a global context Blaser 1995b, Barr 1997, Thistlethwaite and Engel 1998, Kärkkäinen 2004, Migliore 2004, Jones and Lakeland 2005).

A Fundamental Theology of Power

The experience of *power* and *powerlessness* are *fundamental themes* in *North American systematic theology today*, as has been shown in this chapter perusing through denominational, racial, sexual, cultural, and multicultural North America producing its own *indigenous theology* in *basic textbooks*.

Issues of *power* and *powerlessness* serve as a *guiding thread* and a *theological option* in the context of a *critical social reason* (Haight 2001, 46-47, in general Lamb 1982, Lane 1984, O'Brien 1992, Rieger 2007, Taylor 1990, 2011) leading through most contemporary theological and ethical discussions in North America. This chapter has tried to give a *little tour* through North American systematic theology in *basic textbooks*, pointing out the fundamental *microphysics of power and powerlessness* in theology. This shows a determining influence on the *shape* of systematic theology, as a comparison between *North America* and *Europe* easily unveils radical differences in theological landscapes. This cannot be explained only by different cultures, geographies, or ethnic realities. The conscious *choice* to put these issues at the *theological center* is a conscious decision in *fundamental theology*.

Touching on *method*, these questions belong to themes debated in *practical fundamental theologies* (Metz 1980, Lamb 1982, Lane 1984, O'Brien 1992, Wetherilt 1994, Arens 1995a, Haight 2001, McClendon 1986, 1994, 2000, 2002, Rieger 2007, Taylor 1990, 2011). *Socially locating* theologies according to *who* is writing them reflects on the importance of *social location* (Müller 1999, 63–66) in the distribution of *power and powerlessness* in the way modern-day theology is being developed and formulated. No systematic theology in *North America* today, even in the most *basic textbooks* for beginning students, bypasses this fundamental question asked of everyone trying to "think about God" (Sölle 1990, 2002/1990) from that place and space where they are in social life, reflecting consciously and self-critically about the *social place* of the one writing or thinking and on the way this might have a very determinative influence on what is being *said* or what is being *left out*.

In this, *Europe* could learn a great deal from systematic theologies in the *United States*. This dissertation would like to be a contribution to such an *inter-cultural process of learning*.

5

Real Life

METHOD

"'But what does that have to do with real life?' I have come to expect an occasional question like this in courses on systematic theology. I confess that I am often tempted to snap back, 'If you would just abandon your vulgar notions of 'real' life and muster some curiosity you could spare us your question!' Usually, I overcome the temptation and give a little speech instead. If students complain that theology is too 'theoretical', I invite them to consider Kant's argument that nothing is as practical as good theory ... If they object that theologians entertain outdated and therefore irrelevant ideas, I offer them a Kierkegaardian observation that the right kind of non-contemporaneity may be more timely than today's newspaper. I conclude by explaining how ideas that seem detached from everyday concerns may in fact touch the very heart of those concerns ... And yet, when I am done with my disquisition, I have dealt with only half of the worry expressed in my students' skeptical question. We theologians sometimes do teach and write as if we have made a studied effort to avoid contact with the 'impurities' of human lives." (Volf 2002, 245)

"Thus, the practice of narrativity allows for a certain kind of interrelationship or texture among the traditions, communities, and institutions to which we belong and which belong to us. And yet there is also a subjectivity involved, some kind of deliberate

agency that enables one to make choices, to opt for certain plots and not for others, to pursue development of virtues. In other words, narrativity is neither pure social determination nor autonomous individualism, but rather a way to name the practical reality of what we have to face: the ongoing activity of writing our lives . . . To a certain extent, this is merely a Christian anthropological statement: like Augustine in his Confessions, we have to interpret our past in the process of moving forward. But it is intensified in particular ways due to the days in which we live, days in which among other things the presence of women has changed, quite literally, the student bodies in theological education . . . Feminist practices of theological education create narrative agency in the dual sense of providing space for the development of agency and by composing particular narratives for personal and social flourishing. Indeed, in my experience women create through feminist practices of theological education a new experience of subjectivity. Women and men write new narratives for their lives and in this process create new forms of narrative agency." (Chopp 1995a, 34)

"Theology is about waking up. It is amazing what a person who is fully awake can do. A person like Mahatma Gandhi or Pedro Arrupe can make all the difference in the world. Theology pays special attention to the few, the 'Abrahamic minorities' that can change the world by being attentive to the cries of the people. Dom Helder Camara, the bishop of Recife in Northern Brazil for many years, did not get tired of talking about these minorities that can be motivated to become agents of change, artisans for a new humanity . . . Theology is about life, and doing theology is part of living a responsible life. Life is a big school and there are billions of people in its classrooms, the classrooms of the open spaces of our lives." (Sedmak 2002, 1–2)

Finding the Real

Power and Method

Power and *method* are related. Experiences of *power* and *powerlessness* in the everyday world change the way you approach questions on life, meaning, and vision. *North American systematic theology* has long ago realized the importance of questions on *method*. The entrance door to theology may lead you into totally different places. Depending on choices in method, results may turn out differently. What we focus on, who we listen to, what places we visit, which voices we hear or don't hear, all this changes theology in a *paradigmatic way*. Paradigms reveal choices in *method*.

Therefore, this chapter will follow *North American proposals* for a *revision of method* in *teaching and living theology*. North American systematic theology offers many creative and *new visions* for reflection on these questions of method. The issues of *power* and *powerlessness* remain central in these discussions and proposals. The way we *teach* theology already *changes perspectives* on what theology could be all about. The way we introduce and invite students to the vast and limitless *global world* of theological reflection, writing, speaking, singing, praising, mourning, crying, laughing, celebrating, resisting, struggling, opposing, acting, living (Sedmak 2002, 11) already changes the style, the tone, the color, the flavor in the way theology welcomes the traveling student in this global world. *Living in it* may already have a lot to do with *how we got into it*.

Questions of *power* and *powerlessness* shape everything in *method*. The question of *real life* gets posed at its most urgent moment. *Theology* and *real life* should go together. Otherwise, theology becomes play with no real intent for life, or for *changing life*. Theology which does not change people and the earth touched by it, is not theology worth its name as *radical discipleship* following the *way of Jesus* (Herzog 1988, Rieger 1999, Jennings 1992, Hodgson 1994, Chopp and Taylor 1994, Williamson 1999, Finger 1985–1989, 2004, McClendon 1986–2002, Migliore 2004, Augsburger 2006, Taylor 1990, 2011).

In *real life*, *belief* and *conviction* should make a *difference* in the way the world becomes more human. The *powerless* should be empowered in new and hopeful ways, the *powerful* should be called to task for their abuse of might and power, the hopeless should find some hope again, the poor should be uplifted, the broken healed, the hungry fed, the wounded protected, the downtrodden welcomed and included in a community of healing with a *new method*. Method is not just abstract reflection, but has everything to do with the *choices* we make in *teaching* and *living* theology by *following Jesus*.

Theology and Real Life

A *Pentecostal neo-Evangelical*, a *United Methodist feminist radical*, and a *Roman Catholic epistemologist* are talking to each other in heaven or on this earth, debating issues over *real life*. This is at least the way a good joke could start. A good joke or not, *Miroslav Volf* (Volf 1996, 2002, on Miroslav Volf see Hollenweger 1997, 285, 1997a), *Rebecca S. Chopp* (Chopp 1986, 1995a), and *Clemens Sedmak* (Sedmak 2002) could somehow be talking someday, if they have not already done so, to each other. Not just in quotes, epigrams, and introducers, but in *real life*.

Asking questions like "But what does that have to do with real life?" (Volf 2002, 245), may be quite symptomatic of a kind of *academic world* having lost some touch with real life. Maybe not all, but at least some of it. For most beginning students it still seems that *systematic* or even more so *dogmatic theology* is a world of its own, mainly a *foreign territory* first to be discovered, getting ever more elevated in linguistic altitude and colloquial distance from the normal day-to-day folks we usually chat with around the neighboring street or village corner. After all, who knows exactly what the latest inner-trinitarian academic and literary rumblings on processions, interpenetrations, and the variously described to-and-fro movements of trinitarian theologies may have to do with real life, let alone even everyday democracy (Moltmann 1991). And yet all this is part of what students normally get introduced to in *systematic or dogmatic theology*.

A lot has to do with *method*, and with the way theology is being written and taught. Writing and teaching theology as if we were "writing our lives" (Chopp 1995a, 34) could change everything. After all, in its best sense of the word, theology "is about life", as we are "waking up" (Sedmak 2002, 1–2). The most intriguing thing about it: everyone, child, youth, adult, senior, worker, secretary, janitor, teacher, scholar, may be joining the class in a big and open classroom called *real life*. "Life is a big school and there are billions of people in its classrooms, the classrooms of the open spaces of our lives" (Sedmak 2002, 2).

Theology in the Open Classroom

> *I used to be teaching confirmation kids as teenagers according to some more or less given classical or more modern curriculum. Back then in Geneva, with young teenagers speaking both German and French and growing up bilingual as Swiss German teenagers in a French environment, I remember translating texts, stories, sections out of teacher's books, and selected excerpts out of some daily newspapers. The format of a class lesson got to be more or less the same. Introducing a topic, giving some input from texts, stories, photographs. Having the teenagers split up in*

small groups, if possible with only six of them. And then getting the teenagers to come back, resume, summarize, talk and debate, get bored or goof off, look interested or play the rebellious. For years I used to teach that way.

Even in the next town where I got to be pastor in a middle-sized village in Swiss German and sub-urban countryside about a half an hour away from cosmopolitan Zurich I started off with the same classical and modern pedagogy. Week after week I prepared my lesson, structured various learning experiences, got texts, photographs, materials for discussion, group and individual work assignments ready-made and planned, determining the likely sequence of the plenary session as well as the time frame for all this, in order to enter a world of frustrated pedagogy each week again.

Until I came across Wolfgang Hinte's intriguing and provoking book on non-directive or self-determining pedagogy (Hinte 1980, 1990). And until I got to face reality that, in spite of all this great amount of spent energy, somehow things did not work out. Most of all, the teenagers themselves made me think again, up to the point that someday I just started the class with no lesson plan at hand, but only teenagers speaking out their own world and thematic sensitivity.

Things got quite chaotic at first, with phases of anarchy and helplessness, despair over a despairing teacher and despairing students, hardly grown-up teenagers, 15-16-year olds, who had never really learned how to decide on their own what to learn and what to see, what to discover and what to envision as their own and most personally chosen projects, themes for discussion, movies to look at, music to listen to, texts to write, poetry to compose, songs to sing, interviews to make, newspapers to produce, and ultimately, as their last and final act of youthful and self-actualizing creativity, wild and never in this or that way possibly imagined confirmation worship services to prepare.

The teaching style got to be known, gossiped around, talked about, privately debated, publicly commented, silently rejected, loudly encouraged, and still constantly transformed as the years went on. In the meantime confirmation kids as teenagers had learned how to own their own learning, deciding, choosing, exploring, reading, researching, writing, interviewing, typing, composing, planning, experiencing, editing, exhibiting, and putting it all on Macintosh, in learning how to play half-way amateur

Real Life

> *journalists for some local youth magazine in town. In the end several self-composed newspaper editions for each year were published, even being sold at the local postal office right next to something like a daily Playboy magazine couched as newspaper or other public reading pleasures of the day.*
>
> *Out of the experience a whole photo exhibition in a local pub was organized, interviews with national celebrities made possible, and teenagers formerly on drugs and recovering in therapy becoming for a short while printed his/stories. Even a 50-year old prostitute made it to the printed page with her interview and touching Christmas card thanking teenagers for having taken a compassionate interest in her life and story, as they were sitting with her and a social worker in a counseling center in Berne just listening. Around all this, as an overarching theme like a rainbow shining over the thunderstorm, the title of Miroslav Volf's touching book Exclusion and Embrace (Volf 1996).*
>
> *Systematic theology right there, most subjective, personal, and experiential, hanging as a meditative photo exhibit in front of Mexican-food-eating local villagers, quietly sitting for sale in the racks of the postal office as a self-edited youth magazine, and drumming on African drums in a musical confirmation worship service in memory also of a young teenager who had died, less than a year before, on a heroin overdose. Systematic theology right there in the midst of life, lively, provocative, creative, unusual, and speaking or writing, typing or editing, in ever new and creative form. Theology outside of the classroom, and yet in the midst of real life.*

Theology has to do with *life*, and life is never confined to a normal classroom. Most often, classrooms turn into laboratory protection devices leaving *real life* outside. Therefore, it is high time that theology, like any other meaningful *learning* in this world, *move out*, virtually or in reality, to other places than our mostly closed-off and closed-in institutionalized classrooms (on the pedagogy of open classrooms Stephens 1974, Nyberg 1975, Zimmer/Niggemeyer 1986, Shor 1992, Arnold/Schüssler 1998, Hof 2009).

The *neighboring community*, life experiences, stories and memories, newspaper articles and local histories, city spots, world events and art galleries, movie theaters and concert halls, peace demonstrations and community projects, all this and more may be part of a new kind of systematic theology *leaving the classroom*. Everything may become a part of an *open curriculum* (Hinte 1990, Shor 1992, English and Hill 1994, Pinar, Reynolds, Slattery, Taubman 1995, Hof 2009) or a *pedagogy of hope* (Ayers 2001, 2004a, 2004b, Simon 1992, Greene 1995, Ayers and Miller 1998, hooks 2003, McLaren 1995, 2005, Giroux 1997, 2011) in conversation with a systematic theology that wants to be sensitive to human concerns in its curriculum (for a postmodern curricular perspective on theology and education Pinar, Reynolds, Slattery, Taubman 1995a, Hodgson 1999). Classrooms, from the local school to the university lecture room, *open themselves* to *the subjective, the experiential, the personal* (in open pedagogy Hinte 1980, 1990, Kösel 1993, in college/university and adult education Arnold/Schüssler 1998, Shor 1992, Usher, Bryant and Johnston 1997, Jarvis 2004). A neighboring community, city places, world events, autobiographical material, and other personal and social experiences *teaching peace and social justice* (Ayers and Ford 1996, Ayers, Hunt, and Quinn 1998, hooks 2003, McLaren 1995, 2005) are no longer relegated to a spectator seat in the way systematic theology sees itself.

Curriculum as Auto/Biographical Text

Curriculum comes from the *Latin* root *currere*, meaning "to run the course or the running of a course", its metaphorical closeness to the life-course of one's personal *auto/biography* being most prevalent and revealing, as North American and postmodern educator *William F. Pinar* and associates point out in a voluminous historical and longitudinal research project on curriculum theory (Pinar, Reynolds, Slattery, Taubman 1995, 515). Looked at in this metaphorical context, curriculum could be renamed as an *autobiographical and biographical text* (Pinar, Reynolds, Slattery, Taubman 1995, 515–566) telling the story of the one who has experienced true and meaningful learning.

Instead of a purely technical, cognitive, and behavioral approach to a curriculum and its contents, planning human learning accordingly, a more *existential and personal approach* may give the image a whole new ring. Curriculum understood as *life journey*, biographical, autobiographical, and personal, will need a different kind of place and space in *open classrooms* in touch with the surrounding world. In openly permeable and porous classrooms students and faculty are creating *new spaces of learning* even outside of four walls enclosing it, encouraging "relations among school knowledge, life history, and intellectual development in ways that might function self-transformatively" (Pinar, Reynolds, Slattery, Taubman 1995, 515). Curriculum as *theological text* (Pinar, Reynolds, Slattery, Taubman 1995a) could profit a great deal as well from a curriculum *opening itself* to the personal, subjective, and experiential outside of a traditional classroom.

As *William F. Pinar* and his associates (Pinar, Reynolds, Slattery, Taubman 1995a), put it, envisioning a new kind *of postmodern curriculum as theological text*:

> "Those who understand curriculum as theological text understand education as wedded to the most profound issues of the human heart and soul ... Other theological issues include those mystical-ecological yearnings for union with the source of life, the nature of morality in an evil world, and those mythico-imaginative longings of the human spirit . . . Curriculum as a postmodern theological text invites us to a search for truth wherein our destination remains unknown ... Just as the history of curriculum thought can be portrayed as tumultuous movements of creation, crisis, and transformation, so too can the effort to understand curriculum as theological text be characterized as processive movement of body, mind, and spirit in the spiral of procreation, death, and resurrection. The significance of such a ritual is embedded in Native American experience. A Pueblo priest and clan chief, Santiago Rosetta, advises that 'spirit' plays as important a role in human wellness and illness as do mind and body. As a medical student, Carl Hammerschlag, recalls meeting Santiago in the Santa Fe Indian Hospital. Hammerschlag writes: 'Santiago tried to teach me if you are going to dance, you have to move. You can't watch the dance; you can't listen to it or look at it. You have to do it to know it. He told me that he could teach me his steps, but I would have to hear my own music' ... From this perspective body, mind, and spirit are interrelated. The 'wholeness' of this view contradicts the modern experience of fragmentation and isolation and suggests a new theological perspective from which to explore curriculum."
> (Pinar, Reynolds, Slattery, Taubman 1995a, 659–660)

Letting the World Come In

Theology taught and lived in such an *open classroom*, with a holistically minded curriculum letting the world outside *come in*, may take on a whole new shape, color, form, and consistency. Hardened positions and old battle lines sometimes get slowly softened just simply by a one-to-one contact with *real life, real people,* and a *real face.* Meeting a gay evangelical couple and other Christians at some bible study group meeting during a weekday night may make your whole theological world look *different,* more so than just reading about it. Facing confirmation kids as teenagers on heroin may make your sporadic reading of Miroslav Volf's *Exclusion and Embrace* (Volf 1996) somehow come deeply *alive.*

Looking outside of university walls may turn out to be a highly therapeutic move for academia getting back in touch with real life. *Theology* developed in an *open classroom* will be trying to find a *new educational form*, attentive to and inclusive of a neighboring community as well as of those little and big stories, moving experiences, life-changing encounters, poetic memories, upsetting responses, and serious or only funny concerns of students and teachers alike in sharing a common theological space and room open to be rearranged and explored in new ways. And *going outside* will be just as important a part of the curriculum as staying protected and secluded inside.

Theology In Touch with Life

Instead of teaching theology, *academic theology* as well, as a common and highly "studied effort to avoid contact with the 'impurities' of human lives" (Volf 2002, 245), *theology* in an *open classroom—systematic, dogmatic,* or *fundamental*—will become more messy, contaminated, emotional, and experiential, but at the same time also more lively as being *in touch with life.* Life has a way to break out of neat categories and prescribed tables of contents. Basic textbooks, core lecturing classes, advanced seminars, term papers, reading materials, and life exposures may need a whole revision in the way systematic theology is being taught today.

This could open up a whole *new way of learning* in theology, creating "new forms of narrative agency" (Chopp 1995a, 34), as learning—another word for writing your own life—should not be reduced to some lonesome and individualistic monologue from a pulpit or lectern or from silently lecturing pages. Learning in the *global world* will more and more become a creatively-chaotic *networking* along and across many places and spaces, haphazardly mixing locations here and there, no longer being stuck or prisoner to only one particular place. Data transfer—another word for human learning—in the *information age* will make learning more democratic, letting students and confirmation kids as teenagers have a more personal access to self-chosen knowledge, explorative learning, and the subsequent *revisioning of traditions*. What will be considered *learning* and the canons of learning is open for negotiation again.

Life as an *open classroom* in an *open education setting* of a *neighboring universe* is inviting everyone to join the crowd on its walk and trekking along a *life cycle of unending learning*. Theology looked at this way may become intriguing again, getting some of the most basic *human conversation* going. Child and professor, artist and technician, musical star and politician, unemployed and overemployed, drug addict and celebrity, CEO and volunteer activist, teacher and screenwriter, believer and agnostic can thereby find a new way of talking to each other about *real life* again.

Doing Theology as Wounded People

Systematic theology in the *global age* will need to become more *messy* and *sensitive*, getting hands dirty and hearts touched, in contact with the human defilement of simple *dirt* (on theology and dirt, in a New Testament social-science perspective Countryman 1988). Impurities are part of life, even theological life. Instead of being afraid of being contaminated, defiled, and messed up by what people really go through in life, systematic theology will need to *come down and out* from high altitudes and aseptic waiting rooms to walk and sit with people and confirmation kids *where they are*. Like in those years when teenagers in a sleeping-village at the age of 14 got to play around with heroin and other life-endangering shit.

Doing this, theology may discover that most of us are *wounded* somehow. Some more, some less, but all in some way. This may create a new kind of compassionate *theological community building* across common dividing lines, as we recognize that most of us "do theology as wounded people", knowing that in most normal lives no one "can go through life without getting wounded. No human soul leaves life without wounds, humiliations, and experiences of injustice and rejection. We all carry wounds" (Sedmak 2002, 9). Human conversation coming out of one's own *open wounds and scars* in the midst of a *cry* (Aguirre 1997, Smith 1992, Herman 1997, Sölle 2001, Faulde 2002, Park 2004) usually turns out to be the best starter for *soul-connecting* and *community-building conversation*, both in systematic theology and in real life.

The Community of the Weak

Theology in New Places

Even *academia* may reconsider the *open classroom of life* (Sedmak 2002, 2) as a new location to teach beyond not just physically restricting lecture halls and seminar rooms. The *cafeteria* as a new theological lecture hall, the *shopping mall* as a new home for public theological debate, the *city park* as a new playground for theology in engaging plural and *postmodern conversations* (on hermeneutics as conversation, modern and postmodern Tracy 1987, 1993), all these and other *new academic spaces and places* may be reconsidered in getting theology—*systematic, dogmatic,* or *fundamental*—out into the near and far community, on benches on the schoolyard, the marketplace, the riverside, the pebble beach, and other recreation areas, proclaiming in conversation as "artisans for a new humanity" (Sedmak 2002, 1) our most fundamental and human "solidarity-in-hope" (Tracy 1987, 114).

Rosemary Cowan (Cowan 2003), in her biographical-thematic introduction to African American social philosopher/radical theologian *Cornel West* (West 1982–2010, West and Glaude 2004, see his autobiography 2010), describes this new function and role of the "*multicontextual* public intellectual who reaches beyond the public of the academy to the publics of TV talk-shows, grassroots political organizations, and prisons" (Cowan 2003a, 107). *New places* for theology require a new kind of theologian ready to go outside of protected classrooms in classical academia, border-crossing into various and multiple contexts and places in which to speak and act. The pub, the street, the newspaper editorial room, the schoolyard, the traffic light, the soccer field, the homeless shelter, and many other places and spaces qualify for new contexts in theology where an *organic intellectual* (Cowan 2003a, 115–117, Widl 2000, 185–186, and McGrath 2002, 144–155) will "link the life of the mind with a sense of political engagement" (Cowan 2003a, 116).

Theology in new places will need new and activist, with the *everyday world of ordinary folks* involved and *organically engaged* intellectuals "willing to go further in their academic pursuits by attempting to make their work accessible to those located outside the academy" (Cowan 2003a, 115). This will have a determining influence on *theological method.* The place where we start from and wherein we learn and move will change the way we write and do our communal and personal theology.

Theology Accessible to All

Method in theology (in Roman Catholic fundamental theology Kinast 1996, 1999, 2000, Sedmak 2002, Mueller 1984, 1988, 2007), looked at in this creatively spatial way, becomes an *open field* or *space* of experimentation with old and new ways and traditions, words and images. Finding the many foot- and fingerprints of God in the world, as God has already walked ahead of us, in a *fundamental theology of the traces of God* (Neusch 2004) is the *new task* systematic theology is faced with leading outside of its traditional academic walls. French fundamental theologian *Marcel Neusch* describes this *open space* of theology in his *introduction to fundamental theology* (Neusch 2004):

> "Theology only assumes its task fully if it is able to show that the Christian fact has a universal significance, and that this universality is justified by the common destiny of humankind. To give up this task would mean to enclose oneself in a sentiment and to take its share in making the Christian experience incommunicable. However, the claim of the Christian experience is to open up a space of meaning and life accessible to all." (Neusch 2004, 237)

To open up a space of meaning and life *accessible to all* will require a different kind of *theological method*. North American systematic theology is practicing such a kind of *new theological method*, if only in first and still very fragmentary ways.

Choosing Your Method

Contemporary students in theology have a *choice in method* (for Protestants Jennings 1976, 1985a, McClendon 2000, Yoder 2007, for Roman-Catholics Kinast 1996, 1999, 2000, Sedmak 2002, Mueller 1984, 1988, 2007) almost as varied as going to the supermarket or ordering from Amazon. And yet, consciously *choosing your method* in theology is important. A particular method in theology may guide you to one place that other methods leave out or pass by inattentively on the route taken to get from one place to another. *First thoughts* on *first steps* considered, first decisions taken, and first destinations chosen, are not necessarily a waste of time, but say a lot already about what kind of theology you believe in or write about. Selecting your colors and sketching the silhouette of your drawing or painting does make a first difference where your artistic work is taking you. True, later turnings and revisions, setbacks and dead-end streets may still change the direction of your artwork or manuscript, and yet some of it has already been settled in style and method, next to some human idiosyncrasy that habit seems to take over more so than what we would like.

North American and Roman Catholic systematic theologian *J. J. Mueller* (Mueller 1984, 1988, 2007) together with pastoral theologian *Robert L. Kinast* (Kinast 1996, 1999, 2000) list some *nine* possible styles of contemporary theological method. From transcendental, existential, empirical to socio-phenomenological, from ministerial, spiritual, feminist, inculturation to practical, every possible route is open to be taken. *Rahner* and *Lonergan, Macquarrie* and *Tillich, Tracy* and *Meland, Schillebeeckx* and *Sobrino*, among others, represent the first crowd. *Patton* and the *Whiteheads, Cobb* and *Shea, Chopp* and *McFague, Schreiter* and *Bevans* or *Isasi-Diaz*, and *Arens* with *Browning*, again together with others, join the ranks in the second round.

As systematic and fundamental theologian *J.J. Mueller* (Mueller 1984) puts it, method is only and nothing more than a simple tool, and yet it is important to think for a moment why we are using this particular tool instead of another one:

> "A method is a tool. Like a good multi-purpose screwdriver, a method improves upon what weak fingers and fragile fingernails cannot do. A method extends our abilities, improves upon our limitations, reminds us of forgotten procedures, and allows others to see how we arrived at our conclusions . . . Method is not something that we reflect on as such; usually we concern ourselves with finding solutions to immediate problems. But whenever we ask ourselves how we arrived at the answer, then we are raising the method question." (Mueller 1984, 1)

And yet, method is at the same time more than just a simple tool, betraying already our particular coloring in systematic or fundamental theology. As such method could be looked at as a *mini-theology* or a three-minute movie preview *in nuce* of what we really believe in and what is important to us. Not surprisingly then, method in the *history of theology* has a way to reveal radical changes in the way theology has been and is being done. A simple comparison of old and new methods can be just as revealing about the latest *paradigm changes* (Küng and Tracy 1989, Küng 1988, Sedmak 2002) in theology as reading a whole book.

In the words again of Jesuit systematic theologian *J. J. Mueller*, recounting the various *changes in method* just over the last few centuries, thereby pointing to the most obvious and radical changes in the way theology nowadays is being done:

> "In the past, systematic theology was uniform in method. Scripture, for instance, was used to support the teachings (doctrines and dogmas). Scripture appeared as a proof text and not something to be studied for itself. At the end of the nineteenth century, the philosophy of Thomas Aquinas and the Scholastics who followed him was virtually the only acceptable basis for theology. In the first half of the twentieth century, historical investigations unearthed a variety of differences within Thomism itself and opened up the possibility of diversity as part of the Catholic Christian tradition. By the time of Vatican II, the recognition of a plurality of methods arrived. The 1970's was a decade of books on method which indicated a new transition in how theology was done. Indeed, a real change was taking place that will have far-reaching consequences for theology both in this century and in the one to come." (Mueller 1984, 2)

Radical pluralism as a result of an ongoing critical reflection on the way theology is being done is only one visible and obvious aspect of the modern-day situation in theological method. Another one is the irruption and new appearance of *different and other voices* in the theological open arena. Feminist, black, hispanic, Asian, Native, gay, lesbian, and other voices are now speaking their own words in formulating theological method.

Context, Lived Experience, and Practical Action

A New Way of Doing Theology

Common to all of these *newer* and *older ways* in reflecting theological method in North America today is a critical awareness and a new sensitivity for the *specific contexts, lived experience*, and the importance of *practical action* for theology to be relevant. Across the various and many plural methodologies, one finds a common denominator in the way theology nowadays is being developed, imaging the way most people think in real life anyway.

Robert L. Kinast (Kinast 1996, 1999, 2000), North American and Roman Catholic pastoral theologian at the *Center for Theological Reflection*

The Community of the Weak

in *Indian Rocks Beach, Florida*, and influenced by *David Tracy's* model of a *mutually critical correlation* between *classical text* and *modern context* in systematic theology (Tracy 1975–1994, on David Tracy see McEnhill and Newlands 2004, 263–266), resumes the state of the art in thinking about the way people normally think in practical as well as theological terms:

> "*Theological reflection* has become the term for a distinct form of theologizing that has emerged over the last twenty-five years. Yet the term itself does not reveal very much about this form of theologizing. The word theo-*logy* implies some type of reflective activity, while the object of theological reflection—God—is an all-encompassing topic . . . The distinctiveness of this form of theologizing is better suggested by other terms that are sometimes uses—*contextual theology, experiential theology, praxis theology*. Theological reflection works out of specific contexts rather than working with generic truths. It draws upon lived experience as much as classic texts. It aims at practical action, not theoretical ideas. Its distinctiveness is further conveyed by the several sources that have contributed to its development—Latin American liberation theology, feminist theology, Black and Hispanic/Latino theology, catechetical theology, clinical pastoral education, spiritual renewal and ecumenical dialogue . . . What all these sources and synonyms have in common is a deceptively simple threefold movement. It begins with the lived experience of those doing the reflection; it correlates this experience with the sources of the Christian tradition; and it draws out practical implications for Christian living. On the surface this is a natural, commonsense way of functioning. It reflects the way most people think practically." (Kinast 2000, 1–2)

What may appear rather simplistic, easy, and even self-evident is not so self-consciously being made aware of in other academic contexts. A comparison of continents may be revealing again.

Theology in an *open classroom*, letting the world *come in* like fresh and moving air after opening the surrounding windows, is a theological concept *European contexts* are still mostly unfamiliar with, at least in many academic teaching places. *Lectures* are still considered the most important teaching form for imparting the basics, with *seminars* and *papers* as the only places of dialogue to exchange impressions over topics, and *general exams* the final proof for curricular learning in a postmodern world.

Context, lived experience, and *practical action* most often will have to wait for most of the extended curricular course of personal and social time until sometime afterwards, when studies are over, assignments written, curricula run through, papers finished, exams passed, knowledge acquired. Whether, however, as Pueblo priest and clan chief *Santiago Rosetta* ponders, you have already understood how to dance, if you have never danced yourself, remains an open *curricular question* (Pinar, Reynolds, Slattery, Taubman 1995a, 660).

Open Learning in a Global World

European academic teaching and learning has still, in spite of encouraging theoretical concepts, practical models, well-researched experiments, and experiential wisdom on *renewed forms* in *adult education* and *self-determined living learning* (on self-directed open learning Hinte 1980, 1990, on subjective learning Kösel 1993, on alternative postmodern adult and university learning Arnold/Schüssler 1998, English and Hill 1994, Usher, Bryant and Johnston 1997, Jarvis 2004) remained in *basic structure* and form, delivery, class activity, out-of-class tutorials and learning experiences, for the most part *conservative* and very minimally *experimental* (for a fundamental critique of German university education as non-experimental Arnold/Schüssler 1998, 49–62, Hof 2009).

In this *postmodern world*, however, we seem to live in an educationally and experientially *open world*, accessible to all as *real*, a world of ever increasing knowledge where according to calculations of the *Brooks Foundation* at *Stanford University* in *Palo Alto, California*, from the year 1800 to the middle of the 20th century the bulk of human knowledge has multiplied by ten times and the amount of accessible knowledge in this world is doubled every five years as the educational story of the human race goes on (for these figures Arnold/Schüssler 1998, 65). In the 15th century the educational elite in Europe could limit current knowledge to maybe a thousand books, nowadays each year about six million publications are produced globally, 17000 each day. Every five minutes a new medical discovery is made, every three minutes a new physical connection is uncovered, and in every minute a new chemical formula is invented (Arnold/Schüssler 1998, 65).

University teaching and learning in such an ominously limitless and *global world* will need a new vision of *empowering global learning* opening itself to the *outside* and to the *margins* of classical places of academic teaching and learning (on university learning in global, new, and open experimental places Arnold/Schüssler 1998, 49–62, 120–132). As German educational researchers *Rolf Arnold* and *Ingeborg Schüssler* put it

(Arnold/Schüssler 1998), criticizing most European university teaching, academic educational knowledge needs to move away from a simple and one-dimensional *storage knowledge (Speicherwissen)* to a more holistic and global approach of *methodological (Methodenwissen)*, *reflective (Reflexionswissen)*, and *personal (Persönlichkeitswissen)* knowledge (Arnold/Schüssler 1998, 59–60, also Hof 2009).

Didactically, this has clear structural consequences for the way academic teaching and learning is commonly organized. Learning in this postmodern age will need to become more *self-determined, experiential, living, open, imaginative,* and *life-long* (Greene 1995, Ayers and Miller 1998, Ayers 2001, 2004a, 2004b, hooks 2003, Hof 2009) even in academic lecture halls and seminar rooms, opening up university doors and celebrity halls of fame to a new kind of creative *learning culture* that lets the world come in.

Human learning (Kösel 1993, Holzkamp 1995, Arnold/Schüssler 1998, Hof 2009) will turn into a *creative flow* (Csikszentmihalyi 1990, 1993, 1996) of subjective interacting with others and the fully environing human *globe*, exploring the world on our own. Such living learning crosses boundaries and *deconstructs* classical structures of educational teaching and learning (Arnold/Schüssler 1998, 62), moving away from traditional concepts of teaching and learning as ready-made product manufactured to be received. A *pedagogy* of opening up *possibilities* (Arnold/Schüssler 1998, 120–132, Simon 1992, hooks 2003, Ayers 2004a-b, McLaren 1995, 2005 Giroux 1990, 1997, 2011) is *subject-oriented* (Kösel 1993, Holzkamp 1995, Arnold/Schüssler 1998, Hof 2009), starting with the *subjective*, the *experiential*, the *personal.*

Learning How to Dance While Walking with Your Feet

Experiential learning in this *open curriculum way—the curriculum* being *the way*—could learn from the educational vision of *Brazilian* and Roman Catholic *Clodovis Boff* in his *feet-on-the-ground theology* (Boff 1987), written while walking *on foot* on his five-month missionary journey through western Brazil and its jungle, meeting rubber-gatherers, children, women, farmers, and other faces under God's open sky. Here theology suddenly has a face, a name, a place, a smell, a time, a taste. Theology as fundamental and foundational theology *walking along* "over the fertile earth. An earthy theology, like a stretch of land pregnant with the seeds of future life" (Boff 1987, xi).

Poetic language accompanying the way, as *Clodovis Boff* invites theology to a new kind of *methodological dance*:

> "'Feet-on-the-ground', in the first place, because this is a theology moving along over the fertile earth. An earthy theology, like a stretch of land pregnant with the seeds of future life . . . 'Feet-on-the-ground', secondly, because this theology is worked out first with the feet. This sort of theological thinking starts with the feet, moves through the whole body, and rises to the head. There are some things you can grasp only by going there and seeing for yourself. This theology says what it has seen and heard as it moved about in the midst of the people . . . Finally, 'feet-on-the-ground' means that it takes into account the life of those who go around with their feet on the ground. Of those who live on the rock bottom of history, the poor and the oppressed. Those who have been knocked down on the ground, but who keep getting up. A theology of the poor, worked out with them, one that is theirs." (Boff 1987, xi–xii)

This is *theological music* people can dance to, starting with your tapping and slip-sliding feet, rhythms moving up your whole body, melodiously rising to your head. At the same time it is a most *fundamental theological statement* about a different kind of *method* in the way theology can be done. As such a challenge, a wake-up call, a prompting vision to open some closed doors and locked-up academic rooms in need of some fresh air moving in. Learning how to dance while walking with your feet may be a new way of describing *fundamental theology*.

Theological Education Reconsidered

Feet-on-the-ground theology may be a challenge to *systematic theology* in many ways in these postmodern times. Most definitely it is a reminder that *systematic theology in the twentieth and twenty-first century* does not necessarily have to be written in only *one particular form*. The *variety of species* and colors, art forms and literary styles, poetic liberties and musical likes and dislikes (Sedmak 2002, 11) may need to be expanded a little bit, even in old continental *Europe* where the first and as it seems *most lasting genres* in classical forms of *theological reflection* seem to have their educational home of origin (Farley 1983, Muller 1991, Kelsey 1993, Bayer 1994, Sedmak 2002, Mueller 2007).

The Community of the Weak

The debate on *theological education* and its possible *new forms* is only just now being opened, most recently again in pioneering ways in the *United States* (Wheeler and Farley 1991, Chopp 1995a, Banks 1999, Hodgson 1999, Jones and Paulsell 2002), but with challenging repercussions also for an old home continent. A more open dialog between the continents of all places in this world could open up a new vision for contemporary theology in its academic and local context. The *postmodern variety* of many forms in the way people all over the globe *do and live theology* (Sedmak 2002, Mueller 2007) will have to become the generally accepted ground rule in this dialog.

Basic curriculum decisions, questions of modern teaching methods, new technologies of Internet and Intranet, the diversion and dissemination of knowledge, information, and learning on a global scale, as well as the fact that human learning in postmodern times will no longer be able to be channeled in only *one particular educational way*, will have far-reaching consequences for theology in general and its educational transmission in particular. This will make discussions on the *future of theological education* in a *global context* most interesting, and most pertinent.

Method and *curriculum* in *theological education* (Pinar, Reynolds, Slattery, Taubman 1995a) has a lot to do with *first decisions* in *fundamental theologies* as to what is ultimately *fundamental* and *ground-laying* in considering the new architectural form of a future kind of systematic theology. That new buildings will be built is most certain. That new architectural styles and experiments will be tried out is to be expected. *Fundamental theology* has the privilege to be that kind of an academic discipline where such basic questions can be asked and played with while the music goes on.

A Fundamental Theology of Method Flowing

Context, lived experience, and *practical action* (Kinast 2000, 1) are the new thematic *summary words* of North American systematic theology today. In a rather summary way one could say that most debates and discussions, battles and proposals, revisions and retrievals in North American systematic theology of these days are somehow centering in one way or another around these few basic and fundamental *root words*. This can be upheld both for those engaging battles encouraging further elaborating on these new fundamentals, as well as for those openly or secretly developed rebuttals in outright disapproval of any such revisioning attempts. Transference and counter-transference work both directional ways even in the human as well as theological or analytical soul.

As such, there could be a new kind of *fundamental theology* developed from these words. Clarifying, circumscribing, deepening and expanding while focusing on these *basic associative words* may open up a whole new panoramic view on what the entrance door for a new kind of systematic theology in the *twenty-first century* could be.

In the *moving* and *flowing*, meandering and resting, rushing and running *dynamics of theology* (Haight 2001), another word of North American and Jesuit fundamental theologian *Roger Haight* to describe *fundamental theology* (Haight 2001, 1), the images of movement, life, event, source, water, river, lake, ocean, wind, storm, and waves may give a more dynamic sense of what could be considered basic nurture and nature in theology. From this, the often more sedentary and sedimentary discipline of *fundamental theology* (O'Collins 1981, O'Donovan and Sanks 1989, Dulles 1992, Schüssler Fiorenza 1984, Fries 1996, Muller 2001), suggesting some firmly erected *basement images* of cemented and sedimented stability, could maybe even be re-imagined and re-drawn on canvas a bit more *poetically* (for a more poetic fundamental theology Wetherilt 1994, Haight 2001, Mueller 2007).

To have God stay *in movement* (Wetherilt 1994, 147–149) and *fundamental theology* thereafter, is one creative and poetic concern of North American feminist theologian *Ann Kirkus Wetherilt* (Wetherilt 1994), trying to get away from the static rigidity of *the Word* and old and used words and images that have become lifeless. Instead, she encourages *fundamental theologies*, while listening to the various echoes of God, to become more dynamic and poetic:

> "A theological metaphor of a static and unitary Word cannot incorporate the voices of God that echo in the lives of diverse beings and the earth on which they live. The written text, and its successor, electronic data storage, will contribute to voicing God in the world to the extent that those who generate such texts understand their voices to be but one expression of revelation. In the midst of the day-to-day lives of multiple communities and individuals, and especially in their relationships with one another, God is voiced through struggle and celebration, self-defense and education, spirited worship and birthing a baby, writing poetry and planting maize." (Wetherilt 1994, 149)

The Community of the Weak

Ann Kirkus Wetherilt's poetic images for a new kind of fundamental theology could easily join company with words of *Tillichian* Jesuit and fundamental theologian *Roger Haight*:

> "Theology must consistently appeal to the experience of contemporary culture and ask: What can this symbol possibly mean today? What should it mean? How can it illumine and empower Christian life? Responding to these questions involves a free, imaginative, and creative enterprise, one that constantly tries to create a new language that moves from within contemporary culture and discloses the meaning of the tradition to it. Only a free and creative imagination can responsibly preserve the meaning of tradition in new situations." (Haight 2001, 234)

Roman Catholic *Avery Dulles* (Dulles 1992), no suspect for giving up the basic fundamentals in theology, encourages systematic and fundamental theologians to become post-critical, innovative, and creative, in touch with the *tacit dimensions* of the Christian faith that allow for new ways to look at things:

> "Postcritical theology, aware of the tacit dimension, avoids the rationalism of critical and counter-critical apologetics ... It does not seek to argue people into faith by indisputable evidence. On the other hand, it avoids the fideism that substitutes emotion or blind choice for cognition in the sphere of religion. The postcritical theologian points to the necessity of conversion as a self-modifying act that enables one to look at the world with new eyes." (Dulles 1992, 13–14)

Conversion as a self-modifying act that lets us see the world and the people around us in a different and new light is *holistic, actional,* and *aesthetic* all in one, integrating our natural environment, who we are in the midst of others, what we have experienced so far, and how we may be encouraged to act in the future.

Creativity is another word for this kind of a *conversion* and *social transformation* (on social transformation, creativity, and conversion in practical fundamental theology Lamb 1982) necessary for a new kind of systematic theology. It is like a new birth in a new way of looking at the world. There is noting static about it. It is fluid, flushing down like water, always changing while integrating new experiences and imaginative pictures into a flow of collecting personal narratives. It is more than just an informative change in cognitive thinking or a concluding closure of an argumentative mathematical proof line. It brings together our human context, lived experience, and practical action in an act of *new faith* and hopeful *prophetic imagination* (Jennings 1976, Fischer 1983, Chopp 1995a, 108–110, Brueggemann 1978, 2001).

Seeing the world with *new eyes* is more than just getting the math exercise or the multiple-choice exam of dogmatics right. It may change your whole life, or at least help you to survive your whole life. As *Rebecca S. Chopp* puts it: "Imagination, the ability to think the new, is an act of survival" (Chopp 1995a, 108).

North American Theology in Context, Experience, and Action

Contemporary North American systematic theology seems to be circling around these three attracting *new words*: *context, lived experience*, and *practical action* (Kinast 2000, 1). The assigning of first importance, the artist's decision what to put in the spotted foreground and what to place in the shaded background, the haphazard mixing of all three, with sometimes here, and sometimes there a new *café mélange* being served each time, is up to each individual author or collective of authors, but the ingredients seem to stay.

Even as miniature a *clash of theological civilizations* as the one most intensely being fought in North American theology today between *postliberals* (Lindbeck 1984, Hauerwas 1983, Placher 1989, 1994, 2001, Webster, Tanner, and Torrance 2009) and *revisionist theologies* (Tracy 1975–1994, Hodgson 1994, Chopp and Taylor 1994, Jennings 1976–2003, Jones and Lakeland 2005) could be artistically placed somehow and somewhere in this semantic triangle with different locations for each position in place. Whether in *transferal* acceptance in coming nearby and getting close or in *counter-transferal* rejection in moving away and finding one's distance, somehow North American systematic theology still seems to gravitate around an indefinable center with three corners.

David G. Kamitsuka (Kamitsuka 1999), teaching at *Oberlin College*, presents an encouraging vision of possible future *inter-movement engagement* between these still fighting *co-inhabitants* of a postmodern theological world in a triangular playground:

> "Although there are many differences among liberation, postliberal and revisionary perspectives on a spectrum of methodological and constructive issues, I have suggested some ways in which to recast those differences so as to open trajectories for fruitful future intermovement engagement. Each movement's

The Community of the Weak

> approach has its strengths and weaknesses, its insights and oversights. I have tried to draw from what I believe are the strengths and insights of each in order to formulate proposals for theological practice better able to respond to contemporary culture's ecclesial, intellectual and social challenges."
> (Kamitsuka 1999, 173)

Even here, in a hopeful vision of new coalitions across the dividing lines, we find the common *triangular ground* of the basic necessity to formulate a theological practice, to respond to an environing culture, and to integrate all this in a personal and communal faith response within a particular social context.

Context may be the near or far ecclesial community and the intratextual biblical world for some, the social and cultural location of one's neighborhood for others. But both will need to listen to what historical sciences, social sciences, cultural studies, literary studies, people's history, deep ecology, social constructivism, and postmodern geography will tell.

Lived experience may be the cultural-linguistic narratives of personal and communal faith for some, the biographical, ethnographical, and geographical memories and life (his)stories for others. But both sides on the dividing line will need to listen to feminist theory, American studies, postmodernism, poststructuralism, critical psychology, and postcolonial history.

Practical action may be liturgical, intra-communal, missional, and diaconal for some, political, social, emancipatory, and transformative for others. Both, however, across all artificially constructing dividing lines, will need to listen to political science, critical theory, social analysis, community organization, critical pedagogy, postmodern organization theory.

Finding Answers to Simple Questions

Context has to do with the simple question in what kind of a *natural environment*, nature and neighborhood, social network and housing project, friends and enemies, morning sunset and evening ocean strip, junk-yard and high-security building, garbage street and high-class jet-set you live, asking the initial question on *who we are*, where we come from, who our friends are, where we live, what skin color we have, what gender, sexual, or musical preference we have, what kind of a job we have or don't have, how rich or poor we are, what we like and what we don't like, what we have and what we don't have, and where we have finally landed and settled in on our own and most personal life curriculum. The intelligent guess will be that your *systematic theology* will turn out accordingly.

Lived experience has to do with everything so far and even more. It tells your own and *most personal story*. Where you were born, who your mom and dad are, if you have mom and dad. Who your siblings are. Where you grew up in. What schools you went to, or did not go to. If you know how to read. Who your first boyfriend or girlfriend was. What your first job was. When you lost your job last. Where you got knocked down. What your first life breakdown was with everything seeming to fall apart, if you ever had such a thing. When and where you got your first degrees, diplomas, accreditation. What you have and have not seen and heard and felt and run up against in life so far. Exhilarating peek moments, moving sunsets, touching looks, upsetting images, resting secrets, excruciating soul pain, public glamour, civic shame, accompanied tragedies, lived with beauties, broken up relationships. Again an intellectual guess is that all this too will make a difference the way you write *systematic theology*.

And finally, *practical action* has to do with everything that makes people *move* and *act* on what they have learned in their own life curriculum. Theology in particular has a renown history of leaving words sit and wait. To act on what you say and witness to, to let yourself be moved and transformed by people, words and images, concepts and theologies. To join others in dreaming up a better world. To let your words resonate in what you actually do and speak up for, mingle in and risk your reputation for. To join in with a peace demonstration, a housing project, a civic hall public debate, a letter to the editor, a protest march, a peace brigade, a nature protection activity. To let your words take form and color, smell and taste, shape and momentum, a face and a name, a place and a time that actually makes it look like that you *act on what you preach and teach*. All this, and more, so the repeated guess is, will change the way you do, live, and write your *systematic theology*.

North American systematic theology in these days claims that *context*, *lived experience*, and *practical action* do make a difference in the way you write your theology. The following parts of this dissertation will show whether this claim can be upheld unreservedly.

Issues of *power* and *powerlessness* shape fundamental *methods*. This can be seen most visibly in the *fundamental paradigmatic changes* in North American systematic theology in these days. Method has changed North American systematic theology *from the bottom up* in most radical ways, looking in different directions, taking other routes, meeting other people than used to be the academic case. Now *new people, new places, new voices* are moving into the center of the theological stage. A *change in method* leads to a *change in theology* as well, be it systematic, fundamental, dogmatic, ethical, pastoral, and practical.

Method is *the way* people take to learn about life. The *curriculum* is a way through life. In theology as well. *Choices in curriculum* are choices about life and the way we take through life. On the way, following the curricular path, we may meet people here and there. Depending on *where we live*, who we meet, with whom we congregate—our *social place and location* and the *vision* in which we experience both (on social location in theology Müller 1999, 63–66)—our way through life will be *different*. To become aware of this, is already a question of looking at your own *power* or *powerlessness* in life, and where you stand with others, *methodologically* and *theologically*, in the distribution of both.

REFLECTION

I used to think theology had a lot to do with words and books. Foremost, one book. But ultimately, while browsing through thousands of books as Christian faith is increasingly looking like a religion of books, students do get the slowly dawning impression that theology and all its aftermath—lectures, seminars, papers, dissertations, publications—has a lot to do with books. And lots of words.

It used to be that theology was thinking about the Word. From there, many words followed. Primary was, so students were taught, the given word. Everything had started with the utterance of some creative word, calling the world into existence, calling the harbinger of good news to speak his many and touching words. After this, everything else turned out to be a footnote.

It seems as if theology is in love with words. Over centuries the same old words multiplied endlessly not just from the pulpit, lectern, or television preaching desk. Words here and there everywhere. Every Sunday morning or evening throughout the whole entire world words preached, proclaimed, exposited, declared. Words sung, read, written, preached, typed, engraved, digitalized. Solemn words. Memorable phrases, repeated idioms. A proliferation of endless word production all along a history of Christian faith in the course of more now than two-thousand years.

Real Life

After almost twenty-eight years of pastoral ministry I am getting wary of words. Or just simply tired. Solemn proclamations here, pontifical declarations there. Theological paper work all around me. Magazines, church minutes, local press declarations, synod presentations, church board preparatory documentation, regional ecclesiastical social statements, national conference mission summaries, global ethical purpose guidelines. A proliferation of digital or ink-jet or old-style typewriter paperwork all over the theological and informational globe. Theology turning into gigabytes and megabytes in an information-overloaded world.

Looking back, however, I realize how little words alone have changed me. Words can come and go. Words can be overheard, muffled, forgotten, deleted, put in storage, classified, shelved, left on the counter, in the library, on a closed computer screen from which you can walk away.

Experience, however, has another quality and intensity. Experience is what stays with you even when you go on. Even when you try to forget, even when you turn off your screen or reformat your memory board. Experience is that which cannot be erased or written over it. Experience is like a scar that does not go away.

In this experience is more than experiment or simple and tactile sensation for a short while. In a short-lived day and age too many things are considered experiential that only last so long until the next flash of impressions and download of overload information hits you. Experience has more of an in-depth quality that keeps you remembering even after things and impressions, moments and flashes have passed. Experience is that which writes in your soul and body and cannot be erased because it has become part of you.

There are many moments and memories that have become part of me like that. Some of my first memories have to do with experiences in my childhood. My first friendship with soccer team colleagues playing in the neighborhood and speaking French. Even before I went to school at the age of seven I got a taste for what it means to listen and not recognize your own language. Later on I vividly remember that moment with a tenant in the house of my mom standing outside of our door and calling my mom all kinds of names that men in a town like ours obviously used to call single mothers in the 60's and 70's. I also remember listening around the age of eleven to anonymous phone calls getting even more explicit and sexually violent. I even found the

245

The Community of the Weak

tape I had made of all this as I was cleaning up my mom's place after she had died recently. Somehow it inscribed a particular kind of sensitivity in me to watch for those who get hurt.

Life went on, and joy and pain kept writing further and cyclical short stories. Cyclical in the sense of an eternal return of similar and already known themes and forms that get repeatedly engraved or drilled into the ground of your soul creating a black hole ever more deep. One builds on the other or drills even deeper using the already existent hole. Faces and times change, places and moments vary, but themes reoccur and add on to the already existing pattern deepening conviction, outrage, and marvel.

When I was seventeen or eighteen I wanted to become a pastor looking for the scum of society. Drug addicts, alcoholics, the homeless and other marginal people. Those marginal ones that were treated like my mom and others I got to know in the course of my further life curriculum as a child of a single mom in a society that frowned upon such people like my mom. At the time it was reading David Wilkerson's book The Cross and the Switchblade. I had decided I wanted to be a pastor like him.

Almost twenty years later, being in pastoral ministry in a midsized village near a larger city back in Switzerland, I turned out to be just that in the cyclical nature of human experience letting Paulo Freire's generative themes in one's personal life and story reappear. Not even so much out my own choice, more by human tragedy and necessity, I turned out to become the drug pastor of a whole region, known and ultimately famous or infamous for taking sides with those who got and get treated like shit at any human telephone. In the year 1993 a 14-year-old confirmation kid in my class died because of a heroin overdose at an open drug dealing place a few miles away. After that I started looking after those marginal ones I already had a life-long taste and feeling for what it might possibly mean. After years of subsequently highly disputed ministry, public slander, personal attacks, strategic maneuvers, political lobbying, ecclesiastical betraying, youth solidarity, and media celebrity, I got kicked out by a highly publicized public vote out of my eight years of local ministry.

Memories that will not go away. Almost three hundred teenagers, mostly still in school, sitting in a local Reformed church worshipping while mourning the death of a 14-year-old. The same teenagers then sitting outside afterwards and left alone, hardly

Real Life

any adults, no church community taking them in their arms or encircling them with a human embrace.

Months later, in the same local Reformed church, almost three hundred adults sitting again in the same benches. This time, for most of them, a more than two-hour witch hunt against a local pastor to be burned. As intruding outsiders and observing guests on the balcony more than seventy teenagers who had come to show their solidarity with a local pastor after a demonstration outside of the church doors. In the meantime, more than seventy teenagers and others having to watch some of the adult Church members of a church no longer worthy its name acting like this place and space, time and moment, was no church anymore.

Memories that stay like scars. Still every moment present and visible, alive and as if just happening yesterday. Like those sunset moments sitting at a mountain lake somewhere in Southern Germany with another 14-year-old teenager telling the first time in honesty that he too is taking heroin. Then, weeks of presence, absence, runaways, closed homes, legal search warrants, and finally being put away in a youth home that saves his life. Years later still, while meeting the teenager now grown to be an adult, deep moments of remembering those special times, little moments, moving turns, funny episodes, upsetting unknowns.

In contrast, another moment of memory and eternal return, as churches and church officials seem to return a lot on themselves. An official church hearing in the presence of opponents and friends, kids and adults, lawyers and clerks, tape-decks and paperwork, accusations and rebuttals, 15-minute statements and counter-statements. A 17-year-old youth taking the defense of a local pastor while shaking, shivering, moving, trembling. A trembling voice trying to say something personally meaningful und heartfelt in the midst of administrative meaninglessness and heartlessness. At the end, words not really heard, a trembling unrecognized, a plea of defense overridden, put aside, termed irrelevant. After this, a whole community in public war for the next four years, with kids and adults collecting signatures, writing letters, calling in meetings, speaking their own fragile words. All to no avail. A whole community in the end unredeemed and torn apart by one public helpless vote.

Several months later. Two confirmation teenagers who just got confirmed looking for a local pastor who had just been kicked out. On their bikes, two 16-year old girls trying to find a pastor and show some concern. Over the same period of several months that these girls had been looking all over for a pastor, no other pastor colleague, female and male, of a whole region had ever taken up the telephone to try to find out how it is and how it feels to be a famous but kicked out pastor.

Some years later. Actually several years later. Five days after September 11 in the year 2001. The Twin Towers of the World Trade Center had just fallen on television screen only a few days earlier. On the 16th of September the highly publicized photographs and TV-news spots of an impressive and colorful, lively and musical human peace chain across a city neighborhood on a Sunday afternoon. A neighborhood looked at by some as the Bronx of Zurich, by others as one of the most multi-cultural hotchpotch places around, and again by others as a sleeping-town suburbia of Zurich. Almost nine hundred people had gathered to join and give hands.

Africans, Asians, Americans, Swiss, Jews, Buddhists, Muslims, Hindus, Christians, Roman Catholics, Protestants, atheist, believers, artists, journalists, kids, youth, babies, seniors, women, men, country musicians from the US, visual artists from Swiss mountain areas, a black-and-white-mixed Roman-Catholic and Protestant Gospel choir singing old spirituals in the Roman Catholic sanctuary. The local bishop speaking words of greetings and concern after September 11. Buddhists, Jews, Muslims, and Christians speaking short messages about a culture of peace desperately needed also after September 11.

The project had started a long time before September 11. Beginning in the year 2000, planned as an opening symbolic and political, cultural and artistic sign for the just started Decade for a Culture of Peace against Violence of the United Nations and the World Council of Churches proclaimed for the years 2001–2010, the human chain for peace had been projected and planned already months before. Preceding the actual public act an exhibition in several public and ecclesiastical places opened the theme with drawings and paintings of children showing the realities of war over the last sixty years or more since the Spanish civil war in Europe. Nagasaki, Hiroshima, Vietnam, Auschwitz, Rwanda, El Salvador, Afghanistan. Drawings were hanging down right in front of the waiting lines of a local post office or in the windows of some local senior home.

Real Life

> *The human peace chain, reaching in distance almost a whole kilometer, was to be the grand finale. Children's drawings were accompanying the artistic energy released through the actual invitation to all age-groups in view of the human peace chain to produce and draw, paint and sketch artistic peace flags in the Tibet-tradition in an unlimited creative way. On that particular Sunday, with television cameras present, newspaper journalists on the spot, radio speakers reporting, peace flags in all colors and forms were connecting kids, youth, and seniors, Jews and Arabs, Christians and atheist, artists and house wives.*
>
> *At the end, two US country singers, having taken one of the first airlines out of Atlanta after September 11, singing to a multitude of a highly mixed peace chain audience, with a title song on 'Hands in Hands' especially composed for that particular day.*
>
> *Various experiences retold, relived while writing about it one more time, as if it needed to be retold over and over again. Many more experiences that could be added. All of them shaping, influencing, changing, rattling, upsetting, soothing, reframing, translating, transforming my most personal theology. What I think today would not be the same without these images of memory. What I believe or play with believing in old and new ways in theology would not be the same without these moments of standstill and movement, breakdown and recovery, beauty and ugliness, violence and tenderness, magnitude and solitude, sunset sitting and mourning sermon, musical tune and artistic flag.*
>
> *Theology after all these experiences and many more had changed and is still continuing to change. Experiences like these and others speak a louder word and language, speech and lecture, presentation and proclamation, sermon and simple message than most silent books. Experiences like these and others give you and your systematic theology the color you have.*

A Fundamental Theology of Experience

Power and Experience

Power and *powerlessness* are most often moments you *experience*, not books you talk about. The *poor* experience power and powerlessness in those moments when reality breaks apart and living becomes difficult. The *abused* experience power and powerlessness in the bruises of physical or psychological violence that nobody takes at heart. Teenagers at the age of 14 taking heroin in some local village in Switzerland in the 1990's experience power and powerlessness in the distribution of *exclusion and embrace* (Volf 1996), either finding a place to be, or chased around from one social space to the next. *Children at war* experience power and powerlessness in the death of their life dreams, *women* experience power and powerlessness in the social security office treating them as special. *Nature*, cultures, cities, habitats experience power and powerlessness when humans stomp over them and destroy every part of it.

North American systematic theology in a *social and postmodern age* (Haight 2001, Mueller 2007, Rieger 2007, Taylor 1990, 2011) has become most sensitive to these experiences of *power* and *powerlessness*. Experience itself has become the most important theme in fundamental, systematic, ethical, and practical theology. Experience lies at the bottom of all our human walking. *Following Jesus on the way* in *radical discipleship as theology* (McClendon 1986, 1990, 1994, 2000, 2002, Augsburger 2006) first and foremost takes seriously the experiences of people. The experiences of the poor, the socially excluded, the suffering, the left-alone, the broken, the aching. *North American systematic theology* in these days has developed a special hearing for these silent and loud, powerful and powerless voices *out of experience.*

Experience First

Experience, that most particular and *personal coloring* of *who we are* and have become, shapes or rattles, confirms or rejects, revises or deepens, turns over or sets into new place any conceptual theology, whether we want it or not. Bringing our own most personal experience into the conversation with theological tradition, in the words of Roman Catholic and feminist theologian *Ann O'Hara Graff* (O'Hara Graff 1995), is like "walking into the dark, the unexplored worlds in which we have lived, but not fully, because they have not borne their proper names. Now, as we name our experience more adequately, we bring its truthfulness into the arena of interpretation" (O'Hara Graff 1995, 84–85).

Experience is like a *new-born child* in need of a *name*. Birth is first, naming second. Experience is primary, interpreting follows, even though in the course of life's messy mix of interpreting and experiencing both may get mixed up once and a while, letting interpreting take the lead, while experience follows.

Dealing with our most personal experience by *naming* and *interpreting* it is both *prophetic* and *mystic*, clarifying and silencing, making things clearer and letting the dark take over again. Therefore, there is no simple and linear movement from experience to interpretation and back, as if experience only provides the raw material for following dissection and analysis to lift all secrets.

To quote *Ann O'Hara Graff*, as she expounds the interchange between human experience and our attempt to make sense of what experience may want to tell us in and through our own interpretations. She describes this mutual walk as a prophetic and mystic way entailing also a personal risk of having to change or become new:

> "With it we walk into the dark again, where we will see God, Jesus the Christ, life, death, resurrection, sin, grace, holiness, humanity, earth and mystery in new light. As it is a prophet's journey, so also is it a mystic's way, because we must risk the many new faces of our God when we tell the truth of ourselves as best we can." (O'Hara Graff 1995, 85)

Life and its *accompanying experiences* that want to be understood are more *twirling*, spinning, and circling around a *mysterious center* holding both *experience* and *interpretation* together. At one time our most cherished convictions, coming out of long-time experiences, may be turned over by new experiences that call everything we have trusted in so far into question. At other times experiences startle us, make us uncomfortable and let us think a little afterwards within the *categories* and *concepts* we are used to in order to make sense of what we have just seen. Like seeing a gay evangelical couple leading bible study sometime late night in green-pastured Kentucky. The common categories of deep trust and faith in the same God we call gracious may actually help to understand.

At other times our old categories break open and maybe even break apart. *New experiences* make *new interpretations* possible, *new images, new categories*. This again is like a twirling *dance* moving into the unfamiliar while circling from, into, and out of our most personal experiences in conversation with our theological convictions and traditions. As *Ann O'Hara Graff* puts it in beautifully poetic imagery:

> "When we open new analogies, we touch the sacred nerve, the spine of hope and fear that leads from earth to heaven. Yet to be faithful to ourselves and to our God, we must allow our

analogies to break open and encircle us, to lead us in the dance, from, into and out of ourselves toward the riotous plenty that is God. We must risk the overmuch, trust the unfamiliar." (O'Hara Graff 1995, 85)

Embracing the Musical Side of Theology—By Playing It

There may be hundreds of plausible reasons in *theological education and writing* to put experience *back* and *last* on the reserve shelf of theological libraries, never taking a serious look at it as we delve into intellectual and literary grandiosity of all those giants in theological systems that have been presented to us in the course of our academic studies. In spite of it, *experience* stays and *plays with us* (Kane 2004), like the unintentional play of children discovering the world for the first time, as experience is *our first and most personal deep encounter with the world around us.*

Writer, singer, jazz-pop musician, consultant, activist, and social philosopher *Pat Kane* (Kane 2004) describes the seducing mystery of such a *play-ethic* in a postmodern world:

> "The puritans have been telling us since the Reformation that play is at best trivial, at worst demonic and at the very least *not work.* And if we use the word to describe the boundary-challenging, reality-defying, insanely optimistic, relentlessly experimental activity of children, then we usually think we know what we mean by 'play' . . . Play can be beautiful, silly, perplexing, simple, funny, surreal. It can be distracted or obsessed; and it always seems to slip away from the standard rules of measurement, through being either too inconsequential or too diffuse. But we usually trust that it has been *confined,* at least; kept to the margins of our competently functioning adult society. Play is something childish, something we have put behind us, and something we only allow ourselves to recover in moments of permissible excess . . . And when we do play—enjoying it, not regretting it, letting it take us over—we make our excuses. Surely, play is so exceptional, so beyond the everyday norm, that it can have only a temporary rather than a permanent effect. Surely this is where (and when) we're allowed to *break free* from the ethical, the humdrum—from the anxiety of 'how we should live our lives now.'" (Kane 2004, 3)

To put *experience first* is to *allow the world play with us* the way children allow the world to come in and play with it. It follows the human way and method how we get to know and discover this world around us. Maybe *theology*, in its ominous tendency to keep the world around us *out*, would be well-advised to let experience *come in* again.

Experience could be called the *sound of music* that fills the otherwise mostly silent pages in *academia's written form*. Systematic theology may be well-advised to become a little bit more musical by embracing its *poetic and artistic* side again, as it was initially in its long history (Sedmak 1999, 15–16). Letting some of the softer academic disciplines like poetry, biography, and the visual arts in their sounding music come in. Theology can be done in *many forms and colors* (Sedmak 2002, 11–13). "Theology is taught and written, danced and sung, sculpted and painted, even dreamed and cried" (Sedmak 2002, 11). It is high time therefore to let *the personal* in.

> "Theology is about truth, justice, hope, but finally and personally, it is about our Divine lover who chooses to love in us and in our midst. Our humble exploration of our experience is the music that continues to allow us to hear into the rich silence, the candle light that we hold in the great dark, as the God who alone is Holy dawns upon us." (O'Hara Graff 1995, 85)

Fundamental Theology Beginning with Experience

The fundamental and theological decision in *theological method* to put *experience first* is in no way so self-evident or unambiguous, as the history of ferocious and unending theological debates and battles shows. The thought that human experience in the form and shape of *my most personal story*, my history, memory, and life curriculum may have anything valuable to say in a systematic theology is hardly self-evident.

A recent *fundamental theology* in French (Neusch 2004) closes with a whole chapter on the traces and footprints of God in human experience, using the vivid image of *God preparing the way*, wading and strolling through our most *personal lives* (on traces of God in personal lives Neusch 2004, 217–237). Apart from that, most other *fundamental or systematic theologies* are more or less careful in talking about this highly ambiguous and most often embattled territory called human experience.

British systematic theologian *Alister McGrath* (McGrath 2001) describes in his treatment of *human experience* as possible *source* and beginning for *systematic theology* the reasons for a certain ambiguity in starting theology with experience:

> "'Experience' is an imprecise term. The origins of the word are relatively well understood: it derives from the Latin term *experientia*, which could be interpreted as 'that which arises out of traveling through life'. In this broad sense, it means 'an accumulated body of knowledge, arising through first-hand encounter with life.' When one speaks of 'an experienced teacher' or 'an experienced doctor', the implication is that the teacher or doctor has learned her craft through first-hand application . . . Yet the term has developed an acquired meaning, which particularly concerns us here. It has come to refer to the inner life of individuals, in which those individuals become aware of their own subjective feelings and emotions. It relates to the inward and subjective world of experience, as opposed to the outward world of everyday life." (McGrath 2001, 189)

Understood in this way, experience is described in a far too *individualistic manner*, leaving out all *social, cultural,* and *communal* aspects of what experience is participating in. Experience limited to the subjective inner world as over against the outward realities of a social and global *everyday life* (on a sociology of the everyday as social, cultural, and communal Smith 1987, Gardiner 2000) makes those skeptical voices reappear that have already relegated experiential beginnings in theology to the academic field of lyrics or poetics:

> "But, as Feuerbach emphasizes, human experience might be nothing other than experience of *ourselves*, rather than of God. We might simply be projecting our own experiences, and calling the result 'God', where we ought to realize that they are simply experiences of our own very human natures." (McGrath 2001, 196)

Experience reduced to the *inner world* of pure sentiment and emotion, feeling and impression, will be susceptible to *Alister McGrath's* and *Ludwig Feuerbach's* critique of religion, following clarion calls of *Karl Barth*, whatever one's theological orientation in *fundamental theology* may be. However, a more holistic and *social concept of human experience* calls theology back to the place from where it started, as theology has always been coming out of personal and social experiences all throughout its history.

> "Nevertheless, it must be appreciated that this concern with human experience is not something new; it can arguably be discerned in both Old and New Testaments, and it permeates the writings of Augustine of Hippo. Martin Luther declared

that 'experience makes a theologian', and argued that it was impossible to be a proper theologian without an experience of the searing and terrifying judgment of God upon human sin." (McGrath 2001, 191)

Theology coming out of our most *personal and social experiences* of human sin and human grace lives in a *social landscape made out of relationships, stories, mutual dwellings, and personal and social recollections*. Experience as the *starting point* in our theological beginnings is never simple, but complex and multi-faceted. Nevertheless, it lays the ground and basis from which all our theologies are built and developed.

Patchwork Experience as Social and Political

Human sin and divine judgment are always *social* as well as *personal*, including everything that makes us live in the here and now. Experience is like a *living web, social, communal,* and *cultural*. As such it is a *new social construction* (on social constructivism Burr 1995, Anderson 1997, Griffiths 1995, Kruks 2001, Hacking 2002) which the individual makes of his own world. In this personal world, everything is part of it, friends, enemies, the city, the village, personal history, communal stories, cultural habits, natural environments, political events, world economies. As such it is always an "explicitly political subjective experience" (Griffiths 1995, 72). Experience understood in this *postmodern* way (Anderson 1997, Eickelpasch und Rademacher 2004, 21–54) is no longer simple and easy, but rather messy and patchwork-like, while always *social* and *political*.

Feminist philosopher *Morwenna Griffiths* describes in her book *Feminism and the Self* (Griffiths 1995) this *learning from experience* (Griffiths 1995, 11–72) as a *social construction* of the *self* and its *identity* (for a sociology of identity and selves in postmodernity Eickelpasch und Rademacher 2004, Hacking 2002) taking the form of a *web* or *patchwork* centering around *autobiography* and *life story*:

> "I started the book with a metaphor of webs. I end with an extension of that initial metaphor, a metaphor of patchwork. My argument about the construction of self shows that, like patchwork, making a self is relatively easy, though it always takes time and attention. However, again like patchwork, making a good one is very hard indeed. Understanding which pieces of old cloth will fit into the whole is a difficult and painstaking matter. Like patchwork, the construction of an authentic, autonomous

self depends on the context of each fragment, and where it fits within the overall design. Like patchwork, it is hard to say how many makers there are and where all the pieces come from . . . Trying to reduce all our complexities of self-identity to relatively simple designs and simple stories, of the kind that mainstream philosophy tells, has resulted in inappropriate stories about ways in which to deal with our personal and collective dilemma. It is a simplicity which has contributed to sameness and oppression. Infinitely preferable is the variety, confusion, colour, hotchpotch, kaleidoscope, medley, motley, and harlequin of patchwork selves." (Griffiths 1995, 191)

Human experience may be determined and predetermined by many and various outside and *cultural-linguistic* languages and traditions (Lindbeck 1984), social habits and personal preferences, philosophical predilections and political options, musical styles and artistic tastes. The hotchpotch of outside and inside influences is unlimited. And yet, experience seems to be welcoming us *first* wherever we go, in spite of all our possible unconscious and conscious preconceptions and lived-in cultural traditions, developed prejudices and grown personal or social convictions.

The Personal in Fundamental Theology

Most readers and students in *Europe* will hardly find in *basic textbooks* on systematic or fundamental theology references to *personal experience, critical autobiography* (Griffiths 1995, 68–72), or the *social location* (in North America Herzog 1988, 1–22, in Switzerland Müller 1999, 63–66) of a particular fundamental or systematic theology. Systematic and fundamental theology is considered an academic endeavor, independent of concrete and everyday *personal references*. Apart from a few exceptions (Henning und Lehmkühler 1998, Gollwitzer 1998, Sölle 1995b, 1999b, Hasenhüttl 1985, Moltmann 1999, 2000, Küng 2002), the student will rarely know *who* is writing this kind of a systematic theology in *personal terms*.

Even *Jürgen Moltmann*, one of the more autobiographical systematic theologians, openly acknowledges to have given in to a common tendency to leave out an author's personal world in *academic writing*, reflecting on this in *epilegomena* (Moltmann 1999, 2000) after more than fifty years of prolific and personal writing (Moltmann 1959–2010):

"In this book, I have described the ways my own biography has given me entries into theology—in general, in my own person and in the community of the church and the university; and then in particular, access to the individual theological problems. I have described this process in the introductions to the various chapters, because I have come to see that the biographical dimension is an essential dimension of theological insight. As a student, admittedly, I failed to notice that the determining subject belongs to dogmatics. On the contrary, the pure objectivity of what was said was supposed to guarantee its verifiability at all times by everyone everywhere. It was therefore impossible to tell from the splendid books of my teachers who wrote them, and when, and where. And as the author's subjectivity withdrew, all relatedness to the time receded too. What was allegedly the *Zeitgeist*, 'the spirit of the age', was left to the journalists... It took me some time, and some effort of will, before—at the urging of my wife—I dared to say 'I' in theology too ... In the last thirty years I have come to see that it is much harder to communicate to other people *abstractions* drawn from one's own situation and biography than it is to communicate the concrete truth, however subjectively or contextually it may be formulated. Readers of a book want to know not only what the author has to say, but also how he or she arrived at it, and why they put it as they do." (Moltmann 2000, xviii-xix, 1999, 14–15)

To write *systematic theology* in such a way as "to guarantee its verifiability at all times by everyone everywhere" (Moltmann 2000, xviii) is simply an impossibility put in the context of a *global situation* of the *next Christendom* (Jenkins 2002, 2006). The biographical, the autobiographical, the local and social, the personal and communal will become more and more *the matrix* within which systematic theology will be written. *Context* and *situation* shape theology, one way, or another.

Context in Europe

Roman Catholic *Hans Waldenfels* (Waldenfels 2000) opens his introduction to *fundamental theology* with considerations on the *contextual nature* of all our theological thinking (Waldenfels 2000, 16–101), while at the same time reflecting on the future of theology in a *global world civilization* where the world has become *one world* (Waldenfels 2000, 66–70). Protestant Christian ethicist *Denis Müller* meditates in his theological ethics in a modern world on the *social location* of the theologian in a city like Lausanne in French-speaking Switzerland (Müller 1999, 63–66).

The Community of the Weak

Lutheran *Wilfried Härle* in his basic student textbook *Dogmatik* (Härle 2000) considers *context* as the contemporary *life world* of modern-day hearers of the Christian message (Härle 2000, 168–192), while at the same time rejecting a *contextual dogmatics* (Härle 2000, 181–183). The contemporary and day-to-day *life world* in Wilfried Härle's *Dogmatik* is both *everyday, subjective, historical*, and *present*. Information society, postindustrial divisions of labor, systems of insurances, and the accompanying personal feelings of partial security, wealth, but also the fear of loss, and the search for a fulfilled life, are the social and cultural indicators of a modern-day *social location* of contemporary systematic theology (Härle 2000, 184–190).

And yet, this *social location* as described remains rather *abstract*. The *life world* of many people in this global world takes on quite a different color, less abstract, living in the midst of wealth and poverty, digital overload and school illiteracy, peace and violence, employment and unemployment, personal success and social exclusion, public education and secretive child abuse, fulfilled life and absolute hunger in the midst of misery.

Systematic theology in the European context has not yet integrated the *contextual nature* of all our theological endeavor. *Personal experience, social location, cultural context, ethnographic writing, critical autobiography*, and *inter-cultural learning* are still only background topics in systematic theologies. An academic interest in *narrative theologies, biographical research*, and *ethnographic studies* in systematic theology is only at its beginning, mostly coming out of *feminist* and *practical* concerns (Klein 1994, 1998, Maassen 1993, Taube, Tietz-Buck und Klinge 1995, Kuld 1997, Gutmann 1995, 1998, Gössmann, Kuhlmann, Moltmann-Wendel, Praetorius, Schottroff, Schüngel-Straumann, Strahm und Wuckelt 2002).

Jürgen Moltmann, a life-long practitioner of a personal and academic style in theological thinking in close conversation with *worldwide and inter-cultural contexts*, has hopeful words, almost *prophetic*, about a different kind of *systematic and fundamental theology* in the *European context*:

> "At the beginning of the 1970s there was a theological movement in the United States which called for a 'narrative' theology (over against purely argumentative theology) and then, in the context of this narrative theology, went on to demand 'theology as biography' as well. In 1974 Johann Baptist Metz took this up with a wealth of ideas in an article on 'Theology as Biography.' . . . My own experiences with theological thinking have taught me that the two things belong together in Christian theology: the *telling* of God's history with us, and the *argument* for God's

presence—biographical subjectivity and self-forgetting objectivity. Because the way—the method—belongs to the perception of the thing itself, I have written biographical introductions to the different themes, not for the sale of the personal subject, but as a way leading to insight into the object of enquiry. Because the subject as person comes from a community and talks within a community, this is not the in-turned reference of a solitary ego, for: 'What have you what you have not received?'" (Moltmann 2000, xix, 1999, 15)

Learning from *the personal*, combining *biography* and *argument*, developing or renewing first beginnings in the *narrative and story structure of theology*, taking into consideration one's *social and cultural location* and history, and living all this in the context of a *communitarian and communal concept of academic writing* in a new and *global civilization of one world*, all this and more could be used as a description of what *North American systematic theology* over these last several decades has been trying to do all along, with *Jürgen Moltmann* as trans-Atlantic guest and friend, coworker and highly interested European bystander and sympathetic commentator fitting perfectly into *God's riotous* and *plentiful crowd* (O'Hara Graff 1995, 85).

North American Systematic Theology and Social Location

Social location did not use to be a concern for me until my own social location changed unintentionally. Cruising along in life pleasantly and with hardly any major changes has a tendency to let people forget. Only when things suddenly change some theologies change too. At least in my life theologies did change somehow. Moving from a tenderhearted and scared fundamentalism to a radically social neo-evangelicalism, passing through despairing agnosticism and screaming protest atheism, in order to come out of all these ups and downs as a social postmodern, a patchwork radical, an evangelical liberal, a leftist pietist, a poststructural feminist, a multi-cultural as well as postcolonial Swiss, a playful social deconstructivist, a narrative emancipatory ethicist, and last, but not least, a post-national, post-confessional, post-denominational, and post-European theosociologist, if such a thing as this new play on words even exists.

All along theologies changed me and theologies changed because of me. Sometimes my learned and internalized theologies were changing the ways I would go about doing things. Optional decisions being taken accordingly. The decision to sell Nicaraguan bananas at the back entrance door of a local church in Calvin's Geneva after the sermon of the Sunday worship service was over had a lot to do with my theology. To get in trouble for all this afterwards, with some right wing church members making it a problem, changed my theology equally. I did not turn right wing, though, just even some more radical.

The subsequent and hardly spectacular little signature given outside of some voting booth in Calvin's Geneva for the public collection of signatures supporting the nationwide political initiative "For a Switzerland without an army" turned out not only to change my theology, but also most of the rest of my life. Little did I know then that this little signature alone would make me famous or infamous for the next several years to come. Theology again changed, got intensified, deepened, with new visions, stronger convictions. A pacifism that had already been there during my youth and young adulthood got turned on again. Some of it changed my life, some of it my theology, as much as theology changed some of it too.

The decision some years later to write a little church bulletin article on the first Golf war by asking simple questions about the equal recognition of international law here and there, and the subsequent public and political outcry a little and inconspicuous church bulletin article had created, with normally in Swiss church settings hardly anybody reading a local church bulletin, had a lot to do with my theology. The ensuing public debate, even with pushed up newspaper interest, changed some of my public and private theology as well.

The slow but intentional conviction that someone ought to mingle in with drug addicts, homeless and limitless teenagers at the age of fourteen sniffing and shooting heroin, while being more and more pushed to the corner in a social landscape of some well-to-do suburban village with lots of teachers, medical doctors, lawyers, professors, politicians, and other successfully arrived biographies, this too had a lot to do with my most personal theology. And at the same time, every new moment, every new event, every new impending tragedy or experienced new solidarity gave a new twist to some of its general positioning of my theology.

To stand at the pulpit and utter a few words among many others who had joined the microphone about the creative art of a

Real Life

culture for peace against violence in front of kids, youth, seniors, Jews, Buddhists, Muslims, Christians, artists, journalists, gospel singers, country musicians, and other culturally spirited geniuses, this too had a lot to do with my own and most personal theology.

Theology grows as we grow with it. In the course of a life journey there are many places we stand still and think. This turns out to be a next social location from where we think. Every new place, or any old residence, plays along with what we think. The place we are in gives or takes space in what we think. In some places you might not even find a space to think. Thinking turns out to be ecological. Depending on your habitat it grows this way, or another, or not at all.

The ecology of thinking makes theology ecological. It makes a difference if you sit in a heated university building somewhere in Heidelberg or New Haven and are concerned about information technology, insurance policies, the momentary division of labor, the common search for academic meaning, or the linguistic workings of grammars of culture, or if you sit and live in Spanish-speaking neighborhoods, no water, no heating, no school, no university, but with millions of rootless and homeless, jobless and hopeless migrants and settlers trying to find some little work in a nearby metropolitan city of no name.

Ecology of thinking does make a difference. Thoughts may sit or run, find some rest or get chased around from one place to the next. Thoughts that move and run may turn out different from thoughts that sit and wait. Sitting thoughts have a tendency to create sitting theologies. Changing—social, cultural, personal— locations can help to get some more exercise.

All will depend on where you live in the way how you write and what you write in your theology.

The *social location* of contemporary *systematic, dogmatic,* and *fundamental theology* is a recurring theme in North American theology today. Posing the *fundamental question* of one's own personal and social location from where our theologies are written and developed has become a necessary *first discussion opener* in many theological endeavors in the United States of these days. It is not uncommon in basic textbooks or general works in systematic theology in North America to find at first, before authors even enter into a particular topic at hand, some primary reflections on *who* is

The Community of the Weak

writing, *where* the author is coming from, in what kind of a position and life habitat, biographical place and academic setting the author is living, as well as how this has an influence on what is being said and developed.

North American systematic theologian *Frederick Herzog* opens his introduction to systematic theology or *political dogmatics* (Herzog 1988, Rieger 1999) with these kinds of preliminaries to position himself *socially* as well as *theologically*:

> "With our recent sense of having been catapulted into the global village, a small planet with limited resources, we have experienced a shaking of the foundations of modern Christian thought. For example, we have begun to doubt that systematic theologies still ought to be written. They were based on the modern Christian assumption that an author is able to develop a sufficient picture of Christian teaching based on a systematic principle that is the author's very own. In our time, this literary operation can have disastrous consequences . . . More importantly, Christian existence itself has become questionable . . . What do we mean by Christian existence today? Does Christianity in the West still contribute anything distinctive to the human enterprise? Or do we merely bunch together modern ethical precepts and religious notions available to human beings everywhere and call it Christianity? . . . In any case, we discover ourselves caught in a gigantic struggle over the elementary components of Christian thought. I initially thought that the cutting edge of the new situation was new accountability for Christian teaching. The churches again were compelled to take a stand on Christian doctrine. But a more primal issue imposes itself: How does Christian teaching emerge in the first place? How does a Christian thought develop? We are forced also to offer an analysis of the *location* in which we as Christians live and develop doctrine from our life." (Herzog 1988, 1)

Invisible Companions Writing With Us

> *I am a Swiss, male, middle-aged, white, car-owning, employed, healthy, straight, and half-way normal minister or pastor in the Swiss Reformed Church coming out of the Swiss Reformation of old days (Gordon 2002). For the rest a lot of things don't fit. But this may be secondary or at least peripheral for the moment. Basic material is a normal story in biography. Being born in a clean*

and technologically highly advanced hospital in cosmopolitan Zurich, with a mom fighting for me to live. My mom had chosen Zurich to give birth because she did not want her home town to know and gossip. She also wanted to be surrounded by a Protestant Women's Home for Single Mothers where more women lived like her.

Some months later we went back home again. Life back home was like most lives in the 1950's at the time. Growing up in a neighborhood with many little and big one-family houses, no suburban housing blocks or sky-scrapers, ghetto buildings or rusted-iron shelters. A normal neighborhood with normal neighbors, apart from those who could not handle that a single mother would raise a child. The neighborhood was clean, orderly, quiet, mixed, some rich, some middle class, some secretively not as well-to-do, like my mom. But I had normal meals on the table, mineral water to drink, Swiss chocolate at hand, and a soccer ball or a bike to drive around like any other child. At lunch time we often went to a pubic soup kitchen for workers and other employees in center town. I still remember those long waiting lines reaching outside almost to the street while patiently counting the time until we got served at the self-service restaurant with lots of good food.

I went to school like any normal child. I knew some French already before I sat at the school desk for the first time, having soccer friends in the neighborhood who only spoke French. I was pretty good in school, it seems, partially also because my mom forced me every day to do my homework diligently. She herself, with best grades in school, had never been able to go on to better schools. A women was supposed to look after her brother who failed in school several times. Even with best grades during all her school life my mom was never allowed to get more education and nurture, academic training and professional skill than becoming an accountant for lawyers who all kept making big bucks. I still remember her telling me some of the smaller details about how to play with income tax officials to protect her latest boss. Other than that, my mom was a normal mother raising a single child with no dad around.

Until young adulthood I had never seen, for instance, an African American or most other representatives of a bigger world. In teenager times I had a girlfriend who had spent one year as a high-school language exchange student in Pinochet's Chile. Her stories kept following me, especially when she told us how she

The Community of the Weak

was called in to the government office and the Swiss Consulate after she had played the guitar and sung at some public folk festival with other protest song writers. Later on, as a college student interested in the whole big world, things like that kept intriguing me more and more. But a clear concept of social awareness had not yet developed.

I studied *theology* in a *well-protected life biography*. Some twists and turns were unique, different, particular. As an academically scared fundamentalist and charismatic pietist with a growing feel for social and world problems I ended up as a student in the *United States*. However, unlike most other students around me, I never had to nor could I *work* in taking some job to make some money to pay *tuition fees*. Swiss scholarships and a mom who supported me made life easy and pleasant in the USA. I could have ended like most other students I know in Switzerland. *Degrees finished*, jobs available, ministry positions filled, resting holidays booked, bookshelves stacked, cars registered, social security arrangements made, theologies *put aside*.

But somehow *experience* turned out differently. Though I still qualify for most of these qualifiers listed as well, degrees finished, bookshelves stacked, jobs available, cars registered, social security arrangements made, something made me *stop and think* along these minor and major courses of my life. Somehow, looking back, experiences made me think more so than *books or megabytes*. Though I do sit now at a table quite lonely while writing on my personal *Macintosh*, filling pages with dots and comas, sentences and paragraphs, those many *images and memories*, social times and personal stories of a past lived life *sit with me equally*. They flow and float around me as *invisible companions* while I write, writing with me my most personal life and theology.

Invisible companions are the *social locations* of our theology. What I have experienced, where I have been, the neighborhoods I have lived in, the schools I visited, the grades I got, the kind of friends I had and still have, the places I have seen, the tears I have shed, the joys I have shared, the breakdowns I have been through, the beaches I have walked on, the human tragedies I have witnessed, the social visions I have been part of, all this and more makes *my social location in theology* influencing everything I write.

As North American systematic theologians *Rebecca S. Chopp* and *Mark Lewis Taylor* (Chopp and Taylor 1994) put it, pointing out the *contextual nature* of all our theological endeavor:

> "When we say that theology is *contextual*, we mean that even in a given historical period, theology is specific to a diversity of particular, local situations. In other words, theology is affected both diachronically (by differences due to passage through time) and synchronically (by differences occurring because of situational changes—social, political, cultural, gendered, and so on). For example, theological reflection from an inner-city, African-American community in Los Angeles, addressing tensions there, will be different from that emerging from a Latino or Korean community in the same city; and it will certainly be very different from that done by a suburban, Euro-Anglo community in Chicago as it attempts to address enormously high rates of depression, suicide, and drug use among its adolescents ... Awareness of contextuality leads to the understanding that all knowledge, theology included, reflects not only some general sense of meaning but also specific forms of interests." (Chopp and Taylor 1994, 13)

The *place* from which theology is written is important. Whether we call it *context* (Hall 1989, 69–244, Hodgson 1994, 25–26, Thistlethwaite and Engel 1998, 4–7, Waldenfels 2000, 16–101), *social location* (Herzog 1988, 1–22, Hodgson 1994, 25–26, 73–75, Cone 1997/1975, 36–56, Placher 2003, 35–39, Müller 1999, 63–66), or simply the *contemporary situation* (Tracy 1981, 339–404, Hodgson 1994, 25–26, Williamson 1999, 37–43, Peters 2000, 5–33, Härle 2000, 168–192), the challenge to look at one's determining personal and social background in the way we commonly do theology remains the same.

This determining background—in the *Gestalt*-sense of the word—may be more prominent in coloring everything we do than what we have self-critically recognized so far. In this critical sense, looking at all these *invisible companions* writing with us as we put down in ink or megabytes our reflected life as theology may be the most necessary *first step* in good therapy.

The Community of the Weak

Ecological Thinking

The *place* where I write this right now and at this particular moment is my *social location* (Herzog 1988, 1–22, Hodgson 1994, 25–26, 73–75, Cone 1997/1975, 36–56, Placher 2003, 35–39) in theology, invisibly accompanying every word I type. The place in my life that I find myself in right now and at this particular moment in life is the *oikos*, the *lifeworld* (Peters 2000, 24), the home, the house, the room, the office, the street, the playground, the *places and spaces* that influence my theology. This may be conscious or unconscious, reflected or not. The human *ecology of thinking* (for an ecology of thinking in pedagogy and philosophy Kleber 1993, Kösel 1993, Mertens 1998, Clinebell 1996, Gottlieb 2006) works that way, whether we acknowledge it to ourselves or not. No human writing or thinking is ever done in lonesome isolation and social abstraction. All our ecological and spatial environments play along with our most personal and social activities of learning and knowing. How we think and what we write comes out of an *invisible dialogue* with other environing companions still *alive* or even *dead* in memory. This is true for academic and theological writing as well.

German social ecologist and educational theorist *Gerhard Mertens* underlines the special importance of our *ecological space* (Mertens 1998) in which we live and move for all our human *knowing* and *learning*:

> "If we recognize that education—the reflecting positioning of the person in this world—is not possible by definition in a vacuum without any contact to the environment, and if one considers in addition that the *quality of an environment* with its stimulating or blocking potential has to a great extent a co-determining influence on the *educational possibilities* of persons, this once more underlines the necessity of a human-ecological change of orientation also in the educational sciences." (Mertens 1998, 128)

We all live and move in our most personal human *learning environments* (Mertens 1998, 128) which influence what and how we think and learn. Living is learning. The *ecology of thinking* (on the ecology of thinking Mertens 1998, 101–166, on ecological learning Kösel 1993, Kleber 1993, Hof 2009) requires a new kind of *ecological pedagogy*. Systematic theology as well is not exempt from such a *human ecology* in its living and learning. The *social location* of systematic theology needs to be made transparent and openly accessible to critical analysis. The location in which we learn and develop, grow and get convinced, change and follow our convictions in practical actions needs to be looked at more carefully, especially in the way this place that we live in, this space that we move in, may have a determining influence on the kind of theology we write or don't write.

Ecological thinking on the *social location* of *theological education* will invite systematic theology "to offer an analysis of the *location* in which we as Christians live and develop doctrine from our life" (Herzog 1988, 1). To develop doctrine *from our life* is what systematic theology is all about. Ecological thinking in theology makes us sensitive for the externals, the surroundings, the background, and the backdrop of the picture being painted, as theology is never without its own environment and horizon. All theology is a reflection somehow of *the place in which we live*, the streets we walk on, the buses we take, the train stations we pass, the neighborhoods we see, the people we meet, the nature we move in.

Places of Interest

All theology is *interested* theology, reflecting the common taste, habit, look, and place that theologians live in. The *social setting* in which our theology is being done influences what turns out to be our *systematic theology*.

African American systematic theologian *James H. Cone* (Cone 1997/1975, on James Cone see Musser and Price 1996, 118–126) puts it well and succinctly:

> "Theology is not universal language; it is *interested* language and thus is always a reflection of the goals and aspirations of a particular people in a definite social setting . . . What people think about God cannot be divorced from their place and time in a definite history and culture. While God may exist in some heavenly city beyond time and space, human beings cannot transcend history. They are limited to the specificity of their finite nature. And even when theologians claim to point beyond history because of the possibility given by the Creator of history, the divine image disclosed in their language is shaped by their place in time. Theology is *subjective* speech about God, a speech that tells us far more about the hopes and dreams of certain God-talkers than about the Maker and Creator of heaven and earth." (Cone 1997/1975, 36–38)

In *theology* as well, as in any other *social-linguistic places and spaces* (on postmodern social space Keith and Pile 1993, Pile and Thrift 1995,

Simmons 1993, Sibley 1995, Magnusson 1996, Soja 1989, 2000, 2011), affluent people, educated people, carefree and well-off people will speak a different kind of language than the unemployed, the homeless, the HIV-positive, the sexually abused, the socially rejected. Rejection and exclusion change your language, your idioms, your vocabulary. The acceptance or refusal of human space, emotional place, some personal room, and social grace sketch the personal and social map on which we tread.

Humans walk only where they are welcome, sketching the effective limits of their social and natural environments as *personal and meaningful lifeworlds* (Simmons 1993, 76–116). Language and idiom, vocabulary and linguistic style change accordingly, depending on where you have been given the grace and hospitality to stay for a while. The place in this global world where our most personal life is welcomed becomes our lifeworld, a place where we can stretch our legs and rest for a while, because other people speak our own language. Sometimes a simple *difference in lifeworlds* can make communication almost impossible.

Social geographer and critical theorist *I.G. Simmons* (Simmons 1993) portrays the importance of the *lifeworld* as *natural and social environment* of the human person in *philosophy, hermeneutics, painting, sculpture, photography, literature, journalism, music, cinema, television*, and *architecture*. Reflecting on the environing space and the place and nature we live in may be a *new hermeneutical turn* for the *social and human sciences*, for systematic theology as well.

> "Objective social science has critics. They argue that classification, systemisation and theory-formation are inappropriate to the richness and diversity of the human condition. In the case of environment, the individuals' construction of it, vertically as they grow up and horizontally as they relate to wider groups, can easily be lost. So the idea of the 'lifeworld', centred on a self, provides an alternative. This has been the subject of a great deal of philosophical discourse as well as empirical research, and is given further variety by the work of creative artists, some of whom treat environment, nature and place very seriously." (Simmons 1993, 76)

Taking places seriously may be another way to underline the importance of *social location* in all our philosophical reflecting, *human, social*, or *theological* (Müller 1999, 63–66). Codes and languages, idioms and dialects, metaphors and poetic imagery, prose and narrative, may change accordingly. What is important in some places, turns out utterly irrelevant

Real Life

in others, depending on where reflecting and marveling people grow up, go to school or don't go to school, make their living or sit around unemployed, speak their orders or sing their songs.

Theology as well *changes* depending on where it is being written or sung. The importance of space and a *place to be* is only now becoming a topic of interest in systematic theology, as the marginalized and disenfranchised, the locally and globally excluded, the socially and politically exiled, the spiritually and humanly dispossessed, are reclaiming their own social and political space, as visionaries of a better world that "keep inventing political spaces of their own" (Magnusson 1996, 4). *Inventing new spaces and places* of our own can be another way to describe the imaginative and subversive potential of a systematic theology in touch with its own place and social location. No human boundaries will ever after remain untouched. Humanly drawn-up territories and social maps may have to be revised.

Theology in Different Locations

North American slaves developed their own *secret code and language* trying to write a different kind of systematic theology, linguistically opposing the violence of brutal slave masters and violators. Slave narratives and gospel songs were thereby inventing a new political space of their own. Theology, black and white, turned out to be using a different kind of social vocabulary, depending on how black or white one's social skin would be, making mutual comprehension almost impossible. At the same time the *difference in social location* made theology the *differing factor* in bringing about social and narrative victory.

North American systematic theologian *James H. Cone* describes the narrative and social power of *theology as story* in African American slave narratives and animal tales, gospel songs in *Spirituals* and melodies of *the Blues* (Cone 1991/1972, also Jones 1993, Stewart 1997, Wilson Bridges 2001, Perkinson 2005, West 2010), overcoming a white and Western preoccupation with abstract and rational discourse, making it almost impossible for both theological worlds to meet:

> "What white slave masters would have recognized that the tales of Br'er Rabbit and his triumphs over the stronger animals actually expressed black slaves' conscious hopes and dreams of overcoming the slave masters themselves? Who among the white community would have perceived that in the singing

The Community of the Weak

and preaching about 'crossing the river Jordan and entering the New Jerusalem' black slaves were sometimes talking about Canada, Africa, and America north of the Mason-Dixon line? White slave masters were no brighter than our contemporary white theologians who can see in black religion only what their axiological presuppositions permit them to see. And that vision usually extends no further than some notion of black 'otherworldliness' leading to passivity. But there is something much deeper than that simplistic idea in black religion. Nat Turner's spirit is buried beneath the shouts and the cries. And that spirit will soon rise and claim the eschatological future promised in God's encounter with the community . . . It is difficult to express this liberating truth in rational discourse alone; it must be told in story. And when this truth is told as it was meant to be, the oppressed are transformed, taken into another world and given a glimpse of the promised land. And when they leave the church, they often say to one another what the disciples said after having experienced the Risen Lord: 'Did not our hearts burn within while he talked to us on the road, while he opened to us the scriptures?' (Luke 24:32)." (Cone 1997/1975, 56)

Burning hearts while opening the Scriptures could not be any better a description of a systematic theology sensitive to its own social location. *Differing places of interest* make for *different kinds of systematic and narrative theologies*. North American systematic theology over the last several decades has been developing a self-reflecting *fundamental theology of place and space,* looking at its own *social location and cultural story.*

It does *make a difference* whether or not you *sit comfortably* in some heated or sun-protected seminar room or lecture hall unencumbered by communal or social problems around you, untouched by environing realities or encroaching possibilities of human violence, communal exclusion, social poverty, natural misery, or *soul-wounding tragedy*. Whether in old times, or modern times, the *social location* of your theology does make a difference. *Anselm, Descartes, Kant,* or *Hegel* may lose some of their overdrawn importance if looked at from another local and social-geographical perspective from sun-up to nightfall.

In the words of *James H. Cone* again:

"The difference in the form of black and white religious thought is, on the one hand, *sociological.* Since blacks were slaves and had to work from sun-up to nightfall, they did not have time for the art of philosophical and theological discourse. They, therefore, did not know about the systems of Augustine, Calvin, or

Edwards. And if Ernst Bloch is correct in his contention that 'need is the mother of thought' . . . , then it can be said that black slaves did not *need* to know about Anselm's ontological argument, Descartes's *Cogito, ergo sum,* and Kant's *Ding an sich.* Such were not their philosophical and theological problems as defined by their social reality. Blacks did not ask whether God existed or whether divine existence could be rationally demonstrated. Divine existence was taken for granted, because God was the point of departure of their faith. The divine question which they addressed was whether or not God was with them in their struggle for liberation. Neither did blacks ask about the general status of their personal existence or that of the physical world. The brutal presence of white people did not allow that sort of philosophical skepticism to enter their consciousness. Therefore the classical philosophical debate about the priority of concepts versus things, which motivated Kant and his predecessors' reflective endeavors, did not interest black people. What was 'real' was the presence of oppression and the historical need to strive against it. They intuitively perceived that the problem of the auction block and slave drivers would not be solved through philosophical debate. The problem had to be handled at the level of concrete history as that history was defined by the presence of the slave masters. Slaves therefore had to devise a language commensurate with their social situation. That was why they told stories." (Cone 1997/1975, 50)

The *reality* of slave drivers and slave masters, auction blocks and lynching trees, family break-ups and sexual abuse, racial violence and spiritual bankruptcy, lived and confronted every single day, *did make a difference* in the way *God was seen, theology was being done*, church hymnals were sung, philosophies were invented. The *reality* of a particular *social space* and *place to be*, from which there was hardly any escape, did change theology accordingly. *Reality* (McGrath 2004, 93–169) being *that which we may want to run up against, but it will not move.* Reality enclosed in a social space and place that would not transform. Sometimes telling stories may end up to be the only way such realities can be changed.

The Community of the Weak

Biography and Situation

Situation, Location, and Biography

The dawning recognition that any contemporary systematic and fundamental theology is deeply *experiential* and *personal, contextual* and *local, situational* and *biographical* does not just come out of African American experiences in slavery, brought up by some radical black theologians.

In one way or another, theology did know about this all along its turbulent *social and cultural history* (Kee/Albu/Lindberg/Frost/Robert 1998, Barraclough 2003). Issues of place and location become even more prominent as theology in its history is retold in a *global and world perspective* (Hastings 1999, Ellingsen 1999a-b, Dowley 2002, Norris 2002, Collins and Price 2003). In the *history of Christian thought* theology narrated as a *social story* (Placher 1983, Gonzalez 1987a–c, Lane 1996, McGrath 1998, Anderson 2000, Olson 2001, McEnhill and Newlands 2004) has never developed without at the same time been tied to a particular *social and cultural context*. Simply reading the narratives and stories over centuries of theological reflection reveals the contextual and social nature of all our personal and communal theologies. No theology *falls from the skies* (Casalis 1984) as if untouched by human pain and social struggle, personal longings and communal dreaming. Theology—systematic, fundamental, or dogmatic—is inevitably and at the same time *social theology* (Lamb 1982, Lane 1984, Wetherilt 1994, Haight 2001, Taylor 1990, 2011) mirroring and reflecting the *social matrix* (Banawiratma/Müller 1995, Litonjua 2003) in which it has developed.

Theology, even in its most personal and withdrawn academic corner of abstract elaborating of conceptual new visions, is always done as if the "individual is radically social" (Lane 1984, 1). *The social* creeps in and keeps up coming back from the back corner of our unconscious forgetting that all our thinking and writing somehow has its origin somewhere. No human thought just comes up like this. Places and faces, smiles and tears, biographies and tragedies give birth to new thoughts trying to make sense of it all, the good things and the bad things happening to people. The places where we come from are no abstract inventions but the daily humdrum of *human experiences*. They contain *original blessings* (Fox 1983, Greiner 1998, Keller, 2003, Gottlieb 2006) and *original sins* (Suchocki 1995, Peters 1994, Farley 2004) spreading like diseases or human good tidings. *Structures of sin* and *cultures of meaning* (Litonjua 2003) are present wherever people interact and make up stories to make sense of this world. Like theology, social structures and cultures of meaning "do not drop from heaven, but are social constructions" (Litonjua 2003, 339). Once this is recognized, theology—systematic, fundamental, dogmatic—will become more sensitive to its own social location, present situation, and biographical narration from where it speaks and thinks.

To recognize one's *place of origin* from where we speak and think, act and dream, may be the most therapeutic and renewing contribution *North American systematic theology* has given the world of theological academics at the turn of the millennium. *Context, situation, location,* and *(auto)biography* may become the new keywords to open up fruitful dialogue across continents.

The *Western mainstream*, not just in theological academics, may need the broadening and cleansing through mingling with *new sources* of academic interchange between various creeks and waterfalls, brooks and waterways, floods and ocean waves, making deserts come alive.

As North American systematic theologian *Peter C. Hodgson* (Hodgson 1994) puts it, using the visual imagery of *origins* and *sources*, streams and mainstreams coming out of *new social locations* in theology:

> "Analyses of the role of social location in constructing reality have underscored this point, as have black, liberation, and feminist theologies . . . New streams of interpretation and experience—Asian and African, Latin American, African American, Hispanic, feminist, gay and lesbian—are flowing alongside the Western mainstream. They are mingling their waters with what was one thought to be a pure and holy source but had in fact become polluted, and they are having a cleansing effect." (Hodgson 1994, 25-26)

A Different God

Depending on what kind of a life you live and where you live it, your God may turn out *differently*. At least this is what a *fundamental theology of place and social location* will teach. North American systematic and fundamental theology has uncovered the *social and political unconscious* (Jameson 2002, 1981) in theology, having theological discourse undergo a *political psychoanalysis* (Prilleltensky and Nelson 2002, Parker 1997, Smelser 1998, Bauriedl 1999) and *sociology of scientific knowledge* (Benton and Craib 2001, Williams 2000, Goldblatt 2000, Heuermann 2000) according to its various and differing places and social spaces in which it

The Community of the Weak

is phrased, enacted, and performed. Theology as *social performance* will need to become more reflective of its own *social home-coming* and *home-leaving* in and from a particular place.

That *God turns out differently*, depending what kind of a place—and suffering or no suffering or even inflicting suffering—you live and participate in, is put beautifully by North American systematic and black radical theologian *James H. Cone* (Cone 1997/1975):

> "It is of course possible to assume that black religion and white religion are essentially the same, since white people introduced 'Christianity' to black people. However, that assumption will deprive the theologian of vital insights into black religious thought forms, because it fails to recognize the significant connection between thought and social existence. If Ludwig Feuerbach is correct in his contention that 'Thought is preceded by suffering,' . . . and if Karl Marx is at least partially correct in his observation that 'it is not consciousness that determines life but life that determines consciousness,' . . . then it is appropriate to ask, What is the connection between life and theology? The answer cannot be the same for blacks and whites, because blacks and whites do not share the same life. The lives of a black slave and white slaveholder were radically different. It follows that their thoughts about things divine would also be different, even though they might sometimes use the same words about God. The life of the slaveholder and others of that culture was that of extending white inhumanity to excruciating limits, involving the enslavement of Africans and the annihilation of Indians. The life of the slave was the slave ship, the auction block, and the plantation regime. It involved the attempt to define oneself without the ordinary historical possibilities of self-affirmation. Therefore when the master and slave spoke of God, they could not possibly be referring to the same reality." (Cone 1997/1975, 9-10)

The *recognition* "that all of our thoughts are relative, shaped by our social location and class interests as well as our personal experiences and needs" (Hodgson 1994, 73) has reshaped *contemporary North American systematic theology* in radically new ways, being ever more cognizant of its own particular coloring through *personal experience* and *social place*. Theology in black and white will not turn out the same. God will be different accordingly. It is to the credit of North American theology to have pointed out this *fundamental starting point* in elaborating any contemporary systematic theology.

Involving the Personal and Biographical

Situation and *biography* are important signifiers for any *fundamental theology* laying the foundations from where to start in building our theological artifacts or picture walls. The *contemporary situation* in which we live and move, breathe and craft *our life's biography* is the *place we all start from*, whether we are aware of it or not. The more we become aware of it, the more we can freely play with it, realizing how it plays with us.

Socially analyzing our *own story* and the ways it has influenced our *starting point* in building theologies that are never built from scratch is a therapeutic move to become more *aware*, or as German political psychoanalyst *Thea Bauriedl* would call it, "to critically deal with ourselves" (Bauriedl 1999, 18). From there, all kinds of creative and hopeful as well as *emancipatory* new ways of looking at and acting in this world are possible, once our place where we come from is recognized. *Depth psychology* can turn into *depth sociology* opening new spaces to see why we keep repeating the same old and shortsighted mistakes. Healing can happen, even *theological healing*, if from a political analysis of our limiting visions *new spaces* are opened to see the world in a new way, as we reflect on our own contemporary situation in which we find ourselves.

The *silencing, repressing*, and *splitting off* of important segments and aspects of our personality are not just symptoms of a psyche, but happen all the time even in *academics* where all kinds of living segments of the human soul keep being denied its *psychoanalytic relevancy*. *Theology* would do well if it recognized its own *repressive tendency* in keeping out biography and personality. Opening up systematic theology to the *repressed personal* and *biographical* would maybe even let academic work reappear in its "'own language', its own feelings and wishes" (Bauriedl 1999, 39) to revolutionize theology as a "radical risk of self-exposure to the other that any attempt to analyze the present cultural situation must involve" (Tracy 1981, 339).

Systematic theology as *personal involvement*, risking *self-exposure*, and radical *self-analysis* in view of all those *far and near significant others* in this world calling on us, may be the future challenge we have to face as we try to find out in a world of human oppression and social violence, *soul denial* and *communal destruction* through unlimited use and abuse of *power*, "how more humanness can be achieved, namely through more humanness" (Bauriedl 1999, 327).

The Community of the Weak

Facing the Contemporary Situation

North American theology—systematic, fundamental, ethical, and dogmatic—is facing the demanding challenge to confront the *contemporary situation* (Tracy 1981, 339-404). This contemporary situation has a *human face*, looking at you every day in a new way. As such the *social and theological analysis* of the contemporary situation in which we find ourselves will be a prominent topic of *fundamental theology*. At the same time it will be an intrinsic first step in any *theological* and *hermeneutical method* formulating *how to start* the construction of our theology (Berger 1999, 41-53, Beinert 2004, 11-48).

Often, most visible in the *European context*, preliminary analyses of the *contemporary situation* in which systematic theology nowadays finds itself remain in the *abstract*, sociological, hermeneutical, psychological, and philosophical (Tillich 1951-1963, Grass 1973, 7-74, Härle 2000, 168-192, Berger 1999, 41-53, Lange 2001a, 7-26, Biehl und Johannsen 2002, 25-59, Waldenfels 2000, 31-90, Beinert 2004, 11-48), leaving out the day-to-day experiences of the *everyday world* in what people go through in *suffering* (Berger 1999, 165-168). For some, the contemporary situation is described with *Erich Fromm* as *to have* or *to be* (Biehl und Johannsen 2002, 27-42, following Fromm 1976, 1993). *God* or *money*, this is as close as European *systematic theologies* can get in *social analysis*.

North American systematic theologies have experienced a *wider and deeper shattering* of philosophical, sociological, psychological, and hermeneutical analyses of what the *modern and postmodern contemporary situation* might be in these past and present days (Tracy 1981, 339-404, Hall 1989, 69-244, Chopp and Taylor 1994, 1-24, Williamson 1999, 37-43, Haight 2001, 191-212). *Social analysis, philosophical deconstruction, psychological hermeneutics*, and the *postmodern visual gaze* have not precluded the clearing of the vision to look at the *everyday world* bound on death-dealing ways in love with power and destruction. The vocabulary, the content, the description, the poetic and prosaic phrasing turn out to be *more concrete* in reading *basic textbooks* in North American systematic theology.

North American systematic theologian *Clark M. Williamson* (Williamson 1999), letting a *Tillichian* and *Post-Shoah theology* of the *Jewish way of the blessing of life over death* converse with socially hopeful and resistant elements of *narrative, process,* and *feminist theology*, describes the *contemporary social situation* in which we live and move in doing our systematic theologies with concrete images:

> "The death-dealing ways of the twentieth century, its orientation toward death, are reflected in the realities of world hunger and starvation, ecological disaster, the still-ominous threat of nuclear destruction, the new international economic 'order', classism, racism, sexism, and the continuing bias against the 'other', as reflected in the church's anti-Judaism. Sin is not merely personal, but is related to structural causes, to the powerful impact of economic and political institutions that can be named, an impact that can be resisted, but usually is not. Here, perhaps the greatest personal sin is the refusal to resist the powerful. The name for this kind of sin is not 'pride', but 'sloth', the laziness that puts us to sleep in the face of systemic injustice." (Williamson 1999, 37–38)

Social and personal laziness in theology is that kind of thinking and writing that puts readers to sleep in an *abstract non-involvement* of systematic theologies of the contemporary situation that hold us aloof, remaining *at a safe distance* to what really hurts people, destroys the world, makes children, juniors, seniors, and other men and women *cry*. This may be the most glaring and *fundamental difference* between continents in the way systematic theologies are introduced to the *modern and contemporary world*.

The *death-dealing and life-destructive ways* of the *twentieth and twenty-first century*, the workings of the many faces of *power* (Boulding 1990, Westwood 2002, Kahane 2010) and *powerlessness* (Schmalstieg 1991, Poling 1991, 1996, Keller 2005), be it eco-systemic, labor-oriented, urban, rural, transnational, classist, racist, sexist, and simply *violent* (Williamson 1999, 39–43), do set the tone and the music for *contemporary systematic theologies in North America* which refuse to repress or deny *reality*. Becoming *aware of it*, psychoanalytically and *politically* (Bauriedl 1999, 355–377, Kahane 2010), theologically and culturally (Williamson 1999, 37–43, Hall 1989, 69–244, 1988, Haight 2001, 46–47, Rieger 2007, Taylor 1990, 2011), may be the beginning of a *socially sensitive* and *self-critical theology* that speaks *plain English* about what goes on in this hurting world:

> "In plain English that means that an African American, ghetto-dwelling, single mother suffers not only from racism, but also classism and sexism. Also she lives in the most polluted part of town, downwind from the incineration facility and closest to inground toxic pollutants." (Williamson 1999, 43)

The Community of the Weak

Systematic theology facing *contemporary situations* as *visual* and *tactile* as these and others will no longer be the same. At the same time, descriptions of contemporary situations like these and others *connect different places* that might seem to lie far apart. Neighborhoods here and there *connect,* as you can also find a high percentage of single mothers on social welfare, suffering from *social ostracism* and communal prejudice, *classism* and *sexism,* existential worries and regular unemployment checks, downwind from an incineration facility and a few kilometers away from recently uncovered inground toxic pollutants in a place and ministerial parish somewhere in *outbound Zurich, Switzerland.*

Systematic theology will need to become more attentive to its own *concrete and contemporary situation.* This contemporary situation is diverse and different for each place and person, and yet *highly concrete.* Neighborhoods, family ties, partnerships, group solidarities, personal crises, social problems, political spaces, and global realities are all part of it. But these contemporary situations are *lived and concrete experiences* of an *audible, visual, tactile, sensuous, emotional, personal, and communal kind* that leave indelible marks and unforgetable memories that do not go away. Generalities and philosophies, psychologies and sociologies, hermeneutical theories and poetic literacies will not do.

The Concrete Other

The human faces of the *concrete other,* in the conjoined sense of *Carol Gilligan's* ethics of care and *Emanuel Levinas'* ethics of responsibility (Benhabib 1986, 340–343, 1987, 1995, 1995a, Graham 1996a, Habbel 1994, Sponheim 1993, 1999, 2006, 2011), constitute the intransigent *challenge* of *fundamental theology* to look beyond its protected nest of lonesome and withdrawn intellectual individuality to *the public and open crowd of the common people* who tell their personal and communal stories. The *other person,* as well as *the third* and fourth, or fifth irrupting and interrupting as a *concrete other* in the crowd to make things *political* (Habbel 1994, 130–143), calls systematic theology back to where it came from, namely its own most personal story. Theology as *autobiography* will recognize its own source and place of origin once these stories are told and retold. *Stories* keep being populated by lots of people with no one having to risk to stay alone for very long, as people in stories are constantly being *interrupted* by someone wanting to talk or go for a walk. Theology in conversation with human faces of the concrete other will need to talk and *go for walks.*

Real Life

With the words of feminist social philosopher and critical theorist *Seyla Benhabib,* introducing the idea of the *concrete other* to the North American reception of the *critical theory* of the *Frankfurt School* and its communicative ethicist *Jürgen Habermas*:

> "The standpoint of the 'concrete other', by contrast, requires us to view each and every rational being as an individual with a concrete history, identity, and affective-emotional constitution. In assuming this standpoint, we abstract from what constitutes our commonality and seek to understand the distinctiveness of the other. We seek to comprehend the needs of the other, their motivations, what they search for, and what they desire. Our relation to the other is governed by the norm of *complementary reciprocity.*" (Benhabib 1986, 341, Benhabib 1987, 1995, 1995a, for pastoral theology Graham 1996a, Chinula and Clinebell 2009)

Systematic theology governed by a consequential *complementary reciprocity* with its own *contemporary situation* and *social location* (Müller 1999, 63–66) will listen to people, remember faces, include voices, lift silences, unearth treasures, dig up secrets, empower visions, trigger fantasies, and change accordingly. The *stories* and *memories*, the laughter and tears, the dreams and utopias, the nightmares and fairy tales of the common people we have *lived with* and the places we have *lived in* and keep living in will become the common material for a fundamental theology *in conversation* with the world (Tracy 1987, 1993) and in touch with *God's prospect* of *life* and humans' temptation of *death* (on death-dealing temptations contrasting blessings of life Williamson 1999, 37–43, Hall 1988, Brueggemann 1996, Fox 2002). Systematic and fundamental theology in conversation with the modern world will be *talking* while *walking* (Boff 1987) with other people along our common daily ways and city streets, backpack trails and outbound journeys in *real life* (Volf 2002), thus taking seriously what theologians call the *contemporary human situation.*

Living in the Situation

Quite often the *contemporary situation* is described in *systematic theology* as if it were somewhere here and there, but not in the places where we have lived and keep living ourselves. *Systematic theologies* have an tendency to live *outbound*, as if untouched by what is being said and lived by people on the street. It is high time that theology find its home and place on its own and *human ground*. Unattached, ungrounded, unanchored, theologies have a way to fly above and blow away in touching only the few. But even theologians and theologies are made of *people* and *stories* dwelling and coming out of *somewhere*.

Roman Catholic *David Tracy* (Tracy 1975–1999) describes such an *earthbound oceanic fundamental theology* in need and recognition of a *human place*. Human dwellings, the present moment, make up the air and water from which we breathe and quench our human thirst, in which we move and swim, allowing the human race to keep *remembering, hoping,* and *risking* while living in it. Like all-encompassing ocean waves at sea the *contemporary situation* is the *habitat* that we live and move in—with no escape—, not yesterday, not tomorrow, but *today*:

> "Every theology lives in its own situation. The creative and liberating resources of the tradition provide a horizon of questions which theologians bring to bear upon their interpretations of the situation. In this move, theologians are no different from other cultural critics who bring their own orientations, questions and possible, probable or certain modes of analysis and response to the situation encompassing all. Sometimes, as we have seen, theologians tend to speak of this aspect of the theological task as the role of the 'world' in theology, or as an attempt to 'discern the signs of the times'. 'Discernment' seems a correct word: to discern suggests an imagery of tentativeness, groping, risk-bearing alertness, that self-exposure of an authentically spiritual sensitivity to the anxieties and fears, the possibilities of both kairotic moments and demonic threats . . . Yet even 'discernment' of the 'signs of the times' seems somehow too secure an image for the radical risk of self-exposure to the other that any attempt to analyze the present cultural situation must involve. For no thinker, not least the theologian, dwells in some privileged place from which to view what is happening 'out there'. Like all those creatures who dwell in, not on the sea, we are all in our culture and our history: affected by it at every moment for good or ill, groping at every moment to understand, to discern how to live a worthwhile life in this place, at this moment. With the prophetic passion of a Jeremiah, an Isaiah, an Amos, theologians may confront and denounce their age. But no one escapes it; nor does the authentic prophet wish to. With the foolhardiness of a truly misplaced concreteness, contemporary persons in every age may announce that the ever-elusive now and the all-encompassing ego are all that really matters . . . Then, struggling to live not in but on the sea,

Real Life

we drown: having remembered nothing, hoped for nothing, risked nothing. With the pathos of a Miniver Cheevy we may long for a better, a clearer, a cleaner age but, even if such ever existed, we know it is not ours. The worlds of classical Greece, early Christianity, the medieval, Renaissance and Reformation worlds, the self-confident pre-World War I Europe, 'innocent' pre-World War II America: All have classical resources to be retrieved for this later time and place. Yet all are gone and will not, cannot return. We are in this contemporary situation: soon to be yesterday, soon to endure its own inadequate label, soon to receive the judgment and, incredibly enough, possibly even the nostalgia of later generations and ages. We are responsible for retrieving that past in our memories, our tradition and our lives; we are responsible to the future in our hopes, our actions, our promises. If both memory and hope, nostalgia and fantasy are to live at all, they must live as live options in and for the situation encompassing all." (Tracy 1981, 339–340)

Systematic theology as a *live option* living in and for the *situation* we have our home and place in is the *challenge* posed to any good theology. The *contemporary situation* turns out to be filled with people and faces, stories and memories, anecdotes and epic tragedies, common texts and new places. *Theology—systematic, fundamental, dogmatic, ethical, practical, and pastoral*—is confronted with the task to *join together* these people and places, stories and tragedies, fantasies and memories, letting history, story, tradition, text and context artistically *mix and mingle* into new and creative colors in this new and newly to be lived present and contemporary situation.

Biographies of Grace

In this, *systematic theologies* could become something like visible and detectable *biographies of grace* (Boff 1979, Thistlethwaite and Engel 1998, 16–17). Theology in the contemporary situation is always *biographically conditioned* (Boff 1979, 23–24), whether it is being laid open or kept a secret. We all bring our personal and social upbringings, our neighborhoods we lived in, our schools we visited, our friends we had, our enemies we ran into, our trips and travels we made, our private preferences, our public disclaimers, our musical tastes, our literary heroes, our anecdotal moments, and our epic stories to what we craft as *our own and most personal systematic theology*. The hope is that systematic theology may help to make all of this and more into a *story of grace*.

As North American feminist systematic theologians *Susan Brooks Thistlethwaite* and *Mary Potter Engel* (Thistlethwaite and Engel 1998) put it, introducing their basic textbook on a constructive and global systematic theology in the twentieth and twenty-first century with reflections on the *biographical conditioning* of all our theologies:

> "Theology, its methods, dominant themes, structures, and orders, emerges out of particular contexts. Those who organize and contribute to a book of constructive liberation theologies, therefore, bring their own contexts to it. For instance, the expansive treatment of grace in this book, a category usually treated in a limited section in traditional systematics, reflects the particular experiences of grace of this group of writers. The Latin American liberation theologian Leonardo Boff, in *Liberating Grace*, makes the point that we must not ignore 'biographical conditioning factors' in interpreting . . . The biographies of the participants in this volume—all members of non-dominant groups—are vastly different from those of classical theologians of the past. Paul, Augustine, Martin Luther, and Paul Tillich, as educated male ecclesiastics, were members of three dominant groups in their societies. Women, people of color, and peoples in the Two-thirds world have had less experience of the artificial freedom from daily routine that membership in a dominant group brings. They have tended to take note of the presence of grace in nature, in politics, in human interests, and human growth and development. Theirs is a view of grace less estranged from human life and work. God's movement in the world, these writers would say, is not so extraordinary after all." (Thistlethwaite and Engel 1998, 16–17)

Detecting *God's movement in the world*, being not so extraordinary after all, describes a *systematic theology in movement* and constant attention to what people all over the world on this globe have to tell. *Listening to these stories* is the beginning of good theology. *Biography* and *autobiography* will thereby become the building material for a new kind of *fundamental* and *systematic theology telling stories*. Theological concepts will be filled with *narrative truth* that invites for change and renewal. Only then can systematic theology again be and become what it has always been meant to be, namely a *graceful way of blessing* and a *way of life* (Williamson 1999, 13–44, Boff 1979, Fox 1983, 2002, Bühler 2000).

6

Postmodern

GROUNDING

"In contrast to this austere aesthetic of rigid unity and devotional worship, rap's cutting and sampling offers the pluralistic pleasures of deconstructive and reconstructive art—the thrilling beauty of dismembering (and rapping over) old works to create new ones, dismantling the prepackaged and wearily familiar into something stimulatingly different that often achieves a complex, fragile unity of its own." (Shusterman 1997, 140)

"The emotions that surface in the blues and in jazz celebrate a life that is suppressed and mutilated by modernity, and jazz has as much claim to be considered a medium of resistance as does the art of the high priests of modernism." (Witkin 2003, 179)

Theology, Art, and Messy Texts

Theology and Power in Social Postmodernity

Theology in *social postmodernity* needs a *new grounding*. At the same time, we live in a modern and postmodern world where *old fundamentals* no longer hold. The former structural architecture of *fundamental theology*, suggesting some basic foundation on which to build a system of belief and conviction, is being replaced by postmodern *collage* and *bricolage*.

The Community of the Weak

Theology has become an *artistic sampling and cutting*, rapping and mixing of many tunes and notes, standards and references to create a *new postmodern sound*. This chapter will be one more contribution to such a new sound. A chapter most *personal*, full of *emotions* in the midst of *messy texts* which try to prepare some *new grounding* for a *postmodern theology in social ways*.

Art, experience, autobiography, and *border-crossing* will be the general *new themes* to lay some *basic groundwork* for a new melody in theology. Theology nowadays is in many ways like *art*, touching souls and moving hearts while inviting for a *social imagination* that may change the world. Theology is also deeply *experiential*, coming out of deep moments of memory, pain, hope, living which are the tunes and tones of a new kind of theology. Theology, furthermore, is most basically, as proposed here and there in this text in many places, *autobiography*, speaking into words the soul and heart of the one writing. When autobiographies meet, a new world is created which is called *community*. Communities build theologies and join in *common hope*. Theology may be nothing more and nothing less than weaving together *people* in common hope. Finally, theology nowadays needs the vision and the courage, the fantasy and the carnival of *border-crossing*, transgressing old boundaries, disciplines, and commonly assumed non-assumptions. Theology in postmodern times will be more colorful like a *clown*.

This chapter proposes *a different kind of theology*. A theology *artistic*, imaginative, coming out of a deep *cry*, longing for social fantasy and transformation. A theology *experiential*, with experience being that traveling moment in life where you go from one place to the next, on the way with a *wayfaring God* accompanying you in every place. A theology *autobiographical*, in touch with one's own life stories found in common places. Autobiography is nothing else but the writing on paper what has been written into your soul. And, theology *border-crossing*, as you go along your humanly destined way, from one continent to another, from one home to the next, from one community of people to another one. Always in search of the carnival of *laughter* and *dancing* of those who join in a *common hope*.

In all this, *power* and *powerlessness* come along too, accompanying every step you take. And yet, reflecting on it, renaming it, recoloring it may give it a *new tone* as well, showing its omnipresent presence in the midst of everything along the way. *Theology* and *power* in this *social postmodern way* may even get *redeemed* in a mutually relational way. In this way, this

Postmodern

chapter lays the *groundwork* for the final two chapters where *power* will become *hopeful* and *musical* in a creative new way.

Creativity will be the new word for *power*. Creativity joining people, cultures, musical styles, communities, visionaries, ecologies, creativities in the way *Keith Jarrett* or *John Coltrane* may at some point in playing the sound of music join heaven and earth in *jazzy-creative new ways*. The social postmodern may need theologians who *play theology like jazz*, jamming and resisting, composing and dreaming along with companions in love of rap and Dixie, free-style and fusion, rhythm and blues. This chapter is one attempt to start the tune.

Theology as Art

Theology as an intellectual exercise may be considered a *personal work of art*. It not only touches on the question of the *social role* of the intellectual in contemporary society (Osborne 2002a, 167–169, Brooker 2001, 120–122, Andermahr, Lovell, and Wolkowitz 1997, 110–111, Jacoby 2000, Goldfarb 1998, McGowan 2002, West 2008, 2010), but it also reopens the never conclusively settled question of the use or possible uselessness of theological and academic knowledge in being either *liberating* or *life-disempowering* (in theology Wood 2001, Plaskow 1999, Hodgson 1999, Sedmak 2002, in the social sciences Cowan 2003a, for philosophy as a life art Schmid 1998, 297–303).

At the same time, theology as a *creative art work* may be like painting a picture, composing a symphony or *playing jazz* (Welch 1999, 16–26, McClendon 2000, 165–179, Pederson 2001, Wells 2004, Welch 2005, Perkinson 2005, Gelinas 2009), creatively and spiritually engaging in a kind of *theological image making* along soul-shaking tunes and rhythmic notes reconnecting with an age-old and socially resistant *freedom tradition* called *jazz* (Witkin 2003, 179–183, Cooke 1997, Collier 1995, 1997, Adams 1999, on leadership jazz De Pree 1992).

Or, to follow the picture and the musical melody, theology may simply rediscover itself as imaginative *art work* (Apostolos-Cappadona 1998, Ulanov and Ulanov 1999, Pederson 2001, Dyrness 2001, Taylor 2008) expressed, painted, modeled, and prefigured in many memorable instances throughout history through pictures and images speaking theology in the language of the visual (Sedmak 1999, 15–16, 2002, 11–13, Dyrness 2001, Garcia-Rivera 1999, 2003).

The Community of the Weak

With the poetic words of religious epistemologist *Clemens Sedmak* describing the limitless variety and diversity of artistic and linguistic *colors* and *forms* in theology:

> "... the more we know about theology, the more we come to appreciate its many forms and colors ... There are many forms of theology. Theology is taught and written, danced and sung, sculpted and painted, even dreamed and cried. Think of Karl Barth's famous theological dream—the dream that he was to examine Mozart in dogmatics ... Theology can be done with gestures: embracing, kneeling, blessing . . . Movies, novels, buildings, paintings show implicit theologies..." (Sedmak 2002, 11)

Saying this, I am very much aware of the ambiguity of such a claim. Theology both in its *classical* and *hermeneutical sense* is usually not so much associated with *playful human creativity*, but with a given and to be critically interpreted historical meaning as revelation found in ancient holy texts. Nevertheless, there seems to me no better way to describe the imaginative *craft of theology* (Dulles 1992, Sedmak 1999, 2002, Hilpert/Leimgruber 2008).

The times of a critical mind just looking back to a given past are left behind. *Postcritical* (Williamson 1999, 1) as they may become—as both neo-process systematic theologian *Clark M. Williamson* and Roman-Catholic *Avery Dulles* predict—theological writers in various places are invited to rediscover the creative dimension of theology which "seeks to reunite the creative with the cognitive, the beautiful with the true" (Dulles 1992, 15). This leaves most if not all things open for reexamination.

Theology in the form of writing a book or a dissertation may very well be undertaken in view of some *imaginative purpose* (on theology as creative imagination Chopp 1995a, 108–110), even though academic research and conceptual rigor are certainly more admired within the scientific community. My own reason for writing follows such a personal approach.

As a theological writer I am trying to find a *new and creative style* in theology that is not afraid to *say "I"* (on the creative courage to "say I" in theology Sölle 1995a, in feminist theory on autobiography Stanley 1992). The *courage to say "I"* can turn out to be highly relevant for theology and ethics, allowing *human fantasy and creativity* more space as a power for social transformation of the world. This is my personal conviction. The creatively daring courage to say "I" can also abolish human boundaries of the seemingly impossible, both *personal* and *political*.

Dorothee Sölle recalls the *subversive creativity of Jesus*:

> "When Jesus in the manner in which we have described says 'I', he lifted the so-called natural limitations of human life. His fantasy accepted no limits. In the power of his world-transforming fantasy he set aside the boundaries of nations, of social classes, of education, of sexual distinctions, of religions. Indeed, whatever it might mean in the language of myth, he conquered that boundary which more than any other imprisons us, the boundary between life and death" (Sölle 1995a, 55–56)

The *crossing of boundaries* may be the permanent good reason for *good theology*.

A *work of art* is more than just a transient glimpse into personal stories and experiences of the artist. It is both an object to be looked at for the viewer or the reader and a subject of its own, *telling a personal and social history*. Biographical und *personal elements* are always part of the *history of art* (Taborelli 1998, Lucie-Smith 1995, Hunter, Jacobus, and Wheeler 2000), particularly if looked at through the critical lens of *social history* and *feminist criticism* (Schneider 1999). Works of art always have a recognizable context in the life of the artist or the author.

There is a *social purpose* to art, as anarchist and pacifist *Leo Tolstoy* has pointed out: "Art is a human activity consisting in this, that one man consciously by means of certain external signs, hands onto others feelings he has lived through, and that others are infected by those feelings and also experience them . . ." (Tolstoy 1994, 59, on Leo Tolstoy see Lyas 1997, 59–66). Feelings are shared with others to be touched by similar experiences. Variously conflicting modern theories of art—be it representational, emotive-expressive, hermeneutical, marxist, feminist, post-colonial, poststructuralist or postmodern – find their common focus, as *Ken Wilber* would say, in what has been *"lived through"* (for various modern theories of art Wilber 1998, 96–138, on Ken Wilber see Visser 2002).

Such experiences need not be spectacular or exceptional. They can be quite *ordinary and common*, as American pragmatist *John Dewey* has pointed out, connecting the work of art with simply "discovered qualities of ordinary experience". This opens the door for *non-elitist concepts of art and aesthetics* (Dewey 1934, referred to in Korsmeyer 1998, 18, on John Dewey and art Alexander 1987, Shusterman 2001).

Anything experiential can be art. Whatever happens may be art. John Dewey's experiential and non-elitist art theory has strongly influenced *performance art* and *"Arte Povera"* favoring a focus on the ordinary, poor, and neglected (on performance art and Arte Povera Schneider 1996, 215–220, Butin 2002, 31–36). This allows us to open our eyes and ears to more than what is usually considered to be art (for postmodern and non-elitist concepts of art, including popular culture, music, rap, hip-hop Shusterman 2000). *Postmodern concepts of art* follow such an inclusive and non-elitist tradition as they propose highly eclectic and interdisciplinary perspectives in approaching art (on postmodern, eclectic, and interdisciplinary concepts of art Welsch 1990, 1996a, in entertainment theology Taylor 2008).

Theology Personally Lived

Works of art compare with *theological writing* on a *personal and experiential level*. Theological writers most often prefer to be theoretical and objective, disconnected from personal experience, feeling, and sensitivity that make up the fabric of life. My purpose for writing is to present an alternative vision. Theological writing may become *the creative expression of a living work of art*. Writing may be transformed into what woman writer and poet *Anais Nin* calls a "personal life deeply lived" (Nin 1975, 140–170). As a poet and writer she has presented such an artistic and literary expression of her life in her well-known *diaries from 1914–1974* (for biographies on Anais Nin and her diaries Benstock 1988, DuBow 1992, Fitch 1993, Salber 1995, Duxler 2002).

Written documents can become such a deeply personal work of art attempting to disclose the author's own stories and experiences along *autobiographical lines*. Theological writing thus conceived becomes a way of sharing and disclosing what has been lived through and has become part of the life experience of an author, written as a work of art out of creative disturbance and restlessness. "And what I discovered, when the diaries came out, were the thousands of women in lonely little towns who had no one to share their aspirations with; who had some creative disturbance and restlessness . . ." (Nin 1975, 33, on autobiography and feminist theory Stanley 1992).

Whether diary or biography, poetry or academic monograph, all of these forms in writing share one thing in common: they are deeply grounded in previously *lived through emotions and personal stories* which provide the experiential background for a literary work. This may be

Postmodern

claimed in a wider sense for any literary work "in which the history of painting, of mores, of places, of people is harmoniously interwoven, and following the Ariadne thread of one life deeply enough will allow us to discover many lives and imperishable depths of experience" (Nin 1966, 33).

Messy Texts

Even the *social sciences* are nowadays—in postmodern and post-empirical times—considered a *creative art form* (n the social sciences as creative and postmodern art form Nisbet 1976, Brown 1977–1995, Denzin 1989, 1997a, 2003). *Experiential self-reflection* is becoming acceptable in *"messy texts"* (for "messy texts" in postmodern cultural theory/sociology Denzin 1997a, XVII–XVIII) in which personal impression and social scientific argumentation are freely stitched together in a creative and imaginative textual quilt (in postmodern ethnography Krieger 1991, Ellis and Bochner 1996, Denzin 1989, 1997a, 2003).

Systematic theology as well may be looked at as an *imaginative social science* (for theology as social and imaginative Lane 1984, Lamb 1982, Sedmak 2001, 2002, Moltmann 2000, Coste 2000, 2002), as theology in general can be considered a *human and social science* (for theology as a human and social science Bärenz 2000, 28). The postmodern feel for the aesthetic and social dimension of religion may explain why theology and philosophy find their encyclopedic place, for instance in the new *Brockhaus* on "world culture" in the 20th century, right next to and after art, film, literature, and music (Brockhaus-Redaktion 1999, 520–577).

My own theological writing tries to be an experiential and, hopefully, in all modesty, *prophetic act of subversive imagination* remembering the past in order to creatively transform the present. Sometimes imagination needs to be radically and prophetically *decolonized* (for the decolonization of imagination Pieterse and Parekh 1995) in order to create a better future. Theological writing may become such a form of socially subversive and prophetic imagination, as rediscovered in the *biblical tradition* (Brueggemann 1978, 1989, 1991a, 1991b, 1993, 2001a) and in *systematic* and *practical theology* (Jennings 1976, Kaufman 1981, Green 1989, 1999, Ulanov and Ulanov 1999, Ritter 2000).

The social and ethical importance of *creative image making* in religion is forcefully captured by *Douglas John Hall*, as he reminds us that "nothing has been as influential in the creation of images of the human, historically speaking, as religion" (Hall 1986, 14).

The Community of the Weak

David Tracy adds to this the analogy between *art* and *systematic theology*:

> "In an analogous fashion, religion, like art, discloses new resources of meaning and truth to anyone willing to risk allowing that disclosure to 'happen'. It will happen, the systematic-as-hermeneutical theologians believe, by faithful attendance to, and thereby involvement in and interpretation of, the truth-disclosure of genuinely new possibilities for human life in any classical religious tradition of taste, tact, and common (communal) sense." (Tracy 1981, 67)

Socially Imagining a Better World

Theology for Social Change

Social imagination can be a powerful tool for *social change* (Mills 1959, Lakoff and Johnson 1980, Cooey 1994, Brueggemann 2001a). What we know about the world, and what we believe the world can become, is crucial for how we see and understand ourselves as individuals and communities.

Walter Brueggemann leads us through a theological reading of biblical texts enlarging our *social imagination for a better world*:

> "Everything is at stake because how we judge it to be in heaven is the way we imagine it on earth. If our mistaken notion leads us to an impassive, self-sufficient God in heaven, then the model for humanity, for Western culture, for ourselves, is that we should also be self-sufficient, impassive, beyond need, not to be imposed on. Willy-nilly, we will be made in the image of some God. The one for whose image we have settled, is a sure, triumphant God, who runs no risks, makes no commitments, embraces no pain that is definitional. Against that, the covenanting God of the Bible protests and invites us to protest." (Brueggemann 1994, 46)

Expectant *hope* and memories of *pain* are deeply influencing the way we see and look at the world (on memories of hope and pain in biblical theology Brueggemann 1992a, 1992b). Body and mind are involved. Religious imagination weaves together what we have experienced, what we feel, suffer, know, and believe. *Body and emotion,* telling about our deepest hope and pain, strongly shape imagination and fantasy in politics and

Postmodern

epistemology (Brooker 2001, 18–20, Csordas 1994, Johnson 1987, Lutz and Abu-Lughod 1990, Bendelow and Williams 1998).

Feminist radical theologian/thealogian *Paula M. Cooey* reminds us of the determining importance of *embodied imagination:*

> "We have ample evidence that the work we do as theologians and thealogians is imaginative construction, particularly, though not exclusively, the construction of deity; thus we map the faces of our own values . . . Yet, we have only begun to map the theological and thealogical significance of bodies, either for imagination or for the imaginative construction of religious symbols." (Cooey 1994, 128–129)

Theology Ethical and Biographical

Religious imagination very often takes an *ethical and biographical form*, whether as a memorable event, a powerful image, or an impressive moment of some *personal encounter* (for fundamental theology out of a personal encounter Taylor 1990, on hermeneutical implicature Schrag 1986, 1997). And some silently told biographies can even radically change our lives, as we let other people and their pain get close to us and touch our hearts and souls.

> "As we seek continually to substantiate through history these briefly glimpsed, necessarily plural, and always provisional images, the images serve nevertheless to beckon us onward toward a more just future. The provisional image lies for me right now in the brown eyes, the toothy grin, and the large nose of Alicia Partnoy, speaking softly the unspeakable to roughly six hundred first-year college students and their associated faculty on a hot autumn day at Trinity University in San Antonio. Alicia Partnoy, once disappeared, reappeared and lived to tell about it." (Cooey 1994, 129)

Alicia Partnoy was a university student, poet, and mother of a small child when she disappeared in 1977 under the military regime in Argentina, only to reappear years later after surviving violent prison experiences and physical torture.

Other *biographical images* could easily be added, taken from memorable experiences in the everyday world, breathing into theology a life and concrete shape of its own, socially and politically subversive, as we *imagine God and the world* in creative new ways (Jennings 1976, 1985, Kaufman

1981, 1993, 2000, 2006, in pragmatic historicism Davaney 2000). *Human experience* and *theological reflection* will be closely interwoven in my own writing, searching for a creativity which opens itself to the workings of various aspects of *emotional intelligence,* quite often left out in modern academic, cultural, and theological work (on emotional reason/intelligence in cultural creativity Ray and Anderson 2000, on theological work as creative/communal O'Connell Killen and De Beer 1994, Cochrane 1999, Sedmak 2002).

"Everything Starts With a Good Cry"

Theology and Human Experience

In talking about *human experience* we describe *our own social context* (on language, human experience, and social context Giglioli 1982, Edwards 1995, Holmes 1992, Kress 2001). A growing sensitivity for feminine language and the workings of power in the social construction of shifting identities has released a diversity of possible linguistic ways of self-expression in the field of academics (for feminist linguistics Lakoff 1975, Kramarae, Shulz and O'Barr 1984, Hodge and Kress 1993, Talbot 2001, Samel 2000). In talking about ourselves, we disclose personal and social reasons for what we say, remember, defend, focus on, or argue about. All this connects and roots us back to our own, most private and personal experience.

Traditionally, a strong academic interest in the importance of *human experience* for *theological reflection* has been shown in *Roman Catholic fundamental theology,* both in North America and Canada (in North America O'Collins 1981, 32–52, Schüssler Fiorenza 1984, 296–301, Gelpi 1978, 1994, Mueller 2007, in Canada Lacelle et Potvin 1983), as well as in German speaking Europe (Döring 1992, Sedmak 1995, 30–62, 2000, 30–162, Waldenfels 2000, 154–180, Wagner 2003, 24, 150–155). *Protestant theologies* of the Word most often have closed off the vision for the non-linguistic and experiential (on human and religious experience in Protestant theology Sundermeier 1999a, Gelder 1992, 1–14, Schürger 2002). This, in spite of living in a sociologically named *experience society* (Schulze 2001).

Roman Catholic *Edward Schillebeeckx,* among others, has put human experience at the *center* of biblical traditions, predominantly found in the history of Jesus. *Disclosure experiences* can occur in conversation with biblical traditions, critically correlated with human experience in contemporary society. *Fundamental theology* as *hermeneutical and critical theory of human praxis* allows us through Schillebeeckx a new appreciation of human experience in the process of revelation (Schillebeeckx and Van Iersel 1979, Schillebeeckx 1979-2004, in autobiographical interviews Schillebeeckx 2004, on Edward Schillebeeckx the reader Schreiter 1987, followed by Schreiter and Hilkert 1989, Hilkert and Schreiter 2002, Gibellini 1995, 312-335).

This has opened the way, predominantly in North America, for *Process theology* in Roman Catholic theological circles (Lee 1974, Cargas and Lee 1976, Gelpi 1978, Cousins 1994, Bracken and Suchocki 1997, Keller and Daniell 2002), while Europe is only starting to open up to *Process theology's* influence (Faber 2003, Gounelle 1981, 2000). An ensuing *critical dialogue* with *Edward Schillebeeckx* among his students and followers has further strengthened the basic importance of human experience in fundamental theology (Schreiter and Hilkert 1989, Iwashima 1982, Bowden 1983, Kennedy 1993a, 1993b, Hilkert and Schreiter 2002). Others have critically pursued and enlarged his approach, using it as a stepping stone for a *biographical feminist theology* (Maassen 1993, Gössmann 2002, 102-106).

An equally partisan interest in human experience can be found in *feminist theologies*, both in *North America* (Young 1990, Hogan 1995, O'Hara Graff 1995, Isasi-Diaz 1996, Rodriguez 1996, Solberg 1997, Parsons 2002) and in *German speaking Europe* (Sölle 1978, Schaumberger 1991, Maassen 1993, Klein 1994, 1998, Stuart 1997, Gössmann 2002, 102-106). Historical and cultural differences of *experience* are being transgressed and integrated in *postcolonial and post-traditional solidarities* (Kwok Pui-lan 1997, 2005, Keller, Nausner, and Rivera 2005).

Postbarthian, postliberal, and *postmodern Protestant theologies* as well have reopened the Pandora's box of a still undecided debate between students of *Paul Tillich* and followers of *Karl Barth*. A vote in favor of "human experience as Word of God" (Driver 1977, 1981, on Paul Tillich and the legacy of a Chicago theology of culture in modernity and postmodernity Bulman 1981, Musser and Price 1996, 449-459, Dorrien 2006, 123-143) has led to new areas of research and writing on a *theology of culture in postmodernity*. In good posttillichian manner, in interdisciplinary cooperation with *cultural studies*, human experience is being socially deconstructed and reconstructed with the help of *Jacques Derrida, Michel Foucault, Jacques Lacan, Emmanuel Lévinas*, as well as *radical French feminism*.

The Community of the Weak

Political theologies of liberation in times of a radically fragmented *modern and postmodern shaking of foundations* (Taylor 1986, Tillich and Church 1999) in postderridian and postlacanian deconstructions of the logocentric self need to redefine the meaning of *solidarity* and the politics of *identity* in view of a new social vision in fundamental and systematic theology (on solidarity and a politics of identity in fundamental and systematic theology Hopkins 1993, Hopkins and Davaney 1996, Batstone, Mendieta, Lorentzen and Hopkins 1997, Sedmak 1995–2003, Rieger 1998, 2007, Taylor 1990, 2011). Afro-American and womanist, Asian-American, hispanic, gay and lesbian voices are thereby bringing in their own *personal and political experiences* to formulate a *new systematic vision* (Chopp and Taylor 1994, Thistlethwaite and Engel 1998, Evans 1992, Gonzalez 1990, Isasi-Diaz 1993, Thomas/Wondra 2002, Schürger 2002).

Culture, Language, and Experience

The academic debate in systematic theology on the relationship between *culture, linguistics,* and *human experience,* started by *George Lindbeck*, may never be determinatively resolved (Lindbeck 1984, Tilley 1995, 89–113, McGaughey 1997, 172–194, Kamitsuka 1999, Goh 2000, Eckerstorfer 2001). Human experience is socially and culturally predetermined by various "storied communities of tradition" (Rosenwald and Ochberg 1992). And although there is in my view no convincing necessity to give communal priority to an intratextual norm—be it biblical or church tradition—in order to formulate a contemporary systematic theology, in *postchristian times* (Horster 1999) it is certainly a timely and helpful reversal of priorities to point out:

> "This conclusion is paradoxical: Religious communities are likely to be practically relevant in the long run to the degree that they do not first ask what is either practical or relevant, but instead concentrate on their own intratextual outlooks and forms of life." (Lindbeck 1984, 128)

In *postmodern times* (Sim 2001, Ritzer 1997, Bertens 1995, for theology Lakeland 1997, Ward 2005, Penner 2005, Smith 2006, 2008, Taylor 1990, 23–45, 1997, 2011) however, such clearly storied communities of tradition are no longer available (on the breaking-up of community Bounds 1997) as they are radically fragmented into various *hybrid and syncretistic cultures.*

Terrence W. Tilley and *Stuart Kendall*, strongly distancing themselves from *Lindbeck's* overly simplistic and "premodern" (Tilley 1995, 106) cultural-linguistic worldview of faith communities, remind us: "Thought in the postmodern age requires acceptance of the problem of difference . . ." (Tilley 1995, 108). People in these times no longer live in a world of a presumed unity and simplicity. Wherever people try to live together in community there is a great diversity of taste, opinion, tradition, conviction, emotion, and hopeful vision.

> "Hence, the idea of the community has become quite complex in postmodernity. It is not clear that Lindbeck's cultural-linguistic approach has accounted for this complexity. The problem is not that the 'community' doesn't exist, but rather that several interrelated, overlapping, diverse, yet dependent communities exist simultaneously within the same space. Indeed, each of us inhabit or dwell in multiple communities." (Tilley 1995, 105, for a feminist critique of George Lindbeck see Welch 1990, 103–106)

The world nowadays is much more complex and ambiguous, as we are constantly challenged to recognize and accept "the play of differences in our writing, our language, but also in our world, in our communities" (Tilley 1995, 106).

Theology and Power

Furthermore, these *multiple communities* are made up of individuals and groups of people with *very unequal possibilities* to express themselves and to name their experiences within a given interpretive framework. As Christians living all over the world and embedded in very diverse social locations we do share a *common language* as we listen to *biblical stories* that have been and continue to be handed to us, shaping the way we experience and make sense of our *present lives*.

And yet, as South African systematic theologian *James R. Cochrane* points out, openly questioning Lindbeck's over-simplistic social and political worldview from a radically revised cultural-linguistic and communitarian liberation perspective, "the language game is plural, contested, fraught with the effects of systematic distortion and always imbued with unequal relations of power" (Cochrane 1999, 155–156).

Feminist poststructural theologian *Sharon Welch* notes:

> "Lindbeck's reliance on the cultural-linguistic approach evades two fundamental problems: (1) the determinative effect in theological work of the theologian's own social and political location within this cultural-linguistic matrix and (2) the possibility that the 'grammar of faith' is itself oppressive." (Welch 1990, 106)

Frederick Herzog poses the crucial question:

> "Lindbeck's cultural-linguistic model, however, does not deal any less with universal concepts, though emphasizing not experiential but linguistic processes . . . Where is the social location of such a project?" (Herzog 1999, 226)

Actual social and political questions in *experiences of injustice and systemic differences of power* according to someone's *social location* (in biblical studies Segovia and Tolbert 1995a, 1995b, in Christian ethics Müller 1999, 63–66, in theology De La Torre 2004) in a given human community are not at all addressed in postliberalism, as it leaves out any talk about a "world of difference and power structures" (Tilley 1995, 106). *Radical sinfulness* and *systematic distortion* (Habermas 1970, Arens 1995a, 1997, Schüssler Fiorenza 2006) are present in all intratextually constructed worldviews and have an influence on whether individuals and communities are capable of critically stepping out of their tempting *hermeneutical blindness* to "the hybris of those privileged in the power hierarchy" who self-deceivingly "defend their 'orthodoxy' as normative over 'heterodoxy'" (McGaughey 1997, 193). This painfully omnipresent and contradictory world of *socially unequal and culturally hybrid experiences in secular and faith communities* cannot be left out so easily.

> "Whether such communities can be structured so simply as 'intratextual' communities and thus render their members free of the world is another question, one which seems unlikely, at best." (Tilley 1995, 113)

There could be some loosening of the tension between presumably opposing positions, if the *experiential-expressive* and the *cultural-linguistic* are not set in opposition to each other (Lindbeck 1984, 30–45). Liberation, postliberal, and revisionary theologies need to listen more carefully to each other and to *the power dynamics of culture* in order to overcome only seemingly exclusive positions (Taylor 1990, 23–75, also Brown 1994, Lints 1993, Stell 1993, Herzog 1999, Kamitsuka 1999, Goh 2000 where the various models are not set against each other) and to creatively imagine "another way to live which eschews the power of violence" in "communities of a Power which makes for Righteousness" (Tilley 1995, 113).

Theology Post-Constantinian

A *systematic theology in the 21st century* which is sensitive to the *many faces* and workings of *power* (Boulding 1990) in different *communities of this world* most probably will need to form various *rainbow epistemological "coalitions"* (Wetherilt 1994)—be it postliberal, postmodern, poststructural, postfeminist, postcolonial, or simply postcritical—, but the meaning of these terms needs to be told in various *personal stories mutually shared in community* (Albrecht 1995, Walton 1994, Cochrane 1999, Sawyer 2003).

Coalitional thinking in our *theological epistemology* may therefore be the new and creative world music for the future, as feminist fundamental theologian *Ann Kirkus Wetherilt* notes:

> "Coalition often is talked about only in the context of explicit political action. If action, named as resistance struggle against structures of domination, is an integral part of the construction, validation, and expression of knowing for the communities involved, then understandings of coalition must also be expanded to include all aspects of such knowledge production and valorization. The development of a theo-ethic that is committed to hearing and giving voice to multiple standpoints requires engagement in coalition for the production of knowledge in the academy as well as in the day-to-day struggle." (Wetherilt 1994, 126)

We may also have to learn in a new way—as a *marginalized and post-Constantinian church with no power* moving into the *21st century* (Hall 1995, Murray 2004, Frost 2006)—from those *theological and communitarian anarchists* in the *Radical Reformation of the 16th century* (Williams, 1992, Snyder 1995, Klaassen 1973, Littell 1958, Stayer 1976, 1991, Goertz 1988, 1993, 1996, Finger 2004, Augsburger 2006).

The *Radical or Left Wing Reformation* represented an epistemologically subversive and countercultural questioning of a *logocentric alliance of power and logos*. The critique of the alliance between religious and secular worldviews—the historical dominion of the sword to advance religious conviction—goes back to *Anabaptist* ethical and theological roots (on the Anabaptist theological and ethical roots as regards to war and power

Stayer 1976, Stassen und Gushee 2003, Finger 2004). This anarchist critique of the alliance between Word and power in the context of a *theology of radical discipleship* may open up new avenues for contemporary debates (for a Radical Reformation mission theology in postmodern times Murphy 1999 and Murray 2004).

Theology of Discipleship

A *theology of discipleship* (Segovia 1985, Barnes 1995, Metz 1978, Sedmak 2000, 108–162, Augsburger 2006) listening to the marginal strands of this left wing tradition will be an important contribution to the actual debates on theological epistemology, as "the descendants of the Radical Reformation have continued to give priority to discipleship over dogma" (McClendon 1986, 20, quoting Myers 1994, 110). We can find here a *visionary historical precedence* that may have *faithful successors* nowadays among *deconstructivist* as well as *reconstructivist postliberals* against a *Mennonite, Quaker,* or *Baptist/baptist* background (Liechty 1990, Yoder 1994, Myers 1994, Murphy 1994, 1999, McClendon 1986, 1994, 2000, 2002, Finger 2004).

With the Quaker theologian *Ched Myers* we may note:

> "As an historical generalization it is fair to say that the more social status and privilege the church has assumed in a given social order, the more its theological discourse has taken on a defensive, apologetic and abstract character. Conversely, when the church has had less status, or was willing to risk losing it, its theology has tended to be more offensive, critical, and practical." (Myers 1994, 109)

Any serious attempt to recreate a biblical, theological, and ethical vision for the world will always fall back on fragile and unique *personal and social experiences in community* (on community in biblical theology Hanson 1986, Banks 1994, in systematic theology Grenz 1994, 1998, Clapp 1996, Cochrane 1999, Kirkpatrick 2001, in practical theology Walton 1994, Dudley 2002, Sawyer 2003, Marsh 2005). Experiences that have shaped us in who we are today.

> "It is here that we must finally return to the problem of God. Integral to the construction of meaning and purpose is the construction of an image of God, an image which stands ahead of us, calling us to acts of justice and reconciliation, a God who meets us in those times of quiet meditation when we are most

centered on the creative, transcending and loving promptings of the soul and spirit." (Liechty 1990, 100)

Painfully reminded of the *human experience of suffering* and unfulfilled visions of human salvation and reconciliation in the world, a theology of the *life-giving Spirit* will not be able to divorce communal experiences from systematic theological formulation (Blaser 1978, Moltmann 1992, 17–77, Kitamori 1974, Koyama 1974, 115–125, Sölle 1975, Dantine 1976, 125–253, Wallace 2002). It may be necessary sometimes to feel and *embrace the pain* (Brueggemann 1992a, 1992b, 1997, Sölle 2001), to fall apart, and to weep and cry in order to relearn to confess and resist with our own theological formulations (on weeping, crying, confessing, and resisting Smith 1992). Theology without pain is in great danger of losing itself, its soul and its spirit. "*Everything starts with a cry*", good theology as well (on "everything starts with a cry" Aguirre 1997).

Communal Knowing from Experience

Theology Walking

Most often *systematic theology* in *Europe*—I am here writing as a European—has become an *artificial language game* prisoner of its own *academic context*, based on the assumption that academic writing should remain unrelated to *extracurricular events* and *social contexts*. Theological writing conceived this way becomes an *enclosed reflection* by an individual working within a limited world of books and authors in a secluded environment. Relevant events in the *life of the author* are rarely considered adequate references for academic writing, especially in *systematic theology*.

To read in theological writings about *places of birth, stories of childhood, biographical turning points, personal engagements,* and *courageous coming-outs*, or any other personally revealing and disclosing *confessions*, is rather seldom in European circles, with only a few minor exceptions (for places of origin, stories, biographies, and the coming-out of the personal in German systematic theology Biehl und Johannsen 2002, 13–20, Henning und Lehmkühler 1998, Schneider 1997, Weinrich 1999, Schürger 2002, Sedmak 1995–2003).

It is rather exceptional to find someone like *Jürgen Moltmann* conclude his innumerable contributions to the major loci in systematic theology after more than fifty years with a closing work on *epilegomena* instead of *prolegomena*. In these closing reflections and retrospective summaries of important turning points in a lifetime of systematic writing, we find an encouraging academic freedom to *mix the autobiographical with the theological* (Moltmann 1999, 2000). "It has taken me some time and effort until through the prompting of my wife I also dared to say 'I' in theology" (Moltmann 1999, 14).

This is no small step in a *European context* celebrating the *detached author* in matters of *academia*. "You could not see from the great books of my teachers who had written them when and where" (Moltmann 1999, 14). Theology, however, is *a personal path to walk on*, not a detached idea to contemplate from a safe and abstracting *distance*.

> "I have realized over the last thirty years that abstractions from one's own situation and life history are much less able to be communicated to others than the concrete truth, however subjectively or contextually it may be formulated." (Moltmann 1999, 15)

It is a *personal path* to be discovered *step by step*.

> "The path only became clear while walking. And my attempts to walk are of course determined by the personal-biographical, the political-contextual, and the historical kairos in which I live." (Moltmann 1999, 11)

Theology Traveling

Systematic theology with *open hearts, moving feet* and *working hands* in the context of *communal human experiences* will always be more of a *God-walk* and less of a *God-talk* (John 14:6, on theology as God-walk Herzog 1988, Williamson 1999, Schneider 1990, Schneider 1997, 14–16, Rieger 2011). Theology is a *practical way* (Volf 2002, Volf and Bass 2002) on which people walk, talk, sing, chant, pray, suffer, move and act, with their *feet on the ground* walking (Boff 1987, *Vamos Caminando* 1983, Rieger 2011), while not losing too many words which change nothing. Biblical faith as fundamental theology is *action-oriented* (Arens 1995a, Haight 2001, Taylor 1990, 2011), changing the hearts of those walking, proclaiming theology *along the way* with people and their faith and ethics changing. The biblical image of *the way* needs to be remembered in writing *fundamental* and *systematic theology* (Biehl und Johannsen 2002, 63–65, 182–189, Geffré 1983, 263–280, Sedmak 1999, 157, 2000, 108–162, Waldenfels 2000, 376–382, 2002, 23–26, 1994, 167–187).

Postmodern

Theology on such a *practical way* does and should not proclaim *cheap grace*, empty talk, and non-consequential intellectual play. Theology in the social tradition of *Dietrich Bonhoeffer* and lived as *radical discipleship* (Bonhoeffer 1954, 1960, 1995, 120-185, on Bonhoeffer see De Gruchy 1991, 1999, Green 1999, Mottu 2002) will never stand still and unmoved on useless talk. Theologians quite often have a way of talking a lot, while standing still. *Biblical truth* as *Christopraxis* (Taylor 1990, Arens 1995a) is a *practical journey* to walk on in a world in desperate need of change. "Truth is to be done and can be done . . ." (Arens 1995a, 1). *Christian discipleship* is *doing the truth* as we are *travelling along the way* that our faith calls us to *follow* in the midst of those many and various conflicts of this world (Gollwitzer 1982, 174-193). *Experience* is the *melody* we sing as we are *walking*.

Experiential Moving

Experience—in *German* the word *Erfahrung* includes the verb *fahren (moving, driving)*—is like *travelling*, going on a journey through life time, moving from one place to the next, taking memories along the way, getting in touch with our story as we are looking back (on experience in philosophy as travel Schnädelbach 2002, 109, in theology Sundermeier 1999a, Schürger 2002). "Experience is what the person had to face as dangers on a journey and what he keeps in his memory as a result of that journey" (Biehl und Johannsen 2002, 66).

The *Bible* tells many stories about *travel*. "Jahwe was formerly a 'wayfaring God' and his people a 'pilgrim people'. People are constantly on the move, travelling. This is why the Bible is also a book about experience" (Biehl und Johannsen 2002, 63). Experience as *visiting* and *walking* in moving through *life worlds* finds a new and *prime place* in *systematic theology*, both *Protestant* (Biehl und Johannsen 2002, 63-78, Fischer 2002, 309-313, Lange 2001a, 27-51, Gelder 1992, 1-14, Schürger 2002, 11-88) and *Roman Catholic* (Sedmak 1995, 30-62, 2000, 30-162, Wagner 2003, 24, 150-155).

Theology undertaken as *experiential walking* will not be, as pointed out by Roman Catholic fundamental theologian *Clemens Sedmak*, a lonely and secluded endeavor, cut off and well protected from the daily walks of *everyday people and everyday language*. Systematic theology as *practical* (Sedmak 1999, 157-165, 2002, 6-20) will put behind the ivory tower of lonely reading and writing and typing in books and papers, screens and megabytes for the *marketplace*—or with Protestant Christian ethicist *Denis Müller* the Rue du Bourg or St. Laurent in Lausanne (Müller 1999, 66)—of public talk and private gossip in sharing life with *real people*. "Theology as community work of a people on pilgrimage, not as a product of a lonely spirit in an ivory tower—that would be the vision" (Sedmak 1999, 157).

Theologians nowadays are called to become *pilgrims* and *pioneers of old*, now as then *leaving home* as *travelling world explorers*, packing their backpack, ready to visit new places (Sedmak 2002, 16), taking only as little as needed for *little theologies* (Sedmak 2002, 119–157).

The way North American Roman Catholic and fundamental theologian *John J. Mueller* remembers and projects the *spirit of pilgrims*:

> "They have pulled up stakes, harnessed the wagons, and set off for new and unknown territories. Theology is moving, unsettled, searching for and discovering new territories and peoples." (Mueller 1988, 95, quoted in Sedmak 2002, 120)

Theology walking along *streets* and *corners*, places and pubs, greeting people here and there, travelling, strolling along paths and alleys, will try "to make out of the sitting theology in the ivory tower . . . a walking theology on the marketplace" (Sedmak 1999, 165). *Systematic theology visiting the marketplace* will chat and listen, laugh and joke around, as people are telling their daily stories, bumping into each other in their *daily walks* on a *lifelong journey* along a social map of shared joyful or painful experience. *Theology moving*, yet *grounded*, little, yet *rooted*, itinerant, yet *worldly*.

> "The little theologies we are advocating are moving, unsettled—in the way Jesus was moving, unsettled as an itinerant preacher—yet rooted firmly in the God who is the ground of being and world process." (Sedmak 2002, 120)

Systematic theology as *experiential, social,* and *colloquial* will not rejoice in "making out of ten books an eleventh" or think it may be enough "to make a few footnotes to Paul" (Sedmak 1999, 165). The goal of systematic theology as *practical* (Volf and Bass 2002) should not be one more and further big book with big notes and big words.

Little experiences, little concepts, little stories, and *little memories*—but personally experienced—should guide and lead fellow travelers along a life journey towards some loose-end future, carrying along a light backpack with, as *Robert McAfee Brown* would say, a loose-leaf notebook instead of *Thomas Aquinas'* or *Karl Barth's Summa*. A toolbox and a backpack, not

Postmodern

a library, will be the future for systematic theology as practical (Sedmak 2002, 120).

Systematic theology as *practical* will try to teach and learn a more creative kind of *artisanship for a new humanity* (Sedmak 2002), with theologians as *village cooks* (Sedmak 2002, 17–20), bumping into people in the streets, joining the village crowd at dawn, preparing a meal at the village fire, mixing ingredients and human stories, as systematic theologians of a practical future will move and walk in a *mix or marriage* "between theology and experience, between theology and the lifeworld, between theology and social theory" (Sedmak 1999, 165), trying to *make sense* out of all those many and various *personal, social, and political experiences of people* they have *lived and walked with*.

Experience as *travel* (on a philosophy of travel De Botton 2002, on theology travelling Rieger 2011) is always *social and political* (Schnädelbach 2002, 109–145) as well. Experience is that *melody* that resonates in everything we *think* and *do*.

Theology Political

Theological writers have been slow to recognize the importance or relevance of *theological epistemology as a social and political question*. Deconstructivist systematic theologian *Charles Winquist*, describing the *academic logos*, notes:

> "The framing of a discourse is the enfranchisement of a voice ... Liberation and revolution are often about voice, about being allowed to speak. The diverse politics of liberation are not just about politics. They are also about epistemology and, conversely, epistemology is always also about politics." (Winquist 1995, 50)

Feminist epistemologies have pointed out the *social conditioning* of the ways we think we know this world. Epistemologies as theories about how we know what we know are being rewritten from a *feminist perspective* (Alcoff and Potter 1993, Duran 1991, 1998, Code 1998, Tanesini 1999, Gamble 2001). *Truth, knowledge, science,* and the social significance of theory and academic work are being reformulated in new ways, pointing out the *social location* (Smith 1987, 1990, Harding 1991, 1998, Gamble 2001) as well as the *social construction* (Minnich 1990, Code 1991, Rose 1994, Gamble 2001) of all our knowledge, culture, and scientific endeavor. *German speaking Europe* is catching on in the discussion (Nagl-Docekal

1999, Schneider 1998, 228–236, Becker-Schmidt und Knapp 2003), while *feminist theologies of the cross* in *North America* are opening up new ways of thinking about knowing *how we know* (for a feminist theology of the Cross in epistemological terms Solberg 1997).

Feminist historian of philosophies of science *Helen E. Longino* notes that "feminist rethinking of the subject of knowledge reinforces views about the conditioned nature of subjectivity and is well accommodated by a contextualist and social analysis of justification" (Longino 1999, 349, also Longino 1990). Social philosopher *Frederick Schmitt* introduces *social epistemology* which "studies the bearing of social relations, interests, roles, and institutions—what I will term 'social conditions'—on the conceptual and normative conditions of knowledge." (Schmitt 1999, 354, on social epistemology Schmitt 1994).

Theology as of Everyday

Feminist epistemologies, recognizing the *social construction of knowledge* (Smith 1987, 1990, 2005) and the *community-oriented* nature of empirical thinking, base themselves on *everyday experience* (Smith 1987, 1990, 2005, Gardiner 2000, Highmore 2002a, 2002b), both political and personal. As feminist sociologist *Dorothy E. Smith* (Smith 1987, 1990, 2005, on Dorothy E. Smith see Gardiner 2000, 180–206) points out, this requires a whole new way of *artistic thinking and writing* in the social sciences. "We have not known, as poets, painters, and sculptors have known, how to begin from our own experience, how to make ourselves as women the subjects of the sociological act of knowing . . ." (Smith 1987, 69).

Placing our *day-to-day experiences* of *"the everyday world as problematic"* (Smith 1987) at the center of social research and writing (Gardiner 2000, Highmore 2002a, 2002b, Schäfer 1998, Brüsemeister 2000), getting sensitive to the everyday world in all its *concreteness*, constitutes no small "Copernican shift" (Smith 1987, 99) in *historical, sociological, cultural, philosophical*, as well as in *theological thinking* (in fundamental theology Sedmak 1995, 30–62, 2000, 30–162, 2002, in Christian ethics Bondolfi, Heierle und Mieth 1983, McClendon 1986 and 2002).

The *everyday world* leads us back to the commonly shared *first place* from where we all start while looking at our past and present lives, "the place from within which the consciousness of the knower begins, the location of her null point" (Smith 1987, 88).

Thinking about her own *everyday experiences*, an *experiential sociological writer* does not just abstract and conceptualize, but also *smells, tastes, hears* and *feels* the world.

> "... like everyone else she also exists in the body, in the place in which it is ... the place where she confronts people face to face in the physical mode in which she expresses herself to them and they to her as more and other than either can speak. Here there are textures and smells. The irrelevant birds fly away in front of the window. Here she has flu. Here she gives birth. It is a place she dies in. Into this space must come as actual material events, whether as the sounds of speech, the scratchings on the surface of paper that is constituted as document, or directly anything she knows of the world. It has to happen here somehow if she is to experience it at all." (Smith 1987, 82)

Feminist philosopher of science *Jane Duran* notes:

> "Thus much of what we know about the world encourages us to believe that women are natural empiricists and that a feminist epistemology would not be based on speculation or pure ratiocination; rather, it would be a theory of knowledge based on everyday life." (Duran 1998, 114)

Women living an *interconnected life in community* are more naturally "immersed in the world of the sensuous, the concrete, and the material ..." (Duran 1998, 115). This is not an exclusively *feminist approach*, but can be connected with *other traditions in epistemology*.

> "The future development of feminist epistemology depends on our capacity to continue to interpret, construct, and connect points of view in such a way that what women see and know can be shared by all." (Duran 1991, 260)

The *American pragmatist tradition* provides a home for such an *experiential and community-oriented social critique* of philosophies of science (in feminist theory and philosophy of science Seigfried 1996).

> "The pragmatists originally asked us to divorce ourselves from the tradition of a priori speculation that had been the hallmark of philosophy up to that point ... As has been repeatedly argued here, it is that tradition, with its distanced and detached voice, that has denied the experience of so many and that has, indeed, failed to be consonant with the experience of most human beings." (Duran 1998, 182)

The Community of the Weak

Theology Communal

Feminist epistemologies are both *radical communitarian social critiques* and *experiential reformulations* of the *personal* and the *political*. "If there were a way to try to develop a feminist epistemology, the notion of *community* might be a key" (Duran 1998, 113).

Both *feminist epistemologies* and *communitarian critiques* of traditional methods of *political* (on communitarianism and feminist theory Frazer and Lacey 1993) and *theological* reflection (on theology and communitarianism Albrecht 1995, Wetherilt 1994, Bounds 1997, Solberg 1997, Keller 2003) are opening up new vistas for *academic writing*. *Communal experiences, personal stories, and life events* are receiving new attention in academic research, both in method and content (for social research and experience Hughes 2002a, in feminist social research Levesque-Lopman 1988, Diezinger et. al. 1994, Gamble 2001). *Multicultural social and political sciences* are retelling the material dialectic of experience in *post-colonial ways* (Sekyi-Otu 1996, Harding 1998, Gamble 2001).

Lived through human experience is no longer relegated to the expendable outskirts of academic research, only allowed as an illustration for a general theoretical argument. For several decades now *human experience* has become the *focal starting point* of academic research in feminist theory, Afro-American studies, political science, sociology, legal studies, and theology in view of the *"radical historicity of human subjectivity"* (Albrecht 1995, 62) present in any academic work.

Feminist theologian *Gloria Albrecht* pleads for an *epistemology* in the context of a *communitarian liberation theology of the church*:

> "Women's stories of women are only beginning to be told publicly. In the absence of women's stories, publicly told by women und heard by all, women have struggled to give voice to their own experience of experience." (Albrecht 1995, 65)

I would like to follow a similar path. To *"give voice to one's own experience of experience"* has rightfully become the *starting point* of theological writing attempting to be relevant. Without such a grounding in human experience, theological reflection most often ends up to be sterile, aloof and gnostic.

Experience as conceived in *feminist* and *radical social ways* is most basically *personal* and *political*. *Power* and *powerlessness* are involved in both. The *social construction* of language, identity, the person, and experience participates in the distribution of power and powerlessness at any time. *Theology* needs to reconsider the *importance of experience* in personal, social, and political ways. *North American systematic theology* is leading the way.

Whose Experience Counts in Theological Reflection?

Theology Optional

The opening question of North American and Roman Catholic systematic and fundamental theologian *Monika Hellwig*, "Whose experience counts in theological reflection?" (Hellwig 1982), stands at the beginning of any theological writing. Choosing a *particular human experience* as a starting point for theological reflection is at the same time a *political* and a *personal choice* of a specific *theological option* (Jennings 1976, O'Brien 1992, McFarland 1998, Roberts 2000), both in *fundamental* (Klinger 1990, Sedmak 1995–2003) and *systematic theology* (in Roman Catholic dogmatics Hasenhüttl 1974, 1979, 38–49, 2001a, 2001b, Wagner 2003, 24, 150–155, in Protestant systematics Biehl und Johannsen 2002, 63–78, Blaser 1978, Moltmann 1999/2000, Schürger 2002, 11–88).

Giving special value to *subjective and personal experiences* honors authors and bygone traveling companions on a life journey quite removed from the limited worlds of books and papers, dissertations, and academic monographs. *Personal experiences and memories* make up the fabric of communal theological writing, thus honoring a variety of spirits still present beyond limited academic boundaries. *Theological writing* which sees "this question as the pervasive and truly revolutionary one in contemporary theology" (Hellwig 1982, 46) includes *human voices and faces* otherwise unseen and unheard if relegated to the background of academic work.

Personally experienced pain and joy create a *web of memories and expectations* of an individual, memories and expectations which again shape and guide whatever an author considers to be relevant. This is true for my own writing. I have never been able to disconnect whatever I have learned or read or written in my *theological thinking* from what I have experienced in *real life*.

During many years of *pastoral ministry* in different churches in *Switzerland*, theological themes have come up like an accompanying melody leading the way. *Real life experiences* and *academic theological reflection* have been influencing each other in an intimate way. The relationship between these *two life partners* may never be fully comprehended, since there is no simple or one-sided movement from one to the other (on experience and biography in Roman Catholic dogmatics Wagner 2003, 24, 150–155, Schneider 1990, Schneider 1997, in Protestant systematic theology Schürger 2002).

Theology Interdependent

The predominantly *male debate* between *postliberal George Lindbeck* (Lindbeck 1984, on George Lindbeck see Musser and Price 1996, 271–277) and his *cultural-linguistic* model of *human experience*, which is always and already preshaped by cultural symbols, stories, and communal traditions, and *liberal defenders*, viewing human experience as the pre-theological foundation of theological reflection according to an *experiential-expressive* model of religion, seems to remain within a one-sided and still premodern (Tilley 1995, 89-113) understanding of the relationship between *human experience* and *cultural symbols* and how they influence each other in the life of an individual or a community (on the relationship between theological tradition, human experience, culture, and community Brown 1994).

As *Wesley Kort* points out:

> "Lindbeck's project of severing religious doctrines from ties to subjective sources and referents and of locating them in the life of the Christian community is also a project to protect and preserve the objectivist or referential standing or thrust of doctrine. This unbalanced or incomplete use of postmodern discourses . . . is questionable. What goes for the subjectivist side goes for the objectivist, too. To employ postmodern modes of thought is to cut discourses from the security and stability of both poles . . ." (Kort 1992, 37–38, quoted in Tilley 1995, 107)

In my own life, both *human experience* and *theological symbols* have influenced and corrected each other, one shaping, questioning, or reframing the other, in a dynamic and mutual, quite often conflictual, but always *co-equal partnership* and *friendship* of a lively and tension-filled relationship of *interdependence* (Brown 1994). Neither side has ever been clearly separated or autonomously broken off from the other, a *dualistic concept* tied, as it seems, to old patriarchal and "premodern retreats to authority" (Tilley 1995, X) in theological epistemology. "In short, postliberalism, at least in its 'clean' versions, seems to be a bastion of premodern thought in a post-modern world" (Tilley 1995, 109).

Postmodern

Theology Polyphonic

Feminist theologian *Catherine Keller* presents a more convincing—and creatively *postmodern*—model for an *epistemology* which is *relational and non-dualistic*, weaving together the past with the future and tradition with human experience:

> "Love of what already is makes conscious the matrix of connection; in desire, love faces the future. Both the relations from which I come and the possibilities—for new modes of relatedness—toward which I be-come encounter me in and as my inmost Self." (Keller 1986, 213)

In a similar way, Brazilian woman liberation theologian *Ivone Gebara* pleads for an *inclusive epistemology* of the *"polyphonic and multicolored"* (Gebara 1999, 65), freely painting a new picture of theological epistemology that favors *ecofeminist, interdependent, process-oriented, gender-based*, and *affective ways of knowing* (Gebara 1999, 19–65). Premodern, modern, and/or postmodern in our various ways of looking at life, we may have to go back to the unifying and *earthbound spiritual awareness* that—in spite of our many and conflicting cultures, languages, and histories of traditions—humanly *we all breathe the same air*.

> "For this reason, an inclusive epistemology welcomes the great multiplicity of all religious experiences as different expressions of a single breath, a single pursuit of oneness." (Gebara 1999, 65)

Theology Coalitional

New—and more coalitional—modes of thinking (on coalitional thinking in the social sciences Clarke 1989, in feminist fundamental theology Wetherilt 1994) are asked for in order to overcome simplified *dualistic oppositions* between the past of *communal tradition* and the present as well as the future of *human experiences* (Keller 1986, Stell 1993, Brown 1994, McGaughey 1997, Gebara 1999, Haight 2001). *Artificial dichotomies* in methodology will not help. "Such dichotomies . . . make for wonderful rhetoric. But they shed little disclosive light on the human condition constituted out of a tension between a life-world shaped by a linguistic heritage and the sufferings and actions of the past that is challenged with responsible actions in a yet to be realized future" (McGaughey 1997,

190-191). *Individuals* and *communities* of the past and the present continue to confront us with raised voices to be heard in manifold ways.

A *postliberal "hermeneutics of restoration"* à la Lindbeck needs the self-critical and complementary vision (Brown 1994) of a *socially* and *politically* sensitive *"hermeneutics of suspicion"* (McGaughey 1997, 191). In a world of *systematic distortions* (Habermas 1970, Arens 1995a, 1997, Schüssler Fiorenza 2006) through *violence* and *exclusion* in the process of communication between the past and the present *human traditions* are no longer beyond suspicion. Too often traditions have been blind to their own inherent violence, excluding differences of voices, looking away from the suffering in many visible and invisible places.

> "The prescription for the loss of appreciation of the tradition is not a return to 'communal enclaves' of particularity, but, rather, an appropriate embracing of the hermeneutical situation and the need for imaginative variation. There is more light yet to break forth, there is more time to blossom forth, there are alternative social systems and networkings of solidarity yet to be achieved, but above all there is a crying need to rigorously experientially understand both the claims and the distortions of the past. There is a performance test for judging the adequacy if not the truth of a religious proposition, but it is not Lindbeck's statistical test of normative consensus in the religious practices of a community. Rather, it is the performative test of what enhances life, what builds up community and solidarity and tears down walls of destructive prejudice and misunderstanding as a consequence of isolationism, protectionism, and xenophobias." (McGaughey 1997, 194)

Theology Multi-Colored

Pleading for a *feminist fundamental theology* that listens to *the postmodern diversity* of contemporary human voices echoing God, Ann Kirkus Wetherilt notes: "A theological metaphor of a static and unitary Word cannot incorporate the voices of God that echo in the lives of diverse beings and the earth on which they live" (Wetherilt 1994, 149). A *radically revised methodology* in *fundamental theology* points the way to a more *multi-voiced systematic theology*, sensitive to various forms of exclusion and marginalization in the dominant academic discourse. The leading question needs to be asked right at the beginning, developing a *methodology for systematic theology* that will be more *inclusive* and *multi-colored*, carefully listening to those many and variously conflicting voices inscribed in bodies and emotions, languages and convictions of different people and their different human experiences in this world.

> "How might we develop a methodology through which the multiple voices of diverse cultures—and diverse people *within* cultures—could engage in theo-ethical dialogue with one another in the service of new possibilities for living together in the increasingly fragile world which we share?" (Wetherilt 1994, 7–8)

Theology Inclusive

More valued *coalitional and interdependent thinking* in systematic theology could very well overcome many presumed but only artificially created oppositions. Brazilian feminist theologian *Ivone Gebara* (Gebara 1999) pictures such a *new theological methodology* based on an *inclusive cosmology* of a *community of all living things*:

> "We need, little by little, to construct new styles of knowing that are intimately related to our new cosmologies . . . and to our new and more unified visions of reality and anthropologies. We need to overcome dualistic and hierarchical divisions among our ways of knowing and to underline the connections and the interdependencies among them . . . Ecofeminist epistemology is not, then, a fashionable mode of thought that can be put on like a new hat; neither is it knowledge that can be acquired like a new book. It is a stance, an attitude, a search for wisdom, a conviction that unfolds in close association with the community of all living beings." (Gebara 1999, 22–23)

Theology Interlacing

An *artistically woven hermeneutic* of *co-equal* and *mutually interdependent friendship* (Raymond 1986, Hunt 1991, Stuart 1995, 1997, Moltmann-Wendel 2000)—instead of *parental authority*—between *tradition* and *human experience* will always be "aware how vital a friend tradition is to experience . . ." (Stuart 1997, 70). Tradition and experience are forever thrown together in an *inseparable "web of life"* out of which many and various human melodies are repeatedly recomposed to join in the great *"dance of life"* (Welch 1990, 160).

Postliberal Baptist theologian *Elizabeth Barnes* (Barnes 1995) seems to be more in touch with the feminine complexity of such a tender relationship as she recomposes *Lindbeck's* one-sided focus on *biblical narratives* to include *contemporary experiences* in modern art, film, literature, and biographical stories of discipleship. *Non-foundational systematic theology* in postliberal times may become an *artistic weaving and interlacing* of various *stories of committed discipleship*, both past and present, that shape us in the way we see the world. In telling these stories, *systematic theologians* will quite naturally "interlace the biblical narratives with humankind's multitudinous narratives so that transformation occurs and a true story is told" (Barnes 1995, 9). The *artistic movement* in the relationship between *human experience* and *biblical narrative* is like that of a *creative dance*.

> "Interlacing is artistic. It is a kind of dance. It is a kind of artistic weave, a back-and-forth movement like that of the dance or the weaver's shuttle, joining biblical narratives and other narratives, now giving, now taking, interlocking, mutually enriching and expanding each the other. Mystery, surprise, delight, creation and re-creation; all these and more emerge as the interlacing proceeds." (Barnes 1995, 10)

Human experience and *theological reflection* are invited to stay closely together in an adventurous and open relationship with each other, living and *dancing together*, while feeling at home in a *common house of language and tradition* (Brown 1994), here and then giving birth to an ever renewed style of theology that will be personally and socially relevant for these postliberal and *posttraditional times* (Küng and Tracy 1989, Hall 1995, Stuart 2004, in trendy ecclesiologies Frost 2006). *Tradition* will be a common *house* to live in, ready for the birth of new things, sometimes newly painted, quite often differently arranged, most frequently creatively remodeled, in constant and renewed renovation for possible new doors, new windows, or new wallpaper, and, most certainly, new visions. Tradition filled with life, because amazing people are filling it with a *new spirit*.

Mindful of people like *Jacques Gaillot*, who as *Roman Catholic French bishop* in Paris, officially deposed in 1995 by the Vatican for some non-existing diocese in the Algerian desert, filled a house full of multicultural squatters with traditioning *new life* (autobiographical in telling the story Gaillot 1996), as he joined them as *homeless and church-less Roman Catholic bishop* at the *rue du Dragon* in *Paris*, sharing not just the tradition of the *Eucharist*, but his whole *everyday life* with them (Gaillot 1996, 17–24). One possible way *theological reflection* reflecting *tradition* may in the future *spiritually inhabit places* and streets just around the corner, fighting *death*, while giving new birth to *life*.

Theology Spiritual

The *theological symbol of the Spirit*—understood in an *incarnate and communal way*—opens a promising and inclusive route to keep both *theological reflection* and *human experience* related.

As *Jürgen Moltmann* notes:

> "Life in God's Spirit is *life against death*. It is not life against the body. It is life that brings the body's liberation and transfiguration. To say 'yes' to life means saying 'no' to war and its devastations. To say 'yes' to life means saying 'no' to poverty and its humiliations. There is no genuine affirmation of life in this world without the struggle against life's negations." (Moltmann 1992, 97–98)

Choosing between life and death can only be translated in concrete and *experiential terms* (Sölle 1981, Hall 1988, Richard 1983, Gutierrez 1991, Moltmann 1997, Bärenz 2000a). As a *fundamental theme* in *biblical* (Brueggemann 1996, Schottroff und Schottroff 1991) as well as in *systematic theology* (Moltmann 1992, 1997, Schneider 1992a–b, in practical theology Bärenz 2000a) it presents before us the clear necessity of an *ethical choice*.

The *power of the Spirit* works through earthly symbols and human languages, ordinary events and extraordinary happenings, *touching experiences and living traditions*. Conflict and reconciliation, evil and laughter, tragedy and healing, squatting and celebrating the Eucharist in churches and communities retell the social and *subversive stories of the Spirit of life* (Gaillot 1996, for subversive Church history Holl 1998, in pneumatic theology Snook 1999, Wallace 2002). A concrete and ethical *choice* for *life* against *death* in systematic theology has a powerful and determinative influence on the way books are written.

The Community of the Weak

Theology Newly Phrased

Personal and social contexts influence the writing of a book. The same is true of my own modest attempt to write down personal memories in view of new images and formulations in systematic theology. *Theological writing* partakes in the *Spirit of Life* who is *concrete* and *physical*. I hope to be able to show that *systematic theology* need not be gnostic, aloof or a language game in a purely spirited world without a concrete body and soul. In search of a *new religious language* personal truth is always *concrete* (Sölle 1969).

Dorothee Sölle pleads for such a *new language* that breaks the ice of the soul:

> "Scientific language dominates by forcing people to use its language and no other. In this sense the living space for a human language becomes smaller and more private. The person caught between scientific and everyday language is not assisted by its formulations. What the language of the classicists achieved for a long time and what Brecht attempted in our century, namely, expanding an intermediate area where people can express themselves humanly and holistically, seems more and more difficult. In this precarious situation, religious language also degenerates into advertising jargon on the one hand ('Give Jesus a try') and abstract theology on the other. Franz Kafka said: 'A book must be like an ax in order to break the ice of the soul.'" (Sölle 1993, 81–82)

Systematic theology can be an artistic expression of a *personal life deeply lived*. Written in such a *personal style*, systematic theology will be *narrative and poetic* (Taylor 1990, 1–22, Say 1990, Chopp 1989, 1995b, Sölle 1999b, Waldenfels 2000, 387–389, 2002, 67–90) "Without the narrative element, which includes retelling myths and narrating particular experiences, theology dries up" (Sölle 1993, 83). We live in a *common house of language*, yet each member of the house has his or her own *unique and personal story*. Sharing this story is the beginning of good theology. Theology written in such a personal and experiential style can be *empowering* and *leading to hope*. There may be a certain weakness in poetic and narrative language, but it also expresses a truly *biblical vision*.

> "Whenever we escape the language of domination and attempt another language—that is, learn to hear, understand, and speak another language—the linguistic creation, the new development of language, is a source of power and an encouragement that

extends far beyond analytical and critical knowledge... To sing of peace, in the midst of war, I believe, was the secret of the people in the New Testament, who trembled under a comparable misanthropic empire and sang their different songs. Thus they 'lived poetically' and shared with each other a different language." (Sölle 1993, 83)

Theological writing in such a *personal and experiential style* can lead to a profound *spiritual transformation* both for the author and the reader. It can open up a *new vision* of *biblical hope* in the *Spirit of Life*. "And whatever we mean by the word 'spirit'—let us just say with Tillich, that it involves for each of us our ultimate concern—it is in that simple awestruck moment, when great art enters you and changes you, that spirit shines in this world just a little more brightly than it did the moment before" (Wilber 1998, 136). It can even perform *little miracles* of "hearts alive, bodies restored, communities, families, the world—like the lame man, jumping up, leaping, singing, and praising God" (Brueggemann 1996, 157).

Theology as Autobiography

I was born out of wedlock. My life began as an illegitimate child of a working-class woman in a complicated triangle socially frowned upon, and yet frequently to be found even in well-respected circles. More than forty years ago, such a triangle still had dramatic consequences in a social environment which looked down on children and mothers outside of the ordinary. Birth had been given, in secret and without the approval of convention or tradition. Custody rights were withheld for a period of two years, a probation time during which a single working mother had to prove to be fit to raise a child on her own. The challenges of life had to be mastered with an absent and well-to-do father. Societal prejudice, legal barriers and open communal rejection of a life style outside of traditional form created a mix of feeling special and being different.

Only later did I hear from my mother, that my future could have taken another direction, had she followed the legal advice of a medical doctor who suggested to her—in line with the intentions of my biological father—to put me up for adoption in France. The French state adopted children out of wedlock, most of which would end up in their adult life in the foreign legion

> *as mercenaries of war. Experiences of prejudice and exclusion, rejection and the struggle for recognition are even today coloring different moments and memories while looking back. At the same time, I am grateful to realize that this required defining my identity as a patchwork of unconventional life scripts. Those of my mom, those of my own history, written with other coloring pencils than those of most normal kids in school.*

Theology as Memory

There may be more to tell, yet some of these *first memories* will reappear as basic tune or *musical motif* recurrently played and improvised on as life goes on. Only now do I realize how much these *first experiences* have shaped me in the way I see myself today. Lived through feelings, memories, values, beliefs, fears, wishes, and concrete choices have grown together in a life tree of *past memories and present experiences*. All this helps me to become aware of my *deepest and most personal roots*. It also helps me to tell *my own life story* to myself in order to understand and to put things together. Loose ends and shifting identities may be tied together or captured in a passing moment of self-reflection while looking back.

Memories shape and *define identities. Experiences* are the *storehouses of personal stories, narratives and life events.* Only later in life can it happen that we are suddenly reminded of old stories as we face new choices. *Past themes*, which have accompanied our life, continue to shape personal choices. Such *generative themes* (on generative themes in radical and political education Freire 1984, 1994, Araujo Freire and Macedo 1998, McLaren and Lankshear 1994, Shor 1992, hooks 2003, Ayers 2004, Jarvis 2004, Hof 2009) have both a *personal, educational, and political importance* for the human as well as religious development of an individual living in community (Mette 1994, 122–124, Scharer 1995, Hagleitner 1996, Schipani 1988, Groome 1998, Groome and Horell 2003), becoming more and more pronounced and *determinative for one's life* as they are continuously relived in different personal experiences.

As such they act like a *spiral movement*, reminding us of *past themes* as we move from one experience to the next, influencing language and vocabulary, emotion and conviction, ethical reasoning and moral sensitivity. We are born into a *linguistic and cultural world* predating us (Lindbeck 1984). And yet, at the same time, experience redefines words and convictions, emotions and personal logics, as we try to make sense of what we see, hear, taste and feel in the course of our lives.

Theology as Narrative

Systematic theology will become *autobiography* (Taylor 1990, 1–22, Metz 1980, 219–228, 1992/1977, 211–219, Hollenweger 1990, 11–29, Schneider 1997, Weinrich 1999, Waldenfels 2000, 87–90) as soon as the *narrative quality* of *human knowledge* and *reasoning* is recognized and laid open (Hinchman and Hinchman 1997, Venema 2000, Brooker 2001, 146–148, Bell 2002, 109–134). Theology as the telling of traditioning stories and life changing *biblical* and *modern biographies* is to a great extent and at its core *theological narrativity* (Metz 1973, Crites 1989, Chopp 1995b, Bradt 1997, Kitzberger 2002).

Stephen Crites (Crites 1989) makes a strong call for the *experiential and ethical importance of narrative* in the *modern and postmodern university*:

> "Still, the humanities have kept the story alive in the university... So long as the story retains its primary hold on the imagination, the play of immediacy and the illuminating power of abstraction remain in productive tension. But when immediacy and abstract generality are wrenched out of the story altogether, drained of all musicality, the result is something I can only call, with strict theological precision, demonic. Experience becomes demonically possessed by its own abstracting and contracting possibilities, turned alien and hostile to experience itself." (Crites 1989, 86)

In *postmodern times*, new *human and sacred stories* will bring about a "revival of ethical authority" and will make it possible "to recover a living past, to believe again in the future, to perform acts that have significance for the person who acts. By so doing, it restores a human form of experience" (Crites 1989, 88).

The *telling of stories* seems to be God's way of speaking to humans anyway, as *Edward Schillebeeckx* recalls in a little philosophical incident: "A small boy is said once to have remarked, 'People are the words with which God tells his story'" (Schillebeeckx 1989, XIII). *Narratives and stories of discipleship* (in fundamental and systematic theology Metz 1973, 1978, Tilley 1985, Stroup 1981, Barnes 1995, McClendon 1990, 1986, 1994, 2000, 2002, in dissident Mennonite spirituality Augsburger 2006) will radically restructure the way *systematic theology* is formulated in *posttraditional and postchristian times* (Metz 1980, 163–168, 205–228, 1992/1977, 161–164, 197–219, Taylor 1990, 1–22, Sedmak 1995–2003), as authors of systematic theologies will dare to join others in what feminist theologian *Rebecca S. Chopp* calls the creatively musical art of *"composing their lives"* (Chopp 1995b, 22, also Pederson 2001, both referring to Bateson 1990).

Roman Catholic *John Shea* (Shea 1978) puts it beautifully:

> "If GOD made man because he loves stories, creation is a success. For humankind is addicted to stories. No matter our mood, in reverie or expectation, panic or peace, we can be found stringing together incidents, and unfolding episodes. We turn our pain into narrative so we can bear it; we turn our ecstasy into narrative so we can prolong it ... We tell our stories to live ... And, quite simply, we are the stories God tells. Our very lives are the words that come from his mouth." (Shea 1978, 7–8)

Theology as Autobiography

Behind a *theological system* there is a *person* choosing to write about his or her most personal interests. Quite often, the *personality* of the author of theological writings remains hidden behind abstracting words and concepts. And yet, even the most innocent word-choice in writing betrays personal flavor and *autobiographical background*. *Human knowing* is fundamentally shaped by *autobiography* (Taylor 1990, 1–22, Schneider 1997, Weinrich 1999, Waldenfels 2000, 87–90).

Autobiography self-implies a writer in what he says, allowing readers to move *closer*, as radical North American systematic and cultural-political theologian *Mark L. Taylor* underlines: "Putting autobiographical elements into theology is one way to redress the often-lamented distance of theology from peoples' religious, cultural, and political experiences" (Taylor 1990, 2). Academic writers have no good reason not to get closer to where *real people* in *real life* are at.

European Roman Catholic fundamental theologian *Johann Baptist Metz's* notes *dogmatic theology's* widespread and "systematized fear of contagion from life that was not understood" (Metz 1980, 219, quoted in Taylor 1990, 2). *Life* is what is important to us, even if not always understood. What we consider *important* or relevant to be talked about, painful or joyful to tell others, *worthwhile* or crucial to look at, goes back to where we come from. *Systematic theology* needs to rediscover such a *personal standpoint* from where it writes from (on theology as story and narrative Meyer zu Schlochtern 1979, 49–56, Arens 1988, Schneider 1997, Weinrich 1999, Waldenfels 2000, 87–90, Kitzberger 2002, Musser and Price 2003, 340–345).

Feminist standpoint epistemologies (Denzin 1997b, 53–89, Harding 1991, Collins 1990, Smith 1987, 1990, Code 1998, Gamble 2001) remind us repeatedly of the *importance of our first experiences*, at birth, during our childhood and adolescence, in our growing up as young adults, along the life span leading us to where and what we live, think and feel today.

Feminist philosopher and social scientist *Patricia Hill Collins* opens her discussion of an *Afro-American standpoint epistemology* by recalling her *childhood* and *adolescence*:

> "When I was five years old, I was chosen to play Spring in my preschool pageant. Sitting on my throne, I proudly presided over a court of children portraying birds, flowers, and the other 'lesser' seasons. Being surrounded by children like myself—the daughters and sons of laborers, domestic workers, secretaries, factory workers—affirmed who I was . . . I loved my part, because I was Spring, the season of new life and hope. All of the grown-ups told me how vital my part was and congratulated me on how well I had done. Their words and hugs made me feel that I was important and that what I thought, and felt, and accomplished mattered. As my world expanded, I learned that not everyone agreed with them. Beginning in adolescence, I was increasingly the 'first', or 'one of the few', or the 'only' African-American and/or woman and/or working class person in my schools, communities, and work settings. I saw nothing wrong with being who I was, but apparently many others did. My world grew larger, but I felt I was growing smaller. I tried to disappear into myself in order to deflect the painful, daily assaults designed to teach me that being an African-American, working class woman made me lesser than those who were not. And as I felt smaller, I became quieter and eventually was virtually silenced." (Collins 1990, XI)

And black radical feminist *bell hooks* remembers:

> "To me, telling the story of my growing up years was intimately connected with the longing to kill the self . . . I wanted to be rid of the girl who was always wrong, always punished, always subjected to some humiliation or other, always crying, the girl

who was to end up in a mental institution because she could not be anything but crazy or so they told her." (hooks 1989, 155)

Little episodes causing joy or pain, lingering memories which cannot be forgotten, memorable moments which contribute to the *puzzle and patchwork* (Anderson 1997, Keupp u.a. 1999, Eickelpasch und Rademacher 2004) of *who we are today*. All of these elements are important building blocks of the biography and autobiography of an author. *Systematic theology* finds a *source* and *standpoint* in those memorable moments in the life of an individual or a community which cannot be forgotten. It is therefore high time, it seems to me, for systematic theology to become more openly *autobiographical* as well as *ethnographical* in a comprehensive sense of those terms.

The *social sciences* have long ago recognized the *interpretive importance* of *autobiography* as *"messy text"* in the form of autoethnography, ethnographic poetics, anthropological and sociological poetry or novels, short stories, New Journalism, performance texts, ethnographic fictions, and narratives of the self (Denzin 1997a, 90–228, 1989, 2003).

> "These messy texts are often grounded in the study of epiphanal moments in people's lives: the birth of a child ..., a sudden death ... The focus is on those events, narratives, and stories people tell one another as they attempt to make sense of the epiphanies or the existential turning-point moments in their lives... Messy texts are many sited, open ended, they refuse theoretical closure, and they do not indulge in abstract, analytic theorizing. They make the writer a part of the writing project." (Denzin 1997a, XVII)

An *ethnographic and autobiographical writer* is at the same time a *social and cultural critic*: "We study those biographical moments that connect us and our private troubles (our epiphanies) to the larger public culture and its social institutions ..." (Denzin 1997a, XVIII).

Autobiography has become an important category in various *social sciences*, both in *German-speaking Europe* (Wagner-Egelhaaf 2000, Fuchs-Heinritz 2000) and in *North America* (Krieger 1991, Okely and Callaway 1992, Ashley, Gilmore, Peters 1994, Currie 1998, Denzin 1989, 1997a, 2003). The *narrative* and *(auto)biographical voice* is redeemed in the social sciences as narrative or qualitative research, ethnography, critical hermeneutics, cultural studies, symbolic interactionism, and postmodern narrative theory (Currie 1998) listen to the authentic voices of poetic and political *interpretive life histories* (Ellis and Flaherty 1992, Hatch and Wisniewski 1995, Lincoln and Tierney 1996, Denzin 1989, 1997a, 2003).

Narrative therapy has pointed out the social, political and therapeutic importance of retelling and reframing one's personal life story (Freedman and Combs 1996, McLeod 1997). Feminists and critical historians underline the necessity of *personal memory work* in order to deal with the hidden past and to *"name silenced lives"* (Haug 1990, 1999, Personal Narratives Group 1989, McLaughlin and Tierney 1993, Rosenthal 1995).

The *personal* has become acceptable in *social science research and writing*. It will only be a matter of time until the *personal* will also become acceptable in *theological academic writing*. Here again, *North American systematic theology* is leading the way.

Theology as Ethnography

Ethnography may become the most promising *dialogue partner* in *North America* for a *systematic theology in the 21st century*. "Ethnography is that form of inquiry and writing that produces descriptions and accounts about the ways of life of the writer and those written about" (Denzin 1997a, XI).

A *multi-perspective postmodern ethnography* (Comaroff and Comaroff 1992, Clough 1992, Willis 2000, Denzin 1989, 1997a, 2003) which looks at narratives of the self, epistemology, cultural politics, modern cinema, literature, and journalism from various perspectives—from the viewpoints of biographical studies, hermeneutics, symbolic interactionism, poststructuralism, feminism, queer theory, communitarianism, Afro-American studies, cultural studies, as well as post-colonialism (Denzin and Lincoln 2002)—will radically change the way *systematic theology* has been written so far.

"The theologian, like the ethnographer . . ." (Lindbeck 1984, 115, quoted in Smith 1994a, 117), is asked in these *postmodern times* (Clifford and Marcus 1986, Clifford 1988, Clough 1992, Marcus 1998, Willis 2000, Denzin 1989, 1997a, 2003) to contribute to an *ethnographic systematic theology* that is both *local, experiential,* and *global* at the same time (Schreiter 1985, 1997, Smith 1994a, 1994b, Sedmak 1995–2003). Questions of social identity in the context of one's personal biography are central in this approach. "Local theologies of the ethnographic variety of contextual approach strive to answer questions of identity especially" (Schreiter 1985, 13).

The Community of the Weak

Autobiography in *systematic theology* goes back to *historical precedence* (on biography and theology McClendon 1990, Tilley 1985, Sparn 1990, Kuld 1997). The *Confessions* of *Augustine* (354–430) serve as a model for *autobiographical theology* (Saint Augustine 1991, see Stroup 1981, 175–198, Luther 1990, Kuld 1997, 122–147). Baptist systematic theologian *James McClendon* (McClendon 1986, 1990, 1994, 2000, 2002) notes:

> "Biography is of course one form of story—a form distinguished by being always a human story, and always (in intention) a true story. Perhaps these two marks of biography make it a form of story well suited to Christian faith. In favor of this conclusion is the recurrence of the form (or its predecessors) in earliest Christianity: the *Confessions* of Augustine, the *Acts* of the martyrs (and of the Apostles), and, even more central than these, the various *Gospels* of Jesus Christ each tell a human story." (McClendon 1990, 159, on biographical theology as story Stroup 1981, 175–198)

Theology Writing Our Lives

Feminist systematic theologian *Rebecca S. Chopp* (1986, 1989, 1995a/b) points out the *narrativity* of autobiography as a rediscovered form of *reflective awareness* in feminist educational and theological writing, having accompanied the history of theology for a long time:

> "Perhaps it is because narrativity has a practical character that the term has a long resonance within the history of Christian practices. As I have already suggested, theology, at least since Augustine, has been attuned to narrative as a kind of Christian activity. The Christian belief in baptism and the resultant responsibility that one has to live in grace is envisioned as a type of narrativity. From the medieval confessional to the pietist class meeting, the reflective awareness and the narrative direction of the believer's life is emphasized." (Chopp 1995b, 33)

Feminists have long ago rediscovered the value of *autobiography* as a *theological* and *political-poetic voice* for today (The Mudflower Collective 1985, 87–142, Say 1990, Kitzberger 2002, Taube, Tietz-Buck und Klinge 1995, Maassen 1993, Klein 1994, 1998), telling personal life stories as *(auto)biographical theology* (Moltmann-Wendel 1997, Bührig 1999, Sölle 1999b, 2001). Autobiography as a theological as well as an *artistic "act of creation"* (Chopp 1995b, 22) changes the way systematic theology is being

Postmodern

written. *New voices and stories* are shared among different writers in communal writing.

A more personal *resonance* in what is being talked and written about touches the common people in a *new kind of systematic theology* that relearns a *new vocabulary* and a *new language*. Systematic theology joins in the art of autobiography in that "not only do we have to compose our lives anew but that the very art of composing, the ongoingness of creation, is itself going to be a central theme in our lives" (Chopp 1995b, 22). Theological writing thus conceived becomes the most personal and creative form of *"writing our lives"* (Chopp 1995b, 34).

Mark L. Taylor in his *Remembering Esperanza* (Taylor 1990) forcefully presents to us such a *personal and autobiographical approach to systematic theology*, writing his own life in using his *earliest childhood memories* as a basis for a radical cultural-political theology in the North American context:

> "Esperanza used to pick me up, hold me tight, and tickle me. She was a fourteen-year-old girl of the Zapotec village of Teotitlan del Valle, in southern Mexico's province of Oaxaca. She lived just down the street on which my anthropologist father and family lived for a year when I was five." (Taylor 1990, 1)

Using social philosopher *Calvin O. Schrag's* concept of *"hermeneutical self-implicature"* in his *Communicative Praxis and the Space of Subjectivity* (Schrag 1986, 115–138, 1997), *Mark L. Taylor* creatively rewrites systematic theology as *politically radical autobiography*, constantly and openly addressing and revealing *"the 'who' of discourse"* (Taylor 1990, 3). Remembering the fourteen-year-old *Esperanza* serves as a way of re-membering and putting together old and powerful memories in view of current urgencies in contemporary systematic theology, allowing for some *communicative space* between the reader and the writer in which "a critical weaving of autobiographical elements into theological reflection—what Metz calls *'theological biography'*—plays a crucial role in mitigating theology's slide into objectively atrophied forms of teaching" (Taylor 1990, 4, on theological biography Metz 1980, 219–228, Schneider 1997, Weinrich 1999, Sölle 1999b, 2001, Schürger 2002). This has a determinative effect on the way books are written—especially in *systematic theology*—, "because no longer can we write books, in this view, without attending to the located selves entailed in the writing" (Taylor 1990, 16).

Theology may become a *poetic window glass* looking into one's own *soul* and *story*, be it his- or her-story.

323

The Community of the Weak

Theology Looking Through Windows

Autobiography in *systematic theology* allows us to listen more carefully and respectfully to the *poetics of experience* (Gunn 1982) as we follow authors into the vast and mysterious landscape of their own *human subjectivity* (Ellis and Flaherty 1992, Smith 1988, Critchley and Dews 1996, Kruks 2001, Zima 2000), empowering authors and readers to take seriously their own experiences as utmost and innermost *personal subjectivity*. Autobiography invites people in to *come and see* those personal places and locations that were visited on a life-long and personal journey, both *socially* as well as *theologically* (Metz 1980, 32–48, 60-83, 136–153, 229–237, Waldenfels 2000, 87–90, Mette 1994, 156–172, Bärenz 2000a). Systematic theology in the 21st century may turn out to be more *personal* and *autobiographical* (Taylor 1990, 1–22, Metz 1980, 219–228, 1992/1977, 211–219, Hollenweger 1990, Schneider 1997, Weinrich 1999, Kitzberger 2002) in its literary and academic style.

As Roman Catholic pastoral theologian *Reinhold Bärenz*, formerly in *Lucerne, Switzerland*, now in *Rome*, comments on the courage to introduce *the subjective* into the *scientific* in our *academic work*: "The turn to the subject and to the inclusion of subjectivity into science also encouraged me to work in a different theological style" (Bärenz 2000, 27). Theology will need to reintroduce the subjective, the personal, and the communal, as it used to be the case in the *early church writings* where *poetry* and *imagery* served as a basis for theology (Bärenz 2000a, 27).

A *subjective theology* telling the *story* of the one writing and speaking will need to become more transparent about who the *author* is who is writing. Only then can hearts be touched, bodies be healed, and eyes see. Such a *subjective theology* will be openly *biographical*, as Reinhold Bärenz describes the need for a new *hermeneutics of life* as a basis for a new kind of theology:

> "Life itself is a *locus theologicus*, a theology-generating place. This is also true in view of the person of the pastoral theologian himself, in view of the context of his biography and his theology or pastoral theology which is inseparably connected to it. What has been said in view of the dependence of pastoral theology on 'history', is also true in the same way in view of the 'story' of the individual pastoral theologian. In the current discussion on philosophy of science there seems to be a consensus that biographical contextuality need no diminish scientific quality. On the contrary: It can increase it." (Bärenz 2000, 25)

Theology—both as systematic and pastoral—is asked to produce *cultural texts* which can become *"windows on lived experience"* (in ethnographic research Ellis and Flaherty 1992, 6–11), freely interspersed with self-reflecting *subjectivity*, personal impression, and human emotion. These texts need to be more accessible to different people who can see the connection to their own lives and *lifeworlds* in what is being talked about (Sedmak 1995, 30–62, 2000, 30–162, Schneider 1997, Weinrich 1999, Bärenz 2000a).

Theology Rewriting the Self

Auto/Ethnography is a serious invitation to the theologian to *rewrite the self and the social* in a more personal way (Krieger 1991, Ellis and Bochner 1996, Reed-Danahay 1997, Bochner and Ellis 2002, Fuchs-Heinritz 2000). Postmodern sociologist and cultural ethnographer *Norman K. Denzin* (Denzin 1989, 1997a, 2003) describes this *new language* for the *social sciences*:

> "Perhaps we need to invent a new language . . . This new language, post-structural to the core, will be personal, emotional, biographically specific, minimalist in its use of theoretical terms. It will allow ordinary people to speak out, and to articulate the interpretive theories that they use to make sense of their lives. This new language will express the personal struggles of each writer as he or she breaks free of the bonds that connect to the past. This language will be visual, cinematic, kaleidoscopic rhizomatic, rich, and thick in its own descriptive detail, always interactive as it moves back and forth between lived experience and the cultural texts that shape and write that experience . . ." (Denzin 1996, 146)

Ethnographic theological language that listens to the *local wisdom of society's marginal circles and communities of faith* needs to be more personal, emotional, biographically specific, poetic, visual, cinematic, kaleidoscopic, rich, and *thick in its description* (on being thick in ethnographic description in theology Cochrane 1999, Sedmak 2002), as systematic theology is transformed into *experiential poetry and narration*, changing hearts, moving people.

> "In the midst of the day-to-day lives of multiple communities and individuals, and especially in their relationships with one another, God is voiced through struggle and celebration,

self-defense and education, spirited worship and birthing a baby, writing poetry and planting maize." (Wetherilt 1994, 149)

Contextual Theology and Multicultural Identity

People telling about their own personal lives in a global village use many languages. Biographies are no longer tied to one place, one language or one culture alone. People move, travel, and converse in different languages. Cultures get freely mixed in a person's life. Sometimes it happens accidentally, more often it is deliberately chosen. I spoke French as a Swiss-German young child even before I went to school. The kids in the neighborhood with whom I played soccer almost every day and night happened to speak French. Very early I had to learn about a multicultural world, even though at that time I hardly knew what this really meant.

Years later I crossed the Atlantic ocean in order to transgress cultural and linguistic boundaries again. This time it turned out to be more lasting, as I returned to Switzerland after more than 4 years university training in the US, now speaking English at home every day and sharing my life with an American woman as my wife. Linguistic and cultural worlds get personally married and mixed together, symbolic for what is happening to a global world at large. It may be that systematic theology in Europe is still acting like a spinster or a bachelor waiting to finally fall in love, while the world has long ago turned upside down. At least this is how it appears to me when I look at the lack of communication and sharing in systematic theology between two vast continents trying to speak globally to a local world.

Theology as Hybrid

In my own life, many worlds and languages have come together to form a *patchwork* of many identities, a *hybrid cultural identity* (on hybridity in cultural studies Papastergiadis 2000, 168–195, Nash 2000, 79–84, Ashcroft, Griffiths, and Tiffin 1998, 118–121, Ha 1999, 121–136, Chambers 1990, 1994, Lutter und Reisenleitner 1998, 127–129, Lewis 2008, Marchart

Postmodern

2007) which is no longer that clear and pure. The clarity and purity of culture or language has never attracted me very much.

> *Things have become messier over these years. I still like reading a lot of American—actually more so than European—theological or sociological books. I enjoy listening to a French radio station while driving my car from one place to the other or visiting Geneva where I got ordained as a Protestant pastor. I turn on our CD-player at home to hear Latin or Central American folk-songs in order to reconnect with my own political and radical past. And I preach or counsel regularly in Swiss-German or German on the pulpit or in my study as a pastor in a Reformed inner-city church in Zurich, while here and there still feeling homesick for some spectacular places in California where I loved walking with my wife on the beach.*

Home is no longer one place. Cultural anthropologist *Michael Jackson* gets to the core feeling of this century: "Ours is a century of uprootedness. All over the world, fewer and fewer people live out their lives in the place where they were born" (Jackson 1995, 1). Having to live as a *migrant traveler* (Chambers 1990, 1994) or *new mestiza* (Anzaldua 1987) in various cultural and linguistic places has become an important experience for many people in how they feel about themselves.

As such, this may not be something totally new. *Biblical faith* was *born out of wedlock* (on the infancy narrative of Jesus suggesting a birth out of wedlock Schaberg 1990) and in adoration of a *hybrid and socially migrant baby child* in a manger located in between many places, cultures, and languages (on migration and hybridity in the social-cultural world of Jesus Malherbe 1983, Stambaugh and Balch 1986, Malina 1993, 1996, Pilch and Malina 1998, Pilch 1999, Malina 2001, Jennings 2003). Biblical faith, looked at from a *multicultural and social scientific perspective* (Carter and Meyers 1996, Esler 1994, Rohrbaugh 1996, Robbins 1996a, 1996b, Malina 2001), has always been a socially highly subversive and *homeless hope of migrant nomads* (on homelessness as the metaphor of biblical discipleship Elliott 1981), being forced to move from one place to the next. Recently rediscovered *cross-cultural readings of the Bible* (Blount 1995, Segovia and Tolbert 1995a, 1995b, 1998, Malina 2001) are in no way foreign to a biblical and systematic theologian who knows his or her place as a *stranger in diaspora of exile* (Ogletree 1985, McGaughey 1997, Frost

2006) to be both everywhere and nowhere in this world (Segovia 1995a, 1995b, Rieger 2011).

Theology in Diaspora

Constantly shifting identities of a life story lived out in many *cultural diasporas* (Nash 2000, 79–84, Ha 1999, 121–136, Butin 2002, 110–114) can only form a temporary unity, being very diverse from one moment to the next. Already in *premodern and biblical times* people had to find a way to gather together the scattered pieces of various *broken identities*. Life has shown itself to be no different for others or for me *today*. Identities continue to be a *mess*. However, there is something in this premodern and postmodern mess and *multicolored quilt* of a world with *no place to feel at home* that seems to be still truly me, in a world that "has made go-betweens of us all" in "an age of trespass and travel" where "frontiers no longer contain those born within them" (Jackson 1995, 4).

It is not surprising that my concept of systematic theology as well has radically changed over these years. *Systematic and fundamental theology in the 21st century* as I see it most likely will be *local and global, contextual, hybrid, migrant, multicultural, and multilingual* (Schreiter 1985, 1997, Arens 1995b, Waldenfels 2000, 17–25, Sedmak 1995–2003, Blaser 1972–2004). A pluri- and multicolored polyphony of *polycentric voices* (Metz 1987, Bühlmann 1987, Hollenweger 1986, 1990, Collet 2002) needs to be listened to.

It also needs more *humor*, the lightness of being, and the *multicolored festivity and absurdity* of the *carnival* (Cox 1969, Nigg 1956, Lee 1995) in the tradition of the *wild Jesus* (Frost and Hirsch 2009) where many ludicrous masks are allowed to be worn in order to question and *deconstruct* (Matthiae 1999) the politically unitarian and monolithic approach of an old, serious, official, and *feudal academic discipline*. A social and political critique deconstructing various forms of *self-assuming power* has always been part of the *festivity and fantasy of the carnival* as the *feast of the fool* (Cox 1969).

Theology Carnivalesque

Hybrid personalities—like those of the *clown* or the *fool* in the *Middle Ages*—point to the socially disruptive and transfiguring power of *multivocal* language situations and personal narratives, described by the linguistic and cultural theorist *Mikhail Bakhtin* as *carnivalesque* (on Mikhail Bakhtin see Gardiner 2000, 43–70):

> "The idea of a polyphony of voices in society is implied also in Bakhtin's idea of the carnivalesque, which emerged in the Middle Ages when 'a boundless world of humorous forms and manifestations opposed the official and serious tone of medieval ecclesiastical and feudal culture'. . ." (Ashcroft, Griffiths, and Tiffin 1998, 118)

Hybridity as *social and political concept* (Osborne 2002a, 157, Papastergiadis 2000, 168–195, Nash 2000, 79–84, Ashcroft, Griffiths, and Tiffin 1998, 118–121, Lutter und Reisenleitner 1998, 127–129, Ha 1999, 121–136, Butin 2002, 110–114) is a form of *linguistic resistance*, the way clowns are playing the fool in a world in which many things are simply taken for granted. "The language of hybridity becomes a means for critique and resistance to the monological language of authority" (Papastergiadis 2000, 182).

Learning how to be a *modern clown* or a *fool* with many conflicting identities in himself or herself, while not afraid to transgress cultural and linguistic boundaries, may very well be the most important *qualification* for writing *good systematic theology in postmodern times*. It may also not be accidental—in theological retrospective—that the guiding symbol for my multilingual ordination worship service in the *chapel* of the *World Council of Churches* in *Geneva* many years ago was such a *clown*.

Theology Border-Crossing

A *personal identity "in-between"* different cultures and languages quite often creates a strong feeling of *homelessness* in the individual. This however may be healthy for developing a contextual *pilgrim theology* (in South African fundamental theology McGaughey 1997) wherever we decide to settle down for a while. As *migrant nomads* (Braidotti 1994) in modern and postmodern times, feeling at home in the closure and openness of many places (in cultural anthropology Jackson 1989, 1995), *postmodern theologians* will be more sensitive to the widespread radical fragmentation of individuals and communities who cannot find their way *back home*.

The *"impossible homecoming"* (Chambers 1994, 1–8), in which we realize that no place is home anymore, can be an important therapeutic opening to the realities of the world where everybody has become a *stranger* in exile (Ogletree 1985, McGaughey 1997, Frost 2006) in ever

The Community of the Weak

changing personal and social contexts, histories, languages and cultures. Becoming aware of our own never ending *homelessness* in an omnipresent *postmodern diaspora culture* may contribute to an increasing sensitivity and "responsibility toward Otherness" (Nash 2000, 79), in that we find ourselves to be strangers wherever we go. *"Being other and different"* from others will not be foreign to us and our systematic theology, as we know the other to be a *close stranger* within ourselves (Sponheim 1993, Farley 1996, Arens 1995b, Ramminger 1998, Sundermeier 1996, Schürger 2002).

This may also make us more *sensitive* and *empathic* toward the various *dramas* of *lost homes and broken histories,* as we remain in touch with people having to work through past and present social exclusions from previously familiar places and identities, facing *radical evil* and *systemic violence* that continue to *smash personal and social histories to pieces* (in theology Peters 1994, Farley 1990, Poling 1991, 1996, Gestrich 1996, in the social sciences Staub 1989, Kleinman, Das, and Lock 1997, Cohen 2001):

> "To be forced to cross the Atlantic as a slave in chains, to cross the Mediterranean or the Rio Grande illegally, heading hopefully North, or even to sweat in slow queues before officialdom, clutching passports and work permits, is to acquire the habit of living between worlds, caught on a frontier that runs through your tongue, religion, music, dress, appearance and life. To come from elsewhere, from 'there' and not 'here', and hence to be simultaneously 'inside' and 'outside' the situation at hand, is to live at the intersections of histories and memories ... It is simultaneously to encounter the languages of powerlessness and the potential intimations of heterotopic futures. This drama, rarely freely chosen, is also the drama of the stranger. Cut off from the homelands of tradition, experiencing a constantly challenged identity, the stranger is perpetually required to make herself at home in an interminable discussion between a scattered historical inheritance and a heterogeneous present."
> (Chambers 1994, 6)

The *hybrid stranger* is a powerful emblem for ourselves and all our modest attempts to *write a systematic theology* in a most *personal way*. "That stranger, as the ghost that shadows every discourse, is the disturbing interrogation, the estrangement, that potentially exists within us all" (Chambers 1994, 6).

Contextual theology (Schreiter 1985, 1997, Waldenfels 2000, 17–25, Bevans 2002, Blaser 1972–2004) starts with the healthy and unsettling recognition that the *borders* and *boundaries* between worlds and cultures *run through ourselves*, as we find ourselves already to be *multivocal, multilingual*, and *multicultural*.

"*Border dialogues/crossings*" (Chambers 1990, Giroux 1992, Giroux and McLaren 1994, Welsch 1996b, Lewis 2008, Marchart 2007) need to start foremost *in ourselves*. A *contextual theology* deserving its name needs to start with those *frontiers* running *through ourselves*, sensitive to our own *lost homes* and *broken stories*, colored by memories of pain and laughter, dramatic absurdity and liberating humor. Systematic theology needs to go back to the *travelling circus* in order to quietly listen to *border-crossing clowns* and their *carnivalesque power* of laughter (for laughter as the last hope of the fool Cox 1969).

Writing conceived this way is a *patchwork collection* of inner and outer voices, brought together as a *personal and poetic testimony* in dialogue with our own inner and outer *borderlands* (Anzaldua 1987, Ha 1999, 118–121):

> "Writing is not natural. This is its drama. It is an inscription that tries to come alive, that calls for dialogue. When it becomes unstable, unsure of its ground, when there is no longer the illusion that words, sentences and phrases can by themselves, as though by their mere presence, establish a design, then language represents a collection of voices and traces, brought together into a particular mix of which the text is a record, a testimony." (Chambers 1990, 115)

Systematic theology written across the *borderlands* of this modern and postmodern world will be a *personal testimony* to mixed voices and cultures, languages and personal stories within and without ourselves, a *radically destabilizing experience* described by *Gloria Anzaldua* (Anzaldua 1987) as the painful and restless human dilemma of the *mestiza*, the Mexican-American Indian woman caught between various cultures, *alien in all*:

> "Being tricultural, monolingual, bilingual or multilingual, speaking a patois, and in a state of perpetual transition, the *mestiza* faces the dilemma of the mixed breed . . ." (Anzaldua 1987, 78)

The Community of the Weak

The challenge for the *postmodern theologian* will be very similar to the experience of the *new mestiza*, having to cope with clashing contradictions *within herself or himself*.

> "The *new mestiza* copes by developing a tolerance for contradictions, a tolerance for ambiguity. She learns to be an Indian in Mexican culture, to be Mexican from an Anglo point of view. She learns to juggle cultures. She has a plural personality, she operates in a pluralistic mode—nothing is thrust out, the good, the bad, and the ugly, nothing rejected, nothing abandoned. Not only does she sustain contradictions, she turns the ambivalence into something else." (Anzaldua 1987, 79)

A *multicultural and contextual theology* in postmodern times will need to relearn how to live in the *borderlands* of this world and to join its *"dance of cultures"* (Breidenbach und Zukrigl 1998) without rejecting or abandoning anyone or anything *within and without ourselves* (Volf 1996). My own theological writing is trying to be such a personal and daring attempt to keep ears and hearts open to these many voices, languages, and cultures *in- and outside of myself*.

Power in the Borderlands

Power and *powerlessness* today are inscribed in the day-to-day experiences of people, communities, nations, and habitats across the *borderlands* of the postmodern world. Theology as *art, experience, autobiography,* and *multicultural border-crossing* can contribute to the *border-crossing healing* of the world.

For this to happen, *new communities, new cultures,* and *new ecologies* of all living things have to be envisoned and *lived* in reality (on communities as ecologies of hope Granberg-Michaelson 1991, Sawyer 2003). In the temptation of *violence* in a postmodern world, theology could bring a *new hope*. The new hope for a different kind of *creation* and a *communal world*. In order to become *healing* in this, theology has to learn a new language, the language of *culture*. The artistic challenge of theology is *cultural*. The experiential calling of theology is *communal*. The autobiographical task of theology is *redemptive*, reconciling a broken world. And the border-crossing movement of theology in this postmodern world is *creative*, giving birth to new communities of *postmodern healing* in a segregated world.

New communities—postmodern, healing, border-crossing (Granberg-Michaelson1991, Sawyer 2003)—like this will *empower* people and *heal* souls. In new communities like this, *power* and *powerlessness* are reconfigured in new and healing ways. Power will no longer destroy, abuse, wound, and break the soul. Power and powerlessness will be shared in new *postmodern ecclesiologies* where people find a *human embrace* (Volf 1996).

Communities of the weak, the *powerless* who empower the wounded, the broken. Thus, *power* will become *creative* and healing in new ways. The challenge will be to create new kinds of communities where *difference*, *ambiguity*, and *fragment* will flow in *border-crossing ways*. *Postmodern communities and churches* could become places of *diversity* where healing embraces the excluded, the left-alone, the broken. In communities like this, teenagers at the age of 14 taking heroin in some local village in the 1990s in Switzerland will no longer be *on the run* from one place to the next. Teenagers like this in *new communities* like this will find places and faces of *healing* in *community* (Granberg-Michaelson 1991, Sawyer 2003).

Theology as *art, experience, autobiography*, and *border-crossing* will work for the *healing* of *nations* and *communities*. The challenge is *postmodern*. The vision is *biblical*, and *theological*. The temptation and the invitation is *power*. Power used, or abused. Power empowering or destroying. The choice is ours. We are called to live and respond to the *ethical challenge* of *shalom* in the in-betweens of *borderlands* in a postmodern world. In the *community of all living things* power can become *creative, peace-learning, border-crossing* artistically biographies of many diverse and conflicting living things.

Out of this *border-crossing hope* of *theology* whole communities, whole nations, the whole earth can *heal* in *God's reconciling and inclusive redemption* across all our humanly constructed *borderlands* (Anzaldua 1987). In a peacefully joining, reconciling, border-crossing, polyphonic multicultural, inter-racial, inter-generational, inter/intra-faith, inter-life-stylish, and even inter-musical world in *communities of the weak* (Granberg-Michaelson 1991, Sawyer 2003) where people and all living things are experiencing the *power* of *God's multicolorful and communal earth* (Fox 1983-2002, Page 1996, 2000, Grey 2003, Keller 2005, Sponheim 1999, 2006, 2011).

7

Culture

KOINONIA

"Theology is often identified with the productions of educated elites such as clergy and academics. When that identification is made, theology is equated with writings in which conceptual precision and logical coherence are at a premium. These writings are produced in primary conversation with other writings of a similar sort, and they tend to be read only by people with the same educational background and institutional support for sustained intellectual pursuits as their authors. As such a highly specialized intellectual activity, theology seems irrelevant to the common concerns of most people. Putting theology into the cultural context of a Christian way of life challenges this view of theology; it makes theology much more an integral part of daily life . . . Such a revised understanding of theology follows the anthropological shift in the understanding of culture away from associations with high culture. Culture is not primarily located in the intellectual or spiritual achievements of the community—its great works of art, philosophy, or literature. Instead, culture refers to the whole social practice of meaningful action, and more specifically to the meaning dimension of such action—the beliefs, values, and orienting symbols that suffuse a whole way of life. This meaning dimension of social action cannot be localized in some separate sphere specifically devoted to intellectual or spiritual concerns. It accompanies all social action as a constitutive aspect of it . . . "
(Tanner 1997, 69–70)

"According to Williams, 'culture in all its early uses was a noun of process: the tending of something, basically crops or animals.' This is the sense behind such words as horticulture; vini/viticulture, and agriculture. Beginning in the eighteenth century, the idea of cultivation was transferred to humans and with it was born the notion of a cultivated person. This had distinct class overtones and was closely related to the idea of civilization. That idea has not completely died out, for culture is still often associated with 'great works' that are housed in libraries and museums or performed on stage. Poetry and literature, painting and sculpture, symphony and opera, theater and dance—these were, and still are to a large extent, what most people think of when they think of culture. Not so long ago, these were the things you went to college to learn about. To be a cultured person you had to know about them and know how to appreciate them. In addition, especially among the upper classes, it was thought essential that students complete their education with a European tour to absorb the great works of Western culture. Moreover, Western culture was held to be the epitome of civilization. When combined with a belief that culture is an evolutionary, unidirectional, and progressive phenomenon that all peoples are striving for, one can sense the way assumptions about class and race and gender were reinforced by such a tour." (Delaney 2004, 12)

"Theologians, no less than other intellectuals, have come to view human beings as historical creatures located within the complex matrices of particular cultures and social worlds. Gone, whether forever or for the moment, are the universalisms of both Enlightenment reason and nineteenth- and twentieth-century theological liberalism. Over against notions of rationality and experience as ahistorical, commonly structured, and temporally invariant, there have emerged assumptions of the located, particular, pluralistic, and thoroughly historical nature of human existence, experience, and knowledge . . . The cultural domain within which human life is now interpreted as so thoroughly ensconced has also taken on a particular character. Increasingly, culture has come to refer to a multitextured network of relations or total way of life encompassing the myriad relations, institutions, and practices that define a historical period or specific geographical location or formative community or subgroups within larger fields. In contrast to earlier notions of culture as the deposit or accumulation of knowledge or meaning produced by elites, or

The Community of the Weak

as a body of beliefs and values shared by all members of a group such as a nation or religious community, culture now is viewed as the dynamic and contentious process by which meaning, and with it power, is produced, circulated, and negotiated by all who reside within a particular cultural milieu." (Brown, Davaney, Tanner 2001, 5)

Culture may be pretty basic. When you teach 14-year-old confirmation teenagers in a local village somewhere in Switzerland in the 1990s, then culture becomes most prominent as the first meeting point and collision point. A point at which interests may meet, liking the same music, liking the same movies in the cinema, liking even, maybe, the same cloths, the same hairstyle, the same colors, posters, nature scenes, sport heroes, musical industry stars. A point at which interests and understandings may collide, as some people just don't like the same things you do. Pink Floyd, Sting, Mercedes Soza are already out, old-fashioned, even Michael Jackson does not move all hearts anymore, however, noisy Hot Chili Pepper, Rap and Trance, Techno and newly-revived Punk, and maybe somewhere a romantic Céline Dion breaking waves for the Titanic, make the musical, artistic, and religiously pedagogical rounds. Then, as a teacher, you have your first little culture shock, though not with Céline Dion, but maybe with some other sound.

Comes to it the additional problem, that what you may consider serious, high class culture, with some deeper meaning in it, may not in any way seduce the common folk. Action movies yes, but not some where you may have to think a little bit. Most favorably the latest Horror Picture Show, in its many and various commercial CD-versions. Sarafina or Cry Freedom on South Africa may keep young teenagers awake, even Nell with Jodie Foster, Rain Man, Dancing with Wolves, or Forrest Gump. Even Hair or The Day After. But once you go a little bit beyond it and try some so-called high culture—seemingly—the juvenile and junior boredom goes and comes most expectedly with it.

Biographies intrigue. Nelson Mandela, Martin Luther King, Princess Diana, Steve Biko, St. Francis, maybe for a short while even Dietrich Bonhoeffer or Mother Teresa. Beyond that the biographies and literacies of teenagers at the age of 14 in a local village somewhere in Switzerland in the 1990s may vary and differ with what you may consider literacy. The in-breaking of another little shock wave of cultural diversity.

Culture

How much more will the cultural shock wave hit if you realize that teenagers in a local village at the age of 14 somewhere in Switzerland in the 1990s are smoking pot, have a joint, take a pill or more, hang around, listen to Punk and Techno, dress all black, color their hair, goof around, drop out of school, steal and commit break-ins, get homeless, are put away in juvenile homes, just to run away from it. And that some of these teenagers even smoke, sniff, or take heroin in any possible form. The culture shock moves in and stays for a quite definite while.

Teaching religious education in moments like that may become adventurous, fragmenting, shattering, but also creative, lively, and unusual, unused-to, nontraditional, experimental. And being a soul friend, a counselor, a companion to teenagers at the age of 14 in moments like this may be the most challenging border crossing across cultures you have ever dared treading on in your own biography. Diving into another culture, sub-cultural in this case, may take a while, but may be just as upsetting your common frameworks of cognition, experience, understanding, as any other cross-cultural social anthropology. In addition, in moments like that you have no time to think all too cognitively, as you are suddenly, from one day to the other, facing teenagers facing you, with some of these teenagers being part of your own confirmation class. And one of them just died.

Then, the in-breaking culture shock becomes life-changing, life-threatening, challenging, disquieting, upsetting, reshuffling old concepts and coordinates in new shapes, asking for some new paradigm or some new cognitive map to make sense of this newly in-breaking world. Some reject it. Some run away. Some look away or just don't want to look at it. Some would rather call in the army to clean up the social problem than to live with it. Others move by as social bystanders wondering. And some others actually take and collect all their personal and social courage to face it.

Facing it means learning a new language. Getting to know new rituals, new symbols, new social places and hiding spaces, new musical styles and hair combs. Facing it also means taking part in new celebrations and musical rhythms, even if it is only a drumming base. Facing it means putting aside for a moment one's own cognitive map that used to make sense of the world, but now seems to be confusing, actually even leading astray. Facing it also means listening, looking, remaining silent, watching, learning. Facing it means going along, taking walks, driving

The Community of the Weak

somewhere, sitting at sunset on some beautiful and peaceful lake while talking together until some young teenager at the age of 14 confesses and discloses to you that it is taking heroin.

Then, the intercultural work begins. The social work and cultural challenge, the political task and ethical calling, to get a whole local community accept its own members in its midst. In some fundamental ways, it becomes a most theological challenge. The theological challenge to envision and dream up, to create and invite to, to incarnate and witness to an ecclesial and true community (Hodgson 1988, 1994, 293-304, Peck 1987) of the free and equal, the communicative and empathic, the non-exclusionary and inclusive, the communing and embracing (Volf 1996), the reconciling and forgiving where people can be and where teenagers like this at the age of 14 and taking heroin can heal.

Communal healing as a theological challenge in moments like this would need some vision and sense for the ecology of the spirit, the healing and Holy Spirit making communities whole again. Only then would people have realized that the healing of teenagers taking heroin at the age of 14 in some local village in Switzerland in the 1990s was not just some peripheral task and duty for social workers, youth state prosecutors, juvenile homes, youth counselors, school teachers, local pastors, and other general specialists in unspecialized fields like this, but that the challenge—social, ethical, and theological—was a challenge for the community as a whole.

The challenge for the people and a local village was to become a communio or koinonia, a community of the free and equal, the inclusive and emphatic, an ecology of the non-violent and cross-cultural, the border crossing and border-lifting where no one—teenagers and any others—would be shunned or segregated, looked down upon or disrespected, devalued or disregarded, ostracized and excluded. Most sadly, however, like most often in moments like this, it turned out quite differently.

A whole community turned into a war zone. People excluded, teenagers pushed aside. Local pastors slandered. Sacrificial mechanisms of exclusion and violence seducing the spirits. A community turning into a society of pieces, shambles, the wounded. No longer capable and able to face and commune with each other. Racism, sexism, classism, ageism re-enacted in new ways, in new forms, with a new vocabulary in a local village.

Building Postmodern Communities

Power and Community

Theology's most honorable task and calling is the *building of community*. *Communities of the weak* (Granberg-Michaelson 1991, Sawyer 2003) where people get *healed*. However, communities have a way sometimes to turn into the opposite of healing and embracing places, transforming into *wounding nightmares*. Social exclusion, prejudice, violence, racism, sexism, classism, and ageism meet most often on Sunday mornings. The temptation for communities to become *violent* and *excluding* (Volf 1996) is always there. *The abuse of power* (Poling 1991, 1996, Keller 2005) most often takes on an *ecclesiological face*. *Power* and *powerlessness* then get distributed in social and theological space, including some, excluding many, violently chasing people away, teenagers, others, those not considered to belong into *God's gracious reign*.

This chapter will present an *alternative vision for a healing world*. Facing the *postmodern*, facing the broken, facing the reality of a *fragmenting world* where things and people are *shattered* into a *spectrum* (Kliever 1981) of many colors. The variety of colors can be *empowering, luring, enthralling, exciting*, inviting to a *rainbow world* (Wetherilt 1994) of many colors. The task for the colors will be *to learn how to live in peace*. The *shalom* (in biblical theology Brueggemann 1976, 2001, in Christian ethics Hauerwas 1983, Hauerwas and Wells 2006) of biblical dwellings is our common task. In a postmodern world, *to learn how to live in peace* may become the most important task for *theology*. Teenagers at the age of 14 taking heroin in the 1990's in some local village in Switzerland deserve to live in peace. However, communities may need to learn what this could mean. The temptation for *violence* is easy. The invitation to a *postmodern living* as a *koinonia or oikos of people and cultures building community in peace* is more difficult.

Power and *powerlessness* in a *social and postmodern world* have been the guiding thread of this dissertation. In this chapter a *new vision* is presented. The vision of a socially postmodern world in which *communities of the weak* can heal the broken (Granberg-Michaelson 1991, Clapp 1996, Harmer 1998, Sawyer 2003, Marsh 2005). Power and powerlessness get redefined as the power of *creativity* in *building community* (Peck 1987). Community can be inclusive, welcoming, healing, caring, living values of justice and peace in its midst.

The Community of the Weak

This is the *biblical vision of community*, as described most powerfully in an overview on the great variety of *radical ethnic and multicultural Christian communities* on the *margins* of contemporary North America: "*Christian community* may be defined as *a group of people coming together with intentionality to live the gospel values of inclusiveness, justice, and caring in order to create a transformed world*" (Sawyer 2003, 16).

Power in such communities can be *healing*. Power can call people and all living things into *true community*, joining the lost, bringing back the forgotten, forgiving the unforgiven. Power can be redefined as the envisioning of a different world where people get healed. A world where the broken are mended, the wounded attended, the bruised relieved, the excluded inclued, the ostracized welcomed, the slandered renamed, the hopeless encouraged, the *powerless empowered*. This chapter will attempt to dream a *different dream*—communally postmodern, gracious, and colorful *in peace*. The way *God's rainbow* reminds us of our calling *to live in peace* every time God's open sky reveals all its colors on this earth.

In the words of African American theologian and researcher on *alternative and radical multicultural Christian communities* in our postmodern times *Mary R. Sawyer* in her *The Church on the Margins: Living Christian Community* (Sawyer 2003):

> "Christian community cares for the earth and cares for the earth's disenfranchised people, being co-creators with the one and agents of empowerment with the other... Christian community seeks transformation... Transformation is radical by its very nature; it goes to the root of what is oppressive and dehumanizing. It therefore involves risk-taking; Christian community is not for the faint of heart. Furthermore, Christian community is dynamic: it is ever changing, ever cognizant of changing times, changing power relationships, and changing needs... Christian community is experiential; it invites and honors and depends on experiences of Spirit. Christian community is relational; it is characterized by empathy, compassion, patience, forgiveness ... Finally, Christian community is intrinsically loving... people who live out such a love also get to live in that new world—in community." (Sawyer 2003, 16–17)

Culture

Segregating the World

Racism, sexism, classism, ageism may stand for and illustrate any and many ways the world is still being segregated, stratified, and *socially divided* by people (on social stratification Payne 2000, Bottero 2005, Brown 1995, Bieling 2000), *breaking up communites*. *Segregating the world* seems to be a common and uncommon human way to somehow make sense of a confusing world. In itself, it is a *cognitive map* for people to split up the personal and global world into parts so things seem a little bit more tidy and manageable. However, it gets messy once these *cognitive categories* turn social. Having a certain race, a certain sex, a certain belief, a certain social place in life, and a certain age in itself is harmless. But once these categories become a way to *distribute and divide up life*, it becomes most harmful. A *socially dividing racism of life*—whatever its social division may be, *sex, gender, race, belief, class, social skill, literacy, education, employment, health, age, ethnicity, nationality* (in biblical theology McKenzie 1997)—makes some people more important, more valuable, *more worthwhile* in life than others. A *social racism of life* tears up the human fabric of communal living and makes the *ecology of community* disappear.

North American Old Testament scholar *Steven L. McKenzie* (McKenzie 1997) describes the promise of a *biblical vision* for an *ecology of community* living *the different*:

> "Unity with diversity is as important for the church today as it was for the New Testament church. The temptation for Christians of all eras is to require conformity. Perhaps it is human nature for individuals to be uncomfortable with people different from themselves. Hence, the tendency, since the Judaizers, has been for Christians to form congregations made up of homogeneous members—people of the same race and social level, who dress alike, think alike, even look alike. Thus, it is no accident that churches in the United States have basically formed along racial lines. But the New Testament describes Christians in terms of unity, not uniformity. There is no doctrine of segregation in the New Testament. Its credo is not 'separate but equal'; it is 'different but united'. Christians of all races and ethnicities (not to mention social levels and genders) are equal in God's eyes." (McKenzie 1997, 131–132)

Segregating the world breaks apart human ties, communal bonds, global networks, and *earth community's* (Rasmussen 1996, Gebara 1999, Grey 2003) *interdependence* between all living things. As such it is a symptom of *violence*. When in 1993 a confirmation teenager at the age of 14 died of an overdose of heroin at some drug dealing place near an abandoned cargo train station somewhere in Switzerland, the human community and its solidarity had failed somehow at their most basic level. The *ecology of the Spirit* (Moltmann 1992, 1997, Page 1996, 2000, Grey 2003), the *web of life holding us tight and protected*, loved and included, welcomed and *embraced* (Volf 1996), had somehow failed. Church and local community, politicians and pastors, school teachers and social workers, all had failed somehow in providing a network, a *spiritual commune* or *communio* that would have reached out hands and hearts before things went bad.

In that sense, the death of a 14-year-old teenager taking heroin in a local village somewhere in Switzerland in the 1990s showed the spiritual and social bankruptcy of a society and community of individuals in a *segregated* and *segregating world* where people have never learned how to be and become a *true community* (Peck 1987). The *atomistic individual, unencumbered by any neighbor*, by any face and faces looking at you, only focused on the *pure individual*, leads to such early deaths on an abandoned cargo train station. Here, the *communitarian* and *feminist critique* of the *modern and liberal self*, the unencumbered individual, and the *isolated person* (Little 2002, Delanty 2003, Eberly 1994, Moon 1993, Tam 1998, Selznick 1992, Frazer and Lacey 1993, in pastoral theology Graham 1992, Clinebell 1996, Chinula and Clinebell 2009) shows its dead-serious social and personal consequences when society is becoming increasingly just a haphazardly thrown together conglomeration of lonely and isolated individuals that have nothing shared or in common with each other any longer.

Segregating the world seems to be the *usual and learned way* people relate in and to this *modern world*. Separating visual and cognitive, audible and tactile impressions into various categories, appears to be the socialized way. And yet, what is called for in this *postmodern world* is the *new skill* to become more *inclusive*, more uniting, more assembling impressions, categories, and dispersed parts and pieces. This applies to *communal living* in this postmodern world as well. The skill to live life in and as an *inclusive community* is an art still to be discovered and learned. It is not something happening haphazardly just so.

As communitarian *Henry Tam* (Tam 1998) puts it, inscribing the need for the development of new and *inclusive communities* in a much broader *social and political context*:

"One of the most enduring legacies of the 1989 revolutions may turn out to be the final resolution of the dilemma left us by Friedrich Nietzsche in the late nineteenth century: he claimed that we must either follow some unquestionable authority and live the life we are told to live, or throw authority aside completely and each of us decide the way we want to live . . . There can be no doubt that the rejection of authoritarian rule by the people of Eastern Europe and the former Soviet Union should be repeated with all other political regimes and fundamentalist groups which still strive to force others to comply with their demands, when these have no co-operative validation. But this should not lead to the embrace of the free market utopia of individualists, which in practice brings with it the relentless division of communities into the economically powerful and those who live in perpetual insecurity. The key to overcoming this dilemma rests with all citizens, with our commitment to live authentically by the faith we place in our common values, and thus to play our part in the building of inclusive communities." (Tam 1998, 268)

Assembling the World in Community

This would mean, giving up *segregating the world* into parts and pieces, social classes and age groups, sexual preferences and racial distinctions. It would mean *assembling the world* into a new shape, a *new picture* made up of a *variety and multiplicity* in the way human beings live in this world. At the same time, it would mean becoming highly sensitive to the *distribution of power* in this new world. Learning to live and move in an *inclusive community* will need the sensitivity to spot fissures and dividing walls still in place invisibly or visibly dividing people, so that communities learn and practice *new common values* in how to "remove the barriers to people attaining love, wisdom, justice and fulfillment" (Tam 1998, 262).

It is here, where *feminist theory* and *communitarian social ethics* meet. The *embodied self* in a *new community of poets* (Chopp 1989, 84–98) is never alone. I live and breathe because other people live alongside me. They talk to me, give me new ideas, make me dream and hope of some other and better world. I feel the sharing and the care, the common living and acting, the reciprocal solidarity in hope and despair. In this, *feminism* and *communitarianism* unite in a common song of a better world.

As feminist *Elisabeth Frazer* and *Nicola Lacey* (Frazer and Lacey 1993) point out the open convergence of both: "The ideals of solidarity and reciprocity fostered by value-communitarianism resonate with significant themes in feminist ethics and politics, themes which stress mutuality, interdependence, collective values of sharing, responsibility and care ... " (Frazer and Lacey 1993, 123).

The commonalities seem to go even further, reaching the most fundamental level of *human knowing and acting*, in the way people are *assembling* categories and reflective concepts in socially making sense of this world.

> "In communitarian theory our relations to others and our affective ties are incorporated in the political realm in a way which is welcome to feminists. Both social constructionism and value-communitarianism push us towards just the contextualised, concretised model of rationality and reflection presupposed by this approach to ethics. That is, our affective ties and embodied experience feed into our ethical and rational decisions." (Frazer and Lacey 1993, 123)

In *new communities* like this there will be more *affective imaging* of the social, leading to more holistic concepts of living together in and beyond diversity. In *postmodern communities* (on postmodern communities Delanty 2003, 131–148) like this *the social imaginary* will take a new lead, as community is always a new and social construction created by those who want to join in a common experiment to build a *polyphony of community*. Imagining new kinds of communities can create new social worlds as real as those usually known to us.

As community sociologist *Gerard Delanty* (Delanty 2003) puts it, listing new and possible kinds of *postmodern community* that will change the world in concrete and quite real ways:

> "Because community is imagined does not mean that it is not real. We need to abandon the distinction between real versus imagined community. Territorial kinds of community are different from the new expressions of post-traditional community—virtual communities, New Age communities, gay communities, national and ethnic communities, religious communities—which are also reality-creating forces. Such new kinds of community have a powerful capacity to define new situations and thereby construct social reality." (Delanty 2003, 194)

Communities like this will be *postmodern* as a new kind of *"community beyond unity"* (Delanty 2003, 131–148), integrating other already existing modern and postmodern forms of multicultural *"community and difference"* (Delanty 2003, 92–110) and *Habermasian* communicative *"communities of dissent"* (Delanty 2003, 111–130). In that sense, learning how to live in *true community* (Peck 1987) in the postmodern age will not be as easy and cozy as it used to be in modern times, and yet it will also be more challenging and promising.

The promise and *social vision* will be a different *way of relating* as people are learning the new skills of *border crossing* (Giroux 1992, Giroux and McLaren 1994, McLaren 1995, 2005, Welch 1999, 2000, 2005, Rieger 2011) human differences, social divisions, societal stratification, and fragmentation, accepting the basically fractured nature of all our human communities. "Postmodern community is a 'fractured community' that emerges along with the creation of non-foundational, heterogeneous societies . . . ", being a lot more "nomadic, highly mobile, emotional and communicative" (Delanty 2003, 132). And yet, the deep human need to *belong* in some place and social space, virtual or temporal, local or global, remains.

As postmodern community theorist *Gerard Delanty* (Delanty 2003) describes the *deep need* even in postmodern times of humans *to belong somewhere*:

> "The idea that we are living in a postmodern society has been a topic much discussed in recent times. In the postmodern society group membership is more fluid and porous than in modern society. The old certainties of class, race, nation and gender that were the basis of the kind of society that emerged with industrialization have become contested categories in what is now an age of multiple belongings. But the postmodern age is also an insecure age which, in calling into question the assumptions of modernity, has made the problem of belonging more and more acute. The quest for belonging has occurred precisely because insecurity has become the main experience for many people. Even the very notion of society has been called into question, along with all kinds of fixed reference points and fixed identities." (Delanty 2003, 131)

Church as a Postmodern Community

Assembling the world in community is therefore no peripheral social undertaking, but responds to a *basic and deep human need* in postmodern society.

The Community of the Weak

The *Christian church* could be such a place and social space of *belonging* as a new kind of *postmodern community* (on church as a postmodern and post-Constantinian community Granberg-Michaelson 1991, Albrecht 1995, Clapp 1996, Bounds 1997, Grey 1997a, 1997b, Page 2000, Young 2000, Kirkpatrick 2001, Sawyer 2003, Marsh 2005, Mannion 2007) *assembling* and *healing* the diverse, the multiplied, the segregated, the stratified, the divided, the disseminated, the excluded, and the fractured. This would be a new and an old most challenging *mark* of the church as *one*, *holy*, *apostolic*, and *catholic* (on the marks of the church in postmodern times Hodgson 1988, 37–44, 1994, 293–304). *Fundamental theology* as *social theology* (Lamb 1982, Lane 1984, Wetherilt 1994, Arens 1995a, Haight 2001, Storrar and Donald 2003, Taylor 1990, 2011) will retrieve the image of human community as a place of inclusion and healing, justice and communicative living where people are protected from violence. Assembling and healing the excluded is a most fundamental challenge for a *postmodern church* today.

Fundamental theology conceived as *social theology* renews the communitarian concept of church in a *new and inclusive way*. As Christian ethicist and practical theologian *William Storrar* and *World Council of Churches* Faith and Order Commission member *Peter Donald* from the *Centre for Theology and Public Issues* at the *University of Edinburgh* in *Scotland* put it (Storrar and Donald 2003), every theology turns *social* inasmuch as it is lived and reflected *in community*:

> "Social theology within this project refers to that sphere of experience which both informs and tests the reflective process, namely the making of human community. The word becomes flesh in the context of social relations—church, parliament, bowling club, family, to name but a few. If an active commitment is presupposed, it is the commitment to community." (Storrar and Donald 2003, 3)

In a *postmodern place and social space* like this teenagers in a local village somewhere in Switzerland taking heroin in the 1990s would feel more welcome and more hospitably *included* and *embraced* (on exclusion and embrace in communal ecclesiology for postmodern times Volf 1996). *Church as a postmodern community* would be more fragile, more fractured, and more sensitive to those that have been fractured, fragmented, and broken themselves, along the classical dividing lines of social stigma and communal segregation. A church like this would be on the move, *making space and giving room for nomads*. There would be an *open space*, a *communicative freedom*, a *nomadic* and *emotional understanding* for what some teenagers on drugs go through—the excluded of modern and postmodern times— who are constantly *on the move* from one place to the next.

A *nomadic church* would become a *home for nomads*, nobodies, and no-persons that are most often kept outside renovated or newly built church walls. Teenagers at the age of 14 taking heroin somewhere in a local village in Switzerland in the 1990s would experience a *postmodern place and social space* called *church, communio, koinonia*, or *ecclesia* where people know and believe with feminist, postmodern, and Roman Catholic theologian *Mary C. Grey* (Grey 1997a, 1997b) that "'to be is to relate', to be in process, movement, it is in the quality of the *community as prophet* that our hope must be situated" (Grey 1997a, 62). In a place like this, church would be *assembling the world in community*, living up to its basic calling in "'gathering the fragments'" (Grey 1997a, 71) of broken people in this world, inviting everyone to believe in the power to imagine and "dream great dreams" (Grey 1997a, 70).

Then, *church* and any other human place would become a *new place*. A place, to use North American Old Testament scholar *Walter Brueggemann's* poetic and postmodern imagery, where the world is

> "... no longer a closed arena of limited resources and fixed patterns of domination, no longer caught in endless destructive power struggles, but able to recall that lyrical day of creation when the morning stars sang for joy, a world no longer bent on hostility, but under God's presence as a place where creatures 'no longer hurt or destroy.'" (Brueggemann 1993, 51, as quoted in Grey 1997a, 71)

Nomadic Theology across Race, Sex, Class, and Age

Theology as well—*systematic, fundamental, dogmatic, ethical, pastoral*— may become more *nomadic* in a postmodern place and church like that. The *nomadic subject* (on the nomadic subject in cultural and feminist anthropology Braidotti 1994) could become the normal visitor of our churches and our theologies. People may look for an open door, go in, stroll around, take a seat, look around, and slowly move out again to go on with their lives. *Church* and *theology* in this postmodern age will have to face and reflect on the *contemporary existential situation* of all of us having become a "multicultural individual, a migrant who turned nomad"

The Community of the Weak

(Braidotti 1994, 1), with no place really to stay, constantly on the move from one place to the next. And nomadic existence need not entail long trips and extended travel. It can happen right inside of you.

As postmodern feminist and nomadic thinker *Rosi Braidotti* (Braidotti 1994) describes it, the *nomadic traveler* may not even move away from home:

> "Though the image of 'nomadic subjects' is inspired be the experience of peoples or cultures that are literally nomadic, the nomadism in question here refers to the kind of critical consciousness that resists settling into socially coded modes of thought and behavior. Not all nomads are world travelers; some of the greatest trips can take place without physically moving from one's habitat. It is the subversion of set conventions that defines the nomadic state, not the literal act of traveling." (Braidotti 1994, 5)

And yet, *traveling* is part of *nomadic existence*, though it may not move far away, it may not even change place. But traveling in one's mind across the various categories of *race, sex, class, ethnicity*, and *age* is already a world trip. *Theology* that becomes *nomadic* will keep traveling constantly in its mind, moving from one place to the next, even if staying at home. Too much theology is written without the *experience of travel*. Too much theology has *stayed at home* without allowing the bigger world move in. The result of theology conceived in this way, staying home and keeping the world outside, is usually a kind of *sedentary stability*, mono-cultural boredom, and textual uniformity.

Most *basic textbooks* in *theology—systematic, fundamental, dogmatic—*in *German-speaking European contexts* seem to have stayed at home for most of their existing lives. No sense of a radical *nomadic existence*, no little or big picture of a bigger world, no moving and traveling moments getting the reader to *other places*.

In contrast, most *North American basic textbooks* in *theology—systematic, fundamental, dogmatic—*have lost their original homes. The *nomadic existence* can be sensed at all corners, the *traveling mind*, even with some the traveling feet, can be followed at every moment. The simultaneous interaction of crisscrossed categories across the lines of *race, sex, class, ethnicity, handicap*, even *age*, permeates most of theology's literary texture. In that sense, *contemporary North American systematic theology* has in this day and age truly become *nomadic*.

> "The nomad is my own figuration of a situated, postmodern, culturally differentiated understanding of the subject in general and of the feminist subject in particular. This subject can also be describes as postmodern/industrial/colonial, depending on one's locations. In so far as axes of differentiation such as class, race, ethnicity, gender, age, and others intersect and interact with each other in the constitution of subjectivity, the notion of nomad refers to the simultaneous occurrence of many of these at once." (Braidotti 1994, 4)

Nomads have met people of another *race*, another *sex*, another *class*, another *age*. Their thinking and acting therefore can no longer stay the same. Usually, meeting other people changes some of your mind, leading to some other way and path to go through life. This helps "to think through and move across established categories and levels of experience: blurring boundaries without burning bridges" (Braidotti 1994, 4). *Theology as a nomad* will move across those categories and boundaries to find a new place where everyone is welcome.

At the same time, nomads do live *in community*, in between, and going through life. *Communities of nomads* will be *postmodern*. *Theology* for *communities of nomads* will also be *postmodern*, since there is no longer just *one culture*, one race, one sex, one class, one age living in it.

> "Being a nomad, living in transition, does not mean that one cannot or is unwilling to create those necessarily stable and reassuring bases for identity that allow one to function in a community. Rather, nomadic consciousness consists in not taking any kind of identity as permanent. The nomad is only passing through; s/he makes those necessarily situated connections that can help her/him to survive, but s/he never takes on fully the limits of one national, fixed identity. The nomad has no passport—or has too many of them." (Braidotti 1994, 33)

The challenge of *postmodern nomadism* for *theology—systematic, fundamental, dogmatic—*is a *new language* that gets created along the way as people of various walks of life meet in transition between different places. This will be a more *poetic language*, a more *mixed language*. "A related feature of this style is the mixture of speaking voices or modes: I deliberately try to mix the theoretical with the poetic or lyrical mode. These shifts in my voice are a way of resisting the pull toward cut-and-dried, formal, ugly, academic language" (Braidotti 1994, 37).

The Community of the Weak

A Fundamental Theology of Postmodern Nomadism

The social categories of *race, sex, class, ethnicity, handicap*, and *age* have become prominent *nomadic concepts* in *North American systematic theology today*. There is not one *basic textbook* that does not in some way address these necessary issues involved in crossing humanly-made boundaries. A *fundamental theology of postmodern nomadism* seems to accompany most theological endeavors at formulating a *new kind of systematic theology* in the United States. In this, North American systematic theology is taking a leading role in the contemporary context of a world theology.

At the same time, this may become the *theological groundwork* for a *new kind of postmodern ecclesiology*. Theology always gets *practical* once it is lived in *concrete communities*. In the day-to-day challenges of communal living, in the concrete transformation of theological ideas into ethical acting, in the *practical translation of theoretical concepts* into *heart and soul theology*, the usefulness of what theologians normally brood and think upon shows its *social and personal relevance*.

In facing teenagers at the age of 14 taking heroin in some local village somewhere in Switzerland in the 1990s, *theology—systematic, fundamental, dogmatic, pastoral*—shows itself either helpless or life-changing. The concept of a *nomadic theology* does help. In times of communal breakdowns all that remains may be the living of nomadic existence, both pastorally and theologically. The categories of *race, sex, class, ethnicity*, and *age* do apply, though more *metaphorically* (On race, class, gender, age, ethnicity in metaphorical sociology Rigney 2001). *Race, sex, class, ethnicity*, and *age* as social and *metaphorical categories* do stand for the irruption of *the other*, the one that is different, that is perplexing, that is upsetting our common world. In that sense, what blacks, women, gays, the poor, Hispanics, the handicapped, and the young experience in one place, can be experienced somewhere else *as if* one was *metaphorically* the other.

North American sociologist *Daniel Rigney* (Rigney 2001) defines the *interchangeable character* of *social metaphors*, applying them for a *global and socially imaginary perspective* on society in general:

> "Metaphor is a mode of thought wherein we interpret one domain of experience through the language of another. A metaphor, or implied comparison, figuratively identifies one object of thought (A) with another (B), creating a fusion of images and associations between the two and inviting us to view one *as if* it were the other . . . " (Rigney 2001, 3)

Culture

Kids at the age of 14 taking heroin in a local village somewhere in Switzerland in the 1990s may not be *black*, and yet they are treated like coloreds. These kids may not be experiencing *sexism*, and yet their world is filled with labeling mechanisms. These kids may not fit *classism*, and yet the social division and segregation act all the way, just as brutally. These kids may not qualify *ethnically*, and yet the social stratification takes its toll. And after all, these kids do represent a *generation issue*, but it seems the least virulent issue of all. But what qualifies and unites in all of these metaphorical and social moments of "one *as if* it were the other . . . " (Rigney 2001, 3) is the fact that kids are experiencing the most dramatic *violence* and *exclusion* in as much a radical way.

A *fundamental theology of postmodern nomadism* will approach these young teenagers in a different way. Aware of the nomadic existence of all our human ways, the *nomadic theologian* facing teenagers at the age of 14 taking heroin in a local village somewhere in Switzerland in the 1990s may start with a basic "critical consciousness that resists settling into socially coded modes of thought and behavior", as he or she is being called to minister to these teenagers and to get ready for quite some trip, knowing that not "all nomads are world travelers; some of the greatest trips can take place without physically moving from one's habitat. It is the subversion of set conventions that defines the nomadic state, not the literal act of traveling" (Braidotti 1994, 5). Starting with this kind of an attitude may at least start the trip.

Along the trip, the *nomadic theologian* will face all the signs of a *"postmodern kairos"* (on the postmodern kairos in systematic theology Hodgson 1994, 64–66) that theology knows all along as part and parcel of the *basic signature of our times*. Sitting on a bench in the schoolyard late at night with teenagers taking heroin at the age of 14 triggers all the ambiguities of life. Simple words do not hold anymore. One's basic theology *crumbles*. Listening to teenagers in that kind of a life situation makes most *fundamental theology* lose its basis. Suddenly, the *grounding foundations fall*. Witnessing the exclusionary mechanisms of *social ostracism*, village slander, open disregard, emotional wounding, communal segregation, and *systemic violence* makes all idealistic concepts of *ecclesial solidarity* evaporate. At some point, *theology* gets *nomadic*, having lost its own secure home. Suddenly, you become one of them, one of these teenagers who wander from one place to the next.

In moments like this, sitting on a bench late at night, or driving on a moped looking for some runaway teenager, or taking off a whole day to some amusement park in Germany to finally hear at some lakeshore at sunset that a teenager is really taking heroin, lets you evaluate what your basic *fundamental theology* is all about. Then, the *postmodern signature of these times* hits you full blow, having to learn, as North American feminist theologian *Rebecca S. Chopp* describes it, a new kind of "openness rather than closure in the face of the experienced ambiguities of life; solidarity through and across radical differences; embodiment as a basis for overcoming fragmentariness; and liberation in the face of systemic oppression" (quoted in Hodgson 1994, 65, Chopp 1989). Along the way, witnessing and accompanying all that, *your whole existence* becomes *nomadic* too, thrown right into the beginning of some never ending "nomadic journey" (Braidotti 1994, 39).

Taking on the decision to become a *pastor and companion to marginal teenagers at the social periphery of society*, segregated, ousted, ostracized, can be *dangerous, facing the unknown*, with no concept or sense of destiny and destination. The decision may be just intuitive, with the sudden determination "to go". Again, it turns out *nomadic*, even in the intellect, since in deciding to cross the dividing line and join the segregated crowd, being "an intellectual nomad is about crossing boundaries, about the act of going, regardless of the destination" (Braidotti 1994, 22–23). Once the decision has been taken, there is *no more way back* anymore. You join the crowd and get going on the way. *Transitions and passages*, with no sense of a predetermined destination, and some *feeling of lost homelands*, accompany you. A *feeling of instability* takes over, coloring your *whole life*.

Rosi Braidotti pictures it well, this *nomad's new and transitory relationship to the earth* and anything he or she does, gathers, acts, and lives:

> "The nomadic style is about transitions and passages without predetermined destinations or lost homelands. The nomad's relationship to the earth is one of transitory attachment and cyclical frequentation; the antithesis of the farmer, the nomad gathers, reaps, and exchanges, but does not exploit." (Braidotti 1994, 25)

Nomadic Thinking in Theology

Nomadic thinking creeps into your *fundamental theology* as you meet teenagers at the age of 14 taking heroin. Your whole basis in *theology—systematic, fundamental, dogmatic, ethical, practical, pastoral*—is slowly crumbling, going through a *postmodern kairos* forcing you to reconsidered.

A *post-idealistic theology* (Casalis 1984, Metz 1980, 1981, 1998, Lamb 1982, Lane 1984, Downey 1999, Arens 1995a, Haight 2001, Sedmak 2002, Mueller 2007, Rieger 2007, Taylor 1990, 2011) becomes attractive and meaningful again, as all remnants of idealism blow away, being proven to be too much light-weight. Your theology turns out a lot more *earthy, bottom-line, groundwork*, even if you keep on being on the move, never again secure or safe in any particular and remaining place. Theology becomes *ambiguous, plural, unstable*. Former dreams and illusions, securities and certainties pass away. The need to readjust your whole cognitive thinking is hitting you. In that sense, the challenge is most fundamental, most central, most existential, also *most threatening*.

Interpreting the world in order to *change it* becomes a new and more complicated challenge, but also more modest, more silent, more humble. Your hope still wants to change it, as the world needs to be changed. Teenagers at the age of 14 taking heroin need a different world, a world that changes. And yet, the thinking of *nomads* will help you to go step by step, moving from one place of hope to the next. A *fundamental theology of postmodern nomadism* is a *theology of hope* in spite of it.

In the memorable words of North American and Roman Catholic fundamental theologian *David Tracy* (Tracy 1987), calling for a *new thinking* facing the *basic ambiguity* of all our human and theological endeavors in these *postmodern and nomadic times*:

> "Einstein once remarked that with the arrival of the atomic age everything had changed except our thinking. Unfortunately the remark is true. Perhaps contemporary reflections on interpretation, with their emphasis on plurality and ambiguity, are one more stumbling start, across the disciplines, to try to change our usual ways of thinking. It is true that the point is not to interpret the world but to change it. But we will change too little, and that probably too late, if we do not at the same time change our understanding of what we mean when we so easily claim to interpret the world. Our Western dreams of domination, mastery, and certainty are over. The hope that interpretation will show us a way to resist is a fragile hope in a nuclear age. It may be less than we deserve, but it may also be more than we usually allow ourselves to envision, much less act upon . . . As for the rest, there is no release for any of us from the conflict of interpretations if we would understand at all. The alternative is not an escape into the transient pleasures of irony or a flight into despair and cynicism. The alternative is not a new kind of innocence or a passivity masking apathy. Whoever fights for hope fights on

behalf of all of us. Whoever acts on that hope, acts in a manner worthy of a human being. And whoever so acts, I believe, acts in a manner faintly suggestive of the reality and power of that God in whose image human beings were formed to resist, to think, and to act. The rest is prayer, observance, discipline, conversation, and actions of solidarity-in-hope. Or the rest is silence." (Tracy 1987, 114)

Theology Traveling Along Social Metaphors

Traveling as *postmodern nomads* along the *social-metaphorical categories* (Rigney 2001) of *race, sex, class, ethnicity, handicap*, and *age*, symbolic or metaphorical social categories that make up most of today's most brutal reasons for exclusion, division, segregation, stratification, ostracism, slander, prejudice, and violence, makes you *look for hope*. Facing teenagers at the age of 14 taking heroin requires hope, because you cannot afford staying in apathy, irony, or the innocence of passivity. At most, it may make you silent, but a silence in solidarity. *Fundamental theology* may need some moment of silence, before it starts from scratch developing *new social categories* along the nomadic path. Fundamental theology will need to *reformulate itself* along these new categories. Here, *North American systematic theology* is leading the way.

A *fundamental theology of postmodern nomadism* needs to learn from teenagers like that, and from the experience of *social exclusion* along these social categories that still make up most of our modern and postmodern world. This is true, regardless of people's place in life and where people are at, regardless whether one is really black, really gay, really poor, really foreign, really handicapped, really young, or stigmatized in other ways, like teenagers at the age of 14 taking heroin in some local village somewhere in Switzerland in the 1990s. The *mechanisms* are the same, with repeated *experiences of exclusion* of "one *as if* it were the other" (Rigney 2001, 3). A *postmodern nomadic theology—systematic, fundamental, dogmatic, ethical, pastoral*—that stays sensitive to these *metaphorical mechanism* of the distribution of *power* and *powerlessness* in the social interchange of *communal living* in any particular place will not remain the same (on power and powerlessness in metaphors Rigney 2001).

A *fundamental theology of postmodern nomadism* traveling along these *social-metaphorical categories* of *race, sex, class, ethnicity, handicap, age*, will join the crowd of those who have long ago recognized that we

Culture

need a *new way of thinking*, most probably more *nomadic*, more fluid in cognition, more *border crossing*, more *homeless*, more *transdisciplinary* (Braidotti 1994, 36), similar in the ways "contemporary reflections on interpretation, with their emphasis on plurality and ambiguity, are one more stumbling start, across the disciplines, to try to change our usual ways of thinking" (Tracy 1987, 114).

Theology then, in a *social postmodern way* (Chopp and Taylor 1994, Hodgson 1994, Barr 1997, Thistlethwaite and Engel 1998, Williamson 1999, Peters 2000, Inbody 2005, Jones and Lakeland 2005, Rieger 2007, Taylor 1990, 2011), becomes modest, but also *resistant*. It will resist all attempts to put people into prison categories, to place people outside of life, to divide and segregate the world into neat categories excluding some. *Theology* then—*systematic, fundamental, dogmatic, ethical, pastoral*— will become *countercultural* and *political, ecological* and *communitarian*, resisting all forms of life-destruction by presenting a new image, a new language, and a *new social* and *earth vision* for a *postmodern fundamental theology*—*emancipatory, dialogical, ecological*—of "liberation from life-destroying practices" (Hodgson 1994, 66).

Fundamental Theology and Abstractions

Life-destruction begins and grows and expands in our *abstractions*, in our *thinking*, in our *fundamental theologies*. Therefore, our abstractions, our thinking, our fundamental theologies are the ones that need revision. *Depending on where you start* in putting together your cognitive map, life gets messy or it gets healed. A *social healing of our fundamentals* may be called for. *Fundamental theology* could be one of these *healers* in a broken world, starting right at the fundamentals. It could help us deal with our *life-destructive fundamentals*, revisioning our abstractions for the sake of "reconstituting of hope for all victims" (Taylor 1990, 243) in this cognitively and practically *messed-up world*.

As North American and Protestant cultural-political theologian *Mark Kline/Lewis Taylor* closes on his fundamental theology of *Remembering Esperanza* (Taylor 1990), presenting a *postmodern and socially resistant cultural-political theology* for *North American praxis*:

> "Throughout this work a key theme pertaining to connections between oppressions has been that of *abstraction*: abstracting from the woman/ mother in sexism; from the body and same-gender friendships in hetero-realism; from one's self and

> finitude in racism; from the earth and a sharing of its resources in classism. A fully reconciliatory emancipation from the oppressions that are built up around this abstracting practice must seek to ally the different emancipatory tasks that focus on different forms of oppressing abstractions. With the emergence of an alliance of such emancipatory strategies, there begins to occur a 'remembering Esperanza'—a reconstituting of hope for all victims who are dismembered by the abstracting practices of oppression . . . Re-membering Esperanza, therefore, is far more than resistance to the abstractions that oppress women; it is also to practice with equal seriousness a resistance to those related abstractions of a white supremacism that oppresses African Americans, of a hetero-realism that subjugates gay and lesbian persons, and of the classism that impoverishes the underclasses. Until this *full* emancipatory practice becomes our churches' christopraxis, North American churches will more be the tools of oppression than the agents of reconciliatory emancipation. Until then, our calling is to struggle, celebrate and pray in the way of *Christus Mater*." (Taylor 1990, 243, 245)

To *struggle, celebrate* and to *pray* in the way of *Christus Mater* may be just as much part and parcel of a *social ministry* to teenagers at the age of 14 taking heroin in some local village somewhere in Switzerland in the 1990s. The *life-destructive abstractions* are the same. The oppressive constructions and cognitive social maps *excluding life* work the same. The need for a *christopraxis* in churches and communities preaching and living, modeling and embodying in practice the "reconstituting of hope for all victims who are dismembered by the abstracting practices of oppression" (Taylor 1990, 243) is also the same.

A *fundamental theology of postmodern nomadism* invites us to such a kind of *basic rethinking* on what we really believe in in the face of those many and life-destructive metaphorical realities and cognitive imageries—"one *as if* it were the other" (Rigney 2001, 3)—of *race, sex, gender, class, ethnicity, handicap, age,* and *juvenile drug addiction* that can mess up or heal whole theologies and communities.

Fundamental Theology in New Categories

Fundamental theology will have to be reformulated along these *new categories*. The topics of *race, sex, gender, class, ethnicity, age* are only some of the *social indicators* pointing to the more comprehensive issues of *power* and *powerlessness* in theological beginnings. The place where you begin from—the basic theme of fundamental theology—may be determinative for where you get to. Depending on your beginnings, your endings may be quite various. Fundamental theology then will become a *practical fundamental theology* (Metz 1980, Lamb 1982, Lane 1984, Peukert 1984, Schüssler Fiorenza 1984, Wetherilt 1994, Arens 1995a, Haight 2001, Sedmak 2002, Rieger 2007, Taylor 1990, 2011) of various alliances that seeks "to ally the different emancipatory tasks that focus on different forms of oppressing abstractions" (Taylor 1990, 243).

Oppressing abstractions enter *fundamental theology* already at the *first beginnings*. To become sensitive to this, to reflect self-critically on it, to reconstruct its *theological method* and language, its *theoretical structure* and thematic architecture in view of this *new sensitivity* for *power* and *powerlessness* in its various forms of *exclusion*, segregation, stratification, violence, and radical extinction, and to develop a *new kind of fundamental theology* creatively responsive to this kind of human und non-human *suffering* all over the world and in local communities, will be its new and honorable calling. Gone are the times when fundamental theology has only served as a an aristocratic and introductory first tour in the various exquisite rooms and flashy halls of an honorable mansion or kingly estate called theology.

Urgently needed in these times is a *fundamental theology* that revisions itself most radically and *reconstructs theology from scratch*, with a high *social and artistic, personal and practical, ethical and pastoral sensitivity* for the "reconstituting of hope for all victims who are dismembered by the abstracting practices of oppression" (Taylor 1990, 243). Then, all of theology in its various *encyclopedic forms* (Farley 1982, 1983, Jennings 1976, 1985a, Bayer 1994, Davey 2002, Mueller 2007, Hilpert/Leimgruber 2008)—*biblical, historical, systematic, fundamental, dogmatic, ethical, pastoral, practical*—could become more of a *life-changing theory* with a *world-changing practice*, with *fundamental theology* leading the way.

Cultural Studies and Theologies of Culture

The New Theme of Culture

It seems that contemporary *North American systematic theology* has discovered the wide and fascinating field of *cultural studies*. Looking at the more *secular departments* of a *university bookstore* in the *Unites States* in these days will show a whole wall or more filled with the field of *cultural studies*. There is no end to what cultural studies are diving into, finding ever new areas of research and writing for university scholars.

The academic and political interest in *cultural studies* (on cultural studies as an academic new area of research and teaching in North America Sardar and Van Loon 1997, Surber 1998, Barker 2000, 2002, 2004, Lewis 2008, in Europe Lutter und Reisenleitner 1998, Teske 2002, Hepp 2004, Marchart 2007) moves meanderingly from communication studies, literary studies, media studies, cinema studies, popular culture, popular music, youth culture, and MTV to architecture, fashion design, life style, the Internet, modern art, and the sociology of the everyday, from Marxism, post-Marxism, critical theory, the New Left, *Gramsci, Adorno, Foucault, Lyotard, Derrida, Jameson, West, hooks, Said, Spivak, Minh-ha*, poststructuralism, postmodernism, postcolonialism, feminism, postfeminism, and women studies to men studies, queer studies, ethnic studies, native studies, from critical social theory, critical pedagogy, multicultural pedagogy, critical psychology, critical social psychology, critical sociology to deconstruction, symbolic interactionism, social constructionism, systems theory, discourse theory, semiotics, and radical philosophy. There is not one area of research that could not find a home in and within the big wide world of *cultural studies*.

Theology as well has picked up the ball, with *early attempts* (Nelson 1976, Greeley 1988) hardly noticed, but *newer attempts* becoming more prominent (Tanner 1997, Hopkins and Davaney 1998, Brown, Davaney, Tanner 2001, Dyrness 1997, 2001, Friesen 2000, Cobb 2005, Lynch 2005, Staub 2008, Taylor 2008). Some of it has already been prepared by early visionaries, either coming out of *Paul Tillich's* and a *cultural-anthropological* world (on cultural anthropology relating to theology/religion after Paul Tillich see Taylor 1986a and 1990) or the vast field of *African American history and story* (Smith 1994b, Murphy 2000). Others, most prominently *Evangelicals*, have recently found their way into the limitless field of everything that seems to be *popular*, be it popular culture, art, or the picturesque and action-loaded world of literature, music, and movies (Dyrness 1997, 2001, Detweiler and Taylor 2003, Cunningham 2002, Staub 2008, Taylor 2008, Johnston 2000, 2007, Detweiler 2008). *Culture* and *theology*, in good company with revived *father-figures* like *Paul Tillich* (Tillich 1964) who have prepared the way for a younger and interested generation, seem to become the hit topics in *systematic theology* in the *North American context* in these days (on culture and systematic theology Dyrness 1997, 2001,

Culture

Chopp and Taylor 1994, Williamson 1999, McClendon 2000, Peters 2000, Placher 2003, Jones and Lakeland 2005, De La Torre 2004, Taylor 1990, 2011).

Culture seems to be the *new theme* for *theology—systematic, fundamental,* and *dogmatic*—in North America. Inculturation in theology has been a theme already in the early 1980's when *Latin American theologies, African theologies, Asian theologies,* and *Native theologies* of any other place and geographical location in this global world hit and flushed to the shore of the different mainlands of the *European* (on Asian, African, and Latin American theologies reaching Europe Waldenfels 1982, 433–471, Witvliet 1985, Chenu 1987, Blaser 1990b, Gibellini 1995, 336–402, Rowland 1999, Parratt 2004) and the *North American continent* (Ferm 1986a-b, 1988, Hennelly 1995, Ford and Muers 2005, Livingston and Schüssler Fiorenza 2006).

The *new theme*, however, is its *neighborly closeness* as a theological topic. No longer is there talk about some cultural-anthropological problem in *inculturating* the Christian message in a *foreign culture*. No longer is the topic mostly related to questions of *mission theology, third world theologies,* or *inter-cultural communication* between contextual theologies from different continents. And no longer has the topic only a peripheral importance at the fringe of systematic, fundamental, or dogmatic theology when it gets to a *theology of religions* or the question of *contextualization* in a particular place. Rather, the *new theme* is hitting closer home, challenging theology right at the center of its theological reflection.

Culture and *theology* are the most fundamental themes as regards to the reopened question of the possible or impossible future of Christian faith in its identity and relevance as theology—*systematic, fundamental,* and *dogmatic*—in the days to come. The *new theme* has moved right back into homeland, asking some disturbing questions on whether theology has not missed waking up to a changing modern and postmodern *cultural world*.

The Postmodern Cultural World

We do live in a *postmodern cultural world* (in the social sciences Giles and Middleton 1999, Smith 2001, Featherstone 2007, in theology Detweiler and Taylor 2003, Cobb 2005, Lynch 2005, Staub 2008, Taylor 2008, Dyrness, Kärkkäinen, Martinez, and Chan 2008). Walking through any town or city, turning on the television, browsing through the newspaper and looking for the page on cultural events, listening through CDs in a music store, and checking on the latest cinema program, everything shows us the *radical fragmentation of culture* in these days.

What used to be *high culture*, has stepped down to become just one more normal CD among many others and millions. The former *difference* between the Opera house and the bar next door has lost its convincing aura, as both of them are now contributing to some important cultural event. What used to be relegated into some hidden and insider backstage café to play its tunes in *jazz* or *pop* is now filling whole soccer stadiums or music halls. What used to be frowned upon as dirt and unruly spraying on walls has now become much visited *graffiti art*. What used to be separated and segregated into the two big worlds of classical music and entertainment noise is now being mixed in *classical rock*. The mixing and blending of every possible style, the never ending cultural interchange of old and new, avant-garde and baroque, Gregorian and Techno, Gospel and Rap, *Beethoven* and *Madonna*, *Miles Davis* and *Eminem*, *Sting* and *Keith Jarrett*, show one thing, at least in music, namely the endless proliferation of boundless *deconstruction* of any structural limit in *cultural style*.

And yet, this world *makes us into who we are*. A little bit as confusing as visiting and looking at some music store. The proliferation and *radical fragmentation* of musical styles is in the midst of our own most personal souls, in that which makes us *be ourselves*, in our dreams, our preferences, our day-dreams, our love songs. There is no more just *one melody* playing in us. There are *many* now, as many as can be sung. We have become *many* now, not just in musical style, but in this most definitely.

Cultural theorists and personal artists like *Craig Detweiler*, mass communications professor, screenwriter, *Los Angeles Film Studies Center* teacher, now on staff at *Pepperdine University*, and musician, painter, and popular culture theologian *Barry Taylor* teaching at *Fuller Theological Seminary* in *Pasadena, Southern California*, describe it beautifully in their *A Matrix of Meanings: Finding God in Pop Culture* (Detweiler and Taylor 2003, also Detweiler 2008, Taylor 2008, following Johnston 2000, 2007) what *music*, popular or otherwise, seems to be all about for us and our human soul:

> "Pop music is everywhere. When I was young, one had to seek it out in specific places. Now, we live in a world immersed in music. Music surrounds us every time we walk into a store. Banana Republic, Pottery Barn, and Starbucks sell CDs designed as background music for summer barbecues and beach parties.

Culture

> A genre was even developed for a single form of transport: elevator music ... Identity often starts with music categories: punk, techno, hip-hop, goth, and headbanger. English rock star Morrissey remembers listening to a Top 30 show as a six-year-old. After every Tuesday's show, he would run to the typewriter to compile 'my own personal Top 30, which totally conflicted with how the world really was ... ' Morrissey joined millions of others who follow the musical charts to work out life ... "
> (Detweiler and Taylor 2003, 126–127)

To follow the musical charts *to work out life*, this may be a short summary for the theological significance of *music*. Music gives us identity, shapes us in who we are, or reflects it back to us. And sometimes, the world around may quite radically *conflict* with who we are in the Top 30s. Like teaching teenagers at the age of 14 as a local pastor in a confirmation class, and hardly anybody knows who *Pink Floyd* is. When you play *Sting*, some will say you are old-fashioned. When you feel tears with *Mercedes Soza's Gracias a la Vida*, these same teenagers in front of you may not feel anything.

Moments like that are the beginning of a healthy recognition that we do live in a *postmodern world*. And on top of it, you start to realize that you have all this modern and postmodern confusion and collision, cultural radical fragmentation, endless stylish proliferation, and musically incommensurable variety or dissonance, difference and differance, even *within you*. From *Bach* to *Sting*, *Emerson Lake and Palmer* to *Keith Jarrett*, *Carlos Santana* to *John McLaughlin*, *Trance* to *Bad Boys*, and *Gospel* to *New Age*, *Janet Jackson* to *Céline Dion*, all of this and more is in you and makes you into who you are.

Culture becomes a signifier for the *postmodern mess*. Since what goes on outside of you, or inside of your musical ear or heart, is what goes on in your mind too, in your thinking, in your reflecting, in your conceiving, in your constructing the most fabulous *philosophy, sociology, psychology, ethnology, epistemology,* and even *theology*. Your own theology—*systematic, fundamental,* and *dogmatic*—in these postmodern days may also have become a *postmodern mess*, just as *incommensurable* in musical and cognitive style as any CD store nowadays.

Theology too may have become no longer just *one melody*, but *many*, being *radically fragmented* into bits and pieces that a DJ could mix. In theology too, there may be in you this endless mixing and blending of every possible style, the never ending cultural interchange of old and new, avant-garde and baroque, Gregorian and Techno, Gospel and Rap,

The Community of the Weak

Beethoven and *Madonna*, *Miles Davis* and *Eminem*, *Sting* and *Keith Jarrett*, showing one thing, now in theology too, namely the eternally continuous proliferation of a boundlessly radical *deconstruction* of any structural limit in cultural style. God may be a DJ, or your theology may turn out like one at least.

Mixing the Postmodern Mess

In that sense, *culture* and *theology* intersect and coalesce in describing and facing the same, namely the *postmodern mess*. Looking at it in this way, *the postmodern* may turn into a new kind of *symphony*. Blending, cut and paste, and bricolage, or cafeteria style, whether in musical production or theological construction, need not necessarily end in unaesthetic noise. There could be something *new* coming out of it, quite beautiful and hip. And, as a matter of fact, we already do live in a world like that.

To quote again Christian *Evangelicals* and postmodern cultural theorists *Craig Detweiler* and *Barry Taylor* on the postmodern hip:

> "*Blending, cut and paste, bricolage, cafeteria* are all words that have been employed to describe the postmodern approach. The fragmented collages of Pablo Picasso hinted at the coming collision. Hip-hop music introduced the art of sampling. Now, DJs are considered musicians whether or not they play an instrument. The Wachowski Brother's masterful trilogy *The Matrix* merged comic books, science fiction, Japanese anime, martial arts, mathematics, Eastern philosophy, and Western religion into something utterly new. That story ends with *The Matrix Revolutions*. But the postmodern shift is actually about 'retrolutions'. It doesn't shout, 'Out with the old, in with the new.' It rejects *recent* history but embraces our *cumulative* history. The old, or rather the ancient, serves as the new foundation. This 'retrolution' presents 'aspects of the future through terms set by the past, in order to make it palatable' today . . . We think of postmodernity as expressing a 'consciousness of pluralisms'. The veritable flood of ideas and information resulting from democratization and globalization has demanded 'blending'. Commentator Marshall McLuhan anticipated our global village, made smaller and more accessible by advancements in travel, technology, and science. At the same time, access to new ideas, values, and perspectives has exploded. The Internet allows instant access to virtually anything. Our understanding of time and space, geographical and political boundaries, has broadened and blurred. Previously

elusive portions of the Vatican library can be toured at any time, from anywhere, by anyone with a computer and a phone line. Its vast contents can be discussed with any number of other interested parties around the globe without ever leaving the comfort of home. We find ourselves living in a world in which radically diverse worldviews emerge within the same society as alternative lifestyles, and belief systems exist side by side in ways not experienced before." (Detweiler and Taylor 2003, 29–30)

It is both beautiful and amazing to read this from two *Evangelicals* celebrating the *postmodern mess*. But as said already before, the *plurality and radical diversity* of musical styles found nowadays in any CD store around the corner and blended by a skilled and visionary DJ into *symphony* need not become a mess. *Bach* and *Trance* do go together, even if your ear and musical heart has to get used to it a little bit. The same is true in *philosophy, sociology, psychology, ethnology*, and last but not least, *theology*. *Retrolutions*, making the future through the past more palatable for today, cut and pasted in bricolage, while blending a new coffee at the cafeteria, can taste *exquisitely new* in theology as well. And again, it will be a matter of getting used to it to see its new symphony as *God's DJ* is blending and mixing, sampling and cutting and pasting a new sound.

Theology in a *postmodern cultural world* may become more like *God's DJ*, mixing and scratching, blending and pasting together the postmodern mess in fragmentary ways. Like in *Pablo Picasso*, collage may turn into art, and theology in a fragmentary way may turn into a raving and grooving new sound.

Cultural Studies

Cultural studies as an academic discipline are an exploding field of inquiry (in North America Sardar and Van Loon 1997, Surber 1998, Barker 2000, 2002, 2004, Lewis 2008, in Europe Lutter und Reisenleitner 1998, Teske 2002, Hepp 2004, Marchart 2007). The new field has entered into the general *university curriculum* in a bombastic way. This is most particularly true for the whole *Anglo-Saxon world—England, Australia, New Zealand—*, but especially so for most *North American academic institutions*. More and more themes of inquiry are establishing themselves in the field, with no end in view on what else and what more could become a fascinating and ever more expanding area of scholarly interest for some culturally and critically studying minds. Cultural studies are part of the new Top

10 in academic studies, at least in the *Anglo-Saxon world*. Media studies, communication studies, popular culture, literary studies, feminism, postcolonialism, and social theory, all of these and others feed into the general interest of *cultural studies* looking at our most basic and *everyday world*.

Cultural studies are part of the *postmodern turn* that our world has taken. This *new culture* shows itself most clearly and visually, as North American and Roman Catholic *Roger Haight* points out in his fundamental theology *Dynamics of Theology* (Haight 2001)—following *Paul Lakeland* (Lakeland 1997)—in various forms of "architecture and life-style and popular culture. But it is accompanied by principles and axioms formulated by literary critics, philosophers, and theologians" (Haight 2001, 238). The *cultural turn*, however, is what makes it most interesting and omnipresent. The present and future can be described in *Roger Haight's fundamental* and *theological* words as "a culture of war, disruption, and relativism. The whole has been torn into fragments; the universal is an assembly of disconnected parts" (Haight 2001, 239).

A *postmodern fundamental theology* needs to take seriously this emerging shape and character, feel and ambiance of a *new cultural world*. Theology in this kind of radically dispersed world will have to speak and act *differently* in order to attend to the fact that our world has become in some way or another *new*. Following the words of a *Jesuit* facing *the postmodern* who has accepted the fact that "western culture is moving into a period that is new, that shares significant differences from what went before, and which consequently calls forth new value responses and new interpretations of traditional ideas. Thus one reason why the term 'postmodern' may still perform a valuable function lies precisely in its appeal to a *novum*; it jars the imagination into attending to what is new and different in our current situation" (Haight 2001, 239–240).

Cultural studies try to attend to this *novum* of a different and new world facing us, looking at it at its utmost proximity in our *everyday world*. Not the far and farther away cultural worlds of other peoples, nations, tribes, and ethnic groups and places are of interest, but our own most personal and social worlds in which we have our daily life and moving. And these *daily, personal,* and *social worlds* in which we live and have our moving have become quite complicated and confusing. Sex and work, politics and art, leisure and sports, music and cinema, television and the newest fashion, advertising and celebrities, literature and religion, community and identity, poverty and solidarity, all qualify for the analytic and critical interest of cultural studies.

Culture and Popular Culture

Most confusing is already the beginning term of *culture* (for various definitions of culture and pop culture Surber 1998, Giles and Middleton 1999, Smith 2001, Delaney 2004, Lewis 2008). *Cultural studies* deal with culture in all its various forms, both *high* and *popular*, blurring all previously categorized and segregating forms. What culture really is or used to be, high and popular, nobody seems to know anymore. And yet it's there and shapes our daily lives ever more.

Cultural theorists *Craig Detweiler* and *Barry Taylor* (Detweiler and Taylor 2003, Dettweiler 2008, Taylor 2008) introduce in their *A Matrix of Meanings* the purpose of the book as a *cultural studies reader* (Detweiler and Taylor 2003, 19). And so it is, since it covers almost everything cultural studies would cover, in addition written from a clearly fascinating *theological perspective*. Their definition of *culture*—high and popular—is pretty simple:

> "What is popular culture? Most of us have a rough idea from the very phrase itself, but some clarification will help for the sake of our own discussion. Scholars generally make distinctions between popular culture and high or 'elite' culture. High culture traditionally merited the most academic and scholastic attention. The word *culture* was reserved for human works of only the highest sophistication and quality. A symphony orchestra qualified, while a rock group did not. Analysts of popular culture use broader definitions of the word *culture*, making fewer value, taste, or quality judgments. Movies, cartoons, comic books, T-shirts, ball gowns, symphonies, and rock bands *all* constitute 'culture'." (Detweiler and Taylor 2003, 17–18)

What used to be commonly and uncommonly separated is now fusing together. The *classical* is joining the *popular*. Jazz is playing *Bach*. Pop is imitating *Beethoven*. The Gothic is included in the postmodern. The bricolage of architectural, musical, and any other life-style has become common practice, blending and mixing everything in the new cultural mixer to make a new drink. At the bottom of it, giving it its common ground and spirit, is the feel for the *unlimited creative*. *Culture* and *creation* go together, even in its most theological term.

As theologian of culture and *Evangelical* Dean of *Fuller Theological Seminary* in *Southern California William A. Dyrness* (Dyrness 1997, 2001) puts it: "Culture is what we make of creation" (Dyrness 1997, 58). And who says that God may not like jazz or Techno? It's as creative as any other classical, modern, or postmodern gig. Later on, *William A. Dyrness* gives us a little bit more in defining *culture* from where it came from in its first theological, metaphorical, and etymological trip.

> "Culture is itself a metaphor that has come to stand for what humans have made of their particular corner of the earth. *Culture* comes from the Latin *cultura*, which means 'to cultivate', and which probably for medieval believers recalled Adam's cultivation of the Garden of Eden ... So this figurative language relates, not accidentally, to cultivating or rearing a plant or crop or even certain animals. Like all metaphors, however, it has its limits. It illumines the intimate relationship between human activity and the earth, but because of the unique historical context out of which it has arisen, it has also been used to restrict that understanding to human and social processes." (Dyrness 1997, 62)

Culture can be used restrictively or inclusively for the *human creative spirit* that is following in the creation of *God's creative Spirit*. Widening it may make the image and metaphor a lot more open and promising, with even comic books and T-shirts, graffiti walls and DJ art qualifying for it. *Theology* as well, in some way, is *culture*, or at least participates in it. Theology has a particular style, or at least used to have it. Whether its particular *classical style* still *reaches the masses*, like *popular culture* would be defining itself (Detweiler and Taylor 2003, 18), remains an open and questionable question. From there it would be helpful to ask the question whether there is only one style for theology to be itself, or if there may not be more in it.

The project of people like *Craig Detweiler* and *Barry Taylor* "to create a theology *out of* popular culture rather than a theology *for* popular culture. We want to join the theologizing already occurring *within* popular culture, outside the reaches of the traditional academy or religion" (Detweiler and Taylor 2003, 16), is at least worth pondering on to reconsider what theology may be all about in *postmodern times*.

A question for any basic and *fundamental theology* to seriously reconsider.

The Lingua Franca of the Postmodern World

The importance of *culture* and *popular culture* is especially worth reconsidering for any *theology—systematic, fundamental*, or *dogmatic—*in these modern and postmodern times in view of the fact that *popular culture* is becoming "the lingua franca of the postmodern world, a point often missed by scholars" (Detweiler and Taylor 2003, 21).

There is a *new literacy* that is emerging, more *democratic*, less elitist, and definitely more *popular*. Knowledge and wisdom, information and input, culture and civilization take on a whole new shape when people start to take it into their own hands, freely mixing it. A *new canon* of necessary, meaningful, and life-changing knowledge is composed like a canvas to be painted on or a musical piece to be composed from scratch. "This new canon draws from a broader range of influences and from a wider range of source materials, including classic literature and classic movies, songs, and even comic books. The new literacy is democratic, much less elitist, and decidedly influenced by the effects of mediatization" (Detweiler and Taylor 2003, 21).

In addition, *knowledge* now becomes a lot more *accessible to all*, not necessarily only and exclusively through academic and institutionalized channels. *Theology* will have to reconsider itself there too.

To quote again *Craig Detweiler* and *Barry Taylor* on the *diversification* and *plural access to learning* in these *postmodern times*, creating a whole *new type of a student*:

> "Information can now be accessed in any number of ways—computers, the Internet, video, television—and literacies are developed that are often far beyond the grasp of those raised in a more print-based culture. The next wave of students is capable of reading these visual texts and is more comfortable with fast-moving, fragmented pieces of information than were previous generations. Consequently, learning through popular culture allows them to draw on their existing literacies and analyze and think critically." (Detweiler and Taylor 2003, 21)

Learning through popular culture is a new challenge for *systematic theology* in these postmodern times. It is almost like *learning a new language*, the *lingua franca* of these changed times. Language evolves and becomes more pictorial, digital, visual, tactile, and cultural. To refuse to learn this new language, to claim to stay in old print-based cultures, may be a sign of retrograde elitism, but will not move the message of theology, *the Good News* after all, into the hearts of people raised in this postmodern world. We may have to learn a whole new language, easier, simpler, *more colloquial*. Learning the language of the people in the streets may be a good beginning.

The Community of the Weak

In some ways we find ourselves catapulted back into the *first century* when Christians had to translate their message into *street-level language*. The *New Testament* was this kind of a street-level language, the *Koine Greek*, the dialect of the people on the street, instead of the *Attic Greek* that only the educated spoke and understood. The language and the images, the texts and the clips, the colors and the designs, the stories and the artifacts of *popular culture* in our times may be nothing less than the new *Koine Greek* to be learned in *systematic theology* as well, so people can hear and understand.

> "If the Christian world continues in its scholastic mode, viewing popular culture as degraded and superficial, then the gap between church and culture will continue to widen. Our theological propositions will become increasingly redundant to a culture being influenced by other forces. The Gospels were written for 'the people'. Educated Greeks in the first century communicated in Attic Greek, a high cultural form that excluded many. But the writers of the Gospels preferred Koine Greek, a 'street-level' language that communicated to the masses. We must go back to that street-level discussion, where our faith was forged." (Detweiler and Taylor 2003, 23)

Cultural studies could therefore become the *new language program* for *systematic theology* in the years to come. The combination of *culture* and *theology* is a still hardly explored wide open continent. A *fundamental theology of culture* will need some *language training* in a few unexpected places. No longer is going to the Opera, to the symphony hall, to the theater, to the literary reading house the only possibility to get a feel for people's culture. Going weekly to the movies, reading comic books and getting into *The Matrix*, but also listening to some or more CDs your kids or young teenagers listen to, watching MTV, turning on the television, and going to some techno or hip-hop party can become an important *prolegomena to theology*.

Sitting on a bench or the schoolyard with teenagers at the age of 14 taking heroin in some local village somewhere in Switzerland in the 1990s did give me a crash course in language training at its most basic *street-level*. Leveling with them, being on the same wave length, learning a different language, was more educational than many lectures and seminar debates in university halls. It took a while, it took some regular practice, but language does change once you are faced with young teenagers living on the street. And *theology changes too*.

Diving into the *popular culture* of these teenagers—their language, visions, images, idioms, rituals, concepts, worries, smiles, festivities, beliefs, communities, solidarities—was like that of a *cultural anthropologist* doing *field work*. Except that you don't just leave and go away once the research project is almost complete. You stay and get *closer*, get touched and moved all the way. The *ethnographic gaze* (on the ethnographic gaze in North America Coffey 1999, Willis 2000, Brewer 2000, Denzin 1989, 1997a, 2003, Denzin and Lincoln 2002, O'Reilly 2005, in Europe Seipel, Rieker 2003) gets hooked and pulled into it and you *stay*.

Doing Cultural Theology From Below

In all this, a *new perspective* may be most important, namely a *new look "from below"*. Most often, theology has stayed hidden behind the pulpit, at the lectern, in the seminar room or in some university hall. *Cultural studies* may get students outside and among the people. Since an *everyday culture* is definitely not to be found in elite high cultural and academic estates alone, but more so on the street where the people are working, moving, living, dancing, painting, playing, theology in this way, leaving its own most renown academic halls, may get more *street-level* too. In that way, *unheard voices*, voices that most often get silenced, forgotten, and push out of sight and out of the way, may be heard in theology and academics again, with *the postmodern* moving in from below.

> "There has been a tendency in academic environs to engage with only what can be view as high culture. Academia seems to be intoxicated with 'ideas from above'—with the view that the best ideas, and those most worthy of study, emanate from the intelligentsia and trickle down to the rest of society (a very old way of viewing things in our opinion). But much has changed in Western culture in the past one hundred years, not the least of which is the onset of postmodernism with its 'from below' perspective about ideas and values. Jean-François Lyotard, one of the key thinkers in the field, suggests that a hallmark of the postmodern age is that previously unheard voices can be heard and can influence society... In an age of expanding democracy, the people's voice of choice became pop culture." (Detweiler and Taylor 2003, 21–22)

A *fundamental theology of popular culture* could become a new kind of *cultural-political theology of liberation* in the *contemporary postmodern context*, working in and through *popular culture* at the "reconstituting of hope for all victims who are dismembered by the abstracting practices of oppression" (Taylor 1990, 243, Rieger 2007, Taylor 2011). This opens up a whole wide open and new field of *theological and pastoral reflection* on *power* and *culture*, *victimization* and *empowerment* in culture, *violence* and *non-violence* in culture, and the social potential of culture to *creatively change the world* in order to make it a better place.

Cultural studies from its beginnings have always had this *political drive* to make the world a better place. The subversive potential of *creative culture* belongs to its history. Cultural studies follow in the traces of envisioned *political protest, social imagination,* and *creative transformation* of the everyday world in the way people and artists adapt, subvert, and change what they are faced with. As a discipline, cultural studies have been born "in dissent outside the traditional centers of power" (Detweiler and Taylor 2003, 19). This connects it to a *political theology* that sees itself as *practical fundamental theology* (Metz 1980, Lamb 1982, Lane 1984, Peukert 1984, Wetherilt 1994, Arens 1995a, Haight 2001, Sedmak 2002, Rieger 2007, Taylor 1990, 2011) in a *modern and postmodern age*. These open connections, though, between the two poles of cultural studies and political action—aside from a few exceptions (Hopkins and Davaney 1996, Brown, Davaney, Tanner 2001, Hopkins 2005, Lynch 2005, Cobb 2005, Taylor 1990, 2011)—have not been made as yet as visible, but are certainly and readily waiting to be made and developed.

Learning from Cultural Studies' History

Cultural studies look at the *political* in *contemporary culture* in a most pertinent way. This has been part of its *subversive history* ever since its beginning (on the history of cultural studies Surber 1998, 233–267, Brantlinger 1990, Turner 1996, Brooker 1998, Hartley 2003, Lutter und Reisenleitner 1998, 17–49, Hepp 2004, 78–108, Kramer 1997, Teske 2002, Marchart 2007, Lewis 2008).

As North American cultural philosopher and chronicler of British, French, and North American cultural studies *Jere Paul Surber* (Surber 1998) from the *University of Denver* points out in his summary overview of the history of cultural studies: "First, from its very beginning, cultural studies was decisively oriented toward the analysis and critique of *concrete cultural productions and institutions* and their political ramifications" (Surber 1998, 233). This has not changed ever since, even if further radical movements and orientations have been included like feminism, poststructuralism, postmodernism, and postcolonialism.

At the same time, cultural studies have become a truly *international story*, with cross-fertilization across many continents. Beginning in *Britain* in the 1950s, in particular at the *University of Birmingham*, it has in the meantime become a truly cross-cultural and international movement.

As *Jere Paul Surber* puts it, connecting the different continents and movements up to the most recent time in the convergence of an *international movement*:

> "While cultural studies as a concerted and identifiable movement is generally associated with developments at certain British universities, especially the University of Birmingham, in the 1950s, it would be a mistake to view it simply as a British contribution to contemporary critical discourse for several reasons. First, at quite an early stage, it began to draw on other critical discourses developed on the Continent (and, to a lesser degree, in the United States), especially those of the Frankfurt School, structuralism, and later, postmodernism. Second, many of its characteristic themes and emphases were already emerging independently in other countries such as France, the United States, Australia, and Canada, resulting in a good deal of cross-fertilization. Finally, although cultural studies in each country has retained something of its own characteristic set of emphases and preferred approaches due to the differing cultural configurations characteristic of each national region, the growth of an international economy, the internationalization of the media, and new possibilities for international communication among researchers have resulted in a tendency toward a certain degree of convergence of the various regional discourses of cultural studies." (Surber 1998, 234–235)

Cultural studies have become a *lingua franca* on an international scale in interpreting the postmodern world to itself. *Theology* in postmodern times will have to become as *international* too, developing a *theology of culture* just as cross-cultural and analytic, critical and political as cultural studies has become, integrating some of the most *radical social and political movements in a cross-cultural way*. Theology is still far away from this kind of a cross-cultural dialogue and integration. Cultural studies could show it the way.

Filmmaker and communication theorist *Craig Detweiler* and musician-theologian *Barry Taylor* in their collaborative *theology of popular culture* in *A Matrix of Meanings* (Detweiler and Taylor 2003) recall the history and trajectory of *cultural studies* up to the most recent times, adding an *integrative* and *artistic dimension* to it:

> "This book falls within the broad and growing field known as cultural studies. Richard Hoggarth's 1957 book, *The Uses of Literacy*, is generally acknowledged as cultural studies' starting point... Hoggarth focused on working-class-life, offering a personal, subjective response to the changes coursing through postwar England. He criticized the imported American culture that threatened to colonize the British working classes through the growing mass media. From the beginning, cultural studies has championed the underclass, criticized capitalism, and berated America's dominance. Hoggarth founded the Centre for Contemporary Cultural Studies in 1964. The University of Birmingham and scholars such as Stuart Hall became the locus for most of the subsequent intellectual debate on the subject. Assuming Hoggarth's focus on politics and economics, scholars 'read' pop culture from Marxist, feminist, and post-colonial perspectives. London's Routledge Press published most of the seminal overviews central to the discipline. Cultural studies have analyzed cultural practices in relationship to power structures, hoping to understand and undercut the dominant structures that undergird the cultural assumptions in capitalist society. It has trained people to read the signs and decode pop cultural texts to promote new forms of representation. Semiotics emerged as the study of pop culture's signs and symbols... While we acknowledge our debt to pioneers such as Walter Benjamin, bell hooks, and Teresa de Lauretis, we seek to move beyond the politicized categories established in our field. With the fall of communism and the rise of postmodern feminism and queer theory, cultural studies has fragmented into an exhausting variety of subcategories rooted in competing agendas. How ironic that a discipline born in dissent outside the traditional centers of power would dissolve into a debate of elites connected almost exclusively to the academy. We seek to integrate and move past the fragmenting fields of dissent. Our cultural studies deals with politics, acknowledges gender, emphasizes narrative, and appreciates the subjective response of individual readers. But we hope to offer more than a critique. We want to encourage an appreciation for the arts and artists that create our pop cultural artifacts." (Detweiler and Taylor 2003, 18–19)

Working towards the *integration* of the *aesthetic* with the *political*, the appreciative with the oppositional, and the artistic with the communal could be a common task for both *cultural studies* and *theology—systematic, fundamental,* or *dogmatic*—in the future. Making theology learn from the *artistic*, without giving up its *oppositional drive*, letting the *aesthetic* combine with the *political*, and the *creative* with the *communal* (on combining the artistic with the oppositional, the creative with the political and communal Fox 2002), could be a new definition for *theological method* as well. Some first attempts have been made (on basic textbooks in systematic theology combing the artistic with the political in North America Thistlethwaite and Engel 1998, Baker-Fletcher and Baker-Fletcher 1997, in Europe Biehl und Johannsen 2002, Schneider-Flume 2004), but more could be tried in this creative way.

Theology Speaking a New Cultural Language

The *weaving together* of *cultural studies* and *systematic theology*, the bringing together of an appreciation for *popular culture* and the *creative skill* in theological architecture in systematics, and the mixing and blending of various tunes and tones, melodies and rhythms along the continuum of pop culture, modern literature, comics, movies, CDs, songwriters, and artistic performances, with *theological loci* of the traditional university curriculum is something still to be waited for. But it will definitely make theology more *popular*, in all of the neutral and positive senses of this word. A systematic theology that tries to be more popular does not need to be superficial, nor does it have to simply speak after people's mouth. Rather, a *systematic theology* that tries to connect with *the popular* and its emerging *culture* may just now and for the first time learn how to *communicate* with the people in the *lingua franca* of this and the coming day and age.

In this, *theology* will learn from the *history of cultural studies* (Detweiler and Taylor 2003, 18–19, Turner 1996, 11–77, Surber 1998, 233–267, Brantlinger 1990, Brooker 1998, Hartley 2003, Lutter und Reisenleitner 1998, 17–49, Hepp 2004, 78–108, Kramer 1997, Teske 2002, Marchart 2007, Lewis 2008) since its beginning that *the cultural* always implies *the political*, and that any aesthetic or artistic world—which culture and theology both are—is always part of a distribution of human and social *power*, with some in this life and world having more, and others having less. The

The Community of the Weak

critical look at this distribution of possibilities for life, hope, and power—the *power to be* and *to be creative* (Fox 2002)—is most important.

Again, from the history of cultural studies *contemporary theology* can learn to look both ways, both at the popular and the political, with an *empathic* as well as a *critical eye*. The tools for *criticism* are there, Marxism, critical theory, feminism, postfeminism, postmodernism, antiracism, postcolonialism, deconstruction, semiotics, philosophy, and critical social theory. The potential for *appreciative ecstasy* is provided by the simple, endless, and boundless creative fantasies of modern and contemporary artists in the popular.

A *theology* in tune with the *cultural* and *popular* may become a *new dialect*, even a *new academic style*. Too often academic styles in theology have taken their model from old and print-based cultures, focusing mostly on textual forms. *Text* today, however, is everything, in postmodern ways, even picture books, comic books, MTV, cinema, a musical song, a rock concert, performance art, or a still life. *Theology* nowadays will have to study the *languages and images* of these many and various *social texts* floating all around us. And these texts may not be all too textual anymore, but mostly *visual, audible,* and *tactile*. But they speak nevertheless, and sometimes even more and more powerfully than the many and old and print-based classical textual forms.

Doing this, *theology—systematic, fundamental,* and *dogmatic*—as an academic discipline may also reflect on its own tendency to still and mostly affiliate itself with *high cultural forms* in a world where the majority of the people sitting in the pews or walking into churches live and move in their daily *low or popular culture* that most often is not very close to what church is all about. Teenagers at the age of 14 taking heroin in some local village somewhere in Switzerland in the 1990s most certainly have no comprehension for the high culture of abstract theological language most often learned in the *academy*. Their world is punk, hip-hop, *Jim Morrison*, the *Doors*, shit, the movie-musical *Hair*, maybe *Jesus Christ Superstar*, surprisingly *South Africa* in *Cry Freedom*, but most definitely not *Bach*, a classical organ, a hymnal, or a church choir. Talking about God to teenagers like this needs a whole *new textual and visual, musical and artistic dialect*, for theology and a social empathy in joining the world of teenagers like this as well. *Cultural studies* teaching theology a *new language* and sensitivity for the *popular* can help.

Through this, *theology* becomes more *ecological* and *communitarian*, listening to the communities and *lifeworlds* of the people around us.

Culture

Ecology is everything around us that moves and has its being in the *Spirit of Life* (Moltmann 1992, 1997, Gebara 1999, Page 1996, 2000, Grey 2003, Fox 2002, Gottlieb 2006). Life is punk, hip-hop, *Sting, Keith Jarrett,* but also *Bach*, symphonies, high literature, interrupted by comic books, action movies, rock concerts, graffiti walls, and art galleries. All this and more is part and parcel of our wider and all-encompassing *ecology of human life* in which all our *theologies—systematic, fundamental,* and *dogmatic—*are living and moving and kicking as well.

A *fundamental theology in postmodern cultures* will need to become more *ecological* and *communitarian,* sharing and living in the *everyday world* that people in these postmodern times live in. *Popular culture,* and any *culture,* will be seminal terms for a new dialogue between theology and other interdisciplinary fields in the academy. At the same time, getting closer in human touch with the various forms of *popular culture* (Detweiler and Taylor 2003, Lynch 2005, Cobb 2005, Staub 2008, Taylor 2008, Johnston 2000, 2007, Detweiler 2008) in the places and spaces where people are finding *visual and narrative meaning,* will be most important for a new theology diving into *postmodern ethnological and ecological fieldwork,* for instance in joining some techno party and dancing along a DJ's tune, since God could be the DJ playing the world (on popular culture, pop church, and the next, most likely visual and tactile, iconic and digital generations Beaudoin 1998, Harvey 1999, Sweet 1999, 2001, 2007, for the consequences in ecclesiology Frost 2006, Frost and Hirsch 2009, Hirsch 2006, Hirsch and Ferguson 2011, Hirsch and Catchim 2011).

Ecological Theology and Power

Theology Out of the Ecology of Life

Fundamental theology in a *postmodern age* will need to become more *ecological* (on theology and ecology Wright and Kill 1993, Scharper 1998, Sponheim 1999, Gebara 1999, Bouma-Prediger 1995, 2001, Page 1996, 2000, Grey 2003, Hart 2004, Fox 2002, Gottlieb 2006). Ecological in the sense that theology needs to look at its own place and environment where it is developed. An *ecological perspective* on all its ways of knowing and acting will give theology a broader field of vision from where to speak and write. A fundamental theology with an ecological perspective will be more attentive in its cognitive field to the *relational,* the *connected,* the *interdependent,* the *interdisciplinary,* and the *embedded.* Any abstract thought, any cognitive vision, any reflective perspective is always part of a larger whole in which it lives and develops in its academic thinking.

In that way, theologians could become *embedded intellectuals*—what Italian Marxist and cultural theorist *Antonio Gramsci* and African American neo-pragmatist liberation theologian *Cornell West* call *organic intellectuals* (Widl 2000, 185–186, McGrath 2002, 144–155, Cowan 2003, 115–117, 2003a, West 2010)—, fully participating in the *social and cultural world* in which they work and live, act and suffer, hope and develop their human and social activity. Gone should be the times when theology has only been conceived somewhere in a protected study room and lecture hall without any shaping contact with the *outer and rushing world*.

Ecological theology, embedded in the *daily struggles of life*, is looking for what cultural and critical theorist *Henry A. Giroux* (Giroux 1992, Giroux 1981–2011) calls the *specific intellectual* or the *engaged intellectual*, as "Foucault's notion of the specific intellectual taking up struggles connected to particular issues and contexts must be combined with Gramsci's notion of the engaged intellectual who connects his or her work to broader social concerns that deeply affect how people live, work, and survive" (Giroux 1992, 82).

A *theology—systematic, fundamental,* and *dogmatic*—participating in the fullness and *ecology of life* will look around with open eyes, taking in impressions, moments, stories, narratives, and the poetry and artistry of life. Theology that way will no longer just remain prisoner of its own specialized language, mostly dry and mono-lingual, but will open its vocabulary and images, its idioms and academic literacy to the *plentitude of interruptions and interludes*, irruptions and introductions of shapes and colors, forms and melodies of the cultural, the natural, the social, the personal, the musical, the artistic, and the political. Theology then will become *multilingual, multicultural,* and *multi-contextual*, mixing and blending various social locations and personal home-comings.

A *theology* that mostly stays at home, hardly ever interrupted in writing hundreds or thousands of pages, will not be very close to the real in life. In *real life* somebody knocks at your door, calls you out, maybe just for tea or coffee, interrupts you with his or her problems, challenges you to join a just, peaceful, and worthwhile cause. A *theology—systematic, fundamental,* and *dogmatic*—coming out of *social movements—peace movements, ecological movements, human rights movements, social justice movements, gender movements, cultural movements*—has always been moving and touching others a lot more than theologies staying at home.

Finding words in theology after having gone through particularly moving moments and places in life, maybe *hurt*, or overjoyed, maybe *touched*, or wounded, maybe *embraced*, or broken, will give theology and its many formulations a whole new true-ringing tone and style. Truth usually has some *color*, some taste, some emotion, some vivid and personal face.

Some *North American systematic theologies* have come out of such *moving political times, revisioning systematic theology* in its integrity as a *social God-walk* (Herzog 1988, Rieger 1999, 2011), instead of a God-talk, walking in movements for *civil rights* or other walks. Others have taken a more personal experience of a *missionary memory* and *geographical location* to develop a new cultural-political and fundamental theology for the North American context *Remembering Esperanza* (Taylor 1990, in a political theology Taylor 2011). Both *ecological theologies* develop theology *socially* and *ethnographically* out of personal, social, and experiential memories that make up an *ethnology* in the *ecology of life* shaping theology in a most radical way. Theology then gets embedded in personal experience, lived-through joy and suffering, personally seen hurts and wounds, breakdowns and uplifting moments.

Writing theology from personal experiences with 14-year-old teenagers taking heroin in some local village somewhere in Switzerland in the 1990s gives it a different tone and color too. Themes and interests change, the particular focus of your theology will get moved, conclusions get rearranged, phrases and idioms get turned around, and the question of the relevance and identity, meaning and shape of your whole theology and ministry gets newly phrased. Theology then gets *contextual, existential, local*, and *ecological*, in that it gets related, connected, dependent, and disciplined through while embedded in a place that makes your life and theology turn to be *different* from how it had become if you had never seen and lived in this same place. The *places* that you have seen and been in your life will change the way you do theology. In that sense, all our theologies turn out to be *embodied, embedded, enmeshed*, and part of the whole *ecology* that we *live in*.

Theology Getting Creative

Theology seen in this *embedded way*, participating in all our *ecological walks and ways*, will also open itself to the full range of the *creative* all around us, participating in *God's creation* by *being creative* itself (Moltmann 1993/1985, Pederson 2001, Fox 2002, Detweiler and Taylor 2003,

Staub 2008, Gelinas 2009). Former Roman Catholic and now Episcopal theologian of creation spirituality *Matthew Fox* (in publications Fox 1983-2002) from *San Francisco* describes it beautifully and poetically in his book *Creativity* (Fox 2002) how *the creative* of human fantasies and the envisioning of ever new ways and paths is deeply embedded in the *creativity of a whole universe* that constantly keeps *recreating itself,* following and continuing thereby in *God's creative act*. "When the Bible declares that we are made in the 'image and likeness' of the Creator, it is affirming that creativity is at our core just as it lies at the core of the Creator of all things ... An ancient Mesoamerican poet tells us that God dwells in the heart of the artist and the artist draws God out of his or hear heart when the artist is at work" (Fox 2002, 28).

Drawing God out of our hearts in the *creative act of thinking and writing, reflecting and acting,* could be a new way to describe the task of *theology—systematic, fundamental,* and *dogmatic*. Fundamental theology in particular could become more of an artistry than a textual mass of literacy.

The *universe* is thoroughly *creative,* as *modern science* teaches us, ever moving between death and life, change and birth. As *Matthew Fox* puts it: "Today's science is also instructing us in the origins of creativity and finding that the whole universe is permeated with the power of change and birth" (Fox 2002, 40). *Rebirthing theology* therefore is just following what the universe is doing anyway. Putting back *the creative* into *theology—systematic, fundamental,* and *dogmatic—*is therefore a universal calling. It may even be the necessary ingredient for survival of theology and human life in general. *Creativity* and *imagination, vision* and *hopeful border crossing* across all boundaries is a way of *empowerment,* giving theology back to the people to *create and recreate a better world*. "Creativity and imagination are not frosting on a cake: They are integral to our sustainability. They are survival mechanisms. They are of the essence of who we are. They constitute our deepest empowerment" (Fox 2002, 31).

Empowering people to become *life-creative* in order to make our global place a better world could become a new purpose for *fundamental theology.* No longer is it needed to stay in the *defensive* (in classical textbooks on fundamental theology O'Collins 1981, O'Donovan and Sanks 1989, Dulles 1992, Fries 1996, Joest 1988, Wagner 1996, Schmidt-Leukel 1999, Werbick 2000, Beinert 2004, Petzoldt 2004, Neusch 2004) or the *communicative* (Metz 1980, Peukert 1984, Schüssler Fiorenza 1984, Arens 1995a, Waldenfels 2000, Mueller 2007) position to give good reasons for our faith. Instead, *theology—systematic, fundamental, dogmatic, ethical, practical, pastoral*—could become so *visionary*, so *creative*, so *artistic*, and so *life-changing* (Tracy 1987, Wetherilt 1994, McClendon 2000, Haight 2001, Garcia-Rivera 1999, 2003, Gonzalez 2003, Sedmak 2002, 2003, Detweiler and Taylor 2003, Taylor 2008, Taylor 1990, 2011) that its reasons and attractions for faith go with it as the world and its human and non-human habitats change accordingly and attractively. Theology that convinces in its beauty, in its *artistic touch*, and most fundamentally in its *creative vision for a better place and a better world to live in*—a new kind of *creative ecology of living*—, may be more attractive and enticing than any hundreds and thousands of megabytes or gigabytes of simple text.

A theology developed within the *creative ecology of living* will be *rooted* and *connected* to *the earth*. The earth is everything. And the earth is made up of everything, as diverse and multicolored as it could possibly be. Our waking up in the morning, the washing of our face, our daily bread, our regular walk, human faces, natural places, moments to relax, people we meet, kids we hear, friends we chat with. *This our earth is everything*, composed of all and more of all these elements. And this earth is radically committed to an utmost *diversity*. "Nature is so committed to creativity that it 'abhors uniformity'. The world-as-machine metaphor that dominated the modern era got us to think and act in uniform and standardized processes as machines do. But this is not the way of the natural world. Nature is biased in favor of diversity" (Fox 2002, 44). In quite other words, *nature* seems to be *postmodern* itself.

This our earth is the beach, the mountain range, the desert flower, the snow-filled plain, ocean waves. Colors and musical sounds, loudness and silence, busy shopping malls, quiet forest trails. City halls and rock stadiums, movie nights and ethnic dinner tables, art exhibits and meditation circles. A social project to help the poor, a peaceful vision to unite the separated, a cultural exhibit to show the pain of war, a human chain for a culture of peace where people give and hold hands. A youth cellar to harbor the drug-addicted. And any other creative moment that meets us on the way.

As creation spiritualist and ecological fundamental theologian *Matthew Fox* (Fox 1983-2002) from the *University of Creation Spirituality* in *San Francisco* puts it, spreading out the *composing elements* that make up our daily world:

> "There is music and poetry in the universe itself—surely we hear it on planet earth. I am writing this chapter at a friend's house in San Francisco near the ocean. During a lunch break, I walked

along the cliffs overlooking the bay and the Golden Gate Bridge amidst blooming flowers, singing birds, buzzing insects, singing winds, rushing waves. Who can deny the music and song, the color and shadow, the shape and richness that nature makes? Creativity begins here." (Fox 2002, 43)

Fundamental Theology Artfully Composing

All this can be the *composing material* for developing a new kind of *fundamental theology* out of *the creative*. Theology could become more like *composing a symphony* or a picture wall, an artistic sculpture or a performance play, a rock concert or even a city visit. Theology *lived and acted upon* could become more like pictures or photographs of an exhibition inviting the public to come and marvel, to walk through and stand still, to reflect and get active as well. Theology in this *artistic* and *imaginative, envisioning* and *world-forming way* could become a highly *creative art work*, a social action, a cultural event, a picture exhibit, a multimedia moment, a local campaign, a community project, a global initiative, all in their own way disclosing the *artistic and social beauty* of what theology is and may be all about. A *fundamental theology of the creative* would be *creatively proclaiming* what theology in its most basic and *elementary fundamentals* believes in.

North American feminist and fundamental theologian *Ann Kirkus Wetherilt* in her *That They May Be Many* (Wetherilt 1994), a kind of *feminist fundamental theology for the postmodern age*, comes closest to this vision of a *new theological style*. Echoing *the voices of God* in the voices of women, the poor, the excluded, and any other voices of the rejected, she develops a whole *new and critical feminist approach* to theological language, theological method, the dominance of the Word in theology, revelation, authority, the magisterial teaching office, human knowing and reflecting, philosophical epistemology, creativity, community, identity, praxis, and coalitional thinking and acting. *The creative* takes a prominent place in her thinking. The renewal of *theological method and language* will go through a recognition of the importance of *the creative* in any *theology—systematic, fundamental*, and *dogmatic*.

Referring to the groundbreaking research and writing on *female thinking and knowing* in an old classic on feminist epistemology, *Women's Ways of Knowing* (Belenky, Clinchy, Goldberger, and Tarule 1986), Ann

Culture

Kirkus Wetherilt describes the potential, but also the still marginally kept effect of the *artistic* and *creative* in *academic thinking and teaching*:

> "Some of the transformations called for by the authors of *Women's Ways of Knowing* are beginning to emerge in academia. Colleges and universities are instituting more cross-disciplinary courses and programs. Individual teachers and scholars are incorporating works of fiction, poetry, music, and other creative expression into classes other than those specifically devoted to the study of literature or other identifiable art forms. Sometimes this inclusion extends to the forms in which students may express their integration of course material. These trends within feminist epistemologies resonate with the challenges evoked by engaging diverse women's voices and thus add insight and support to the development of a metaphor of voices . . . But many of the new insights emerging from these still-embryonic epistemological shifts have yet to find their way into dominating theo-ethical discourse. A friend and colleague was *failed* in a course in her M.Div. program for handing in a creative, artistic, interpretive project instead of the traditional academic paper—to a self-proclaimed 'feminist' professor. The student had taken seriously the professor's verbalization of the need for thought and creativity, feeling and emotion, to be more integrated in the academy . . . The mere addition of more voices is not sufficient to challenge basic authoritarian structures when rigid boundaries between creativity and action and 'legitimate' academic work remain intact . . . " (Wetherilt 1994, 86–87)

Composing theology in the way *artists* or *action performers* create and compose their art work could be a new way to do *theology—systematic, fundamental,* and *dogmatic—*, more actional, visual, tactile, and communal. Theological categories would then be translated into *narrative images, visual pictures, actional projects,* and *communal events.*

Creatively Knowing and Thinking

Crossing these rigid boundaries and integrating *action, project, art,* and *creativity* into the theological curriculum, even in *systematic, fundamental,* and *dogmatic theology,* will be a necessary and new challenge for teaching and writing, researching and projecting in the theological academy. *Creative knowing and thinking* in theology (Wetherilt 1994, 97–104, Pederson 2001, Perkinson 2005, also Haight 2001, Sedmak 2002, Mueller 2007) is more than just adding a few poetic lines, a few narrative stories, or a few music, art, and movie references to a class or one's theology. *Creative knowing and thinking* opens up whole new ways of integrating knowledge, class material, phantasy, vision, empowerment, action, and social creativity in *actional projects* of a comprehensive unity. Knowing and *learning*—most particularly in a globalized academy of the postmodern age—will be a lot more *actional, project-oriented,* and *community-involving* (on project-oriented community-involvement in theology Wetherilt 1994, 105–116), translating what we believe and reflect on in our theologies into concrete *actions, projects* and *creative art works*, socially and culturally, communally and individually.

As *Ann Kirkus Wetherilt* puts it, calling for an academic revalorization of *embodied knowledge*, integrating *action* and *feeling, knowledge* and *vision*, a type of knowledge that communities of wisdom outside of the academy have long practiced:

> "An embodied approach to knowing insists upon recognition of the multiple modes of construction, validation, and expression of that which constitutes knowledge/truth/wisdom. Such an approach, long affirmed by many communities that have been excluded from the so-called traditional avenues of knowledge production, allows for the incorporation of multiple voices and perspectives into theo-ethical discourse. The challenge of embodied knowing, with its transgression of the boundaries of thought and feeling, body and mind/spirit, reflection and action, demands similar transgression of some of the boundaries between the more 'traditional' conceptions of knowledge." (Wetherilt 1994, 97)

The power of *symbol* and *creativity, action* and *project*, needs to be rediscovered in theology, opening itself up to more nontraditional ways of learning and speaking the Word in these postmodern days. Sometimes, *symbolic action* and *project-turned creativity* can speak stronger and louder than many normal and often repeated traditional words.

In the words of *Ann Kirkus Wetherilt* on the power and transforming impact of imaginative symbols and *actional creativity*, found throughout the *history of religious communities*:

> "Imagination and creativity are deeply embedded in the religious impulses of all cultures. One has only to look at the work of the 'great master' of Western culture to discern the overwhelming presence of religious themes, whether in painting,

sculpture, music, fiction, or poetry. Museums around the world are being challenged to return 'art works' from indigenous cultures to their rightful owners, for whom they have profoundly religious significance. A piece of sculpture named *Christa* can invoke intense and conflictual theological debate because of the power of symbol and creativity." (Wetherilt 1994, 97)

To reclaim this social power of *symbol, action, creativity,* and *transforming project* for *fundamental theology* would be a worthwhile task for future theologies. Translating our basic concepts in theology into *actional pictures, images, stories,* and social or cultural *art works* would be following in the steps of God's creative and continuous modeling of this world, reshaping it, reinventing it, redrawing it, recreating it, reimagining it. God gets so concrete and *ecological* when it gets to transforming and artistically recreating the world. "God is voiced through struggle and celebration, self-defence and education, spirited worship and birthing a baby, writing poetry and planting maize" (Wetherilt 1994, 149). And God may be voiced through a *fundamental theology of the creative* that translates its fundamentals and basics into artistic and social, communal and actional *poetic imagery*.

Creatively Actional

A *fundamental theology* in the context of a *creative ecology of living*, involved in all these day-to-day events and moments, stories and happenings of what *the earth, the sky, Gods* and *mortals go through* (on the earth, the sky, Gods, and mortals McDaniel 1989, 1990 1995, 2000) and suffer every day, will be *actional*. No human ecology works without *action, movement, change, history, story*, and *basic transformations* every day. A still water or lake dies after a certain time if there is no movement and refreshing change once in a while. The same is true for humans and mortals of diverse kinds. We participate, as North American Jesuit and postmodern fundamental theologian *Roger Haight* puts it, in the ever changing "social historicity of human existence" (Haight 2001, 3). Human and earthly *life time* is *dynamic*, changing, moving, and a *creative ecology of living* shares in the movements of time and space, story and future, forever flushed along in the flowing stream of "constant change and novelty" (Haight 2001, 4). This life-dynamic, moving, and flowing understanding of theology is also "the condition for the possibility of creative theology" (Haight 2001, 5).

Theology then becomes quite *ecologically* a kind of *creative thinking and acting* along the streams of a flowing life.

In this, *social and ecological living* in any place and time is *actional*. Both in that people are *acted upon*, and that people respond and *act* themselves to others acting on them. "From the first moment of existence and at every moment in it the human person is acted upon. The person is at it were a center of relationships through which a whole host of influences and actions are operative at every imaginable level" (Haight 2001, 4). People live and learn through their *actions*. More so, and most permanently through what they *do* and *suffer*, create and see or make happening.

Learning in that sense, in *theology* as well, will be most lasting and relevant if it is done *in action*. This is why the *creative* and *actional* seem to have such a permanent and lasting impact on people, more so and more powerfully and intensely, more deeply and on a soul-level, than most endless books and multiplied papers, never finished dissertations and well-meaning manifestos. The *learning effect* of action seems to outdo every other form of learning and thinking, and this may be just simply due to our human constitution in that people learn about the world better and more permanently in acting and doing rather than in endless contemplating what may or may not be the world.

Action is *moving, implicating,* and *visual energy*. It is dynamic and *project-oriented*. People act on ideas and turn them into projects to let ideas put on shoes and coats to get out of the house or study or lecture hall and *move*—even run—forward, changing some things in this world quite practically and visually, even dramatically. There is a *dramatic pragmatism* in action without being pragmatic in philosophy. But there is a definite thrust to *make ideas work* and walk, model and paint, craft and construct the world in a different and recognizable way. To *see* and *hear, watch* and *witness* peace and justice, hope and mercy, prophetic speech and reconciliatory talk, creation and the apocalyptic, sacrifice and forgiveness, nonviolent courage and communitarian care, inclusive community and spirited creativity take on *real form and living shape*, concrete color and visual practice is always more convincing for bystanders and participating insiders than most of these same topics or *loci* being treated in abstract dogmatic care.

Jesuit *Roger Haight* in his fundamental theology *Dynamics of Theology* (Haight 2001) describes the dynamic power of *action* with images and concepts from nineteenth century's French Roman Catholic *Maurice Blondel* (Blondel 1893/1984), taking it as a *fundamental dimension* for his revisioning of prolegomena to systematic theology. Action leads to envisioning new ways in life and translates these new ideas into a *project*. It *empowers* people at the same time, as "conceiving human existence as action gives one's thinking a vitalistic or energistic cast. Human life is action; it is for action; its purpose is to discover and create. Human existence is a project" (Haight 2001, 8). A *project* is a *creative act*, in that it invites people to join, gather, congregate, to share fantasies, brain-storm novelties, think out new ideas and *change the world*. Along the way, *theology* gets *practical, participatory, visionary, empowering*, and *imaging* new ways for individuals and whole communities to *live and act* in this world.

Making *theology* into a *project*, even *systematic, fundamental*, or *dogmatic theology*, could mean getting out of the classroom into the environing *ecology* of the close and farther surroundings of our world in order to develop a *concrete project* with local people in the neighborhood or our personal communities who want to *see* theology walk and work, compose and paint, craft and construct, model and sketch, empower and *change the globe*. This could be a community action, an educational program, a church meeting, a peace project, a shelter facility, a youth cellar, a cultural event, an artistic performance, a political campaign, or a global initiative, all translating and *incarnating theology into the concrete and visual, local and experiential places of people's homes and houses, habitats and communities* in theology's environing surroundings of an *ecology of life*. An in that sense, theology would no longer live a secluded and non-ecological life.

Within Ecological Suffering

Having theology open itself and move to places of the *ecology of life* will make it also more sensitive to what people really feel and *suffer* in *real life*. What people *suffer* and go through—in actions and reactions responding and suffering the actions of others—in the *creative ecology of living this life* has a more lasting memory than any other story or paper, literacy or lecture content. And it seems, that this life is quite often and mainly *disorder, disruption, destruction* when looked at empathically, at least when we look at—and don't look away or simply try to forget or tune out—the common daily life for a majority of people in this world.

Just contemplating, reflecting, abstracting, and rephrasing the world without getting a feel and taste for what *people* and *the earth* actually *go through, suffer, get acted upon*, and *act themselves*, maybe just simply out of sheer desperation, will not be enough human and earthly learning in order to recreate and renew theology as well as this *ecological world* in need of radical change, as Roman Catholic *Edward Schillebeeckx* (Schillebeeckx 1979) describes it: "It is only through the ethical critique of the history of humankind's accumulated suffering that in a paradoxical yet real fashion contemplation and action can be intrinsically connected with a possible realization of meaning" (Schillebeeckx 1979, 622).

Roger Haight introduces *suffering* as *foundational* for any *fundamental theology* in these *modern and postmodern times*, having his fundamental theology in *Dynamics of Theology* (Haight 2001) begin right in its entering chapter with the recognition that *the world* for most people and other mortals is a world of *human and ecological disorder*, if not disaster, since every violent and uncreative breaking up and tearing open of the intricately flowing and forever weaving *web of life* is somehow breaking up the creative order and flow of human and earthly life:

> "Finally, historical, social, human existence is not characterized primarily by order but by disorder. This foundational insight has been the deepest contribution of liberation theology to Christian theology. Social existence for the far greater portion of the human race today can only be characterized as primarily negative in terms of the criteria of human suffering. The point of departure for a theology attuned to the social, historical condition of human existence cannot be positive; it must be a negative experience that reacts against the outrages to the *humanum* which history itself presents before us. . . . Moreover, the negative aspect of our common social historical situation in the world today highlights the apologetic character that theology must assume. Theological understanding cannot prescind from the actual situation of so many human beings who are victims of social suffering." (Haight 2001, 5)

Beginning *fundamental theology* with the overwhelming recognition, the *wounding pain*, and the upsetting sensitivity for the ecological *disorder of life* in all its various forms and sufferings will make *the creative* in *God's creation* ever more *resistant, oppositional, visionary*, imaginative, and lively in trying to *weave, heal*, and *reconcile* the broken web to create a different and re-created world. The artist's eye and heart cannot suffer torn pieces and fractured forms, broken lines and broken hearts.

The *demonic* (Fox 2002, 35–37) upsets any *creative mind*, having to watch the destruction of life, as humans and others can use their imaginative vision and world-changing strength "for blessing or for curse, for life or for death . . . " (Fox 2002, 35). Creatively birthing the *dysfunctional*, the malicious, the evil, this is our potential too. It belongs to the skills of creative living too. The scary thing about is that we humans have become so good at it.

Creating suffering in other people, in other souls, bodies, minds, and hearts, as well as in everything that lives and moves on this earth, seems to be a *human artistic skill* just as ponderous as creating new life. "Our planet does not know other species that can accomplish nearly the destruction we can when we put our minds to it. Our capacity for dysfunction, for destruction, for malice, for evil is unparalleled among the creatures of the earth" (Fox 2002, 35). Any thematic start in *fundamental theology* in an *ecological age* where everything and everyone is deeply related and dependently indebted, but als *vitally endangered and lively threatened* to and by any other, needs to seriously take notice of this basic human capacity before continuing.

Creatively Empowering

Theology—systematic, fundamental, and *dogmatic—*, recognizing itself as embedded in all of life, and faced with the permanent temptation that life gets *destroyed*, will be called to become more *empowering* both in its thinking and in its acting.

Power and *empowerment* can be looked at and newly defined as the *relational capacity to be creative in life*. Both of these connected concepts, *the relational* and *power*, go together. Power does not have to be associated with simple and easy *dominion*, dominance, oppression, suppression, or the social and political possibility to act against and in spite of the will of others, as sometimes traditionally and sociologically conceived. A concept of power described in this warlike atomistic way is mostly *antagonistic* instead of inclusive and inviting into a more open and creative relationship. *Power* in the *creative sense* is opening possibilities, inviting, luring, envisioning, and composing *new ways of looking at life*, like *composing a symphony*, a *project*, an *art work*, or a *social vision*.

An *ecological spirituality* in theology (McDaniel 1989–2000, Fox 1983–2002, Grey 2003, Keller 2003, Gottlieb 2006) will be most relevant for the times to come. Recognizing its *social context*, sensing its *ecological human place*, and witnessing in and through *human and earth communities* may be the new and challenging task for *theology—systematic*,

The Community of the Weak

fundamental, and *dogmatic*—in these years to come. A theology that stays atomistic and remains in abstract lecture halls, unrelated to its social and natural habitat, uninterested by what real people around it suffer and may be going through, will lose more and more of its relevance. *Theology* will have to become more *community-oriented*, moving down and out of high academic lecture halls, mingling and mixing with the people, sharing lives and moments, joining crowds and visions, shaking hands and faces, exchanging concepts and ideals, forging projects and healing separations. Theology will have to recognize its own *relational place* in which it lives and moves and has its being.

North American process theologian and *World Council of Churches* Church and Society member *Jay B. McDaniel* (McDaniel 1989–2000) describes the *ecological and relational nature* of all our *thinking and acting*, congregating and living so that all common separations of *Them-Against-Us* disappear, showing a more complex and *interdependent community of all living things*:

> "What, then, is the alternative 'ecological' perspective? It is a *relational* point of view in which emphasis is placed on the reality of internal relations. One living being is 'internally related' to others if the organism's relations to those others are partly constitutive of the organism's own essence. In process theology these relations are not abstract spatial properties such as 'above' and 'below'; they are, rather, concrete acts of 'taking into account' the other entities from the point of view of the entity at issue. Even as living beings have a power for independent creativity and sentience in the present, process thinkers argue, and even as they have intrinsic value as realities for themselves, they are internally related to the past and to the surrounding world. Either consciously or unconsciously they 'feel' or 'take into account' the past and the surrounding world from a particular experiential perspective, and in so doing they are dependent upon that past and that world. In many respects the specific character of their relations to others are imposed upon them; in some respects they are chosen; but in all respects the relations are part of, rather than apart from, the identities of the entities at issue. Living beings, animals and plants alike, are individuals-in-community rather than individuals-in-isolation ... Relationality also applies in a more general way to communities. A 'community' may be an atom, molecule, living cell, animal body, ecosystem, bioregion, or, in its more distinctively human manifestations, a family, neighborhood, town, city, ethnic tradition, or nation.

Its members will include human and non-human individuals that are voluntarily or involuntarily bound together as mutual participants in one another's destinies. Indeed, the human family is a community of sorts, as is the earth itself and the cosmos as a whole. To say that relationality applies to communities is to say that communities are what they are in relation to other communities, and that, particularly at this stage in history with reference to life on earth, their destinies are interdependent. The web of life is best conceived as a collective 'we' in which, ontologically speaking, there are no 'theys.'" (McDaniel 1990, 27–28)

Becoming Communal

Theology in all its various forms will no longer be able to stay *un-ecologically secluded* and lonely somewhere in a back-room among piled-up books and papers, articles and dissertations. Rather, it will become most radically *communal*. A *theological academic culture* that models the lonely atomistic soul, the atomistic student, the atomistic teacher, the atomistic scholar, and the atomistic university on a lonely island away from any other world or community will not teach nor encourage an *ecological vision* for the *common community of all living things*, starting with the common people and other common signs of creative life right next door. Such an atomistic concept of theology adds to and fuels the atomistic view of the world, dividing and separating the world into segments, disciplines, academic degrees, and unrelated spaces in communities. The contrary would be needed. Old separations of disciplines and academic locations should be dissolving, new forms of *communal theology-making* should be encouraged.

Otherwise, the *separating mind* will continue, even in theology, keeping alive a *group soul feeling*, dividing everything into the *'we'* against the *'they'*, which, as *Jay B. McDaniel* portrays quite vividly, will ultimately destroy the world:

> "In other circles it is not so much the *individual soul* that is viewed atomistically as it is the *group soul*. The result of a group soul mentality is often ethnocentrism, in which the value of a seemingly self-contained and independent 'we' is celebrated over against a stereotyped and objectified 'they'. Particular instances include religious intolerance, in which a 'we' who know the right path to salvation are distinguished from a 'they' who are ignorant; racial bigotry, in which a 'we' who are racially pure

are distinguished from a 'they' who are racially impure; sexual chauvinism, in which a 'we' who are of superior gender are differentiated from a 'they' who are not; East-West policy regarding nuclear war, in which a 'we' who inhabit one land consider the possibility of winning a nuclear exchange with a 'they' who inhabit another land; and class domination, in which a 'we' who are economically and politically advantaged either oppress or exercise paternalistic control over a 'they' who are poor or oppressed. In each instance the 'we' is a collective atom, a group soul, separated from, and celebrated over against, another collective atom, called the 'they'." (McDaniel 1990, 26–27)

Empowering theology in an *ecological age* will be *feeling the other* as if he or she were part of oneself. This entails that theology needs to get out of academic halls and meet life were it is to be able to *feel* and *see* people and other living things. This life will be found in the neighborhood, in the city, on the street, in the subway, on a schoolyard, at the crosswalk, in the community hall, in an art gallery, at a rock concert, at the jazz club, in the public park, at the homeless shelter. Theology getting *ecological* will change *relationally* into a *feeling theology* that keeps thinking—as it goes on and develops its many concepts—of these different people and experiences it just made and met. Personal biography, local stories, communal tragedies, global sufferings will become the new *natural habitat* for an *ecological fundamental theology* in the postmodern age. This may even mean to give up your job or leave your home and live somewhere else to live closer where the *real life* really is.

Developing an *empowering theology* would be based on *empathic thinking* all long, as we read and collect, teach and learn, listen and write, lecture and note, excerpt and summarize, construct and develop our various theologies, always aware of the need and necessity to become conscious of the *omnipresent presence* of every other living thing, so we "learn to feel the presence of other living beings and of the natural world as if they are part of us. We must feel their presence as if their destinies and our own are intertwined, as if their interests and our own are identified. Stated in biblical terms, we must learn to love our neighbors as ourselves, realizing that our neighbors are part of ourselves" (McDaniel 1990, 29).

Becoming Sensual

A *fundamental theology* in touch with its own most personal and social *habitat*, its relationships, neighborhoods, communities, and global places, will at last become *erotic with the earth* and everything living in it, while finding therein its most spiritual *power*. The power to *feel* and *sense* everything as somehow *connected*. People, races, gender, ages, convictions, the earth. They all find a peaceful place in a larger vision of relations. No longer is the argumentative most needed. No longer is a separating mind mostly called for. No longer are analytic dissections the only way to unite the living. Rather, in an *erotic moment*, we discover our love for everything that is.

This makes *fundamental theology* a lot more *sensual*, with verbs like *touch*, *sound*, *feel*, *see*, and *smell* complementing and guiding our thinking. A *biocentric spirituality* in theology is needed, right at the beginning when theologies get constructed. Sitting on a bench with teenagers at the age of 14 taking heroin in some local village somewhere in Switzerland in the 1990s did change my sensory vision in theology. You touch human misery, you hear the sound of music, you feel the need for an embrace, you see the hidden fear of exclusion, you smell the forbidden danger. All this changes your theology immediately. Sitting on a bench in the midst of an *ecology of misery*, with little moments of amazing solidarity, touching care, and moving faces, you start to rethink your whole theology. The senses make you reconsider what the earth and God may mean.

In moments like this, *theology* needs to get *rooted* again, when sometimes theology has a tendency to lift off. You get called to get back to the *fundamentals* of what makes life *worth living*. A *fundamental theology of the creative ecology of the living* will be more in touch with its own senses and reconnect with these earthly moments. It all starts there, before we develop our most intricate and complex, smart and convincing theologies. It may be needed at times to feel this primary place again and to stay there for a while.

As North American process theologian *Jay B. McDaniel* (McDaniel 1989) describes it poetically, inviting theology to a *biocentric spirituality* that stretches our imagination on metaphors for God and the world to its utmost limit in an *ecological fundamental theology*:

> "In addition to an intellectual recognition of our rootedness in the Earth, however, a biocentric spirituality can also involve a sensual—indeed, an erotic—love of the Earth, cognizant of the fact that the Earth is God's body. In feeling drawn toward healthy soil—enjoying its touch, its smell, and its visual appearance—we caress the very God whose body is that soil. In breathing clean air—enjoying the sensation of inhalation and exhalation—we breathe the very God whose body is that air. In drinking clean

The Community of the Weak

water—enjoying its freshness against our palates—we drink the very God whose body is that water. And in journeying into the wilderness areas—feeling the pulsations of life unmanipulated by humans—we journey into the very God whose body is that wilderness. As our senses join soil, air, water, and wilderness, they join God. A biocentric spirituality can be a spirituality of touch, sound, and smell as well as thought." (McDaniel 1989, 91–92)

Spreading Life

Fundamental theology empowering people in this way will *spread life* and not death all around it. *Rooted* in a power beyond itself, *theology—systematic, fundamental,* and *dogmatic*—can connect and *root people back* in this power in creative ways, presenting images and metaphors for that which gives people hope and encouragement to move on in their lives and act accordingly. To have theology take on an *encouraging function* may be something new and old in academic circles.

The *academy* in the wake of *historical* and *technological consciousness* has lost some of its *life-changing* and *hope-instilling* purpose, especially in theology where the contents of disciplines in view of societal acceptance in a modern university context have too often adopted an *objectivist and factual approach* to knowledge, skill, and wisdom.

However, *university disciplines* in all areas of *human knowledge* could recover some of their *empowering vision* that used to be at the basis of initial concepts of universal knowledge at the inauguration of the *university educational system,* in particular in the field of *theology* (for a more sapiential, poetic, biographical, communal, ecological, transformative habitus in theological education Farley 1983, Chopp 1995, Banks 1999, Jones and Paulsell 2002, Villafane, Jackson, Evans, and Evans 2002, in entertainment theology and untamed missional discipleship Taylor 2008, Hirsch and Hirsch 2010). Too often *theology* has given in to a *modern concept of university education* that has turned *instrumental,* instead of *sapiential,* promoting a "technological view of education" (Farley 1983, 153), the technology of assimilating limitless masses of knowledge and information for some practical and professional use. *Education* as *empowerment* and as a "ministry of hope" (Jones and Paulsell 2002, 120–134) has often been lost. And yet, finding *hope* has to do with the capacity and *empowerment* to be able to *spread life* and to see life being spread all around us. *Fundamental theology* could be such a *recovery of hope* in *spreading life* all around, if it rediscovers its *basic rootedness in life*.

Power comes from *being rooted* and *revived*—having been given *roots* and *wings* (McDaniel 1995)—, embedded and encouraged in this kind of *sensual ecological spirituality* that senses the touch, smell, sound, vision, and thought of the earth. *To have power* does not imply to have dominion and precedence, dominance and preeminence over others or the earth. Rather, it is a kind of *tender power* that *empowers* others, encourages others to be encouraged themselves, living in a community of dreamers who share all they have in dreaming while joining their visions for a better world.

A *power* like this is *tender, careful, communitarian, ecological,* and yet just as *sturdy, determined, and intentional* as any emergence of life against death. Where life wants to grow, to spread, to diversify and expand into all directions of the earth, there is a tender sturdiness that can be more powerful than any weapons and death. Power then will be *personal, social, communitarian, ecological,* and *political* as well.

Power then also gets implanted in a *community of change* that co-creates the world. Theology can no longer stay isolated and outside of day-to-day moments of life. If all of theology—academic and colloquial—participates in the *relationality of life* (McDaniel 1990, 1–32, 163–179, also McDaniel 2000), theology will have to *go out* and look for other places where it finds a new sense and purpose, meaning and destiny. Theology will profit from this *out-going exposure to real life*, more so than it may think. Because in moments like this theology gets *ecological* and starts to join the process of *spreading life*, spreading and planting the most basic values and visions that theology can teach and which may *change the world*.

As North American process theologian *Jay B. McDaniel* describes this *rooting* and *implanting* of theology and ourselves in a *local place* to which we belong.

> "The beginnings of such rootedness lie in acquiring a 'sense of place' . . . Inasmuch as we enjoy a sense of place, we will know about the flora and fauna of our bioregions; we will understand their geographical and biological history; we will appreciate local culture and history; we will be sensitive to local landscapes and forms of life. A sense of place involves amazement at the particular and awe for the ordinary. Only when we accept

responsibility for the places we live will the world achieve any degree of inclusive *shalom* . . . An inner sense of place is not enough. We need to behave in ways that mirror and express our solidarity with the places in which we live, for example, through community development. From a Christian point of view, we are not simply isolated individuals; our well-being is partly dependent on the well-being of the communities of which we are a part, and vice-versa." (McDaniel 1995, 68)

Transforming Communities

A *fundamental theology* that is intentional on *spreading life* in those places where it finds itself may decide, for instance, to participate in local *community development projects*, furthering *peace-making* (on ecological peace-making in community projects McDaniel 1995, 59–74 and Gornik 2002) in places where people live right next door, providing *hope-filled theological images and metaphors, narratives and parables* for grassroots and local democracy, political decentralization, respect for diversity, non-violence, post-patriarchal values, personal and social responsibility, global responsibility, future focus, ecological wisdom, and community-based economics (McDaniel 1995, 68–69).

Theology would then get out *on the street* into the neighborhood and develop a *project*, a social vision, a *community event*, a cultural moment, a political campaign, modeling "education as communal cooperative activity" (Chopp 1995a, 111, also Chicago Theological Seminary's Urban project in Thistlethwaite and Cairns 2003/1994). Theology would in this way participate in *transforming the city* and *communities* (Greenway and Monsma 2000, Villafane, Jackson, Evans, and Evans 2002, Gornik 2002, Dudley 2002, for ecological and social action pastoral care Clinebell 1996, Chinula and Clinebell 2009, Clinebell and McKeever 2011), wherever this may be.

North American feminist theologian *Rebecca S. Chopp* has given this *social vision* of *theological education* in *cooperative and communal ways* shape and content in her *Saving Work* (Chopp 1995a), underlining the need for more *community-oriented theologies* which transform and change the way people live together in the Spirit. This new community of the Spirit as *ekklesia*—not limited to the church alone—"works through the lives of women and men for the realization of new life for all, including the earth" (Chopp 1995a, 52).

Theology lives and moves and has its being in *ecological and social habitats* that need to be taken into account in our theological reflection and education. And if, as it is argued, the primary focus of theological education is not just found in the right ordering of cognitive ideas, but also and just as much in the learning and living of *right relationships*, an *ecology of justice*, then a *fundamental theology* of the *creative ecology of living* will have to become attentive to the fact that the *building and transforming of community* may be a primary issue in theological prolegomena, both theoretically and practically:

> "Education may well be about 'what we do' as well as 'what we say'. If theological education is about merely the ordered learning of cognitive ideas, then finding the right curriculum will solve all the current problems in theological education. But if knowing God is as much a matter of right relationships as it is a mastery of correct ideas, then the present crises of theological education cannot be fixed merely by reordering the curriculum. New relationships of imagination, of justice, of dialogue must be formed in the midst of a pluralistic world and new forms of relating, teaching, and community building will have to be developed. The *how* of learning is directly related, in this notion of theological education as a process, to the *what* of learning. Indeed, the task for the subjects of theological education may be as much the doing of new forms of relationships to God, self, others, traditions, and society as it is the articulation of right ideas." (Chopp 1995a, 111)

Finding *power* in new and *right relationships*—relationships to family members, co-students, local communities, global worlds—that empower people and all other living things of the earth, makes theology into a *process* that *creates new things*. The creative part of theology needs to be emphasized more, especially its *social creativity* that envisions and participates in the creation of new social worlds.

A *fundamental theology* with a *mission*, a concrete task, a *communal goal*, a *social vision*, will not stay in the lecture hall or seminar room for long. It will go out into the community and *transform ideas into projects*, based on a model of "theological education that is wholly or partly field-based, and that involves some measure of doing what is being studied" (Banks 1999, 141).

Australian and Evangelical *Robert Banks* (Banks 1999), teaching at *Fuller Theological Seminary* in *Southern California*, calls this approach *missional*. Theology follows a mission, not just in its practical disciplines, but in all other disciplines as well, interdisciplinary and cross-cultural across academic and local spaces. Theology becomes *hands-on* in that it gets translated into *communal projects* and *cultural events* that involve and empower everyone, even spaces and places outside campus and the official curriculum.

> "One year at Fuller Seminary we decided to make 'reconciliation' the theme, partly because of its overall theological centrality, and partly because it is a pressing issue in racially torn and economically divided Los Angeles. Where this was a major feature of a course, professors were urged to look for ways of relating it to issues inside and outside the campus. This took place across the three schools in the seminary—Theology, Psychology, and World Mission. Where other courses touched on the theme, professors were encouraged to highlight it in some way. The seminary president made it the focus of his first address to students in the new academic year, and weekly chapel services included it in sermons. It was also the chosen theme of an annual film festival in the city cosponsored by the seminary, and an annual festival of the arts in the seminary. The theme also appeared during a month devoted to African-American history and concerns, and was the subject of several student-organized brown-bag lunches, and several issues of the weekly student publication." (Banks 1999, 234)

Theology in this *missional model* (on theology in the missional mode Banks 1999, 129–186, also Villafane, Jackson, Evans, and Evans 2002, Gornik 2002, on missional church Frost 2006, Frost and Hirsch 2009, Hirsch 2006, Hirsch and Hirsch 2010, Hirsch and Ferguson 2011, Hirsch and Catchim 2011) takes its human tent and puts it up in other places than what is usually expected, getting into an excursion and field-trip mode to reach out into the world. Theology gets *public* this way, bringing theology into the public places and streets of the city—as *New York Theological Seminary* used to practice under *George W. Webber*, taking theological courses into the streets of *New York City* (Banks 1999, 176, for New York Theological Seminary's street theological education Pazmino 1988). Theology in this way makes itself *public*—the way *Fuller Theological Seminary* moved out of campus into the artistic public on the fundamental Christian theme of reconciliation—in a *creative* and *artistic way*, going into civic places in using film and art festivals, chapel sermons, weekly student publications, brown-bag lunches, and any other traditional or creative media way to carry across a particular message.

Culture

Creative Public Theology Poetically Transforming the World

Theology—systematic, fundamental, and *dogmatic—*in these *postmodern urban times* may become more *creative* and *public* (Petersen 1995, Banks 1999, Jones and Paulsell 2002), more transient, on the move, always somewhere else, but deeply relevant to a place, a community, a neighborhood, a village, a city, a globe in need of a creatively transforming word. Theology in these *postmodern urban times* will be asked to become *transforming* the *public,* transforming *villages, neighborhoods, communities, cities* in creatively transforming *the world* (on theology transforming villages, neighborhoods, communities, cities, and the world Greenway and Monsma 2000, Villafane, Jackson, Evans, and Evans 2002, Gornik 2002, Sider, Olson, and Rolland Unruh 2002, Jacobsen 2001, Dudley 2002, Childs 2006).

A *creative public theology* (Petersen 1995, Banks 1999, Jones and Paulsell 2002) like this will *move out into the streets* and develop "curriculum around student-related and more general concerns, holding classes in an on-site ministry setting and addressing local concerns with the help of a reflective practitioner. All these connect theology and life more closely ... " (Banks 1999, 176).

New themes and *social skills* will be needed, skills that theology will have to integrate as well. These will be skills needed for reflecting and acting in the *ecology of public life,* regarding basic skills in *social action, community development, community change, project development, peacemaking,* and *conflict resolution* (on basic skills in social action, community development, community change, project development Greenway and Monsma 2000, Jacobsen 2001, Dudley 2002, Villafane, Jackson, Evans, and Evans 2002, Gornik 2002, Sider, Olson, and Rolland Unruh 2002, on peace-making and conflict transformation Schrock-Shenk and Ressler 1999, Evans, Evans, and Kraybill 2000a-b, Weaver and Biesecker-Mast 2003, Lederach 1999, 2004).

> "The task of engaging in 'transforming education' requires the development of skills vital to the public life and civic responsibility of the urban church. Programmatic tools of transformation are skills of theological and social analysis, congregational and community organization, community development, civic and social spirituality, and multicultural community conflict resolution." (Villafane, Jackson, Evans, and Evans 2002, 196–197)

Fundamental theology living and moving and having its being in the midst of its own *ecology of life* will be *world-transforming* if it moves out into the social and earthly habitats of common life in order to transform communities, neighborhoods, villages, cities, and the globe. Theology then becomes skill-oriented and transformative, process-oriented and project-focused. Projecting theology out into the open field of *social visions* and *communal dreams, public hopes* and *local artistry* may give it back some *roots* in home-coming as well as *wings* to take off in a life-changing way (on roots and wings and visions McDaniel 1995, 2000).

These *earthly roots* and *heavenly wings* may help us as theologians to "become better dreamers, better listeners, better homemakers, better laughers, better sleepers. Even better theologians" (McDaniel 2000, 160). Theology staying *earth-bound* has always had more of a ring of the real. At the same time, theology gains in color and form.

Fundamental Theology Getting to Know Things Ecologically

Human knowing in *theology* will change accordingly. Getting in touch with earth-grounded life may mean getting next to a cleaning lady on her knees in order to scrub the floors with her, recognizing holistically "that there are many ways of knowing: musical, bodily, shamanic, domestic, poetic, mathematical, scientific, emotional, and theological" (McDaniel 2000, 160). *Human knowing* is deeply *ecological*.

Everything *participates* in *how we know this world*. We know through the pain of our body, the fears of our soul, the daily chores of domestic living, the poetic vision of a sunset, the mathematical structure of our logics, the scientific skill of human invention and discovery, the emotional backdrop of our projecting, and the theological crafting of our hopes. In it we come to recognize that *all our human knowing interconnects with everything*, from the smallest flower growing on a sidewalk to the biggest life project that we head on to.

Epistemology, or the reflection on our human knowing, as eco-feminist Roman Catholic and liberation theologian *Ivone Gebara* (Gebara 1999) from *Brazil* puts it, "is nothing more than an invitation to think about how we know ourselves and the things that surround us in our everyday lives" (Gebara 1999, 20). These things of our everyday lives belong to our most human *ecology*. Flowers are part of it. The fresh air. The soft voice of a little and smiling child next door. Work or no work. Food or no food. Social friends or no friends. Everything that makes up our human living enters into the ways we know humanly. Even *telling your most personal story* is *epistemology*. People who know will know holistically, with food and flowers, stories and sufferings always being part of it. "They then have begun to see that certain expressions, such as 'you are what you eat' or 'I love flowers', are ways of knowing or recognizing the interdependence between the life of plants or the flowers and our own lives. This is knowing; this is epistemology!" (Gebara 1999, 20).

Theological epistemology in the *ecology of life* and in *fundamental theology* can no longer be reduced to *one particular way of human knowing* (on the diversity of eco-feminist epistemology Gebara 1999, 19–65). There is more to life and human knowing than argument, intellect, synthetic judgment, analytic dissection, and contradictory juxtaposition. There is also the transformative binding and molding, welding and weaving of a *poetic mind* that unites the separate, binds the loose ends, narrates the seemingly opposite, creating a kind of *koinonia of knowing*. In this koinonia of knowing everything is connected or is being connected. In this it can learn a great deal from *ecofeminist epistemology* that tries to develop "a stance, an attitude, a search for wisdom, a conviction that unfolds in close association with the community of all living beings" (Gebara 1999, 23).

Story-telling is one such way to unite the often separate. *Narrative thinking* combines things that usually have been segmented and dissected, analyzed and separated most violently and argumentatively. The narrative has a poetic way to think more peacefully and non-violently. Knowing non-violently creates a community of the living and invites to a *different kind of epistemology*. "Participants thus begin to describe how they tell the stories of their lives, and come to see that this too is epistemology" (Gebara 1999, 20). *Telling stories* invites into a *community of story-telling*. It excludes dominion and conquest, competition and violence, as it introduces "the notion of communion with, rather than conquest of, the earth and space" (Gebara 1999, 52). *Sharing space* in telling stories *lets others be*.

In this *non-violent koinonia of knowing*—with no need to keep up our *separating minds* active—we may peacefully discover how God is present in everything, in the smallest grasshopper, the most beautiful lily, the soul-shaking jazz tune, the glittering spring snow, and the committed cleaning woman scrubbing earthly floors, finding and letting God and the world be. God who is more than our human and most often *separating words*.

Epistemology and *theology* lived in this *non-violent and non-separate way* will be *contextual, holistic, affective,* and *inclusive* (Gebara 1999, 61–65), relating everything to everything in new and *poetic ways*. "The thing to do, then, is to relate subjectivity to objectivity, individuality to collectivity, transcendence to immanence, tenderness to compassion and solidarity, plants to humanity, and animals to humanity, based on a perspective that is all-encompassing and intimately interwoven" (Gebara 1999, 53).

As North American ecological theologian *Jay McDaniel* (McDaniel 2000) describes the non-verbal and interconnected ways of our human knowing in a *process theological epistemology*.

> "Let it be because we are better able to find the God who is more than words: the God who is found in the very presence of healthy food, the cleaning woman, jazz, and spring snow. And who is found in the presence of a mysterious and womblike Love who hears us when we say 'Dear God, I want you', 'Dear God, I need you', 'Dear God, I am so sorry', or 'Dear God, it is all so beautiful' . . . the encircling Presence who hears prayers and who is found in jazz and the cleaning woman. I have spoken of the presence of this God as God's Breathing. I have suggested that, if we listen to this Breathing in a deep way, we will want to get down on our knees next to the cleaning women and scrub the floors. We might also want to help her stand up, stretch, and go home. This, too, is the Great Work. It is bodily and domestic and ordinary and holy . . . To live from the Center: this is what it comes to. It is the Way of Jesus and the Buddha. Of Mother Teresa and the Dalai Lama. Of the cleaning woman and the jazz musician. Of the lilies and the grasshoppers. It is eternal life, moment by moment. It is all that really matters. Even the stars pray." (McDaniel 2000, 160)

Fundamental Theology Living in Koinonia

Fundamental theology can contribute to this *new community of all living things* as a *socially transforming theology* by providing *basic metaphors and images*, concepts and guiding terms for *transformation of communal living*.

One such *fundamental term* will be *koinonia*, translated into many concrete and social images. *Community* as *biblical koinonia* is more than just casual city or village community. It has a *deep-meaning* going beyond common social categories. It includes fellowship, communion, collaboration, sharing, partnership, and solidarity embedded in a *life-affirming* and *inclusive spirituality*.

North American Hispanic theologian and Pentecostal Evangelical *Eldin Villafane* from *Gordon-Conwell Theological Seminary* describes in his collaborative and case-study-based urban theology Transforming the City (Villafane, Jackson, Evans, and Evans 2002) the power of *koinonia* in the *postmodern city* most beautifully, referring to the collaborative inter-denominational, inter-faith, and inter-agency program of urban development in *Los Angeles*, the *Los Angeles Metro-Strategy*, as a *new form of theological koinonia*:

> "The postmodern city challenges both the church and urban theological education to commit to a wholistic urban *koinonia*. In Scripture, particularly in Pauline writings, *koinonia* is a rich and fruitful word-concept yielding multiple meanings. It can mean fellowship or communion with, or participation in something, as well as collaboration, sharing, giving, distribution, and partnership . . . It speaks to us of solidarity and community. In biblical Christianity *koinonia* is a mark of maturity—of true spirituality . . . The Los Angeles Metro-Strategy challenges both the local parish and all urban theological education programs to an enlarged vision of collaboration—of *koinonia*. The city as *koinonia*, if anything, speaks to a collaboration that is as *large* as the city, as *wide* as the programs serving it, and as *deep* as its confessional representatives. In the interest of serving the city as agents of justice and *shalom*, an urban *koinonia* must be demonstrated that transcends the parochial interest of individual seminaries, churches, denominations, or religious traditions . . . This presents a great challenge to our urban theological programs and institutions, which should, nay *must*, be in collaboration with the many and diverse: neighborhoods or communities of service; congregations and faith traditions dotting our cities; grassroots parachurch organizations and service agencies; municipal institutions; and public and private delivery systems in our cities. The *shalom* of our cities demands from all its benevolent actors no more and no less than this kind of wholistic *koinonia*—in truth, an authentic spirituality." (Villafane, Jackson, Evans, and Evans 2002, 197–199)

This is *fundamental theology* at its best, integrating the *communal* and the *local* with the *theological* in new ways, while making theology *socially creative* and *transforming the world*. Fundamental theology infuses into a public discussion its own theological concept of *shalom* and *koinonia*, guiding and giving support to a social and political process of *community-building, community development, political action,* and *communal living*.

This is a kind of *fundamental theology* that is *empowering* and *creative*, giving conceptual support to practical action, community change, and street concerns (on theology becoming community- and street-oriented Banks 1999, Jacobsen 2001, Gornik 2002, Dudley 2002). Theology is thus moving out into the streets *to put up its tent* or its provisionary home among the people and live there for a while, becoming *missional* in "replacing comfortable intellectual and therapeutic approaches to learning by the uncertainties of public communal discipleship" (Banks 1999, 133), accompanying the people in their human and social struggles, suggesting *metaphors for social action*, inviting peace-making visions into communal pain over past and present break-ups, and bringing the separated and segregated back into a human *oikos* and *koinonia* of mutual support, ecological care, communal solidarity, and social protest against all attempts *to let death win over life*.

Dogmatic Relevance: Oikos and Koinonia of Cultures

Finding Back Home in Peace

A *theological home-coming* in the *contemporary and postmodern world* is not the same anymore than what it used to be in other times. The world has become complex, confusing, conflicting to such an extent that a theological or any other home-coming may sometimes seem almost inconceivable. Too many *radical diversities*, too much *hurt and pain* over past and present human separations, social segregations, ideological battlefields, and *communal split-ups* have made it seem almost impossible and unreal that humans may be able *to come back home* and *live together* in a complex reality of *colorful and multi-dimensional peace* (on community-peace Nagler 2001, Neufeld Redekop 2002, Weaver and Biesecker-Mast 2003, Lederach 1999, 2004).

Since *peace* as communal and biblical *shalom* in this broken *postmodern world* (for biblical theology Brueggemann 2001, 1976, in systematic theology Duchrow and Liedke 1989, Stotts 1973, Panikkar 1995, Nouwen 1998, Wink 2000, Enns 2001, 2003, Enns, Holland, and Riggs 2004) has become a lot more *complex, multidimensional*, being lived and played in a more complicated *polyphony* or *polychronicity* (Lederach 1999, 78), some have rather decided to give up on it.

And yet, *communal peace-making* in this conflict-ridden world may become the most demanded and looked for *social skill* of *theology* in the times to come. *Learning how to live peacefully and non-violently* in this *polyphony and polychronicity of creation* will be the new challenge for theology as well.

A fundamental theology of the ecology of living will uphold the beauty of creation, the vulnerability of each living thing, and the ethical calling of every human and non-human face and form looking at us. To contribute to such an ecological theology of creation in postmodern times will need a *fundamental theology of conflict* and *conflict transformation*.

Here *Mennonite* theologians and *conflict scholars* in the *Anabaptist tradition* have opened the way to look at everything and everyone *created* in God's world in non-violent ways (in the radical Anabaptist-Mennonite tradition of conflict transformation Schrock-Shenk and Ressler 1999, Evans, Evans, and Kraybill 2000a–b, Neufeld Redekop 2002, Lederach 1999, 2004).

As Mennonite *sociologist of conflict* and theologian of peace and reconciliation *John Paul Lederach* puts it in his beautiful *The Journey to Reconciliation* (Lederach 1999, also Lederach 2004), contrasting and juxtaposing hopeful stories and visions of a non-violent creation with the day-to-day realities of looking into the face of real creation: "Each morning, I am almost fearful of opening the newspaper to find out what happened the night before. With these realities around us, it takes a blind eye or crass nerves to write about reconciliation. Maybe it takes faith and hope" (Lederach 1999, 13).

Faith and *hope* are exactly those mysterious and life-changing domains of *fundamental theology* that tries to give reasons to the world for its hope (1 Peter 3:15, referred to in O'Collins 1981, 24, Wagner 1996, 1, Schmidt-Leukel 1999, 12, Waldenfels 2000, 20–21). It may be high time that these reasons take on a *conflict-transforming and people-redeeming shape*, telling their story and their stories about why Christians believe that the world can be saved.

Telling Stories of No More Wounding

Creation is *one big story-book*, narrating and picturing, painting and composing how people and all living things could live together without being wounded or wounding others. Even if most daily newspapers and story books, diaries and history books, committee reports and personal memories tell other things, with stories having turned most violent, most painful, and most destructive in their human and non-human endings, in our Christian faith and hope *theology—systematic, fundamental,* and *dogmatic—*tells its own story in stories with hopeful reasons to believe that things can be transformed differently.

A *theology of creation* in this way will be *story-theology* at its best, telling one story after another about how created living things have learned how to stop hurting each other, and instead, have begun to creatively dance with each other in colorful harmony.

> "Stories are different from definitions, exegeses, or theoretical explanations. They can take on the qualities of a person, someone we interact with and learn from, someone we struggle and disagree with, someone who affirms and challenges us. Stories engulf both our hearts and minds. We talk a lot about stories in mediation and the work of conflict transformation. We believe in the need to tell and hear stories. We work to create a space that honors the experience shared in people's stories." (Lederach 1999, 14)

Joining in the Dance of Life

Creating a space for people's stories follows an *ecological path* through the many and diverse places and spaces of human and non-human living in that it listens to the *groaning* (Romans 8:22) and *rejoicing* of creation as it moves along. *Theology* then becomes a *journey*, a path, a trail, walking step by step into a better future where, hopefully, people and all living things learn how to *commune* with each other in *truth, justice, mercy, hope,* and *peace*. A peaceful living in creation would mean a new heaven and a new earth transformed. *Shalom*, peace, and a *reconciled living* will then be multiple, polychronic, and systemic, with everything and everyone related and connected with the other, joining in the melodious *dance of life*.

As North American Mennonite *John Paul Lederach* (Lederach 1999, 2004) describes the *systemic dance* of a *reconciled world* and creation along the many and various tunes and tones, melodies and beats, lines and shapes, times and places of *truth, justice, mercy, hope,* and *peace* in a polychronicity of *peaceful ecological living* where each one finds his or her voice to reach his or her true and *creative potential*:

> "The key to polychronic approaches comes in two elements: *multiplicity* of activities and *simultaneity* of action, doing several things at the same time. We need to develop lenses that permit us to see reconciliation and time from a polychronic frame of reference. This requires a *systemic* rather than a *linear* perspective on people, relationships, activities, and context . . . With a systemic view, we see people and relationships within a context,

a social fabric that is dynamic, interdependent, and evolving. We do not place primary focus on pinpointing the cause, as if that sets in motion a linear reaction. We try to understand the overall system and how change in any one aspect will change all the others. In other words, we have a polychronic, systemic view of reconciliation... Like a dance, we simultaneously have activities taking place related to the past (Truth), the present (Justice and Mercy), and the future (Hope and Peace). Each contributes and each can change the view of the others and the impact of the others. Each needs a voice. Each depends on the others to reach full potential." (Lederach 1999, 78–79)

In places like this, *people dance with each other*, putting aside old armors, by-gone hatreds, kept-up enmities, and broken stories. In places like this people and all living things rejoice in each other, joining in the *dance of life* (Lederach 1999, 79) that needs protecting.

Creation then becomes a *feast* (Fox 2002, Kaufmann 2000, 2006, Moltmann 1993/1985, 1992, 1997, 2003, 2010), maybe even the *feast of fools* (Cox 1969) and *wild spirits* (on the creational wild spirits Fox 2002, 145–153), having found solace and a safe place in the midst of laughter and tears over put-aside wars and inflicted destructions. Since after all, even our most volatile conflicts and volcanic irruptions may be nothing else and nothing more than the creatively moving *energy* of our own creation. *Energy* in itself is moving, changing, transforming the world. It is our choice whether we use it for *mercy, justice, truth, hope,* and *peace,* or for *hurting.* "A polychronic approach to time and reconciliation calls for a view of Truth, Justice, Mercy, Peace, and Hope as personal and social *energies*" (Lederach 1999, 79).

Energies can be used in various ways, both *helpful* and *conflictual.* *Creative energy* is part and parcel of *creation,* both in harmony and in conflict. "In the Beginning ... Was Conflict" (Lederach 1999, 110–117), inasmuch as "creation is rooted in *passion* and *caring*" (Lederach 1999, 111). Whether we use our creative energies for passion and caring, or for wounding and hurting, is *our choice.*

Learning how to live in the social matrix and systemic ecology of all these creative human and non-human energies may be the most challenging task for a *theology of creation* that encourages *radical diversity.* *Variety and diversity* have been present at creation since its back-projected beginnings. "Differences and distinctions permeate the creation account. In the first chapter of Genesis, the phrase 'of every kind' appears ten times, referring to seeds, plants, birds, fish, and animals. I am left with the overall picture of a rain forest, full of almost infinite varieties of life, or of a coral reef teeming with diverse creatures" (Lederach 1999, 112–113). Learning how to live in our own modern and postmodern rain forest or coral reef *peacefully* will be the challenge.

Learning the Postmodern Living Together

Creation may be *just right next door* when you get out of the house and stroll through your neighborhood. Creation is everything that is simply there. Some of it pleases, some of it enervates. Some of it appears beautiful, some of it looks miserable. In all of it there is *life energy* looking at you. We may be looking away, as we are passing beggars on the street. We may be peeking secretly at someone's misery. We may be stopped by the *images of violence or mercy. Everything nowadays is part of our creation. Creation* that has been there *ever since*, and creation that we have *created.* It all falls together into that place and time in which we live and move and have our being. Creation is both *past* and *present*, as well as lying in the *future*.

As German systematic theologian *Jürgen Moltmann* (Moltmann 2003) puts it *dogmatically, biblically,* and *poetically*:

> "The final syllable of the German word for creation, *Schöpfung*, indicates the *completed* process of creative activity and its result. Consequently when we talk about creation, we instinctively think, theologically speaking, about the original state of the world and the beginning of all things, imagining them as a condition that was once finished, complete in itself and perfect. Belief in creation echoes the Creator's judgement over his creation: 'Behold, it was very good' . . . Unfortunately we cannot, like our Creator, come to rest at this point. For experience tells us: 'Behold, it is unfortunately not very good at all.' It has been spoilt; it is 'corrupt', says the Bible (Gen. 6.5, 11). This discrepancy between the judgment of faith and the judgment of experience has led people to place the 'very good creation' ahead of history." (Moltmann 2003, 34–35)

Creation is an *ethical challenge* to form and transform the world, both past, present and future. Creation is *continuously renewing itself* through our own *human creative act.* We participate in every moment in some creative movement of God's Spirit, be it the writing of a text, the listening to a child laughing, the attentiveness to some hurting soul, or the imaginative painting of some new and more equitable world. Creation is found in all our human places and spaces that we live in.

The *challenge of creation* will then be to *let it be*, to let others be, to have others protected, encircled, invited, *included*. Inclusion as a creative act in the midst of war and conflict, battle and wounding, is the called-for vision for a new *postmodern living together*, whether in one's personal home, familiar relationships, civic duties, local neighborhoods, or in the global world. The *"very good" creation* in the midst of broken and fragmented, torn and shattered worlds of *violence* in and around us still lies ahead of us, waiting our *creative co-creating* with God for it to be born (Moltmann 2003, 35).

Living and ministering as a local pastor in a village in the 1990s somewhere in Switzerland facing the breaking up of community around the disputed question of 14-year-old teenagers taking heroin and playing with death brings up the whole *postmodern world* as broken and fragmented, torn and shattered as any world could be in moments like this. Nothing holds anymore, no basic foundations on which to tread, no more grand narratives that could explain or hold together everything. No more common values and denominators that might bind and weld together people in a *non-violent ecology of all living things*. Instead, the simple temptation to solve things and communal problems like this *violently* creeps up in every place dealing with it. In the media, in the city hall, in the village council, in neighborhood gossip, church bulletins, school boards, and in any other places where a community is faced with a *postmodern break-up* of possibilities to still understand a *common world*.

Peace as *shalom* in a situation of ethical and theological calling like this would mean a *postmodern living together* in spite of it all. It would mean learning the new vocabulary of non-violent living. It would mean to develop a new kind of *postmodern fundamental and dogmatic theology of peaceful living*. All this still needs developing. The theme of *creation* and *creativity* would be at the center. A *social home-coming* for people in postmodern times will need a highly creative new way of building *true community* (Peck 1987). A community that is not falling into pseudo-mutuality, fear of conflict, nor exclusion of the other. In places like this the power and skill of *communal creativity* (Fox 2002) will envision new forms of living together where even teenagers taking heroin at the age of 14 in some local village somewhere in Switzerland in the 1990s will find a safe and embracing place to feel at home and be *cared for*.

The Community of the Weak

In places like this no human and non-human being will be *wounded*. In places like this no member of a community will be excluded, slandered, broken, having his or her right and reason for existence being taken. In places like this a new and *postmodern koinonia or oikos in God's plural world* will protect every sign of life, whatever its need and pain, beauty and creative artistry, as every living being in a place like this in some way reflects the chaos and order of creation. All living things in a place like this participate in the *koinonia-life* of the Spirit hovering over them, feeling the *pulse of creation* (Sponheim 1999, 2006, 2011) ever more transforming life, individuals, communities, and the entire world.

The Interruption of the Other

The ethical question and social challenge how human places and communities are dealing with the radical *interruption* of *the other*—with those that are different, broken, queer, special, marked, and wounded—, will be most determinative for a *fundamental theology of creation* in the future (on the interruption of the other Sponheim 1999, 42–65). Teenagers taking heroin at the age of 14 in some local village somewhere in Switzerland in the 1990s are *the other* upsetting and breaking open a modern and postmodern world. The world will no longer be the same once these young teenagers are being taken seriously. But the choice remains an ethical one between simply choosing *violence* or creatively working for a *postmodern peace*. The face of *the other* is facing us as we meet teenagers like this on the street. The ethical challenge is the fundamental question—touching as much on remakings of *sociology* as on revisions of *fundamental theology*— whether our modern communities turning *postmodern* can hold out and *creatively embrace* the human and non-human pain of broken realities, conflictual break-ups, and interrupting disturbances.

As North American and Lutheran systematic theologian *Paul R. Sponheim* (Sponheim 1993, 1999, 2006, 2011) puts it in his social theology of creation as creative transformation of the world in *The Pulse of Creation* (Sponheim 1999), using Jewish philosopher *Emmanuel Levinas* as fundamental reference for the irruption and interruption of *the other* in our quiet and undisturbed lives:

> "'The given is other' . . . In interruption, by the Creator's will the human person encounters one who is truly different, who in Levinas's language 'disturbs the being at home with oneself' . . . The person is called to be human 'together' with others . . .

> The other is unconditionally given, so that to be is to be related to that which is other. Thus does the Creator equip the creature. The creature is not left alone. God does not create windowless monads, and God will not be evicted from God's universe. The gift, the givenness, of the other is the promise of creation."
> (Sponheim 1999, 88–89)

Teenagers at the age of 14 taking heroin in some local village somewhere in Switzerland in the 1990s are the ethical and theological challenge of *the other* disturbing a community in its undisturbed life. The challenge is to become a community where nobody is evicted, where all see themselves in close relationship to each other, becoming a *caring community* that has learned how to live together with others, even if we seem and remain strange and strangers to each other. In caring communities we recognize that "to be a creature is to be face-to-face with the other(s)." (Sponheim 1999, 141). A caring community would see 14-year-old teenagers in the same way. These others like teenagers at the age of 14 are the *marginalized others* waiting to be heard and seen.

North American systematic theologian *Paul R. Sponheim* recalls the biblical image of *the stranger*, the one who stands as a silent challenge to the Christian conscience in a world of the *powerful* and the *powerless*, being excluded, evicted, enslaved:

> "At this point the Christian will be particularly engaged, because she knows how often God's blessing comes to and through the stranger (e.g., Deut. 14:28–29; 26:10–13; Luke 4:25–27; 14:16–24) . . . In this journey the 'other' will be not just agent, but end. *What* we work for will surely call for opposition to rising tides of ethnocentrism and heterosexism, open in hate crimes and cloaked in immigration policy. We cannot leave unaddressed the unresolved American racial paradox represented by a Thomas Jefferson who could write the celestial sentences of the Declaration of Independence, while owning more than a few slaves on the earth of Monticello. Earth is not only a metaphor. Seen in wider focus, the planet stands as a silent witness and mute neighbor to challenge the Christian conscience . . . "
> (Sponheim 1999, 142)

The Community of the Weak

The Koinonia and Oikos of God's Plural World

The dogmatic relevance of *oikos* and a *koinonia of cultures* is found at this crossroad of broken possibilities. Coming home into the *oikos* of God's plural place of a variety of cultures, filling the house with new life as its old and new members learn how to live a *nonviolent, multi-cultural,* and *postmodern koinonia,* this will be the challenge. both for theology and human living together. *Creation* and the peaceful living together of all living things is the dogmatic vision for this. Creation may be chaotic, forever moving and changing, most diverse, and unpredictable. And yet there is a particular kind of beauty, artistic order, and patterned interconnection, that shows itself even in the midst of the *creatively chaotic*. To look at creation in this *chaotic dogmatic tradition* may be a new way to look at it, and yet it is strengthened and doubled by the images and narratives of a *new science* telling its own *new story* of creation (on the new science and the new stories of creation McGrath 1999, Barbour 2000, Toolan 2001, Wiseman 2002, Moltmann 2003, Edwards 2004, Sponheim 1999, 2006, 2011).

As North American systematic theologian *Peter C. Hodgson* (Hodgson 1994, also Hodgson 2007) puts it in his revision of dogmatic theology *Winds of the Spirit,* underlining the creative process of a chaotic evolving of creation in dogmatic terms:

> "The new science of 'chaos' has shown that the most diverse, flexible, and unpredictable dynamic systems at the same time reveal the most intricate and beautiful patterns of order . . . Those who wish to affirm the often wild, wondrous, fecund diversification found in nature and to resist imposing a premature purpose on an essentially open process are surely right, but at the same time they recognize that things are interconnected in the most radical way; and some believe that the creative process has a strangely serendipitous, even quasi-teleological, quality . . . At the heart of creation is a mystery that evokes awe from scientist and theologian alike. It is from such awe that faith in God as Creator has arisen." (Hodgson 1994, 17)

Musically transposed to *human living together* this may mean that the *chaotic* and *conflictual* in creation is actually *the natural*. The creative involves the birthing of the conflictual. And the creative unites the dissolving conflictual. Both happen. Both are part of this mystery called human and non-human life. Whether in the *scientific world* of cosmological narratives and stories how things actually happened and still happen, or in the *human world* of how humans and other living things actually tick, there is the similarity, if not equivocal analogy.

Or as Mennonite sociologist *John Paul Lederach* (Lederach 1999, 2004) puts it in his *theology of conflict and creation*, comparing the *chaotic* and moving of human living with the *ordered* and unified of *working ants* that we hopefully keep being different from:

> "The question is probing the issue of our natural inclinations as we think about building the perfect world. What regularly emerges is our temptation to put robot workers in the ideal factory. The place would work mechanically and without a hitch. People would be asked to do a particular job, but not to think, dream, or make many choices. All the choices are already made. People are asked to follow instructions and make the product . . . How interesting and ironic that such a place is set up to eliminate diversity and choice! It also eliminates conflict. Read major novels about the future, like *1984* or *Brave New World*. See how the authors conceive of paradise as a place where conflict does not exist. To achieve such a condition in these worlds, the author wipes out diversity and individuality, to restrict imagination and choice. In other words, it is the *exact opposite* of God's creation commitments: Godlikeness in each, unique diversity for all, and freedom throughout . . . On the sixth day, God looked over this creation and said, 'It is very good.' Quite frankly, it was a mess, a dynamic, rich, and wonderful mess. In my view, this is the central point of the creation commitments. The very elements that make human experience rich and dynamic, the characteristics missing in the experience of ants, are the elements that make conflict inevitable. Conflict is natural." (Lederach 1999, 115–116)

A *koinonia and oikos of cultures* in *God's plural world* will *include the diverse*, it will welcome the stranger, it will embrace the wounded, heal the broken, listen to the slandered, take in the excluded, *bringing all things in creation together back home in peace*. This *creative home-coming in peace* will not exclude diversity, variety, the human face of the other. It will learn how to live in non-violent diversity, restoring the broken and the estranged. "*Our mission* is to align ourselves with God, who is working to bring all things together, to *reconcile* all of creation and particularly a broken, estranged humanity. This is the 'universal restoration' destined to bless all families of the earth (Acts 3:20–26; Col. 1:20)" (Lederach 1999, 160). Taking in teenagers at the age of 14 who take heroin in some local village somewhere in Switzerland in the 1990s into a *non-violent home of new living* is one way to enact this vision. And *conflict* moves in with it.

A *postmodern koinonia and oikos of cultures* in which *no one is wounded, hurt*, and *broken*, no one is slandered, shunned, and excluded, is something and some place *still to be created*, dreamed of, painted, narrated, envisioned, and developed, as it is not yet here to be. But little elements creep up in places here and there. It comes and goes, like the *winds of the Spirit* (Hodgson 1994). Its vision is *new, radical, visionary, and highly creative*. It requires colorful fantasy, social imagination, and creative endurance.

It calls for a *theology—systematic, fundamental*, and *dogmatic*—that *trains* and *encourages* people in *ecological living* where everything and everyone is connected with each other in its and their utmost *diversity*. The *postmodern dream* is there, remaining an ever luring incentive to keep on dreaming about creatively opening places and spaces, homes and houses, church buildings and youth cellars, communities and villages, neighborhoods and cities, regions and countries, nations and continents where *the dream* is "to heal our broken communities across the globe" (Lederach 1999, 166). Then creation would rejoice in exaltation.

Dreaming Creation

Creation redeemed will remain a *dream*. And yet we are called to be and keep on being *dreamers* (on being dreamers in conflict transformation Lederach 1999, 190–202, as an artful moral imagination Lederach 2004). To dream about and keep on dreaming about a human community in which teenagers at the age of 14 taking heroin in some local village somewhere in Switzerland in the 1990s would be embraced, and not excluded (on exclusion and embrace Volf 1996), remains a beautiful dream. It turned out differently, most violently. And yet, little and big moments did get born. Moments when young teenagers could see the dream, could feel the enclosure, could sense a new world. It may be true that we "seem to have a scarcity of dreamers these days" (Lederach 1999, 191). And yet dreams keep coming up, day and night. *Theology* could learn from the *craft of dreaming*. Since in some ways theology may be nothing else but a form of creative dreaming, picturing the invisible, painting the hopeful, singing the unheard off, healing the incurable, forgiving the unforgivable, envisioning the incredible. Theology may become a *dream-catcher* or *dream-keeper* of a particular sort.

As creation sociologist and conflict theologian *John Paul Lederach* (Lederach 1999, 2004) puts it, referring to the poetic imagery of *Langston Hughes*:

> "'The Dream Keeper' calls us to bring all of our dreams, so they can be protected from the 'too-rough fingers of the world'. In 'Dreams', the author advises us to 'hold fast to dreams', for without them life is 'frozen' and 'barren', grounded like a 'broken-winged bird' . . . " (Lederach 1999, 191, referring to Hughes 1994)

Fundamental theology in a *postmodern age* will be well advised to listen to and take seriously its own *dreams*. *Dreaming creation* in non-violent forms, dreaming communities in mutual understanding, dreaming nations in peaceful living, may be a dream. And yet theology in its fundamentals opens the dream. The dogmatic relevance of a theology of creation lies at this crossroad. Creation will have to be reconsidered as an *oikos and koinonia of cultures in peace*. Theology may contribute to this vision, having biblical and dogmatic images at hand. Some of these dogmatic and theological dreams may even be paradoxical, as any hope against hope remains in paradox. Foolish, powerless, weak it may be, and yet transforming the world, as we express *our belief*.

> "I believe in the God of history, the God of creation, the God of love and compassion, the God of immeasurable power. This God has chosen to work through the weak and foolish . . . I believe in the God of Shalom, who invites us to be a part of the new kingdom dream. There human energies are spent on healing the sick, housing the homeless, and feeding the hungry. There we choose not the weapons of destruction to resolve our differences but the God-given gifts of reason and speech, and the overwhelming coals of love and compassion (cf. Rom. 12:20)." (Lederach 1999, 201)

Dreaming creation in dogmatic terms sees the world as "*a community of creation*" (Moltmann 1993/1985, 3–4) where all living things are in *fellowship with each other*. It is a *totality* where nothing can be dealt with separately. Nothing can be broken off, taken aside, separated and segregated away from everything else. Dreaming about creation in the dogmatic tradition requires *integrating and integral thinking* (Moltmann 1993/1985, 3–4), especially in these modern and postmodern times where the *natural sciences* and *philosophical thinking* have become more sensitive to the intricate community of all living things. To describe this community of all living things, poetic modeling and creative thinking will be needed. The *story of creation* is nowadays told *poetically* even by scientists describing the *new cosmologies* as a process that is ultimately indescribable, and therefore requires poetic description (on new cosmologies Swimme and Berry 1992, Swimme 1996, Berry 1999, Haught 2000, Toolan 2001, 127–191, Edwards 2004).

German systematic theologian *Jürgen Moltmann* (Moltmann 1993/1985) describes the need for integrating and integral ways of thinking about a *doctrine of creation*:

> "The methods of an ecological doctrine of creation of this kind cannot be one-dimensional. It must use multifarious ways of access to the community of creation, and make people aware of them. We find these approaches in both tradition and experience, in science as well as in wisdom, in intuition but also in deduction. We shall try to look critically at theological traditions in the doctrine of creation. But I should also like to take up new, post-critical scientific methods and ways of thinking. And the approaches of poetic perception and intuition must be integrated as well. The doctrine of creation that emerges will not be one that merely builds up concepts and tries to find definitions, on the philosophical model, important though that is. It will also take up and use symbols, which mould the unconscious and guide awareness in a way which is unknown to the conscious mind. Finally, there is an expectant and creative imagination in the spheres of the potential and the future which we have to call poetic. If we were to exclude this from a doctrine of creation, we could not talk about 'the future of creation' at all. Theology always includes the imagination, fantasy for God and his kingdom. If we were to ban the images of the imagination from theology, we should be robbing it of its best possession. Eschatologically oriented theology is dependent on a messianic imagination of the future, and sets this imagination free." (Moltmann 1993/1985, 4)

Power Creative and Ecological

From this, a *new concept of power* can be envisioned, with power *empowering* the *ecology of living*. Power is no longer the atomistic capability of an autonomous individual to do whatever he or she wants to do against all odds and human or social barriers. Power becomes *communal*, as it empowers people *to live in true community* (Peck 1987). The *koinonia or oikos of cultures in God's plural world* is called into existence by some reality beyond the real, enlivened and made possible, created and protected, kept alive and furthered by this creative and creating *Spirit of Life* empowering everything, be it churches, communities, individuals, and the whole of creation (on the Spirit of Life in creation, communities, and churches Moltmann 1992, 1992/1977, 1993/1985, 1997, 2003, 2010).

Gathering in the presence of God in *friendship* and *fellowship* (for a theology of friendship and fellowship Moltmann-Wendel 2001) may be the *new form of human power* more powerful than weapons and armies, economic strategies and political policies. At least from a theological perspective, *power* will be the *power and strength of the weak* (Sölle 1984) gathering in hope against all hope, while participating in the "uprisings of life against the many forms of death" (Sölle 1984, 76). Power in this creative way is like a composition, an art work, a symphony, a novel, a social project. It empowers *vision and hope* to become *reality*.

Power understood in *biblical* and *theological terms* (in biblical and systematic theology on God and power Migliore 1983, Case-Winters 1990, Schmalstieg 1991, Jennings 1992, Pasewark 1993, Firer Hinze 1995, Rigby 1997, Dawn 2001, Griffin 2004, Keller 2005, Wink 1984–2009, Sponheim 1993–2011) is both *creative* and *ecological, communal* and *political*, weaving together in a musical or poetic moment the *interdependent, connected, mutual,* and *non-violent* (on the creative, interdependent, connected, mutual, and non-violent character of the power of Jesus—over against principalities and powers—in biblical and systematic tradition Wink 1984–2009). Power is never dominion or domination, but always a *new creation* giving hope and space.

Power is the continuously enlivening *art of creation*, the hopeful and visionary *art of life* (on a philosophy of life as an art form—following Michel Foucault—see Schmid 1998, on Michel Foucault see Brown 2000) composing new things and melodies, paintings and life projects, social visions and political agendas, communal hopes and global longings, participating in the never-ending and creative stirrings of life in the ecology of our human living (on activity, pulse, and sacred longings of God's creation Snook 1999, Page 1996, 2000, Grey 2003, Sponheim 1999, 2006, 2011). The power of the Spirit of Life will be "renewing the earth" *ecologically* (Snook 1999, 128) as if it were redrawing and re-sketching creation at its beginning, giving it space and light and the breath of life. This Spirit of Life, renewing and redrawing, is *God in creation* (Moltmann 1993/1985,

1992, 1997, 2003), in that "the whole creation is alive with the breath or Spirit of God" (Snook 1999, 1).

Ecology is *God's place* or *oikos* of *earthly dwelling*, the *koinonia of all living things*, empowering everything and everyone. In this *koinonia of living* power encourages the dreaming of life. Empowering visions, luring desires, creative compositions, artistic fantasies, visionary projects, they all move and enliven human hearts to change the face and shape of the earth. Power in this way is *ecological* in that it connects, weaves together, composes, and assembles the disparate and separate, unifying the broken, gathering the dispersed. A power like this is not destructive, antagonistic, oppressive, or dominant. It serves, instead of uses, human life, earthly life, global life. It reconciles separations, heals the wounded, brings together the estranged in a new koinonia of all living things, a *koinonia of peace* (Brueggemann 1976, 2001). In it there are no losers or winners, but only *companions*, having *culturally disarmed* (Panikkar 1995).

As Roman Catholic intercultural theologian *Raimon Panikkar* (Panikkar 1995, 2009), teaching at the *University of California, Santa Barbara*, puts it, coining "the word '*ecosophy*' to denote the *wisdom of the earth* itself: "In true reconciliation, there are neither victors nor vanquished. All come out winners, because the whole, of which we make up a part, is respected" (Panikkar 1995, 100). A *koinonia of peace* with humans and the earth putting aside its cultural and political, social and communal warfare, its arms, its strategies, its policies and ideologies, its theories and theologies to win over arguments most exclusively, to exclude life most permanently and ban alternatives most normatively, to succeed most successfully and assert itself most powerfully, will need the ecological modesty of a deep "desire for peace" of "pacifying in itself" (Panikkar 1995, 102–103).

Pacifying in itself, the earth and human desire will have to learn how to live *non-violently* in this *earth community* (Rasmussen 1996, Gebara 1999, Page 1996, 2000, Grey 2003, Gottlieb 2006) that makes up our natural habitat. Earth could then become something like a hopeful sign of the *Shalom Church* envisioned in biblical images (for a „Shalom Church" in biblical imagery Brueggemann 2001, 151–165). The Shalom Church being that place and space of living together in peace around a *common table*. The table of fellowship and sharing in everything that the earth produces. *Wine, bread, hope*, and *community*.

As North American Old Testament scholar *Walter Brueggemann* (Brueggemann 2001) describes the *new koinonia of table fellowship*, an

Culture

ecological kind of table fellowship sharing its dreams, around the *power of the weak*, in memory of *Jesus*:

> "So we may live by the joy of Jesus, who rejoiced at upsetting newness. We may live by the risk of Jesus, who emptied himself. We may live by the power of Jesus, which other folks thought to be weakness. He always surprised them by drawing power from perceived weakness. We may live by the dreams of Jesus, which are not unlike the dreams of Martin Luther King, Jr.—eloquent fantasies about a new age surely to surge among us. All of that—joy, risk, power, and dreams—all of that was about a new age being born among us; we dare not and need not settle in, either grimly or complacently, on the old age, which is passing away. Of course, that is nonsense, and the world knows that—the world that crucified Jesus, the older brothers who sent the dreamer Joseph off to slavery—because the world cannot abide such dreams. False dreams are so scary. We are invited to stay close to Jesus and draw on the sources of ministry and resilience that he used. We are invited to stay with the bold one, to take care not to get sucked in by any of the timid ones. Until I reflected on it, I thought the imagery of vine-branches was stale if not static. But it is a radical business, inviting us to stay connected to God and therefore not be connected elsewhere. And if we belong to the grape family, our business is grapes—perhaps the wine of the new kingdom—and we are not permitted to produce briers or even eggplant or okra, but only the wine of the new age." (Brueggemann 2001, 156)

Sharing in the Ecological Peace of God

Sharing in the wine of the *new kingdom* is sharing in the *ecological peace of God*. This peace is *earthly, communal, sensual, artistic, creative, nourishing,* and *community-building*. It invites the world to some new table, the *communion table of Jesus* having lived many visionary *shaloms* at tables. "The shalom from the table means to embody a kind of wholeness and freedom and justice that the world does not recognize or even know it exists" (Brueggemann 2001, 158). This *ecological shalom* prefigured at the many tables Jesus used to invite people to and commune with the excluded, the frowned upon, may seem strange, unheard of, even unreal. And yet it prefigures the *new kingdom,* even though if may seem outright *foolish*. "It is sheer foolishness to eat with publicans and tax-collectors. It is indefensible nonsense to touch lepers, to dance with the dead and bring them to life. But that is what he did and why he got killed, and it is the work he left us to do" (Brueggemann 2001, 161).

Power then is a *gift*. Like the gift of good wine at the table. Like the morning sun waking us. Like the smile on the face of a child welcoming us. *Power is not control*, not dominion, not mastery. *It is given. It grows, it expands, it moves and enlivens the living.* It is like a seed opening. It is like a set table inviting us. It connects and brings together people, memories, stories, ideas, projects, hopes, visions. It opens up wide spaces and places, wild images and bold dreams. *It makes people move again* while hoping anew. *It empowers the powerless*. It enlivens the dead. It raises up the hopeless and gives them a new vision. In all of it, it does not tear apart the fabric of the living, but adds to it, inviting everyone and everything living to yield to the *creative and creating dance* and its musically poetic melody. "*Shalom* is precisely the capacity to yield to the gift of power, which comes unexpectedly and unexplained and, therefore, is neither understood nor managed by us. But capacity to receive and yield is not what we nurture or value. We stress rather consistently control, mastery, and competence. And the more we master, control, and manage, the less we can yield to the gift" (Brueggemann 2001, 160).

Creative Empowering

This *ecological peace of God* calls back the forgotten, the unvalued, the left out. It *empowers* those with no power. It encourages the broken-hearted. It uplifts those that have been downtrodden, so that the *mighty* may fall from their *thrones* (on the mighty falling from their thrones New Testament terms Walsh 1987). The biblical concept of *Shalom* includes this kind of *transforming power*. Creation is power. *Creation* is empowering, as creation happens in every new and creative moment where people and other living things find their own hopeful vision. Hope is the birth of the creative in some human or non-human soul, leading to limitless dreaming about how the world could change. Dreaming is hope, hope empowered. And power may be nothing more than the *Spirit of creation* (Moltmann 1992, 1997, 1993/1985, 2003, Fox 2002, Edwards 2004) moving, hovering, luring, drawing, envisioning, and prompting life to grow.

Empowerment is a *biblical term* as well as a *social vision* (on empowerment in biblical and systematic theology Weber 1989, Walsh 1987, Heyward 1982, 1995, Brock 1988, Walker 1991, Jennings 1992, Purvis

1993, Mackey 1994, Sanders 1995, Wink 1984-2009). It may all have started in *Africa*, as African American Methodist and social ethicists *Theodore Walker, Jr.* from *Southern Methodist University* in *Dallas, Texas* reminds us in his African-American social ethics of empowerment *Empower the People* (Walker 1991): "We have learned from Scripture that long before the common era, an African by the name of Moses confronted another African called Pharaoh" (Walker 1991, 20). The Exodus was the most primal act of *social empowerment* for a people. African American spirituality and preaching is in constant memory of this primal act of *creative empowerment*. "From our pulpits we have learned that God was not concerned simply that the people be free to go, but more inclusively, that God was concerned that the people might be free to go serve God" (Walker 1991, 20).

In its creative act, *empowerment* makes people *authors* of their own lives and their own dreams, putting pencils and pens and brushes and visions into their hands to write about and paint a new world, out of personal authority and dignity. In the words of North American womanist and Christian ethicist *Cheryl J. Sanders* (Sanders 1995) at *Howard University*: "Empowerment is the process by which an individual or group conveys to others the authority to act. Although empowerment finds meaningful application in politics, economics, and social relations, in this discussion it is most highly valued as a spiritual transaction that both invokes and responds to the divine presence as mediated through human interaction" (Sanders 1995, 4). Empowerment is deeply *spiritual*, connecting us with the Spirit that makes things alive, individuals and whole communities.

Empowerment is a *project*, a new vision for a different world, a different kind of life. It this, it is *creative* and *artistic*, creating a new world. Power is not some mechanical or strategic act, some distributive measurement of strength and weakness, dominance and submission. Rather, it is the *spirit of art* (on power as creative art Starhawk 1987, Fox 2002), *dancing with power* (Starhawk 1987, 194–195) as we are recreating the world for some divine and human purpose, for some *artistic new vision* that lures the world into beauty and justice, peace and communal living.

As North American peace activist, eco-feminist, and Goddess spiritualist *Starhawk* (Starhawk 1987) puts it: "We can feel that power in acts of creation and connection, in planting, building, writing, cleaning, healing, soothing, playing, singing, making love, We can feel it in acting together with others to oppose control" (Starhawk 1987, 10). Power in the creative mode is everything else but control or dominance. It lures the world into *creative beauty* (Fox 2002).

Empowerment is a *creative act* (in Christian social ethics Walker 1991, Sanders 1995, in the social sciences Mayo 2000, Herriger 2002) opening up *spaces* to paint a new world, *God's world*. It is a different way of valuing things, healing things and people, as people and all living things experience "*empowerment* to restore and heal and *guidance* to risk for the unvalued of the world whom God has not ceased to value" (Brueggemann 2001, 161). In this, it is restoring a broken creation, healing a wounded world, mending the bent and torn fabric of life.

Empowerment theo-ethics (Page 1996, 2000, Grey 2003, Sponheim 1993, 1999, 2006, 2011) chooses *different values*, opts for different themes and concerns, and takes sides for different kinds of people and signs of life in a broken world. It participates in God's creative act of creation, both at its beginning, and into an open future, knowing that God has bound him- or herself to creation to continue his or her creative work. "In knowing this divine freedom binding itself to the creation, the Christian has cause to amplify the verb with which we began by speaking of empowerment. In God's unfailing presence there is power" (Sponheim 1999, 113). This power is *transforming*, moving, changing things and the world, as it is "*God's* transforming action" (Sponheim 1999, 88).

Earth Healing

Power *unites* the separate. It is *inclusive* and *world-healing* (on power as inclusive and world-healing Ruether 1992, McFague 1997, Page 1996, 2000, Grey 2003, Gottlieb 2006). *Earth healing* participates in God's creative act of primal creation. It reconciles the broken pieces, yearning for peace in the midst of hatred and global violence. A power that divides and segregates the world is a power of dominion and domination, wanting to rule and win rather than serve and commune. The power that ecological living envisions is *embracing, connecting,* and *reconciling*.

As ecofeminist Roman Catholic and liberation theologian *Mary C. Grey* (Grey 2003) describes in her *Sacred Longings*, an *ecotheology* of *earth reconciliation*, the "*reconnecting* with the earth", the *sacred eros* longing for the unifying of all living things, as "a satisfying, healing and joyful process" (Grey 2003, 209):

> "Reconnecting with the earth means at the same time *reconciliation* with the earth, a journey of turning toward the earth in humility and repentance. In the process faith communities—at the moment mostly confined to individualistic notions of repentance—become true to their original vision and calling to live justly with creation. They begin to speak and live out truth from the heart. Through a sense of the preciousness of creation's giftedness, they receive the transformative possibilities of living more simply. Compassion for the entire ecological community becomes mobilized. Again, the emergence of a new monasticism. . . . Reconciliation is both a symbol of healed creation, a vision that enables and inspires action for a future state of being, and something that one already tastes and lives from now. Something that touches our deepest yearnings, for we struggle with reconciled hearts . . . But our yearning selves, longing for peace, struggle with the fact that there are many groups nurtured to hate, whose existence depends on this narrow identity overcoming other identities, for whom vengeance is the only operative reality. . . . It is often a world where hatred has been deliberately created in communities long accustomed to relating as neighbors." (Grey 2003, 209–210)

Hatred and *violence* as well are *creations* of the *human and communal mind*. Whole communities can be *torn, broken*, and radically *destroyed* by the *creation of hatred*. Then, "reconciliation is a process for the long haul, a process where re-membering and being willing to let go of certain memories, learning to respect difference, and commitment to the freedom of the other are integral ingredients in the commitment. The *perichoretic* movement of compassion able to embrace difference and otherness is relevant here" (Grey 2003, 210). Life has a way to take its time to *heal wounded scars and broken moments*. And yet, there is this mysterious, mystical flow wanting to unite the separate paths, reaching out to the other, even the enemy, to reconnect and heal the broken toll. This may be the *Spirit, life, erotic longing, repenting forgiveness,* leading all to the same: the reunification of broken-off pieces in the unity of life. *Compassion* may be the other word for this spiritual power, uniting the broken and healing the nations.

> "In the end it is only this vision that keeps us going and restores heart to our culture. The vision is not of returning to Eden, whence the fertile river flows, . . . but of the restored city, of a reconciled Jerusalem, where 'the leaves of the tree are for the healing of the nations' (Rev. 22.1) and the crystal waters of life flow through the streets. Treading the ecomystical path, our wild, sacred longings for a healed cosmos are kept alive

by the Spirit as Wild Bird: she keeps our hearts restless for a time when the deserts are once again fertile, when sacred rivers flow, and the long suffering of vulnerable desert peoples is at an end. *Longing for water is longing for life and for a world that is flowing and juicy with fruitfulness.* The desiring heart expands with boundless compassion in myriad communities around the globe, and the dawn of a transformed world is on the horizon." (Grey 2003, 211)

To find *communities* of this kind of a *sacred longing* is the beginning of a *new creation*. Communities can become the healing of nations, people, generations. The *koinonia* and *oikos* of cultures in God's plural world is a challenge for the earth's community to be transformed into a place and human space where people can learn and experience the *perichoretic compassion* embracing *the different* and *the other* (on the perichoretic—Trinitarian in its image—compassion embracing the other and the different Volf 1996).

This *learning process* starts in small places, in local villages, city neighborhoods, local churches, and communal living on a small scale. Facing 14-year-old teenagers taking heroin in some local village somewhere in Switzerland in the 1990s is such a human challenge to become a *koinonia* and *oikos* of *shalom* in God's plural world. The *culture shock* is right there. The intercultural barriers go right through the same ethnic and communal social group. The overwhelming threat of a presence unheard-of is not any less demanding and challenging as any other in-breaking of strange and estranged cultural norms.

A New Creation

To learn how to live in *peace* in a place like this, would be the beginning of a *new creation*. To learn how to embrace as a *true community* (Peck 1987, Volf 1996, Kirkpatrick 2001, 2003) the open vulnerability of teenagers at the age of 14 taking heroin in some local village in Switzerland in the 1990s would be the beginning of a *fundamental theology* that is in touch with its own sacred longings for a *world in peace*. A world where "sacred rivers flow, and the long suffering of vulnerable desert peoples is at an end" (Grey 2003, 211).

The *dogmatic relevance* of this *koinonia* and *oikos* of cultures *at peace* in God's plural world is this creative and sacred dream. The dream of a *healed cosmos*, of a sacred longing, of a restored heart to our cultures, "through the healing of broken connections: to be reconciled to our deepest selves, with each other and with the earth" (Grey 2003, 211).

A *fundamental theology* of the *koinonia* and *oikos* of cultures in God's plural world will have to develop a *new vocabulary* more in touch with the *"longing for life and for a world that is flowing and juicy with fruitfulness"* (Grey 2003, 21). A fundamental theology like that will be more down-to-earth, colloquial, common, and *natural* (McFague 1997). It will also open up its deepest desires, its hidden erotic dreams, its cover-up sensuous longings. Its language will change accordingly, becoming more *poetic*, and less prosaic. The argumentative will give way to the *connective* (for the connective over against the argumentative in fundamental theology Wetherilt 1994, 147–149), connecting the dispersed and separate into the flow of a common narrative and image creating a new place. A *holistic, affective,* and *inclusive epistemology* (Gebara 1999, 62–65) will guide its path on its earthly way.

In the same way as *true communities* (Peck 1987) need to learn the skills of inclusive thinking, affective sensitivity, and holistic vision, *theology* as well—*systematic, fundamental, dogmatic, ethical, pastoral*—will have to become more *communitarian* and *community-building* in this way. A theology of creation has *dogmatic relevance* for all theological disciplines. It will change the way theology is being done. The *inclusive*, the *affective*, and the *holistic* need to move into theology's *oikos* and *koinonia* of scholars and students, writers and readers as well. Learning how to live together in postmodern peace in a *koinonia* and *oikos* of cultures in God's plural world starts right there where people do theology. The transferal to communities is the next step. *Fundamental theology* itself will need to become its *own house*, its own fellowship and *friendship of various cultures* and themes, colors and nations, learning how to live in a *bio-diversity* of *artistic play*.

A New Kind of Power

Then, *power* can be redefined as well, in the way *North American systematic theology* has tried to contribute to a *new concept of power* over these last several decades.

Power in the *koinonia* and *oikos* of cultures in God's plural world will be *relational* and *creative, artistic* and *actional*. It will encourage people and all living things to flow and flourish, to co-create and co-paint a new world. In this, it will *empower* people and get empowered as well, since empowerment is always inclusive in changing most everything, the one empowered and the one empowering as well. It is a *creative partnership* with the ecology of all living things. With everything connected, power changes everything.

In the words of African American and womanist theologian *Cheryl J. Sanders* in her *Empowerment Ethics* (Sanders 1995), describing the mutual empowering that requires a *costly justice* at the base of all longings for power:

> "Empowerment ethics posits norms and principles for people in charge, people who are serious about their accountability to others in the form of justice. Dietrich Bonhoeffer, the Christian theologian who lost his life while taking a stand against Adolf Hitler in Nazi Germany, warned against 'cheap grace' in *The Cost of Discipleship* . . . The moral predicament of some modern African American Christian intellectuals suggests a 'cheap justice' of demanding repentance and restitution from the oppressing group in the name of God, without fostering a corresponding self-critique on the part of either the oppressed or those who claim to speak for them. Cheap justice is manifested in the lives of empowered individuals who verbalize prophetic claims on behalf of the oppressed, but who distance themselves physically, emotionally, and politically from the oppressed group, freely imbibing the elite privileges, status, and material benefits offered by the very same structures and networks they oppose with words . . . Costly justice, on the other hand, is a sacrificial struggle on the part of empowered individuals who maintain creative partnerships with the oppressed and who identify unambiguously with the best interests of the oppressed group. Costly justice is grounded in the ongoing vision and work of persons whose moral outlook and spiritual principles have been forged in the communal historical experience of oppression." (Sanders 1995, 8)

Power in this concept is *grounded, physical, emotional,* and *political*. It shares in the daily lives of people who are kept powerless. It is *communal* and *spiritual*, being forged and molded by the realities of life. It comes out of an *ecology of powerlessness* that makes words ring true. Those who speak about empowerment know what it means to use these words. Otherwise, words have a tendency to disconnect from reality. Power here is connected, in creative partnership and communication with those who lack power and hope for a healing word. It becomes creative in sacrificial struggle, costly in grace and justice, *healing* in that it empowers from within.

Creative power in the ecology of all living things participates in *God's creative power* changing everything. The smallest change of tone, color, warmth, breeze, the smallest change of shape, form, face, the smallest or monumental revolution of life on earth is sign and symbol for God's creative power. Humans share in it by trying to *change the world*. Not as rulers, not as kings, not as domineering lords of all, but as *co-creative companions* walking along with all the others, humans and other living things, on the way toward a healing and healed creation.

Healing is the *ultimate power*. Healing all the broken pieces, reconnecting broken people, reconciling damaged stories, while our deepest "longing for life and longing for God come together in a resting place where desires are satisfied and fulfilled in justice for vulnerable communities and the earth's own economy" (Grey 2003, 211–212). The *oikos* and *koinonia* of cultures in God's plural world may be this *healing place*.

Finding the Healing Place—In Dancing

In a *healing place* like this young teenagers at the age of 14 taking heroin in some local village somewhere in Switzerland in the 1990s would *feel at home*, safely protected and warmly welcomed. No more wounding, no more hurting, no more running from one place to the next. A community of all, trying to live the *Shalom* of all living things. A *healing community* having turned into a *true community* (Peck 1987, Granberg-Michaelson 1991, Harmer 1998, Sawyer 2003, Marsh 2005) where the world is joining in one great and festive *dance* (Moltmann 1993/1985, 304–307). No more exclusion, everyone joining. All faces laughing, all tears disappeared. All wounds healing. All separations united. All hatred vanished.

German systematic theologian *Jürgen Moltmann* describes *the world as dance* most beautifully in his *God in Creation* (Moltmann 1993/1985), referring to *African, Indian,* and *Christian traditions*, ancient, patristic, and modern, as a symbol and metaphor for the *ecology of life* in which we all have our own and most particular place:

> "The special thing about this dance metaphor is the link between space and time forged by rhythm. In the rhythmic vibrations and movements of the dance steps, space is measured in terms of time, and time in terms of space. In the movements of the dance, the antithesis is united and the unity divided. Union and disunion alternate and are one in their alternation. In the rhythm of the dance the antitheses are reconciled. So in

> the dancing, pulsating energies of the world, heaven and earth, eternity and time, life and death are one. And the One is again divided into eternity and time, into heaven and earth, into life and death ... In San Marco in Florence Fra Angelico painted the dance of the angels with the redeemed in paradise on the way to the ecstasy of the beatific vision. The well-known Shaker song 'The Lord of the Dance' goes back to these ancient and patristic metaphors about the world as dance, and the Logos as the leader of the dance which moves the world. The eternal perichoresis of the Trinity might also be described as an eternal round danced be the Triune God, a dance out of which the rhythms of created beings who interpenetrate one another correspondingly rise like an echo." (Moltmann 1993/1985, 306–307)

Power, newly conceived, may be like a *human dance*, inviting everyone and every living thing to *join creation* in all its creative melodies.

Pablo Picasso has a beautiful *painting on peace* as a *human dance*, with variously colored figures circling around a center of peace in the shape of a dove. The picture invites everyone to the *human dance*. *Power* then, in this human dance, will not *wound* the other, hurt or destroy. Power then will not break up communities and humanly vulnerable hearts. *Power* then will *heal, create*, and invent a *new world* where people and all living things may *live in peace*, and where the *Spirit of life* as *Wild Bird* will keep "our hearts restless for a time when the deserts are once again fertile, when sacred rivers flow, and the long suffering of vulnerable desert peoples is at an end" (Grey 2003, 211). And when *suffering* is finally *redeemed* and *healed* and *at its end*.

Releasing Power—To the Sound of Music

Power and *powerlessness* have been the guiding thread of this dissertation to its end. In a world turned *postmodern* and *social* (Page 1996, 2000, Grey 2003, Rieger 2007, Taylor 1990, 2011), this dissertation has tried to present a *new vision* for power and powerlessness in community in a postmodern world. The postmodern calls for a *new vocabulary*, new images, new narratives, and a *new vision* in order to *change the world*. Church in the postmodern world owes it to the next generation in *exile* or *on the untamed verge* (Frost 2006, Hirsch and Hirsch 2010, Hirsch and Ferguson 2011, Hirsch and Catchim 2011).

The postmodern has not been interpreted as *ironic*, or *playful*, or endlessly deconstructed. Rather, the postmodern has been seen as the *great invitation* to a celebration of the plural, the different, the ambiguous, and at the same time as the *great temptation* to solve the postmodern dilemma or trilemma with the simple use of *violence* in the *abuse of power* (Poling 1991, 1996, Schmalstieg 1991, Gaillot 1997, 2002). The experience of young teenagers at the age of 14 taking heroin in some local village somewhere in Switzerland in the 1990s has shown how tempting violence remains.

Power can release *other visions*. This dissertation has been an attempt to open up some *new images*, more *communal*, more *healing*, more *border crossing*, more *inclusive*, more *theological* in its invitation to a *dance of healing*. Dancing to the power of healing may be one way to play the music. Theology could become more *musical*. The power in it would suggest that *rhythm and blues*, or *jazz and fusion* may not be so far from *God's* initial *sound of music*.

8

Music

ALL THAT JAZZ

"Because the human race is one, a fundamental anthropological character engenders all kinds of common dimensions in human existence as such, but always analogous in their concreteness. Thus one must immediately ask, whose subjectivity is being analyzed, from what standpoint, toward what end? The social constitution of the individual and the social construction of the interpretation of reality by each one put all essays at universal assertion in the parentheses of particularity. But in the end, this does not destroy the unity of the human race (Christianity, creation), nor the value of attempts to find a formal universal structure of knowing (Lonergan), nor a common drive toward transcendence (Augustine, Blondel, Rahner), nor the ability to establish within historical life anthropological constants (Nussbaum, Schillebeeckx). These efforts help establish the bonds of human communication. But they are not to be confused on the level of specific content with a totalizing human story that supercedes pluralism." (Haight 2001, 240–241)

"A theological metaphor of a static and unitary Word cannot incorporate the voices of God that echo in the lives of diverse beings and the earth on which they live. The written text, and its successor, electronic data storage, will contribute to voicing God in the world to the extent that those who generate such texts understand their voices to be but one expression of revelation. In the midst of the day-to-day lives of multiple communities and individuals, and especially in their relationships with one another, God is voiced through struggle and celebration, self-defense and education, spirited worship and birthing a baby, writing poetry and planting maize. As these many voices of justice—echoes of God—come into increasing dialogue with each other, possibilities are enhanced for the coming of the kin-dom, now and forever." (Wetherilt 1994, 149)

"Teaching theology is not about conveying the right way of doing theology. Studying theology is not about getting to know the theological method. On the contrary, the more we know about theology, the more we come to appreciate its many forms and colors . . . There are many forms of theology. Theology is taught and written, danced and sung, sculpted and painted, even dreamed and cried. Think of Karl Barth's famous theological dream—the dream that he was to examine Mozart in dogmatics; think of the use of dreams in discernment processes or the newly discovered importance of dreams in religious communities. Or consider the beauty of the ability to cry . . . Theology can be done with gestures: embracing, kneeling, blessing . . . Movies, novels, buildings, paintings show implicit theologies . . . Local theological expressions may be found in sculpture and drama . . . Even silence might be an adequate way of doing theology . . . When we take a look at the theological activities, we find a number of related activities: teaching and preaching, counseling and planning, writing and discussing, studying and exchanging. The desk, the lectern, and the discussion table are part of the whole project of doing theology, as are the conference hall, the counseling room, the living room, the dining room, and even the shade of a tree. Thinking of diverse examples of doing theology broadens our view." (Sedmak 2002, 11–13)

New Themes, New Tunes, New Chords

Theology Jazzy

The purpose of this work has been *creative rumbling*. Writing theology in a new way and a *new key* may be promising for the future. Especially, since theology has had a strong tendency to repeat itself in endless ways. The skillful art of wild and intuitive *improvisation* is certainly not the most familiar mode theology has come to us across its many centuries. Most of it has stayed *classical*, in music and in style. Theology has a liking for the classical, the structural, the unitary, the architectural, the composed, be it *baroque* or *Gothic*, *Romantic* or *modern*. As we all know, classical music is beautiful. But it is not the only style in the world to play. "A theological metaphor of a static and unitary Word cannot incorporate the voices of God that echo in the lives of diverse beings and the earth on which they live" (Wetherilt 1994, 149).

Fundamental theology could be a place in the encyclopedic landscape of the many and various theological disciplines where new things, new themes, new tunes, and new chords can be tried out, experimented with, improvised, and newly arranged. Like a *jam-session* in a jazz club, theology could be more funky, free-style, and jazzy. There is no reason to believe that God only likes classical. *Bach, Mozart, Beethoven, Brahms, Chopin*, even *Arnold Schönberg* may resonate beautifully in heaven's classical auditorium, and yet *Ella Fitzgerald, Miles Davis, John McLaughlin, Bill Evans, Chuck Corea*, or *Keith Jarrett* sound just as incredible and beautiful in heaven's open space. There is no need to become particular. God may like many and various styles. Even if the sound of music unites us in a common play, there are more melodies and tunes, rhythms and chords than the human heart may hear.

To listen to a *symphony* of *thoughtfully composed architecture*, highly structured thematic tones, and intricately interdependent and interrelating choruses may be mind-boggling, and touching or overwhelming each listening human heart. It helps to bind hearts together in a common moment of formal universal structures of knowing (*Lonergan*), or a common drive toward transcendence (*Augustine, Blondel, Rahner*) of the human race. And yet: "These efforts help establish the bonds of human communication. But they are not to be confused on the level of specific content with a totalizing human story that supersedes pluralism" (Haight 2001, 240–241). Pluralism is with us to stay, both in music and in other prosaic or artistic human ways.

This is most true for *theology—systematic, fundamental*, and *dogmatic*—in heaven's open place. If God ever follows and gets the gist of it in what we say and write, compose and develop, put to paper and store on hard disc, he or she may enjoy a variety of theologies in place. Both narrative and argumentative, both structural and chaotic, both systematic and mosaic, both linear and cyclical, both classical and jazzy, both dissecting and assembling, both analytical and synthetic, both prosaic and poetic, both separating and unifying, both nomadic and architectural. There is no need to believe that God is boring and only likes one style. So, what makes us think that if God likes variety, theology could not take and enjoy it as well? "There are many forms of theology. Theology is taught and written, danced and sung, sculpted and painted, even dreamed and cried" (Sedmak 2002, 11). This *variety* is for us to portray.

Fundamental theology is dealing with *method, style, content*, and *basics* of theology. Foundational questions are being asked. Fundamental issues are being debated. The question of method and style is a foundational one. Depending on one's choices, the architectural composition of theology turns out differently. Some will build a *Medieval* or *modern cathedral* with the most elaborate and complex structures of definitional thought and conceptual reflection, skillfully crafting and chiseling every concept, terminology, definition, and philosophy, juxtaposing and analyzing, synthesizing and summarizing most complex intellectual worlds. Theology becomes a *symphony*, with orchestras and pianos playing *Rachmaninoff*, or *George Gershwin*, with every tune and note carefully placed, intensely thought through, and systemically phrased.

Others may play it more *popular*, building a *tavern* or a *theater*, a *jazz club* or a *musical hall* for the common folk. With easier arrangements and architecture, more conducive and inviting to the popular soul. They prefer jazz, blues, soul, folk, rock, pop, hip-hop, techno, playing DJ all along. They rap over and recompose existing notes. They prefer simple tunes, subtle compositions and designs, playing easily digestible chords. The systematic and complex turns into narrative, the conceptually intricate turns visual, the elaborately composed turns into mosaic, the prosaic becomes poetic, the philosophical colloquial, the definitional pictorial, the abstract actual and practical. Both deserve our admiration, the Medieval or modern cathedral and the postmodern tavern or musical hall where people of all walks of life find their own most common and deepest sense in life.

Theology—systematic, fundamental, and *dogmatic—*could be more like this, playing *jazz* or acting as heaven's DJ cutting and sampling *techno* or *rap*. "In contrast to this austere aesthetic of rigid unity and devotional worship, rap's cutting and sampling offers the pluralistic pleasures of deconstructive and reconstructive art—the thrilling beauty of dismembering (and rapping over) old works to create new ones, dismantling the prepackaged and wearily familiar into something stimulatingly different that often achieves a complex, fragile unity of its own." (Shusterman 1997, 140). *Rapping* over theoretical and theological tones could be the new postmodern way to recollect the old with the new for an ever newer artistic way.

The Community of the Weak

Theology could become *rap* or *jazz* once in a while. *Jazz* has a way to combine the artistic, the elaborate, and *the resisting postmodern* and subversively *free*. In a modern world that keeps people down and under, the emotions of jazz may sometimes be the only place where the *Spirit of life* is breaking out to touch the free. "The emotions that surface in the blues and in jazz celebrate a life that is suppressed and mutilated by modernity, and jazz has as much claim to be considered a medium of resistance as does the art of the high priests of modernism" (Witkin 2003, 179, on leadership jazz De Pree 1992, on theology and Christian ethics as jazz Pederson 2001, Wells 2004, Welch 1999, 2005, McClintock Fulkerson 2005, Perkinson 2005, Gelinas 2009). Even though most modern and postmodern—like premodern—theology still plays *classical*, there could be new ways envisioned to make theology more *jazzy*. Jazz could become a metaphor for a new kind of *theology—systematic, fundamental*, and *dogmatic*.

Jazz as Metaphor

African American black liberation theologian and neo-pragmatist philosopher of religion *Cornel West* (West 1982–2010, Yancy 2001, West and Glaude 2004, see Musser and Price 1996, 505–512, Cowan 2003, West 2010), formerly at *Harvard University*, now at *Princeton University*, describes the conceptual *metaphor* of *jazz* in almost postmodern terms, referring to *Malcolm X's* performances to listening audiences, with jazz being a powerful symbol for *black cultural hybridity* that opens up new ways of feeling and thinking, speaking and writing, reflecting and acting in this world, both culturally, politically, socially, and theologically. Jazz becomes a metaphor for a *way of being* in this world (on jazz as a metaphor Cowan 2003, 25–29 and Cornel West's autobiography West 2010):

> "Furthermore, the cultural hybrid character of black life leads us to highlight a metaphor alien to Malcolm X's perspective—yet consonant with his performances to audiences—namely, the metaphor of jazz. I use the term 'jazz' here not so much as a term for a musical art form, as for a mode of being in the world, an improvisational mode of protean, fluid, and flexible dispositions toward reality suspicious of 'either/or' viewpoints, dogmatic pronouncements, or supremacist ideologies. To be a jazz freedom fighter is the attempt to galvanize and energize world-weary people into forms of organization with accountable leadership that promote critical exchange and broad reflection. The interplay of individuality and unity is not one of uniformity and

unanimity imposed from above but rather of conflict among diverse groupings that reach a dynamic consensus subject to questioning and criticism. As with a soloist in a jazz quartet, quintet or band, individuality is promoted in order to sustain and increase the *creative* tension with the group—a tension that yields higher levels of performance to achieve the aim of the collective project." (West 1994, 150–151, West 2010)

Jazz is a poetic image for a new way of thinking and acting in this world. It could become a new image for doing *theology* as well, *improvisational, fluid*, and *protean* in style. It tries to overcome traditional and academic 'either/or' categories and common ways of argumentative and dissecting thinking. It is *narrative*, the way any standards and melodies in jazz become a newly told and reinvented story that needs to be developed, expanded, enlarged, and resumed as common improvisation goes on.

It is *inclusively combining*, letting music be a *communicative event* where different players play and interplay with each other sympathetically or competitively. In the end, it is a big *dialogue*, making the world of music become consent. With no need for structural uniformity or cultural unanimity, but with a *cross-cultural creativity* that overcomes borders and boundaries in hybrid events.

In jazz there is no more Jew, nor Gentile, man or woman, free or slave (Galatians 3:28). Jazz is a kind of *critical democracy* (West 1994, 145, West 2005) with *border-crossing* tastes for black and white, male or female. "This kind of critical and democratic sensibility flies in the face of any policing of borders and boundaries of 'blackness', 'maleness', femaleness', or whiteness' (West 1994, 151).

Jazz is *hybrid*, in that it shares the story of *black culture, black religion,* and *black music* in general: a "*cultural hybrid character in which the complex mixture of African, European, and Amerindian elements are constitutive of something that is new and black in the modern world*" (West 1994, 144–145). *Theology* becoming more *jazzy* will also become more *hybrid*, mixing and messing up the common theological and everyday world.

At the same time, the musical traditions of the *blues* and *jazz* are also deeply *humanist*, sensitive to all of human emotion. The sensitivity for *pain and hurt* is part of it. In a comfort-oriented society negating pain and hurt it is a constant challenge and calling to remain sensitive to those living in hurtful moments. The musical tradition of the *blues* keeps this social memory going. In itself it is a *subversive task* for theology and social theory to remember pain and hurt.

The Community of the Weak

As North American biographer *Rosemary Cowan* (Cowan 2003, on Cornel West also Musser and Price 1996, 505–512, Yancy 2001, and West 2010) from *California State University, Stanislaus* describes it in her critical monograph on *Cornel West*, who "ascribes particular importance to the subversive and oppositional resources found within blues-music and the blues-based music of jazz" (Cowan 2003, 27, also Gelinas 2009).

> "West wants to inject a blues sensibility based on a sense of the tragic into American discourse; this entails facing up to the American past, in the form of subversive remembrance rather than sentimental nostalgia. Evil must be named and unmasked if it is to be overcome, and so West's response to the tragic is to *wrestle* with evil rather than simply accept it as the destiny of the way things are . . . Like the earlier spirituals, the blues captures the cry of the oppressed; it recognizes human possibility and human frailty and thus has a tragic base that rejects sentimentality. The blues is written out of pain and keeps details of one's painful experiences alive, yet attempts to transcend the pain; it expresses the agony of life as well as the possibility of overcoming evil through endurance." (Cowan 2003, 26–27)

Telling Its Individual Story

As *Cornel West* puts it in his Afro-American revolutionary theology of liberation *Prophesy Deliverance!* (West 1982), underlining the humanist tradition of *blues, jazz, spirituals*, and *gospel*:

> "The best example of the Afro-American humanist tradition is its music. The rich pathos of sorrow and joy which are simultaneously present in spirituals, the exuberant exhortations and divine praises of the gospels, the soaring lament and lyrical tragicomedy of the blues, and the improvisational character of jazz affirm Afro-American humanity. These distinct art forms, which stem from the deeply entrenched oral and musical traditions of African culture and evolve out of the Afro-American experience, express what it is like to be human under black skin in America. Afro-American musicians are Afro-American humanists *par excellence*. They relish their musical heritage and search for ways to develop it. This search proceeds without their having to prove to others that this heritage is worth considering, or that it is superior to any other. Rather, the Afro-American musical heritage develops and flourishes by using both its fertile

roots and its elements from other musical traditions—from the first religious hymns and work songs through Scott Joplin, Bessie Smith, Louie Armstrong, Mahalia Jackson, Ella Fitzgerald, Duke Ellington, Coleman Hawkins, Lester Young, Billie Holiday, Charlie Parker, Dizzy Gillespie, Ulysses Kay, Miles Davis, Ornette Coleman, John Coltrane, and contemporary black music ... The heritage remains vibrant, with innovation and originality ensuring continual growth. Indeed, it has become one of the definite elements in American culture." (West 1982, 85–86)

Theology could learn from all these jazzy-thinking musicians as well. *Fundamental theology*, as developed in this present work, could become more *improvisational* and vibrant, the way *jazz* makes you move your feet and hips and start to dance. Theology could become, like in this present attempt at writing *theology—systematic, fundamental,* and *dogmatic*—in a *new creative style*, a kind of *musical dialogue* and *literary story* telling classical standards in new and unheard-off ways. Theology then would become more *narrative*, less argumentative, less systematic, less dogmatic, less structural, but more *impromptu* and more content. It would be less arguing, systematizing, contradicting, debating, rebutting. It would be more colluding, connecting, combining, unifying, reconciling, and home-bringing, without forcing things into uniformity or conformity. It may even be less academic, and yet more wisdom-like in making theology move out into the street or on the dance floor, *telling or dancing its individual story*.

As *Rosemary Cowan* (Cowan 2003) summarizes this type of a *jazz-like thinking* in her monograph on *Cornel West*, with descriptions that apply just as much to a new way of *doing theology* as proposed and developed in this present theological work, telling its own and most personal story:

> "Jazz celebrates individual invention, resiliency, agency, spontaneity, reinterpretation, and a capacity to make the music in the pressure of the moment. It is many-voiced and is a frame through which multiple expressions can be projected. Jazz relies on individual assertion and improvisation, on creative unity and group coordination, and so while it tells an individual story, it arrives at an overall coherence; in fact, full-throated individuality of expression *enhances* the collectivity." (Cowan 2003, 28)

The Community of the Weak

Playing Blues in the Tragic

At the same time, *theology—systematic, fundamental*, and *dogmatic*—may need more sensitivity to human *hurt* and *pain*. Theology out of pain, out of human scarring and emotional or physical wounds, has a way of being more authentic and touching, the way the *blues* touches human souls and hearts wherever it is being played.

As *Cornel West* puts it, referring to the black musical tradition and the blues of people like *Louis Armstrong, Duke Ellington, Charlie Parker, Bettie Smith, Ella Fitzgerald, Mahalia Jackson*, or *Billie Holiday*, this "rich tradition of black music is not only an artistic response to the psychic wounds and social scars of a despised people; more importantly, it enacts in dramatic forms the creativity, dignity, grace and elegance of African-Americans..." (West 1993b, 25).

The black musical tradition, in its *popular culture* style, keeps people *alive*, in the midst of hurt and pain, keeps bodies moving and vibrant, while dancing and loving. "I'm talking about people who help keep me alive ... when we talk about popular culture we're talking about its materiality at the level of producing and sustaining human bodies. Or at least at times convincing that body not to end its vitality and vibrancy, not to kill oneself. That's in part what culture does; it convinces you not to kill yourself, at least for a while" (West 1993a, 98–99).

Theology, like *black music*, may be nothing more than a violent opposition to the *tragic* in life, opposing the absurdity of human pain and hurt, mostly inflicted by people on people. Theology could turn to be *blues theology* of *blues people* in search of love und justice in compassion. "My own work and life have always unfolded under the dark shadows of death, dread and despair in search of love, dialogue and democracy. I am first and foremost a blues man in the world of ideas—a jazz man in the life of the mind—committed to keeping alive the flickering candles of intellectual humility, personal compassion and social hope while living in our barbaric century" (West 1999, xv). This battle with the tragic is the groundwork on which to build. Above it are human hope and social fantasy, trying to change the world. Music is one way to do it. Theology may be another way.

As *Cornel West* puts it, describing himself as a *Chekhovian Christian* in a tragicomic world, in the tradition of Russian writer *Anton Chekhov*, portraying the battle with the tragic in comic-hopeful and musical ways:

> "My Chekhovian Christian viewpoint is idiosyncratic and iconoclastic. My sense of the absurdity and incongruity of the world is closer to the Gnosticism of Valentinus, Luria or Monoimos than that of historic religious orthodoxies—yet, unlike them, it retains a deep sense of history. My intellectual lineage goes more through Schopenhauer, Tolstoy, Rilke, Melville, Lorca, Kafka, Celan, Beckett, Soyinka, O'Neill, Kazantzakis, Morrison, and, above all, Chekhov (all great dramatic poets of death, courage and compassion) than most theologians and philosophers. And, I should add, it reaches its highest expression in music—as in Brahms's *Requiem* and Coltrane's *A Love Supreme*. Music at its best achieves this summit because it is the grand archeology into and transfiguration of our guttural cry, the great human effort to grasp in time (with the most temporal of the arts) our deepest passions and yearnings as prisoners of time. Profound music leads us—beyond language—to the dark roots of our scream and the celestial heights of our silence." (West 1999, *xvii*)

Theology getting in touch with the dark roots of our *scream*, hearing the guttural cry, voicing the deepest passions and yearnings, all this is *blues theology* of *blues people*, getting *jazzy* or *funky* once and a while, even rapping over the world of music, as much as the world of ideas. This present theological work has been an attempt to *play jazz theologically*, with a mixture between *pain* and *hurt*, *hope* and *resistance*, and *faith* (West 1993, 2008, 2010). In good blues and jazz tradition, it has played its standards in emotional new ways, "committed to keeping alive the flickering candles of intellectual humility, personal compassion and social hope while living in our barbaric century. I am primarily a dramatist of philosophical notions and historical narratives that partake of blood-drenched battles on a tear-soaked terrain in which our lives and deaths are at stake" (West 1999, *xv*).

Becoming a *dramatist* of philosophical notions may be a good description for the kind of *fundamental theology* this work has tried to present.

A New Fundamental Theology

Fundamental Theology in a New Key

In the present theological work there has been an attempt at writing *fundamental theology* in a *new key*. New themes, new debates, new references, and new walking partners in the social sciences, cultural studies, ethnography, and art and music theory have contributed to a different feel and style that may not be so familiar in traditional academic circles. And yet, it all finds its common center in a *theology as autobiography*. This too has a look most particular, unusual, and different. And yet, it serves as a guiding thread and a *new theological program* that has been followed as consistently as possible all through the various chapters. Every chapter has been another attempt at improvisational play and interplay between standards and new themes.

Theology—systematic, fundamental, and *dogmatic*—can be written in new ways. This has been an attempt and a serious proposition to do things a little differently. There is no engraved rule that academic writing has to be only one way. There is no general law that says that theology can only come in one shape. There is the common *habitus* of the argumentative, the abstract, the systematic-conceptual, the highly philosophical and definitional, over against the narrative, the concrete, the fluid and pictorial, the colloquial and free-flowing, as opposing categories in play. The proposition of this particular approach to theology as developed in the chapters presented is a *new melody*, a *new style*, and a *new fundamental theology*.

Inasmuch as *fundamental theology* deals with questions of method, style, criteria, basics, and interdisciplinary border-crossings to lay the *groundwork* for *doing theology*, both *thematically* (O'Collins 1981, Schüssler Fiorenza 1984, O'Donovan and Sanks 1989, Dulles 1992, Fries 1996, Haight 2001, Wagner 1996, Schmidt-Leukel 1999, Waldenfels 2000, Werbick 2000, Verweyen 2000, Sedmak 2003, Mueller 2007) and *socially* (Metz 1980, Lamb 1982, Peukert 1984, Lane 1984, Tracy 1987, Wetherilt 1994, Arens 1995a, Sedmak 2002, Rieger 2007, Taylor 1990, 2011), the present attempt has been a timid proposition of a new kind of fundamental theology. Method, style, basics, and interdisciplinary border-crossings have been at the center of attention in various previous chapters, next to thematic discussions on some of the most recent challenges facing *systematic, fundamental,* and *dogmatic theology* in a *postmodern and ecological new age*. The guiding thread and reference of *power* and *powerlessness* as fundamental themes in *North American systematic theologies* has served as a *focusing prism* to look at and highlight the fundamental issues in beginning theology in this postmodern time.

Fundamental theology both in *European* and *North American contexts* has mostly stayed within *Roman Catholic domains*, due to a longer and more established historical tradition justifying the separation of an introducing discipline that others put into prolegomena to systematic theology. However, both in *North America*, and most recently in *German-speaking Europe*, fundamental theology has become a *Protestant issue* as well, even if it is not always given this particular and explicit name (for new models of German fundamental theologies in the Protestant tradition Joest 1988, Moltmann 1988, Marquardt 1988, Ott 1994, Bayer 1994, Hollenweger 2000, Petzoldt 2004, Honecker 2005).

In *North America, fundamental theology* has not been taken up in *Protestant circles* in name, but has been developed under other thematic names (Lints 1993a, Wetherilt 1994, Ogden 1996, Cochrane 1999, McClendon 2000, Grenz and Franke 2001, Vanhoozer 2002, McGrath 2004, Rieger 2007, Taylor 1990, 2011). The present attempt at a new kind of fundamental theology in the postmodern time could be considered a first attempt at a truly *Protestant fundamental theology* with an *international, intercultural, inter-confessional, inter-contextual,* and *interdisciplinary intent*.

Fundamental Theology in Narrative Style

Theology can be written out of *drama*. Then, it takes another style. "I am primarily a dramatist of philosophical notions and historical narratives that partake of blood-drenched battles on a tear-soaked terrain in which our lives and deaths are at stake" (West 1999, *xv*). *Dramatists* of philosophical notions make highly abstract concepts of fundamental theology down-to-earth and *dramatic*, concrete, and filled with daily and *narrative examples*.

The *concrete example* of a community facing young teenagers at the age of 14 taking heroin in some local village somewhere in Switzerland in the 1990s has been the guiding thread pulling everything together. Conceptual notions, philosophical themes, sociological images, cultural debates, and theological loci in doctrine and fundamentals have been purposefully combined in a *narrative style* trying to weave together a textual pattern that creates a whole new picture or texture. Theology becomes more mosaic, and yet it has more color, more contrast, and more concrete taste.

In this, it shares in style and content in what North American feminist theologian *Rebecca S. Chopp* calls in her *Saving Work* (Chopp 1995a), a contribution to revisions and new models in contemporary theological education in *North America*, the *practice of narrativity* (Chopp 1995b). Theological education in postmodern times needs a different style of theology, as encouraged by feminists after the *shaking of all foundations*. *Narrativity* as a personal, communal, and theological concept means "the active agency of writing one's own life: the ongoing construction of one's own life in the context of human and planetary relations" (Chopp 1995b, 21). Theology then becomes *communal* and *individual*, *social* and *personal*, empowering people in their particular lives.

Theology as *narrativity* gets *concrete, experiential, contextual, personal, biographical* and *autobiographical*. It helps people become *artists of their own lives* (on philosophy as life art Schmid 1998), with narrators turning into life-telling composers, musicians, sculptors, painters, writers, biographers, as they are playing with words and phrases "composing their lives" (Chopp 1995b, 22, referring to Bateson 1990, on theology as creative life art and jazz Pederson 2001, Perkinson 2005, Gelinas 2009). Old meanings and symbols are being re-written, with old and new images and concepts mixed and reconstructed in creative new ways. "The traditional narratives, the rules and roles, the pleasures and pains, no longer fit contemporary cultural and political reality. The act of creating oneself in the midst of social and interpersonal relations requires new meanings, symbols, characters, images, and plots" (Chopp 1995b, 22).

Fundamental theology as written and developed in this present proposal defends the *option* both in *method* and in *style* that "theology, at least since Augustine, has been attuned to narrative as a kind of Christian activity. The Christian belief in baptism and the resultant responsibility that one has to live in grace is envisioned as a type of narrativity. From the medieval confessional to the pietist class meeting, the reflective awareness and narrative direction of the believer's life is emphasized" (Chopp 1995b, 33).

To write *fundamental theology* in a predominantly *narrative style*, has a long tradition, though marginalized in common academic circles. Most often the argumentative and systematic, the paraphrasing and juxtaposing of concepts and positions, schools and authors is emphasized. The ensuing textual result most often is conflictual, opposing, contradicting, and contra-posing variously *separated* worlds of ideas. The present work has tried to do the opposite. It has tried to *narratively bring together* lone strangers, turned-off enemies, and lost or forgotten souls meandering helplessly and sometimes highly unconnected in philosophical, theological, and sociological space.

The present work has tried to do theology *ecologically* by looking at what life has provided us with concepts, notions, ideas, and stories that make up our *postmodern theological habitat*. It has tried not to *exclude* or *oppose* anything, but rather to include and invite all living things. This approach thinks and writes more *inclusively*, combining and connecting, adding and expanding, bringing together and gathering what life and theology in all their bio-diversity have to tell. It therefore becomes more *narrative*, telling about what life and theology may be all about. A *fundamental theology* like this tries to create *wide open spaces* in which people can be and live. It may be like an open playground inviting fantasy, with enough sand for everyone to build unbelievable and creative dreams.

A Jazzy Fundamental Theology

As such, the present proposal and theological work is more a *jazzy fundamental theology* than anything else. It plays theology in various new keys and chords, tunes and melodies that may be most relevant for a future fundamental theology as well. The *choice of method* already can be grounds for open discussion, rebuttal, or admiration, depending on one's likes and dislikes in academic circles. The general intent of this work has been to write theology in a *newly creative way*, basically writing theology in *jazzy tunes* while pursuing "the ongoing activity of writing our lives" (Chopp 1995a, 34).

Theology in this way becomes *jazzy, improvisational, imaginative*, and *communicatively free*, "involved in the creation of physical spaces, in the way we relate to one another, in how we choose what is studied, and what is read" (Chopp 1995b, 43). A *fundamental theology of education* (for a postmodern and critical theology of education Hodgson 1999) creating spaces for people to live and play will encourage *improvisation, narrative, poetry*, and *play* (for narrative, improvisation, poetry, and play Kane 2004, in Christian ethics Wells 2004). Theology will then be played like in a lively *jam-session* in a local jazz club, with jazz musicians playing their standards in ever new and imaginative ways. "The theme of imagination includes the conditions of possibility for subjects to place themselves in new roles, stories, and patterns. The development of the imagination is necessary if subjects are to write their lives in new ways" (Chopp 1995b, 43). Jazz musicians write their lives every time they intone a new melody, telling a new story on old and familiar themes. They create new *narratives* every time, as well as a *communicative space* to live and play (Pederson 2001, Perkinson 2005, Gelinas 2009).

The Community of the Weak

North American systematic theologian *Peter C. Hodgson* describes this *jazzy space* in his fundamental theology of education *God's Wisdom* (Hodgson 1999, on postmodern critical pedagogy Shor 1992, Giroux 1982-2011 McLaren 1995, 2005, Denzin 2003, Ayers 2004b, hooks 2004, Hof 2009), the *community of freedom* living a *transformative postmodern pedagogy* in following *Jesus*:

> "*Christian* theology of education takes its orientation on the paradigmatic figure of Jesus of Nazareth, who incarnates God's Wisdom in his teaching and practice, his way of living and dying. The central image of his teaching was that of a new and radically open community of freedom in which God's Wisdom prevails as opposed to the foolishness and weakness of human wisdom. This divine Wisdom overthrows the dominant logic of the world (hierarchical, authoritarian, juridical, dualistic) in favor of a new logic, that of grace, love, and freedom, of uncoerced and fully reciprocal communicative practices." (Hodgson 1999, 140)

Writing our lives in a more *jazzy way* has been at the center of this new way of writing a fundamental theology in dialogue with other voices. *Jazz* as a *metaphor* (West 1993a, 98-99, 1993b, 25, 1994, 144-145, 150-151, 1999, xv, xvii, Cowan 2003, 25-29, Gelinas 2009) invites theology to become more *jazzy*, living an *improvisational community of freedom* in its own writing. Dualistic and hierarchical logics may be replaced by a *new logic* of *narrative weaving*, the way artists and jazz musicians compose a new material or musical story. In this, this work has only been a first and most modest initial attempt, as a starting tune to be followed and improvised on as ground-laying standards for others to develop who like its beginning and tone-setting rhythms and chords, beats and melodies, its jazzy-bluesy "polyphonic, rhythmic effects and antiphonal vocal techniques, of kinetic orality and affective physicality . . . " (West 1988, 177).

Like with *jazz* and *blues* : some like it, and some don't. But it's still good music.

North America and Europe

This *fundamental theology* has been trying to be *border-crossing*, a fundamental task for the discipline, both interculturally and internationally, in getting *North America* and *Europe* a little bit closer in virtual distance. The *cross-fertilization* of North American and European systematic theologies is still a task ahead of us, with the hope that some day some new type of *theological world music* may start to resonate and fill the atmospheric space, mostly still silent at the present time, especially in Europe. The general tendency to do theology still and only within continental bounds needs some questioning as to whether this is nowadays an adequate and responsible academic work and thinking in a *global world*.

The proposal of this present work is that theology will profit from a *globalization* in perspective in *systematic, fundamental*, and *dogmatic theology* as well, as some other theological disciplines like *practical* and *pastoral theology* seem to have discovered (on globalization in practical/pastoral theology in Europe Nipkow, Rössler und Schweizer 1991, in North America Wilson, Mofokeng, Poerwowidagdo, Evans, Evans 1996, Heitink 1999, Chinula and Clinebell 2009, Clinebell and McKeever 2011).

Theological debates in *North America* have hardly been noticed on the *European continent*, except for discussions mainly in French-speaking areas on *postmodernity* (Gisel et Evrard 1996, Gisel 1995), *postliberalism* (Lindbeck 1984, 1994, Boss, Emery et Gisel 2004, Eckerstorfer 2001), *process theology* (Gounelle 1981, 2000, Faber 2000, 2003), and *Stanley Hauerwas' communitarian ethics* (Müller 1999, 50–52, Troisième Cycle en éthique de Suisse romande, May 4–5, 2006 with Stanley Hauerwas at the University of Lausanne). Apart from the global impact of *feminist theologies* (Parmentier 1998, Gerber 1987, Jakobs 1993, Volkwein 1999, Kalsky 2000, Leicht, Rakel, Rieger-Goertz 2003), some gaze at *black, womanist* (Blaser 1972, Chenu 1977, 1984, Gibellini 1995, 371–402, Wollrad 1999, Kalsky 2000), and *American Hispanic theologies* (Fornet-Betancourt 2002), most other recent theological currents and revisions in North American systematic theology have remained almost invisible to the European eye. With the notable exception of the work of *Klauspeter Blaser* at the *University of Lausanne* (on North American theology Blaser 1995a, on contemporary and postmodern theology Blaser 1995b, 1997, 1999).

The attempt presented in this dissertation to have *North American systematic theology* set the agenda for dialogue for a future *intercontinental, intercultural, inter-contextual, inter-confessional*, and *interdisciplinary fundamental theology on a global scale* will have to be judged by others as successful or at least promising if it contributes to more *intercontinental theological dialogue* in the future to come. North American systematic theology does offer fascinating and challenging *new themes* for a systematic, fundamental, and dogmatic theology in this postmodern age.

The Community of the Weak

The *fundamental theology* exposed in these present pages attempts to turn around the general forgetfulness in *intercultural dialogue* between *Europe* and *North America*. With the conviction that North America has to offer a great deal to basic questions in contemporary *theology*—be it *systematic, fundamental,* and *dogmatic*. The reader of these pages will have to judge for himself or herself, if theology in *North America*, as some still seem to believe, really does not exist.

New Themes

This *fundamental theology* has been developed around several *new themes* that seem to set the agenda for theology in the future to come. Instead of starting theology and its groundwork with classical topoi like method, sources, structure, theology and human knowing, theology and experience, theology and the sciences, religion, the critique of religion, religious language, revelation, tradition, Jesus, the church, theory and praxis, this present work has tried to find other paths and other open windows to get the by-standing stranger and peeking voyeur interested in the probably never ending human endeavor of *academic theology*.

In this, the present work in all its chapters has tried to be *creative*, following North American and Roman Catholic fundamental theologian *Avery Dulles*' suggestion in his *The Craft of Theology* (Dulles 1992) to develop theology in such a way as "to reunite the creative with the cognitive, the beautiful with the true" (Dulles 1992, 15). Whether this has been successful, others will have to judge. Yet the intent has been to make theology more *artistic* and *personal*. The common reluctance of authors in theology to hide personality and aesthetic taste, individual liking and musical preference behind a mountain of academic speech is not shared by the present author writing these pages. Especially, since it is my conviction that theology would gain in relevance and accessibility, in power and persuasion if it became more *personal,* laying open your deepest soul.

The present work is one attempt to prove this claim in actual form. Theology could become more of a kind of artistic and passionately involving work for *artisans for a new humanity* (on theology—fundamental, systematic, ethical, and pastoral—as artisanship for a new humanity Sedmak 2002) where people sense what *torments* and *touches* an author. Both beauty and misery, compassion and loneliness, outcry and serenity should be felt in pages written. Theology would gain in *life-changing power,* if you could tell what makes an author laugh and cry. In this sense, these pages have also tried to constantly remain close and true to my personal *experience*, even where abstract concepts and theoretical rumblings have been played. After all, the fame and claim of academic theologians lies in their endless and famous or infamous capabilities to forever *play* (for a philosophy of play Kane 2004) with every single word humans say.

And yet, life, in all its seriousness and happiness, is not just constantly playing. There may be moments, like when you have to put to rest, quite unexpectedly, a 14-year-old teenager that had just died, that will not seem like *play*.

Then, sentences like these of religious epistemologist and Roman Catholic fundamental theologian *Clemens Sedmak* (Sedmak 2002) take on a whole new and *real* taste: "We do theology as wounded people, sometimes because of our wounds. No one can go through life without getting wounded. No human soul leaves life without wounds, humiliations, and experiences of injustice and rejection. We all carry wounds" (Sedmak 2002, 9). Out of these wounds in life some of the best theologies have been written.

A Theology of Wounded Healers

This is why this *fundamental theology*, as proposed in these pages, has repeatedly kept alive the memories and images of *pain* and *experience*. Pain and experience draw a picture and put down on paper or a canvass those moments of deep memory that you may never forget, engraved and inscribed in your soul for as long as you live. Some experiences never go away. Some stay with you as long as you have and hear your breath, like a recurring melody that does not recede in the silence of space. Having to lead the funeral service of a 14-year-old confirmation teenager of your own class that just died of an overdose of heroin is a moment you will never forget. And on top of it, losing your job because of solidarity with teenagers like these, repeated years later again, because of this one and only unforgiven story, is an experience that never fades away. At the same time, hurtful moments like these could be a *new source* of true theology, as painful and hurtful as they may be.

As *Clemens Sedmak* (Sedmak 2002) puts it, addressing the *wounded healers* (in pastoral theology Nouwen 1994, in Asian American Han-theology Park 2004, also Hernandez 2006) as being some of the best theologians in life:

The Community of the Weak

> "We do theology not because of hope in a magically liberated sorrow-free and happy life. We do theology because we hope that wounds may be the source of strength . . . We do theology because of wounded people who have touched us. Jesus surrendered his power and became vulnerable, defenseless and wounded . . . We do theology because people suffer. Doing theology is a way to attend to the wounds of our time. There are the wounds of ignorance and stupidity, the wounds of broken promises and unrealized dreams, the wounds of innocent suffering and of guilt, the wounds of open questions and burning concerns. We all do theology as wounded healers, as people in need of healing and comfort, and as people who can share the life-giving strength of our wounds. . . . We could not do theology without this trust in the power of our wounds and the wounds of our fellow creatures. This is the power of the poor in history, the power of the children, the power of the powerless." (Sedmak 2002, 9–10)

Finding the *power* of the *hurting* and *powerless*, this has been the recurring melody in these pages of *fundamental theology* in a new age. The new age, in all its pain and happiness, is *cultural, postmodern, ecological,* and *power-broken*. Power has a way to *break* people and whole communities, dreams and whole life-plans, visions and whole soul-yearnings, solidarities and whole communal feelings. *Power* can be *violent*, haphazardly destroying the meek, the dreamers, the sensitive, the hopeful, the beautiful. Power has a way to raze and stomp everything to the ground, regardless of victims and broken souls, screaming emotions and outcrying bodies. And yet, *power* can also be meek, soft, tender, gentle, *life-saving*. To find out the determinative *difference*, this may be theology's most honorable calling.

Culture, Postmodernism, Ecology, and Power

This *fundamental theology* in a new key has tried to play and do theology across the new themes of *culture, postmodernism, ecology,* and *power*. Guiding thread and recurring reference has been the upsetting experience of 14-year-old teenagers taking heroin in some local village somewhere in Switzerland in the 1990s, with a local pastor—the present author—trying to minister theologically to this situation. These experiences have made my theology a lot more *experiential*. Even some of the most cognitive concepts have become reframing companions guiding my understanding of what happened, what I did, and what I believe in. Theology ever since has taken a concrete and experiential turn. Theological concepts get *thickly inscribed* in what one goes through.

Behind it all lies the burning question for *theology* and its methodology—*systematic, fundamental, dogmatic, ethical, pastoral*—North American feminist theologian *Ann Kirkus Wetherilt* poses right at the beginning of her beautiful book *That They May Be Many* (Wetherilt 1994): "How might we develop a methodology through which the multiple voices of diverse cultures—and diverse people *within* cultures—could engage in theo-ethical dialogue with one another in the service of new possibilities for living together in the increasingly fragile world which we share?" (Wetherilt 1994, 7–8). A multiple world having to live together is no easy task. Understandings are fragile, broken. The modern has turned postmodern, with no more story or stories that hold. And yet, people and whole communities still have to live together. To find the possibilities, to find a new language, to bring together the dispersed and broken in new voices heard, this may be the most challenging task for a new kind of *fundamental theology*.

The present world is most *cultural*, and in this *divided*, in that people realize they don't understand each other anymore, not just in music, taste, or clothing. Even teenagers at the age of 14 and adults do not share the same cultural world anymore. The world has become modern, or even *postmodern*, with no more common story that we share. The common and familiar is breaking and broken, with whole communities realizing that they don't share the same world anymore. In a *kairos* like this, theology is called for to find a *new language* that *heals* the world. Healing the nations, healing the broken, healing the separate and divided, where communities fall, this could be a new task for theology to face. The healing won't happen with a *power* as commonly understood. Rather, a whole new concept of *ecological power* will have to be developed. Ecology being that *oikos* or *koinonia* of all living things that have to learn how to live together in nonhurting ways. The wounded may show the way, having been wounded on life's brutal ways. And yet, the wounded may know what *communities of the weak* can change, in that *power* is redefined in new and creative ways.

Fundamental theology in the twenty-first century is confronted with the issues of *culture, postmodernism, ecology*, and *power*. Within the parameters of these four themes a contemporary fundamental theology will have to be developed in the future. The more surprising it is, therefore, that textbooks on fundamental theology in *Europe* do not touch on these issues in an extensive or explicit way. Some refer to the global challenge of *context* and *culture* (in Roman Catholic fundamental theology Waldenfels 2000), with side-excursions on *popular culture* (Müller 1998), others face the *kairos* of a *postmodern world* simply in passing (Müller 1998, Werbick 2000). Exceptional are approaches to issue of *ecological thinking* (on the ecology of life and life worlds Waldenfels 2000) and the head-on *confrontation* with the theological and socio-political question of *power* and *powerlessness* in fundamental theology (in political, practical/pastoral fundamental theologies Peukert 1984, Schmalstieg 1991, Arens 1992, 1995a, Heitink 1999, Sölle 2001, Metz 1980, 1992/1977, 2006, Moltmann 1999, 2000, 2010).

The difference in comparison with *North America* is striking. In *North American systematic theology*, both *fundamental* and *dogmatic*, the basic theological issues of *culture, postmodernism, ecology*, and *power* have taken up an enormous and all-determining space in literature and discussion. The issue of *culture/pop culture* is omnipresent (Smith 1994b, Tanner 1997, Hopkins and Davaney 1996, Brown, Davaney, and Tanner 2001, Dyrness 1997, 2001, Cobb 2005, Taylor 2008, Taylor 1990, 2011). The *postmodern* challenges all theological systems, *Roman Catholic, Protestant*, and *Evangelical* (Tracy 1987, Hodgson 1994, Chopp and Taylor 1994, Tilley 1995, Grenz 1996, Lakeland 1997, Grenz and Franke 2001, Vanhoozer 2003, Riggs 2003, Penner 2005, Ward 2005, Smith 2006, 2008, Dyrness, Kärkkäinen, Martinez, and Chan 2008). The *ecological turn* in theological thinking has taken over *Young Evangelicals* and *liberals, Roman Catholics* and *Protestants* (Scharper 1998, McDaniel 1989–2000, Bouma-Prediger 1995, 2001, Fox 1983–2002, Gottlieb 2006). Issues of *power* and *powerlessness*, exclusion and embrace, oppression and survival, extinction and enlivening those who are being kept out from life and vision, have tormented and deeply concerned North America in most *fundamental* theological debates (Lamb 1982, Lane 1984, Tracy 1987, Jennings 1992, Hodgson 1994, Chopp and Taylor 1994, Volf 1996, Batstone, Mendieta, Lorentzen, and Hopkins 1997, Keller 2005, Rieger 1998–2011, Taylor 1990, 2011).

A *fundamental theology* of the future will have to face these four common terms. In a globalized world where *cultures* collide, where narratives of the *modern and postmodern* fall, where communities and whole *ecological* networks of life break, and where people and other living things still suffer under the abuse of *power*, an *intercultural, international, interconfessional, inter-contextual*, and *interdisciplinary fundamental theology* will have to think about some *healing word* (Granberg-Michaelson 1991,

Sawyer 2003, Park 2004, Marsh 2005) healing the nations, mending the wounded, bringing together the estranged, and reconciling the world.

A dialog between *North America* and *Europe* could be most interesting here in finding new words and new themes, creating new and inter-continental *coalitions* for the sake of a new world. A new world in desperate need of some *empowering word* that gives its reasons for its hope and vision (1 Peter 3:15), as *fundamental theology* is determined to do.

The present theological work has attempted to take visitors on a *first tour* to this new and wide open field of unlimited theological vision in *North America*, always with a view to keep *Europe* in mind. The visited landscape is immense and over-powering, as *North America* is in general for anyone visiting for the first time. And yet, the invitation stands to join two continents that so far have stayed separate, for the loss of each one. The fascinating challenge to get *North America* and *Europe* in *systematic theology* into more extended dialog still lies ahead of us. And yet, first attempts can be made to get the two uneven lovers or visitors of *theology—systematic, fundamental,* and *dogmatic*—into the same and common bed.

Communities of the Weak

Then would *new communities* be built, both *theologically* and in *communal reality* (for visions of community in dissident spirituality changing the world, peace-making, communal, socially activist, community-involved, caring for justice and peace, the koinonia of the earth, rooted in discipleship-faith theology Peck 1987, Jackson 1987, Banks 1994, Harmer 1998, Dudley 2002, Sawyer 2003, Marsh 2005, Augsburger 2006). *New communities* built both academically and globally, of all those who share this promising vision of a new kind of *power* in the midst of daily and global *powerlessness*, in the *community of the weak*. Then, even teenagers at the age of 14 taking heroin in some local village somewhere in Switzerland in the 1990s could find some hope and reason for a new world. A new world, where no one is excluded, but where everyone is *embraced* (Volf 1996) in this *sacred presence* empowering new visions in a *community of the weak*.

In the poetic words of North American feminist *Ann Kirkus Wetherilt* (Wetherilt 1994), envisioning *new communities* in theology and *communal living*, coalitional, divine, incarnational, and in sacred dialogue, to create a new and more *just* and *sane world* where nobody is hurt (as envisioned, never perfectly, in the Mennonite intentional community Reba Place Fellowship and Church in Evanston north of Chicago, with

The Community of the Weak

its story told in Jackson 1987, having celebrated in August 2007 a 50-year anniversary, and in other marginal and "beloved communities" Sawyer 2003, Kirkpatrick 2001, Marsh 2005):

> "The experiences and expressions of many . . . , experiences and expressions ignored, deplored, or aborted by those manning the bastions of ecclesial and other pseudoholy power, provide glimpses of the divine reality that is beyond Word (or words) and that shines through in the treasured 'sacred texts' that are primary resources for this study. This sacred presence, this incarnation of the holy, must not continue to be silenced through the unwillingness or assumed inability of persons from diverse communities and social locations to dialogue and work in coalition with one another in the day-by-day struggle for a more just and sane world." (Wetherilt 1994, 12)

Bibliography

Abeldt, S., and W. Bauer, editors. 2000. "... was es bedeutet, verletzbarer Mensch zu sein": Erziehungs-wissenschaft im Gespräch mit Theologie, Philosophie und Gesellschaftstheorie. Mainz: Matthias-Grünewald.
Abrams, M. H. 1999. *A Glossary of Literary Terms*. New York: Harcourt Brace.
Achtemeier, P. J., editor. 1985. *Harper's Bible Dictionary*. San Francisco: Harper & Row.
Adam, A. K. M., editor. 2000. *Handbook of Postmodern Biblical Interpretation*. St. Louis: Chalice.
Adams, R. 2003. *Social Work and Empowerment*. Third Edition. New York: Palgrave Macmillan.
Adams, S. 1999. *Jazz: A Crash Course*. New York: Simon & Schuster.
Adams, W. P. 2000. *Die USA im 20. Jahrhundert*. Oldenbourg Grundriss der Geschichte 29. Munich: R. Oldenbourg.
Aguirre, L. P. 1997. *Tout commence par un cri*. Paris: Les Editions Ouvrières.
Ahmed, S. 1998. *Differences that Matter: Feminist Theory and Postmodernism*. New York: Cambridge University Press.
Albanese, C. L. 1998. *America: Religions and Religion*. Third Edition. Belmont: Wadsworth.
Albrecht, G. 1995. *The Character of Our Communities: Toward an Ethic of Liberation for the Church*. Nashville: Abingdon.
Alcoff, L. M. 1996. *Real Knowing: New Versions of the Coherence Theory*. Ithaca: Cornell University Press.
———, and E. Potter, editors. 1993. *Feminist Epistemologies*. New York: Routledge.
Alexander, T., editor. 1987. *John Dewey's Theory of Art, Experience and Nature*. Albany: State University of New York Press.
Alt, J. A. 2002. *Das Abenteuer der Erkenntnis: Eine kleine Geschichte des Wissens*. Munich: C. H. Beck.
Ambler, R. 1990. *Global Theology: The Meaning of Faith in the Present World Crisis*. Philadelphia: Trinity.
Ammicht, Quinn R. 1999. *Körper—Religion—Sexualität: Theologische Reflexionen zur Ethik der Geschlechter*. Mainz: Matthias-Grünewald.
———, and E. Tamez, editors. 2002. "The Body and Religion." *Concilium*. International Journal for Theology 38. London: SCM.
Andermahr, S., T. Lovell, and C. Wolkowitz. 1997. *A Concise Glossary of Feminist Theory*. London: Arnold.
Anderson, B. W., editor. 1984. *Creation in the Old Testament*. Philadelphia: Fortress.
———. 1994. *From Creation to New Creation*. Overtures to Biblical Theology. Minneapolis: Fortress.

Bibliography

———. 1994a. "The Tower of Babel: Unity and Diversity in God's Creation." In *From Creation to New Creation*, 165–78. Overtures to Biblical Theology. Minneapolis: Fortress.

Anderson, W. P., editor. 2000. *A Journey through Christian Theology: With Texts from the First to the Twenty-First Century*. Minneapolis: Fortress.

Anderson, W. T., editor. 1995. *The Truth About The Truth: De-confusing and Reconstructing the Postmodern World*. New York: Jeremy P. Tarcher/Putnam.

———. 1997. *The Future of the Self: Inventing the Postmodern Person*. New York: Jeremy P. Tarcher.

———. 2004. *All Connected Now: Life in the First Global Civilization*. Boulder: Westview.

Angus, I., and S. Jhally, editors. 1989. *Cultural Politics in Contemporary America*. New York: Routledge.

Anzaldua, G. 1987. *Borderlands/La Frontera: The New Mestiza*. San Francisco: Aunt Lute.

Apostolos-Cappadona D., editor. 1998. *Art, Creativity, and the Sacred: An Anthology in Religion and Art*. New York: Continuum.

Appiah, K. A., and H. L. Gates, editors. 1996. *The Dictionary of Global Culture*. New York: Penguin.

Appignanesi, R. and C. Garratt. 1995. *Postmodernism For Beginners*. Cambridge: Icon.

Aquino, M. P. 1993. *Our Cry for Life: Feminist Theology from Latin America*. Maryknoll: Orbis.

Araujo Freire, A. M., and D. Macedo, editors. 1998. *The Paulo Freire Reader*. New York: Continuum.

Arènes, J. 2001. *Dépasser sa violence*. Paris: Les Editions Ouvrières.

Arens, E. 1988. "'Wer kann die grossen Taten des Herrn erzählen?' (Ps 106,2): Die Erzählstruktur christlichen Glaubens in systematischer Perspektive." In *Erzählter Glaube—erzählende Kirche*, edited by R. Zerfass, 13–27. Quaestiones Disputatae 116. Freiburg: Herder.

———. 1992. *Christopraxis: Grundzüge theologischer Handlungstheorie*. Quaestiones Disputatae 139. Freiburg: Herder.

———, editor. 1994. *Gottesrede—Glaubenspraxis: Perspektiven theologischer Handlungstheorie*. Darmstadt: Wissenschaftliche Buchgesellschaft.

———. 1995a. *Christopraxis: A Theology of Action*. Minneapolis: Augsburg Fortress.

———, editor. 1995b. *Anerkennung der Anderen: Eine theologische Grunddimension interkultureller Kommunikation*. Quaestiones Disputatae 156. Freiburg: Herder.

———. 1997. "Interruptions: Critical Theory and Political Theology Between Modernity and Postmodernity." In *Liberation Theologies, Postmodernity, and the Americas*, edited by D. Batstone, E. Mendieta, L. A. Lorentzen, and D. N. Hopkins, 222–42. New York: Routledge.

———. 2000. "Theologie als Wissenschaft. Die Bedeutung des handlungstheoretischen Ansatzes von Helmut Peukert." In *". . . was es bedeutet, verletzbarer Mensch zu sein": Erziehungswissenschaft im Gespräch mit Theologie, Philosophie und Gesellschaftstheorie*, edited by S. Abeldt and W. Bauer, 13–27. Mainz: Matthias-Grünewald.

———. 2003. "Bildung braucht Verständigung: Potenziale und Perspektiven der Universität." In *Geistesgegenwärtig: Zur Zukunft universitärer Bildung*, edited by E. Arens, J. Mittelstrass, H. Peukert, and M. Ries, 63–84. Luzern: Exodus.

———. 2007. *Gottesverständigung: Eine kommunikative Religionstheologie.* Quaestiones Disputatae. Freiburg: Herder.
———, editor. 2010. *Zeit denken: Eschatologie im interdisziplinären Diskurs.* Quaestiones Disputatae. Freiburg: Herder.
———, J. Mittelstrass, H. Peukert, and M. Ries, editors. 2003. *Geistesgegenwärtig: Zur Zukunft universitärer Bildung.* Luzern: Exodus.
Armesto, F. F. 2003. *Ideas That Changed the World.* New York: Dorling Kindersley.
Armstrong, J. H., editor. 1996. *The Coming Evangelical Crisis.* Chicago: Moody.
Arnold, H. L., and H. Detering, editor. 2001. *Grundzüge der Literaturwissenschaft.* Munich: Deutscher Taschenbuch.
Arnold, R., and I. Schüssler. 1998. *Wandel der Lernkulturen: Ideen und Bausteine für ein lebendiges Lernen.* Darmstadt: Wissenschaftliche Buchgesellschaft.
Aronowitz, S. 1988. *Science as Power: Discourse and Ideology in Modern Society.* Minneapolis: University of Minnesota Press.
Aronson, E., T. D. Wilson, and R. M. Akert. 1994. *Social Psychology: The Heart and the Mind.* New York: HarperCollins.
———. 2004. *Sozialpsychologie.* 4., aktualisierte Auflage. Munich: Pearson Studium.
Ashcroft, B., G. Griffiths, and H. Tiffin, editors. 1998. *Key Concepts in Post-Colonial Studies.* New York: Routledge.
Ashley, K., L. Gilmore, and G. Peters, editors. 1994. *Autobiography and Postmodernism.* Amherst: University of Massachusetts Press.
Ashley, J. M. 1998. *Interruptions: Mysticism, Politics, and Theology in the Work of Johann Baptist Metz.* Notre Dame: University of Notre Dame Press.
Askew, T. A., and P. W. Spellman. 1984. *The Churches and the American Experience: Ideals and Institutions.* Grand Rapids: Baker.
Augsburger, D. 2006. *Dissident Discipleship: A Spirituality of Self-Surrender, Love of God, and Love of Neighbor.* Grand Rapids: Brazos.
Axelrod, A., and C. Phillips. 2004. *What Every American Should Know About American History: 200 Events That Shaped the Nation.* Avon: Adams.
Ayers, W. 2001. *To Teach: The Journey of a Teacher.* 2nd ed. New York: Columbia University, Teachers College Press.
———. 2004a. *Teaching the Personal and the Political: Essays on Hope and Justice.* New York: Columbia University, Teachers College Press.
———. 2004b. *Teaching Toward Freedom: Moral Commitment and Ethical Action in the Classroom.* Boston: Beacon.
———, and P. Ford, editors. 1996. *City Kids—City Teachers: Reports from the Front Row.* New York: The New Press.
———, J. A. Hunt, and T. Quinn, editors. 1998. *Teaching for Social Justice. A Democracy and Education Reader.* New York: The New Press.
———, and J. L. Miller, editors. 1998. *A Light in Dark Times: Maxine Greene and the Unfinished Conversation.* New York: Columbia University, Teachers College Press. Bach, A., editor. 1999. *Women in the Hebrew Bible: A Reader.* New York: Routledge.
Bachmann, M. 2002. *Göttliche Allmacht und theologische Vorsicht: Zu Rezeption, Funktion und Konnotationen des biblisch-frühchristlichen Gottesepithetons pantokrator.* Stuttgart: Katholisches Bibelwerk.
Bacik, J. J. 1989. *Contemporary Theologians.* Chicago: Thomas More.

Bibliography

Badham, R. A., editor. 1998. *Introduction to Christian Theology: Contemporary North American Perspectives*. Louisville: Westminster John Knox.

Bahr, H. E. 1992. *Revolte gegen den Todestrieb: Die grossen Glaubensthemen*. Freiburg: Herder.

Bailey, T. A., and D. M. Kennedy, editors. 1994. *The American Spirit: United States History as Seen by Contemporaries*. Eighth Edition. 2 Vols. Lexington: D. C. Heath.

Bailie, G. 1995. *Violence Unveiled: Humanity at the Crossroads*. New York: Crossroad.

Baker, M. D. 1999. *Religious No More: Building Communities of Grace and Freedom*. Downers Grove: InterVarsity.

Baker-Fletcher, K., and G. K. Baker-Fletcher. 1997. *My Sister, My Brother: Womanist and Xodus God-Talk*. Maryknoll: Orbis.

Bal, M., F. Van Dijk Hemmes, and G. Van Ginneken. 1988. *Und Sara lachte... Patriarchat und Widerstand in biblischen Geschichten*. Münster: Morgana Frauenbuchverlag.

Balasuriya, T. 1984. *Planetary Theology*. Maryknoll: Orbis.

Ballard, P., and J. Pritchard. 1996. *Practical Theology in Action: Christian Thinking in the Service of Church and Society*. London: SPCK.

Banawiratma, J. B., and J. Müller. 1995. *Kontextuelle Sozialtheologie: Ein indonesisches Modell*. Freiburg: Herder.

Bandstra, B. L. 2004. *Reading the Old Testament: An Introduction to the Hebrew Bible*. Third Edition. Belmont: Thomson/Wadsworth.

Banks, R. 1994. *Paul's Idea of Community: The Early House Churches in their Cultural Setting*. Rev. ed. Peabody: Hendrickson.

———. 1999. *Reenvisioning Theological Education: Exploring a Missional Alternative to Current Models*. Grand Rapids: Eerdmans.

Barbour, I. G. 2000. *When Science Meets Religion: Enemies, Strangers, or Partners?* San Francisco: HarperSanFrancisco.

Bärenz, R. 2000. *Die Wahrheit der Fische: Neue Situationen brauchen eine neue Pastoral*. Freiburg: Herder.

———. 2000a. "Hermeneutik des Lebens." In *Die Wahrheit der Fische: Neue Situationen brauchen eine neue Pastoral*, 11–37. Freiburg: Herder.

Barker, C. 2000. *Cultural Studies: Theory and Practice*. Thousand Oaks: Sage.

———. 2002. *Making Sense of Cultural Studies: Central Problems and Critical Debates*. Thousand Oaks: Sage.

———. 2004. *The SAGE Dictionary of Cultural Studies*. Thousand Oaks: Sage.

Barnes, B. 1995. *The Elements of Social Theory*. Princeton: Princeton University Press.

Barnes, E. 1995. *The Story of Discipleship: Christ, Humanity, and Church in Narrative Perspective*. Nashville: Abingdon.

Barnes, M. H., editor. 2001. *Theology and the Social Sciences*. College Theology Society Annual Volume 46. Maryknoll: Orbis.

Barr, W. R., editor. 1997. *Constructive Christian Theology in the Worldwide Church*. Grand Rapids: Eerdmans.

Barraclough, G., editor. 2003. *The Christian World: A Social and Cultural History of Christianity*. London: Thames & Hudson.

Barry, P. 2002. *Beginning Theory: An Introduction to Literary and Cultural Theory*. New York: Manchester University Press.

Bartchy, S. S. 1992. "Table Fellowship." In *Dictionary of Jesus and the Gospels*, edited by J. B. Green and S. McKnight, 796–800. Downers Grove: InterVarsity.

———. 2002. "The Historical Jesus and Honor Reversal at the Table." In *The Social Setting of Jesus and the Gospels*, edited by W. Stegemann, B. J. Malina, and G. Theissen, 175–83. Minneapolis: Fortress.
Barth, H. M. 2001. *Dogmatik—Evangelischer Glaube im Kontext der Weltreligionen: Ein Lehrbuch*. Gütersloh: Chr.Kaiser/Gütersloher.
Barton, S. C. 1995. "Historical Criticism and Social-Scientific Perspectives in New Testament Study." In *Hearing the New Testament: Strategies for Interpretation*, edited by J. B. Green, 61–89. Grand Rapids: Eerdmans.
Bass, D. C., editor. 1997. *Practicing our Faith: A Way of Life for a Searching People*. San Francisco: Jossey-Bass.
Bateson, M. C. 1990. *Composing a Life*. New York: Plume.
Batstone, D., E. Mendieta, L. A. Lorentzen, and D. N. Hopkins, editors. 1997. *Liberation Theologies, Postmodernity, and the Americas*. New York: Routledge.
Bauckham, R. 1993. "Moltmann, Jürgen." In *The Blackwell Encyclopedia of Modern Christian Thought*, edited by A. E. McGrath, 385–88. Oxford: Blackwell.
———. 1995. *The Theology of Jürgen Moltmann*. Edinburgh: T. & T. Clark.
———. 1997. "Jürgen Moltmann." In *The Modern Theologians: An Introduction to Christian Theology in the Twentieth Century*, edited by D. F. Ford, 209–224. Oxford: Blackwell.
Baudler, G. 1992. *God and Violence: The Christian Experience of God in Dialogue with Myths and Other Religions*. Springfield: Templegate.
———. 2001. *Ursünde Gewalt: Das Ringen um Gewaltfreiheit*. Düsseldorf: Patmos.
Bauer, J. B., editor. 1985. *Entwürfe der Theologie*. Graz: Styria.
Bauman, Z. 1993. *Postmodern Ethics*. Oxford: Blackwell.
———. 1995. *Life in Fragments: Essays in Postmodern Morality*. Oxford: Blackwell.
Baumann, R. 1989. *"Gottes Gerechtigkeit"—Verheissung und Herausforderung für diese Welt*. Freiburg: Herder.
Bauriedl, T. 1999. *Auch ohne Couch: Psychoanalyse als Beziehungstheorie und ihre Anwendungen*. Stuttgart: Klett-Cotta.
Bayer, O. 1994. *Theologie*. Handbuch Systematischer Theologie. Vol. 1. Gütersloh: Gütersloher.
Becker-Schmidt, R., and G. A. Knapp. 2003. *Feministische Theorien zur Einführung*. 3rd ed. Hamburg: Junius.
Bedford, N. E. 1995. *Jesus Christus und das gekreuzigte Volk: Christologie der Nachfolge und des Martyriums bei Jon Sobrino*. Concordia Reihe Monographien. Volume 15. Aachen: Augustinus.
———. 2006. "Speak 'Friend', and 'Enter': Friendship and Theological Method." In *God's Life in Trinity*, edited by M. Volf and M. Welker, 33–43. Minneapolis: Fortress.
Bedford-Strohm, H. 2001. *Schöpfung*. Ökumenische Studienhefte 12. Bensheimer Hefte 96. Göttingen: Vandenhoeck and Ruprecht.
Behrens, R. 2004. *Postmoderne*. Wissen 3000. Hamburg: Europäische Verlagsanstalt.
Beinert, W. 1990. *Heilender Glaube*. Mainz: Matthias-Grünewald.
———, editor. 1995. *Glaubenszugänge: Lehrbuch der Katholischen Dogmatik*. 3 vols. Paderborn: Ferdinand Schöningh.
———. 2004. *Kann man dem Glauben trauen? Grundlagen theologischer Erkenntnis*. Regensburg: Friedrich Pustet.

Bibliography

Belenky, M. F., B. M. Clinchy, N. R. Goldberger, and J. M. Tarule. 1986. *Women's Ways of Knowing: The Development of Self, Voice, and Mind.* New York: Basic Books.

Bell, D. 1993. *Communitarianism and Its Critics.* Oxford: Oxford University Press.

Bell, R. H. 2002. *Understanding African Philosophy: A Cross-Cultural Approach to Classical and Contemporary Issues.* New York: Routledge.

Bellis, A. O. 1994. *Helpmates, Harlots, Heroes: Women's Stories in the Hebrew Bible.* Louisville: Westminster John Knox.

Bendelow, G., and S. J. Williams, editors. 1998. *Emotions in Social Life: Critical Themes and Contemporary Issues.* New York: Routledge.

Bendit, R., and A. Heimbucher. 1979. *Von Paulo Freire lernen: Ein neuer Ansatz für Pädagogik und Sozialarbeit.* Munich: Juventa.

Benhabib, S. 1986. *Critique, Norm, and Utopia: A Study in the Foundations of Critical Theory.* New York: Columbia University Press.

———. 1987. "The Generalized and the Concrete Other: The Kohlberg-Gilligan Controversy and Feminist Theory." In *Feminism as Critique: Essays on the Politics of Gender in Late-Capitalist Societies,* edited by S. Benhabib and D. Cornell, 77–95. Cambridge: Polity.

———. 1995. *Selbst im Kontext: Kommunikative Ethik im Spannungsfeld von Feminismus, Kommunitarismus und Postmoderne.* Frankfurt: Suhrkamp.

———. 1995a. "Der verallgemeinerte und der konkrete Andere: Die Kohlberg/Gilligan-Kontroverse aus der Sicht der Moraltheorie." In *Selbst im Kontext: Kommunikative Ethik im Spannungsfeld von Feminismus, Kommunitarismus und Postmoderne,* 161–91. Frankfurt: Suhrkamp.

———, and D. Cornell, editors. 1987. *Feminism as Critique: Essays on the Politics of Gender in Late-Capitalist Societies.* Cambridge: Polity.

Benson, P., editor. 1993. *Anthropology and Literature.* Urbana: University of Illinois Press.

Benstock, S., editor. 1988. *The Private Self: Theory and Practice of Women's Autobiographical Writings.* Chapel Hill: University of North Carolina Press.

Benton, T., and I. Craib. 2001. *Philosophy of Social Science: The Philosophical Foundations of Social Thought.* New York: Palgrave.

Berger, A. A. 2003. *The Portable Postmodernist.* Walnut Creek: Altamira.

Berger, K. 1988. *Hermeneutik des Neuen Testaments.* Gütersloh: Gütersloher Verlagshaus Gerd Mohn.

———. 1999. *Hermeneutik des Neuen Testaments.* Tübingen: A. Franke.

Bernasconi, R., editor. 2001. *Race.* Blackwell Readings in Continental Philosophy. Malden: Blackwell.

Berquist, J. L. 1992. *Reclaiming Her Story: The Witness of Women in the Old Testament.* St. Louis: Chalice.

Berry, P., and A. Wernick, editors. 1992. *Shadow of Spirit: Postmodernism and Religion.* New York: Routledge.

Berry, T. 1999. *The Great Work.* New York: Bell Tower.

Berten, I. 1990. *Christ pour les pauvres: Dieu à la marge de l'histoire.* Paris: Cerf.

Bertens, H. 1995. *The Idea of the Postmodern: A History.* New York: Routledge.

———. 2001. *Literary Theory: The Basics.* New York: Routledge.

Berthrong, J. H. 1999. *The Divine Deli: Religious Identity in the North American Cultural Mosaic.* Maryknoll: Orbis.

Best, S. 2003. *A Beginner's Guide to Social Theory.* Thousand Oaks: Sage.

Bibliography

Best, S., and Kellner D. 1991. *Postmodern Theory: Critical Interrogations.* London: Macmillan.

———. 1997. *The Postmodern Turn.* New York: Guilford.

Betz, H. D. 1995. *The Sermon on the Mount: A Commentary of the Sermon on the Mount, including the Sermon on the Plain (Matthew 5:3—7:27 and Luke 6:20–49).* Hermeneia. Minneapolis: Fortress.

Betz O., editor. 1980. *Zugänge zur religiösen Erfahrung.* Düsseldorf: Patmos.

Beumer, J. 1998. *Henri Nouwen: Sein Leben—sein Glaube.* Freiburg: Herder.

Bevans, S. B. 2002. *Models of Contextual Theology.* Rev. and exp. ed. Maryknoll: Orbis.

The Bible and Culture Collective and E. A. Castelli, editors. 1995. *The Postmodern Bible.* New Haven: Yale University Press.

Biehl, P., and F. Johannsen. 2002. *Einführung in die Glaubenslehre: Ein religionspädagogisches Arbeitsbuch.* Neukirchen-Vluyn: Neukirchener.

Biehl, P., and K. Wegenast, editors. 2000. *Religionspädagogik und Kultur: Beiträge zu einer Theorie kulturell vermittelter Praxis in Kirche und Gesellschaft.* Neukirchen-Vluyn: Neukirchener.

Bieling, H. J. 2000. *Dynamiken sozialer Spaltung und Ausgrenzungen—Gesellschaftstheorien und Zeitdiagnosen.* Münster: Westfälisches Dampfboot.

Bierhoff, B. 1993. *Erich Fromm: Analytische Sozialpsychologie und visionäre Gesellschaftskritik.* Opladen: Westdeutscher.

Bierhoff, H. W., and M. J. Herner. 2002. *Begriffswörterbuch Sozialpsychologie.* Stuttgart: W. Kohlhammer.

Bigsby, C., editor. 2006. *The Cambridge Companion to Modern American Culture.* New York: Cambridge University Press.

Birch, B. C. 1991. *Let Justice Roll Down: The Old Testament, Ethics, and Christian Life.* Louisville: Westminster John Knox.

Bird, P. A. 1997. *Missing Persons and Mistaken Identities: Women and Gender in Ancient Israel.* Minneapolis: Fortress.

Biser, E., F. Hahn, and M. Langer, editors. 1999a. *Der Glaube der Christen: Ein ökumenisches Handbuch.* Vol. 1. Munich: Pattloch/Calwer.

———, editors. 1999b. *Der Glaube der Christen: Ein ökumenisches Wörterbuch.* Vol. 2. Munich: Pattloch/Calwer.

Blaser, K. 1972. *Wenn Gott schwarz wäre . . . Das Problem des Rassismus in Theologie und christlicher Praxis.* Zürich: Theologischer Verlag Zürich.

———. 1978. *Gottes Heil in heutiger Wirklichkeit: Überlegungen—Beispiele—Vorschläge.* Frankfurt: Otto Lembeck.

———. 1980. *Le monde de la théologie.* Collectif. Geneva: Labor et Fides.

———. 1983. *La Mission: dialogues et défis.* Geneva: Labor et Fides.

———. 1985. *Esquisse de la Dogmatique.* Lausanne: Université de Lausanne.

———. 1987. *Karl Barth 1886-1968: Combats—Idées—Reprises.* Bern: Peter Lang.

———. 1990a. *Une Eglise, des confessions.* Geneva: Labor et Fides.

———. 1990b. *Le Conflit Nord-Sud en théologie.* Lausanne: Edition du Soc.

———. 1991. *Volksideologie und Volkstheologie: Ökumenische Entwicklungen im Lichte der Barmer Theologischen Erklärung.* Munich: Chr. Kaiser.

———. 1995a. *Les théologies nord-américaines.* Geneva: Labor et Fides.

———. 1995b. *La théologie au XXè siècle: Histoire—Défis—Enjeux.* Lausanne: L'Age d'Homme.

Bibliography

———, editor. 1995c. *La théologie, sa théorie, ses expressions, sa pertinence: un dossier de textes.* Lausanne: Université de Lausanne.

———. 1996. "Variété des théologies postmodernes et crise des 'fondationalismes'" In *La théologie en postmodernité,* edited by P. Gisel and P. Evrard, 191–211. Actes du 3è cycle de théologie systématique des Facultés de Théologie de Suisse romande. Geneva: Labor et Fides, 191-211.

———. 1997. *Dossier dogmatique: Manuel couvrant les principaux lieux de la doctrine chrétienne.* Lausanne: Université de Lausanne.

———. 1999. *Variétés des théologies postmodernes.* Cours donné au semestre d'hiver 1998/1999. Lausanne: Université de Lausanne.

———. 2000. *Signe et instrument: approche protestante de l'Eglise.* Fribourg: Editions Universitaires Fribourg Suisse.

———. 2002. *Thèmes, théories et textes de la Tradition Chrétienne: outils de base pour l'étude de la théologie.* CD-ROM. Lausanne: Université de Lausanne.

———. 2003a. *Le Christianisme social: une approche théologique et historique.* Paris: Van Dieren.

———. 2003b. *Coup de foudre.* Geneva: Labor et Fides.

———. 2004. " La théorisation des pratiques." In *Précis de Théologie Pratique,* edited by G. Routhier G. and M. Viau, 205–19. Théologies Pratiques. Montreal: Novalis/Lumen Vitae.

Blasi, A. J., P.-A. Turcotte, J. Duhaime, editors. 2002. *Handbook of Early Christianity: Social Science Approaches.* Lanham: Rowman & Littlefield.

Bleicher, J. 1990. *Contemporary Hermeneutics: Hermeneutics as Method, Philosophy and Critique.* New York: Routledge.

Bloesch, D. G. 1978. *Essentials of Evangelical Theology: God, Authority, and Salvation.* Vol. 1. San Francisco: Harper & Row.

———. 1979. *Essentials of Evangelical Theology: Life, Ministry, and Hope.* Vol. 2. San Francisco: Harper & Row.

Blondel, M. 1893/1984. *Action: Essay on a Critique of Life and a Science of Practice.* Notre Dame: University of Notre Dame Press.

Blount, B. K. 1995. *Cultural Interpretation: Reorienting New Testament Criticism.* Minneapolis: Augsburg Fortress.

Bochner, A. P., and C. Ellis, editors. 2002. *Ethnographically Speaking: Autoethnography, Literature, and Aesthetics.* Ethnographic Alternatives Books Series. Vol. 9. Walnut Creek: AltaMira.

Boff, C. 1987. *Feet-On-The-Ground Theology: A Brazilian Journey.* Maryknoll: Orbis.

———. 1987a. *Theology and Praxis: Epistemological Foundations.* Maryknoll: Orbis.

Boff, L. 1976. *Kleine Sakramentenlehre.* Düsseldorf: Patmos.

———. 1979. *Liberating Grace.* Maryknoll: Orbis.

———. 1997. *Cry of the Earth, Cry of the Poor.* Maryknoll: Orbis.

———, editor. 1999. *Prinzip Mitgefühl: Texte für eine bessere Zukunft.* Freiburg: Herder.

———. 2001. *The Prayer of Saint Francis: A Message of Peace for the World Today.* Maryknoll: Orbis.

Böhnisch, L. 1996. "Der Soziale Raum und das Sozialräumliche in der Pädagogik." In *Pädagogische Soziologie: Eine Einführung,* 147–76. Munich: Juventa.

Böhnisch, L., and R. Münchmeier. 1987. "'Raumorientierung' als theoretische und konzeptionelle Perspektive." In *Wozu Jugendarbeit? Orientierungen für Ausbildung, Fortbildung und Praxis,* 89–117. Munich: Juventa.

———. 1990. *Pädagogik des Jugendraums: Zur Begründung und Praxis einer sozialräumlichen Jugendpädagogik*. Munich: Juventa.
Bolaffi, G., R. Bracalenti, P. Braham, and S. Gindro, editors. 2003. *Dictionary of Race, Ethnicity, and Culture*. Thousand Oaks: Sage.
Bond, H. K., S. D. Kunin, and F. A. Murphy, editors. 2003. *A Companion to Religious Studies and Theology*. Edinburgh: Edinburgh University Press.
Bondolfi, A., W. Heierle, and D. Mieth, editors. 1983. *Ethos des Alltags: Festgabe für Stephan H. Pfürtner zum 60. Geburtstag*. Zürich: Benziger.
Bonhoeffer, D. 1954. *Life Together*. New York: Harper and Brothers.
———. 1960. *The Cost of Discipleship*. New York: Macmillan.
———. 1992. *Ethik. 1940–1943*. Edited by I. von Tödt, H.E. Tödt, E. Feil, and C. Green. Gütersloh: Chr. Kaiser.
———. 1995. *Ethics. 1940–1943*. Edited by Bethge E. New York: Simon & Schuster.
Borg, M. J. 1998. *Conflict, Holiness, and Politics in the Teachings of Jesus*. Harrisburg, PA: Trinity.
Boss, M., G. Emery, and P. Gisel, editors. 2004. *Postlibéralisme?: la théologie de George Lindbeck et sa réception*. Geneva: Labor et Fides.
Bottero, W. 2005. *Stratification: Social Division and Inequality*. New York: Routledge.
Bottomore, T. 2002. *The Frankfurt School and Its Critics*. New York: Routledge.
Boulding, K. E. 1990. *Three Faces of Power*. Newbury Park: Sage.
Boulton, W. G., T. D. Kennedy, and A. Verhey, editors. 1994. *From Christ to the World: Introductory Readings in Christian Ethics*. Grand Rapids: Eerdmans.
Bouma-Prediger, S. 1995. *The Greening of Theology: The Ecological Models of Rosemary Radford Ruether, Joseph Sittler, and Jürgen Moltmann*. The American Academy of Religion. Atlanta: Scholars.
———. 2001. *For the Beauty of the Earth: A Christian Vision for Creation Care*. Grand Rapids: Baker Academic.
Bounds, E. M. 1997. *Coming Together, Coming Apart: Religion, Community, and Modernity*. New York: Routledge.
Bourdieu, P. 1991. *Language and Symbolic Power*. Edited by John. B. Thompson. Cambridge: Polity.
Bowden, J. 1983. *Edward Schillebeeckx: In Search of the Kingdom of God*. New York: Crossroad.
Boyer, P. S., C. E. Clark, J. F. Kett, N. Salisbury, H. Sitkoff, and N. Woloch. 1996. *The Enduring Vision: A History of the American People*. 3rd Edition. Lexington: D. C. Heath.
Braaten, C. E., and R. W. Jenson, editors. 1984. *Christian Dogmatics*. 2 Vols. Minneapolis: Fortress.
Bracken, J. A., and M. Suchocki, editors. 1997. *Trinity in Process: A Relational Theology of God*. New York: Continuum.
Bradstock, A., and C. Rowland, editors. 2002. *Radical Christian Writings: A Reader*. Malden: Blackwell.
Bradt, K. M. 1997. *Story as a Way of Knowing*. Kansas City: Sheed & Ward.
Brady, I., editor. 1991. *Anthropological Poetics*. Savage: Rowman & Littlefield.
Brah, A. 1996. *Cartographies of Diaspora: Contesting Identities*. New York: Routledge.
Braidotti, R. 1994. *Nomadic Subjects: Embodiment and Sexual Difference in Contemporary Feminist Theory*. New York: Columbia University Press.

Bibliography

Brantlinger, P. 1990. *Crusoe's Footprints: Cultural Studies in Britain and America*. New York: Routledge.
Braun, W. 1995. *Feasting and Social Rhetoric in Luke 14*. Cambridge: Cambridge University Press.
Breidenbach, J., and I. Zukrigl. 1998. *Tanz der Kulturen: Kulturelle Identität in einer globalisierten Welt*. Munich: Antje Kunstmann.
Breidlid, A., F. C. Brogger, Y. T. Gulliksen, and T. Sirevag, editors. 1996. *American Culture: An Anthology of Civilization Texts*. New York: Routledge.
Brenner, A., editor. 1993. *Genesis: The Feminist Companion to the Bible*. Vol. 1. Sheffield: Sheffield Academic.
Brewer, J. D. 2000. *Ethnography*. Buckingham: Open University Press.
Brock, R. N. 1988. *Journeys by Heart: A Christology of Erotic Power*. New York: Crossroad.
———, and R. A. Parker. 2001. *Proverbs of Ashes: Violence, Redemptive Suffering, and the Search for What Saves Us*. Boston: Beacon.
Brockhaus-Redaktion, editor. 1999. *Auf dem Weg zur "Weltkultur": Das zwanzigste Jahrhundert*. Brockhaus—Die Bibliothek. Kunst und Kultur. Vol. 6. Leipzig: F. A. Brockhaus.
Bronfen, E., B. Marius, and T. Steffen, editors. 1997. *Hybride Kulturen: Beiträge zur anglo-amerikanischen Multikulturalismusdebatte*. Tübingen: Stauffenburg.
Brooker, P. 2001. *A Concise Glossary of Cultural Theory*. London: Arnold.
Brooker, W. 1998. *Teach Yourself Cultural Studies*. London: Teach Yourself.
Brooks, A. 1997. *Postfeminisms: Feminism, Cultural Theory, and Cultural Forms*. New York: Routledge.
Brouwer, S. 1993. *Conquest and Capitalism, 1492-1992*. Carlisle: Big Picture.
Brown, A. L. 2000. *On Foucault: A Critical Introduction*. Belmont: Wadsworth.
Brown, D. 1994. *Boundaries of Our Habitations: Tradition and Theological Construction*. Albany: State University of New York Press.
———, S. G. Davaney, and K. Tanner, editors. 2001. *Converging on Culture: Theologians in Dialogue with Cultural Analysis and Criticism*. New York: Oxford University Press.
Brown, R. 1995. *Prejudice: Its Social Psychology*. Cambridge: Blackwell.
Brown R. H. 1977. *A Poetic for Sociology: Toward a Logic of Discovery for the Human Sciences*. New York: Cambridge University Press.
———. 1987. *Society as Text: Essays on Rhetoric, Reason, and Reality*. Chicago: The University of Chicago Press.
———. 1989. *Social Science as Civic Discourse: Essays on the Invention, Legitimation, and Uses of Social Theory*. Chicago: The University of Chicago Press.
———, editor. 1995. *Postmodern Representations: Truth, Power, and Mimesis in the Human Sciences and Public Culture*. Urbana: University of Illinois Press.
Browning, D. S. 1991. *A Fundamental Practical Theology: Descriptive and Strategic Proposals*. Minneapolis: Fortress.
Browning, G., A. Halcli, and F. Webster, editors. 2000. *Understanding Contemporary Society: Theories of the Present*. Thousand Oaks: Sage.
Brueggemann, W. 1976. *Living Toward a Vision: Biblical Reflections on Shalom*. New York: United Church Press.
———. 1978. *The Prophetic Imagination*. Philadelphia: Fortress.

———. 1982. *Genesis*. Interpretation: A Bible Commentary for Teaching and Preaching. Atlanta: John Knox.
———. 1989. *Finally Comes The Poet: Daring Speech for Proclamation*. Minneapolis: Augsburg Fortress.
———. 1991. *Interpretation and Obedience: From Faithful Reading to Faithful Living*. Minneapolis: Augsburg Fortress.
———. 1991a. "The Third World of Evangelical Imagination." In *Interpretation and Obedience: From Faithful Reading to Faithful Living*, 9–27. Minneapolis: Augsburg Fortress.
———. 1991b. "Monopoly and Marginality in Imagination." In *Interpretation and Obedience: From Faithful Reading to Faithful Living*, 184–204. Minneapolis: Augsburg Fortress.
———. 1992. *Old Testament Theology: Essays on Structure, Theme, and Text*. Edited by Patrick D. Miller. Minneapolis: Fortress.
———. 1992a. "A Shape for Old Testament Theology, II: Embrace of Pain." In *Old Testament Theology: Essays on Structure, Theme, and Text*, edited by Patrick D. Miller, 22–44. Minneapolis: Fortress.
———. (1992b). "The Rhetoric of Hurt and Hope: Ethics Odd and Crucial." In *Old Testament Theology: Essays on Structure, Theme, and Text*, edited by Patrick D. Miller, 45–66. Minneapolis: Fortress.
———. 1993. *The Bible and Postmodern Imagination: Texts under Negotiation*. Minneapolis: Augsburg Fortress.
———. 1994. *A Social Reading of the Old Testament: Prophetic Approaches to Israel's Communal Life*. Minneapolis: Augsburg Fortress.
———. 1996. *The Threat of Life: Sermons on Pain, Power, and Weakness*. Edited by C. L. Campbell. Minneapolis: Augsburg Fortress.
———. 1997. *Theology of the Old Testament: Testimony, Dispute, Advocacy*. Minneapolis: Augsburg Fortress.
———. 2001. *Peace*. Understanding Biblical Themes. St. Louis: Chalice.
———. 2001a. *The Prophetic Imagination*. 2nd ed. Minneapolis: Fortress.
———. 2002. *Reverberations of Faith: A Theological Handbook of Old Testament Themes*. Louisville: Westminster John Knox.
Brüsemeister, T. 2000. *Qualitative Forschung: Ein Überblick*. Wiesbaden: Westdeutscher.
Büchele, H. 1996. *Eine Welt oder keine: Sozialethische Grundfragen angesichts einer ausbleibenden Weltordnungspolitik*. Mainz: Matthias-Grünewald.
Buchholz, R. 2001. *Körper—Natur—Geschichte: Materialistische Impulse für eine nachidealistische Theologie*. Darmstadt: Wissenschaftliche Buchgesellschaft.
Buggle, F. 2004. *Denn sie wissen nicht, was sie glauben—Oder warum man redlicherweise nicht mehr Christ sein kann: Eine Streitschrift*. Aschaffenburg: Alibri.
Bühler, P. 2000. *La grâce première : prédestination et providence. Dossier de l'encyclopédie du Protestantisme*. Geneva: Labor et Fides.
Bühlmann, W. 1987. *Weltkirche: Neue Dimensionen—Modell für das Jahr 2001*. Graz: Styria.
Bührig, M. 1999. *Spät habe ich gelernt, gerne Frau zu sein: Eine feministische Autobiographie*. Stuttgart: Kreuz.
Buhle, M. J., P. Buhle, and D. Georgakas, editors. 1990. *Encyclopedia of the American Left*. Urbana: University of Illinois Press.
Buhle, M. J., and H. J. Kaye, editors. 1994. *The American Radical*. New York: Routledge.

Bibliography

Bulman, R. F. 1981. *A Blueprint for Humanity: Paul Tillich's Theology of Culture.* Lewisburg: Bucknell University Press.

Buri, F. 1970. *Gott in Amerika: Amerikanische Theologie seit 1960.* Vol. 1. Bern: Paul Haupt.

———. 1972. *Gott in Amerika: Religion, Theologie und Philosophie seit 1969.* Vol. 2. Bern: Paul Haupt.

Burr, V. 1995. *An Introduction to Social Constructionism.* New York: Routledge.

Burston, D. 1991. *The Legacy of Erich Fromm.* Cambridge: Harvard University Press.

Butin H., editor. 2002. *DuMonts Begriffslexikon zur zeitgenössischen Kunst.* Köln: DuMont Literatur und Kunst.

Callinicos, A. 1999. *Social Theory: A Historical Introduction.* Cambridge: Polity.

Cameron, J. 1992. *The Artist's Way: A Course in Discovering and Recovering your Creative Self.* London: Pan.

———. 1996. *The Vein of Gold: A Journey to Your Creative Heart.* New York: Putnam.

———. 2002. *Walking in this World: Practical Strategies for Creativity.* New York: Putnam.

Campbell, N., and A. Kean. 1997. *American Cultural Studies: An Introduction to American Culture.* New York: Routledge.

Caputo, J. D. 1987. *Radical Hermeneutics: Repetition, Deconstruction, and the Hermeneutical Project.* Bloomington: Indiana University Press.

———, and M. Yount, editors. 1993. *Foucault and the Critique of Institutions.* University Park: The Pennsylvania State University Press.

Cargas, H. J., and B. Lee, editors. 1976. *Religious Experience and Process Theology: The Pastoral Implications of a Major Modern Movement.* New York: Paulist.

Carmody, D. L. 1995. *Christian Feminist Theology: A Constructive Interpretation.* Cambridge: Blackwell.

Carmody, J. 1983. *Ecology and Religion: Toward a New Christian Theology of Nature.* Ramsey: Paulist.

Carson, F. 2001. "Feminism and the Body." In *The Routledge Companion to Feminism and Postfeminism,* edited by S. Gamble, 117–28. New York: Routledge.

Carter, C. E., and C. L. Meyers. 1996. *Community, Identity, and Ideology: Social Science Approaches to the Hebrew Bible.* Winona Lake: Eisenbrauns.

Casalis, G. 1984. *Correct Ideas Don't Fall from the Skies: Elements for an Inductive Theology.* Maryknoll: Orbis.

Case-Winters, A. 1990. *God's Power: Traditional Understandings and Contemporary Challenges.* Louisville: Westminster John Knox.

Castelli, E. A. 1994. "Allegories of Hagar: Reading Galatians 4:21-31 with Postmodern Feminist Eyes." In *The New Literary Criticism and the New Testament,* edited by E. Malbon Struthers, 228–50. Sheffield: Sheffield Academic.

Castells, M. 1996–1999. *The Information Age: Economy, Society, and Culture.* 3 Vols. Oxford: Blackwell.

Castro, E. 1985. *Freedom in Mission—The Perspective of the Kingdom of God: An Ecumenical Inquiry.* Geneva: WCC.

Cauthen, K. 1986. *Systematic Theology: A Modern Protestant Approach.* Lewiston: Mellen.

Cavallaro, D. 2001. *Critical and Cultural Theory: Thematic Variations.* New Brunswick: Athlone.

Cavanaugh, W. T. 1998. *Torture and Eucharist: Theology, Politics, and the Body of Christ.* Malden: Blackwell.

———. 2003. *Theopolitical Imagination.* Edinburgh: T. & T. Clark.

Cenkner, W., editor. 1996. *The Multicultural Church: A New Landscape in U. S. Theologies.* New York: Paulist.

Chambers, I. 1990. *Border Dialogues: Journeys in Postmodernity.* New York: Routledge.

———. 1994. *Migrancy, Culture, Identity.* New York: Routledge.

Chenu, B. 1977. *Dieu est noir: Histoire, religion et théologie des Noirs américains.* Paris: Centurion.

———. 1984. *Le Christ noir américain.* Paris: Desclée de Brouwer.

———. 1987. *Théologies chrétiennes des tiers mondes: Théologies latino-américaine, noire américaine, noire sud-africaine, africaine, asiatique.* Paris: Centurion.

———, and Neusch M. 1995. *Théologiens d'aujourd'hui: Vingt portraits.* Paris: Centurion.

Childs, J. M. 2006. *Ethics in the Community of Praise: Faith, Formation, and Decision.* Minneapolis: Fortress.

Chilton, B. 1996. *Pure Kingdom: Jesus' Vision of God.* Grand Rapids: Eerdmans.

Chinula, D. M., and H. J. Clinebell. 2009. *Building King's Beloved Community: Foundations for Pastoral Care and Counseling with the Oppressed.* Eugene: Wipf & Stock.

Chopp, R. S. 1986. *The Praxis of Suffering: An Interpretation of Liberation and Political Theologies.* Maryknoll: Orbis.

———. 1989. *The Power to Speak: Feminism, Language, God.* New York: Crossroad.

———. 1995a. *Saving Work: Feminist Practices of Theological Education.* Louisville: Westminster John Knox.

———. 1995b. "Shaking the Foundations: The Practice of Narrativity." In *Saving Work: Feminist Practices of Theological Education*, 19–44. Louisville: Westminster John Knox.

———, and M. L. Taylor, editors. 1994. *Reconstructing Christian Theology.* Minneapolis: Augsburg Fortress.

Christian, C. M. 1995. *Black Saga: The African American Experience.* Boston: Houghton Mifflin.

Chryssochoou, X. 2004. *Cultural Diversity: Its Social Psychology.* Malden: Blackwell.

Ciompi, L. 1999. *Die emotionalen Grundlagen des Denkens: Entwurf einer fraktalen Affektlogik.* Göttingen: Vandenhoeck & Ruprecht.

Clapp, R. 1996. *A Peculiar People: The Church as Culture in a Post-Christian Society.* Downers Grove: InterVarsity.

———. 2000. *Border Crossings: Christian Trespasses on Popular Culture and Public Affairs.* Grand Rapids: Brazos.

Clarke, M. E. 1989. *Ariadne's Thread: The Search for New Modes of Thinking.* New York: St. Martin's.

Clements, W. M., and H. J. Clinebell. 1995. *Counseling for Spiritually Empowered Wholeness: A Hope-Centered Approach.* New York: Routledge.

Clifford, J. 1988. *The Predicament of Culture: Twentieth-Century Ethnography, Literature, and Art.* Cambridge: Harvard University Press.

———, and G. L. Marcus, editors. 1986. *Writing Culture: The Poetics and Politics of Ethnography.* Berkeley: University of California Press.

Bibliography

Clinebell, H. J. 1984. *Basic Types of Pastoral Care and Counseling: Resources for the Ministry of Healing and Growth.* Nashville: Abingdon.

———. 1996. *Ecotherapy: Healing Ourselves, Healing the Earth.* New York: Routledge.

———, and B. C. McKeever. 2011. *Basic Types of Pastoral Care and Counseling.* 3rd Edition. Nashville: Abingdon.

Clough, P. T. 1992. *The End(s) of Ethnography: From Realism to Social Criticism.* Newbury Park: Sage.

Coates, J. 1986. *Women, Men, and Language.* New York: Longman.

Cobb, J. B. 1989. "Theologie in den Vereinigten Staaten: Woher und wohin?" *Evangelische Theologie* 49, 200–213.

———. 2002. *Postmodernism and Public Policy: Reframing Religion, Culture, Education, Sexuality, Class, Race, Politics, and the Economy.* Albany: State University of New York Press.

Cobb, K. 2005. *The Blackwell Guide to Theology and Popular Culture.* Blackwell Guides in Theology. Malden: Blackwell.

Cochrane, J. R. 1999. *Circles of Dignity: Community Wisdom and Theological Reflection.* Minneapolis: Augsburg Fortress.

Code, L. 1991. *What Can She Know? Feminist Theory and the Construction of Knowledge.* Ithaca: Cornell University Press.

———. 1998. "Epistemology: Voice and Voicelessness: A Modest Proposal?" In *Philosophy in a Feminist Voice: Critiques and Reconstructions,* edited by J. A. Kourany, 204–30. Princeton: Princeton University Press.

Coffey, A. 1999. *The Ethnographic Self: Fieldwork and the Representation of Identity.* Thousand Oaks: Sage.

Cohen, S. 2001. *States of Denial: Knowing about Atrocities and Suffering.* Cambridge: Polity.

Cohn-Sherbok, L. 1998. *Who's Who in Christianity.* New York: Routledge.

Colbert, D., editor. 1997. *Eyewitness to America: 500 Years of American History in the Words of Those Who Saw It Happen.* New York: Vintage.

Coleman, R. J. 1972/1980. *Issues of Theological Conflict: Evangelicals and Liberals.* Grand Rapids: Eerdmans.

Coll, R. A. 1994. *Christianity & Feminism in Conversation.* Mystic: Twenty-Third.

Collet, G. 2002. *". . . bis an die Grenzen der Erde": Grundfragen heutiger Missionswissenschaft.* Freiburg: Herder.

Collier, J. L. 1995. *Jazz: The American Theme Song.* New York: Oxford University Press.

———. 1997. *Jazz: The American Saga.* New York: Holt.

Collins, M., and M. A. Price. 2003. *The Story of Christianity: 2000 Years of Faith.* New York: DK.

Collins, P. H. 1990. *Black Feminist Thought: Knowledge, Consciousness, and the Politics of Empowerment.* New York: Routledge.

Comaroff, J., and J. Comaroff. 1992. *Ethnography and Historical Imagination.* Boulder: Westview, 1992.

Comblin, J. 1988. *Cry of the Oppressed, Cry of Jesus: Meditations on Scripture and Contemporary Struggle.* Maryknoll: Orbis.

———. 2004. *People of God.* Maryknoll: Orbis.

Cone, J. H. 1969. *Black Theology and Black Power.* New York: Seabury.

———. 1970. *A Black Theology of Liberation.* Philadelphia: Lippincott.

———. 1990/1970. *A Black Theology of Liberation.* Twentieth Anniversary Edition. Maryknoll: Orbis.
———. 1991. *Martin & Malcolm & America: A Dream or a Nightmare.* Maryknoll: Orbis.
———. 1991/1972. *The Spirituals and the Blues: An Interpretation.* Maryknoll: Orbis.
———. 1997/1975. *God of the Oppressed.* Rev. ed. Maryknoll: Orbis.
Connor, S., editor. 2004. *The Cambridge Companion to Postmodernism.* New York: Cambridge University Press.
Conyers, A. J. 1988. *God, Hope, and History: Jürgen Moltmann and the Christian Concept of History.* Macon: Mercer University Press.
Cooey, P. M. 1994. *Religious Imagination and the Body: A Feminist Analysis.* New York: Oxford University Press.
———, S. A. Farmer, and M. E. Ross, editors. 1987. *Embodied Love: Sensuality and Relationship as Feminist Values.* San Francisco: Harper & Row.
Cooke, M. 1997. *The Chronicle of Jazz.* New York: Abbeville.
Cooper, D. E. 2003. *World Philosophies: An Historical Introduction.* 2nd edition. Malden: Blackwell.
Corley, K. E. 1993. *Private Women, Public Meals: Social Conflict in the Synoptic Tradition.* Peabody: Hendrickson.
Cormie, L. 1978. "The Hermeneutical Privilege of the Oppressed." *Catholic Theological Society of American Proceedings* 33, 155-181.
Cortina, M., and M. Maccoby, editors. 1996. *A Prophetic Analyst: Erich Fromm's Contribution to Psychoanalysis.* London: Jason Aronson.
Cory, C. A., and D. T. Landry, editors. 2000. *The Christian Theological Tradition.* Upper Saddle River: Prentice-Hall.
Coste, R. 1997. *Théologie de la paix.* Cogitatio Fidei 203. Paris: Cerf.
———. 2000. *Les dimensions sociales de la foi: Pour une théologie sociale.* Cogitatio Fidei 217. Paris: Cerf.
———. 2002. *Les fondements théologiques de l'Evangile Social.* Cogitatio Fidei 226. Paris: Cerf.
Countryman, L. W. 1988. *Dirt, Greed, and Sex: Sexual Ethics in the New Testament and their Implications for Today.* Minneapolis: Fortress.
Cousins, E. H. 1994. *Christ of the 21st Century.* New York: Continuum.
Couture, P. D., and R. J. Hunter, editors. 1995. *Pastoral Care and Social Conflict: Essays in Honor of Charles V. Gerkin.* Nashville: Abingdon.
Cowan, R. 2003. *Cornel West: The Politics of Redemption.* Cambridge: Polity.
———. 2003a. "The Multicontextual Public Intellectual." In *Cornel West: The Politics of Redemption,* 102–26. Cambridge: Polity.
Cox, H. 1965. *The Secular City: Secularization and Urbanization in Theological Perspective.* New York: Macmillan.
———. 1969. *The Feast of Fools: A Theological Essay on Festivity and Fantasy.* Cambridge: Harvard University Press.
Craig, G., and M. Mayo, editors. 1995. *Community Empowerment.* London: Zed.
Crelinsten, R. D., and A. P. Schmid, editor. 1994. *The Politics of Pain: Torturers and Their Masters.* Boulder: Westview.
Critchley, S., and P. Dews, editors. 1996. *Deconstructive Subjectivities.* Albany: State University of New York Press.

Bibliography

Crites, S. 1989. "The Narrative Quality of Experience." In *Why Narrative? Readings in Narrative Theology,* edited by S. Hauerwas and G. L. Jones, 65–88. Grand Rapids: Eerdmans,

Croatto, S. 1987. *Biblical Hermeneutics: Toward a Theory of Reading as the Production of Meaning.* Maryknoll: Orbis.

Crosby, M. H. 1981. *Spirituality of the Beatitudes: Matthew's Challenge for First World Christians.* Maryknoll: Orbis.

Crossan, J. D. 1991. *The Historical Jesus: The Life of a Mediterranean Jewish Peasant.* San Francisco: HarperCollins.

———. 1994. *Jesus: A Revolutionary Biography.* San Francisco: HarperCollins.

———, and J. L. Reed. 2002. *Excavating Jesus: Beneath the Stones, Beneath the Texts.* San Francisco: Harper SanFrancisco.

Crowther, J., and K. Kavanagh, editors. 1999. *Oxford Guide to British and American Culture.* New York: Oxford University Press.

Cruikshank, B. 1999. *The Will to Empower: Democratic Citizens and Other Subjects.* Ithaca: Cornell University Press.

Csikszentmihalyi, M. 1990. *Flow: The Psychology of Optimal Experience.* New York: HarperCollins.

———. 1993. *The Evolving Self: A Psychology for the Third Millennium.* New York: HarperCollins.

———. 1996. *Creativity: Flow and the Psychology of Discovery and Invention.* New York: HarperCollins.

Csordas, T. J., editor. 1994. *Embodiment and Experience: The Existential Ground of Culture and Self.* Cambridge: Cambridge University Press.

Culpepper, R. A. 1995. "The Gospel of Luke: Introduction, Commentary, and Reflections." In *The New Interpreter's Bible: Luke, John,* edited by L. E. Keck, 1–490. Nashville: Abingdon.

Cunningham, D. S. 2002. *Reading is Believing: The Christian Faith through Literature and Film.* Grand Rapids: Brazos.

Currie, M. 1998. *Postmodern Narrative Theory.* New York: St. Martin's.

Dabney, D. L. 2000. "Moltmann, Jürgen." In *The Oxford Companion to Christian Thought,* edited by A. Hastings, A. Mason, and H. Pyper, 444–45. Oxford: Oxford University Press.

Daly, M. 1973. *Beyond God the Father: Towards a Philosophy of Women's Liberation.* Boston: Beacon.

Dantine, W. 1976. *Hoffen–Handeln–Leiden: Christliche Lebensperspektiven.* Göttingen: Vandenhoeck & Ruprecht.

Dassmann, E. 1993. *Augustinus: Heiliger und Kirchenlehrer.* Stuttgart: Kohlhammer.

Davaney, S. G. 2000. *Pragmatic Historicism: A Theology for the Twenty-First Century.* Albany: The State University of New York Press.

Davey, M. 2002. *Mastering Theology.* Palgrave Master Series. New York: Palgrave.

Dawn, M. J. 2001. *Powers, Weakness, and the Tabernacling of God.* Grand Rapids: Eerdmans.

Day, P. L., editor. 1989. *Gender and Difference in Ancient Israel.* Minneapolis: Fortress.

De Botton, A. 2002. *The Art of Travel.* London: Penguin.

De Gruchy, J. W., editor. 1986. *Cry Justice! Prayers, Meditations, and Readings from South Africa.* Preface by Bishop Desmond Tutu. Cape Town: Lux Verbi.

―――, editor. 1991. *Dietrich Bonhoeffer: Witness to Jesus Christ.* The Making of Modern Theology: Nineteenth- and Twentieth-Century Texts. Minneapolis: Fortress.

―――. 1999. *The Cambridge Companion to Dietrich Bonhoeffer.* Cambridge: Cambridge University Press.

De La Torre, M. A. 2002. *Reading the Bible from the Margins.* Maryknoll: Orbis.

―――, editor. 2004. *Handbook of US. Theologies of Liberation.* St. Louis: Chalice.

―――, and E. D. Aponte. 2001. *Introducing Latino/a Theologies.* Maryknoll: Orbis.

De Pree, M. 1992. *Leadership Jazz.* New York: Dell.

Dean, W. 2004. *American Spiritual Culture: And the Invention of Jazz, Football, and the Movies.* New York: Continuum.

Dear, J. 1994. *The God of Peace: Toward a Theology of Nonviolence.* Maryknoll: Orbis.

―――. 2000. *Jesus the Rebel: Bearer of God's Peace and Justice.* Franklin: Sheed & Ward.

Degenhardt, H. J. 1965. *Lukas—Evangelist der Armen: Besitz und Besitzverzicht in den lukanischen Schriften.* Stuttgart: Katholisches Bibelwerk.

Deinet, U. 1999. *Sozialräumliche Jugendarbeit: Eine praxisbezogene Anleitung zur Konzeptentwicklung in der Offenen Kinder- und Jugendarbeit.* Opladen: Leske + Budrich.

Delacampagne, C. 2004. *Die Geschichte der Sklaverei.* Düsseldorf: Patmos/Artemis & Winkler.

Delaney, C. 2004. *Investigating Culture: An Experiential Introduction to Anthropology.* Malden: Blackwell.

Delanty, G. 2003. *Community.* New York: Routledge.

Della Porta, D., and M. Diani 1999. *Social Movements: An Introduction.* Oxford: Blackwell.

Denzin, N. K. 1989. *Interpretive Biography.* Newbury Park: Sage.

―――. 1996. "The Epistemological Crisis in the Human Disciplines: Letting the Old Do the Work of the New." In *Ethnography and Human Development: Context and Meaning in Social Inquiry,* edited by R. Jessor, A. Colby, and R. A. Shweder, 127–51. Chicago: University of Chicago Press.

―――. 1997a. *Interpretive Ethnography: Ethnographic Practices for the 21st Century.* Thousand Oaks: Sage.

―――. 1997b. "Standpoint Epistemologies." In *Interpretive Ethnography: Ethnographic Practices for the 21st Century,* 53–89. Thousand Oaks: Sage.

―――. 2003. *Performance Ethnography: Critical Pedagogy and the Politics of Culture.* Thousand Oaks: Sage.

―――, and Y. S. Lincoln, editors. 2002. *The Qualitative Inquiry Reader.* Thousand Oaks: Sage.

Deschner, K. 1972. *Abermals krähte der Hahn: Eine Demaskierung des Christentums von den Evangelisten bis zu den Faschisten.* Reinbek: Rowohlt Taschenbuch.

―――. 1988. *Der gefälschte Glaube: Eine kritische Betrachtung kirchlicher Lehren und ihrer historischen Hintergründe.* Munich: Knesebeck & Schuler.

―――. 2002. *Der Moloch: Eine kritische Geschichte der USA.* Überarbeitete Neuausgabe. Munich: Wilhelm Heyne.

―――, and H. Herrmann. 1993. *Der Anti-Katechismus: 200 Gründe gegen die Kirchen und für die Welt.* Munich: Goldmann.

Detweiler, C. 2008. *Into the Dark: Seeing the Sacred in the Top Films of the 21st Century.* Cultural Exegesis. Grand Rapids: Baker Academic.

Bibliography

———, and B. Taylor. 2003. *A Matrix of Meanings: Finding God in Pop Culture.* Engaging Culture. Grand Rapids: Baker Academic.
Deuser H., G. M. Martin, K. Stock, and M. Welker, editors. 1986. *Gottes Zukunft— Zukunft der Welt: Festschrift für Jürgen Moltmann zum 60. Geburtstag.* Munich: Chr. Kaiser.
———, and D. Korsch, editors. 2004. *Systematische Theologie heute: Zur Selbstverständigung einer Disziplin.* Gütersloh: Gütersloher Verlagshaus.
Dewey, J. 1934. *Art as Experience.* New York: Putnam.
Dietrich, W., and C. Link. 1995. *Die dunklen Seiten Gottes: Willkür und Gewalt.* Vol. 1. Neukirchen-Vluyn: Neukirchener.
———. 2000. *Die dunklen Seiten Gottes: Allmacht und Ohnmacht.* Vol. 2. Neukirchen-Vluyn: Neukirchener.
Diezinger, A. et al., editors. 1994. *Erfahrung mit Methode: Wege sozialwissenschaftlicher Frauenforschung.* Freiburg: Kore.
Dillmann, R., and C. Mora Paz. 2000. *Das Lukas-Evangelium: Ein Kommentar für die Praxis.* Stuttgart: Katholisches Bibelwerk.
Dodd, N. 1999. *Social Theory and Modernity.* Cambridge: Polity.
Döring, H. 1992. "Theologie im Medium der Erfahrung." In *In Verantwortung für den Glauben: Beiträge zur Fundamentaltheologie und Ökumenik. Festschrift für Heinrich Fries,* edited by P. Neuner and H. Wagner, 47–65. Freiburg: Herder.
Dorrien, G. 2000. *The Barthian Revolt in Modern Theology: Theology without Weapons.* Louisville: Westminster John Knox.
———. 2006. *The Making of American Liberal Theology: Crisis, Irony, and Postmodernity 1995–2005.* Louisville: Westminster John Knox.
Douglas, T. 1995. *Scapegoats: Transferring Blame.* New York: Routledge.
Dowley, T., editor. 2002. *Introduction to the History of Christianity: First Century to the Present Day—A Worldwide Story.* Minneapolis: Fortress.
Downey, J. K., editor. 1999. *Love's Strategy: The Political Theology of Johann Baptist Metz.* Harrisburg: Trinity.
Doyle, D. M. 1992. *The Church Emerging form Vatican II.* Mystic: Twenty-Third Publications.
———. 2000. *Communion Ecclesiology: Vision and Versions.* Maryknoll: Orbis.
Driver, T. F. 1977. *Patterns of Grace: Human Experience as Word of God.* San Francisco: Harper & Row.
———. 1981. *Christ in a Changing World: Towards an Ethical Christology.* London: SCM.
Dröge, M. 2000. *Kirche in der Vielfalt des Geistes: Die christologische und pneumatologische Begründung der Kirche bei Jürgen Moltmann.* Neukirchen-Vluyn: Neukirchener.
Dube, M. W. 2000. *Postcolonial Feminist Interpretation of the Bible.* St. Louis: Chalice.
DuBow, W. 1992. "The Political Power of the Personal Word: Anais Nin's Diaries in Their 1960's and 1970's Cultural Context." Ph.D. Dissertation, University of North Carolina.
Duchrow, U., and G. Liedke. 1989. *Shalom: Biblical Perspectives on Creation, Justice, and Peace.* Geneva: WCC.
Dudley, C. S. 2002. *Community Ministry: New Challenges, Proven Steps to Faith-Based Initiatives.* Bethesda: Alban Institute.
Duling, D. C. 2003. *The New Testament: History, Literature, and Social Context.* 4th ed. Belmont: Thomson/Wadsworth.

Dulles, A. 1992. *The Craft of Theology: From Symbol to System.* New York: Gill and Macmillan.
Dumais, M. 1995. *Le Sermon sur la Montagne: Etat de la recherche—Interprétation—Bibliographie.* Sainte-Foy, Québec: Letouzey & Ané.
Duncan, R., and J. Goddard. 2003. *Contemporary America.* New York: Palgrave Macmillan.
Dunn, J. D. G., and J. W. Rogerson, editors. 2003. *Eerdmans Commentary on the Bible.* Grand Rapids: Eerdmans.
Duran, J. 1991. *Toward a Feminist Epistemology.* Lanham: Rowman & Littlefield.
———. 1998. *Philosophies of Science/Feminist Theories.* Boulder: Westview.
Durand, A. 1992. *La cause des pauvres: Société, éthique et foi.* Paris: Cerf.
———. 1995. *J'avais faim . . . Une théologie à l'épreuve des pauvres.* Paris: Desclée de Brouwer.
Dussel, E. 1995. *The Invention of the Americas: Eclipse of "the Other" and the Myth of Modernity.* New York: Continuum.
———. 1998. *The Underside of Modernity: Apel, Ricoeur, Rorty, Taylor, and the Philosophy of Liberation.* Amherst: Humanity.
Duxler, M. B. 2002. *Seduction: A Portrait of Anais Nin.* Boulder: Edgework.
Dyrness, W. A. 1997. *The Earth is God's: A Theology of American Culture.* Maryknoll: Orbis.
———. 2001. *Visual Faith: Art, Theology, and Worship in Dialogue.* Engaging Culture. Grand Rapids: Baker Academic.
———, V. M. Kärkkäinen, J. F. Martinez, and S. Chan, editors. 2008, *Global Dictionary of Theology: A Resource for the Worldwide Church.* Downers Grove: IVP Academic.
Eagleton, M., editor. 1996a. *Feminist Literary Theory: A Reader.* Oxford: Blackwell.
———. 1996b. *Working with Feminist Criticism.* Oxford: Blackwell.
Eagleton, T. 1996. *Literary Theory: An Introduction.* Oxford: Blackwell.
Ebach, J. 1998. *Weil das, was ist, nicht alles ist.* Theologische Reden 4. Frankfurt: Gemeinschaftswerk der Evangelischen Publizistik.
———. 1998a. "Wir sind *ein* Volk: Wörter und Namen in 1. Mose 11,1-9." In *Weil das, was ist, nicht alles ist*, 108–30. Theologische Reden 4. Frankfurt: Gemeinschaftswerk der Evangelischen Publizistik.
Eberly, D. A., editor. 1994. *Building a Community of Citizens: Civil Society in the 21st Century.* Lanham: University Press of America.
Ebertz, M. N. 1987. *Das Charisma des Gekreuzigten: Zur Soziologie der Jesusbewegung.* Tübingen: Mohr.
Eckerstorfer, A. 2001. *Kirche in der postmodernen Welt: Der Beitrag George Lindbecks zu einer neuen Verhältnisbestimmung.* Salzburger Theologische Studien. Vol. 16. Innsbruck: Tyrolia.
Edwards, D. 1983. *Human Experience of God.* New York: Paulist.
———. 2004. *Breath of Life: A Theology of the Creator Spirit.* Maryknoll: Orbis.
Edwards, J. 1995. *Language, Society, and Identity.* Oxford: Blackwell.
Ehrman, B. D. 2004. *The New Testament: A Historical Introduction to the Early Christian Writings.* 3rd ed. New York: Oxford University Press.
Eichler, U., and I. Müllner, editor. 1999. *Sexuelle Gewalt gegen Mädchen und Frauen als Thema der feministischen Theologie.* Gütersloh: Kaiser/Gütersloher.
Eickelpasch, R., and C. Rademacher. 2004. *Identität.* Einsichten Soziologische Themen. Bielefeld: Transcript.

Bibliography

Eigenmann, U. 1998. *"Das Reich Gottes und seine Gerechtigkeit für die Erde": Die andere Vision vom Leben.* Luzern: Exodus.

Elias, J. L. 1976. *Conscientization and Deschooling: Freire's and Illich's Proposals for Reshaping Society.* Philadelphia: Westminster.

Elizondo, V. 1988. *The Future is Mestizo: Life Where Cultures Meet.* Bloomington: Meyer-Stone.

Ellingsen, M. 1999a. *Reclaiming Our Roots—An Inclusive Introduction to Church History: The Late First Century to the Eve of the Reformation.* Vol. 1. Harrisburg: Trinity.

———. 1999b. *Reclaiming Our Roots—An Inclusive Introduction to Church History: From Martin Luther to Martin Luther King, Jr.* Vol. 2. Harrisburg: Trinity.

Elliott, J. H. 1981. *A Home for the Homeless: A Sociological Exegesis of 1 Peter, Its Situation and Strategy.* Philadelphia: Fortress.

———. 1995. *Social Scientific Criticism of the New Testament.* London: SPCK.

Ellis, C., and A. P. Bochner, editors. 1996. *Composing Ethnography: Alternative Forms of Qualitative Writing.* Ethnographic Alternatives Series. Vol. 1. Walnut Creek: AltaMira/Sage.

Ellis, C., and M. G. Flaherty, editors. 1992. *Investigating Subjectivity: Research on Lived Experience.* Newbury Park: Sage.

English, F. W., and J. C. Hill. 1994. *Total Quality Education: Transforming Schools Into Learning Places.* Thousand Oaks: Corwin.

Enns, F., editor. 2001. *Dekade zur Überwindung von Gewalt: Impulse.* Frankfurt: Otto Lembeck.

———. 2003. *Friedenskirche in der Ökumene: Mennonitische Wurzeln einer Ethik der Gewaltfreiheit.* Göttingen: Vandenhoeck & Ruprecht.

———, S. Holland, and A. K. Riggs, editors. 2004. *Seeking Cultures of Peace: A Peace Church Conversation.* Scottdale: Herald.

Erickson, M. J. 1998. *Christian Theology.* Grand Rapids: Baker.

Erskine, N. L. 1994. *King Among the Theologians.* Cleveland: Pilgrim.

———. 2005. *From Garvey to Marley: Rastafari Theology.* Gainesville: The University Press of Florida.

Esler, P. F. 1987. "Table-fellowship." In *Community and Gospel in Luke-Acts: The Social and Political Motivations in Lucan Theology,* 71–109. New York: Cambridge University Press.

———. 1994. *The First Christians in their Social Worlds: Social-Scientific Approaches to New Testament Interpretation.* New York: Routledge.

———, editor. 2001. *Early Christian World.* 2 Vols. New York: Routledge.

Espeja, J. 1987. *L'Eglise, mémoire et prophétie.* Paris: Cerf.

Espin, O. O., and M. H. Diaz, editors. 1999. *From the Heart of Our People: Latino/a Explorations in Catholic Systematic Theology.* Maryknoll: Orbis.

Estell, K., editor. 1994. *African America: Portrait of a People.* Detroit: Visible Ink.

Eurich, C. 1993. *Aufruf zu einem neuen Orden: Gemeinsam für die Schöpfung—gegen Ohnmacht und Resignation.* Stuttgart: Kreuz.

Evans, A. F., R. A. Evans, and R. S. Kraybill. 2000a. *Peace Skills: A Manual for Community Mediators.* San Francisco: Jossey Bass.

———. 2000b. *Peace Skills: Leader's Guide.* San Francisco: Jossey Bass.

Evans, C. A. 1990. *Luke.* New International Biblical Commentary. Peabody: Hendrickson.

Evans, J. H. 1992. *We Have Been Believers: An African-American Systematic Theology.* Minneapolis: Augsburg Fortress.
Faber, R. 2000. *Prozesstheologie: Zu ihrer Würdigung und kritischen Erneuerung.* Mainz: Matthias-Grünewald.
———. 2003. *Gott als Poet der Welt: Anliegen und Perspektiven der Prozesstheologie.* Darmstadt: Wissenschaftliche Buchgesellschaft.
Fackre, G. 1984. *The Christian Story: A Narrative Interpretation of Basic Christian Doctrine.* Rev. ed. Grand Rapids: Eerdmans.
———. 1996. *The Christian Story: A Narrative Interpretation of Basic Christian Doctrine.* 3rd ed. Grand Rapids: Eerdmans.
Fant, C. E., Musser D. W., Reddish M. G. 2001. *An Introduction to the Bible.* Rev. ed. Nashville: Abingdon.
Farb, P. and Armelagos G. 1980. *Consuming Passions: The Anthropology of Eating.* Boston: Houghton Mifflin.
Farley, E. 1982. *Ecclesial Reflection: An Anatomy of Theological Method.* Philadelphia: Fortress.
———. 1983. *Theologia: The Fragmentation and Unity of Theological Education.* Philadelphia: Fortress.
———. 1990. *Good and Evil: Interpreting a Human Condition.* Minneapolis: Augsburg Fortress.
———. 1996. *Deep Symbols: Their Postmodern Effacement and Reclamation.* Valley Forge: Trinity.
Farley, W. 1990. *Tragic Vision and Divine Compassion: A Contemporary Theodicy.* Louisville: Westminster John Knox.
———. 1996. *Eros for the Other: Retaining Truth in a Pluralistic World.* University Park: Pennsylvania State University Press.
———. 2005. *The Wounding and Healing of Desire: Weaving Heaven and Earth.* Louisville: Westminster John Knox.
Farmer, W. R., A. LaCocque, and S. McEvenue, editors. 1998. *The International Bible Commentary: A Catholic and Ecumenical Commentary for the Twenty-First Century.* Collegeville: Liturgical.
Faulde, C. 2002. *Wenn frühe Wunden schmerzen: Glaube auf dem Weg zur Traumaheilung.* Mainz: Matthias-Grünewald.
Faulstich, P., and C. Zeuner. 1999. *Erwachsenenbildung: Eine handlungsorientierte Einführung in Theorie, Didaktik und Adressaten.* Munich: Juventa.
Feagin, J. R. 2000. *Racist America: Roots, Current Realities, and Future Reparations.* New York: Routledge.
———, and Vera H. 2001. *Liberation Sociology.* Boulder: Westview.
Featherstone, M. 2007. *Consumer Culture and Postmodernism.* Theory, Culture & Society. 2nd ed. Thousand Oaks: Sage.
———, and Lash S., editors. 1999. *Spaces of Culture: City—Nation—World.* Thousand Oaks: Sage.
Felder, C. H., editor. 1991. *Stony the Road We Trod: African American Biblical Interpretation.* Minneapolis: Fortress.
Ferm, D. W., editor. 1982. *Contemporary American Theologies: A Book of Readings.* New York: Seabury.
———. 1986a. *Third World Liberation Theologies: An Introductory Survey.* Maryknoll: Orbis.

Bibliography

———, editor. 1986b. *Third World Liberation Theologies: A Reader.* Maryknoll: Orbis.
———. 1988. *Profiles in Liberation: 36 Portraits of Third World Theologians.* Mystic: Twenty-Third.
———. 1990. *Contemporary American Theologies: A Critical Survey.* Rev. ed. San Francisco: Harper & Row.
Fernandez, E. S. 1994. *Toward a Theology of Struggle.* Maryknoll: Orbis.
———, and F. F. Segovia, editors. 2001. *A Dream Unfinished: Theological Reflections on America from the Margins.* Maryknoll: Orbis.
Fernsehen, D. R. S., editor. 1989. *Wer hat dich so geschlagen? Widerborstige Meditationen: Sölle—Wallraff—Rinser—Küng.* Zürich: Schweizer.
Ferro, M., editor. 2003. *Le livre noir du colonialisme XVIe—XXIe siècle: de l'extermination à la repentance.* Paris: Robert Laffont.
Fewell, Nolan D. 1998. "Changing the Subject: Retelling the Story of Hagar the Egyptian." In *Genesis: A Feminist Companion to the Bible,* edited by A. Brenner, 182–94. Second Series. Sheffield: Sheffield Academic.
Figueroa, D. 1989. *Paulo Freire zur Einführung.* Hamburg: Junius.
Figueroa Deck, A. 1992. *Frontiers of Hispanic Theologies in the United States.* Maryknoll: Orbis.
Fineberg, J. 2000. *Art Since 1940: Strategies of Being.* 2nd ed. London: Laurence King Publishing.
Finger, T. N. 1985. *Christian Theology: An Eschatological Approach.* Vol. 1. Scottdale: Herald.
———. 1989. *Christian Theology: An Eschatological Approach.* Vol. 2. Scottdale: Herald.
———. 2004. *A Contemporary Anabaptist Theology: Biblical, Historical, Constructive.* Downers Grove: IVP Academic.
Finlayson, G. J. 2005. *Habermas: A Very Short Introduction.* New York: Oxford University Press.
Finzsch, N., J. O. Horton, and L. E. Horton. 1999. *Von Benin nach Baltimore: Die Geschichte der African Americans.* Hamburg: Hamburger Edition.
Firer, Hinze C. 1995. *Comprehending Power in Christian Social Ethics.* The American Academy of Religion. Atlanta: Scholars.
Fischer, H. 2002. *Protestantische Theologie im 20. Jahrhundert.* Stuttgart: Kohlhammer.
Fischer, I. 1994. "'Go and Suffer Oppression' said God's Messenger to Hagar." In *Violence against Women,* edited by E. Schüssler Fiorenza and M. S. Copeland , 75–82. *Concilium.* Maryknoll: Orbis.
———. 1994a. *Die Erzeltern Israels: Feministisch-theologische Studien zu Genesis 12-36.* Berlin und New York: Walter de Gruyter.
———. 1994b. "Trennungserzählungen von Hagar und Ismael." In *Die Erzeltern Israels: Feministisch-theologische Studien zu Genesis 12-36,* 259–337. New York: de Gruyter, .
———. 2000. *Gottesstreiterinnen: Biblische Erzählungen über die Anfänge Israels.* Stuttgart: Kohlhammer.
———. 2000a. "Sara, Hagar und Abraham: Szenen einer Ehe unter der Verheissung." In *Gottesstreiterinnen: Biblische Erzählungen über die Anfänge Israels,* 18–71. Stuttgart: Kohlhammer.
Fischer, G., and P. Riedesser. 1999. *Lehrbuch der Psychotraumatologie.* 2nd ed. Munich: Ernst Reinhardt.

Fischer, K. R. 1983. *The Inner Rainbow: The Imagination in Christian Life*. Ramsey: Paulist.
Fitch, N. R. 1993. *Anais: The Erotic Life of Anais Nin*. Boston: Little, Brown.
Flam, H. 2002. *Soziologie der Emotionen*. Konstanz: UVK Verlagsgesellschaft.
Flax, J. 1990. *Thinking Fragments: Psychoanalysis, Feminism, and Postmodernism in the Contemporary West*. Berkeley: University of California Press.
Flynn, E. 2000. *Foundations of Catholic Theology*. Franklin: Sheed & Ward.
Foner, E. 1998. *The Story of American Freedom*. New York: Norton.
———, editor. 1997. *The New American History*. American Historical Association. Rev. and exp. ed. Philadelphia: Temple University Press.
Ford, D. F., editor. 1989. *The Modern Theologians: An Introduction to Christian Theology in the Twentieth Century*. 2 Vols. Cambridge: Basil Blackwell.
———, editor. 1993. *Theologen der Gegenwart*. Deutsche Ausgabe ediert und übersetzt von Christoph Schwöbel. Paderborn: Ferdinand Schöningh.
———, editor. 1997. *The Modern Theologians: An Introduction to Christian Theology in the Twentieth Century*. 2nd ed. Malden: Blackwell.
———, and R. Muers, editors. 2005. *The Modern Theologians: An Introduction to Christian Theology Since 1918*. 3rd ed. Malden: Blackwell.
Ford, M. 1999. *Wounded Prophet: A Portrait of Henri J. M. Nouwen*. London: Darton, Longman and Todd.
Fornet-Betancourt, R., editor. 2002. *Glaube an der Grenze: Die US-amerikanische Latino-Theologie*. Freiburg: Herder.
Forrester, D. B. 1988. *Theology and Politics*. New York: Basil Blackwell.
———. 2000. *Truthful Action: Explorations in Practical Theology*. Edinburgh: T. & T. Clark.
Foster, H., editor. 1983. *The Anti-Aesthetic: Essays on Postmodern Culture*. Port Townsend: Bay.
Foucault, M. 1980. *Power/Knowledge: Selected Interviews and Other Writings 1972-1977*. Edited by C. Gordon. New York: Harvester Wheatsheaf.
Fox, M. 1983. *Original Blessing: A Primer in Creation Spirituality*. Santa Fe: Bear.
———. 1988. *The Coming of the Cosmic Christ: The Healing of Mother Earth and the Birth of a Global Renaissance*. San Francisco: HarperSanFrancisco.
———. 1990. *A Spirituality Named Compassion*. San Francisco: HarperCollins.
———. 1991. *Creation Spirituality: Liberating Gifts for the Peoples of the Earth*. San Francisco: HarperSanFrancisco.
———. 1995. *Wrestling with the Prophets: Essays on Creation Spirituality and Everyday Life*. San Francisco: HarperSanFrancisco.
———. 1999. *Sins of the Spirit, Blessings of the Flesh: Lessons for Transforming Evil in Soul and Society*. New York: Three Rivers.
———. 2000. *One River, Many Wells: Wisdom Springing From Global Faiths*. New York: Jeremy P. Tarcher/Penguin.
———. 2002. *Creativity: Where the Divine and the Human Meet*. New York: Jeremy P. Tarcher.
Fox, R. W. 2004. *Jesus in America: Personal Savior, Cultural Hero, National Obsession*. San Francisco: Harper SanFrancisco.
Frankemölle, H., editor. 2000. *Lebendige Welt Jesu und des Neuen Testaments*. Freiburg: Herder.

Bibliography

Franklin, J. H., and A. A. Moss. 1998. *From Slavery to Freedom: A History of African Americans*. Seventh Edition. 2 Vols. New York: McGraw-Hill.

Frazer, E., and N. Lacey. 1993. *The Politics of Community: A Feminist Critique of the Liberal-Communitarian Debate*. New York: Harvester Wheatsheaf.

Fredrickson, G. M. 2002. *Racism: A Short History*. Princeton: Princeton University Press.

Freedman, D. N., editor. 2000. *Eerdmans Dictionary of the Bible*. Grand Rapids: Eerdmans.

Freedman, J., and G. Combs. 1996. *Narrative Therapy: The Social Construction of Preferred Realities*. New York: Norton.

Freire, P. 1984. *Pedagogy of the Oppressed*. New York: Continuum.

———. 1985. *The Politics of Education: Culture, Power, and Liberation*. Massachusetts: Bergin & Garvey.

———. 1994. *Pedagogy of Hope: Reliving Pedagogy of the Oppressed*. New York: Continuum.

Fretheim, T. E. 1994. "The Book of Genesis: Introduction, Commentary, and Reflections." In *The New Interpreter's Bible: Genesis to Leviticus*. Vol. 1: *General and Old Testament Articles, Genesis, Exodus, Leviticus*, edited by L. E. Keck, 319–674. Nashville: Abingdon.

Frey, C. 1999. *Einführung in die Philosophie: Für Studierende der Theologie*. Waltrop: Hartmut Spenner.

———, editor. 2000. *Repetitorium der Dogmatik*. 7. Auflage. Waltrop: Hartmut Spenner.

Frey, E. 2004. *Schwarzbuch USA*. Frankfurt: Eichborn.

Fries, H. 1996. *Fundamental Theology*. Washington: Catholic University of America Press.

Friesen, D. K. 2000. *Artists, Citizens, Philosophers—Seeking the Peace of the City: An Anabaptist Theology of Culture*. Scottdale: Herald.

Fromm, E. 1942. *The Fear of Freedom*. London: Routledge & Kegan Paul.

———. 1949. *Man for Himself: An Enquiry into the Psychology of Ethics*. London: Routledge & Kegan Paul.

———. 1956. *The Sane Society*. London: Routledge & Kegan Paul.

———. 1973. *The Anatomy of Human Destructiveness*. Greenwich: Fawcett.

———. 1976. *To Have or To Be*. London: Abacus.

———. 1993. *The Art of Being*. London: Constable.

Frost, M. 2006. *Exiles: Living Missionally in a Post-Christian Culture*. Grand Rapids: Baker.

———, and Hirsch A. 2009. *Rejesus: A Wild Messiah for a Missional Church*. Peabody: Hendrickson.

———. 2011. *The Faith of Leap: Embracing a Theology of Risk, Adventure, and Courage*. Grand Rapids: Baker.

Frymer-Kensky, T. 2002. *Reading the Women of the Bible*. New York: Schocken.

Fuchs, O. 1990. *Heilen und Befreien: Der Dienst am Nächsten als Ernstfall von Kirche und Pastoral*. Düsseldorf: Patmos.

———. 1993. *Stigma: Gezeichnete brauchen Beistand*. Frankfurt: Josef Knecht.

———. 2003. "Das Weiheamt im Horizont der Gnade—Die Dimension des Lebenszeugnisses als Dynamik des priesterlichen Dienstes." In *Den Himmel offen*

halten: Priester sein heute, edited by G. Augustin and J. Kreidler, 102–25. Freiburg: Herder.
Fuchs-Heinritz, W. 2000. *Biographische Forschung: Eine Einführung in Praxis und Methoden*. Wiesbaden: Westdeutscher Verlag.
Fuellenbach, J. 1995. *The Kingdom of God: The Message of Jesus Today*. Maryknoll: Orbis.
———. 2002. *Church: Community for the Kingdom*. Maryknoll: Orbis.
Fuller, S. 2002. *Knowledge Management Foundations*. Boston: Butterworth-Heinemann.
Funk, R. 1978. *Mut zum Menschen: Erich Fromms Denken und Werk, seine humanistische Religion und Ethik*. Stuttgart: Deutsche Verlags-Anstalt.
———. 1999. *Erich Fromm—Liebe zum Leben: Eine Bildbiographie*. Stuttgart: Deutsche Verlags-Anstalt.
———, H. Johach, and G. Meyer. 2000. *Erich Fromm heute: Zur Aktualität seines Denkens*. Munich: Deutscher Taschenbuch.
Fürer, P. 1993. *Was die Kirchen verheimlich(t)en*. Langnau am Albis: Agnos.
Füssel, K., D. Sölle, F. Steffensky. 1993. *Die Sowohl-als-auch-Falle: Eine theologische Kritik des Postmodernismus*. Luzern: Exodus.
Gabriel, K. 1992. *Christentum zwischen Tradition und Postmoderne*. Quaestiones Disputatae 141. Freiburg: Herder.
Gaillot, J. 1996. *Ce que je crois*. Paris: Editions Desclée de Brouwer.
———. 1997. *Sonnenaufgang in der Wüste—Ich wähle die Freiheit*. Küsnacht/Zürich: Edition K. Haller.
———. 2002. *Machtlos, aber frei*. Küsnacht/Zürich: Edition K. Haller.
Galeano, E. 1973. *Open Veins of Latin America: Five Centuries of the Pillage of a Continent*. New York: Monthly Review.
Galilea, S. 1984. *The Beatitudes: To Evangelize as Jesus Did*. Maryknoll: Orbis.
Gallagher, M. P. 1997. *Clashing Symbols: An Introduction to Faith-and-Culture*. London: Darton, Longman and Todd.
Gamble, S., editor. 2001. *The Routledge Companion to Feminism and Postfeminism*. New York: Routledge.
Gammie, J. G. 1989. *Holiness in Israel*. Overtures to Biblical Theology. Minneapolis: Fortress.
Ganoczy, A. 1974. *Sprechen von Gott in heutiger Gesellschaft: Weiterentwicklung der "Politischen Theologie."* Freiburg: Herder.
———. 1976. *Der schöpferische Mensch und die Schöpfung Gottes*. Mainz: Matthias-Grünewald.
———. 1987. *Schöpfungslehre*. Leitfaden Theologie 10. Düsseldorf: Patmos.
Garcia-Rivera, A. R. 1999. *The Community of the Beautiful: A Theological Aesthetics*. Collegeville: Liturgical.
———. 2003. *A Wounded Innocence: Sketches for a Theology of Art*. Collegeville: Liturgical.
Gardiner, M. E. 2000. *Critiques of Everyday Life*. New York: Routledge.
Garrett, J. L. 1990. *Systematic Theology: Biblical, Historical, and Evangelical*. Vol. 1. Grand Rapids: Eerdmans.
———. 1995. *Systematic Theology: Biblical, Historical, and Evangelical*. Vol. 2. Grand Rapids: Eerdmans.
Gates, H. L., and C. West. 2000. *The African-American Century: How Black Americans Have Shaped Our Country*. New York: Simon & Schuster.

Bibliography

Gaustad, E. S. 1990. *A Religious History of America.* New rev. ed. San Francisco: HarperSanFrancisco.

Gebara, I. 1999. *Longing for Running Water: Ecofeminism and Liberation.* Minneapolis: Augsburg Fortress.

———. 2002. *Out of the Depths: Women's Experience of Evil and Salvation.* Minneapolis: Augsburg Fortress.

Geffré, C. 1983. *Le christianisme au risque de l'interprétation.* Cogitatio Fidei 120. Paris: Cerf.

Gelder, K. 1992. *Glaube und Erfahrung: Eine kritische Auseinandersetzung mit Gerhard Ebelings "Dogmatik des christlichen Glaubens" im Kontext der gegenwärtigen evangelisch-theologischen Diskussion.* Neukirchen-Vluyn: Neukirchener.

Gelfert, H.-D. 2002. *Typisch amerikanisch: Wie die Amerikaner wurden, was sie sind.* Munich: C. H. Beck.

Gelinas, R. 2009. *Finding the Groove: Composing a Jazz-Shaped Faith.* Grand Rapids: Zondervan.

Gelpi, D. L. 1978. *Experiencing God: A Theology of Human Emergence.* New York: Paulist.

———. 1988. *Inculturating North American Theology: An Experiment in Foundational Method.* American Academy of Religion Studies in Religion 54. Atlanta: Scholars.

———. 1994. *The Turn to Experience in Contemporary Theology.* Mahwah: Paulist.

———. 2001. *Gracing of Human Experience: Rethinking the Relationship Between Nature and Grace.* Collegeville: Liturgical.

Gerber, U. 1987. *Die feministische Eroberung der Theologie.* Munich: C. H. Beck.

Gergen, M. M., editor. 1988. *Feminist Thought and the Structure of Knowledge.* New York: New York University Press.

Gerkin, C. V. 1991. *Prophetic Pastoral Practice: A Christian Vision of Life Together.* Nashville: Abingdon.

———. 1997. *An Introduction to Pastoral Care.* Nashville: Abingdon.

Gestrich, C. 1996. *Die Wiederkehr des Glanzes in der Welt: Die christliche Lehre von der Sünde und ihrer Vergebung in gegenwärtiger Verantwortung.* Tübingen: Mohr (Siebeck).

Gibellini, R. 1994. *Panorama de la théologie au XXè siècle.* Paris: Cerf.

———. 1995. *Handbuch der Theologie im 20. Jahrhundert.* Regensburg: Friedrich Pustet.

Gibert, P. 2002. *L'espérence de Caïn: La violence dans la Bible.* Paris: Bayard.

Giesen, H. 1995. *Herrschaft Gottes—heute oder morgen? Zur Heilsbotschaft Jesu und der synoptischen Evangelien.* Regensburg: Friedrich Pustet.

Giglioli, P. P., editor. 1982. *Language and Social Context.* London: Penguin.

Giles, J. and Middleton T. 1999. *Studying Culture: A Practical Introduction.* Oxford: Blackwell.

Gilkey, L. 1969. *Naming the Whirlwind: The Renewal of God-Language.* New York: Bobbs-Merrill.

———. 1985. "Events, Meanings and the Current Tasks of Theology." *Journal of the American Academy of Religion* 53 (December 1985), 717–34.

Gill, R., editor. 1995. *Readings in Modern Theology: Britain and America.* London: SPCK.

Girard, M. 1994. *Le pauvre, sacrement de Dieu: méditation biblique et théologique.* Montréal: Médiaspaul.

Girard, R. 1986. *The Scapegoat*. Baltimore: Johns Hopkins University Press.

———. 2001. *I See Satan Fall Like Lightening*. Maryknoll: Orbis.

Girardet, G. 1978. *Lecture politique de l'Evangile de Luc*. Bruxelles: Editions Vie Ouvrière.

Giroux, H. A. 1981. *Ideology, Culture, and the Process of Schooling*. Philadelphia: Temple University Press.

———. 1983. *Theory and Resistance in Education: A Pedagogy for the Opposition*. New York: Bergin & Garvey.

———. 1988a. *Teachers as Intellectuals: Toward a Critical Pedagogy of Learning*. New York: Bergin & Garvey.

———. 1988b. *Schooling and the Struggle for Public Life: Critical Pedagogy in the Modern Age*. Minneapolis: University of Minnesota Press.

———. 1990. *Curriculum Discourse as Postmodernist Critical Practice*. Geelong: Deakin University Press.

———, editors. 1991. *Postmodernism, Feminism, and Cultural Politics: Redrawing Educational Boundaries*. Albany: State University of New York Press.

———. 1992. *Border Crossings: Cultural Workers and the Politics of Education*. New York: Routledge.

———. 1994. *Disturbing Pleasures: Learning Popular Culture*. New York: Routledge.

———. 1996. *Fugitive Cultures: Race, Violence, and Youth*. New York: Routledge.

———. 1997. *Pedagogy and the Politics of Hope: Theory, Culture, and Schooling*. Boulder: Westview.

———. 2000. *Impure Acts: The Practical Politics of Cultural Studies*. New York: Routledge.

———. 2003. *Public Spaces, Private Lives: Democracy Beyond 9/11*. Lanham: Rowman & Littlefield.

———. 2011. *On Critical Pedagogy*. Critical Pedagogy Today. New York: Continuum.

———, and Giroux S. S. 2004. *Take Back Higher Education: Race, Youth, and the Crisis of Democracy in the Post-Civil-Rights Era*. New York: Palgrave Macmillan.

———, and McLaren P., editors. 1994. *Between Borders: Pedagogy and the Politics of Cultural Studies*. New York: Routledge.

———, and Simon R. I., editors. 1989. *Popular Culture, Schooling, and Everyday Life*. New York: Bergin & Garvey.

Gisel P., editor. 1995. *Encyclopédie du Protestantisme*. Paris: Cerf.

———, and P. Evrard, editors. 1996. *La théologie en postmodernité*. Actes du 3è cycle de théologie systématique des Facultés de théologie de Suisse romande. Geneva: Labor et Fides.

Glebe-Möller, J. 1987. *A Political Dogmatic*. Philadelphia: Fortress.

Goertz, H. J. 1988. *Die Täufer: Geschichte und Deutung*. Munich: C. H. Beck.

———. 1993. *Religiöse Bewegungen in der frühen Neuzeit*. Enzyklopädie Deutscher Geschichte. Vol. 20. Munich: R. Oldenbourg.

———. 1996. *The Anabaptists*. New York. Routledge.

Goffman, E. 1963. *Stigma: Notes on the Management of Spoiled Identity*. Englewood Cliffs: Prentice-Hall.

Goh, J. C. K. 2000. *Christian Tradition Today: A Postliberal Vision of Church and World*. Louvain: Peeters.

Bibliography

Göhlich, M., editor. 1997. *Offener Unterricht, Community Education, Alternativschulpädagogik, Reggiopädagogik: Die neuen Reformpädagogiken—Geschichte, Konzeption, Praxis.* Basel: Beltz.

Goldblatt, D., editor. 2000. *Knowledge and the Social Sciences: Theory, Method, Practice.* The Open University. New York: Routledge.

Goldfarb, J. C. 1998. *Civility and Subversion: The Intellectual in Democratic Society.* New York: Cambridge University Press.

Goldstein P. 1990. *The Politics of Literary Theory: An Introduction to Marxist Criticism.* Tallahassee: The Florida State University Press.

Goleman, D. 1995. *Emotional Intelligence: Why it can matter more than IQ.* New York: Bantam.

———, Kaufman P., and Ray M. 1993. *The Creative Spirit.* New York: Plume.

Gollwitzer, H. 1982. *An Introduction to Protestant Theology: In the Tradition of Barth and Bonhoeffer, a Theology of Freedom and Solidarity.* Philadelphia: Westminster.

———. 1998. *Skizzen eines Lebens.* Aus verstreuten Selbstzeugnissen gefunden und verbunden von Friedrich-Wilhelm Marquardt, Wolfgang Brinkel und Manfred Weber. Gütersloh: Chr. Kaiser/Gütersloher.

Gombrich, E. H. 1995. *The Story of Art.* London: Phaidon.

Gomez, M. 1994. *Theologie des Lebens: Botschaft der Hoffnung aus El Salvador.* Munich: Claudius.

Gonzalez, J. L. 1987a. *A History of Christian Thought: From the Beginnings to the Council of Chalcedon.* Vol. 1. Rev. ed. Nashville: Abingdon.

———. 1987b. *A History of Christian Thought: From Augustine to the Eve of the Reformation.* Vol. 2. Rev. ed. Nashville: Abingdon.

———. 1987c. *A History of Christian Thought: From the Protestant Reformation to the Twentieth Century.* Vol. 3. Rev. ed. Nashville: Abingdon.

———. 1990. *Manana: Christian Theology from a Hispanic Perspective.* Nashville: Abingdon.

———. 1992. *Out of Every Tribe and Nation: Christian Theology at the Ethnic Roundtable.* Nashville: Abingdon.

———. 1999. *Christian Thought Revisited: Three Types of Theology.* Rev. ed. Maryknoll: Orbis.

———. 2002. *The Changing Shape of Church History.* St. Louis: Chalice.

———. 2005. *A Concise History of Christian Doctrine.* Nashville: Abingdon.

———. 2005a. *Essential Theological Terms.* Louisville: Westminster John Knox.

———, and Z. M. Perez 2002. *An Introduction to Christian Theology.* Nashville: Abingdon.

Gonzalez, M. A. 2003. *Sor Juana: Beauty and Justice in the Americas.* Maryknoll: Orbis.

Good, J., and I. Velody, editors. 1998. *The Politics of Postmodernity.* New York: Cambridge University Press.

Good, M. J., P. Brodwin, B. Good, and A. Kleinman. 1992. *Pain as Human Experience: An Anthropological Perspective.* Berkeley: University of California Press.

Gordon, B. 2002. *The Swiss Reformation.* Manchester: Manchester University Press.

Gornik, M. R. 2002. *To Live in Peace: Biblical Faith in the Changing Inner City.* Grand Rapids: Eerdmans.

Gossai, H. 1995. *Power and Marginality in the Abraham Narrative.* Lanham: University Press of America.

Gössmann, E., H. Kuhlmann, E. Moltmann-Wendel, I. Praetorius, L. Schottroff, H. Schüngel-Straumann, D. Strahm, and A. Wuckelt, editors. 2002. *Wörterbuch der feministischen Theologie*. Gütersloh: Gütersloher.

Gottlieb, R. S., editor. 1993. *Radical Philosophy: Tradition, Counter-Tradition, Politics*. Philadelphia: Temple University Press.

———. 2006. *A Greener Faith: Religious Environmentalism and Our Planet's Future*. New York: Oxford University Press.

Gottwald, N. K., and R. A. Horsley, editors. 1993. *The Bible and Liberation: Political and Social Hermeneutics*. Maryknoll: Orbis.

Goudineau, H., and Souletie J. L. 2002. *Jürgen Moltmann*. Invitations aux théologiens. Paris: Cerf.

Gounelle, A. 1981. *Le Dynamisme Créateur de Dieu: Essai sur la Théologie du Process*. Cahier spécial de la revue *Etudes Théologiques et Religieuses*. Paris: Van Dieren Editeur.

———. 2000. *Le Dynamisme Créateur de Dieu: Essai sur la Théologie du Process*. Nouvelle édition, revue et augmentée. Paris: Van Dieren Editeur.

Gourgues, M. 1997. *Les paraboles de Luc: D'amont en aval*. Montréal: Mediaspaul.

Graham, E. L. 1995. *Making the Difference: Gender, Personhood and Theology*. London: Mowbray.

———. 1996. *Transforming Practice: Pastoral Theology in an Age of Uncertainty*. London: Mowbray.

———. 1996a. "'Concrete' and 'Generalized' Others." In *Transforming Practice: Pastoral Theology in an Age of Uncertainty*, 153–55. London: Mowbray.

Graham, L. K. 1992. *Care of Persons, Care of Worlds: A Psychosystems Approach to Pastoral Care and Counseling*. Nashville: Abingdon.

Granberg-Michaelson, K. 1991. *Healing Community*. Geneva: WCC.

Grass, H. 1973. *Christliche Glaubenslehre*. Part 1. Theologische Wissenschaft 12/1. Stuttgart: Kohlhammer.

———. 1974. *Christliche Glaubenslehre*. Part 2. Theologische Wissenschaft 12/2. Stuttgart: Kohlhammer.

Grassi, J. A. 2002. *Informing the Future: Social Justice in the New Testament*. Mahwah: Paulist.

Greeley, A. M. 1988. *God in Popular Culture*. Chicago: Thomas More.

Green, C. J. 1999. *Bonhoeffer: A Theology of Sociality*. Grand Rapids: Eerdmans.

Green, G. 1989. *Imagining God: Theology and the Religious Imagination*. Grand Rapids: Eerdmans.

———. 1999. *Theology, Hermeneutics, and Imagination: The Crisis of Interpretation at the End of Modernity*. Cambridge: Cambridge University Press.

Green, J. B. 1995. "'To Proclaim Good News to the Poor': Mission and Salvation." In *The Theology of the Gospel of Luke*, 76–101. New York: Cambridge University Press.

———. 1997. *The Gospel of Luke*. New International Commentary on the New Testament. Grand Rapids: Eerdmans.

Green, K., and J. LeBihan. 1996. *Critical Theory and Practice: A Coursebook*. New York: Routledge.

Greene, M. 1995. *Releasing the Imagination: Essays on Education, the Arts, and Social Change*. San Francisco: Jossey-Bass.

Bibliography

Greenfield, P. M. 1997."Culture as a Process: Empirical Methods for Cultural Psychology." In *Handbook of Cross-Cultural Psychology,* edited by J. W. Berry, Y. H. Poortinga, and J. Pandey. 2nd ed. Boston: Allyn and Bacon.
Greiner, D. 1998. *Segen und Segnen: Eine systematisch-theologische Grundlegung.* Stuttgart: Kohlhammer.
Gremmels, C., and W. Huber, editors. 2002. *Religion im Erbe: Dietrich Bonhoeffer und die Zukunftsfähigkeit des Christentums.* Gütersloh: Chr. Kaiser/Gütersloher.
Grenz, S. J. 1993. *Revisioning Evangelical Theology: A Fresh Agenda for the 21st Century.* Downers Grove: InterVarsity.
———. 1994. *Theology for the Community of God.* Grand Rapids: Eerdmans.
———. 1998. *Created for Community: Connecting Christian Belief with Christian Living.* Grand Rapid: Baker.
———. 1996. *A Primer on Postmodernism.* Grand Rapids: Eerdmans.
———. 2000. *Renewing the Center: Evangelical Theology in a Post-Theological Era.* Grand Rapids: Baker Academic.
———, and J. R. Franke 2001. *Beyond Foundationalism: Shaping Theology in a Postmodern Context.* Louisville: Westminster John Knox.
———, and R. E. Olson 1992. *20th-Century Theology: God & the World in a Transitional Age.* Downers Grove: InterVarsity.
Grey, M. C. 1993. *The Wisdom of Fools? Seeking Revelation for Today.* London: SPCK.
———. 1997a. *Prophecy and Mysticism: The Heart of the Postmodern Church.* Edinburgh: T. & T. Clark.
———. 1997b. *Beyond the Dark Night: A Way Forward for the Church?* London: Cassell.
———. 2003. *Sacred Longings: Ecofeminist Theology and Globalization.* London: SCM.
Griffin, D. R. 2004. *God, Power, and Evil: A Process Theodicy.* Louisville: Westminster John Knox.
———, W. A. Beardslee, and J. Holland. 1989. *Varieties of Postmodern Theology.* Albany: State University of New York Press.
Griffiths, M. 1995. *Feminism and the Self: The Web of Identity.* New York: Routledge.
Groome, T. H. 1998. *Sharing Faith: A Comprehensive Approach to Religious Education and Pastoral Ministry—The Way of Shared Praxis.* Eugene: Wipf and Stock.
———, and H. D. Horell, editors. 2003. *Horizons and Hopes: The Future of Religious Education.* Mahwah: Paulist.
Gruber, F. 2001. *Im Haus des Lebens: Eine Theologie der Schöpfung.* Regensburg: Friedrich Pustet.
Gruber, M. I. 1998. "Genesis 21.12: A New Reading of an Ambiguous Text." In *Genesis: A Feminist Companion to the Bible,* edited by A. Brenner, 172–79. Second Series. Sheffield: Sheffield Academic.
Grünwaldt, K. 2002. *Auge um Auge, Zahn um Zahn? Das Recht im Alten Testament.* Mainz: Matthias-Grünewald.
Gudorf, C. E. 1992. *Victimization: Examining Christian Complicity.* Philadelphia: Trinity.
Guelich, R. A. 1982. *Sermon on the Mount: Foundation for Understanding.* Waco: Word.
Gundry-Volf, J. M., and M. Volf. 1997. *A Spacious Heart: Essays on Identity and Belonging.* Harrisburg: Trinity.
Gunn, J. V. 1982. *Autobiography: Toward a Poetics of Experience.* Philadelphia: University of Pennsylvania Press.

Günter, A., editor. 1996. *Feministische Theologie und postmodernes Denken: Zur theologischen Relevanz der Geschlechterdifferenz*. Stuttgart: Kohlhammer.
Gunton, C. E., editor. 1997. *The Cambridge Companion to Christian Doctrine*. New York: Cambridge University Press.
Guthrie, S. C. 1994. *Christian Doctrine*. Rev. ed. Louisville: Westminster John Knox.
Gutierrez, G. 1991. *The God of Life*. Maryknoll: Orbis.
Gutmann, H. M. 1995. *Die tödlichen Spiele der Erwachsenen: Moderne Opfermythen in Religion, Politik und Kultur*. Freiburg: Herder.
———. 1998. *Der Herr der Heerscharen, die Prinzessin der Herzen und der König der Löwen: Religion lehren zwischen Kirche, Schule und populärer Kultur*. Gütersloh: Chr. Kaiser/Gütersloher.
Ha, K. N. 1999. *Ethnizität und Migration*. Grundbegriffe der Sozialphilosophie und Gesellschafts-theorie. Einstiege 9. Münster: Westfälisches Dampfboot.
Habbel, T. 1994. *Der Dritte stört: Emmanuel Levinas – Herausforderung für Politische Theologie und Befreiungstheologie*. Mainz: Matthias-Grünewald.
Habermas, J. 1970. "On Systematically Distorted Communication." *Inquiry* 13 (1970) 205–18.
———. 1985. *Die Neue Unübersichtlichkeit*. Kleine Politische Schriften V. Frankfurt: Suhrkamp.
———. 1987. *The Philosophical Discourse of Modernity: Twelve Lectures*. Cambridge: MIT Press.
———. 1989. *The New Conservatism: Cultural Criticism and the Historians' Debate*. Edited and translated by Shierry Weber Nicholsen. Cambridge: MIT Press.
———. 2002. *Religion and Rationality: Essays on Reason, God, and Modernity*. Edited and with an introduction by Eduardo Mendieta. Cambridge: Polity.
———. 2002a. "Israel or Athens: Where does Anamnestic Reason Belong? Johannes Baptist Metz on Unity amidst Multicultural Plurality." In *Religion and Rationality: Essays on Reason, God, and Modernity*, edited and with an introduction by Eduardo Mendieta, 129–38. Cambridge: Polity.
Hackett, J. A. 1989. "Rehabilitating Hagar: Fragments of an Epic Pattern." In *Gender and Difference in Ancient Israel*, edited by P. L. Day, 12–27. Minneapolis: Fortress.
Hacking, I. 2002. *Was heisst 'soziale Konstruktion'? Zur Konjunktur einer Kampfvokabel in den Wissenschaften*. 3rd ed. Frankfurt: Fischer.
Hägglund, B. 1993. *Geschichte der Theologie: Ein Abriss*. Gütersloh: Chr. Kaiser/Gütersloher.
Hagleitner, S. 1996. *Mit Lust an der Welt—in Sorge um sie: Feministisch-politische Bildungsarbeit nach Paulo Freire und Ruth C. Cohn*. Mainz: Matthias-Grünewald.
Haight, R. 2001. *Dynamics of Theology*. 2nd ed. Maryknoll: Orbis.
Hall, D. J. 1986. *Imaging God: Dominion as Stewardship*. Commission on Stewardship, National Council of the Churches of Christ in the U. S. A. Grand Rapids: Eerdmans.
———. 1988. *The Stewardship of Life in the Kingdom of Death*. Rev. ed. Grand Rapids: Eerdmans.
———. 1989. *Thinking the Faith: Christian Theology in a North American Context*. Minneapolis: Augsburg Fortress.
———. 1993. *Professing the Faith: Christian Theology in a North American Context*. Minneapolis: Augsburg Fortress.
———. 1995. *The End of Christendom and the Future of Christianity*. Harrisburg: Trinity.

Bibliography

———. 1996. *Confessing the Faith: Christian Theology in a North American Context.* Minneapolis: Augsburg Fortress.

Halpern, R., and E. Dal Lago, editors. 2002. *Slavery and Emancipation.* Blackwell Readers in American Social and Cultural History. Malden: Blackwell.

Hamilton, V. P. 1990. *The Book of Genesis: Chapters 1–17.* New International Commentary on the Old Testament. Grand Rapids: Eerdmans.

———. 1995. *The Book of Genesis: Chapters 18–50.* New International Commentary on the Old Testament. Grand Rapids: Eerdmans.

Hanks, T. 2000. *The Subversive Gospel: A New Testament Commentary of Liberation.* Cleveland: Pilgrim.

———. 2000a. "Luke: Good News for the Poor and for Women." In *The Subversive Gospel: A New Testament Commentary of Liberation*, 37–54. Cleveland: Pilgrim.

Hanson, B. C. 1997. *Introduction to Christian Theology.* Minneapolis: Fortress.

Hanson, K. C., and D. E. Oakman 1998. *Palestine in the Time of Jesus: Social Structures and Social Conflicts.* Minneapolis: Fortress.

Hanson, P. D. 1986. *The People Called: The Growth of Community in the Bible.* San Francisco: Harper & Row.

Harding, S. 1991. *Whose Science? Whose Knowledge? Thinking from Women's Lives.* Ithaca: Cornell University Press.

———. 1998. *Is Science Multicultural? Postcolonialisms, Feminisms, and Epistemologics.* Bloomington: Indiana University Press.

Harding, V. 1990. *Hope and History: Why We Must Share the Story of the Movement.* Maryknoll: Orbis.

Hardt, M., and A. Negri 2000. *Empire.* Cambridge: Harvard University Press.

———. 2004. *Multitude: War and Democracy in the Age of Empire.* New York: Penguin.

Härle, W. 2000. *Dogmatik.* 2nd rev. ed. New York: Walter de Gruyter.

Harmer, C. M. 1998. *The Compassionate Community: Strategies The Work for the Third Millenium.* Maryknoll: Orbis.

Harrington, M. (1962/1981). *The Other America: Poverty in the United States.* New Edition. New York: Penguin.

Harris, J. H. 1991. *Pastoral Theology: A Black-Church Perspective.* Minneapolis: Fortress.

Harris, S. L. 2006. *The New Testament: A Student's Introduction.* 5th ed. New York: McGraw-Hill.

Hart, J. 2004. *What Are They Saying About Environmental Theology?* Mahwah: Paulist.

Hart, K. 2004. *Postmodernism: A Beginner's Guide.* Oxford: Oneworld.

Hart, R. L. 1968/2001. *Unfinished Man and the Imagination: Toward an Ontology and a Rhetoric of Revelation.* Louisville: Westminster John Knox.

Hartley, J. 2003. *A Short History of Cultural Studies.* Thousand Oaks: Sage.

Hartley, J. E. 2000. *Genesis.* New International Biblical Commentary. Peabody: Hendrickson.

Hartman, J. E., and E. Messer-Davidow, editors. 1991. *(En)Gendering Knowledge: Feminists in Academe.* Knoxville: The University of Tennessee Press.

Harvey, B. A. 1999. *Another City: An Ecclesiological Primer for a Post-Christian Word.* Harrisburg: Trinity.

Harvey, D. 1990. *The Condition of Postmodernity: An Enquiry into the Origins of Cultural Change.* Cambridge: Blackwell.

Hasenhüttl, G. 1974. "Erfahrung als Ort der Theologie." In *Praktische Theologie heute*, edited by F. Klostermann and R. Zerfass, 624–37. Munich: Chr. Kaiser.

———. 1979. *Kritische Dogmatik*. Graz: Styria.

———. 1985. *Freiheit in Fesseln: Die Chance der Befreiungstheologie*. Freiburg: Walter.

———. 2001a. *Glaube ohne Mythos: Offenbarung, Jesus Christus, Gott*. Vol. 1. Mainz: Matthias-Grünewald.

———. 2001b. *Glaube ohne Mythos: Mensch, Glaubensgemeinschaft, Symbolhandlungen, Zukunft*. Vol. 2. Mainz: Matthias-Grünewald.

Hasker, W. 2008. *The Triumph of God over Evil: Theodicy for a World of Suffering*. Strategic Initiatives in Evangelical Theology. Downers Grove: IVP Academic.

Hastings, A., editor. 1999. *A World History of Christianity*. London: Cassell.

———, A. Mason, and H. Pyper, editors. 2002. *Christian Thought: A Brief History*. New York: Oxford University Press.

———, A. Mason, and H. Pyper, editors. 2003. *Key Thinkers in Christianity*. New York: Oxford University Press.

Hatch, J. A., and R. Wisniewski, editors. 1995. *Life History and Narrative*. Washington: Falmer.

Hauerwas, S. 1983. *The Peaceable Kingdom: A Primer in Christian Ethics*. Notre Dame: University of Notre Dame Press.

———, and S. Wells, editors. 2006. *The Blackwell Companion to Christian Ethics*. Malden: Blackwell.

———, N. Murphy, and M. Nation, editors. 1994. *Theology Without Foundations: Religious Practice and the Future of Religious Truth*. Nashville: Abingdon.

Haug, F. 1990. *Erinnerungsarbeit*. Hamburg: Argument.

———. 1999. *Vorlesungen zur Einführung in die Erinnerungsarbeit: The Duke Lectures*. Hamburg: Argument.

Haugaard, M., editor. 2002. *Power: A Reader*. Manchester: Manchester University Press.

Haught, J. F. 2000. *God after Darwin: A Theology of Evolution*. Boulder: Westview.

Hawthorn, J. 2001. *A Glossary of Contemporary Literary Theory*. London: Arnold.

Hayes, D. L. 1996. *And Still We Rise: An Introduction to Black Liberation Theology*. New York and Mahwah: Paulist.

Heideking, J., and V. Nünning 1998. *Einführung in die amerikanische Geschichte*. Munich: C. H. Beck.

Heimbach-Steins, M. 2001. *Einmischung und Anwaltschaft: Für eine diakonische und prophetische Kirche*. Ostfildern: Schwabenverlag.

Heitink, G. 1999. *Practical Theology: History—Theory—Action Domains*. Grand Rapids: Eerdmans.

Hekman, S. J. 1990. *Gender and Knowledge: Elements of a Postmodern Feminism*. Cambridge: Polity.

Hellwig, M. K. 1982. *Whose Experience Counts in Theological Reflection?* The 1982 Père Marquette Theology Lecture. Milwaukee: Marquette University Press.

———. 1983. *Jesus—The Compassion of God: New Perspectives on the Tradition of Christianity*. Collegeville: Liturgical.

Hendrickx, H. 1986. *A Time for Peace: Reflections on the Meaning of Peace and Violence in the Bible*. Quezon City: Claretian.

Hendriks, J. 2001. *Gemeinde als Herberge: Kirche im 21. Jahrhundert—eine konkrete Utopie*. Gütersloh: Chr. Kaiser/Gütersloher.

Hendry, J. 1999. *An Introduction to Social Anthropology: Other People's Worlds*. London: Macmillan.

Bibliography

Hennelly, A. T. 1995. *Liberation Theologies: The Global Pursuit of Justice*. Mystic: Twenty-Third.

Henning, C., and K. Lehmkühler, editor. 1998. *Systematische Theologie der Gegenwart in Selbst-darstellungen*. Tübingen: Mohr Siebeck.

Hepp, A. 2004. *Cultural Studies und Medienanalyse: Eine Einführung*. 2nd ed. Wiesbaden: VS Verlag für Sozialwissenschaften.

Herman, J. L. 1997. *Trauma and Recovery: The Aftermath of Violence—From Domestic Abuse to Political Terror*. New York: Basic.

Hernandez, W. 2006. *Henri Nouwen: A Spirituality of Imperfection*. Mahwah: Paulist.

Heron, A. I. C. 1980. *A Century of Protestant Theology*. Philadelphia: Westminster.

Herriger, N. 2002. *Empowerment in der Sozialen Arbeit: Eine Einführung*. Stuttgart: Kohlhammer.

Hershberger, M. 1999. *A Christian View of Hospitality: Expecting Suprises*. Scottdale: Herald.

Herzfeld, M. 2001. *Anthropology: Theoretical Practice in Culture and Society*. Malden: Blackwell.

Herzog, F. 1972. *Liberation Theology: Liberation in the Light of the Fourth Gospel*. New York: Seabury.

———. 1980. *Justice Church: The New Function of the Church in North American Christianity*. Maryknoll: Orbis.

———. 1982. "Dogmatik in Nordamerika." In *Theologische Realenzyklopädie*, edited by G. Krause and G. Müller, 104–16. Vol. 9. New York: Walter de Gruyter.

———. 1988. *God-Walk: Liberation Shaping Dogmatics*. Maryknoll: Orbis.

———. 1999. "The End of Systematic Theology." In *Theology from the Belly of the Whale: A Frederick Herzog Reader*, edited by J. Rieger, 224–35. Harrisburg: Trinity.

———. 1999a. "Dogmatics in North America." In *Theology from the Belly of the Whale: A Frederick Herzog Reader*, edited by J. Rieger, 236–51 Harrisburg: Trinity.

Herzog, W. R. 1994. *Parables as Subversive Speech: Jesus as Pedagogue of the Oppressed*. Louisville: Westminster John Knox.

———. 2000. *Jesus, Justice, and the Reign of God: A Ministry of Liberation*. Maryknoll: Orbis.

Hetherington, K. 1998. *Expressions of Identity: Space, Performance, Politics*. Thousand Oaks: Sage.

Heuermann, H. 2000. *Wissenschaftskritik: Konzepte—Positionen—Probleme*. Tübingen und Basel: A. Franke.

Heyward, C. 1982. *The Redemption of God: A Theology of Mutual Relation*. Lanham: University Press of America.

———. 1995. *Staying Power: Reflections on Gender, Justice, and Compassion*. Cleveland: Pilgrim.

Higgins, G. C. 2009. *Wrestling With the Questions: An Introduction to Contemporary Theologies*. Minneapolis: Fortress.

Highmore, B. 2002a. *Everyday Life and Cultural Theory: An Introduction*. New York: Routledge.

———, editor. 2002b. *Everyday Life Reader*. New York: Routledge.

Hilkert, M. C., and R. J. Schreiter, editors. 2002. *The Praxis of the Reign of God: An Introduction to the Theology of Edward Schillebeeckx*. 2nd ed. New York: Fordham University Press.

Hill, A. F., and E. C. Jordan, editors. 1995. *Race, Gender, and Power in America: The Legacy of the Hill-Thomas Hearings*. New York: Oxford University Press.

Hill, B. R. 2003. *Exploring Catholic Theology: God, Jesus, Church, and Sacraments*. Mystic: Twenty-Third.

Hillerbrand, H. J., editor. 2004. *The Encyclopedia of Protestantism*. 4 Vols. New York: Routledge.

Hilpert, K., and S. Leimgruber, editor. 2008. *Theologie im Durchblick: Ein Grundkurs*. Grundlagen Theologie. Freiburg: Herder.

Hinchman, L. P., and S. K. Hinchman, editors. 1997. *Memory, Identity, Community: The Idea of Narrative in the Human Sciences*. New York: State University of New York Press.

Hindess, B. 1996. *Discourses of Power: From Hobbes to Foucault*. Cambridge: Blackwell.

Hinkelammert, F. J. 1989. *Der Glaube Abrahams und der Ödipus des Westens: Opfermythen im christlichen Abendland*. Münster: Edition Liberacion.

Hinte, W. 1980. *Non-direktive Pädagogik: Eine Einführung in Grundlagen und Praxis des selbstbestimmten Lernens*. Opladen: Westdeutscher.

———. 1990. *Non-direktive Pädagogik: Eine Einführung in Grundlagen und Praxis des selbstbestimmten Lernens*. Wiesbaden: Deutscher Universitäts-Verlag.

Hirsch, A. 2006. *The Forgotten Ways: Reactivating the Missional Church*. Grand Rapids: Brazos.

———, and T. Catchim. 2011. *The Permanent Revolution: Apostolic Imagination and Practice for the 21st Century Church*. San Francisco: Jossey-Bass.

———, and D. Ferguson. 2011. *On the Verge: A Journey into the Apostolic Future of the Church*. Grand Rapids: Zondervan.

———, and D. Hirsch. 2010. *Untamed: Reactivating a Missional Form of Discipleship*. Grand Rapids: Baker.

Hitzler, R., and A. Honer, editors. 1997. *Sozialwissenschaftliche Hermeneutik: Eine Einführung*. Opladen: Leske+Budrich.

Hodge, R., and G. Kress. 1993. *Language as Ideology*. New York: Routledge.

Hodgson P. C. 1971. *Jesus—Word and Presence: An Essay in Christology*. Philadelphia: Fortress.

———. 1974. *Children of Freedom: Black Liberation in Christian Perspective*. Philadelphia: Fortress.

———. 1976. *New Birth of Freedom: A Theology of Bondage and Liberation*. Philadelphia: Fortress.

———. 1988. *Revisioning the Church: Ecclesial Freedom in the New Paradigm*. Philadelphia: Fortress.

———. 1989. *God in History: Shapes of Freedom*. Nashville: Abingdon.

———. 1994. *The Winds of the Spirit: A Constructive Christian Theology*. Louisville: Westminster John Knox.

———. 1999. *God's Wisdom: Toward a Theology of Education*. Louisville: Westminster John Knox.

———. 2001. *Christian Faith: A Brief Introduction*. Louisville: Westminster John Knox.

———. 2007. *Liberal Theology: A Radical Vision*. Minneapolis: Augsburg Fortress.

———, and R. H. King, editors. 1985. *Christian Theology: An Introduction to Its Traditions and Tasks*. 2nd rev. enl. ed. Philadelphia: Fortress.

———, and R. H. King, editors. 1994. *Christian Theology: An Introduction to Its Traditions and Tasks*. 3rd ed. Minneapolis: Fortress.

Bibliography

Hoekendijk, J. C. 1964. *Die Zukunft der Kirche und die Kirche der Zukunft.* Stuttgart: Kreuz.
Hof, C. 2009. *Lebenslanges Lernen: Eine Einführung.* Stuttgart: W. Kohlhammer.
Hogan, L. 1995. *From Women's Experience to Feminist Theology.* Sheffield: Sheffield Academic.
Holdenried, M. 2000. *Autobiographie.* Stuttgart: Reclam.
Holifield, E. B. 1992. "Nordamerikanische Theologie." In *Evangelisches Kirchenlexikon: Internationale theologische Enzyklopädie,* edited by E. Fahlbusch, J. M. Lochman, J. Mbiti, J. Pelikan, and L. Vischer, 775–83. Vol 3: L-R. Göttingen: Vandenhoeck & Ruprecht.
Holl, A. 1998. *The Left Hand of God: A Biography of the Holy Spirit.* New York: Doubleday.
Hollenweger, W. J. 1986. "Intercultural Theology." *Theology Today* 43, 28-35.
———. 1990. *Erfahrungen der Leibhaftigkeit: Interkulturelle Theologie.* Munich: Chr. Kaiser.
———. 1997. *Charismatisch-pfingstliches Christentum: Herkunft, Situation, Ökumenische Chancen.* Göttingen: Vandenhoeck & Ruprecht.
———. 1997a. *Pentecostalism: Origins and Developments Worldwide.* Peabody: Hendrickson.
———. 2000. *Der Klapperstorch und die Theologie: Die Krise von Theologie und Kirche als Chance.* Kindhausen: Metanoia.
Holloway, J. 2002. *Change the World Without Taking Power: The Meaning of Revolution Today.* London: Pluto.
Holmes, J. 1992. *An Introduction to Sociolinguistics.* New York: Longman.
Holzkamp, K. 1995. *Lernen: Subjektwissenschaftliche Grundlegung.* Frankfurt: Campus.
Honecker M. 2005. *Glaube als Grund christlicher Theologie.* Stuttgart: Kohlhammer.
hooks, b. 1989. *Talking Black, Thinking Feminist, Thinking Black.* Boston: South End.
———. 2003. *Teaching Community: A Pedagogy of Hope.* New York: Routledge.
Hopkins, D. N. 1993. *Shoes That Fit Our Feet: Sources for a Constructive Black Theology.* Maryknoll: Orbis.
———. 1999. *Introducing Black Theology of Liberation.* Maryknoll: Orbis.
———. 2000. *Down, Up, and Over: Slave Religion and Black Theology.* Minneapolis: Fortress.
———. 2005. *Being Human: Race, Culture, and Religion.* Minneapolis: Fortress.
———, and S. G. Davaney, editors. 1996. *Changing Conversations: Religious Reflection and Cultural Analysis.* New York: Routledge.
Höring, P. C. 2000. *Jugendlichen begegnen: Jugendpastorales Handeln in einer Kirche als Gemeinschaft.* Stuttgart: Kohlhammer.
Horsley, R. A. 1994. *Sociology and the Jesus Movement.* 2nd ed. New York: Continuum Publishing Company.
Horster, D. 1999. *Postchristliche Moral: Eine sozialphilosophische Begründung.* Hamburg: Junius.
Huber, W. 1993. *Die tägliche Gewalt: Gegen den Ausverkauf der Menschenwürde.* Freiburg: Herder.
———. 1996. *Violence: The Unrelenting Assault on Human Dignity.* Minneapolis: Fortress.
———, and H. R. Reuter. 1990. *Friedensethik.* Stuttgart: W. Kohlhammer.

Hugger, P., and U. Stadler, editors. 1995. *Gewalt: Kulturelle Formen in Geschichte und Gegenwart*. Zürich: Unionsverlag.
Hughes C. 2002. *Key Concepts in Feminist Theory and Research*. Thousand Oaks: Sage.
———. 2002a. "Experience." In *Key Concepts in Feminist Theory and Research*, 151–73. Thousand Oaks: Sage.
Hughes, L. 1994. *The Dream Keeper and Other Poems*. New York: Alfred A. Knopf.
Humm, M. 1994. *A Reader's Guide to Contemporary Feminist Literary Criticism*. New York: Prentice Hall.
Hungs, F. J. 1991. *Handbuch der theologischen Erwachsenenbildung*. Munich: J. Pfeiffer.
Hunt, M. 1991. *Fierce Tenderness: A Feminist Theology of Friendship*. New York: Crossroad.
Hunter, S., J. Jacobus, and D. Wheeler. 2000. *Modern Art: Painting, Sculpture, Architecture*. 3rd rev. ed. New York: Harry N. Abrams.
Huntington, S. P. 1996. *The Clash of Civilizations and the Remaking of World Order*. New York: Touchstone.
Imbach, J. 1990. *Kleiner Grundkurs des Glaubens*. Düsseldorf: Patmos.
Inbody, T. L. 1997. *The Transforming God: An Interpretation of Suffering and Evil*. Louisville: Westminster John Knox.
———. 2005. *The Faith of the Christian Church: An Introduction to Theology*. Grand Rapids: Eerdmans.
Isasi-Diaz, A. M. 1993. *En La Lucha—In the Struggle: A Hispanic Women's Liberation Theology*. Minneapolis: Augsburg Fortress.
———. 1996. "Experiences." In *Dictionary of Feminist Theologies*, edited by L. M. Russell and J. S. Clarkson, 95–96. Louisville: Westminster John Knox.
———. 1996a. *Mujerista Theology: A Theology for the Twenty-First Century*. Maryknoll: Orbis.
———. 2004. *En La Lucha/In the Struggle: Elaborating a Mujerista Theology*. 2nd ed. Minneapolis: Fortress.
———, and F. F. Segovia, editors. 1996. *Hispanic/Latino Theology: Challenge and Promise*. Minneapolis: Fortress.
Isherwood, L., editor. 2000. *The Good News of the Body: Sexual Theology and Feminism*. New York: New York University Press.
Isin, E. F. 2002. *Being Political: Genealogies of Citizenship*. Minneapolis: University of Minnesota Press.
Iwashima, T. 1982. *Menschengeschichte und Heilserfahrung: Die Theologie von Edward Schillebeeckx als methodisch reflektierte Soteriologie*. Düsseldorf: Patmos.
Jackson, D., and N. Jackson. 1987. *Glimpses of Glory—Thirty Years of Community: The Story of Reba Place Fellowship*. Elgin: Brethren.
Jackson, M. 1989. *Paths Toward a Clearing: Radical Empiricism and Ethnographic Inquiry*. Bloomington: Indiana University Press.
———. 1995. *At Home in the World*. Durham: Duke University Press.
Jacobsen, D. A. 2001. *Doing Justice: Congregations and Community Organizing*. Minneapolis: Fortress.
Jacoby, R. 2000. *Last Intellectuals: American Culture in the Age of Academe*. New York: Basic.
Jacquin, P., D. Royot, and S. Whitfield. 2000. *Le peuple américain: Origines, immigration, ethnicité et identité*. Paris: Editions du Seuil.

Bibliography

Jakobs, M. 1993. *Frauen auf der Suche nach dem Göttlichen: Die Gottesfrage in der feministischen Theologie*. Vol. 1. Münster: Morgana Frauenbuchverlag.

———. 2003. *All that Jazz: Die Geschichte einer Musik*. Leipzig: Reclam.

Jameson, F. 2002/1981. *The Political Unconscious: Narrative as a Socially Symbolic Act*. New York: Routledge.

Janowski, B., and M. Welker, editor. 2000. *Opfer: Theologische und kulturelle Kontexte*. Frankfurt: Suhrkamp.

Janzen, J. G. 1991. "Hagar in Paul's Eyes and in the Eyes of Yahweh (Gen 16): A Study in Horizons." *Horizons of Biblical Theology* 13, 1–22.

Janzen, W. 1994. *Old Testament Ethics: A Paradigmatic Approach*. Louisville: Westminster John Knox.

Jarvis, P. 2004. *Adult Education and Lifelong Learning: Theory and Practice*. 3rd ed. New York: Routledge.

Jeanrond, W. G. 1988. *Text and Interpretation as Categories of Theological Thinking*. New York: Crossroad.

———. 1991. *Theological Hermeneutics: Development and Significance*. New York: Crossroad.

———. 1995. *Call and Response: The Challenge of Christian Life*. Dublin: Gill & Macmillan.

———, and J. L. Rike, editors. 1991. *Radical Pluralism and Truth: David Tracy and the Hermeneutics of Religion*. New York: Crossroad.

Jenkins, P. 2002. *The Next Christendom: The Coming of Global Christianity*. New York: Oxford University Press.

———. 2003. *A History of the United States*. 2nd ed. New York: Palgrave Macmillan.

———. 2006. *The New Faces of Christianity: Believing the Bible in the Global South*. New York: Oxford University Press.

Jenkins, R. 2002. *Pierre Bourdieu*. Key Sociologists. Rev. ed. New York: Routledge.

Jennings, T. W. 1976. *Introduction to Theology: An Invitation to Reflection Upon the Christian Mythos*. Philadelphia: Fortress.

———. 1982. *Life as Worship: Prayer and Praise in Jesus' Name*. Grand Rapids: Eerdmans.

———. 1985. *Beyond Theism: A Grammar of God-Language*. New York: Oxford University Press.

———, editor. 1985a. *The Vocation of the Theologian*. Philadelphia: Fortress.

———. 1992. *Loyalty to God: The Apostles' Creed in Life and Liturgy*. Nashville: Abingdon.

———. 2003. *The Insurrection of the Crucified: The "Gospel of Marc" as Theological Manifesto*. Chicago: Chicago Theological Seminary Exploration Press.

Jenson, R. W. 1997. *Systematic Theology: The Triune God*. Vol. 1. New York: Oxford University Press.

———. 1999. *Systematic Theology: The Works of God*. Vol. 2. New York: Oxford University Press.

Jessor, R., A. Colby, and R. A. Shweder, editors. 1996. *Ethnography and Human Development: Context and Meaning in Social Inquiry*. Chicago: University of Chicago Press.

Jilesen, M. 2003. *Gott erfahren—wie geht das? Psychologie und Praxis der Gottesbegegnung*. Freiburg: Herder.

Jinkins, M. 2001. *Invitation to Theology*. Downers Grove: InterVarsity.

Joas, H. 1996. *The Creativity of Action*. Cambridge: Polity.
Jochum, R., and C. Stark, editor. 1991. *Theologie für gebrannte Kinder: Beiträge zu einer neuen politischen Theologie*. Freiburg: Herder.
Joest, W. 1988. *Fundamentaltheologie*. Theologische Wissenschaft 11. 3rd ed. Stuttgart: Kohlhammer.
———. 1995. *Dogmatik: Die Wirklichkeit Gottes*. Band 1. 4th ed. Göttingen: Vandenhoeck & Ruprecht.
———. 1996. *Dogmatik: Der Weg Gottes mit dem Menschen*. Band 2. 4. Auflage. Göttingen: Vandenhoeck & Ruprecht.
Johnson, C., and B. Adelman. 2000. *King: The Photobiography of Martin Luther King Jr.* New York: Penguin Putnam.
Johnson, L. T. 1991. *The Gospel of Luke*. Sacra Pagina. Vol. 3. Collegeville: Liturgical.
Johnson, M. 1987. *The Body in the Mind: The Bodily Basis of Meaning, Imagination, and Reason*. Chicago: Chicago University Press.
Johnson, W. S. 1997. *The Mystery of God: Karl Barth and the Postmodern Foundations of Theology*. Louisville: Westminster John Knox.
Johnston, R. K. 2000. *Reel Spirituality: Theology and Film in Dialogue*. Engaging Culture. Grand Rapids: Baker Academic.
———, editor. 2007. *Reframing Theology and Film: New Focus for an Emerging Discipline*. Cultural Exegesis. Grand Rapids: Baker Academic.
Jones, A. C. 1993. *Wade in the Water: The Wisdom of the Spirituals*. Maryknoll: Orbis.
Jones, G. L., editor. 2004. *The Blackwell Companion to Modern Theology*. Blackwell Companions to Religion. Malden: Blackwell.
———, and S. Paulsell, editors. 2002. *The Scope of Our Art: The Vocation of the Theological Teacher*. Grand Rapids: Eerdmans.
Jones, J. J. 2002a. *A Grammar of Christian Faith: Systematic Explorations in Christian Life and Doctrine*. Vol. 1. Lanham: Rowman & Littlefield.
———. 2002b. *A Grammar of Christian Faith: Systematic Explorations in Christian Life and Doctrine*. Vol. 2. Lanham: Rowman & Littlefield.
Jones, P. 2003. *Introducing Social Theory*. Cambridge: Polity.
Jones, S. 2000. *Feminist Theory and Christian Theology: Cartographies of Grace*. Guides to Theological Inquiry. Minneapolis: Fortress.
———, and P. Lakeland, editors. 2005. *Constructive Theology: A Contemporary Approach to Classical Themes*. Minneapolis: Fortress.
Jones, W. P. 1989. *Theological Worlds: Understanding the Alternative Rhythms of Christian Belief*. Nashville: Abingdon.
Judovitz, D. 2001. *The Culture of the Body: Genealogies of Modernity*. Ann Arbor: The University of Michigan Press.
Jung, P. B., and S. Jung, editors. 2003. *Moral Issues and Christian Responses*. Belmont: Wadsworth/Thompson Learning.
Jüngel, E. 1976. *The Doctrine of the Trinity: God's Being is in Becoming*. Grand Rapids: Eerdmans.
———. 1983. *God as the Mystery of the World: On the Foundation of the Theology of the Crucified One in the Dispute Between Theism and Atheism*. Grand Rapids: Eerdmans.
———. 1990. *Wertlose Wahrheit: Zur Identität und Relevanz des christlichen Glaubens*. Munich: Chr. Kaiser.

Bibliography

Kahane, A. 2010. *Power and Love: A Theory and Practice of Social Change.* San Francisco: Berrett-Koehler.
Kahl, J. 1968. *Das Elend des Christentums oder Plädoyer für eine Humanität ohne Gott.* Reinbek: Rowohlt Taschenbuch.
Kaiser, N., editor. 1994. *Selbst bewusst: Frauen in den USA.* Leipzig: Reclam.
Kalsky, M. 2000. *Christaphanien: Die Re-Vision der Christologie aus der Sicht von Frauen in unterschiedlichen Kulturen.* Gütersloh: Chr. Kaiser/Gütersloher.
Kamitsuka, D. G. 1999. *Theology and Contemporary Culture: Liberation, Postliberal, and Revisionary Perspectives.* Cambridge: Cambridge University Press.
Kane, P. 2004. *The Play Ethic: A Manifesto for a Different Way of Living.* London: Macmillan.
Kantzenbach, F. W. 1988a. *Christentum in der Gesellschaft: Kleine Sozialgeschichte des Christentums. Band 1. Alte Kirche und Mittelalter.* Saarbrücken-Scheidt: Rita Dadder.
———. 1988b. *Christentum in der Gesellschaft: Kleine Sozialgeschichte des Christentums. Band 2. Reformation und Neuzeit.* Saarbrücken-Scheidt: Rita Dadder.
Kanyoro, M. R. A., editor. 1997. *In Search of a Round Table: Gender, Theology, and Church Leadership.* Geneva: WCC.
———, and W. S. Robins, editors. 1992. *The Power We Celebrate: Women's Stories of Faith and Power.* Geneva: WCC.
Kärkkäinen, V. M. 2002a. *An Introduction to Ecclesiology: Ecumenical, Historical, and Global Perspectives.* Downers Grove: InterVarsity.
———. 2002b. *Pneumatology: The Holy Spirit in Ecumenical, International, and Contextual Perspective.* Grand Rapids: Baker Academic.
———. 2003. *Christology: A Global Introduction.* Grand Rapids: Baker Academic.
———. 2004. *The Doctrine of God: A Global Introduction.* Grand Rapids: Baker Academic.
Karris, R. J. 1985. *Luke: Artist and Theologian, Luke's Passion Account as Literature.* New York: Paulist.
Kaufman, G. D. 1968. *Systematic Theology: A Historicist Perspective.* New York: Charles Scribner's Sons.
———. 1981. *The Theological Imagination: Constructing the Concept of God.* Philadelphia: Westminster.
———. 1993. *In Face of Mystery: A Constructive Theology.* Cambridge: Harvard University Press.
———. 2000. *In the Beginning . . . Creativity.* Minnepolis: Augsburg Fortress.
———. 2006. *Jesus and Creativity.* Minneapolis: Fortress.
Kaylor, D. R. 1994. *Jesus the Prophet: His Vision of the Kingdom on Earth.* Louisville: Westminster John Knox.
Keane, J. 2003. *Global Civil Society?* New York: Cambridge University Press.
Kearney, R. 2002. *Strangers, Gods and Monsters: Interpreting Otherness.* New York: Routledge.
Kee, H. C., E. Albu, C. Lindberg, J. W. Frost, and D. L. Robert. 1997. *Christianity: A Social and Cultural History.* 2nd ed. Upper Saddle River: Prentice-Hall.
Keen, R. 2004. *The Christian Tradition.* Upper Saddle River: Prentice-Hall.
Keith, M., and S. Pile, editors. 1993. *Place and the Politics of Identity.* New York: Routledge.
Keller, C. 1986. *From a Broken Web: Separation, Sexism, and Self.* Boston: Beacon.

———. 2003. *Face of the Deep: A Theology of Becoming.* New York: Routledge.
———. 2005. *God and Power: Counter-Apocalyptic Journeys.*
———, and A. Daniell, editors. 2002. *Process and Difference: Between Cosmological and Poststructuralist Postmodernisms.* Albany: State University of New York Press.
———, M. Nausner, and M. Rivera, editors. 2004. *Postcolonial Theologies: Divinity and Empire.* St. Louis: Chalice.
Kelly, M., editor. 1990. *Hermeneutics and Critical Theory in Ethics and Politics.* Cambridge: The MIT Press.
———, editor. 1994. *Critique and Power: Recasting the Foucault/Habermas Debate.* Cambridge: The MIT Press.
Kelsey, D. H. 1993. *Between Athens and Berlin: The Theological Education Debate.* Grand Rapids: Eerdmans.
Kennedy, P. 1993a. *Deus Humanissimus: The Knowability of God in the Theology of Edward Schillebeeckx.* Fribourg: University Press Fribourg Switzerland.
———. 1993b. *Schillebeeckx.* Collegeville: Michael Glazier.
Kerby, A. P. 1991. *Narrative and the Self.* Bloomington: Indiana University Press.
Keupp, H. 1997. *Ermutigung zum aufrechten Gang.* Tübingen: Deutsche Gesellschaft für Verhaltenstherapie.
———. 1999. *Identitätskonstruktionen: Das Patchwork der Identitäten in der Spätmoderne.* Rowohlts Enzyklopädie. Hamburg: Rowohlt Taschenbuch.
Kidwell, C. S., H. Noley, G. E. Tinker. 2001. *A Native American Theology.* Maryknoll: Orbis.
Kinast, R. L. 1996. *Let Ministry Teach: A Guide to Theological Reflection.* Collegeville: Liturgical.
———. 1999. *Making Faith-Sense: Theological Reflection in Everyday Life.* Collegeville: Liturgical.
———. 2000. *What Are They Saying About Theological Reflection?* New York/Mahwah: Paulist.
King, M. L. 1992. *I Have a Dream: Writings and Speeches that Changed the World.* Edited by James Melvin Washington. San Francisco: Harper.
Kirk-Duggan, C. A. 2001. *Refiner's Fire: A Religious Engagement with Violence.* Minneapolis: Fortress.
———. 2001a. *Misbegotten Anguish: A Theology and Ethics of Violence.* St. Louis: Chalice.
Kirkpatrick, D., editor. 1988. *Faith Born in the Struggle for Life: A Rereading of Protestant Faith in Latin America Today.* Grand Rapids: Eerdmans.
Kirkpatrick, F. G. 2001. *The Ethics of Community.* New Dimensions to Religious Ethics Vol. 1. Malden: Blackwell.
———. 2003. *A Moral Ontology for a Theistic Ethic: Gathering the Nations in Love and Justice.* Burlington: Ashgate.
Kitamori, K. 1974. *Theology of the Pain of God.* Richmond: John Knox Press, 1965/1946.
Kitzberger, I. R. 2002. *Autobiographical Biblical Criticism: Between Text and Self.* Leiden: Deo.
Klaassen, W. 1973. *Anabaptism: Neither Catholic nor Protestant.* Waterloo: Conrad.
Klammer, B. 1995. *Projekttheologie: Ein Manifest.* Zürich: Ammann.
Klarer, M. 1999. *An Introduction to Literary Studies.* New York: Routledge.
Kleber, E. W. 1993. *Grundzüge ökologischer Pädagogik: Eine Einführung in ökologisch-pädagogisches Denken.* Munich: Juventa.

Bibliography

Kleden, P. B. 2000. *Christologie in Fragmenten: Die Rede von Jesus Christus im Spannungsfeld von Hoffnungs- und Leidensgeschichte bei Johann Baptist Metz.* Münster: LIT.

Klein, S. 1994. *Theologie und empirische Biographieforschung: Methodische Zugänge zur Lebens- und Glaubensgeschichte und ihre Bedeutung für eine erfahrungsbezogene Theologie.* Stuttgart: Kohlhammer.

———. 1998. "Von den Erfahrungen von Frauen zu feministischer Theologie: Hören und Erzählen als Ermächtigung zu neuem Sein von Frauen und zu einer neuen Rede von Gott." In Meyer-Wilmes H., Troch L., Bons-Storm R. (Eds.). *Feminist Perspectives in Pastoral Theology.* Yearbook of the European Society of Women in Theological Research. Volume 6/98. Mainz: Matthias-Grünewald Verlag, 47-71.

Kleinman, A., V. Das, and M. Lock, editors. 1997. *Social Suffering.* Berkeley: University of California Press.

Klemm, U. 1984. *Anarchistische Pädagogik: Über den Zusammenhang von Lernen und Freiheit in der Bildungskonzeption Leo N. Tolstois.* Siegen-Eiserfeld: Winddruck.

Kliever L. D. 1981. *The Shattered Spectrum: A Survey of Contemporary Theology.* Atlanta: John Knox.

Klinger, E. 1990. *Armut—Eine Herausforderung Gottes: Der Glaube des Konzils und die Befreiung des Menschen.* Zürich: Benziger.

———, W. Knecht, and O. Fuchs, editor. 2001. *Die globale Verantwortung: Partnerschaften zwischen Pfarreien in Deutschland und Peru.* Würzburg: Echter.

Klosinski, L. E. 1988. *The Meals in Mark.* Ann Arbor: University Microfilms.

Knapp, G. P. 1989. *The Art of Living: Erich Fromm's Life and Works.* New York: Peter Lang.

Koenig, J. 1985. *New Testament Hospitality: Partnership with Strangers as Promise and Mission.* Overtures to Biblical Theology 17. Philadelphia: Fortress.

Koffler, J. 2001. *Mit-Leid: Geschichte und Problematik eines ethischen Grundwortes.* Studien zur systematischen und spirituellen Theologie 34. Würzburg: Echter.

Kolchin, P. 1993. *American Slavery: 1619-1877.* New York: Penguin Putnam.

Körner, R. 2004. *Weisheit: Die Spiritualität des Menschen.* Leipzig: St. Benno.

Korsmeyer, C., editor. 1998. *Aesthetics: The Big Questions.* Oxford: Blackwell.

Kort, W. 1992. *Bound to Differ: The Dynamics of Theological Discourses.* University Park: The Pennsylvania State University Press.

Korte, H., and B. Schäfers, editors. 2002. *Einführung in Hauptbegriffe der Soziologie.* Einführungskurs Soziologie. Vol. 1. Edited by H. Korte and B. Schäfers. Opladen: Leske+Budrich.

Koschorke, K., F. Ludwig, and M. Delgado, editors. 2004. *Aussereuropäische Christentumsgeschichte: Asien, Afrika, Lateinamerika 1450-1990.* Neukirchen-Vluyn: Neukirchener.

Kösel, E. 1993. *Die Modellierung von Lernwelten: Ein Handbuch zur Subjektiven Didaktik.* Elztal-Dallau: Laub.

Koyama, K. 1974. *Waterbuffalo Theology.* Maryknoll: Orbis.

———. 1976. *No Handle on the Cross: An Asian Meditation on the Crucified Mind.* London: SCM.

———. 1999. *Waterbuffalo Theology.* Twenty-Fifth Anniversary Edition. Rev. and exp. Maryknoll: Orbis.

Kraimer K. 1994. "Lebenswelt als Konzept." In *Die Rückgewinnung des Pädagogischen: Aufgaben und Methoden sozialpädagogischer Forschung*, 63–194. Weinheim: Juventa.

Kramarae, C., M. Shulz, and W. O'Barr, editors. 1984. *Language and Power*. London: Sage.

Kramer, J. 1997. *British Cultural Studies*. Munich: Wilhelm Fink.

Kramer Silverman, P. 1998a. "The Dismissal of Hagar in Five Art Works of the Sixteenth and Seventeenth Centuries." In *Genesis: A Feminist Companion to the Bible*, edited by A. Brenner, 195–217. Second Series. Sheffield: Sheffield Academic.

———. (1998b). "Biblical Women that Come in Pairs: The Use of Female Paris as a Literary Device in the Hebrew Bible." In Brenner A. edited by. *Genesis: A Feminist Companion to the Bible*. Second Series. Sheffield: Sheffield Academic, 218-232.

Kraus, G. 1994. *Gott als Wirklichkeit: Lehrbuch zur Gotteslehre*. Grundrisse zur Dogmatik. Vol. 1. Frankfurt: Josef Knecht.

———. 1997. *Welt und Mensch: Lehrbuch zur Schöpfungslehre*. Grundrisse zur Dogmatik. Vol. 2. Frankfurt: Josef Knecht.

Kraus, H. J. 1983. *Systematische Theologie im Kontext biblischer Geschichte und Eschatologie*. Neukirchen-Vluyn: Neukirchener.

Kraybill, D. B. 1990. *The Upside-Down Kingdom*. Rev. ed. Scottdale: Herald.

———. 2003/1978. *The Upside-Down Kingdom*. 25th Anniversary Edition. Scottdale: Herald.

Kreisberg, S. 1992. *Transforming Power: Domination, Empowerment, and Education*. Albany: State University of New York Press.

Kreitzer, L. J., and D. W. Rooke, editors. 2000. *Ciphers in the Sand: Interpretations of The Woman Taken in Adultery (John 7.53–8.11)*. Sheffield: Sheffield Academic.

Kress, G. 2001. "Sociolinguistics and social semiotics." In *The Routledge Companion to Semiotics and Linguistics*, edited by P. Cobley, 66–82. New York: Routledge.

Krieg, C., T. Kucharz, and M. Volf, editors. 1996. *Die Theologie auf dem Weg in das dritte Jahrtausend: Festschrift für Jürgen Moltmann zum 70. Geburtstag*. Gütersloh: Chr.Kaiser/Gütersloher.

Krieger, D. J. 1991. *The New Universalism: Foundations for a Global Theology*. Maryknoll: Orbis.

Krieger, S. 1991. *Social Science and the Self: Personal Essays on an Art Form*. New Brunswick: Rutgers University Press.

Kruks, S. 2001. *Retrieving Experience: Subjectivity and Recognition in Feminist Politics*. Ithaca: Cornell University Press.

Kuhn, T. 1970. *The Structure of Scientific Revolutions*. 2nd ed. Chicago: University of Chicago Press.

Kuld, L. 1997. *Glaube in Lebensgeschichten: Ein Beitrag zur theologischen Autobiographieforschung*. Stuttgart: Kohlhammer.

Küng, H. 1988. *Theology for the Third Millennium: An Ecumenical View*. New York: Doubleday.

———. 2002. *Erkämpfte Freiheit—Erinnerungen*. Munich: Piper.

———, and Tracy D., editors. 1989. *Paradigm Change in Theology: A Symposium for the Future*. Edinburgh: T. & T. Clark.

Küster, V. 1999. *Die vielen Gesichter Jesu Christi: Christologie interkulturell*. Neukirchen-Vluyn: Neukirchener.

———. 2001. *The Many Faces of Jesus Christ: Intercultural Christology*. London: SCM.

Bibliography

Kwok, Pui-lan. 1995. *Discovering the Bible in the Non-Biblical World*. Maryknoll: Orbis.

———. 1997. "The Sources and Resources of Feminist Theologies: A Post-Colonial Perspective." In *Sources and Resources of Feminist Theologies* edited by E. Hartlieb and C. Methuen, 5–23. Yearbook of the European Society of Women in Theological Research. Vol. 5/97. Mainz: Matthias-Grünewald.

———. 2005. *Postcolonial Imagination and Feminist Theology*. Louisville: Westminster John Knox.

———, D. H. Compier, and J. Rieger, editors. 2007. *Empire and the Christian Tradition: New Readings of Classical Theologians*. Minneapolis: Fortress.

Lacelle, E. J., and T. R. Potvin, editors. 1983. *L'expérience comme lieu théologique: Discussions actuelles*. Montréal: Fides.

LaCugna, C. M., editor. 1993. *Freeing Theology: The Essentials of Theology in Feminist Perspective*. New York: HarperCollins.

Lakeland, P. 1990. *Theology and Critical Theory: The Discourse of the Church*. Nashville: Abingdon.

———. 1997. *Postmodernity: Christian Identity in a Fragmented Age*. Guides to Theological Inquiry. Minneapolis: Augsburg Fortress.

Lakoff, G., and M. Johnson. 1980. *Metaphors We Live By*. Chicago: The University of Chicago Press.

Lakoff, R. 1975. *Language and Woman's Place*. New York: Harper & Row.

Lamb, M. L. 1982. *Solidarity with Victims: Toward a Theology of Social Transformation*. New York: Crossroad.

Lane, D. A. 1984. *Foundations for a Social Theology: Praxis, Process, and Salvation*. Ramsey: Paulist.

Lane, T. 2006. *A Concise History of Christian Thought*. Rev. and exp. ed. Grand Rapids: Baker Academic.

Lange, D. 2001a. *Glaubenslehre*. Vol. 1. Tübingen: Mohr Siebeck.

———. 2001b. *Glaubenslehre*. Vol. 2. Tübingen: Mohr Siebeck.

Lange, E. 1980. *Sprachschule für die Freiheit: Bildung als Problem und Funktion der Kirche*. Munich: Chr. Kaiser/Burckhardthaus.

Lash, S. 2002. *Critique of Information*. Thousand Oaks: Sage.

Latourelle, R., and R. Fisichella, editors. 2000. *Dictionary of Fundamental Theology*. New York: Crossroad/Herder.

Lechte, J. 2003. *Key Contemporary Concepts: From Abjection to Zeno's Paradox*. Thousand Oaks: Sage.

Lederach, J. P. 1999. *The Journey Toward Reconciliation*. Scottdale: Herald.

———. 2004. *The Moral Imagination: The Art and Soul of Building Peace*. New York: Oxford University Press.

Lee, B. 1974. *The Becoming of the Church: A Process Theology of the Structures of Christian Experience*. New York: Paulist.

Lee, J. 1995. *Clowns for Beginners*. New York: Writers and Readers.

Lee, J. Y. 1995. *Marginality: The Key to Multicultural Theology*. Minneapolis: Fortress.

Lehmann, T. 1996. *Negro Spirituals: Geschichte und Theologie*. Neuhausen-Stuttgart: Hänssler.

Leicht, I., C. Rakel, and S. Rieger-Goertz, editors. 2003. *Arbeitsbuch feministische Theologie: Inhalte, Methoden und Materialien für Hochschule, Erwachsenenbildung und Gemeinde*. Gütersloh: Chr. Kaiser/Gütersloher.

Leitch, V. B., editor. 2001. *The Norton Anthology of Theory and Criticism*. New York: Norton.
Leith, J. H. 1993. *Basic Christian Doctrine*. Louisville: Westminster John Knox.
Leledakis, K. 1995. *Society and Psyche: Social Theory and the Unconscious Dimension of the Social*. Washington: Berg.
Lemert, C., and A. Branaman, editors. 1997. *The Goffman Reader*. Malden: Blackwell.
Lemke, H. 2000. *Freundschaft: Ein philosophischer Essay*. Darmstadt: Wissenschaftliche Buch-gesellschaft.
Leonhardt, R. 2004. *Grundinformation Dogmatik: Ein Lehr- und Arbeitsbuch für das Studium der Theologie*. 2nd ed. Göttingen: Vandenhoeck & Ruprecht.
Lesch, W., and G. Schwind, editors. 1993. *Das Ende der alten Gewissheiten: Theologische Auseinandersetzung mit der Postmoderne*. Mainz: Matthias-Grünewald.
Levesque-Lopman, L. 1988. *Claming Reality: Phenomenology and Women's Experience*. Totowa: Rowman & Littlefield.
Levinas, E. 1969. *Totality and Infinity: An Essay on Exteriority*. Pittsburgh: Duquesne University Press.
———. 1987. *Time and the Other (and Additional Essays)*. Pittsburgh: Duquesne University Press.
Lewis, J. 2008. *Cultural Studies: The Basics*. Thousand Oaks: Sage.
Liechty, D. 1990. *Theology in Postliberal Perspective*. Philadelphia: Trinity.
Lienemann, W. 2000. *Frieden*. Ökumenische Studienhefte 10. Göttingen: Vandenhoeck & Ruprecht.
Lienhard, F. 2000. *De la pauvreté au service en Christ*. Paris: Cerf.
Lincoln, Y. S., and W. Tierney, editors. 1996. *Representation and the Text: Reframing the Narrative Voice*. Albany: State University of New York Press.
Lindbeck, G. A. 1984. *The Nature of Doctrine: Religion and Theology in a Postliberal Age*. Philadelphia: Westminster.
———. 1994. *Christliche Lehre als Grammatik des Glaubens: Religion und Theologie im postliberalen Zeitalter*. Gütersloh: Chr. Kaiser/Gütersloher.
Link, C. 1991a. *Schöpfung: Schöpfungstheologie in reformatorischer Tradition*. Handbuch Systematischer Theologie Band 7/1. Gütersloh: Gütersloher Verlagshaus.
———. (1991b). *Schöpfung: Schöpfungstheologie angesichts der Herausforderungen des 20. Jahrhunderts*. Handbuch Systematischer Theologie. Vol. 7/2. Gütersloh: Gütersloher.
Link-Wieczorek, U., R. Miggelbrink, D. Sattler, M. Haspel, U. Swarat, and H. Bedford-Strohm. 2004. *Nach Gott im Leben fragen: Ökumenische Einführung in das Christentum*. Gütersloh: Gütersloher/Herder.
Lints, R. 1993. "The Postpositivist Choice: Tracy or Lindbeck?" *Journal of the American Academy of Religion* 61, 655–77.
———. 1993a. *The Fabric of Theology: A Prolegomenon to Evangelical Theology*. Grand Rapids: Eerdmans.
Lipp, W. 1985. *Stigma und Charisma: Über soziales Grenzverhalten*. Schriften zur Kultur-soziologie. Berlin: Dietrich Reimer.
Lischer, R. 1995. *The Preacher King: Martin Luther King, Jr. and The Word That Moved America*. New York: Oxford University Press.
Litonjua, M. D. 2003. *Structures of Sin, Cultures of Meaning: Social Science and Theology*. New York: 1stBooks Library.

Bibliography

Littell, F. H. 1958. *The Anabaptist View of the Church: A Study in the Origins of Sectarian Protestantism*. Boston: Starr King/Beacon Hill.

Little, A. 2002. *The Politics of Community: Theory and Practice*. Edinburgh: Edinburgh University Press.

Livingston, J. C., and E. Schüssler Fiorenza, with S. Coakley, and J. H. Evans 2000. *Modern Christian Thought: The Twentieth Century*. Vol. 2. Upper Saddle River: Prentice-Hall.

———. 2006. *Modern Christian Thought: The Twentieth Century*. Vol. 2. 2nd ed. Minneapolis: Fortress.

Loebbert, M. 2003. *Storymanagement: Der narrative Ansatz für Management und Beratung*. Stuttgart: Klett-Cotta.

Lohfink, G. 1988. *Wem gilt die Bergpredigt? Beiträge zu einer christlichen Ethik*. Freiburg: Herder.

Lohfink, N. F. 1987. *Option for the Poor: The Basic Principle of Liberation Theology in the Light of the Bible*. Berkeley: BIBAL.

Long, E. L. 1997. *To Liberate and Redeem: Moral Reflections on the Biblical Narrative*. Cleveland: Pilgrim.

Long, S. D. 2001. *The Goodness of God: Theology, the Church, and Social Order*. Grand Rapids: Brazos.

Longino, H. E. 1990. *Science as Social Knowledge*. Princeton: Princeton University Press, 1990.

———. 1999. "Feminist Epistemology." In *The Blackwell Guide to Epistemology*, edited by J. Greco and E. Sosa, 327–53. Oxford: Blackwell.

Louis, J. H., and J.-O. Heron 1990. *William Penn et les quakers: Ils inventèrent le Nouveau Monde*. Paris: Gallimard.

Löw, M. 2001. *Raumsoziologie*. Frankfurt: Suhrkamp.

Lucie-Smith, E. 1995. *Art Today*. London: Phaidon.

Lundgren, S. 1998. *Fight Against Idols: Erich Fromm on Religion, Judaism, and the Bible*. New York: Peter Lang.

Luther, H. 1990. "Das unruhige Herz: Über implizite Zusammenhänge zwischen Autobiographie, Subjektivität und Religion." In *Wer schreibt meine Lebensgeschichte? Biographie, Autobiographie, Hagiographie und ihre Entstehungszusammenhänge*, edited by W. Sparn, 360–85. Gütersloh: Gütersloher.

Lüthi, K. 1971. *Theologie als Dialog mit der Welt von heute*. Quaestiones Disputatae 53. Freiburg: Herder.

Lutter, C., and M. Reisenleitner. 1998. *Cultural Studies: Eine Einführung*. Vienna: Turia+Kant.

Lutz, B., editor. 2003. *Metzler Philosophen Lexikon: Von den Vorsokratikern bis zu den Neuen Philosophen*. Stuttgart: J. B. Metzler.

Lutz, C. A., and L. Abu-Lughod, editors. 1990. *Language and the Politics of Emotion*. New York: Cambridge University Press.

Lyas, C. 1997. *Aesthetics*. London: UCL Press.

Lynch, G. 2005. *Understanding Theology and Popular Culture*. New York: Wiley-Blackwell.

Lynton, N. 1989. *The Story of Modern Art*. London: Phaidon.

Maassen, M. 1993. *Biographie und Erfahrung von Frauen: Ein feministisch-theologischer Beitrag zur Relevanz der Biographieforschung für die Wiedergewinnung der Kategorie Erfahrung*. Münster: Morgana.

Bibliography

Macey, D. 2000. *The Penguin Dictionary of Critical Theory.* New York: Penguin Putnam.
Mach, Z. 1993. *Symbols, Conflict, and Identity: Essays in Political Anthropology.* Albany: State University of New York Press.
Mackey, J. P. 1994. *Power and Christian Ethics.* Cambridge: Cambridge University Press.
Macquarrie, J. 2001. *Twentieth-Century Religious Thought.* 5th ed. London: SCM.
———. 2002. *Twentieth-Century Religious Thought.* New ed. Harrisburg: Trinity.
Madison, G. B. 1988. *The Hermeneutics of Postmodernity: Figures and Themes.* Bloomington: Indiana University Press.
Magnusson, W. 1996. *The Search for Political Space: Globalization, Social Movements, and the Urban Political Experience.* Toronto: University of Toronto Press.
Maguire, D. C. 1993. *The Moral Core of Judaism and Christianity: Reclaiming the Revolution.* Minneapolis: Fortress; reprinted 2004, Wipf & Stock.
———. 2005. *A Moral Creed for All Christians.* Minneapolis: Fortress.
Malherbe, A. J. 1983. *Social Aspects of Early Christianity.* Philadelphia: Fortress.
Malina, B. J. 1993. *The New Testament World: Insights from Cultural Anthropology.* Louisville: Westminster John Knox.
———. 1993a. *Windows on the World of Jesus: Time Travel to Ancient Judea.* Louisville: Westminster John Knox.
———. 1996. *The Social World of Jesus and the Gospels.* New York: Routledge.
———. 1998. "Feast." In *Handbook of Biblical Social Values,* edited by J. J. Pilch and B. J. Malina, 81–84. Peabody: Hendrickson.
———. 2001. *The Social Gospel of Jesus: The Kingdom of God in Mediterranean Perspective.* Minneapolis: Fortress.
———, and R. L. Rohrbaugh. 1992. *Social-Science Commentary on the Synoptic Gospels.* Minneapolis: Augsburg Fortress.
Mann, B. 2006. *Women's Liberation and the Sublime: Feminism, Postmodernism, Environment.* Studies in Feminist Philosophy. New York: Oxford University Press.
Mannion, G. 2007. *Ecclesiology and Postmodernity: Questions for the Church in Our Time.* Collegeville: Michael Glazier.
Marchart, O. 2007. *Cultural Studies.* Stuttgart: UTB.
Marcus, G. E. 1998. *Ethnography Through Thick and Thin.* Princeton: Princeton University Press.
Markham, I. S. 2003. *A Theology of Engagement.* Malden: Blackwell.
Marquardt, F. W. 1988. *Von Elend und Heimsuchung der Theologie: Prolegomena zur Dogmatik.* Munich: Chr. Kaiser.
Marsden, G. M., editor. 1984. *Evangelicalism and Modern America.* Grand Rapids: Eerdmans.
———. 1987. *Reforming Fundamentalism: Fuller Seminary and the New Evangelicalism.* Grand Rapids: Eerdmans.
———. 2001. *Religion and American Culture.* 2nd ed. Belmont: Wadsworth.
Marsh, C. 2005. *The Beloved Community: How Faith Shapes Social Justice, from the Civil Rights Movement to Today.* New York: Basic.
Martin, R. P. 1989. *Reconciliation: A Study of Paul's Theology.* Grand Rapids: Zondervan.
Martinez, G. 2001. *Confronting the Mystery of God: Political, Liberation, and Public Theologies.* New York: Continuum.
Matsuoka, F., and E. S. Fernandez, editors. 2003. *Realizing the America of Our Hearts: Theological Voices of Asian Americans.* St. Louis: Chalice.

Bibliography

Matthiae, G. 1999. *Clownin Gott: Eine feministische Dekonstruktion des Göttlichen.* Stuttgart: Kohlhammer.

Mauk, D., and J. Oakland. 2002. *American Civilization: An Introduction.* 3rd ed. New York: Routledge.

Mayo M. 2000. *Cultures, Communities, Identities: Cultural Strategies for Participation and Empowerment.* New York: Palgrave Macmillan.

McBrien, R. 1994. *Catholicism.* 3rd ed. Rev. and updated. San Francisco: HarperSanFrancisco.

McClendon, J. W. 1986. *Ethics.* Systematic Theology. Vol. 1. Nashville: Abingdon.

———. 1990. *Biography as Theology: How Life Stories Can Remake Today's Theology.* Philadelphia: Trinity.

———. 1994. *Doctrine.* Systematic Theology. Vol. 2. Nashville: Abingdon.

———. 2000. *Witness.* Systematic Theology. Vol. 3. Nashville: Abingdon.

———. 2002. *Ethics.* Systematic Theology. Vol. 1. 2nd ed. Rev. and enl. Nashville: Abingdon.

———, and J. M. Smith 1975. *Understanding Religious Convictions.* Notre Dame: University of Notre Dame Press.

———. 1994. *Convictions: Diffusing Religious Relativism.* Rev. ed. Philadelphia: Trinity; reprinted 2002, Wipf & Stock.

McClintock Fulkerson, M. 1994. *Changing the Subject: Women's Discourses and Feminist Theology.* Minneapolis: Fortress.

———. 2005. "'They Will Know We are Christians by Our Regulated Improvisation': Ecclesial Hybridity and the Unity of the Church." In *The Blackwell Companion to Postmodern Theology,* edited by G. Ward, 265–79. Malden: Blackwell.

McDaniel, J. B. 1989. *Of God and Pelicans: A Theology of Reverence for Life.* Louisville: Westminster John Knox.

———. 1990. *Earth, Sky, Gods & Mortals: Developing an Ecological Spirituality.* Mystic: Twenty-Third.

———. 1995. *With Roots and Wings: Christianity in an Age of Ecology and Dialogue.* Maryknoll: Orbis.

———. 2000. *Living from the Center: Spirituality in an Age of Consumerism.* St. Louis: Chalice.

McDermott, G., editor. 2010. *The Oxford Handbook of Evangelical Theology.* New York: Oxford University Press.

McDonogh, G. W., R. Gregg, and C. H. Wong, editors. 2001. *Encyclopedia of Contemporary American Culture.* New York: Routledge.

McEnhill, P., and G. Newlands 2004. *Fifty Key Christian Thinkers.* New York: Routledge.

McEvenue, S. 1990. *Interpreting the Pentateuch.* Old Testament Studies. Vol. 4. Collegeville: Liturgical.

McFague, S. 1987. *Models of God: Theology for an Ecological, Nuclear Age.* Philadelphia: Fortress.

———. 1993. *The Body of God: An Ecological Theology.* Minneapolis: Fortress.

———. 1997. *Super, Natural Christians: How We Should Love Nature.* Minneapolis: Fortress.

McFarland, I. A. 1998. *Listening to the Least: Doing Theology from the Outside In.* Cleveland: United Church Press.

McGaughey, D. R. 1997. *Strangers and Pilgrims: On the Role of Aporiai in Theology.* New York & Berlin: De Gruyter.

McGowan, J. 2002. *Democracy's Children: Intellectuals and the Rise of Cultural Politics.* Ithaca: Cornell University Press.
McGrath, A. E. 1993. *Evangelicalism and the Future of Christianity.* London: Hodder & Stoughton.
———. 1996. *A Passion for Truth: The Intellectual Coherence of Evangelicalism.* Downers Grove: InterVarsity.
———. 1997. *Der Weg der christlichen Theologie: Eine Einführung.* Munich: C. H. Beck.
———. 1998. *Historical Theology: An Introduction to the History of Christian Thought.* Malden: Blackwell.
———. 1999. *Science & Religion: An Introduction.* Oxford: Blackwell.
———. 2001. *Christian Theology: An Introduction.* 3rd ed. Malden: Blackwell.
———, editor. 2001a. *The Christian Theology Reader.* 2nd ed. Malden: Blackwell.
———. 2002. *The Future of Christianity.* Malden: Blackwell.
———. 2004. *The Science of God: An Introduction to Scientific Theology.* Edinburgh: T. & T. Clark.
———. 2004a. *Theology: The Basics.* Malden: Blackwell.
———. 2011. *Der Weg der christlichen Theologie: Eine Einführung.* Neue Ausgabe. Giessen: Brunnen.
McKenna, A. J. 1992. *Violence and Difference: Girard, Derrida, and Deconstruction.* Urbana: University of Illinois Press.
McKenna, M. 1994. *Not Counting Women and Children: Neglected Stories from the Bible.* Maryknoll: Orbis.
McKenzie, J. L. 1965. *Dictionary of the Bible.* New York: Macmillan.
McKenzie, S. L. 1997. *All God's Children: A Biblical Critique of Racism.* Louisville: Westminster John Knox.
McKim, D. K. 2001. *Introducing the Reformed Faith: Biblical Revelation, Christian Tradition, Contemporary Significance.* Louisville: Westminster John Knox.
McLaren, B. D. 2006. *A Generous Orthodoxy.* Grand Rapids: Zondervan.
McLaren, P. L. 1995. *Critical Pedagogy and Predatory Culture: Oppositional Politics in a Postmodern Era.* New York: Routledge.
———. 2005. *Capitalists and Conquerors: A Critical Pedagogy against Empire.* Lanham: Rowman & Littlefield.
———, and R. Farahmandpur. 2004. *Teaching against Global Capitalism and the New Imperialism: A Critical Pedagogy.* Lanham: Rowman & Littlefield.
———, and N. Jaramilo 2009. *Pedagogy and Praxis in the Age of Empire: Towards a New Humanism.* Rotterdam: Sense.
———, and C. Lankshear, editors. 1994. *The Politics of Liberation: Paths from Freire.* New York: Routledge.
McLaughlin, D., and W. G. Tierney, editors. 1993. *Naming Silenced Lives: Personal Narratives and Processes of Educational Change.* New York: Routledge.
McLeod, J. 1997. *Narrative and Psychotherapy.* Thousand Oaks: Sage.
McWilliams, W. 1985. *The Passion of God: Divine Suffering in Contemporary Protestant Theology.* Macon: Mercer University Press.
Meeks, W. A. 1986. *The Moral World of the First Christians.* Philadelphia: Westminster.
Meier-Seethaler, C. 2001. *Gefühl und Urteilskraft: Ein Plädoyer für die emotionale Vernunft.* Munich: C. H. Beck.
Ménard, C., and F. Villeneuve, editors. 1995. *Drames humains et foi chrétienne: Approches éthiques et théologiques.* Montréal: Fides.

Bibliography

Mendieta, E., editor. 2004. *The Frankfurt School on Religion.* New York: Routledge.
Mertens, G. 1998. *Umwelten: Eine humanökologische Pädagogik.* Paderborn: Schöningh.
Mette, N. 1994. *Religionspädagogik.* Leitfaden Theologie. Vol. 24. Düsseldorf: Patmos.
———, and H. Steinkamp, editors. 1997. *Anstiftung zur Solidarität: Praktische Beispiele der Sozialpastoral.* Mainz: Matthias-Grünewald.
Metz, J. B. 1973. "A Short Apology of Narrative." *Concilium* 85, 84–96; reprinted in *Love's Strategy: The Political Theology of Johann Baptist Metz,* edited by J. K. Downey, 102–12. Harrisburg: Trinity, 1999.
———. 1978. *Followers of Christ: The Religious Life and the Church.* New York: Paulist.
———. 1980. *Faith in History and Society: Toward a Practical Fundamental Theology.* New York: Seabury.
———. 1981. *The Emergent Church: The Future of Christianity in a Post-Bourgeois World.* London: SCM.
———. 1987. "Im Aufbruch zu einer kulturell polyzentrischen Weltkirche." In *Zukunftsfähigkeit: Suchbewegungen im Christentum,* edited by F.-X. Kaufmann and J. B. Metz, 93–165. Freiburg: Herder.
———. 1992/1977. *Glaube in Geschichte und Gesellschaft: Studien zu einer praktischen Fundamentaltheologie.* Mainz: Matthias-Grünewald.
———. 1997. *Zum Begriff der neuen Politischen Theologie: 1967-1997.* Mainz: Matthias-Grünewald.
———. 1998. "On the Way to a Postidealist Theology." In *A Passion for God: The Mystical-Political Dimension of Christianity,* edited by J. M. Ashley, 30–53. Mahwah: Paulist.
———. 2006. *Memoria passionis: Ein provozierendes Gedächtnis in pluralistischer Gesellschaft.* Freiburg: Herder.
———, L. Kuld, and A. Weisbrod, editors. 2000. *Compassion—Weltprogramm des Christentums: Soziale Verantwortung lernen.* Freiburg: Herder.
———, and J. Reikenstorfer. 2011. *Mystik der offenen Augen: Wenn Spiritualität aufbricht.* Freiburg: Herder.
Meueler, E. 1986. *Erwachsene lernen: Beschreibung, Anstösse, Erfahrungen.* Stuttgart: Klett-Cotta.
———. 1993. *Die Türen des Käfigs: Wege zum Subjekt in der Erwachsenenbildung.* Stuttgart: Klett-Cotta.
Meyer, J. 1998. *Esclaves et Négriers.* Paris: Gallimard.
Meyer, T. 2003. *Was ist Politik?* 2nd ed. Opladen: Leske+Budrich.
Meyer zu Schlochtern, J. 1979. "Erzählung als Paradigma einer alternativen Denkform: Ansätze zu einer 'narrativen Theologie.'" In *Theologische Berichte 8: Wege theologischen Denkens,* edited by J. Pfammatter and F. Furger, 35–70. Zürich: Benziger.
Meyers C., T. Craven, and R. S. Kraemer, editors. 2000. *Women in Scripture: A Dictionary of Named and Unnamed Women in the Hebrew Bible, the Apocryphal/ Deuterocanonical Books, and the New Testament.* Grand Rapids: Eerdmans.
Meyers, E. S., editor. 1992. *Envisioning the New City: A Reader on Urban Ministry.* Louisville: Westminster John Knox.
Middleton, J. R., and B. J. Walsh 1995. *Truth is Stranger Than it Used to Be: Biblical Faith in a Postmodern Age.* Downers Grove: InterVarsity.

Mieth, D. 1978. "What is Experience?" *Concilium* 113, 40–53. *"Revelation and Experience"* issue, edited by E. Schillebeeckx and B. van Iersel. New York: Crossroad.

———. 1995. "Theologie, Profile und Entwicklungstendenzen im internationalen Umfeld." In *Forschungspolitisches Früherkennen*, edited by the Swiss Economic Council, 159. Bern.

Migliore, D. L. 1983. *The Power of God*. Philadelphia: Westminster.

———. 1991. *Faith Seeking Understanding: An Introduction to Christian Theology*. Grand Rapids: Eerdmans.

———. 2004. *Faith Seeking Understanding: An Introduction to Christian Theology*. 2nd ed. Grand Rapids: Eerdmans.

Mildenberger, F. 1972. *Theorie der Theologie: Enzyklopädie als Methodenlehre*. Stuttgart: Calwer.

———, and H. Assel. 1995. *Grundwissen der Dogmatik: Ein Arbeitsbuch*. 4th ed. Stuttgart: Kohlhammer.

Miller, E. L., and S. J. Grenz. 1998. *Fortress Introduction to Contemporary Theologies*. Minneapolis: Fortress.

Miller, P. 1987. *Domination and Power*. New York: Routledge & Kegan Paul.

Mills, C. W. 1959. *The Sociological Imagination*. New York: Oxford University Press.

Minnich, E. K. 1990. *Transforming Knowledge*. Philadelphia: Temple University Press.

Minow, M., and N. L. Rosenblum, editors. 2002. *Breaking the Cycles of Hatred: Memory, Law, and Repair*. Martha Minow Lectures. Edited by Nancy L. Rosenblum. Princeton: Princeton University Press.

Mitchell Corbett, J. 2000. *Religion in America*. 4th ed. Englewood Cliffs: Prentice-Hall.

Mitchem, S. Y. 2002. *Introducing Womanist Theology*. Maryknoll: Orbis.

Mödritzer, H. 1994. *Stigma und Charisma im Neuen Testament und seiner Umwelt: Zur Soziologie des Urchristentums*. Göttingen: Vandenhoeck & Ruprecht.

Molla, S. 1992. *Les idées noires de Martin Luther King*. Geneva: Labor et Fides.

Moltmann, J. 1959. *Die Gemeinde im Horizont der Herrschaft Christi: Neue Perspektiven in der protestantischen Theologie*. Neukirchen-Vluyn: Neukirchener.

———. 1964. *Theologie der Hoffnung: Untersuchungen zur Begründung und zu den Konsequenzen einer christlichen Eschatologie*. Munich: Chr. Kaiser.

———. 1967. *Theology of Hope: On the Ground and the Implications of a Christian Eschatology*. London: SCM.

———. 1969. "Toward a Political Hermeneutic of the Gospel." In *Religion, Revolution, and the Future*, 83–107. New York: Scribner's.

———. 1973. *Theology and Joy*. London: SCM.

———. 1978. *The Passion for Life: A Messianic Lifestyle*. Philadelphia: Fortress.

———. 1980. *Experiences of God*. Philadelphia: Fortress.

———. 1980a. "Why am I a Christian?" In *Experiences of God*, 1–18. Philadelphia: Fortress.

———. 1981. *The Trinity and the Kingdom of God: The Doctrine of God*. London: SCM.

———. 1983. *The Power of the Powerless: The Word of Liberation for Today*. San Francisco: Harper & Row.

———. 1984. *On Human Dignity: Political Theology and Ethics*. London: SCM.

———. 1988. *Was ist heute Theologie? Zwei Beiträge zu ihrer Vergegenwärtigung*. Quaestiones Disputatae 114. Freiburg: Herder.

Bibliography

———. 1988. *Theology Today: Two Contributions Towards Making Theology Present.* London: SCM.

———. 1988a. "An Autobiographical Note by Jürgen Moltmann." In *God, Hope, and History: Jürgen Moltmann and the Christian Concept of History,* edited by A. J. Conyers, 203–23. Macon: Mercer University Press.

———. 1991. *History and the Triune God: Contributions to Trinitarian Theology.* London: SCM.

———. 1992. *The Spirit of Life: A Universal Affirmation.* London: SCM.

———. 1992/1977. *The Church in the Power of the Spirit: A Contribution to Messianic Ecclesiology.* 2nd ed. London: SCM.

———. 1993/1967. *Theology of Hope: On the Ground and the Implications of a Christian Eschatology.* Minneapolis: Fortress.

———. 1993/1974. *The Crucified God: The Cross of Christ as the Foundation and Criticism of Christian Theology.* Minneapolis: Fortress.

———. 1993/1985. *God in Creation: A New Theology of Creation and the Spirit of God.* The Gifford Lectures 1984–1985. Minneapolis: Fortress.

———. 1993/1990. *The Way of Jesus Christ: Christology in Messianic Dimensions.* Minneapolis: Fortress.

———. 1994. *Jesus Christ for Today's World.* Minneapolis: Fortress.

———. 1996. *The Coming of God: A Christian Eschatology.* Minneapolis: Fortress.

———. 1997. *The Source of Life: The Holy Spirit and the Theology of Life.* London: SCM.

———, editor. 1997a. *How I Have Changed: Reflections on Thirty Years of Theology.* Harrisburg: Trinity.

———. 1997b. "Jürgen Moltmann." In *How I Have Changed: Reflections on Thirty Years of Theology,* edited by J. Moltmann, 13–21. Harrisburg: Trinity.

———. 1999. *Erfahrungen theologischen Denkens: Wege und Formen christlicher Theologie.* Gütersloh: Chr.Kaiser/Gütersloher.

———. 1999a. *God for a Secular Society: The Public Relevance of Theology.* Minneapolis: Fortress.

———. 2000. *Experiences in Theology: Ways and Forms of Christian Theology.* London: SCM.

———. 2002 "Gott und Raum." In *Wo ist Gott? Gotteräume—Lebensräume,* edited by J. Moltmann and C. Rivuzumwami, 29–41. Neukirchen-Vluyn: Neukirchener.

———. (2002a). *Wissenschaft und Weisheit: Zum Gespräch zwischen Naturwissenschaft und Theologie.* Gütersloh: Chr. Kaiser/Gütersloher Verlagshaus.

———. 2003. *Science and Wisdom.* Minneapolis: Fortress.

———. (2003a). *Im Ende—der Anfang: Eine kleine Hoffnungslehre.* Gütersloh: Chr. Kaiser/ Gütersloher Verlagshaus.

———. 2004. *In the End—The Beginning: The Life of Hope.* Minneapolis: Fortress.

———. 2009. *A Broad Place: An Autobiography.* Minneapolis: Fortress.

———. 2010. *Sun of Righteousness, Arise!: God's Future for Humanity and the Earth.* Minneapolis: Fortress.

———, and C. Rivuzumwami, editor. 2002. *Wo ist Gott? Gotteräume—Lebensräume.* Neukirchen-Vluyn: Neukirchener.

Moltmann-Wendel, E. 1994. *Mein Körper bin ich: Neue Wege zur Leiblichkeit.* Gütersloh: Gütersloher.

———. 1997. *Autobiography.* London: SCM, 1997.

———. 2000. *Wach auf, meine Freundin: Die Wiederkehr der Gottesfreundschaft*. Stuttgart: Kreuz.

———. 2001. *Rediscovering Friendship: Awakening to the Promise and Power of Women's Friendships*. Minneapolis: Fortress.

Moody, D. 1981. *The Word of Truth: A Summary of Christian Doctrine Based On Biblical Revelation*. Grand Rapids: Eerdmans.

Moon, J. D. 1993. *Constructing Community: Moral Pluralism and Tragic Conflicts*. Princeton: Princeton University Press.

Morley, D., and K. Robins. 1995. *Spaces of Identity: Global Media, Electronic Landscapes, and Cultural Boundaries*. New York: Routledge.

Morrison, T., editor. 1992. *Race-ing Justice, En-gendering Power: Essays on Anita Hill, Clarence Thomas, and the Construction of Social Reality*. New York: Pantheon.

Morse, C. 1994. *Not Every Spirit: A Dogmatics of Christian Disbelief*. Valley Forge: Trinity.

Mott, S. C. 1982. *Biblical Ethics and Social Change*. New York: Oxford University Press.

Mottu, H. 2002. *Dietrich Bonhoeffer*. Invitations aux théologiens. Paris: Cerf.

Mouw, R. J., and S. Griffioen 1993. *Pluralism and Horizon: An Essay in Christian Public Philosophy*. Grand Rapids: Eerdmans.

Mouzelis, N. P. 2008. *Modern and Postmodern Social Theorizing: Bridging the Divide*. New York: Cambridge University Press.

Moxnes, H. 1988. *The Economy of the Kingdom: Social Conflict and Economic Relations in Luke's Gospel*. Philadelphia: Fortress.

Mudge, L. S. 1998. *The Church as Moral Community: Ecclesiology and Ethics in Ecumenical Debate*. New York: Continuum.

———. 2001. *Rethinking the Beloved Community: Ecclesiology, Hermeneutics, Social Theory*. Lanham: University Press of America.

Mueller, J. J. 1984. *What Are They Saying About Theological Method?* Ramsey: Paulist.

———. 1988. *What is Theology?* Wilmington: Michael Glazier.

———. 2007. *Theological Foundations: Concepts and Methods for Understanding Christian Faith*. Winona: Anselm Academic.

Mueller-Vollmer, K., editor. 1988. *The Hermeneutics Reader: Texts of the German Tradition from the Enlightenment to the Present*. New York: Continuum.

Muller, R. A. 1991. *The Study of Theology: From Biblical Interpretation to Contemporary Formulation*. Grand Rapids: Zondervan.

Müller, D. 1992. *Les lieux de l'action: Ethique et religion dans une société pluraliste*. Le champs éthique 22. Geneva: Labor et Fides.

———. 1998. *Les éthiques de responsabilité dans un monde fragile*. Geneva: Labor et Fides.

———. 1999. *L'éthique protestante dans la crise de la modernité: Généalogie, critique, reconstruction*. Paris: Cerf.

———. 1999a. *La morale*. Dossiers de l'Encyclopédie du Protestantisme 4. Paris: Cerf.

———. 2005. *Karl Barth*. Initiations aux théologiens. Paris: Cerf.

Müller, G. L. 1998. *Katholische Dogmatik: Für Studium und Praxis der Theologie*. 2nd ed. Freiburg: Herder.

Müller, J. 1993. *Pastoraltheologie: Ein Handbuch für Studium und Seelsorge*. Graz: Styria.

———. 1993a. "Auf der Seite des Lebens." In *Pastoraltheologie: Ein Handbuch für Studium und Seelsorge*, 16–23. Graz: Styria.

Bibliography

Müller, K. 1994. *Wenn ich "ich" sage: Studien zur fundamentaltheologischen Relevanz selbstbewusster Subjektivität*. Frankfurt: Peter Lang.

———, editor. 1998. *Fundamentaltheologie: Fluchtlinien und gegenwärtige Herausforderungen*. Regensburg: Friedrich Pustet.

Müller, W. W. 2002. *Gnade in Welt: Eine symboltheologische Sakramentenskizze*. Münster: LIT.

Müller-Fahrenholz, G. 1997. *The Art of Forgiveness: Theological Reflections on Healing and Reconciliation*. Geneva: World Council of Churches Publications.

———. 2000. *The Kingdom and the Power: The Theology of Jürgen Moltmann*. London: SCM.

Mullings, L., editor. 2009. *New Social Movements in the African Diaspora: Challenging Global Apartheid*. Critical Black Studies. New York: Palgrave Macmillan.

Münch, R. 1991. *Dialektik der Kommunikationsgesellschaft*. Frankfurt: Suhrkamp.

Murphy, F. X. 1999. *Vatican Council II*. Maryknoll: Orbis.

Murphy, J. W. 1989. *Postmodern Social Analysis and Criticism*. New York: Greenwood.

Murphy, L. G., editor. 2000. *Down By the Riverside: Readings in African American Religion*. New York: New York University Press.

Murphy, N. 1994. "Textual Relativism, Philosophy of Language, and the baptist Vision." In *Theology Without Foundations: Religious Practice and the Future of Religious Truth*, edited by S. Hauerwas, N. Murphy, and M. Nation, 245–70. Nashville: Abingdon.

———. 1996. *Beyond Liberalism and Fundamentalism: How Modern and Postmodern Philosophy Set the Theological Agenda*. Valley Forge: Trinity.

———. 1997. *Anglo-American Postmodernity: Philosophical Perspectives on Science, Religion, and Ethics*. Boulder: Westview.

———. 1999. "Missiology in the Postmodern West: A Radical Reformation Perspective." In *To Stake a Claim: Mission and the Western Crisis of Knowledge*, edited by J. A. Kirk and K. J. Vanhoozer, 96–119. Maryknoll: Orbis.

Murray, S. 2004. *Post-Christendom: Church and Mission in a Strange New World*. Exeter: Paternoster.

Musser, D. W., and J. L. Price, editors. 1992. *A New Handbook of Christian Theology*. Nashville: Abingdon.

———, editors. 2003. *New and Enlarged Handbook of Christian Theology*. Nashville: Abingdon.

———, editors. 1996. *A New Handbook of Christian Theologians*. Nashville: Abingdon.

Myers, C. 1994. "'I Will Ask *You* a Question': Interrogatory Theology." In *Theology Without Foundations: Religious Practice and the Future of Religious Truth*, edited by S. Hauerwas, N. Murphy, and M. Nation, 91–116. Nashville: Abingdon.

Nagl-Docekal, H. 1999. *Feministische Philosophie: Ergebnisse, Probleme, Perspektiven*. Frankfurt: Fischer Taschenbuch.

Nagler, M. N. 2001. *Is There No Other Way? The Search for a Nonviolent Future*. Berkeley: Berkeley Hills.

Nanda, S. 1994. *Cultural Anthropology*. Belmont: Wadsworth.

Nash, K. 2000. *Contemporary Political Sociology: Globalization, Politics, Power*. Oxford: Blackwell.

Naumann, T. M. 2000. *Das umkämpfte Subjekt: Subjektivität, Hegemonie und Emanzipation im Postfordismus*. Tübingen: Diskord.

Neafsey, J. 2006. *A Sacred Voice is Calling: Personal Vocation and Social Conscience.* Maryknoll: Orbis.
Nelson, J. B. 1978. *Embodiment.* Minneapolis: Augsburg.
Nelson, J. W. 1976. *Your God is Alive and Well and Living and Appearing in Popular Culture.* Philadelphia: Westminster.
Nelson-Pallmeyer, J. 2001. *Jesus Against Christianity: Reclaiming the Missing Jesus.* Harrisburg: Trinity.
Neufeld Redekop, V. 2002. *From Violence to Blessing: How an Understanding of Deep-Rooted Conflict Can Open Paths to Reconciliation.* Ottawa: Novalis/Saint Paul University.
Neuhaus, P. 2001. *"Erinnerung" als Brückenkategorie: Anstösse zur Vermittlung zwischen der Politischen Theologie von Johann Baptist Metz und der Tiefenpsychologischen Theologie Eugen Drewermanns.* Münster: LIT.
Neusch, M. 2004. *Les traces de Dieu: Eléments de théologie fondamentale.* Paris: Cerf.
———, and B. Chenu. 1994. *Au pays de la théologie: A la découverte des hommes et des courants.* 2nd ed. Paris: Le Centurion.
Neusner, J., editor. 2003. *World Religions in America.* 3rd ed. Louisville: Westminster John Knox.
Neville, R. C. 1991. *A Theology Primer.* Albany: State University of New York Press.
Newman, R., and M. Sawyer. 1996. *Everybody Say Freedom: Everything You Need to Know About African-American History.* New York: Penguin.
Newsom, C. A., and S. H. Ringe, editors. 1992. *The Women's Bible Commentary.* Louisville: Westminster John Knox.
Newton, K. M. 1990. *Interpreting the Text: A Critical Introduction to the Theory and Practice of Literary Interpretation.* New York: St. Martin's.
Neyrey, J. H., editor. 1991. *The Social World of Luke-Acts: Models for Interpretation.* Peabody: Hendrickson.
———. 1991a. "Ceremonies in Luke-Acts: The Case of Meals and Table-Fellowship." In *The Social World of Luke-Acts: Models of Interpretation,* edited by J. H. Neyrey, 361–87. Peabody: Hendrickson.
———. 1996. "Meals, Food, and Table Fellowship." In *The Social Sciences and New Testament Interpretation,* edited by R. L. Rohrbaugh, 159–82. Peabody: Hendrickson.
Ng, D., editor. 1996. *People on the Way: Asian North Americans Discovering Christ, Culture, and Community.* Valley Forge: Judson.
Nicholson, L., editor. 1990. *Feminism/Postmodernism.* New York: Routledge.
———, and S. Seidman, editors. 1995. *Social Postmodernism: Beyond Identity Politics.* New York: Cambridge University Press.
Niewiadomski, J., and W. Palaver, editors. 1995. *Vom Fluch und Segen der Sündenböcke: Raymund Schwager zum 60. Geburtstag.* Vienna: Kulturverlag.
Nigg, W. 1956. *Der christliche Narr.* Zürich: Artemis.
Nin, A. 1966. *In Favour of the Sensitive Man and other Essays.* London: Penguin.
———. 1975. *A Women Speaks.* London: Penguin.
Nipkow, K. E., D. Rössler, and F. Schweizer, editor. 1991. *Praktische Theologie und Kultur der Gegenwart: Ein internationaler Dialog.* Gütersloh: Gütersloher Verlagshaus Gerd Mohn.
Nisbet, R. 1976. *Sociology as an Art Form.* New York: Oxford University Press.
Nolan, A. 1992. *Jesus Before Christianity.* Rev. ed. Maryknoll: Orbis.

Bibliography

Noll, M. A. 1992. *A History of Christianity in the United States and Canada.* Grand Rapids: Eerdmans.

———. 2000. *Das Christentum in Nordamerika.* Leipzig: Evangelische Verlagsanstalt.

———, N. O. Hatch, G. A. Marsden, D. F. Wells, and J. D. Woodbridge, editors. 1983. *Eerdmans Handbook to Christianity in America.* Grand Rapids: Eerdmans.

Nolland, J. 1989. *Luke 1—9:20.* Word Biblical Commentary. Vol. 35A. Dallas: Word.

———. 1993a. *Luke 9:21—18:34.* Word Biblical Commentary. Vol. 35B. Dallas: Word.

———. 1993b. *Luke 18:35—24:53.* Word Biblical Commentary. Vol. 35C. Dallas: Word.

Noller, A. 1995. *Feministische Hermeneutik: Wege einer neuen Schriftauslegung.* Neukirchen-Vluyn: Neukirchener.

Nordsieck, R. 1994. *Reich Gottes—Leben der Welt: Jesu eigene Botschaft, unter Einbeziehung des Thomas-Evangeliums.* Neukirchen-Vluyn: Neukirchener.

Norris, F. W. 2002. *Christianity: A Short Global History.* Oxford: Oneworld.

Norton, M. B., D. M. Katzman, P. D. Escott, H. P. Chudacoff, T. G. Paterson, W. M. Tuttle, and W. J. Brophy. 1996. *A People and a Nation: A History of the United States.* Brief edition. 4th ed. Boston: Houghton Mifflin.

Nouwen, H. 1994. *The Wounded Healer: Ministry in Contemporary Society.* New ed. London: Darton, Longman and Todd.

———. 1998. *The Road to Peace: Writings on Peace and Justice.* Edited by John Dear. Maryknoll: Orbis.

Nowell, I. 1997. *Women in the Old Testament.* Collegeville: Liturgical.

Nünning, A., editor. 1998. *Metzler Lexikon Kultur- und Literaturtheorie.* Stuttgart: J. B. Metzler.

Nyberg, D., editor. 1975. *The Philosophy of Open Education.* London and Boston: Routledge & Kegan Paul.

O'Brien, J. 1992. *Theology and the Option for the Poor.* Collegeville: Michael Glazier Book.

O'Collins, G. 1981. *Fundamental Theology.* Ramsey: Paulist.

———, and E. G. Farrugia. 2000. *A Concise Dictionary of Theology.* Rev. exp. ed. New York: Paulist.

O'Connell Killen, P., and J. De Beer. 1994. *The Art of Theological Reflection.* New York: Crossroad.

O'Donnell, K. 2003. *Postmodernism.* Lion Access Guides. Oxford: Lion.

O'Donovan, L. J., and T. H. Sanks, editors. 1989. *Faithful Witness: Foundations of Theology for Today's Church.* New York: Crossroad.

Ogden, S. M. 1996. *Doing Theology Today.* Valley Forge: Trinity.

Ogletree, T. W. 1983. *The Use of the Bible in Christian Ethics.* Philadelphia: Fortress.

———. 1985. *Hospitality to the Stranger: Dimensions of Moral Understanding.* Philadelphia: Fortress.

O'Hara Graff, A. E., editor. 1995. *In the Embrace of God: Feminist Approaches to Theological Anthropology.* Maryknoll: Orbis.

Okely, J., and H. Callaway, editors. 1992. *Anthropology and Autobiography.* New York: Routledge.

Oki Ahearn, D., and P. R. Gathje, editors. 2005. *Doing Right and Being Good: Catholic and Protestant Readings in Christian Ethics.* Collegeville: Liturgical.

Olson, R. E. 2001. *The Story of Christian Theology: Twenty Centuries of Tradition & Reform.* Downers Grove: InterVarsity.

———. 2002. *The Mosaic of Christian Belief: Twenty Centuries of Unity and Diversity.* Downers Grove: InterVarsity.
O'Reilly, K. 2005. *Ethnographic Methods.* New York: Routledge.
Ormerod, N. 1997. *Introducing Contemporary Theologies: The What and the Who of Theology Today.* Enl. and rev. ed. Maryknoll: Orbis.
Osborn, L. 1995. *Restoring the Vision: The Gospel and Modern Culture.* New York: Mowbray.
Osborne, R. 2002a. *Megawords: 200 Terms You Really Need to Know.* Thousand Oaks: Sage.
———. 2002b. "Power." In *Megawords: 200 Terms You Really Need to Know,* 215–17. Thousand Oaks: Sage.
———. 2002c. "Space." In *Megawords: 200 Terms You Really Need to Know,* 233–35. Thousand Oaks: Sage.
Ott, H. 1994. *Apologetik des Glaubens: Grundprobleme einer dialogischen Fundamentaltheologie.* Darmstadt: Wissenschaftliche Buchgesellschaft.
———, and K. Otte. 1999. *Die Antwort des Glaubens: Systematische Theologie in 50 Artikeln.* 3rd ed. Stuttgart: Kohlhammer.
Outhwaite, W. 1994. *Habermas: A Critical Introduction.* Key Contemporary Thinkers. Cambridge: Polity.
Owen, D., editor. 1997. *Sociology after Postmodernism.* Thousand Oaks: Sage.
Padilla A., R. Goizueta, and E. Villafane, editors. 2005. *Hispanic Christian Thought at the Dawn of the 21st Century.* Apuntes in honor of Justo L. Gonzalez. Nashville: Abingdon.
Page, R. 1996. *God and the Web of Creation.* London: SCM.
———. 2000. *God With Us: Synergy in the Church.* London: SCM.
Pally, M. 2010. *Die Neuen Evangelikalen in den USA: Freiheitsgewinne durch fromme Politik.* Berlin: Berlin University Press.
Panikkar, R. 1995. *Cultural Disarmament: The Way to Peace.* Louisville: Westminster John Knox.
———. 2009. *The Rhythm of Being: The Gifford Lectures.* Maryknoll: Orbis.
Pannenberg, W. 1991–1998. *Systematic Theology.* 3 vols. Grand Rapids: Eerdmans.
Papastergiadis, N. 2000. *The Turbulence of Migration: Globalization, Deterritorialization and Hybridity.* Oxford: Polity.
Paris, P. J. 1995. *The Spirituality of African Peoples: The Search for a Common Moral Discourse.* Minneapolis: Fortress.
Park, A. S. 2004. *From Hurt to Healing: A Theology of the Wounded.* Nashville: Abingdon.
Parker, I. 1997. *Psychoanalytic Culture: Psychoanalytic Discourse in Western Society.* Thousand Oaks: Sage.
Parmentier, E. 1998. *Les filles prodigues: Défis des théologies féministes.* Geneva: Labor et Fides.
Parmesani, L. 2000. *Art of the Twentieth Century: Movements, Theories, Schools, and Tendencies 1900–2000.* Milano: Skira.
Parratt, J., editor. 2004. *An Introduction to Third World Theologies.* Cambridge: Cambridge University Press.
Parsons, S. F., editor. 2002. *The Cambridge Companion to Feminist Theology.* New York: Cambridge University Press.
Pasewark, K. A. 1993. *A Theology of Power: Being Beyond Domination.* Minneapolis: Fortress.

Bibliography

Patte, D. 1995. *Ethics of Biblical Interpretation: A Reevaluation*. Louisville: Westminster John Knox.

———. 1996. *Discipleship According to the Sermon on the Mount: Four Legitimate Readings, Four Plausible Views of Discipleship, and Their Relative Values*. Valley Forge: Trinity.

Patterson, S. J. 1998. *The God of Jesus: The Historical Jesus and the Search for Meaning*. Harrisburg: Trinity.

Payne, G., editor. 2000. *Social Divisions*. New York: St. Martin's.

Pazmino, R. W. 1988. *The Seminary in the City: A Study of New York Theological Seminary*. New York: University Press of America.

Peck, M. S. 1987. *The Different Drum: The Creation of True Community—The First Step to World Peace*. London: Arrow.

Pederson, A. 2001. *God, Creation, and All That Jazz: A Process of Composition and Improvisation*. St. Louis: Chalice.

Pedraja, L. G. 2003. *Teologia: An Introduction to Hispanic Theology*. Nashville: Abingdon.

Peelman, A. 1995. *Christ Is a Native American*. Maryknoll: Orbis.

Peerman, D., editor. 1968. *Theologie im Umbruch: Der Beitrag Amerikas zur gegenwärtigen Theologie*. Munich: Chr. Kaiser.

Penner, M. B., editor. 2005. *Christianity and the Postmodern Turn: Six Views*. Grand Rapids: Brazos.

Perera, S. B. 1986. *The Scapegoat Complex: Toward a Mythology of Shadow and Guilt*. Toronto: Inner City.

Perez-Esclarin, A. 1978. *Atheism and Liberation*. Maryknoll: Orbis.

Perkinson, J. 2005. "The Jazz of the Spirit: A Poetic Perspective." In *Constructive Theology: A Contemporary Approach to Classical Themes*, edited by S. Jones and P. Lakeland, 270–74. Minneapolis: Fortress.

Persie, M. 1984. *Befreiung und Umkehr für die Zukunft: Paulo Freire, Theologie der Befreiung und praxisverändernde Bildung*. Munich: AG SPAK.

Personal Narratives Group, editor. 1989. *Interpreting Women's Lives: Feminist Theory and Personal Narratives*. Indianapolis: Indiana University Press.

Pesch, O. H. 2008. *Katholische Dogmatik aus ökumenischer Erfahrung*. Vol. 1. Mainz: Matthias-Grünewald.

———. 2010. *Katholische Dogmatik aus ökumenischer Erfahrung*. Vol. 2. Mainz: Matthias-Grünewald.

Peters, T. 1994. *Sin: Radical Evil in Soul and Society*. Grand Rapids: Eerdmans.

———. 2000. *God—The World's Future: Systematic Theology for a New Era*. 2nd ed. Minneapolis: Fortress.

Petersen, R. L., editor. 1995. *Christianity and Civil Society: Theological Education for Public Life*. Maryknoll: Orbis.

Petzoldt, M., editor. 2004. *Evangelische Fundamentaltheologie in der Diskussion*. Leipzig: Evangelische Verlagsanstalt.

Peukert, H. 1984. *Science, Action, Fundamental Theology: Toward a Theology of Communicative Action*. Cambridge: MIT Press.

Phan, P. C., and J. Y. Lee, editors. 1999. *Journeys at the Margin: Toward an Autobiographical Theology in American-Asian Perspective*. Collegeville: Liturgical.

Phillips, D. T. 1998. *Martin Luther King Jr. on Leadership: Inspiration and Wisdom for Challenging Times*. New York: Warner.

Phillips, T. R., and D. L. Okholm, editor. 1996. *The Nature of Confession: Evangelicals and Postliberals in Conversation*. Downers Grove: InterVarsity.

Pieterse, J. N., and B. Parekh, editors. 1995. *The Decolonization of Imagination: Culture, Knowledge, and Power*. London: Zed.

Pilch, J. J. 1999. *The Cultural Dictionary of the Bible*. Collegeville: Liturgical.

———, and B. J. Malina, editors. 1998. *Handbook of Biblical Social Values*. Peabody: Hendrickson.

Pile, S., and N. Thrift, editors. 1995. *Mapping the Subject: Geographies of Cultural Transformation*. New York: Routledge.

Pilgrim, W. 1981. *Good News to the Poor: Wealth and Poverty in Luke-Acts*. Minneapolis: Augsburg.

Pinar, W. F., W. M. Reynolds, P. Slattery, and P. M. Taubman. 1995. *Understanding Curriculum: An Introduction to the Study of Historical and Contemporary Curriculum Discourses*. Counterpoints: Studies in the Postmodern Theory of Education. Vol. 17. New York: Peter Lang.

———. 1995a. "Understanding Curriculum as Theological Text." In *Understanding Curriculum: An Introduction to the Study of Historical and Contemporary Curriculum Discourses*, 606–60. Counterpoints: Studies in the Postmodern Theory of Education. Vol. 17. New York: Peter Lang.

Pinnock, C. H., and R. C. Brow. 1994. *Unbounded Love: A Good News Theology for the 21st Century*. Downers Grove: InterVarsity.

Pinnock, S. K., editor. 2003. *The Theology of Dorothee Soelle*. Harrisburg: Trinity.

Pittman, D. A., R. L. F. Habito, and T. C. Muck, editors. 1996. *Ministry and Theology in Global Perspective: Contemporary Challenges for the Church*. Grand Rapids: Eerdmans.

Pixley, G. V. 1981. *God's Kingdom: A Guide for Biblical Study*. Maryknoll: Orbis.

———, and C. Boff. 1989. *The Bible, the Church, and the Poor*. Maryknoll: Orbis.

Placher, W. C. 1983. *A History of Christian Theology: An Introduction*. Philadelphia: Westminster.

———. 1989. *Unapologetic Theology: A Christian Voice in a Pluralistic Conversation*. Louisville: Westminster John Knox.

———. 1994. *Narratives of a Vulnerable God: Christ, Theology, and Scripture*. Louisville: Westminster John Knox.

———. 2001. *Jesus the Savior: The Meaning of Jesus Christ for Christian Faith*. Louisville: Westminster John Knox.

———, editor. 2003. *Essentials of Christian Theology*. Louisville: Westminster John Knox.

Plaskow, J. 1999. "The Academy as Real Life: New Participants and Paradigms in the Study of Religion." *Journal of the American Academy of Religion* 67, 521–38.

Pleins, J. D. 2001. *The Social Visions of the Hebrew Bible: A Theological Introduction*. Louisville: Westminster John Knox.

Pohl, C. D. 1999. *Making Room: Recovering Hospitality As a Christian Tradition*. Grand Rapids: Eerdmans.

Pöhlmann, H. G. 2002. *Abriss der Dogmatik: Ein Kompendium*. Gütersloh: 6. überarbeitete und erweiterte Auflage. Chr.Kaiser/Gütersloher.

Poling, J. N. 1991. *The Abuse of Power: A Theological Problem*. Nashville: Abingdon.

———. 1996. *Deliver Us From Evil: Resisting Racial and Gender Oppression*. Minneapolis: Augsburg Fortress.

Bibliography

Polkinghorne, D. E. 1988. *Narrative Knowing in the Human Sciences.* Albany: State University of New York Press.
Pope-Levison, P., and J. R. Levison. 1992. *Jesus in Global Contexts.* Louisville: Westminster John Knox.
Preiswerk, M. 1987. *Educating in the Living World: A Theoretical Framework for Christian Education.* Maryknoll: Orbis.
Price, L. 2002. *Theology Out of Place: A Theological Biography of Walter J. Hollenweger.* New York: Sheffield Academic.
Prilleltensky, I., and G. Nelson 2002. *Doing Psychology Critically: Making a Difference in Diverse Settings.* New York: Palgrave Macmillan.
Pröpper, T. 2001. *Evangelium und freie Vernunft: Konturen einer theologischen Hermeneutik.* Freiburg: Herder.
Prothero, S. 2003. *American Jesus: How the Son of God Became a National Icon.* New York: Farrar Straus & Giroux.
Pruyser, P. W. 1983. *The Play of Imagination.* Madison: International Universities Press.
Pugh, J. C. 2001. *The Matrix of Faith: Reclaiming a Christian Vision.* New York: Crossroad.
Purvis, S. B. 1993. *The Power of the Cross: Foundations for a Christian Feminist Ethic of Community.* Nashville: Abingdon.
Quebedeaux, R. 1974. *The Young Evangelicals: Revolution in Orthodoxy.* San Francisco: Harper & Row.
———. 1978. *The Worldly Evangelicals.* San Francisco: Harper & Row.
Raberger, W., and H. Sauer, editors. 2003. *Vermittlung im Fragment: Franz Schupp als Lehrer der Theologie.* Regensburg: Friedrich Pustet.
Rahner, K., and H. Vorgrimler, editors. 2002. *Kleines Konzilskompendium: Sämtliche Texte des Zweiten Vatikanums.* Neuausgabe. Freiburg: Herder.
Rajchman, J., and C. West, editors. 1985. *Post-Analytic Philosophy.* New York: Columbia University Press.
Ramminger, M. 1998. *Mitleid und Heimatlosigkeit: Zwei Basiskategorien einer Anerkennungs-hermeneutik.* Theologie in Geschichte und Gesellschaft. Vol 5. Luzern: Exodus.
Rasmussen, L. 1996. *Earth Community, Earth Ethics.* Maryknoll: Orbis.
Rauchfleisch, U. 1996. *Allgegenwart von Gewalt.* Göttingen: Vandenhoeck & Ruprecht.
Ray, P. H., and S. R. Anderson. 2000. *The Cultural Creatives.* New York: Three Rivers.
Ray, S. G. 2003. *Do No Harm: Social Sin and Christian Responsibility.* Minneapolis: Fortress.
Raymond, J. G. 1986. *A Passion for Friends: Toward a Philosophy of Female Affection.* Boston: Beacon.
Redling, J. 1995. *Kleines USA-Lexikon: Wissenswertes über Land und Leute.* Munich: C. H. Beck.
Reed-Danahay, D. E., editor. 1997. *Auto/Ethnography: Rewriting the Self and the Social.* New York: Berg.
Reineke, M. J. 1997. *Sacrificed Lives: Kristeva on Women and Violence.* Bloomington: Indiana University Press.
Reinhardt, K. 1992. *Öffnung der Schule: Community Education als Konzept für die Schule der Zukunft?* Basel: Beltz.
Reijnen, A. M. 1998. *L'Ombre de Dieu sur terre: Un essai sur l'incarnation.* Lieux théologiques 31. Geneva: Labor et Fides.

Rendtorff, T. 1990. *Ethik: Grundelemente, Methodologie und Konkretionen einer ethischen Theologie.* Vol. 1. 2nd ed. Stuttgart: Kohlhammer.

———. 1991. *Ethik: Grundelemente, Methodologie und Konkretionen einer ethischen Theologie.* Vol. 2. 2nd ed. Stuttgart: Kohlhammer.

Rhodes, L. N., and N. D. Richardson. 1991. *Mending Severed Connections: Theological Education for Communal Transformation.* San Francisco: San Francisco Network Ministries.

Richard, P. 1983. *The Idols of Death and the God of Life.* Maryknoll: Orbis.

———. 1995. "The Hermeneutics of Liberation: A Hermeneutics of the Spirit." In *Reading from this Place: Social Location and Biblical Interpretation in Global Perspective,* edited by F. F. Segovia and M. A. Tolbert, 263-80. Vol. 2. Minneapolis: Fortress.

———. 1998. "The Hermeneutics of Liberation: Theoretical Grounding for the Communitarian Reading of the Bible." In *Reading from this Place: Social Location and Biblical Interpretation in Global Perspective,* edited by F. F. Segovia and M. A. Tolbert, 272-82. Vol. 2. Minneapolis: Fortress.

Richardson, A., and J. Bowden, editors. 1983. *The Westminster Dictionary of Christian Theology.* Philadelphia: Westminster.

Ricoeur, P. 1970. *Freud and Philosophy.* New Haven: Yale University Press.

Rieger, J. 1998. *Remember the Poor: The Challenge to Theology in the Twenty-First Century.* Harrisburg: Trinity.

———, editor. 1999. *Theology from the Belly of the Whale: A Frederick Herzog Reader.* Harrisburg: Trinity.

———. 2001. *God and the Excluded: Visions and Blindspots in Contemporary Theology.* Minneapolis: Augsburg Fortress.

———, editor. 2003. *Opting for the Margins: Postmodernity and Liberation in Christian Theology.* New York: Oxford University Press.

———. 2007. *Christ & Empire: From Paul to Postcolonial Times.* Minneapolis: Augsburg Fortress.

———. 2011. *Traveling.* Minneapolis: Fortress.

Rigby, C. L., editor. 1997. *Power, Powerlessness, and the Divine: New Inquiries in Bible and Theology.* Atlanta: Scholars.

Riggs, J. W. 2003. *Postmodern Christianity: Doing Theology in the Contemporary World.* Harrisburg: Trinity.

Rigney, D. 2001. *The Metaphorical Society: An Invitation to Social Theory.* Lanham: Rowman & Littlefield.

Ringe, S. H. 1995. *Luke.* Westminster Bible Companion. Louisville: Westminster John Knox.

Ritschl, D. 1981. *Theologie in den Neuen Welten: Analysen und Berichte aus Amerika und Australasien.* Munich: Chr. Kaiser.

Ritter, W. H., editor. 2000. *Religion und Phantasie: Von der Imaginationskraft des Glaubens.* Göttingen: Vandenhoeck & Ruprecht.

———, R. Feldmeier, W. Schoberth, and G. Altner. *Der Allmächtige: Annäherung an ein umstrittenes Gottesprädikat.* Göttingen: Vandenhoeck & Ruprecht.

Ritzer, G. 1993. *The McDonaldization of Society.* Thousand Oaks: Pine Forge.

———. 1997. *Postmodern Social Theory.* New York: McGraw-Hill.

———. 2000. *Modern Sociological Theory.* 5th ed. New York: McGraw-Hill.

Bibliography

Rivera, L. N. 1992. *A Violent Evangelism: The Political and Religious Conquest of the Americas*. Louisville: Westminster John Knox.
Roark, D. M. 1972. *Dietrich Bonhoeffer*. Makers of the Modern Theological Mind. Waco: Word.
Robbins, V. K. 1996a. *The Tapestry of Early Christian Discourse: Rhetoric, Society, and Ideology*. New York: Routledge.
———. 1996b. *Exploring the Texture of Texts: A Guide to Socio-Rhetorical Interpretation*. Valley Forge: Trinity.
Roberts, J. H. 2000. *Thinking Theologically in Aotearoa New Zealand*. Aotearoa: ColCom.
Robinson, J. A. T. 1963. *Honest to God*. Philadelphia: Westminster.
Rode, R. 1992. *USA*. Munich: C. H. Beck.
Rodriguez, J. 1996. *Stories We Live/Cuentos Que Vivimos: Hispanic Women's Spirituality*. Mahwah: Paulist.
Rodriguez, J. D., and L. I. Martell-Otero, editors. 1997. *Teologia en Conjunto: A Collaborative Hispanic Protestant Theology*. Louisville: Westminster John Knox.
Roeck, B. 1993. *Aussenseiter, Randgruppen, Minderheiten: Fremde im Deutschland der frühen Neuzeit*. Göttingen: Vandenhoeck & Ruprecht.
Rohls J. 1997a. *Protestantische Theologie der Neuzeit I: Das 19. Jahrhundert*. Vol. 1. Tübingen: Mohr Siebeck.
———. 1997b. *Protestantische Theologie der Neuzeit II: Das 20. Jahrhundert*. Vol. 2. Tübingen: Mohr Siebeck.
———. 2002. *Philosophie und Theologie in Geschichte und Gegenwart*. Tübingen: Mohr Siebeck.
Rohrbaugh, R. L., editor. 1996. *The Social Sciences and New Testament Interpretation*. Peabody: Hendrickson.
Römer, T. 1998. *Dieu obscur: Le sexe, la cruauté et la violence dans l'Ancien Testament*. Geneva: Labor et Fides.
Rose, H. 1994. *Love, Power, and Knowledge: Towards a Feminist Transformation of the Sciences*. Cambridge: Polity.
Rosen, S. 1987. *Hermeneutics as Politics*. New York: Oxford University Press.
Rosenau, P. M. 1992. *Post-Modernism and the Social Sciences: Insights, Inroads, and Intrusions*. Princeton: Princeton University Press.
Rosenberg, T. 1992. *Children of Cain: Violence and the Violent in Latin America*. New York: Penguin.
Rösener, C. 2001. *Vom Brot, das mehr wird durch Teilen: Feministische Theologien aus Nord und Süd im Dialog*. Frankfurt: Otto Lembeck.
Rosenthal, G. 1995. *Erlebte und erzählte Lebensgeschichte: Gestalt und Struktur biographischer Selbstbeschreibungen*. Frankfurt: Campus.
Rosenwald, G. C., and R. L. Ochberg, editors. 1992. *Storied Lives: The Cultural Politics of Self-Understanding*. New Haven: Yale University Press.
Roth, J. S. 1997. *The Blind, the Lame, and the Poor: Character Types in Luke-Acts*. Sheffield: Sheffield Academic.
Rothenbühler, H. 1976. *Der Barfussmessias: Jesus und seine Antwort auf das Hosianna der Geringen*. Biel: Adiatur-Gesellschaft.
Rotzetter, A. 1996. *Im Kreuz ist Leben*. Freiburg: Paulusverlag Freiburg Schweiz.
———. 2000. *Spirituelle Lebenskultur für das dritte Jahrtausend*. Freiburg: Herder.
Rouse, J. 1987. *Knowledge and Power: Toward a Political Philosophy of Science*. Ithaca: Cornell University Press.

Rowland, C., editor. 1999. *The Cambridge Companion to Liberation Theology.* Cambridge: Cambridge University Press.

———, and M. Corner. 1989. *Liberating Exegesis: The Challenge of Liberation Theology to Biblical Studies.* Louisville: Westminster John Knox.

Ruether, R. R. 1983. *Sexism and God-Talk: Toward a Feminist Theology.* Boston: Beacon.

———. 1983/1993. *Sexism and God-Talk: Toward a Feminist Theology.* Boston: Beacon.

———. 1992. *Gaia & God: An Ecofeminist Theology of Earth Healing.* San Francisco: HarperSanFrancisco.

Russell, L. M. 1976. *The Liberating Word: A Guide to Nonsexist Interpretation of the Bible.* Philadelphia: Westminster.

———, editor. 1985. *Feminist Interpretation of the Bible.* New York: Basil Blackwell.

———. 1993. *Church in the Round: Feminist Interpretation of the Church.* Louisville: Westminster John Knox.

Saint Augustine. 1991. *Confessions.* Translated with an introduction and notes by Henry Chadwick. New York: Oxford University Press.

Salber, L. 1995. *Tausendundeine Frau: Die Geschichte der Anais Nin.* Reinbek: Rowohlt.

Samel, I. 2000. *Einführung in die feministische Sprachwissenschaft.* Berlin: Erich Schmidt.

Samuel, V., and C. Sugden, editors. 1984. *Sharing Jesus In the Two Thirds World: Evangelical Christologies From the Contexts of Poverty, Powerlessness, and Religious Pluralism.* The Papers of the First Conference of Evangelical Mission Theologians from the Two Thirds World, Bangkok, Thailand, March 22–25, 1982. Grand Rapids: Eerdmans.

Samuels, A. 1993. *The Political Psyche.* New York: Routledge.

Sanders, C. J. 1995. *Empowerment Ethics for a Liberated People: A Path to African American Social Transformation.* Minneapolis: Fortress.

Sands, K. M. 1994. *Escape from Paradise: Evil and Tragedy in Feminist Theology.* Minneapolis: Fortress.

Sanks, T. H., and J. A. Coleman, editors. 1993. *Reading the Signs of the Times: Resources for Social and Cultural Analysis.* Mahwah: Paulist.

Sardar, Z., and B. Van Loon. 1997. *Introducing Cultural Studies.* Cambridge: Icon.

Sauer, R. 1990. *Mystik des Alltags: Jugendliche Lebenswelt und Glaube.* Freiburg: Herder.

Sauter, G., and M. Welker, editor. 1993. "Systematische Theologie in den USA." *Verkündigung und Forschung* 38/1.

Sawyer, M. R. 2003. *The Church on the Margins: Living Christian Community.* Harrisburg: Trinity.

Say, E. 1990. *Evidence on Her Own Behalf: Women's Narrative as Theological Voice.* Lanham: Rowman & Littlefield.

Scannone, J. C. 1992. *Weisheit und Befreiung: Volkstheologie in Lateinamerika.* Düsseldorf: Patmos.

Scarry, E. 1985. *The Body in Pain: The Making and Un-Making of the World.* New York: Oxford University Press.

Schaberg, J. 1990. *The Illegitimacy of Jesus: A Feminist Theological Interpretation of the Infancy Narratives.* New York: Crossroad.

Schäfer, H. 2004. *Praxis—Theologie—Religion: Grundlinien einer Theologie- und Religionstheorie im Anschluss an Pierre Bourdieu.* Frankfurt: Otto Lembeck.

Schäfer, P. 1998. *Alltag in den Vereinigten Staaten: Von der Kolonialzeit bis zur Gegenwart.* Graz: Styria.

Bibliography

Scharer, M. 1995. *Begegnungen Raum geben: Kommunikatives Lernen als Dienst in Gemeinde, Schule und Erwachsenenbildung.* Mainz: Matthias-Grünewald.
Scharer, M., and B. J. Hilberath. 2003. *Kommunikative Theologie: Eine Grundlegung.* Mainz: Matthias-Grünewald.
Scharper, S. B. 1998. *Redeeming the Time: A Political Theology of the Environment.* New York: Continuum.
Schaumberger, C. 1991. "Erfahrung." In edited by E. Gössmann et al., 73–78. *Wörterbuch der feministischen Theologie.* Gütersloh: Gütersloher.
Schenke, L. u.a. 2004. *Jesus von Nazareth—Spuren und Konturen.* Stuttgart: Kohlhammer.
Scheper-Hughes, N. 1992. *Death without Weeping: The Violence of Everyday Life in Brazil.* Berkeley: University of California Press.
Scherzberg, L. 1995. *Grundkurs feministische Theologie.* Mainz: Matthias-Grünewald.
Schillebeeckx, E. 1974. *The Understanding of Faith: Interpretation and Criticism.* New York: Charles Scribner's Sons.
———. 1979. *Jesus: An Experiment in Christology.* New York: Seabury.
———. 1980a. "Erfahrung und Glaube." In *Christlicher Glaube in moderner Gesellschaft,* edited by F. Böckle, F. X. Kaufmann, K. Rahner, B. Welte, 73-116. Vol. 25. Freiburg: Herder.
———. 1980b. *Christ: The Experience of Jesus as Lord.* New York: Crossroad.
———. 1981. *Interim Report on the Books Jesus and Christ.* New York: Crossroad.
———. 1989. *Church: The Human Story of God.* New York: Crossroad.
———. 1995. *The Language of Faith: Essays on Jesus, Theology, and the Church.* Concilium. Maryknoll: Orbis.
———. 2004. *God is New Each Moment.* New York: Continuum.
———, and B. Van Iersel, editors. 1979. "Revelation and Experience." *Concilium.* International Journal for Theology 113. New York: Crossroad.
Schipani, D. S. 1988. *Religious Education Encounters Liberation Theology.* Birmingham: Religious Education.
———. 2003. *The Way of Wisdom in Pastoral Counseling.* Elkhart: Institute of Mennonite Studies.
Schirato, T., and J. Webb. 2003. *Understanding Globalization.* Thousand Oaks: Sage.
Schmalstieg, D. O. 1991. *Macht-Wechsel: Theologie, Herrschaft, Sprache in Bewegung.* Genf: Michael Servet.
Schmid, P. F. 1998. *Im Anfang ist Gemeinschaft: Personenzentrierte Gruppenarbeit in Seelsorge und praktischer Theologie—Beitrag zu einer Theologie der Gruppe.* Stuttgart: Kohlhammer.
Schmid, W. 1998. *Philosophie der Lebenskunst: Eine Grundlegung.* Frankfurt: Suhrkamp.
Schmidt, H. 1969. *Frieden.* Stuttgart: Kreuz.
Schmidt-Leukel, P. 1999. *Grundkurs Fundamentaltheologie: Eine Einführung in die Grundfragen des christlichen Glaubens.* Munich: Don Bosco.
Schmitt, F., editor. 1994. *Socializing Epistemology: The Social Dimensions of Knowledge.* Lanham: Rowman & Littlefield.
———. 1999. "Social Epistemology." In *The Blackwell Guide to Epistemology,* edited by J. Greco and E. Sosa, 354–82. Oxford: Blackwell.
Schmookler, 1988. *Out of Weakness: Healing the Wounds That Drive Us to War.* New York: Bantam.
Schnädelbach, H. 2002. *Erkenntnistheorie zur Einführung.* Hamburg: Junius.

Schneider, B. 1999. *Penthesilea: Die andere Kultur- und Kunstgeschichte sozialgeschichtlich und patriarchatskritisch*. Bern: Zytglogge.

Schneider, M. 1997. *Theologie als Biographie*. St. Ottilien: EOS.

Schneider, N. 1996. *Geschichte der Ästhetik von der Aufklärung bis zur Postmoderne*. Stuttgart: Reclam.

———. 1998. *Erkenntnistheorie im 20. Jahrhundert: Klassische Positionen*. Stuttgart: Reclam.

Schneider T., editor. 1985. *Der verdrängte Aufbruch: Ein Konzils-Lesebuch*. Mainz: Matthias-Grünewald.

———. 1990. *Auf seiner Spur: Ein Werkstattbuch*. Edited by A. Moos. Düsseldorf: Patmos.

———, editor. 1992a. *Handbuch der Dogmatik: Prolegomena, Gotteslehre, Schöpfungslehre, Christologie, Pneumatologie*. Vol. 1. Düsseldorf: Patmos.

———, editor. 1992b. *Handbuch der Dogmatik: Gnadenlehre, Ekklesiologie, Mariologie, Sakramentenlehre, Eschatologie, Trinitätslehre*. Düsseldorf: Patmos.

———. 1998. *Was wir glauben: Eine Auslegung des Apostolischen Glaubensbekenntnisses*. 5th ed. Düsseldorf: Patmos.

Schneider-Flume, G. 2004.*Grundkurs Dogmatik: Nachdenken über Gottes Geschichte*. Göttingen: Vandenhoeck & Ruprecht.

Schneiders, S. M. 1999. *The Revelatory Text: Interpreting the New Testament as Sacred Scripture*. Rev. ed. Collegeville: Liturgical.

Schoberth, I. 1992. *Erinnerung als Praxis des Glaubens*. Munich: Chr. Kaiser.

Schoonenberg, P. 1992. *Der Geist, das Wort und der Sohn: Eine Geist-Christologie*. Regensburg: Friedrich Pustet.

Schottroff, L. 1995. *Lydia's Impatient Sisters: A Feminist Social History of Early Christianity*. Louisville: Westminster John Knox.

———, and W. Schottroff. 1991. *Die kostbare Liebe zum Leben: Biblische Inspirationen*. Munich: Chr. Kaiser.

———, and W. Stegemann. 1986. *Jesus and the Hope of the Poor*. Maryknoll: Orbis.

———, and M. T. Wacker, editor. 1999. *Kompendium Feministische Bibelauslegung*. Gütersloh: Chr. Kaiser/Gütersloher.

———, S. Schroer, and M. T. Wacker 1998. *Feminist Interpretation: The Bible in Women's Perspective*. Minneapolis: Fortress.

Schottroff, W., and W. Stegemann, editors. 1984. *God of the Lowly: Socio-Historical Interpretations of the Bible*. Maryknoll: Orbis.

Schrag, C. O. 1986. *Communicative Praxis and the Space of Subjectivity*. Bloomington: Indiana University Press.

———. 1997. *The Self after Postmodernity*. New Haven: Yale University Press.

Schreiter, R. J. 1985. *Constructing Local Theologies*. Maryknoll: Orbis.

———, editor. 1987. *The Schillebeeckx Reader*. New York: Crossroad.

———. 1992. *Reconciliation: Mission and Ministry in a Changing Social Order*. Maryknoll: Orbis.

———. 1992a. *Abschied vom Gott der Europäer: Zur Entwicklung regionaler Theologien*. Salzburg: Anton Pustet.

———. 1993. "Christian Theology between the Global and the Local." *Theological Education* 29, 113-126.

———. 1997. *The New Catholicity: Theology between the Global and the Local*. Maryknoll: Orbis.

Bibliography

———. 1998. *The Ministry of Reconciliation: Spirituality and Strategies.* Maryknoll: Orbis.

———, and M. C. Hilkert, editors. 1989. *The Praxis of Christian Experience: An Introduction to the Theology of Edward Schillebeeckx.* San Francisco: Harper & Row.

Schrock-Shenk, C., and L. Ressler, editors. 1999. *Making Peace with Conflict: Practical Skills for Conflict Transformation.* Scottdale: Herald.

Schulze, G. 2001. *The Experience Society.* Thousand Oaks: Sage.

Schupp, F. 1974. *Auf dem Weg zu einer kritischen Theologie.* Quaestiones Disputatae 64. Freiburg: Herder.

Schürger, W. 2002. *Wirklichkeit Gottes und Wirklichkeit der Welt: Theologie im Konflikt der Interpretationen.* Stuttgart: Kohlhammer.

Schüssler Fiorenza, E. 1983. *In Memory of Her: A Feminist Theological Reconstruction of Christian Origins.* New York: Crossroad.

———. 1988. "The Ethics of Interpretation: De-Centering Biblical Scholarship." *Journal of Biblical Literature* 107, 3–17.

———. 1992. *But She Said: Feminist Practices of Biblical Interpretation.* Boston: Beacon.

———. 1994. *Jesus—Miriam's Child, Sophia's Prophet: Critical Issues in Feminist Christology.* New York: Continuum.

———. 1995. *Bread not Stone: The Challenge of Feminist Biblical Interpretation.* Boston: Beacon.

———, editor. 1996. *The Power of Naming: A Concilium Reader in Feminist Liberation Theology.* Maryknoll: Orbis.

———. 1998. *Sharing Her Word: Feminist Biblical Interpretation in Context.* Boston: Beacon.

———. 1999. *Rhetoric and Ethic: The Politics of Biblical Studies.* Minneapolis: Fortress.

———. 2000. *Jesus and the Politics of Interpretation.* New York: Continuum.

Schüssler Fiorenza, F. 1984. *Foundational Theology: Jesus and the Church.* New York: Crossroad.

———. 1992. "The Church as a Community of Interpretation: Political Theology between Discourse Ethics and Hermeneutical Reconstruction." In *Habermas, Modernity, and Public Theology,* edited by D. S. Browning and F. Schüssler Fiorenza, 66–91. New York: Crossroad.

———. 2006. *Beyond Hermeneutics: Theology as Discourse.* New York: Continuum.

———, and J. P. Galvin, editors. 1991a. *Systematic Theology: Roman Catholic Perspectives.* Vol. 1. Minneapolis: Fortress.

———, and J. P. Galvin, editors. 1991b. *Systematic Theology: Roman Catholic Perspectives.* Vol. 2. Minneapolis: Fortress.

———, and J. P. Galvin, editors. 2011. *Systematic Theology: Roman Catholic Perspectives.* 2nd rev. ed. Minneapolis: Fortress.

Schwager, R. 1987. *Must There Be Scapegoats? Violence and Redemption in the Bible.* New York: Harper & Row.

Schwarz, H. 1986. *Responsible Faith: Christian Theology in the Light of 20th-Century Questions.* Minneapolis: Augsburg.

———. 1996. *Schöpfungsglaube im Horizont moderner Naturwissenschaft.* Neukirchen-Vluyn: Friedrich Bahn.

Scott J. W. 1992. "Experience." In J. Butler and J. W. Scott (Eds.). *Feminists Theorize the Political.* New York: Routledge, 22-40.

Scott, P., and W. T. Cavanaugh, editors. 2003. *The Blackwell Companion to Political Theology.* Blackwell Companions to Religion. Malden: Blackwell.

Sedgwick, E. K. 1990. *Epistemology of the Closet.* Berkeley: University of California Press.

Sedmak, C. 1995. "Ich kenne mich nicht aus": *Theologie—Philosophie—Problemtheorie.* Salzburg: Ursula Müller-Speiser.

———. 1999. *Theologie als "Handwerk": Eine kleine Gebrauchsanweisung.* Regensburg: Friedrich Pustet.

———. 2000. *Lokale Theologien und globale Kirche: Eine erkenntnistheoretische Grundlegung in praktischer Absicht.* Freiburg: Herder.

———. 2001. *Sozialtheologie: Theologie, Sozialwissenschaften und der Cultural Turn.* Frankfurt: Peter Lang.

———. 2002. *Doing Local Theology: A Guide for Artisans for a New Humanity.* Maryknoll: Orbis.

———. 2003. *Theologie in nachtheologischer Zeit.* Mainz: Matthias-Grünewald.

———, editor. 2003a. *Was ist gute Theologie?* Salzburger Theologische Studien 20. Innsbruck: Tyrolia.

Segovia, F. F., editor. 1985. *Discipleship in the New Testament.* Philadelphia: Fortress.

———. 1995a. "Toward a Hermeneutics of the Diaspora: A Hermeneutics of Otherness and Engagement." In *Reading from this Place: Social Location and Biblical Interpretation in the United States,* edited by F. F. Segovia and M. A. Tolbert, 57–73. Vol. 1. Minneapolis: Augsburg Fortress.

———. 1995b. "Toward Intercultural Criticism: A Reading Strategy from the Diaspora." In *Reading from this Place: Social Location and Biblical Interpretation in the United States,* edited by F. F. Segovia and M. A. Tolbert, 303–30. Vol. 2. Minneapolis: Augsburg Fortress.

———. 2000. *Decolonizing Biblical Studies: A View from the Margins.* Maryknoll: Orbis.

———, editor. 2003. *Toward a New Heaven and a New Earth: Essays in Honor of Elisabeth Schüssler Fiorenza.* Maryknoll: Orbis.

———, and M. A. Tolbert, editors. 1995a. *Reading from this Place: Social Location and Biblical Interpretation in the United States.* Vol. 1. Minneapolis: Augsburg Fortress.

———, and M. A. Tolbert, editors. 1995b. *Reading from this Place: Social Location and Biblical Interpretation in Global Perspective.* Vol. 2. Minneapolis: Augsburg Fortress.

———, and M. A. Tolbert, editors. 1998. *Teaching the Bible: The Discourses and Politics of Biblical Pedagogy.* Maryknoll: Orbis.

Segundo, J. L. 1993. *Signs of the Times: Theological Reflections.* Edited by A. T. Hennelly. Maryknoll: Orbis.

Seidman, S. 1994. *Contested Knowledge: Social Theory in the Postmodern Era.* Cambridge: Blackwell.

———. 2008. *Contested Knowledge: Social Theory Today.* 4th ed. New York: Wiley-Blackwell.

———, and J. C. Alexander, editors. 2001. *The New Social Theory Reader: Contemporary Debates.* New York: Routledge.

———, and D. G. Wagner, editors. 1992. *Postmodernism and Social Theory: The Debate over General Theory.* Cambridge: Basil Blackwell.

Bibliography

Seifart, A. 1978. *Der Gott der politischen Theologie: Die Entwicklung der Gottesdiskussion vom kämpfenden Nationalgott bis zur christlich motivierten Strategie des Guerillakrieges.* Zürich: Benziger.

Seiffert, H. 1992. *Einführung in die Hermeneutik: Die Lehre von der Interpretation in den Fachwissenschaften.* Tübingen: A. Franke.

Seigfried, C. H. 1996. *Pragmatism and Feminism: Reweaving The Social Fabric.* Chicago: University of Chicago Press.

Seipel, C., and P. Rieker. 2003. *Integrative Sozialforschung: Konzepte und Methoden der qualitativen und quantitativen empirischen Forschung.* Weinheim: Juventa.

Sekyi-Otu, A. 1996. *Fanon's Dialectic of Experience.* Cambridge: Harvard University Press.

Selden R., P. Widdowson, and P. Brooker. 1997. *A Reader's Guide to Contemporary Literary Theory.* New York: Prentice Hall.

Selznick, P. 1992. *The Moral Commonwealth: Social Theory and the Promise of Community.* Berkeley: University of California Press.

Seymour-Smith, C. 1986. *Dictionary of Anthropology.* New York: Palgrave.

Shaw, M. 2003. *War and Genocide: Organized Killing in Modern Society.* Cambridge: Polity.

Shea, J. 1978. *Stories of God: An Unauthorized Biography.* Allen: Thomas More.

Shilling, C. 1993. *The Body and Social Theory.* London: Sage.

Shoemaker, N., editor. 2001. *American Indians.* Blackwell Readers in American Social and Cultural History. Malden: Blackwell.

Shor, I. 1992. *Empowering Education: Critical Teaching for Social Change.* Chicago: The University of Chicago Press.

Shusterman, R. 1997. *Practicing Philosophy: Pragmatism and the Philosophical Life.* New York: Routledge.

———. 2000. *Pragmatist Aesthetics: Living Beauty, Rethinking Art.* 2nd ed. Lanham: Rowman & Littlefield.

———. 2001. "Pragmatism: Dewey." In edited by B. Gaut and D. M. Lopes, 97–106. *The Routledge Companion to Aesthetics.* New York: Routledge.

Sibley, D. 1995. *Geographies of Exclusion: Society and Difference in the West.* New York: Routledge.

Sibony, D. 1997. *Le "racisme", une haine identitaire.* Paris: Editions du Seuil.

Sider, R. J., P. N. Olson, and H. Rolland Unruh 2002. *Churches That Make a Difference: Reaching Your Community with Good News and Good Works.* Grand Rapids: Baker.

Sigrist, C. 1995. *Die geladenen Gäste: Diakonie und Ethik im Gespräch—Zur Vision einer diakonischen Kirche.* Bern: Peter Lang.

Sim, S., editor. 2001. *The Routledge Companion to Postmodernism.* New York: Routledge.

Simmons, I. G. 1993. *Interpreting Nature: Cultural Constructions of the Environment.* New York: Routledge.

Simon, R. I. 1992. *Teaching Against the Grain: Texts for a Pedagogy of Possibility.* Edited by H. A. Giroux and P. Freire. Critical Studies in Education and Culture Series. New York: Bergin & Garvey.

Simpson, G. M. 2002. *Critical Social Theory: Prophetic Reason, Civil Society, and Christian Imagination.* Guides to Theological Inquiry. Minneapolis: Augsburg Fortress.

Simpson, L. C. 2001. *The Unfinished Project: Toward a Postmetaphysical Humanism.* New York: Routledge.

Sitton, J. 2003. *Habermas and Contemporary Society.* New York: Palgrave Macmillan.
Sleeper, C. F. 1992. *The Bible and the Moral Life.* Louisville: Westminster John Knox.
Smart, N. 2000. *World Philosophies.* New York: Routledge.
———, and S. Konstantine. 1991. *Christian Systematic Theology in a World Context.* Minneapolis: Fortress.
Smelser, N. J. 1998. *The Social Edges of Psychoanalysis.* Berkeley: University of California Press.
Smith, A. 1982. *The Relational Self: Ethics & Therapy from a Black Church Perspective.* Nashville: Abingdon.
Smith, C. 1995. *American Evangelicalism: Embattled and Thriving.* Chicago: University of Chicago Press.
Smith, C. M. 1992. *Preaching as Weeping, Confession, and Resistance: Radical Responses to Radical Evil.* Louisville: Westminster John Knox.
Smith, D. E. 1987. "Table Fellowship as a Literary Motif in the Gospel of Luke." *Journal of Biblical Literature* 106, 613-638.
———. 2003. *From Symposium to Eucharist: The Banquet in the Early Christian World.* Minneapolis: Fortress.
Smith, D. E. 1987. *The Everyday World als Problematic: A Feminist Sociology.* Milton Keynes: Open University Press.
———. 1990. *The Conceptual Practices Of Power: A Feminist Sociology of Knowledge.* Boston: Northeastern University Press.
———. 2005. *Institutional Ethnography: A Sociology for People.* Walnut Creek: Altamira Press.
Smith, J. K. A. 2006. *Who's Afraid of Postmodernism?: Taking Derrida, Lyotard, and Foucault to Church.* The Church and Postmodern Culture. Grand Rapids: Baker Academics.
———. 2008. *After Modernity?: Secularity, Globalization, and the Re-enchantment of the World.* Waco: Baylor University Press.
Smith, N. H. 1997. *Strong Hermeneutics: Contingency and Moral Identity.* New York: Routledge.
Smith, P. 1988. *Discerning the Subject.* Minneapolis: University of Minnesota Press.
Smith, P. 2001. *Cultural Theory: An Introduction.* Malden: Blackwell.
Smith, T. H. 1994a. "Ethnography-as-Theology: Inscribing the African American Sacred Story." In *Theology Without Foundations: Religious Practice and the Future of Theological Truth,* edited by S. Hauerwas S., N. Murphy, and M. Nation, 117-39. Nashville: Abingdon.
———. 1994b. *Conjuring Culture: Biblical Formations of Black America.* New York: Oxford University Press.
Smith, P. B., and M. H. Bond. 1998. *Social Psychology Across Cultures.* London: Prentice-Hall.
Smith-Christopher, D., editor. 1995. *Text and Experience: Towards a Cultural Exegesis of the Bible.* Sheffield: Sheffield Academic.
Snook, L. E. 1999. *What in the World is God Doing? Re-Imagining Spirit and Power.* Minneapolis: Augsburg Fortress.
Snyder, C. A. 1995. *Anabaptist History and Theology: An Introduction.* Kitchener: Pandora.
———. 2004. *Following in the Footsteps of Christ: The Anabaptist Tradition.* Maryknoll: Orbis.

Bibliography

Snyder, H. A. 1991. *Models of the Kingdom*. Nashville: Abingdon.
Soares-Prabhu, M. G. 2003. *The Dharma of Jesus*. Edited by D'Sa Francis Xavier. Maryknoll: Orbis.
Sobrino, J. 1978. *Christology at the Crossroads: A Latin American Approach*. Maryknoll: Orbis.
———, and I. Ellacuria, editors. 1996. *Systematic Theology: Perspectives from Liberation Theology*. Maryknoll: Orbis.
Soggin, J. A. 1997. *Das Buch Genesis: Kommentar*. Darmstadt: Wissenschaftliche Buchgesellschaft.
Soja, E. W. 1989. *Postmodern Geographies: The Reassertion of Space in Critical Social Theory*. New York: Verso.
———. 2000. *Postmetropolis: Critical Studies of Cities and Regions*. New York: Wiley-Blackwell.
———. 2011. *Postmodern Geographies: The Reassertion of Space in Critical Social Theory*. 2nd ed. New York: Verso.
Solberg, M. M. 1997. *Compelling Knowledge: A Feminist Proposal for an Epistemology of the Cross*. Albany: State University of New York Press.
Sölle, D. 1969. *The Truth is Concrete*. London: Burns & Oates.
———. 1971. *Politische Theologie: Auseinandersetzung mit Rudolf Bultmann*. Stuttgart: Kreuz.
———. 1974. *Political Theology*. Philadelphia: Fortress.
———. 1975. *Suffering*. Philadelphia: Fortress.
———. 1978. *Death By Bread Alone: Texts and Reflections on Religious Experience*. Philadelphia: Fortress.
———. 1981. *Choosing Life*. Philadelphia: Fortress.
———. 1984. *The Strength of the Weak: Toward a Christian Feminist Identity*. Philadelphia: Westminster.
———. 1990. *Thinking about God: An Introduction to Theology*. Philadelphia: Trinity.
———. 1993. "In Search of a New Religious Language." In *On Earth as in Heaven: A Liberation Spirituality of Sharing*, 81–89. Louisville: Westminster John Knox.
———. 1995. *Creative Disobedience*. Cleveland: Pilgrim.
———. 1995a. "A Person Says 'I.'" In *Creative Disobedience*, 54-59. Cleveland: Pilgrim.
———. 1995b. *Gegenwind: Erinnerungen*. Hamburg: Hoffmann und Campe.
———. 1999a. *Erinnert euch an den Regenbogen: Texte, die den Himmel auf Erden suchen*. Edited by B. Hertel and B. Petersen. Freiburg: Herder.
———. 1999b. *Against the Wind: Memoir of a Radical Christian*. Minneapolis: Augsburg Fortress.
———. 2001. *The Silent Cry: Mysticism and Resistance*. Minneapolis: Fortress.
———, and L. Schottroff. 2002. *Jesus of Nazareth*. Louisville: Westminster John Knox.
———. 2002/1990. *Gott denken: Einführung in die Theologie*. Ungekürzte Taschenbuchausgabe. Munich: Piper.
Song, C. S. 1982. *The Compassionate God*. Maryknoll: Orbis.
———. 1999. *The Believing Heart: An Invitation to Story Theology*. Minneapolis: Fortress.
Sparn, W., editor. 1990. *Wer schreibt meine Lebensgeschichte? Biographie, Autobiographie, Hagio-graphie und ihre Entstehungszusammenhänge*. Gütersloh: Gütersloher.
Spohn, W. C. 2000. *Go and Do Likewise: Jesus and Ethics*. New York: Continuum.

Sponheim, P. R. 1993. *Faith and the Other: A Relational Theology*. Minneapolis: Augsburg Fortress.
———. 1999. *The Pulse of Creation: God and the Transformation of the World*. Minneapolis: Fortress.
———. 2006. *Speaking of God: Relational Theology*. St. Louis: Chalice.
———. 2011. *Love's Availing Power: Imaging God, Imagining the World*. Minneapolis: Fortress.
Stacey, J. 1984. *Groundwork of Theology*. Rev. ed. London: Epworth.
Stambaugh, J. E., and D. L. Balch. 1986. *The New Testament in Its Social Environment*. Philadelphia: Westminster.
Stanley, L. 1992. *The Auto/biographical I: The Theory and Practice of Feminist Auto/biography*. Manchester: Manchester University Press.
———, and S. Wise. 1993. *Breaking Out Again: Feminist Ontology and Epistemology*. New York: Routledge.
Stannard, D. E. 1992. *American Holocaust: The Conquest of the New World*. New York: Oxford University Press.
Starhawk. 1987. *Truth or Dare: Encounters with Power, Authority, and Mystery*. San Francisco: HarperSanFrancisco.
Stark, W. 1996. *Empowerment: Neue Handlungskompetenzen in der psychosozialen Arbeit*. Freiburg: Lambertus.
Stassen, G. H. and D. P. Gushee. 2003. *Kingdom Ethics: Following Jesus in Contemporary Context*. Downers Grove: IVP Academic.
———, D. M. Yeager, and J. H. Yoder. 1996. *Authentic Transformation: A New Vision of Christ and Culture*. Nashville: Abingdon.
Staub, D. 2008. *The Culturally Savvy Christian: A Manifesto for Deepening Faith and Enriching Popular Culture in an Age of Christianity-Lite*. San Francisco: Jossey-Bass.
Staub, E. 1989. *The Roots of Evil: The Origins of Genocide and Other Group Violence*. New York: Cambridge University Press.
———. 2003. *The Psychology of Good and Evil: Why Children, Adults, and Groups Help and Harm Others*. New York: Cambridge University Press.
Stayer, J. M. 1976. *Anabaptists and the Sword*. Lawrence: Coronado.
———. 1991. *The German Peasants' War and Anabaptist Community of Goods*. Montreal: McGill-Queen's University Press.
Stegemann, E. W., and W. Stegemann. 1999. *The Jesus Movement: A Social History of Its First Century*. Minneapolis: Fortress.
Stegemann, W., B. J. Malina, and G. Theissen, editors. 2002. *The Social Setting of Jesus and the Gospels*. Minneapolis: Fortress.
Steinkamp, H. 1991. *Sozialpastoral*. Freiburg: Lambertus.
———. 1994. *Solidarität und Parteilichkeit: Für eine neue Praxis in Kirche und Gemeinde*. Mainz: Matthias-Grünewald.
Stell, S. L. 1993. "Hermeneutics in Theology and the Theology of Hermeneutics: Beyond Lindbeck and Tracy." *Journal of the American Academy of Religion* 61, 678–703.
Stephens, L. S. 1974. *The Teacher's Guide to Open Education*. New York: Holt, Rinehart and Winston.
Stewart, A. 2001. *Theories of Power and Domination: The Politics of Empowerment in Late Modernity*. Thousand Oaks: Sage.

Bibliography

Stewart, C. F. 1997. *Soul Survivors: An African American Spirituality.* Louisville: Westminster John Knox.
Stone, H. W., and J. O. Duke. 1996. *How To Think Theologically.* Minneapolis: Fortress.
Storrar, W., and P. Donald, editors. 2003. *God in Society: Doing Social Theology in Scotland Today.* Edinburgh: Saint Andrew Press.
Stotts, J. L. 1973. *Shalom: The Search for a Peaceable City.* Nashville: Abingdon.
Stout, J. 1988. *Ethics After Babel: The Languages of Morals and their Discontents.* Cambridge: James Clarke.
Strahm, D. 1997. *Vom Rand in die Mitte: Christologie aus der Sicht von Frauen in Asien, Afrika und Lateinamerika.* Theologie in Geschichte und Gesellschaft. Vol. 4. Luzern: Exodus.
Straub, J., editor. 1998. *Erzählung, Identität und historisches Bewusstsein: Die psychologische Konstruktion von Zeit und Geschichte.* Erinnerung, Geschichte, Identität 1. Frankfurt: Suhrkamp.
Stroup, G. W. 1981. *The Promise of Narrative Theology: Recovering the Gospel in the Church.* Atlanta: John Knox Press.
Stuart, E. 1995. *Just Good Friends: Towards a Lesbian and Gay Theology of Relationships.* London: Mowbray.
———. 1997. "Experience and Tradition: Just Good Friends." In *Sources and Resources of Feminist Theologies,* edited by E. Hartlieb and C. Methuen, 49–71. Yearbook of the European Society of Women in Theological Research. Volume 5/97. Mainz: Matthias-Grünewald.
Suchocki, M. H. 1989. *God—Christ—Church: A Practical Guide to Process Theology.* New rev. ed. New York: Crossroad.
———. 1995. *The Fall to Violence: Original Sin in Relational Theology.* New York: Continuum.
Sugirtharajah, R. S., editor. 1995. *Voices from the Margin: Interpreting the Bible in the Third World.* Maryknoll: Orbis.
———. 2001. *The Bible and the Third World: Precolonial, Colonial and Postcolonial ncounters.* New York: Cambridge University Press.
Sullivan, M. 2002. *101 Questions and Answers on Vatican II.* Mahwah: Paulist.
Sundermeier, T. 1996. *Den Fremden verstehen: Eine praktische Hermeneutik.* Göttingen: Vandenhoeck & Ruprecht.
———. 1999. *Was ist Religion? Religionswissenschaft im theologischen Kontext: Ein Studienbuch.* Gütersloh: Chr. Kaiser/Gütersloher.
———. 1999a. "Zur Einleitung: Religion und Erfahrung." In *Was ist Religion? Religionswissenschaft im theologischen Kontext: Ein Studienbuch,* 11–27. Gütersloh: Chr. Kaiser/Gütersloher.
Surber, J. P. 1998. *Culture and Critique: An Introduction to the Critical Discourses of Cultural Studies.* Boulder: Westview.
Sutphin, S. T. 1977. *Options in Contemporary Theology.* Washington: University Press of America.
Swaim, J. C. 1982. *War, Peace, and the Bible.* Maryknoll: Orbis.
Swartley, W. M., editor. 2000. *Violence Renounced: René Girard, Biblical Studies, and Peacemaking.* Telford: Pandora.
Swartz, D. 1997. *Culture & Power: The Sociology of Pierre Bourdieu.* Chicago: The University of Chicago Press.

Sweet, L. 1999. *SoulTsunami: Sink or Swim in New Millennium Culture.* Grand Rapids: Zondervan.

———. 2007. *The Gospel According to Starbucks: Living with a Grande Passion.* Colorado Springs: WaterBrook.

Swimme B. 1996. *The Heart of the Cosmos.* Maryknoll: Orbis.

———, and T. Berry. 1992. *The Universe Story.* San Francisco: HarperSanFrancisco.

Taborelli, G., editor. 1998. *Art: A World History.* New York: Dorling Kindersley.

Takaki, R. 1993. *A Different Mirror: A History of Multicultural America.* Boston: Little, Brown.

Talbot, M. M. 2001. "Feminism and Language." In *The Routledge Companion to Feminism and Postfeminism,* edited by S. Gamble, 140–47. New York: Routledge.

Tam, H. 1998. *Communitarianism: A New Agenda for Politics and Citizenship.* New York: New York University Press.

Tamez, E. 1982. *Bible of the Oppressed.* Maryknoll: Orbis.

———. 1986. "The Woman Who Complicated the History of Salvation." In *New Eyes for Reading: Biblical and Theological Reflections By Women from the Third World,* edited by J. S. Pobee and B. Von Wartenberg-Potter, 5–17. Geneva: World Council of Churches Publications.

———. 1993. *The Amnesty of Grace: Justification by Faith from a Latin American Perspective.* Nashville: Abingdon.

Tanesini, A. 1999. *An Introduction to Feminist Epistemologies.* Oxford: Blackwell.

Tannehill, R. C. 1996. *Luke.* Abingdon New Testament Commentaries. Nashville: Abingdon.

Tanner, K. 1997. *Theories of Culture: A New Agenda for Theology.* Guides to Theological Inquiry. Minneapolis: Fortress.

Tarnas, R. 1991. *The Passion of the Western Mind: Understanding the Ideas That Have Shaped Our World View.* New York: Ballantine.

Taube, R., C. Tietz-Buck, and C. Klinge. 1995. *Frauen und Jesus Christus: Die Bedeutung von Christologie im Leben protestantischer Frauen.* Stuttgart: Kohlhammer.

Taylor, B. 2008. *Entertainment Theology: New-Edge Spirituality in a Digital Democracy* Cultural Exegesis. Grand Rapids: Baker Academic.

Taylor, M. C. 1984. *Erring: A Postmodern A/theology.* Chicago: The University of Chicago Press.

Taylor, M. L. 1986. "In Praise of Shaky Ground: The Liminal Christ and Cultural Pluralism." *Theology Today* 43, 36–51.

———. 1986a. *Beyond Explanation: Religious Dimensions in Cultural Anthropology.* Macon: Mercer University Press.

———. 1990. *Remembering Esperanza: A Cultural-Political Theology for North American Praxis.* Maryknoll: Orbis.

———. 1997. "Vodou Resistance/Vodou Hope: Forging a Postmodernism that Liberates." In *Liberation Theologies, Postmodernity, and the Americas,* edited by D. Batstone, E. Mendieta, L. A. Lorentzen, and D. N. Hopkins, 169–87. New York: Routledge.

———. 2001. *The Executed God: The Way of the Cross in Lockdown America.* Minneapolis: Augsburg Fortress.

———. 2011. *The Theological and the Political: On the Weight of the World.* Minneapolis: Fortress.

Bibliography

———, and G. J. Bekker. 1990. "Engaging the Other in a Global Village." *Theological Education* 26, Supplement 1, 52–85.

Taylor, V. E., and C. E. Winquist, editors. 2001. *Encyclopedia of Postmodernism*. New York: Routledge.

Terrell, J. M. 1998. *Power in the Blood? The Cross in the African American Experience*. Maryknoll: Orbis.

Tesfai, Y., editor. 1994. *The Scandal of a Crucified World: Perspectives on the Cross and Suffering*. Maryknoll: Orbis.

Teske, D. 2002. *Cultural Studies: GB*. Berlin: Cornelsen.

Teubal, S. J. 1990. *Hagar the Egyptian: The Lost Traditions of the Matriarchs*. San Francisco: Harper and Row.

———. 1993. "Sarah and Hagar: Matriarchs and Visionaries." In *Genesis: The Feminist Companion to the Bible*, edited by A. Brenner, 235–50. Vol. 1. Sheffield: Sheffield Academic.

The Mudflower Collective. Cannon K. G., editor. 1985. *God's Fierce Whimsy: Christian Feminism and Theological Education*. New York: Pilgrim Press.

The New American Bible. (2006/1991). With Revised New Testament and Revised Psalms. National Conference of Catholic Bishops and the United States Catholic Conference. Nashville: Catholic Bible Press.

Theissen G. 1978. *Sociology of Early Palestinian Christianity*. Minneapolis: Fortress.

———. 2003. *Jesus als historische Gestalt: Beiträge zur Jesusforschung*. Edited by Annette Merz. Göttingen: Vandenhoeck & Ruprecht.

———, and A. Merz. 1998. *The Historical Jesus: A Comprehensive Guide*. London: SCM.

Thiersch, H. 1992. *Lebensweltorientierte Soziale Arbeit: Aufgaben der Praxis im sozialen Wandel*. Munich: Juventa.

Thiselton, A. C. 2002. *A Concise Encyclopedia of the Philosophy of Religion*. Oxford: Oneworld.

Thistlethwaite, S. B. 1989. *Sex, Race, and God: Christian Feminism in Black and White*. New York: Crossroad; reprinted Wipf & Stock, 2004.

———, and G. F. Cairns, editors. 1994. *Beyond Theological Tourism: Mentoring as a Grassroots Approach to Theological Education*. Maryknoll: Orbis; reprinted Wipf & Stock, 2003.

———, and M. P. Engel, editors. 1998. *Lift Every Voice: Constructing Christian Theologies from the Underside*. Maryknoll: Orbis.

Thomas, O. C. 1994. *Introduction to Theology*. Rev. ed. Harrisburg: Morehouse Publishing.

———, and E. K. Wondra. 2002. *Introduction to Theology*. 3rd ed. Harrisburg: Morehouse.

Thompson A. 2009. *Erich Fromm: Explorer of the Human Condition*. New York: Palgrave Macmillan.

Thornton S. G. 2002. *Broken Yet Beloved: A Pastoral Theology of the Cross*. St. Louis: Chalice.

Thurn, S., and K. J. Tillmann, editors. 1997. *Unsere Schule ist ein Haus des Lernens: Das Beispiel Laborschule Bielefeld*. Hamburg: Rowohlt.

Tidball, D. J. 1994. *Who Are The Evangelicals? Tracing the Roots of Today's Movements*. London: HarperCollins.

Tilley, T. W. 1985. *Story Theology*. Wilmington: Michael Glazier.

———. 1995. *Postmodern Theologies: The Challenge of Religious Diversity.* Maryknoll: Orbis.
Tillich, P. 1951. *Systematic Theology: Reason and Revelation, Being and God.* Vol. 1. Chicago: The University of Chicago Press.
———. 1957. *Systematic Theology: Existence and the Christ.* Vol. 2. Chicago: The University of Chicago Press.
———. 1963. *Systematic Theology: Life and the Spirit, History and the Kingdom of God.* Vol. 3. Chicago: The University of Chicago Press.
———. 1964. *Theology of Culture.* New York: Oxford University Press.
———, and F. F. Church, editors. 1999. *The Essential Tillich.* Chicago: University of Chicago Press.
Tinker, G. E. 1993. *Missionary Conquest: The Gospel and Native American Cultural Genocide.* Minneapolis: Fortress.
Tolstoy, L. 1994. *What is Art?* London: Duckworth.
Tomkins, S. 2005. *A Short History of Christianity.* Grand Rapids: Eerdmans.
Toolan, D. 2001. *At Home in the Cosmos.* Maryknoll: Orbis.
Topel, J. L. 1979. *The Way to Peace: Liberation through the Bible.* Maryknoll: Orbis.
———. 2001. *Children of a Compassionate God: A Theological Exegesis of Luke 6:20-49.* Collegeville: Liturgical.
Toulouse, M. G., and J. O. Duke, editors. 1997. *Makers of Christian Theology in America.* Nashville: Abingdon.
———, editors. 1999. *Sources of Christian Theology in America.* Nashville: Abingdon.
Townes, E. M., editor. 1993. *A Troubling In My Soul: Womanist Perspectives on Evil & Suffering.* Maryknoll: Orbis.
Tracy, D. 1975. *Blessed Rage for Order: The New Pluralism in Theology.* New York: Seabury.
———. 1981. *The Analogical Imagination: Christian Theology and the Culture of Pluralism.* New York: Crossroad.
———. 1987. *Plurality and Ambiguity: Hermeneutics, Religion, and Hope.* San Francisco: Harper & Row.
———. 1989. "Hermeneutical Reflections in the New Paradigm." In *Paradigm Change in Theology: A Symposium for the Future,* edited by H. Küng and D. Tracy, 34-62. Edinburgh: T. & T. Clark.
———. 1993. *Theologie als Gespräch: Eine postmoderne Hermeneutik.* Mainz: Matthias-Grünewald.
———. 1994. *On Naming the Present: God, Hermeneutics, and Church.* Maryknoll: Orbis.
———. 1999. "Fragments: The Spiritual Situation of Our Times." In *God, the Gift, and Postmodernism,* edited by J. D. Caputo and M. J. Scanlon, 170-84. Bloomington: Indiana University Press.
Trask, H. K. 1986. *Eros and Power: The Promise of Feminist Theory.* Philadelphia: University of Pennsylvania Press.
Triandis, H. C. 1994. *Culture and Social Behavior.* New York: McGraw-Hill.
Trible, P. 1984. *Texts of Terror: Literary-Feminist Readings of Biblical Narratives.* Philadelphia: Fortress.
———. 1985. "The Other Woman: A Literary and Theological Study of the Hagar Narratives." In *Understanding the Word: Essays in Honor of Bernhard W. Anderson,*

Bibliography

edited by J. T. Butler, E. W. Conrad, and B. C. Ollenburger, 221–46. Sheffield: JSOT Press.

Trigo, P. 1991. *Creation and History*. Theology and Liberation Series. Maryknoll: Orbis.

Troost, A. 1993. "Reading for the Author's Signature: Genesis 21.1–21 and Luke 15.11–32 as Intertexts." In *Genesis: The Feminist Companion to the Bible*, edited by A. Brenner, 251–72. Vol. 1. Sheffield: Sheffield Academic.

Tück, J. H. 1999. *Christologie und Theodizee bei Johann Baptist Metz: Ambivalenz der Neuzeit im Licht der Gottesfrage*. Paderborn: Ferdinand Schöningh.

Türk, H. J. 1990. *Postmoderne*. Unterscheidung: Christliche Orientierung im religiösen Pluralismus. Mainz: Matthias-Grünewald.

Turner, B. S. 1996. *The Body and Society*. Thousand Oaks: Sage.

Turner, G. 1996. *British Cultural Studies: An Introduction*. 2nd ed. New York: Routledge.

Turner, L. A. 2000. *Genesis*. Readings: A New Biblical Commentary. Sheffield: Sheffield Academic.

Turner, V., and E. Bruner, editors. 1986. *The Anthropology of Experience*. Urbana: University of Illinois Press.

Ulanov, A., and B. Ulanov. 1999. *The Healing Imagination: The Meeting of Psyche and Soul*. Einsiedeln: Daimon.

Uphoff, B. 1991. *Kirchliche Erwachsenenbildung: Befreiung und Mündigkeit im Spannungsfeld von Kirche und Welt*. Praktische Theologie heute. Vol. 3. Stuttgart: Kohlhammer.

Usher, R., I. Bryant, and R. Johnston. 1997. *Adult Education and the Postmodern Challenge: Learning Beyond Limits*. New York: Routledge.

Vaage, L. E., editor. 1997. *Subversive Scriptures: Revolutionary Readings of the Christian Bible in Latin America*. Harrisburg: Trinity.

Valentin, B., editor. 2003. *New Horizons in Hispanic/Latino(a) Theology*. Cleveland: Pilgrim.

Vamos Caminando. Machen wir uns auf den Weg! 1983. Equipo Pastoral de Bambamarca. Freiburg: Exodus.

Van der Bent, A. 1995. *Commitment to God's World: A Concise Critical Survey of Ecumenical Social Thought*. Geneva: WCC.

Van Voorst, R. E. 2004. *Reading the New Testament Today*. Belmont: Thomson/Wadsworth.

VanElderen, M., and M. Conway. 2001. *Introducing the World Council of Churches*. Rev. and enl. ed. Geneva: WCC.

Vanhoozer, K. J. 2002. *First Theology: God, Scripture, and Hermeneutics*. Downers Grove: InterVarsity.

———, editor. 2003. *The Cambridge Companion to Postmodern Theology*. New York: Cambridge University Press.

———. 2005. *The Drama of Doctrine: A Canonical-Linguistic Approach to Christian Theology*. Louisville: Westminster John Knox.

Vanoni, G., and B. Heininger. 2002. *Das Reich Gottes: Perspektiven des Alten und Neuen Testaments*. Die Neue Echter Bibel. Vol. 4. Würzburg: Echter.

Venema, H. I. 2000. *Identifying Selfhood: Imagination, Narrative, and Hermeneutics in the Thought of Paul Ricoeur*. Albany: State University of New York Press.

Venetz, H. J. 2000. *Der Evangelist des Alltags: Streifzüge durch das Lukasevangelium*. Freiburg: Paulusverlag.

Verweyen, H. 2000. *Gottes letztes Wort: Grundriss der Fundamentaltheologie*. 3rd ed. Regensburg: Friedrich Pustet.
Vilanova, E. 1997. *Histoire des théologies chrétiennes: XVIIIe-XXe siècle*. Tome III. Paris: Cerf.
Villafane, E., B. W. Jackson, R. A. Evans, and A. F. Evans. 2002. *Transforming the City: Reframing Education for Urban Ministry*. Grand Rapids: Eerdmans.
Visser, F. 2002. *Ken Wilber—Denker aus Passion: Eine Zusammenschau*. Petersberg: Via Nova.
Voderholzer, R. 2001. *Fundamentaltheologie/Ökumenische Theologie*. Paderborn: Bonifatius.
Vogel, L. J. 1991. *Teaching and Learning in Communities of Faith: Empowering Adults Through Religious Education*. San Francisco: Jossey-Bass.
Volf, M. 1996. *Exclusion and Embrace: Theological Reflections on Identity, Otherness, and Reconciliation*. Nashville: Abingdon.
———. 1996a. "Theology, Meaning, and Power: A Conversation with George Lindbeck on Theology and the Nature of Christian Difference." In *The Nature of Confession: Evangelicals and Postliberals in Conversation*, edited by T. R. Phillips and D. L. Okholm, 45–66. Downers Grove: InterVarsity.
———. 2002. "Theology for a Way of Life." In *Practicing Theology: Beliefs and Practices in Christian Life*, edited by M. Volf and D. C. Bass, 245–63. Grand Rapids: Eerdmans.
———, and D. C. Bass, editors. 2002. *Practicing Theology: Beliefs and Practices in Christian Life*. Grand Rapids: Eerdmans.
———, and M. Welker, editors. 2006. *God's Life in Trinity*. Minneapolis: Fortress.
———, C. Krieg, and T. Kucharz, editors. 1996. *The Future of Theology: Essays in Honor of Jürgen Moltmann*. Grand Rapids: Eerdmans.
Volkwein, K. 1999. *Der Traum einer gemeinsamen Sprache: Feministische Theologie in den USA der siebziger Jahre*. Mainz: Matthias-Grünewald.
Wachterhauser, B. R., editor. 1986. *Hermeneutics and Modern Philosophy*. Albany: State University of New York Press.
Wacker, M. T. 1988. "1. Mose 16 und 21: Hagar—die Befreite." In *Feministisch gelesen: 32 ausgewählte Bibeltexte für Gruppen, Gemeinden und Gottesdienste*, edited by E. R. Schmidt, M. Korenhof, and R. Jost, 25–32. Vol. 1. Stuttgart: Kreuz.
Wagner, H. 1996. *Einführung in die Fundamentaltheologie*. Darmstadt: Wissenschaftliche Buchgesellschaft.
———. 2003. *Dogmatik*. Studienbücher Theologie 18. Stuttgart: Kohlhammer.
Wagner-Egelhaaf, M. 2000. *Autobiographie*. Stuttgart: J. B. Metzler.
Wainwright, G. 1980. *Doxology—The Praise of God in Worship, Doctrine, and Life: A Systematic Theology*. New York: Oxford University Press.
Waldenfels, B. 2000. *Das leibliche Selbst: Vorlesungen zur Phänomenologie des Leibes*. Frankfurt: Suhrkamp.
Waldenfels, H., editor. 1982. *Theologen der Dritten Welt: Elf biographische Skizzen aus Afrika, Asien und Lateinamerika*. Munich: C. H. Beck.
———. 1994. *Phänomen Christentum: Eine Weltreligion in der Welt der Religionen*. Freiburg: Herder.
———. 2000. *Kontextuelle Fundamentaltheologie*. 3rd ed. Paderborn: Ferdinand Schöningh.
———. 2002. *Christus und die Religionen*. Regensburg: Friedrich Pustet.

Bibliography

Walker, T. 1991. *Empower the People: Social Ethics for the African-American Church.* Maryknoll: Orbis.

Wallace, M. I. 2002. *Fragments of the Spirit: Nature, Violence, and the Renewal of Creation.* Harrisburg: Trinity.

———, and T. H. Smith, editors. 1994. *Curing Violence: Essays on René Girard.* Sonoma: Polebridge.

Wallis, J. 1994. *The Soul of Politics: A Practical and Prophetic Vision for Change.* Maryknoll: Orbis.

Walsh, J. P. M. 1987. *The Mighty From Their Thrones: Power in the Biblical Tradition.* Philadelphia: Fortress.

Walther, I. F., editor. 2002. *Kunst des 20. Jahrhunderts: Malerei—Skulpturen und Objekte—Neue Medien—Fotographie.* Köln: Taschen.

Walton, M. 1994. *Marginal Communities: The Ethical Enterprise of the Followers of Jesus.* Kampen: Kok Pharos.

Ward, G. 1997. *Teach Yourself Postmodernism.* Teach Yourself Books. London: Hodder & Stoughton.

Ward, G. 1996. *Theology and Contemporary Critical Theory.* New York: St. Martin's.

———, editor. 1997. *The Postmodern God: A Theological Reader.* Oxford: Blackwell.

———, editor. 2005. *The Blackwell Companion to Postmodern Theology.* Malden: Blackwell.

Warneck, W. 1990. *Friedenskirchliche Existenz im Konziliaren Prozess.* Hildesheim: Georg Olms.

Wartenberg, T. E. 1990. *The Forms of Power: From Domination to Transformation.* Philadelphia: Temple University Press.

———, editor. 1992. *Rethinking Power.* Albany: State University of New York Press.

Wartenberg-Potter, B., editor. 2004. *Was tust du, fragt der Engel: Mystik im Alltag.* Freiburg: Herder.

Wasser, H., editor. 2000. *USA: Wirtschaft—Gesellschaft—Politik.* Opladen: Leske+Budrich.

Waters, J. W. 1991. "Who Was Hagar?" In *Stony the Road We Trod: African American Biblical Interpretation,* edited by C. H. Felder, 187–205. Minneapolis: Fortress.

Watley, W. D. 1985. *Roots of Resistance: The Nonviolent Ethic of Martin Luther King Jr.* Valley Forge: Judson.

Watson, P. 2000. *A Terrible Beauty—The People and Ideas that Shaped the Modern Mind: A History.* London: Phoenix.

Way, P. 2005. *Created by God: Pastoral Care for All God's People.* St. Louis: Chalice.

Wearne, P. 1996. *Return of the Indian: Conquest and Revival in the Americas.* London: Cassell.

Weaver, J. D., and Biesecker-Mast, G., editors. 2003. *Teaching Peace: Nonviolence and the Liberal Arts.* Lanham: Rowman & Littlefield.

Webb, J. B. 2004. *The Complete Idiot's Guide to Christianity.* Indianapolis: Alpha.

Webber, R. H. 2002. *The Younger Evangelicals: Facing the Challenges of the New World.* Grand Rapids: Baker.

Weber, H. R. 1989. *Power: Focus for a Biblical Theology.* Geneva: WCC.

———. 1996. *A Laboratory for Ecumenical Life: The Story of Bossey 1946-1996.* Geneva: WCC.

Webster, J. B. 1990. *Eberhard Jüngel: An Introduction to His Theology.* Cambridge: Cambridge University Press.

———. 1997. "Eberhard Jüngel." In Ford D. F. edited by. *The Modern Theologians: An Introduction to Christian Theology in the Twentieth Century.* Oxford: Blackwell, 52-66.
Webster, J. B., K. Tanner, and I. Torrance, editors. 2009. *The Oxford Handbook of Systematic Theology.* New York: Oxford University Press.
Weedon, C. 1997. *Feminist Practice and Poststructuralist Theory.* 2nd ed. Cambridge: Blackwell.
Weems, R. J. 1988. *Just a Sister Away: A Womanist Vision of Women's Relationships in the Bible.* San Diego: LuraMedia.
———. 1988a. "A Mistress, a Maid, and No Mercy." In *Just a Sister Away: A Womanist Vision of Women's Relationships in the Bible,* 1-21. San Diego: LuraMedia.
———. 1991. "Reading *Her Way* through the Struggle: African American Women and the Bible." In *Stony the Road We Trod: African American Biblical Interpretation,* edited by C. H. Felder, 57-77. Minneapolis: Fortress.
Wegenast, K. 1999. "Zum Verhältnis Systematischer und Praktischer Theologie in Geschichte und Gegenwart 1984." In *Lern-Schritte: 40 Jahre Religionspädagogik 1955-1995,* 208-34. Stuttgart: Kohlhammer.
Wehr, H. 1990. *Erich Fromm zur Einführung.* Hamburg: Junius.
Weinrich, M. 1999. *Theologie und Biographie: Zum Verhältnis von Lehre und Leben.* Wuppertal: Foedus.
Weir, A. 1996. *Sacrificial Logics: Feminist Theory and the Critique of Identity.* New York: Routledge.
Weissberg, R. 1999. *The Politics of Empowerment.* Westport: Praeger.
Welch, S. D. 1985. *Communities of Resistance and Solidarity: A Feminist Theology of Liberation.* Maryknoll: Orbis.
———. 1990. *A Feminist Ethic of Risk.* Minneapolis: Fortress.
———. 1991. "An Ethic of Solidarity and Difference." In *Postmodernism, Feminism, and Cultural Politics: Redrawing Educational Boundaries,* edited by H. A. Giroux, 83-99. Albany: State University of New York Press.
———. 1999. *Sweet Dreams in America: Making Ethics and Spirituality Work.* New York: Routledge.
———. 2000. *A Feminist Ethic of Risk.* Rev. ed. Minneapolis: Fortress.
———. 2004. *After Empire: The Art and Ethos of Enduring Peace.* Minneapolis: Fortress.
———. 2005. "'Lush Life': Foucault's Analytics of Power and a Jazz Aesthetic." In *The Blackwell Companion to Postmodern Theology,* edited by G. Ward, 79-103. Malden: Blackwell.
Welker, M. 1988. *Universalität Gottes und Relativität der Welt: Theologische Kosmologie im Dialog mit dem amerikanischen Prozessdenken nach Whitehead.* 2nd ed. Neukirchen-Vluyn: Neukirchener.
———. 1992. *Gottes Geist: Theologie des Heiligen Geistes.* Neukirchen-Vluyn: Neukirchener.
———. 1994. *God the Spirit.* Minneapolis: Fortress.
———. 1995. *Schöpfung und Wirklichkeit.* Neukirchen-Vluyn: Neukirchener.
Wells, D. F. 1993. *No Place for Truth or Whatever Happened to Evangelical Theology?* Grand Rapids: Eerdmans.
Wells, S. 2004. *Improvisation: The Drama of Christian Ethics.* Grand Rapids: Brazos.
Welsch, W. 1990. *Ästhetisches Denken.* Stuttgart: Reclam.
———. 1996a. *Grenzgänge der Ästhetik.* Stuttgart: Reclam.

Bibliography

———. 1996b. *Vernunft: Die zeitgenössische Vernunftkritik und das Konzept der transversalen Vernunft*. Frankfurt: Suhrkamp.
Wenham, G. J. 1987. *Genesis 1–15*. Word Biblical Commentary. Vol. 1. Waco: Word.
———. 1993. *Genesis 16-50*. Word Biblical Commentary. Vol. 2. Dallas: Word.
Werbick, J. 1992. *Bilder sind Wege: Eine Gotteslehre*. Munich: Kösel.
———. 2000. *Den Glauben verantworten: Eine Fundamentaltheologie*. Freiburg: Herder.
Wersich, R. B., editor. 1996. *USA-Lexikon: Schlüsselbegriffe zu Politik, Wirtschaft, Gesellschaft, Kultur, Geschichte und zu den deutsch-amerikanischen Beziehungen*. Berlin: Erich Schmitt.
West, C. 1982. *Prophesy Deliverance! An Afro-American Revolutionary Christianity*. Philadelphia: Westminster.
———. 1988. *Prophetic Fragments*. Grand Rapids: Eerdmans.
———. 1989. *The American Evasion of Philosophy: A Genealogy of Pragmatism*. New York: Macmillan.
———. 1991. *The Ethical Dimensions of Marxist Thought*. New York: Monthly Review Press.
———. 1993. *Keeping Faith: Philosophy and Race in America*. New York: Routledge.
———. 1993a. *Prophetic Thought in Postmodern Times: Beyond Eurocentrism and Multiculturalism*. Vol. 1. Monroe: Common Courage.
———. 1993b. *Prophetic Reflections—Notes on Race and Power in America: Beyond Eurocentrism and Multiculturalism*. Vol. 2. Monroe: Common Courage.
———. 1994. *Race Matters*. New York: Vintage.
———. 1999. *The Cornel West Reader*. New York: Basic Civitas.
———. 2005. *Democracy Matters: Winning the Fight Against Imperialism*. New York: Penguin.
———. 2008. *Hope on a Tightrope: Words and Wisdom*. New York: Hay House.
———. 2010. *Brother West: Living and Loving Out Loud, A Memoir*. New York: Smiley.
———, and Glaude E. S., editors. 2004. *African American Religious Thought: An Anthology*. Louisville: Westminster John Knox.
West, G. 1995. *Biblical Hermeneutics of Liberation: Modes of Reading the Bible in the South African Context*. Maryknoll: Orbis.
Westwood, S. 2002. *Power and the Social*. New York: Routledge.
———. 2002a. "A Brief History of Power." In *Power and the Social*, 5–28. New York: Routledge.
———. 2002b. "Spatial Power." In *Power and the Social*, 99–113. New York: Routledge.
Wetherilt, A. K. 1994. *That They May Be Many: Voices of Women, Echoes of God*. New York: Continuum.
Wetzel, C. 2001. *Das Reclam Buch der Kunst*. Stuttgart: Reclam.
Wheeler, B. G., and E. Farley, editors. 1991. *Shifting Boundaries: Contextual Approaches to the Structure of Theological Education*. Louisville: Westminster John Knox.
White, L. M. 2004. *From Jesus to Christianity*. San Francisco: HarperSanFrancisco.
White, S. K. 1991. *Political Theory and Postmodernism*. New York: Cambridge University Press.
———, editor. 1995. *The Cambridge Companion to Habermas*. New York: Cambridge University Press.

Whitelam, K. W. 1998. "The Social World of the Bible." In *The Cambridge Companion to Biblical Interpretation*, edited by J. Barton, 35–49. Cambridge: Cambridge University Press.
Wickeri, P. L., J. K. Wickeri, and D. M. A. Niles, editors. 2000. *Plurality, Power, and Mission: Intercontextual Theological Explorations on the Role of Religion in the New Millennium*. London: The Council for World Mission.
Wickler, P., editor. 2004. *Handbuch Mobbing-Rechtsschutz*. Heidelberg: C. F. Müller.
Widl, M. 2000. *Pastorale Weltentheologie—transversal entwickelt im Diskurs mit der Sozialpastoral*. Praktische Theologie heute. Stuttgart: Kohlhammer.
Wiedenhofer S. 1976. *Politische Theologie*. Stuttgart: Kohlhammer.
Wiéner, C. 2000. *Le Dieu des pauvres*. Paris: Les Editions Ouvrières.
Wiggershaus, R. 2004. *Jürgen Habermas*. Rowohlts Monographien. Reinbek bei Hamburg: Rowohlt.
Wilber, K. 1998. *The Eye of Spirit: An Integral Vision for a World Gone Slightly Mad*. Boston: Shambhala.
Wilder, A. N. 1976. *Theopoetic: Theology and the Religious Imagination*. Philadelphia: Fortress.
Will, J. E. 1989. *A Christology of Peace*. Louisville: Westminster John Knox.
Williams, D. S. 1993. *Sisters in the Wilderness: The Challenge of Womanist God-Talk*. Maryknoll: Orbis.
———. 1993a. "Hagar's Story: A Route to Black Women's Issues." In *Sisters in the Wilderness: The Challenge of Womanist God-Talk*, 15–33. Maryknoll: Orbis.
Williams, G. H. 1992. *The Radical Reformation*. 3rd ed. Kirkville: Sixteenth Century Journal Publishers.
Williams, J. G. 1991. *The Bible, Violence, and the Sacred: Liberation from the Myth of Sanctioned Violence*. New York: HarperCollins.
———, editor. 1996. *René Girard: The Girard Reader*. New York: Crossroad.
Williams, M. 2000. *Science and Social Science: An Introduction*. New York: Routledge.
Williams, P. D. 1991. *The Alchemy of Race and Rights*. Cambridge: Harvard University Press.
Williamson, C. M. 1993. *A Guest in the House of Israel: Post-Holocaust Church Theology*. Louisville: Westminster John Knox.
———. 1999. *Way of Blessing, Way of Life: A Christian Theology*. St. Louis: Chalice.
Willis, P. 2000. *The Ethnographic Imagination*. Cambridge: Polity.
Wills D. W. 2002. "Vereinigte Staaten von Amerika." In *Theologische Realenzyklopädie*, edited by G. Müller, 593–639. Vol. 34. New York: Walter de Gruyter.
———. 2005. *Christianity in the United States: A Historical Survey and Interpretation*. Notre Dame: University of Notre Dame Press.
Wilmore, G. S. 1983. *Black Religion and Black Radicalism: An Interpretation of the Religious History of Afro-American People*. 2nd ed. Rev. and enl. Maryknoll: Orbis.
Wilson, H. S., T. Mofokeng, J. Poerwowidagdo, R. A. Evans, and A. F. Evans. 1996. *Pastoral Theology from a Global Perspective: A Case Method Approach*. Maryknoll: Orbis.
Wilson Bridges, F. 2001. *Resurrection Song: African-American Spirituality*. Maryknoll: Orbis.
Wimbush, V. L., and R. C. Rodman, editors. 2001. *African Americans and the Bible: Sacred Text and Social Texture*. New York: Continuum.

Bibliography

Wind, R. 1995. *Befreiung buchstabieren: Basislektüre Bibel.* Gütersloh: Chr. Kaiser/Gütersloher Verlagshaus.
Wink, W. 1984. *Naming the Powers: The Language of Power in the New Testament.* Minneapolis: Fortress.
———. 1986. *Unmasking the Powers: The Invisible Forces That Determine Human Existence.* Minneapolis: Fortress.
———. 1992. *Engaging the Powers: Discernment and Resistance in a World of Domination.* Minneapolis: Fortress.
———. 1998. *When the Powers Fall: Reconciliation in the Healing of Nations.* Minneapolis: Fortress.
———. 1998a. *The Powers That Be: Theology for a New Millennium.* New York: Doubleday.
———, editor. 2000. *Peace Is The Way: Writings on Nonviolence from the Fellowship of Reconciliation.* Maryknoll: Orbis.
———. 2009. *The Human Being: Jesus and the Enigma of the Son of Man.* Minneapolis: Fortress.
Winklmayr, J. 1993. *Lebenswelt Pfarrgemeinde: Zu einer diakonischen Pfarrpastoral.* Vienna: Kultur.
Winling, R. 1983. *La théologie contemporaine: 1945-1980.* Paris: Le Centurion.
Winquist, C. E. 1995. *Desiring Theology.* Chicago: University of Chicago Press.
Wiseman, J. A. 2002. *Theology and Modern Science: Quest for Coherence.* New York: Continuum.
Witkin, R. W. 2003. *Adorno on Popular Culture.* New York: Routledge.
Witvliet, T. 1985. *A Place in the Sun: An Introduction to Liberation Theology in the Third World.* London: SCM.
Wohlmuth, J. 1992. *Jesu Weg—unser Weg: Kleine mystagogische Christologie.* Würzburg: Echter.
Wollrad, E. 1999. *Wildniserfahrung: Womanistische Herausforderung und eine Antwort aus Weisser feministischer Perspektive.* Gütersloh: Chr. Kaiser/Gütersloher.
Wood, M. D. 2001. "Religious Studies as Critical Organic Intellectual Practice." *Journal of the American Academy of Religion* 69, 129–162.
Woods, T. 1999. *Beginning Postmodernism.* Manchester and New York: Manchester University Press.
Wright, N. G., and Kill, D. 1993. *Ecological Healing: A Christian Vision.* Maryknoll: Orbis.
Yancy, G., editor. 2001. *Cornel West: A Critical Reader.* Malden: Blackwell.
Yeatman, A. 1994. *Postmodern Revisionings of the Political.* New York: Routledge.
Yoder, J. H. 1972/1994. *The Politics of Jesus: Vicit Agnus Noster.* 2nd ed. Grand Rapids: Eerdmans.
———. 1994. "Walk and Word: The Alternatives to Methodologism." In *Theology Without Foundations: Religious Practice and the Future of Religious Truth*, edited by S. Hauerwas, N. Murphy, and M. Nation, 77–90. Nashville: Abingdon.
———. 2007. *Preface to Theology: Christology and Theological Method.* Grand Rapids: Brazos.
Young, H. J., editor. 1983. *God and Human Freedom: A Festschrift in Honor of Howard Thurman.* Richmond, IN: Friends United Press; reprinted by Wipf & Stock, 2002.
Young, I. M. 1987. "Impartiality and the Civic Public: Some Implications of Feminist Critiques of Moral and Political Theory." In *Feminism as Critique: Essays on the*

Politics of Gender in Late-Capitalist Societies, edited by S. Benhabib and D. Cornell, 57–76. Cambridge: Polity.

Young, J. U. 1992. *A Pan-African Theology: Providence and the Legacies of the Ancestors.* Trenton: Africa World.

Young, P. D. 1990. *Feminist Theology/Christian Theology: In Search of Method.* Minneapolis: Fortress.

———. 2000. *Re-creating the Church: Communities of Eros.* Harrisburg: Trinity.

Your Kingdom Come. 1980. Mission Perspectives. Report on the World Conference on Mission and Evangelism. Melbourne, Australia, 12–25 May 1980. Edited by the Commission on World Mission and Evangelism. Geneva: World Council of Churches.

Zager, W. 2002. *Bergpredigt und Reich Gottes.* Neukirchen-Vluyn: Neukirchener.

Zalewski, M. 2000. *Feminism After Postmodernism: Theorising Through Practice.* New York: Routledge.

Zeindler, M. 2001. *Gotteserfahrung in der christlichen Gemeinde: Eine systematisch-theologische Untersuchung.* Stuttgart: W. Kohlhammer.

Zerfass, R., editor. 1988. *Erzählter Glaube—erzählende Kirche.* Quaestiones Disputatae 116. Freiburg: Herder.

Zima, P. V. 1995. *Literarische Ästhetik: Methoden und Modelle der Literaturwissenschaft.* Basel: A. Franke.

———. 2000. *Theorie des Subjekts: Subjektivität und Identität zwischen Moderne und Postmoderne.* Tübingen und Basel: A. Franke.

Zimmer, J., and E. Niggemeyer. 1986. *Macht die Schule auf, lasst das Leben rein: Von der Schule zur Nachbarschaftsschule.* Basel: Beltz.

Zinn, H. 1996. *A People's History of the United States: From 1492 to the Present.* 2nd ed. New York: Longman.

———. 2003. *A People's History of the United States: Abridged Teaching Edition.* New York: The New Press.

Zulehner, P. M. 1989a. *Pastoraltheologie: Fundamentalpastoral—Kirche zwischen Auftrag und Erwartung.* Vol. 1. Düsseldorf: Patmos.

———. 1989b. *Pastoraltheologie: Gemeindepastoral—Orte christlicher Praxis.* Vol. 2. Düsseldorf: Patmos.

———. 1990a. *Pastoraltheologie: Übergänge—Pastoral zu den Lebenswenden.* Vol. 3. Düsseldorf: Patmos.

———. 1990b. *Pastoraltheologie: Pastorale Futurologie—Kirche auf dem Weg ins gesellschaftliche Morgen.* Vol. 4. Düsseldorf: Patmos.

———, and J. Brandner. 2002. *"Meine Seele dürstet nach dir" (Psalm 63,2): Gottes-Pastoral.* Ostfildern: Schwabenverlag.

www.ingramcontent.com/pod-product-compliance
Lightning Source LLC
Chambersburg PA
CBHW070651300426
44111CB00013B/2370